HAGUE CONVENTIONS

A compilation of documents

HAGUE CONVENTIONS

A compilation of documents

L. de Beer (ed.)

INTERNATIONAL COURTS ASSOCIATION

Hague conventions, a compilation of documents
L. de Beer (ed.)

ISBN 978-90-5887-073-5

Production:
Claudia Tofan

Published by:

Wolf Legal Publishers (WLP)
P.O. Box 31051
6503 CB Nijmegen
The Netherlands
Tel: +31 24 355 19 04
Fax: +31 84 837 67 00
E-Mail: info@wolfpublishers.nl
www.wolfpublishers.com

Table of Contents

Hague conventions Convention 1899 and 1907

Introduction

The St. Petersburg Declaration (1868) forms the starting point for later international conferences that resulted in the regulation of warfare. It paved the way for the 1899 Hague Conventions and familiarized the participants with the idea of regulating warfare through international agreements involving a large number of member States.[1]

The Hague Conventions are two international treaties negotiated at international peace conferences at The Hague in the Netherlands. The First Hague Conference took place in 1899 and the Second Hague Conference in 1907.[2] These Conventions turned out to be the basic principles of the laws of war into a written document agreed to by a Convention of delegates from all over the world.[3]

1899

For the 1899 conference, the Russians took the initiative. They choose The Hague as the place of the conference, because of the neutrality of the Netherlands in international (war) matters, to convince the superpowers.
The conference was a nameless body. It was only a conference proposed by the Emperor of all the Russias, and invited the Queen of the Netherlands, to meet at the Hague to consider the subjects contained in the Russian rescripts. The public acclaimed it as a Peace Conference, well knowing that the meeting of official delegates to consider the reduction of armament and the means by which peace could be maintained was in the eye of the initiators not meant like a Peace Conference.[4]

At the conference there were three core areas: dispute regulation, reduction of armament and the development of Humanitarian War Law.
One reason underlying the attempts to regulate warfare there was the desire to avoid having wars fought at all by establishing a court of arbitration and imposing States with the duty to first try to resolve an issue by peaceful means. And the other reason was that, in the unfortunate case that States insisted on resorting to warfare, unnecessary suffering should be prevented.
Purely humanitarian concerns were voiced and called upon as reasons for putting these principles at the top of the agenda. If one thinks pressure from a non-governmental organization and media attention surrounding international conferences are a uniquely modern phenomenon, the history of the Hague Peace Conferences might offer some

---

[1] K. Dijkhof, *War, Law and Technology*, WLP 2010, p. 26.

[2] < http://en.wikipedia.org/wiki/Hague_Conventions_of_1899_and_1907>.

[3] K. Dijkhof, *War, Law and Technology*, WLP 2010, p. 19.

[4] James Brown Scott, 'The Hague Peace Conferences of 1899 and 1907 and International Arbitration', 1909, p. 3.

surprising insight. There was broad press coverage with all sorts of pressure groups present, pressing their agenda by attempting contact with the delegates attending the Conference. This pressure was aimed more at preventing war than regulating how war should be fought.

The Hague Conferences were very large assemblies. The official delegates of twenty-six countries attended and took part in the proceedings.[5]

The delegates failed to reach an agreement on the primary object for which it was called namely the limitation or reduction of armament. On the other hand the Final Act, three Conventions and three Declarations were adopted.[6] One of those successes was a purpose for which the First Hague Peace Conference of 1899 was convened; "the revision of the declaration concerning the laws and customs of war elaborated in 1874 by the Conference of Brussels, and not yet ratified" (Russian circular note of 30 December 1898). The Conference of 1899 succeeded in adopting a Convention on land warfare to which Regulations are annexed.

Although the ultimate goal, preventing future wars, and the secondary goal, general arms limitation, weren't reached, it would be wrong to judge the 1899 Hague Peace Conference as a failure. The fundamental foundation of the laws of war 'means to inure the enemy are not unlimited' was codified for the first time.[7] In general, the outcome of the convention was solid. They are still forming the basis for today's laws of war.[8]
A rather significant aspect of the 1899 Conference is the fact, that the Final Acts were signed by the delegates, but ratification of the Final Acts by the states never occurred.

The 1899 Peace Conference ended with a number of clear achievements in addition to some unfinished, ongoing business. The differences revealed in the often fierce debates had not led to insurmountable tensions. Promises were made to review the matters that had not been agreed upon and to make a further attempt to reach agreement on those matters. Those promises were kept and, in 1907, a second Peace Conference was held again in The Hague.[9]

---

[5] James Brown Scott, 'The Hague Peace Conferences of 1899 and 1907 and International Arbitration', 1909, p. 3.
[6] *Laws of war and international law*, WLP 2002, p. 88.
[7] *Laws of war and international law*, WLP 2002, p. 88.
[8] K. Dijkhof, *War, Law and Technology*, WLP 2010, p. 43.
[9] K. Dijkhof, *War, Law and Technology*, WLP 2010, p. 44.

CORRESPONDENCE, INSTRUCTIONS AND REPORTS OF THE UNITED STATES COMMISSION

Peace Conference at the Hague 1899: Rescript of the Russian Emperor* August 24 (12, Old Style), 1898

The maintenance of general peace, and a possible reduction of the excessive armaments which weigh upon all nations, present themselves in the existing condition of the whole world, as the ideal towards which the endeavors of all Governments should be directed.

The humanitarian and magnanimous ideas of His Majesty the Emperor, my August Master, have been won over to this view. In the conviction that this lofty aim is in conformity with the most essential interests and the legitimate views of all Powers, the Imperial Government thinks that the present moment would be very favorable for seeking, by means of international discussion, the most effectual means of insuring to all peoples the benefits of a real and durable peace, and, above all, of putting an end to the progressive development of the present armaments.

In the course of the last twenty years the longings for a general appeasement have become especially pronounced in the consciences of civilized nations. The preservation of peace has been put forward as the object of international policy; in its name great States have concluded between themselves powerful alliances; it is the better to guarantee peace that they have developed, in proportions hitherto unprecedented, their military forces, and still continue to increase them without shrinking from any sacrifice.

All these efforts nevertheless have not yet been able to bring about the beneficent results of the desired pacification. The financial charges following an upward march strike at the public prosperity at its very source.

The intellectual and physical strength of the nations, labor and capital, are for the major part diverted from their natural application, and unproductively consumed. Hundreds of millions are devoted to acquiring terrible engines of destruction, which, though today regarded as the last word of science, are destined tomorrow to lose all value in consequence of some fresh discovery in the same field.

National culture, economic progress, and the production of wealth are either paralyzed or checked in their development. Moreover, in proportion as the armaments of each Power increase, so do they less and less fulfill the object which the Governments have set before themselves.

---

* Handed to diplomatic representatives by Count Mouravieff, Russian Foreign Minister, at weekly reception in the Foreign Office, St. Petersburg, August 24/12, 1898.

The economic crises, due in great part to the system of armaments *a L'outrance,* and the continual danger which lies in this massing of war material, are transforming the armed peace of our days into a crushing burden, which the peoples have more and more difficulty in bearing. It appears evident, then, that if this state of things were prolonged, it would inevitably lead to the very cataclysm which it is desired to avert, and the horrors of which make every thinking man shudder in advance.

To put an end to these incessant armaments and to seek the means of warding off the calamities which are threatening the whole world-such is the supreme duty which is today imposed on all States.
Filled with this idea, His Majesty has been pleased to order me to propose to all the Governments whose representatives are accredited to the Imperial Court, the meeting of a conference which would have to occupy itself with this grave problem.

This conference should be, by the help of God, a happy presage for the century which is about to open. It would converge in one powerful focus the efforts of all States which are sincerely seeking to make the great idea of universal peace triumph over the elements of trouble and discord.

It would, at the same time, confirm their agreement by the solemn establishment of the principles of justice and right, upon which repose the security of States and the welfare of peoples.

Peace Conference at the Hague 1899: Russian Circular January 11, 1899 (December 30, 1898, Old Style)

When, in the month of August last, my August Master instructed me to propose to the Governments which have Representatives in St. Petersburg the meeting of a Conference with the object of seeking the most efficacious means for assuring to all peoples the blessings of real and lasting peace, and, above all, in order to put a stop to the progressive development of the present armaments, there appeared to be no obstacle in the way of the realization, at no distant date, of this humanitarian scheme.

The cordial reception accorded by nearly all the Powers to the step taken by the Imperial Government could not fail to strengthen this expectation. While highly appreciating the sympathetic terms in which the adhesions of most of the Powers were expressed, the Imperial Cabinet has been also able to collect, with lively satisfaction, evidence of the warmest approval which has reached it, and continues to be received, from all classes of society in various parts of the globe.

Notwithstanding the strong current of opinion which exists in favor of the ideas of general pacification, the political horizon has recently undergone a decided change. Several Powers have undertaken fresh armaments, striving to increase further their military forces, and in the presence of this uncertain situation, it might be asked whether the Powers considered the present moment opportune for the international discussion of the ideas set forth in the circular of August 12 (24, O.S.).

In the hope, however, that the elements of trouble agitating political centers will soon give place to a calmer disposition of a nature to favor the success of the proposed Conference, the Imperial Government is of opinion that it would be possible to proceed forthwith to a preliminary exchange of ideas between the Powers, with the object:

(a) Of seeking without delay means for putting a limit to the progressive increase of military and naval armaments, a question the solution of which becomes evidently more and more urgent in view of the fresh extension given to these armaments; and

(b) Of preparing the way for a discussion of the questions relating to the possibility of preventing armed conflicts by the pacific means at the disposal of international diplomacy.

In the event of the Powers considering the present moment favorable for the meeting of a Conference on these bases it would certainly be useful for the Cabinets to come to an understanding on the subject of the programme of their labors.

The subjects to be submitted for international discussion at the Conference could, in general terms, be summarized as follows:

1. An understanding not to increase for a fixed period the present effective of the armed military and naval forces, and at the same time not to increase the Budgets pertaining thereto; and a preliminary examination of the means by which a reduction might even be effected in future in the forces and Budgets above mentioned.
2. To prohibit the use in the armies and fleets of any new kind of firearms whatever, and of new explosives, or any powders more powerful than those now in use, either for rifles or cannon.
3. To restrict the use in military warfare of the formidable explosives already existing, and to prohibit the throwing of projectiles or explosives of any kind from balloons or by any similar means.
4. To prohibit the use, in naval warfare, of submarine torpedo boats or plungers, or other similar engines of destruction; to give an undertaking not to construct, in the future, vessels with rams.
5. To apply to naval warfare the stipulations of the Geneva Convention of 1864, on the basis of the additional Articles of 1868.
6. To neutralize ships and boats employed in saving those overboard during or after an engagement.
7. To revise the Declaration concerning the laws and customs of war elaborated in 1874 by the Conference of Brussels, which has remained unratified to the present day.
8. To accept in principle the employment of good offices, of mediation and facultative arbitration in cases lending them selves thereto, with the object of preventing armed conflicts between nations; to come to an understanding with respect to the mode of applying these good offices, and to establish a uniform practice in using them.

It is well understood that all questions concerning the political relations of States, and the order of things established by Treaties, as in general all questions which do not directly fall within the program adopted by the Cabinets, must be absolutely excluded from the deliberations of the Conference.

In requesting you, Sir, to be good enough to apply to your Government for instructions on the subject of my present communication, I beg you at the same time to inform it that, in the interest of the great cause which my August Master has so much at heart, His Imperial Majesty considers it advisable that the Conference should not sit in the capital of one of the Great Powers, where so many political interests are centered, which might, perhaps, impede the progress of a work in which all the countries of the universe are equally interested.

I have, etc.,
[Signed] COMTE MOURAVIEFF.

Peace Conference at the Hague 1899:
Instructions to the International (Peace) Conference at the Hague

Washington, April 18, 1899

MR. HAY TO HON. ANDREW D. WHITE, HON. SETH LOW, HON. STANFORD NEWEL, CAPT. ALFRED T. MAHAN, U. S. N., CAPT. WILLIAM CROZIER, U. S. A., DELEGATES ON THE PART OF THE PRESIDENT OF THE UNITED STATES.

DEPARTMENT OF STATE,

Gentlemen: You have been appointed by the President to constitute a commission to represent him at an international conference called by His Imperial Majesty the Emperor of Russia to meet at The Hague, at a time to be indicated by the Government of the Netherlands, for the purpose of discussing the most efficacious means of assuring to all peoples the " benefits of a real and durable peace."

Upon your arrival at The Hague you will effect an organization of your commission, whose records will be kept by your secretary, Hon. Frederick W. Holls. All reports and communications will be made through this Department, according to its customary forms, for preservation in the archives.

The program of topics suggested by the Russian minister of foreign affairs for discussion at the Conference in his circular of December 30, 1898, is as follows:
1. An understanding stipulating the nonaugmentation, for a term to be agreed upon, of the present effective armed land and sea forces, as well as the war budgets pertaining to them; preliminary study of the ways in which even a reduction of the aforesaid effectives and budgets could be realized in the future.
2. Interdiction of the employment in armies and fleets of new firearms of every description and of new explosives, as well as powder more powerful than the kinds used at present, both for guns and cannons.
3. Limitation of the use in field fighting of explosives of a formidable power, such as now in use, and prohibition of the discharge of any kind of projectiles or explosives from balloons or by similar means.
4. Prohibition of the use in naval battles of submarine or diving torpedo boats, or of other engines of destruction of the same nature; agreement not to construct the future warships armed with rams.
5. Adaptation to naval war of the stipulation of the Geneva Convention of 1864, on the base of the additional articles of 1868.
6. Neutralization, for the same reason, of boats or launches employed in the rescue of the shipwrecked during or after naval battles.
7. Revision of the declaration concerning the laws and customs of war elaborated in 1874 by the Conference of Brussels, and not yet ratified.

8. Acceptance, in principle, of the use of good offices, mediation, and voluntary arbitration, in eases where they are available, with the purpose of preventing armed conflicts between nations; understanding in relation to their mode of application and establishment of a uniform practice in employing them.

It is understood that all questions concerning the political relations of States and the order of things established by treaties, as in general all the questions which shall not be included directly in the programme adopted by the cabinets, should be absolutely excluded from the deliberations of the Conference.

The first article, relating to the nonaugmentation and future reduction of effective land and sea forces, is, at present, so inapplicable to the United States that it is deemed advisable for the delegates to leave the initiative upon this subject to the representatives of those Powers to which it may properly belong. In comparison with the effective forces, both military and naval, of other nations, those of the United States, are at present so far below the normal quota that the question of limitation could not be profitably discussed.

The second, third, and fourth articles, relating to the non-employment of firearms, explosives, and other destructive agents, the restricted use of existing instruments of destruction, and the prohibition of certain contrivances employed in naval warfare, seem lacking in practicability, and the discussion of these propositions would probably prove provocative of divergence rather than unanimity of views. It is doubtful if wars are to be diminished by rendering them less destructive, for it is the plain lesson of history that the periods of peace have been longer protracted as the cost and destructiveness of war have increased. The expediency of restraining the inventive genius of our people in the direction of devising means of defense is by no means clear, and, considering the temptations to which men and nations may be exposed in a time of conflict, it is doubtful if an international agreement to this end would prove effective. The dissent of a single powerful nation might render it altogether nugatory. The delegates are, therefore, enjoined not to give the weight of their influence to the promotion of projects the realization of which is so uncertain.

The fifth, sixth, and seventh articles, aiming in the interest of humanity to succor those who by the chance of battle have been rendered helpless, thus losing the character of effective combatants, or to alleviate their sufferings, or to insure the safety of those whose mission is purely one of peace and beneficence, may well awake the cordial interest of the delegates, and any practicable propositions based upon them should receive their earnest support.

The eighth article, which proposes the wider extension of good offices, mediation, and arbitration, seems likely to open the most fruitful field for discussion and future action. " The prevention of armed conflicts by-pacific means," to use the words of Count Mouravieff's circular of December 30, is a purpose well worthy of a great international convention, and its realization in an age of general enlightenment should not be impossible. The duty of sovereign States to promote international justice by all wise and effective means is only secondary to the fundamental necessity of preserving their own existence. Next in importance to their independence is the great fact of their interdependence.

Nothing can secure for human government and for the authority of law which it represents so deep a respect and so firm a loyalty as the spectacle of sovereign and independent States, whose duty it is to prescribe the rules of justice and impose penalties upon the lawless, bowing with reverence before the august supremacy of those principles of right which give to law its eternal foundation.

The proposed Conference promises to offer an opportunity thus far unequaled in the history of the world for initiating a series of negotiations that may lead to important practical results. The long-continued and widespread interest among the people of the United States in the establishment of an international court, as evidenced in the historical resume attached to these instructions as Annex A, gives assurance that the proposal of a definite plan of procedure by this Government for the accomplishment of this end would express the desires and aspirations of this nation. The delegates are, therefore, enjoined to propose, at an opportune moment, the plan for an international tribunal, hereunto attached as Annex B. and to use their influence in the Conference in the most effective manner possible to procure the adoption of its substance or of resolutions directed to the same purpose. It is believed that the disposition and aims of the United States in relation to the other sovereign Powers could not be expressed more truly or opportunely than by an effort of the delegates of this Government to concentrate the attention of the world upon a definite plan for the promotion of international justice.

Since the Conference has its chief reason of existence in the heavy burdens and cruel waste of war, which nowhere affect innocent private persons more severely or unjustly than in the damage done to peaceable trade and commerce, especially at sea, the question of exempting private property from destruction or capture on the high seas would seem to be a timely one for consideration.

As the United States has for many years advocated the exemption of all private property not contraband of war from hostile treatment, you are authorized to propose to the Conference the principle of extending to strictly private property at sea, the immunity from destruction or capture by belligerent Powers which such property already enjoys on land as worthy of being incorporated in the permanent law of civilized nations.

I am, etc.,

JOHN HAY.

Annex A
Historical Resume

From time to time in the history of the United States, propositions have been made for the establishment of a system of peaceable adjustment of differences arising between nations. As early as February, 1832, the senate of Massachusetts adopted, by a vote of 19 to 5, a resolution expressing the opinion that "some mode should be established for the amicable and final adjustment of all international disputes instead of resorting to war."

A similar resolution was unanimously passed by the house of representatives of the same State in 1837, and by the senate by a vote of 35 to 5.

A little prior to 1840 there was much popular agitation regarding the convocation of a congress of nations for the purpose of establishing the international tribunal. This idea was commended by resolutions adopted by the legislature of Massachusetts in 1844, and by the legislature of Vermont in 1852.

In February, 1851, Mr. Foote, from the Committee on Foreign Relations, reported to the Senate of the United States a resolution that in the judgment of this body it would be proper and desirable for the Government of the United States whenever practicable to secure in its treaties with other nations a provision for referring to the decision of umpires all future misunderstandings that can notate satisfactorily adjusted by amicable negotiation in the first instance, before a resort to hostilities shall be had.

Two years later Senator Underwood, from the same committee reported a resolution of advice to the President suggesting a stipulation in all treaties hereafter entered into with other nations referring the adjustment of any misunderstanding or controversy to the decision of disinterested and impartial arbitrators to be mutually chosen.

May 31, 1872, Mr. Sumner introduced into the Senate a resolution in which, after reviewing the historical development of municipal law and the gradual suppression of private war, and citing the progressive action of the Congress of Paris with regard to neutrals, he proposed the establishment of a tribunal to be clothed with such authority as to make it a " complete substitute for war," declaring a refusal to abide by its judgment hostile to civilization, to the end that "war may cease to be regarded as a proper form of trial between nations."
In 1874 a resolution favoring general arbitration was passed by the House of Representatives.

April 1, 1883, a confidential inquiry was addressed to Mr. Frelinghuysen, Secretary of State, by Colonel Frey, then Swiss minister to the United States, regarding the possibility of concluding a general treaty of arbitration between the two countries. Mr. Frelinghuysen, citing the general policy of this country in past years, expressed his disposition to consider the proposition with favor. September 5, 1883, Colonel Frey submitted a draft of a treaty, the reception of which was acknowledged by Mr. Frelinghuysen on the 26th of the same month. This draft, adopted by the Swiss Federal Council July 24, 1883, presented a short plan of arbitration. These negotiations were referred to in the President's Annual Message for 1883, but were not concluded.

In 1888, a communication having been made to the President and Congress of the United States by two hundred and thirty-five members of the British Parliament, urging the conclusion of a treaty of arbitration between the United States and Great Britain, and reinforced by petitions and memorials from multitudes of individuals and associations from Maine to California, great enthusiasm was exhibited in its reception by eminent citizens of New York. As a result of this movement on June 13, 1888, Mr. Sherman, from the Committee on Foreign Relations, reported to the Senate a joint Resolution requesting the President to invite, from time to time, as fit occasions may arise, negotiations with any government with which the United States has or may have diplomatic relations, to the end that the differences or disputes arising between the two governments which can not be adjusted by diplomatic agency may be referred to arbitration, and be peaceably adjusted by such means.

November 29, 1881, Mr. Blaine, Secretary of State, invited the Governments of the American Nations to participate in a Congress to be held in the city of Washington, November 24, 1882, " for the purpose of considering and discussing the methods of preventing war between the nations of America." For special reasons the enterprise was temporarily abandoned, but was afterwards revived and enlarged in Congress, and an act was passed authorizing the calling of the International American Conference, which assembled in Washington in the autumn of 1889. On April 18, 1890, referring to this plan of arbitration, Mr. Blaine said:

> “If, in this closing hour, the Conference had but one deed to celebrate, we should dare call the world's attention to the deliberate, confident, solemn dedication of two great continents to peace, and to the prosperity which has peace for its foundation. We hold up this new Magna Charta, which abolishes war and substitutes arbitration between the American Republics, as the first and great fruit of the " International American Conference."

The Senate of the United States on February 14,1890, and the House of Representatives on April 3, 1890, adopted a concurrent resolution in the language reported by Mr. Sherman to the Senate in June, 1888.

July 8, 1895, the French Chamber of Deputies unanimously resolved:
The Chamber invites the Government to negotiate as soon as possible a permanent treaty of arbitration between the French Republic and the Republic of the United States of America.

July 16, 1893, the British House of Commons adopted the following resolution:
Resolved, That this House has learnt with satisfaction that both Houses of the United States Congress have, by resolution, requested the President to invite from time to time, as fit occasions may arise, negotiations with any government with which the United States have or may have diplomatic relations, to the end that any differences or disputes arising between the two governments which can not be adjusted by diplomatic agency may be referred to arbitration and peaceably adjusted by such means; and that this House, cordially sympathizing with the purpose in view, expresses the hope that Her Majesty's Government will lend their ready cooperation to the Government of the United States upon the basis of the foregoing resolution.

December 4, 1893, President Cleveland referred to the foregoing resolution of the British House of Commons as follows:

> It affords me signal pleasure to lay this parliamentary resolution before the Congress and to express my sincere gratification that the sentiment of two great and kindred nations is thus authoritatively manifested in favor of the rational and peaceable settlement of international quarrels by honorable resort to arbitration.
> These resolutions led to the exchange of communications regarding the conclusion of a permanent treaty of arbitration, suspended from the spring of 1895 to March 5, 1898, when negotiations were resumed which resulted in the signature of a treaty January 11, 1897, between the United States and Great Britain.

In his inaugural address, March 4, 1897, President McKinley said:

> Arbitration is the true method of settlement of international as well AS local differences.. It was recognized as the best means of adjustment of differences between employers and employees by the Forty-ninth Congress in 1886, and its application was extended to our diplomatic relations by the unanimous concurrence of the Senate and House of the Fifty-first Congress in 1890. The latter resolution was accepted as the basis of negotiations with us by the British House of Commons in 1893, and upon our invitation a treaty of arbitration between the United States and Great Britain was signed at Washington and transmitted to the Senate for ratification in January last.

Since this treaty is clearly the result of our own initiative, since it has been recognized as the leading feature of our foreign policy throughout our entire national history-the adjustment of difficulties by judicial methods rather than forge of arms-and since it presents to the world the glorious example of reason and peace, not passion and war, controlling the relation between two of the greatest nations of the world, an example certain to be followed by others, I respectfully urge the early action of the Senate thereon, not merely as a matter of policy, but as a duty to mankind. The importance and moral influence of the ratification of such a treaty can hardly be overestimated in the cause of advancing civilization. It may well engage the best thought of the statesmen and people of every country, and I can not but consider it fortunate that it was reserved to the United States to have the leadership in so grand a work.

The Senate of the United States declined to concur in the ratification of the Treaty of Arbitration with Great Britain, but for reasons which might not affect a general treaty directed toward a similar end.

The publication by this Government of the exhaustive " History and Digest of the International Arbitrations to which the United States has been a Party," by the Hon. John Bassett Moore, late Assistant Secretary of State, a work extending through six volumes, marks a new epoch in the history of arbitration. It places beyond controversy the applicability of judicial methods to a large variety of international disagreements which have been successfully adjudicated by individual arbitrators or temporary boards of arbitration chosen by the litigants for each case. It also furnishes an exceedingly valuable body of rules of organization and procedure for the guidance of future tribunals of a similar nature. But, perhaps, its highest significance is the demonstration of the superiority of a permanent tribunal over merely special and temporary boards of arbitration, with respect to economy of time and money as well as uniformity of method and procedure.

A history of the various plans for the realization of international justice shows the gradual evolution of clearer and less objectionable conceptions upon this subject. Those of Bluntschli, Lorimer, David Dudley Field, and Leone Levi have been long before the public, each containing useful suggestions, but impracticable as a whole. Certain rules for the regulation of the procedure of international tribunals of arbitration were discussed by the Institute of International Law at its sessions at Geneva in 1874, and at The Hague in 1875, and provisional rules were finally approved. Another set of rules was proposed by a select committee of lawyers at the Universal Peace Congress, held in Chicago in 1893. Resolutions of a somewhat elaborate nature were adopted by the Inter-parliamentary Conference, composed of British and French members of Parliament, at Brussels in 1895. _In April, 1896, the Bar Association of the State of New York at a special meeting held at Albany adopted a plan for the establishment of a permanent international tribunal. The almost continuous movement of thought in this direction since 1832 has been interrupted only by the late Spanish-American war.

A careful review of all the plans for an international tribunal that have thus far been proposed makes it evident that they have failed from two causes: (1) Too great elaboration and complication, involving too many debatable questions; and (2) the absence of an opportune occasion for proposing them to an authoritative international body.

The plan that is to prove successful, if a sufficient number of sovereign States be disposed to adopt any plan whatsoever for an international tribunal, must combine an adequate grasp of the conditions with an extreme simplicity, leaving much to the cooperation of others and the development of the future.

The introduction of a brief resolution at an opportune moment in the proposed Peace Conference would at least place the United States on record as the friend and promoter of peace. The resolution hereto appended is intended to embody in the briefest and simplest manner the most useful suggestions of all the plans proposed.

Annex B
Plan for an International Tribunal

Resolved, That in order to aid in the prevention of armed conflicts by pacific means, the representatives of the Sovereign Powers assembled together in this Conference be, and hereby are, requested to propose to their respective Governments a series of negotiations for the adoption of a general treaty having for its object the following plan, with such modifications as may be essential to secure the adhesion of at least nine Sovereign Powers.

1. The Tribunal shall be composed of judges chosen on account of their personal integrity and learning in international law by a majority of the members of the highest court now existing in each of the adhering States, one from each sovereign State participating in the treaty, and shall hold office until their successors are appointed by the same body.

2. The Tribunal shall meet for organization at a time and place to be agreed upon by the several Governments, but not later than six months after the general treaty shall be ratified by nine Powers, and shall organize itself by the appointment of a permanent clerk and such other officers as may be found necessary, but without conferring any distinction upon its own members. The Tribunal shall be empowered to fix its place of sessions and to change the same from time to time as the interest of justice or the convenience of the litigants may seem to require, and fix its own rules of procedure.

3. The contracting nations will mutually agree to submit to the International Tribunal all questions of disagreement between them, excepting such as may relate to or involve their political independence or territorial integrity. Questions of disagreement, with the aforesaid exceptions, arising between an adherent State and a non-adhering State, or between two sovereign States not adherent to the treaty, may, with the consent of both parties in dispute, be submitted to the International Tribunal for adjudication, upon the condition expressed in Article 6.

4. The Tribunal shall be of a permanent character and shall be always open for the filing of cases and counter cases, either by the contracting nations or by others that may choose to submit them, and all cases and counter cases, with the testimony and arguments by which they are to be supported or answered, are to be in writing. All cases, counter cases, evidence, arguments, and opinions expressing judgment are to be accessible, after a decision is rendered, to all who desire to pay the necessary charges for transcription.

5. A bench of judges for each particular case shall consist of not less then three nor more than seven, as may be deemed expedient, appointed by the unanimous consent of the Tribunal, and not to include a member who is either a native, subject, or citizen of the State whose interests are in litigation in that case.

6. The general expenses of the Tribunal are to be divided equally between the adherent Powers, but those arising from each particular case shall be provided for as may be directed by the Tribunal. The presentation of a case wherein one or both of the parties may be a non-adherent State shall be admitted only upon condition of a mutual agreement that the State against which judgment may be found shall pay, in addition to the judgment, a sum to be fixed by the Tribunal for the expenses of the adjudication.

7. Every litigant before the International Tribunal shall have the right to make an appeal for reexamination of a case within three months after notification of the decision, upon presentation of evidence that the judgment contains a substantial error of fact or law.

8. This treaty shall become operative when nine sovereign States, whereof at least six shall have taken part in the Conference of The Hague, shall have ratified its provisions.

Peace Conference at the Hague 1899:
General Report of the United States Commission

The Hague, July 31, 1899

THE HONORABLE JOHN HAY, Secretary of State,

Sir: On May 17, 1899, the American Commission to the Peace Conference of The Hague met for the first time at the house of the American Minister, The Honorable Stanford Newel, the members in the order named in the instructions from the State Department being Andrew D. White, Seth Low, Stanford Newel, Captain Alfred T. Mahan of the United States Navy, Captain William Crozier of the United States Army, and Frederick W. Holls, Secretary. Mr. White was elected President and the instructions from the Department of State were read.

On the following day the Conference was opened at the Palace known as "The House in the Wood, " and delegates from the following countries, twenty-six in number, were found to be present: Germany, The United States of America, Austria-Hungary, Belgium, China, Denmark, Spain, France, Great Britain and Ireland, Greece, Italy, Japan, Luxemburg, Mexico, Montenegro, The Netherlands, Persia, Portugal, Roumania, Russia, Servia, Siam, Sweden and Norway, Switzerland, Turkey and Bulgaria.

The opening meeting was occupied mainly by proceedings of a ceremonial nature, including a telegram to the Emperor of Russia and a message of thanks to the Queen of the Netherlands, with speeches by M. de Beaufort, the Netherlands Minister of Foreign Affairs, and M. de Staal, representing Russia.

At the second meeting a permanent organization of the Conference was effected, M. de Staal being chosen President, M. de Beaufort honorary President, and M. van Karnebeek, a former Netherlands Minister of Foreign Affairs, Vice-President. A sufficient number of Secretaries was also named.

The work of the Conference was next laid out with reference to the points stated in the Mouravieff circular of December 30, 1898, and divided between three great committees as follows:

The first of these committees was upon the limitation of armaments and war budgets, the interdiction or discouragement of sundry arms and explosives which had been or might be hereafter invented, and the limitation of the use of sundry explosives, projectiles, and methods of destruction both on land and sea, as contained in Articles 1 to 4 of the Mouravieff circular.

The second great committee had reference to the extension of the Geneva Red Cross Rules of 1864 and 1868 to maritime warfare, and the revision of the Brussels Declaration of 1874 concerning the laws and customs of war and contained in Articles 5 to 7 of the same circular.

The third committee had as its subjects, mediation, arbitration, and other methods of preventing armed conflicts between nations, as referred to in Article 8 of the Mouravieff circular.

The American members of these three committees were as follows: of the first committee, Messrs. White, Mahan, Crozier; of the second committee, Messrs. White, Newel, Mahan, Crozier; of the third committee, Messrs. White, Low and Holls.

In aid of these three main committees sub-committees were appointed as follows:

The first committee referred questions of a military nature to the first sub-committee of which Captain Crozier was a member, and questions of a naval nature to the second sub-committee of which Captain Mahan was a member.
The second committee referred Articles 5 and 6, having reference to the extension of the Geneva Rules to maritime warfare to a sub-committee of which Captain Mahan was a member, and Article 7, concerning the revision of the laws and customs of war, to a sub-committee of which Captain Crozier was a member.
The third committee appointed a single sub-committee, of "examination," whose purpose was to scrutinize plans, projects, and suggestions of arbitration, and of this committee, Mr. Holls was a member.

The main steps in the progress of the work wrought by these agencies, and the part taken in it by our Commission are detailed in the accompanying reports made to the American Commission by the American members of the three committees of the Conference. It will be seen from these that some of the most important features finally adopted were the result of American proposals and suggestions.

As to that portion of the work of the First Committee of the Conference which concerned the non-augmentation of armies, navies, and war budgets for a fixed term and the study of the means for eventually diminishing armies and war budgets, namely Article 1, the circumstances of the United States being so different from those which obtain in other parts of the world and especially in Europe, we thought it best, under our instructions, to abstain from taking any active part. In this connection, the following declaration was made:

The Delegation of the United States of America has concurred in the conclusions upon the first clause of the Russian letter of December 30, 1898, presented to the Conference by the First Commission, namely: that the proposals of the Russian representatives, for fixing the amounts of effective forces and of budgets, military and naval, for periods of five and three years. cannot now be accepted, and that a more profound study upon the part of each State concerned is to be desired. But, while thus supporting what seemed to be the only practicable solution of a question submitted to the Conference by the Russian letter, the Delegation wishes to place upon the Record that the United States, in so doing, does not express any opinion as to the course to be taken by the States of Europe.

This declaration is not meant to indicate mere indifference to a difficult problem, because it does not affect the United States immediately, but expresses a determination to refrain from enunciating opinions upon matters into which, as concerning Europe alone, the United States has no claim to enter. The resolution offered by M. Bourgeois, and adopted by the First Commission, received also the hearty concurrence of this Delegation, because in so doing it expresses the cordial interest and sympathy with which the United States, while carefully abstaining from anything that might resemble interference, regards all movements that are thought to tend to the welfare of Europe. The military and naval armaments of the United States are at present so small, relatively, to the extent of territory and to the number of the population, as well as in comparison with those of other nations, that their size can entail no additional burden of expense upon the latter, nor can even form a subject for profitable mutual discussion.

As to that portion of the work of the first committee which concerned the limitations of invention and the interdiction of sundry arms, explosives, mechanical agencies, and methods heretofore in use or which might possibly be hereafter adopted both as regards warfare by land and sea, namely, Articles 2, 3, and 4, the whole matter having been divided between Captains Mahan and Crozier, so far as technical discussion was concerned, the reports made by them from time to time to the American Commission formed the basis of its final action on these subjects in the first committee and in the Conference at large.

The American Commission approached the subject of the limitation of invention with much doubt. They had been justly reminded in their instructions of the fact that by the progress of invention as applied to the agencies of war, the frequency, and indeed the exhausting character of war had been as a rule diminished rather than increased. As to details regarding missiles and methods, technical and other difficulties arose which obliged us eventually, as will be seen, to put ourselves on record in opposition to the large majority of our colleagues from other nations on sundry points. While agreeing with them most earnestly as to the end to be attained, the difference in regard to some details was irreconcilable. We feared falling into worse evils than those from which we sought to escape. The annexed Reports of Captains Mahan and Crozier will exhibit very fully these difficulties and the decisions thence arising.

As to the work of the Second great Committee of the Conference, the matters concerned in Articles 3 and 6 which related to the extension to maritime warfare of the Red Cross

Rules regarding care for the wounded adopted in the Geneva Conventions of 1864 and 1868 were, as already stated, referred as regards the discussion of technical questions in the committee and sub-committee to Captain Mahan, and the matters concerned in Article 7, on the revision of the laws and customs of war were referred to Captain Crozier. On these technical questions Captains Mahan and Crozier reported from time to time to the American Commission, and these reports having been discussed both in regard to their general and special bearings, became the basis of the final action of the entire American Commission, both in the second committee and in the Conference at large.

As to the first of these subjects, the extension of the Geneva Red Cross Rules to maritime warfare, while the general purpose of the articles adopted elicited the especial sympathy of the American Commission, a neglect of what seemed to us a question of almost vital importance, namely: the determination of the status of men picked up by the hospital ships of neutral states or by other neutral vessels, has led us to refrain from signing the Convention prepared by the Conference touching this subject, and to submit the matter, with full explanation, to the Department of State for decision.

As to the second of these subjects, the revision of the laws and customs of war, though the code adopted and embodied in the third convention commends our approval, it is of such extent and importance as to appear to need detailed consideration in connection with similar laws and customs already in force in the army of the United States, and it was thought best, therefore, to withhold our signature from this Convention, also, and to refer it to the State Department with a recommendation that it be there submitted to the proper authorities for special examination and signed, unless such examination shall disclose imperfections not apparent to the Commission.

In the Third great Committee of the Conference, which had in charge the matters concerned in Article 3 of the Russian circular, with reference to good offices, mediation, and arbitration, the proceedings of the sub-committee above referred to became especially important.

While much interest was shown in the discussions of the first of the great Committees of the Conference, and still more in those of the second, the main interest of the whole body centered more and more in the third. It was felt that a thorough provision for arbitration and its cognate subjects is the logical precursor of the limitation of standing armies and budgets, and that the true logical order is, first, arbitration and then disarmament.

As to subsidiary agencies, while our Commission contributed much to the general work regarding good offices and mediation, it contributed entirely, through Mr. Holls, the plan for " Special Mediation, " which was adopted unanimously, first by the committee and finally by the Conference.

As to the plan for "International Commissions of Inquiry" which emanated from the Russian Delegation, our Commission acknowledged its probable value, and aided in elaborating it; but added to the safeguards against any possible abuse of it, as concerns the United States, by our Declaration of July 25, to be mentioned hereafter.

The functions of such commissions is strictly limited to the ascertainment of facts, and it is hoped that, both by giving time for passions to subside and by substituting truth for rumor, they may prove useful at times in settling international disputes. The Commissions of Inquiry may also form a useful auxiliary both in the exercise of Good Offices and to Arbitration.

As to the next main subject, the most important of all under consideration by the third committee-the plan of a Permanent Court or Tribunal-we were able, in accordance with our instructions, to make contributions which we believe will aid in giving such a court dignity and efficiency.

On the assembling of the Conference, the feeling regarding the establishment of an actual, permanent tribunal was evidently chaotic, with little or no apparent tendency to crystallize into any satisfactory institution. The very elaborate and, in the main, excellent proposals relating to procedure before special and temporary tribunals, which were presented by the Russian Delegation, did not at first contemplate the establishment of any such permanent institution. The American plan contained a carefully devised project for such a tribunal, which differed from that adopted mainly in contemplating a tribunal capable of meeting in full bench and permanently in the exercise of its functions, like the Supreme Court of the United States, instead of a Court like the Supreme Court of the State of New York, which never sits as a whole, but whose members sit from time to time singly or in groups, as occasion may demand. The Court of Arbitration provided for, resembles in many features the Supreme Court of the State of New York, and courts of unlimited original jurisdiction in various other States. In order to make this system effective a Council was established, composed of the diplomatic representatives of the various Powers at The Hague, and presided over by the Netherlands Minister of Foreign Affairs, which should have charge of the central office of the proposed Court, of all administrative details, and of the means and machinery for speedily calling a proper bench of judges together, and for setting the Court in action. The reasons why we acquiesced in this plan will be found in the accompanying report This compromise involving the creation of a Council and the selection of judges, not to be in session save when actually required for international litigation, was proposed by Great Britain, and the feature of it, which provided for the admission of the Netherlands with its Minister of Foreign Affairs as President of the Council, was proposed by the American Commission. The nations generally joined in perfecting the details. It may truthfully be called, therefore, the plan of the Conference.

As to the revision of the decisions by the tribunal in case of the discovery of new facts, a subject on which our instructions were explicit, we were able, in the face of determined and prolonged opposition, to secure recognition in the Code of Procedure for the American view.

As regards the procedure to be adopted in the International Court thus provided, the main features having been proposed by the Russian Delegation, various modifications were made by other Delegations, including our own. Our Commission was careful to see that in this Code there should be nothing which could put those conversant more especially with British and American Common Law and Equity at a disadvantage. To sundry important features proposed by other Powers our own Commission gave hearty support. This was the case more especially with Article 27 proposed by France. It provides a means, through the agency of the Powers generally, for calling the attention of any nations apparently drifting into war, to the fact that the tribunal is ready to hear their contention. In this provision, broadly interpreted, we acquiesced, but endeavored to secure a clause limiting to suitable circumstances the "duty" imposed by the article. Great opposition being shown to such an amendment as unduly weakening the article, we decided to present a declaration that nothing contained in the convention should make it the duty of the United States to intrude in or become entangled with European political questions or matters of internal administration, or to relinquish the traditional attitude of our nation toward purely American questions. This declaration was received without objection by the Conference in full and open session.

As to the results thus obtained as a whole regarding arbitration, in view of all the circumstances and considerations revealed during the sessions of the Conference, it is our opinion that the " Plan for the Peaceful Adjustment of International Differences," which was adopted by the Conference, is better than that presented by any one nation. We believe that, though it will doubtless be found imperfect and will require modification as time goes on, it will form a thoroughly practical beginning, that it will produce valuable results from the outset, and that it will be the germ out of which a better and better system will be gradually evolved.

As to the question between compulsory and voluntary arbitration, it was clearly seen, before we had been long in session, that general compulsory arbitration of questions, really likely to produce war, could not be obtained; in fact, that not one of the nations represented at the Conference was willing to embark in it so far as the more serious questions were concerned. Even as to questions of less moment it was found to be impossible to secure agreement except upon a voluntary basis. We ourselves felt obliged to insist upon the omission from the Russian list of proposed subjects for compulsory arbitration, international conventions relating to rivers, to inter-oceanic canals, and to monetary matters. Even as so amended, the plan was not acceptable to all. As a consequence, the Convention prepared by the Conference provides for voluntary arbitration only. It remains for public opinion to make this system effective. As questions arise threatening resort to arms, it may well be hoped that public opinion in the nations concerned, seeing in this great international court a means of escape from the increasing horrors of war, will insist more and more that the questions at issue be referred to it. As time goes on such reference will probably more and more seem, to the world at large, natural and normal, and we may hope that recourse to the tribunal will finally, in the great majority of serious differences between nations, become a popular means of avoiding the resort to arms. There will also be another effect worthy of consideration. This is the building up of a body of international law growing out of the decisions handed down by the judges. The procedure of the tribunal requires that reasons for such decisions shall be given, and these decisions and reasons can hardly fail to form additions of especial value to international jurisprudence.

It now remains to report the proceedings of the Conference, as well as our own action, regarding the question of the immunity of private property not contraband, from seizure on the seas in time of war. From the very beginning of our sessions it was constantly insisted by leading representatives from nearly all the great Powers that the action of the Conference should be strictly limited to the matters specified in the Russian circular of December 30, 1898, and referred to in the invitation emanating from the Netherlands Ministry of Foreign Affairs.

Many reasons for such a limitation were obvious. The members of the Conference were, from the beginning, deluged with books, pamphlets, circulars, newspapers, broadsides, and private letters on a multitude of burning questions in various parts of the world. Considerable numbers of men and women devoted to urging these questions came to The Hague or gave notice of their coming. It was very generally believed in the Conference that the admission of any question not strictly within the limits proposed by the two circulars above mentioned would open the door to all those proposals above referred to and that this might lead to endless confusion, to heated debate, perhaps even to the wreck of the Conference and consequently to a long postponement of the objects which both those who summoned it and those who entered it had directly in view.

It was at first held by very many members of the Conference that under the proper application of the above rule, the proposal made by the American Commission could not be received. It required much and earnest argument on our part to change this view, but finally the Memorial from our Commission, which stated fully the historical and actual relation of the United States to the whole subject, was received, referred to the appropriate committee, and finally brought by it before the Conference.

In that body it was listened to with close attention and the speech of the Chairman of the Committee, who is the eminent President of the Venezuelan Arbitration Tribunal, nowin session at Paris, paid a hearty tribute to the historical adhesion of the United States to the great principle concerned. He then moved that the subject be referred to a future Conference. This motion we accepted and seconded, taking occasion in doing so to restate the American doctrine on the subject, with its claims on all the nations represented at the Conference.

The Commission was thus, as we believe, faithful to one of the oldest of American traditions, and was able at least to keep the subject before the world. The way is paved also for a future careful consideration of the subject in all its bearings and under more propitious circumstances.

The conclusions of the Peace Conference at The Hague took complete and definite shape in the final act laid before the Delegates on July 29th, for their signature. This Act embodied three Conventions, three Declarations, and seven Resolutions as follows:

First, a Convention for the peaceful adjustment of international differences. This was signed by sixteen Delegations, including that of the United States of America, there being adjoined to our signatures a reference to our declaration above referred to, made in open Conference on July 25, and recorded in the proceedings of that day.

Second, a Convention concerning the laws and customs of war on land. This was signed by fifteen Delegations. The United States Delegation refer the matter to the Government at Washington with the recommendation that it be there signed.

Third, a Convention for the adaptation to maritime warfare of the principles of the Geneva Conference of 1864. This was signed by fifteen Delegations. The United States representatives refer it, without recommendation, to the Government at Washington.

The three Declarations were as follows:

First: a Declaration prohibiting the throwing of projectiles and explosives from balloons or by other new analogous means, such prohibition to be effective during five years. This was signed by seventeen Delegations as follows: Belgium, Denmark, Spain, The United States of America, Mexico, France, Greece, Montenegro, The Netherlands, Persia, Portugal, Roumania, Russia, Siam, Sweden and Norway, Turkey and Bulgaria.
Second, a Declaration prohibiting the use of projectiles having as their sole object the diffusion of asphyxiating or deleterious gases. This, for reasons given in the accompanying documents, the American Delegation did not sign. It was signed by sixteen Delegations as follows: Belgium, Denmark, Spain, Mexico, France, Greece, Montenegro, The Netherlands, Persia, Portugal, Roumania, Russia, Siam, Sweden and Norway, Turkey and Bulgaria.
Third, a Declaration prohibiting the use of bullets which expand or flatten easily in the human body, as illustrated by certain given details of construction. This for technical reasons, also fully stated in the report, the American Delegation did not sign. It was signed by fifteen Delegations as follows: Belgium, Denmark, Spain, Mexico, France,

Greece, Montenegro, The Netherlands, Persia, Roumania, Russia, Siam, Sweden and Norway, Turkey and Bulgaria.

The seven Resolutions were as follows:

First, a Resolution that the limitation of the military charges which at present so oppress the world is greatly to be desired, for the increase of the material and moral welfare of mankind.
This ended the action of the Conference in relation to matters considered by it upon their merits. In addition the Conference passed the following resolutions, for all of which the United States Delegation voted, referring various matters to the consideration of the Powers or to future Conferences. Upon the last five resolutions a few Powers abstained from voting.
The Second Resolution was as follows: The Conference taking into consideration the preliminary steps taken by the federal government of Switzerland for the revision of the Convention of Geneva, expresses the wish that there should be in a short time a meeting of a special conference having for its object the revision of that Convention.

This Resolution was voted unanimously.

Third: The Conference expresses the wish that the question of rights and duties of neutrals should be considered at another Conference.
Fourth: The Conference expresses the wish that questions relative to muskets and marine artillery, such as have been examined by it, should be made the subject of study on the part of the governments with a view of arriving at an agreement concerning the adoption of new types and calibers.
Fifth: The Conference expresses the wish that the governments, taking into account all the propositions made at this Conference, should study the possibility of an agreement concerning the limitation of armed forces on land and sea and of war budgets.
Sixth: The Conference expresses the wish that a proposition having for its object the declaration of immunity of private property in war on the high seas, should be referred for examination to another Conference.
Seventh: The Conference expresses the wish that the proposition of regulating the question of bombardment of ports, cities, or villages by a naval force, should be referred for examination to another Conference.

It will be observed that the conditions upon which Powers not represented at the Conference can adhere to the Convention for the Peaceful Regulation of International Conflicts is to "form the subject of a later agreement between the Contracting Powers." This provision reflects the outcome of a three days' debate in the Drafting Committee as to whether this Convention should be absolutely open, or open only with the consent of the Contracting Powers. England and Italy strenuously supported the latter view. It soon became apparent that, under the guise of general propositions, the Committee was discussing political questions, of great importance at least to certain Powers. Under these circumstances the representatives of the United States took no part in the discussion, but supported by their vote the view that the Convention, in its nature, involved reciprocal obligations; and also the conclusion that political questions had no place in the Conference, and must be left to be decided by the competent authorities of the Powers represented there.

It is to be regretted that this action excludes from immediate adherence to this Convention our sister Republics of Central and South America, with whom the United States is already in similar relations by the Pan-American Treaty. It is hoped that an arrangement will soon be made which will enable these States, if they so desire, to enter into the same relations as ourselves with the Powers represented at the Conference.

This report should not be closed without an acknowledgment of the great and constant courtesy of the Government of the Netherlands and all its representatives to the American Commission as well as to all the members of the Conference. In every way they have sought to aid us in our work and to make our stay agreeable to us. The accommodations they have provided for the Conference have enhanced its dignity and increased its efficiency.

It may also be well to put on record that from the entire Conference, without exception, we have constantly received marks of kindness, and that although so many nations with different interests were represented, there has not been in any session, whether of the Conference or of any of the committees or subcommittees, anything other than calm and courteous debate.

The text of the Final Act of the various Conventions and Declarations referred to therein, is appended to this report.

All of which is most respectfully submitted:
ANDREW D. WHITE, President,
SETH LOW,
STANFORD NEWEL,
A. T. MAHAN,
WILLIAM CROZIER,
FREDERICK W. HOLLS, Secretary.

Peace Conference at the Hague 1899: Report of Captain Crozier to the Commission of the United States of America to the International Conference at the Hague Regarding the Work of the First Committee of the Conference and its Sub-committee

The Hague, July 31, 1899

THE COMMISSION OF THE UNITED STATES OF AMERICA TO THE INTERNATIONAL CONFERENCE AT THE HAGUE

Gentlemen: I have the honor of submitting a resume of the work of the First Committee of the Conference and of its First Sub-Committee, which was the military subdivision, concerning the following subjects, which are mentioned in the second and third numbered articles of the circular of Count Mouravieff of December 30, 1898 (January 11, 1899), namely: powders, explosives, field guns, balloons, and muskets; also the subject of bullets which, although not mentioned in either of the above designated articles of Count Mouravieff's circular, were considered by this Committee, notwithstanding that it would have appeared more logical to consider them under the seventh numbered article of the circular, referring to the declaration concerning the laws and customs of war made by the Brussels Conference in 1874.

The Russian representative on the First Committee was Colonel Gilinsky, and the propositions for discussion were for the most part presented by him in the name of the Russian Government, and upon him generally devolved the duty of explaining the proposals and of supporting them in the first instance.

Powders

By this term was meant the propelling charge of projectiles, as distinguished from the bursting charge. The proposition presented was that which is contained in the second article of the circular, namely: an agreement not to make use of any more powerful powders than those now employed, both for field guns and muskets. There was little discussion on the proposition; in fact, the remarks of the United States Delegate were the only ones made upon the subject, and the proposition was unanimously rejected.

Explosives

By this term was meant the bursting charges of projectiles. Two propositions were made. The first was not to make use of mining shells (*obus brisants on a fougasses*) for field artillery. After a short discussion the proposition was decided in the negative by a vote of eleven to ten. The second proposition was not to make use of any new explosives, or of any of the class known as high explosives for the bursting charges of projectiles. This proposition was also, after a short discussion, lost by a vote of twelve to nine.

Field Guns

The proposition on this subject was for the Powers to agree that no field material should be adopted of a model superior to the best material now in use in any country-those countries having inferior material to the best now in use to have the privilege of adopting such best material. During the discussion, which was extended to some length, the question divided itself into two parts, and two votes were taken upon it. The first was as to whether, in case improvements in field artillery should be forbidden, this interdiction should nevertheless permit everybody to adopt the most perfect material now in use anywhere. The vote upon this question was so accompanied by reservations and explanations, that it was impossible to state what the result of it was-the only thing evident being that the question was not entirely understood by the voting delegates. Consequently, a second vote was taken upon the question whether the Powers should agree not to make use, for a fixed period, of any new invention in field artillery. This question was decided in the negative by a unanimous vote, with the exception of Russia and Bulgaria, which abstained from voting. The Russian Delegate, at a later period, explained that his abstention was due to the fact that the question had taken such a form that its decision in the affirmative would have prevented the adoption of rapid fire field guns, which, in the view that these were of an existing type, he desired to retain for his Government the privilege of adopting.

Balloons

The Sub-Committee first voted a perpetual prohibition of the use of balloons or similar new machines for throwing projectiles or explosives. In the full Committee, this subject was brought up for reconsideration by the United States Delegate and the prohibition was, by unanimous vote, limited to cover a period of five years only. The action taken was for humanitarian reasons alone, and was founded upon the opinion that balloons, as they now exist, form such an uncertain means of injury that they cannot be used with any accuracy; that the persons or objects injured by throwing explosives from them may be entirely disconnected from any conflict which may be in process, and such that their injury or destruction would be of no practical advantage to the party making use of the machines. The limitation of the interdiction of five years' operation preserves liberty of action under changed circumstances which may be produced by the progress of invention.

Muskets

The proposition presented under this head was that no Power should change their existing type of small arm. It will be observed that this proposition differed from that in regard to field guns, which permitted all Powers to adopt the most perfect material now in existence-the reason for the difference being explained by the Russian delegate to be that, whereas there was a great difference in the excellence of field artillery material in use in different countries, they have all adopted substantially the same musket, and being on an equal footing, the present would be a good time to cease making changes. The object of the proposition was stated to be purely economic. It was explained that the prohibition to adopt a new type of musket would not be intended to prevent the improvement of existing types; whereupon there immediately arose a discussion as to what constituted a type and what improvements might be made without falling under the prohibition of not changing it. Efforts were made to effect a concord of views by specifying details, such as initial velocity, weight of projectile, etc., also by the proposition to limit the time for which the prohibition should hold, but no agreement could be secured. The United States delegate stated early in the discussion, on the attitude of the United States toward questions of this class, that our Government did not consider limitations in regard to the use of military inventions to be conducive to the peace of the world, and for that reason such limitation would in general not be supported by the American Commission.

A separate vote was taken upon the question whether the Powers should agree not to make use of automatic muskets, and as this may be taken as a fair example of the class of improvements which, although they may have reached such a stage as to be fairly before the world, have not yet been adopted by any nation, an analysis of the vote taken upon it may be interesting as showing the attitude of the different Powers in regard to such questions. The States voting in favor of the prohibition were Belgium, Denmark, Spain, Holland, Persia, Russia, Siam, Switzerland, and Bulgaria (nine). Those voting against it were Germany, the United States, Austria-Hungary, Great Britain, Italy, Sweden and Norway (six). And those abstaining were France, Japan, Portugal, Roumania, Servia, and Turkey (six.) From this statement it may be seen that none of the great Powers of the world, except Russia, was willing to accept restrictions in regard to military improvements when the question of increase of efficiency was involved, and that one great Power (France) abstained from expressing an opinion upon the subject.

In the Full Committee, after another effort to secure some action in the line of the proposition had failed, it was agreed that the subject should be regarded as open for the future consideration of the different Governments.

A question was also raised as to whether there should be any agreement in regard to the use of new means of destruction, which might possibly have a tendency to come into vogue, such as those depending upon electricity or chemistry. After a short discussion, in which the Russian representative declared his Government to be in favor of prohibiting the use of all such new instrumentalities because of their view that the means of destruction at present employed were quite sufficient, the question was also put aside as one for future consideration on the part of the different Powers.

The United States representative made no objection to these questions being considered as remaining open upon the general ground of not offering opposition to desired freedom of discussion, the attitude of the United States in regard to them having, however, been made known by his statement already given.

Bullets

This subject gave rise to more active debate and to more decided differences of view than any other considered by the Sub-Committee. A formula was adopted as follows:

The use of bullets which expand or flatten easily in the human body, such as jacketed bullets of which the jacket does not entirely cover the core or has incisions in it, should be forbidden.

When this subject came up in the Full Committee the British representative, Major-General Sir John Ardagh, made a declaration of the position of his Government on the subject, in which he described their Dum Dum bullet as one having a very small portion of the jacket removed from the point, so as to leave uncovered a portion of the core of about the size of a pin-head. He said that this bullet did not expand in such manner as to produce wounds of exceptional cruelty, but that on the contrary the wounds produced by it were in general less severe than those produced by the Snider, Martini-Henry, and other rifles of the period immediately preceding that of the adoption of the present small bore. He ascribed the bad reputation of the Dum Dum bullet to some experiments made at Tubingen in Germany with a bullet from the forward part of which the jacket, to a distance of more than a diameter, was removed. The wounds produced by this bullet were of a frightful character, and the bullets being generally supposed to be similar to the Dum Dum in construction had probably given rise to the unfounded prejudice against the latter.

The United States Representative here for the first time took part in the discussion, advocating the abandonment of the attempt to cover the principle of prohibition of bullets producing unnecessarily cruel wounds by the specification of details of construction of the bullet, and proposing the following formula:

The use of bullets which inflict wounds of useless cruelty, such as explosive bullets and in general every kind of bullet which exceeds the limit necessary for placing a man immediately *hors de combat*, should be forbidden.

The Committee, however, adhered to the original proposition, which it voted without acting on the substitute submitted.

The action of the Committee having left in an unsatisfactory state the record, which thus stated that the United States had pronounced against a proposition of humanitarian intent, without indicating that our Government not only stood ready to support but also proposed by its representative a formula which was believed to meet the requirements of humanity much better than the one adopted by the Committee, the United States delegate, with the approval of the Commission and in its name proposed to the Conference at its next full session the above-mentioned formula as an amendment to the one submitted to the Conference by the First Committee. In presenting the amendment he stated the objections to the Committee's proposition to be the following: First, that it forbade the use of expanding bullets, notwithstanding the possibility that they might be made to expand in such regular manner as to assume simply the form of a larger caliber, which property it might be necessary to take advantage of, if it should in the future be found desirable to adopt a musket of very much smaller caliber than any now actually in use. Second, that by thus prohibiting what might be the most humane method of increasing the shocking power of a bullet and limiting the prohibition to expanding and flattening bullets, it might lead to the adoption of one of much more cruel character than that prohibited. Third, that it condemned by designed implication, without even the introduction of any evidence against it, the use of a bullet actually employed by the army of a civilized nation.

I was careful not to defend this bullet, of which I stated that I had no knowledge other than that derived from the representations of the delegate of the Power using it, and also to state that the United States had no intention of using any bullet of the prohibited class, being entirely satisfied with the one now employed, which is of the same class as are those in common use.

The original proposition was, however, maintained by the Conference the only negative votes being those of Great Britain and the United States. It may be stated that in taking the vote it was decided to vote first upon the proposition as it came from the Committee, instead of upon the amendment, notwithstanding the strong opposition of the United States and other Powers to this method of procedure as being contrary to ordinary parliamentary usage and preventing an expression of opinion upon the amendment submitted in the name of the United States Commission.

From this report results the advice that, of the two declarations of the Conference originating in the First Sub-Committee of the First Committee, viz: that concerning the use of balloons and that concerning the use of expanding or flattening bullets, the first only be signed by the United States Commission.

The reports of General den Beer Portugael of the work of the Sub-Committee, and of M. de Karnebeek of that of the full First Committee, are hereto annexed and marked respectively "A" and "B."

I am, gentlemen,

Very respectfully, your obedient servant,

WILLIAM CROZIER,
Captain of Ordnance, U. S. A.
Commissioner.

Peace Conference at the Hague 1899:
Report of Captain Mahan to the United States Commission to the International Conference at the Hague, on Disarmament, etc., with Reference to Navies

THE HAGUE, July 31, 1899

To THE COMMISSION OF THE UNITED STATES OF AMERICA TO THE INTERNATIONAL CONFERENCE AT THE HAGUE

Gentlemen: I beg to make the following report concerning the deliberations and conclusions of the Peace Conference on the questions of disarmament, and the limitations to be placed upon the development of the weapons of war, so far as navies are concerned.

Three questions were embraced in the first four articles of the Russian Letter of December 30, 1898, and were by the Conference referred to a Committee, known as the First Committee. The latter was divided into two sub-committees, which dealt with Articles 2, 3 and 4, as they touched naval or military subjects, respectively. The general drift of these three Articles was to suggest limitations, present and prospective, upon the development of the material of war, either by increase of power, and of consequent destructive effect, in weapons now existing, or by new inventions. Article 1, which proposed to place limits upon the augmentation of numbers in the personnel of armed forces, and upon increase of expenditure in the budgets, was reserved for the subsequent consideration of the full Committee.

As regards the development of material, in the direction of power to inflict injury, there was unanimous assent to the proposition that injury should not be in excess of that clearly required to produce decisive results; but in the attempt to specify limitations in detail, insurmountable obstacles were encountered. This was due, partly to an apparent failure, beforehand, to give to the problem submitted that "*etude prealable technique*," a wish for which, expressed by the Conference to the Governments represented, was almost the only tangible result of the deliberations.

Three propositions were, however, adopted: one, unanimously forbidding, during a term of five years, the throwing of projectiles, or explosives, from balloons, or by other analogous methods. Of the two others, one, forbidding the use of projectiles the sole purpose of which was, on bursting, to spread asphyxiating or deleterious gases, was discussed mainly in the naval sub-committee. It received in that, and afterward in the full Committee, the negative vote of the United States naval delegate alone, although of the affirmative votes several were given subject to unanimity of acceptance. In the final reference to the Conference, in full session, of the question of recommending the adoption of such a prohibition, the Delegation of Great Britain voted " No, " as did that of the United States.

As a certain disposition has been observed to attach odium to the view adopted by this Commission in this matter, it seems proper to state, fully and explicitly, for the information of the Government, that on the first occasion of the subject arising in Sub-Committee, and subsequently at various times in full Committee, and before the Conference, the United States naval delegate did not cast his vote silently, but gave the reasons, which at his demand were inserted in the reports of the day's proceedings. These reasons were, briefly: 1. That no shell emitting such gases is as yet in practical use, or has undergone adequate experiment; consequently, a vote taken now would be taken in ignorance of the facts as to whether the results would be of a decisive character, or whether injury in excess of that necessary to attain the end of warfare, the immediate disabling of the enemy, would be inflicted. 2. That the reproach of cruelty and perfidy, addressed against these supposed shells, was equally uttered formerly against firearms and torpedoes, both of which are now employed without scruple. Until we knew the effects of such asphyxiating shells, there was no saying whether they would be more or less merciful than missiles now permitted. 3. That it was illogical, and not demonstrably humane, to be tender about asphyxiating men with gas, when all were prepared to admit that it was allowable to blow the bottom out of an ironclad at midnight, throwing four or five hundred into the sea, to be choked by water, with scarcely the remotest chance of escape. If, and when, a shell emitting asphyxiating gases alone has been successfully produced, then, and not before, men will be able to vote intelligently on the subject.

The question of limiting armaments and budgets, military and naval, likewise resulted in failure to reach an agreement, owing to the extensive and complicated considerations involved. A general wish was emitted that the subject in its various relations might in the future receive an attentive study on the part of the various Governments: and there was adopted without dissent a resolution proposed in the First Committee, in full session, by M. Bourgeois, the First Delegate of France, as follows:
The Committee consider limitation of the military expenditures which now weigh upon the world is greatly to be desired, for the increase of the moral and material welfare of humanity.

This sentiment received the assent of the Conference also.

The military and naval delegates of the United States Commission bore a part in all the proceedings in Sub- and Full Committee; but, while joining freely in the discussion of questions relating to the development of material, reserve was maintained in treating the subject of disarmament and of limitation of budgets, as being more properly of European concern alone. To avoid the possibility of misapprehension of the position of the United States on this matter, the following statement, drawn up by the Commission, was read at the final meeting of the First Committee, July 17, when the report to be presented to the Conference was under consideration:

The Delegation of the United States of America have concurred in the conclusions upon the first clause of the Russian Letter of December 30, 1898, presented to the Conference by the First Commission, namely: that the proposals of the Russian representatives, for fixing the amounts of effective forces and of budgets, military and naval, for periods of five and three years, cannot now be accepted, and that a more profound study on the part of each State concerned is to be desired. But, while thus supporting what seemed to be the only practicable solution of a question submitted to the Conference by the Russian letter, the Delegation wishes to place upon the Record that the United States, in so doing, does not express any opinion as to the course to be taken by the States of Europe. This declaration is not meant to indicate mere indifference to a difficult problem, because it does not affect the United States immediately, but expresses a determination to refrain from enunciating opinions upon matters into which, as concerning Europe alone, the United States has no claim to enter. The words drawn up by M. Bourgeois, and adopted by the First Commission, received also the hearty concurrence of this Delegation because in so doing, it expresses the cordial interest and sympathy with which the United States, while carefully abstaining from anything that might resemble interference, regards all movements that are thought to tend to the welfare of Europe. The military and naval armaments of the United States are at present so small, relatively, to the extent of territory and to the lumber of population, as well as in comparison with those of other nations, that their size can entail no additional burden of expense upon the latter, nor can even form a subject for profitable mutual discussion.
I have the honor to be Your obedient servant,

A. T. MAHAN,
Captain U. S. Navy and Delegate.

Peace Conference at the Hague 1899: Report of Captain Mahan to the United States Commission to the International Conference at the Hague, Regarding the Work of the Second Committee of the Conference.

The Hague, July 31, 1899

To THE COMMISSION OF THE UNITED STATES on AMERICA TO THE INTERNATIONAL CONFERENCE AT THE HAGUE

Gentlemen: I have the honor to submit to the Commission the following report, which I believe to be in sufficient detail, of the general proceedings, and of the conclusions reached by the Second Committee of the Conference, in relation to Articles 5 and 6 of the Russian Circular Letter of December 30, 1898.

In the original distribution of labor of the Conference, Articles 5, 6, and 7, of the said letter, were attributed to the Second Committee. The latter was divided into two Sub-Committees, to one of which was assigned the Articles 5 and 6, as both related to naval matters. Of this Sub-Committee I was a member, and it has fallen to me especially, among the United States Delegates, to follow the fortunes of the two articles named in their progress through the Sub-Committee, and through the full Committee; but not through the smaller special Committee, the *Comite de Redaction*, to which the Sub-Committee intrusted the formulation of its views. Of that *Comite de Redaction* I was not a member.

These two articles are as follows:
5. Adaptation to naval war of the stipulations of the Geneva Convention of 1864, on the base of the Additional Articles of 1868.
6. Neutralization, for the same reason, of boats or launches employed in the rescue of the shipwrecked during or after naval battles.

The general desirability of giving to hospital vessels the utmost immunity, consistent with the vigorous prosecution of war, was generally conceded, and met, in fact, with no opposition; but it was justly remarked at the outset that measures must be taken to put under efficient control of the belligerents all hospitals ships fitted out by private benevolence, or by neutrals, whether associations or individuals. It is evident that unless such control is explicitly affirmed, and unless the various cases that may arise, in which it may be needed, are, as far as possible, foreseen and provided for, incidents may well occur which will bring into inevitable discredit the whole system of neutral vessels, hospital or others, devoted to the benevolent assistance of the sufferers in war.

The first suggestion, offered almost immediately, was that the simplest method of avoiding such inconvenience would be for the said neutral vessels, being engaged in service identical with that of belligerent hospital vessels to which it was proposed to extend the utmost possible immunity, should frankly enter the belligerent service by hoisting the flag of the belligerent to which it offered its services. This being permitted by general consent, and for purposes purely humanitarian, would constitute no breach of neutrality, while the control of either belligerent, when in presence, could be exercised without raising those vexed questions of neutral rights which the experience of maritime warfare shows to be among the most difficult and delicate problems that belligerents have to encounter.

This proposition was supported by me, as being the surest mode of avoiding difficulties easy to be foreseen, and which in my judgment are wholly unprovided for by the articles adopted by the Conference. The neutral ship is, by common consent, permitted to identify itself with the belligerent and his operations for certain laudable purposes: why not for the time assume the belligerent's flag? The reasoning of the opposition was that such vessels should be considered in the same light as national vessels, and that to require them to hoist a foreign flag would be derogatory (*porterait atteinte*) to the sovereignty of the State to which they belonged. This view prevailed.

The first three meetings of the Sub-Committee, May 25, 30 and June 1, were occupied in a general discussion of the Additional Articles of 1868, suggested by the Russian letter of December 30, 1898, as the basis of the adaptation to naval wars of the Geneva Convention of 1864. In this discussion was also embraced Article 6 of the Russian letter, relating to the neutralization of boats engaged in rescuing the shipwrecked (*naufrages*) that is, men overboard for any cause during, or after, naval battles.

At the close of the second meeting it was decided that the president of the Sub-Committee should appoint the *Comite de Redaction* before mentioned. As finally constituted, this *Comite de Redaction* contained a representative from Great Britain, from Germany, from Russia, and from France. At the close of its third session the Sub-Committee was adjourned to await the report of the *Comite de Redaction*. It again assembled and received the reportof June 13; this beingthe fourth meeting of the Sub-Committee.

The *Comite de Redaction* embodied in ten articles the conclusions of the Sub-Committee. The articles were preceded by a lucid or comprehensive report, the work chiefly of M. Renault, the French member of the *Comite de Redaction*. This report embraces the reasoning upon which the adoption of the articles is supported. A copy of the report and of the articles (marked A) accompanies this letter.

Upon receiving the report and the articles, I pointed out to one of the members of the *Comite de Redaction*, that no adequate provision was made to meet the case of men who by accident connected with a naval engagement, such, for instance, as the sinking of their ship, were picked up by a neutral vessel. The omission was one likely to occur to an

American, old enough to remember the very concrete and pertinent instance of the British yacht *Deerhound* saving the men of the Alabama, including her captain, who were then held to be under the protection of the neutral flag. It requires no flight of imagination to realize that a hostile commander-in-chief, whom it has always been a chief object of naval warfare to capture, as well as other valuable officers, might thus escape the hands of a victor.

At the meeting of the Sub-Committee on June 16, I drew attention to this omission when the vote was reached on Article 6, which provides that neutral vessels of various classes, carrying sick, wounded, or shipwrecked (*naufrages*) belligerents, cannot be captured for the mere fact of this transportation; but that they do remain exposed to capture for violation of neutrality which they may have committed. I had then-unaccountably now to myself-overlooked the fact that there was an equal lack of satisfactory provision in the case of the hospital ships under neutral flags, whose presence on a scene of naval warfare is contemplated and authorized by Article 3. It was agreed that I should appear before the *Comite de Redaction*, prior to their final revision of the report and articles. This I did; but after two hours, more or less, of discussion, I failed to obtain any modification in the report or the articles. When, therefore, on the 15th of June, the matter came before the full Second Commission, I contented myself-as the articles were voted only ad referendum-subject to the approval of the Governments- with registering our regret that no suitable provision of the kind advocated had been made.
The matter was yet to come before the full Committee. Before it did so, I had recognized that the difficulty I had noted concerning neutral vessels other than hospital ships might arise equally as regards the latter, the presence of which was contemplated and authorized, whereas that of other neutral ships might very well be merely accidental. I accordingly drew up and submitted to the United States Commission, three additional articles, preceding these with a brief summary of the conditions which might readily occasion the contingency against which I sought to provide. This paper (annexed and marked B) having received the approval of the Delegation, was read, and the articles submitted to the Second Committee in a full session, held June 20, immediately prior to the session of the Conference, at 4 p.m. the same day, to ratify the work of the Committee. The three additional articles were referred to the *Comite de Redaction* with instructions to report to the full Committee. The ten articles were then reported to the Conference and passed without opposition, under the reserve that the articles submitted by the United States Delegation were still to be considered.

Here matters rested for some time, owing, as I understand to certain doubtful points arising in connection with the three proposed articles, which necessitated reference to home governments by one or more of the delegations. Finally, I was informed that not only was there no possibility of a favorable report, nor, consequently, of the three proposed articles passing, but also that, if pressed to a full discussion, there could scarcely fail to be developed such difference of opinion upon the construction of the ten articles already adopted as would imperil the unanimity with which they had before been received. This information was conveyed by me to the United States Commission, and after full consideration I was by it instructed to withdraw the articles. This was accordingly done immediately by letter, on July 18, to Vice-Admiral Sir John Fisher, Chairman of the *Comite de Redaction*, and through him to the President of the Second Commission.

At the subsequent meeting of the full Conference, July 20, the withdrawal being communicated by the President of the Second Committee, it was explained that this Commission, while accepting the ten articles, and withdrawing its own suggested additions, must be understood to do so, not because of any change of opinion as to the necessity of the latter, but in order to facilitate the conclusion of the labors of the Conference; that the Commission were so seriously impressed with the defects of the ten articles, in the respects indicated, that it could sign them only with the most explicit understanding that the doubts expressed before the Second Committee would be fully conveyed to the United States Government, and the liberty of action of the latter wholly reserved, as to accepting the ten articles.

By this course the ten articles, which else might ultimately have failed of unanimous adoption, have been preserved intact, with several valuable stipulations embodied in them. But while there is much that is valuable, it seems necessary to point out to the Commission that to the hospital ships under neutral flags, mentioned in Article 3, and to neutral vessels in certain employments, under Article 6, are conceded a status and immunities hitherto unknown. While this is the case, there is not, in my opinion, in the articles any clear and adequate provision to meet such cases as were meant to be met by the three articles proposed by the Commission, and which are perfectly conceivable and possible. Upon resection I am satisfied that no necessity exists for the authorization of hospital vessels under a neutral flag upon the scene of naval war, and that the adhesion of our Government to such a scheme may be withheld without injury to any one. As regards Article 6, conceding immunities heretofore not allowed to neutral vessels-for the transport of belligerents has heretofore been a violation of neutrality, without reservation in favor of the sick and wounded-it appears to me objectionable and premature, unless accompanied by reservations in favor of the belligerent rights of capture and recapture. These the articles fail to provide explicitly. For these reasons it is my personal opinion that Articles 3 and 6 should not be accepted by the Government of the United States. If the Delegation concur in this view, I recommend that such opinion be expressed in the general report.

I have the honor to be Your obedient servant,

A. T. MAHAN
Captain U. S. Navy and Delegate.

Peace Conference at the Hague 1899: Paper Read by Captain Mahan Before the Second Committee of the Peace Conference on June 20, 1899

It is known to the members of the Sub-Committee, by which these articles were accepted, that I have heretofore stated that there was an important omission, which I desired to rectify in an additional article or articles. The omission was to provide against the case of a neutral vessel, such as is mentioned in Article 6, picking up naufrages on the scene of a naval battle, and carrying them away, either accidentally or intentionally. What, I asked, is the status of such *combattants naufrages*?

My attention being absorbed by the case of vessels under Article 6, it was not until last night that I noticed that there was equally an omission to provide for the status of *combattants naufrauges*, picked up by hospital ships. In order that nonprofessional men, men not naval officers, may certainly comprehend this point, allow me to develop it. On a field of naval battle the ships are constantly in movement; not merely the movement of a land battle, but a movement of progress, of translation from place to place more or less rapid. The scene is here one moment; a half-hour later it may be five miles distant. In such a battle it happens that a ship sinks; her crew become naufrauges; the place of action shifts; it is no longer where these men are struggling for life; the light cruisers of their own side come to help, but they are not enough; the hospital ships with neutral flag come to help; neutral ships other than hospital also arrive; a certain number of combattants naufrauges are saved on board neutral ships. To which belligerent do these men belong? It may happen that the neutral vessel, hospital or otherwise, has been with the fleet opposed to the sunken ship. After fulfilling her work of mercy, she naturally returns to that fleet. The *combattants naufrauges* fall into the power of the enemy, although it is quite probable that the fleet to which they belong -may have had the advantage.

I maintain that unless some provision is made to meet this difficulty, much recrimination will arise. A few private seamen, more or less, a few sub-officers, may not matter, but it is possible that a distinguished general officer, or valuable officers of lower grade may be affected. This will tend to bring into discredit the whole system for hospital ships; but further, while hospital ships, being regularly commissioned by their own Government, may be supposed to act with perfect impartiality, such presupposition is not permissible in the case of vessels named in Article 6. Unless the status of combattants naufrauges saved by them is defined, the grossest irregularities may be expected- the notoriety of which will fully repay the class of men who would perpetrate them.

As many cases may arise, all of which it is impossible to meet specifically, I propose the following additional articles based upon the single general principle that combattants naufrauges, being ipso facto combatants hors de combat, are incapable of serving again during the war, unless recaptured or until duly exchanged.

Additional Articles Proposed By Captain Mahan

1. In the case of neutral vessels of any kind, hospital ships or others, being on the scene of a naval engagement, which may, as an act of humanity, save men in peril of drowning, from the results of the engagement, such neutral vessels shall not be considered as having violated their neutrality by that fact alone. They will, however, in so doing, act at their own risk and peril.

2. Men thus rescued shall not be considered under the cover of the neutral flag, in case a demand for their surrender is by a ship of war of either belligerent. They are open thus to capture, or to recapture. If such demand is made, the men so rescued must be given up, and shall then have the same status as though they had not been under a neutral flag.

3. In case no such demand is made by a belligerent ship, the men so rescued, having been delivered from the consequences of the fight by neutral interposition, are to be considered hors de combat, not to serve for the rest of the war, unless duly exchanged. The Contracting Governments engage to prevent as far as possible, such persons from serving until discharged.

Peace Conference at the Hague 1899:
Report of Captain Crozier to the Commission of the United States of America to the International Conference at the Hague, Regarding the Work of the Second Sub-committee of the Second Committee of the Conference

The Hague, July 31, 1899

COMMISSION OF THE UNITED STATES OF AMERICA TO THE INTERNATIONAL CONFERENCE AT THE HAGUE

Gentlemen: I have the honor to submit a summary of the work appertaining in the first instance to the Second Sub-Committee of the Second Committee of the Conference. This Sub-Committee was charged with the revision of the declaration concerning the laws and customs of war, prepared in 1874 by the Conference of Brussels but never ratified. It is the subject indicated by article number seven of the circular of Count Mouravieff of December 30, 1898. Although the work of the Conference of Brussels was mentioned in this circular, previous publication of a code of what might be called the laws and customs of war had been made in General Order No. 100 issued from the Adjutant-General's Office of the United States Army in 1863, having been prepared by Dr. Francis Lieber of Columbia University. A graceful allusion to this publication and acknowledgment of its value was made by the chairman of the Sub-Committee, M. de Martens of Russia, at one of its sessions.

A code of the "Laws and Customs of War on Land,"[10] comprising sixty articles, was elaborated by the Sub-Committee and by the Conference. This code, if accepted by the United States, would take the place of those portions of the present instructions for the Government of its armies in the field which are covered by its sixty articles. It would not completely take the place of these instructions for the reasons that certain subjects relating to hostilities are omitted therefrom, some because of their delicacy, such as retaliation, and reprisals, etc., others because they relate to the internal administration of an army and to the methods to be used to enforce observation of the code, as by penalties for violations. An important example of this class of omissions is found in Article 46 of the United States instructions (General Order 100) which forbids, under severe penalties, officers or soldiers from making use of their position or power in a hostile country for private commercial transactions even of such nature as would otherwise be legitimate. In regard to the omitted subjects the declaration is made that while awaiting the establishment of a more complete code of the laws of war, populations and combatants remain under the protection and exactions of the principles of the law of nations as it

[10] The links in this document refer to the Code as Completed. Captain Crozier in his discussion of the Code and his comparison of it to General Order No. 100 is using it in its proposed form.

results from established usage, from the rules of humanity, and from the requirements of the public conscience.

The code in general presents that advance from the rules of General Order No. 100, in the direction of effort to spare the sufferings of the populations of invaded and occupied countries, to limit the acts of invaders to those required by military necessities, and to diminish what are ordinarily known as the evils of war, which might be expected from the progress of nearly forty years' thought upon the subject. It is divided into four sections and each of them into several chapters.

Section I, of three chapters, treats of the personnel of the belligerents.
Chapter I, Articles 1 to 30, prescribes what persons are legitimate combatants and has particular reference to levee en masse.

Article 2 represents the extreme concession to unorganized resistance in prescribing as the sole condition of treatment as legitimate combatants of populations of an unoccupied country suddenly invaded, without time for organization, and taking up arms in its defense, to be that they shall observe the laws and customs of war. During the discussion of this chapter an additional article was proposed for adoption by the representative of Great Britain, to the effect that nothing in it should be understood as tending to diminish or suppress the right of the population of an invaded country to fulfill it patriotic duty of offering to the invaders by all legitimate means the most strenuous resistance.

The article was warmly supported by the representative of Switzerland, but was just as decidedly opposed by the representative of Germany. The proposed article was withdrawn by its author, under appeals from delegates favoring its spirit but deeming it superfluous and calculated to endanger the adoption of the portion of the code under consideration. It is the opinion of the United States representative that the withdrawal was wise, in view of the concession in Article 2 of all that is covered by the one proposed.

Chapter II, Articles 4 to 20, treats of prisoners of war.
Article 4 stipulates that their personal property, with the exception of arms, horses and military papers, shall remain in their possession. The case is not specially covered of large sums of money which may be found on the persons of prisoners or in their private luggage, and referred to in Article 72 of General Order No. 100 in such way as to throw doubt upon the strictly private character of such funds.

Article 6 provides, as does Article 76 of General Order 100, that prisoners of war may be required to perform work, but it goes further, in that it covers the fact and the determination of the rate of payment for such work and the disposition to be made of such pay.

Article 77 of General Order No. 100, which provides for severe penalty, even for death, for conspiracy among prisoners of war to effect a united or general escape or to revolt against the authority of the captors, has no counterpart in the new code. Article 12 of the new code provides that in case of breach of parole the offender shall be brought to trial, but it does not prescribe the death penalty as does Article 124 of General Order No. 100.

Articles 14, 15, 16 and 17 are quite new in their scope.
They provide for the establishment of a bureau of information in regard to prisoners of war and prescribe its duties; also for the extension, under necessary guarantees, of all proper facilities to members of duly organized prisoners' aid societies; for franking privileges for the bureau of information; for exemption from postal and customs charges of letters, orders, money, and packages of or for prisoners of war, and of the possible advance to officers of the pay allowed by their Government in such situation, to be afterward repaid by the latter. It will be observed that in case of adoption of the code by the United States, enabling legislation by Congress will be required for the operation of these four articles.
Chapter III, Article 21, treats of the sick and wounded, and it contains only a reference to the Geneva Convention.

Section II, of five chapters, treats of acts of war. Chapter I, Articles 22 and 23, refers to legitimate means of injuring the enemy, to sieges and to bombardments. Article 23 prohibits the issue of the declaration that no quarter will be given, not making allowance for the special case contemplated in Article 60 of General Order No. 100, of a commander in great straits, such that his own salvation makes it impossible for him to encumber himself with prisoners, nor for the retaliatory measures contemplated by Articles 61, 62, 63, and 66 of General Order No. 100. The death penalty prescribed by Article 71 of the Order, for killing or wounding a disabled enemy, is not found among the provisions of the code.

Article 23 also forbids the destruction or seizure of private property except when imperiously required by the necessities of war. During the discussion of this prohibition the United States representative stated the desire of his Government that it should extend to private property both upon land and sea, and that the revision of the declaration of the Conference of Brussels which the Powers had been invited to make, had been understood to properly include this extension, that he could not accept the decision of the chairman that the Sub-Committee was not competent to consider it, because of the limitation of the revision strictly to the subject of land warfare, although he would not insist upon an immediate decision as to such competence, asking simply that the subject be left open for further treatment by the full Committee and by the Conference. The method of after-treatment, by which the subject was relegated to the consideration of a future Conference, is familiar to the Commission.

Article 25 forbids the bombardment of unprotected cities. It was proposed by the Italian representative that the interdiction should extend to bombardment from the sea as well as from the land, but upon the manifestation of opposition to this extension action was limited to the expression of a hope that the subject would be considered by a future conference; the representative of Great Britain abstaining from this expression because of lack of instruction upon the subject.
Chapter II, Articles 29 to 31, treats of spies. It does not prescribe the punishment to be inflicted in case of capture.

Chapter III, Articles 32 to 34, refers to flags of truce.
Chapter IV, Article 35, to capitulations.
Chapter V, Articles 36 to 41,to armistices.

Section III, of a single chapter, Articles 43 to 46, treats of the delicate subject of military authority upon hostile territory. The omission of some of its provisions was urged by the representatives of Belgium, upon the ground that they had the character of sanctioning in advance rights of an invader upon the soil and of thus organizing the regime of defeat; that rather than to do this it would be better for the population of such territory to rest under the general principle of the law of nations. The provisions were retained upon the theory that, while not acknowledging the right, the possible fact had to be admitted and that wise provision required that proper measures of protection for the population and of restrictions upon the occupying force should be taken in advance.

Article 43 is stronger in its terms than Article 3 of General Order No. 100, in requiring respect by the occupying force, unless absolutely prevented, of the laws in force in the occupied territory.

Article 26 of General Order No. 100, in regard to an oath of allegiance and fidelity on the part of magistrates and other civil officers, may require modification in view of Article 45 of the new code, although this may possibly not be necessary as the latter article mentions only populations.

Articles 48 to 54 refer to contributions and requisitions in money and kind; they are more detailed in their provisions than the articles of General Order No. 100 referring to the same subject, but they do not differ therefrom in spirit and general purport. They express the idea that such contributions are not to be made for the purpose of increasing the wealth of the invader. The provision that the shore-ends of submarine cables might be treated in accordance with the necessities of the occupying force and that restitution should be made and damages regulated at the conclusion of peace, after having at first found entry into the code, was afterward stricken out at the instance of the British representative.

Article 46 forbids the seizure or destruction of works of art or similar objects, and is in this respect more restrictive than Article 36 of General Order No. 100, which permits the removal of such articles for the benefit of the Government of the occupying army and relegates the ultimate settlement of their ownership to the treaty of peace.

Section IV, of a single chapter, Articles 57 to 60, treats of belligerents confined, and of sick and wounded cared for, upon neutral territory, a subject not referred to in General Order No. 100. It provides generally that obligation is imposed upon the neutral to see that such persons shall not take further part in the war, but attention was invited by the United States representative to the fact that for sick and wounded simply passing through neutral territory on their way to their own country, no such provision is made. Because of anticipated difficulty in securing harmony or for other reasons the Committee did not decide the question, and a decision was not demanded by the United States representative, who could see no direct interest of the United States in question, which he had raised only in the interest of good work. During the progress of the work of the Sub-Committee expression was made, upon the initiative of the representative of Luxemburg, of the hope that the question of the regulation of the rights and duties of neutrals would form part of the programme of an early conference. Foreign ambassadors, ministers, other diplomatic agents and consuls, whose treatment is regulated by Articles 8, 9 and 87 of General Order No. 100, are not mentioned in the new code. It is also silent upon the subject of guerillas, armed prowlers, war rebels, treachery, war traitors and guides, treated in Sections 4 and 5 of General Order No. 100.

It is not attempted to make this report a full digest of the proposed code or a complete exposition of its relations with the existing instructions for the government of the armies of the United States in the field-the object is to present such general summary as may indicate that the Convention containing the code is a proper one for the Commission to recommend the acceptance of by the Government of the United States, and also that because of the extent and importance of the subject such acceptance should be preceded by a careful examination of the code by the department of Military Law. The agreement in the Convention to issue to the armies of the Signatory Powers instructions in conformity with the code, is not understood to mean that such instructions shall contain nothing more than is found in the code itself, but that all the provisions of the code shall be met and none of them violated in such instructions. A very complete discussion of the articles of the code is contained in the report of Mr. Rolin, the official reporter of the sub-committee, which is hereto annexed and marked C.

WILLIAM CROZIER,
Captain of Ordnance, U. S. A.
Commissioner.

Peace Conference at the Hague 1899:
Report of Mr. White, Mr. Low, and Mr. Holls, to the American Commission to the International Conference at the Hague, Regarding the Work of the Third Committee of the Conference

The Hague, JULY 31, 1899

COMMISSION OF THE UNITED STATES OF AMERICA TO THE INTERNATIONAL CONFERENCE AT THE HAGUE

Gentlemen: The undersigned members of the Third Commission of the Conference, to which was referred the matter of Arbitration and Mediation, have the honor of submitting the following report regarding the work of that Committee:

The Committee on Arbitration was appointed at the second session of the Conference, held May 20, 1899; and on Tuesday, May 23, the Committee met for the first time under the chairmanship of M. Leon Bourgeois of France. It then discussed merely routine business and adjourned until Friday, May 25. At this meeting it was decided to appoint a sub-committee called the Comite d'Examen, to consist of eight members, for the purpose of drafting a plan for International Arbitration and Mediation. The membership of the Comite d'Examen was proposed by the so-called Bureau of the Full Committee, consisting of the President, Honorary Presidents, and the Vice-President, as follows: M. Chevalier Descamps of Belgium, M. Asser of the Netherlands, M. de Martens of Russia, Professor Born of Germany, Professor Lammasch of Austria, M. Odier of Switzerland, Baron d'Estournelles de Constant of France, and Mr. Holls of the United States of America. The Honorary Presidents of the Committee, Sir Julian Pauncefote of England, Count Nigra of Italy, also took part in the work of the Comite d'Examen, as well as the President of the Conference, Baron de Staal of Russia. The Comite d'Examen held eighteen working sessions, all of its members being present at every session, with two exceptions caused by the absence of M. de Martens at the Venezuelan Arbitration in Paris.

On July 7, 1899, the *Comite d'Examen* presented to the full Committee the project for the peaceable settlement of international disputes, which, after discussion in the full Committee and in the Conference, was, on the 25th of July, unanimously adopted. A copy of this convention is annexed to this report. It consists of sixty-one articles, of which the first contains a general declaration regarding the maintenance of peace. Articles 2 to 8 inclusive relate to good offices and mediation; Articles 9 to 14, to international commissions of inquiry; Articles 15 to 20, o arbitral justice in general; Articles 30 to 57, to the procedure before the said court; and Articles 58 to 61, to the ratification of the convention and the like. All of these articles and the considerations which led to their adoption have been carefully discussed, on behalf of the Committee, by its reporter, M. Descamps, whose report is annexed hereto.

At the opening of the first meeting of the Third Committee of the Conference the Russians proposed a carefully-worked-out scheme:

1. For Good Offices and Mediation.

2. For Arbitrations ad hoc, to which was annexed a code for arbitral procedure.

3. For International Inquiries.

Sir Julian Pauncefote having been given the floor as one of the Vice-Presidents of the Conference, at once suggested a vote upon the principle of a Permanent Tribunal for International Arbitrations.

The Russians, thereupon, instantly gave notice that they also had a plan for a permanent Court which would be submitted in due course. It was thought best to discuss the principle of a permanent court only in connection with a careful discussion of definite plans, and it was therefore then resolved to send all plans bearing on this subject to the *Comite d'Examen*, together with the Russian proposals for Good Offices and Mediation.

At the meeting of the Committee, held Wednesday, May 31, the American project for an international tribunal of arbitration was presented, through the President of the Conference, M. de Staal. At about the same time, or just before, the English and the Russian plans for a permanent tribunal were also submitted. In the *Comite d'Examen* the plan proposed by Sir Julian Pauncefote was taken, by the consent of the Russians and Americans, as the basis of the Committee's work. This plan, however, has been greatly modified and enlarged, by provisions from both the American and the Russian plans, and also by suggestions made in Committee. The plan adopted by the Conference, therefore, while founded on the British proposals so far as the form of the Permanent Court is concerned, is really the work of the *Comite d'Examen*.

Compared with the original American project, it differs from it essentially in the following particulars. The fundamental idea of the American plan was a court which should not only be permanent but continuous in its functions, consisting of not less than nine judges, from whose number special benches might be chosen by the litigants; provision was also expressly made for the possibility of a session of the entire tribunal at one time. The latter idea was absolutely unacceptable to most of the Continental States. One objection raised to it was that there had not yet been sufficient experience in arbitrations to warrant a continuously sitting tribunal, so that if one were provided it would probably have nothing to do during the greater portion of the year, and thus become an object of criticism, if not of ridicule. Another objection found expression in the fear that such a tribunal would assume a dignity and importance for which the nations were not yet prepared. The expense involved in the payment of salaries to judges whose time would be taken, was also a consideration of no little importance, and the payment of permanent salaries was looked upon as being likely to emphasize the undesirable spectacle of an international court with perhaps little to do. The plan of Sir Julian Pauncefote happily avoided these difficulties, while it yet provided a permanent court not altogether unlike the Supreme Court of the State of New York, which consists of a comparatively large number of judges who never sit as a body but who are constantly exercising judicial functions, either alone or in separate tribunals made up from among their number. This organization appears in the perfected plan adopted by the Conference.

The American plan further proposed that the tribunal for which it provided should itself appoint its secretary or clerk and supervise the administration of its own bureau or record office. When the idea of a continuously sitting tribunal was abandoned, another method of administration of the bureau or record office was made necessary. Accordingly, the proposal which has been adopted provides that as soon as nine of the Powers who have acceded to this convention have ratified it, the representatives of the signatory powers accredited to the Government of the Netherlands will meet under the presidency of the Minister of Foreign Affairs of the Netherlands and organize themselves as a permanent Council of Administration, whose first duty it will be to create a permanent Bureau of Arbitration. The Council of Administration will appoint a secretary-general, secure quarters for the court and such assistants as may be necessary, in the shape of archivists and other officials who will sit in permanence at The Hague, and who will constitute the working staff and headquarters of the international system of arbitration. The Hague was selected as the seat of the permanent tribunal, by common consent, no proposition or vote favoring any other place having been received.

The American plan provided for one judge from each adhering country. The British proposal suggested two, and on the motion of the German delegate this number was increased to not more than four. The German delegation stated that their reason for proposing a larger number was that the Great Powers, at least, ought, in their opinion, to nominate as members of the tribunal men of eminence, not only in law, but also perhaps a diplomat and perhaps a military or naval expert. The Powers are not restricted to their own citizens in the choice of judges, and two or more Powers may unite in naming the same person. The judges to be named are to hold office for six years, and during the exercise of their functions and when outside of their own country they are to enjoy diplomatic privileges and immunities.

In place of the provision of the American proposal that the tribunal itself should fix its own rules of procedure, the Committee adopted a code of procedure proposed by the Russian delegation, with slight amendments. This code is almost identical with the rules of procedure adopted for the British and Venezuela Court of Arbitration, now in session at Paris. The authors of these rules were, it is understood, M. de Martens, President of the Court, Mr. Justice Brewer of the United States, and Lord Justice Collins of Great Britain.

The provision contained in the American plan that the cases, counter cases, depositions, arguments, and opinions of the court should, after the delivery of the judgment, be at the disposition of any one willing to pay the cost of transcription, was, by common consent, left as an administrative detail for the consideration of the Council of Administration.

The American proposal that every case submitted to the tribunal must be accompanied by a stipulation signed by both parties, to agree in good faith to abide by the decision, which was also a feature of the Russian proposals, was unanimously adopted; as was also the further American proposal that in each particular case the bench of judges should, by preference, be selected from the list of members of the tribunal. The *Comite d'Examen* was unwilling to make a categorical rule, as suggested in the American plan, that when the tribunal consisted of only three members none of them should be a native, subject, or citizen of either of the litigating States, but, on the other hand, the American objector to tribunals consisting of only one representative of each litigating State and one umpire was embodied in the provision that, except in case of an agreement to the contrary, the tribunal should, in all cases, consist of five members, two being nominated by each State, the four to choose the fifth. This enables the parties to have one representative each on the bench, while the majority of the tribunal may, nevertheless, consist of entirely impartial judges, who may not necessarily agree on all points with either side.

The American proposal regarding the expenses of the tribunal, that the judges should be paid only when on duty, was in effect adopted. The American proposal was the only one which contained provision for a second hearing for the correction of manifest errors. This provision was inserted in the code of procedure in a permissive form, after much opposition.

The American proposal that the Convention should be in force upon the ratification of nine States was adopted, but the restriction as to the character of these States, contained in the American plan, was omitted as unnecessary. It is substantially certain that among the first adhering States there will be eight European or American Powers, of whom at least four have been signatory Powers of the Treaty of Paris of 1856. It should be observed here that this description was made a part of the American Plan, only in order to make it clear that in the opinion of the United States Government the confirmation of a certain number of the Great Powers was essential to success.

The one distinctive feature of the American plan which was rejected on principle was that providing for the cooperation of the highest courts of each country in the selection of members of the Court of Arbitration. This idea proved absolutely unacceptable to the Continental Powers for various reasons, which have been stated to the department in our despatch Number 10. There is no highest court for the entire Empire of Austria-Hungary, and the relations between the different parts of the Empire are not calculated to make joint action by the two highest courts practicable or desirable. This is also true of Sweden and Norway. In Russia the highest court consists of a Senate of one hundred members, whose cooperation in the matter of appointment would contradict all local traditions. Besides this, the organization of the courts of nearly all Continental countries is based upon the traditions of the Roman Law, and those traditions always have excluded the idea of any action on the part of a judicial tribunal, with reference to the selection of a man or men for any particular purpose, even if the latter were judicial in its nature. Furthermore, in several large European States, notably Germany, the rules governing the practice of the law are such as to prevent the members of the highest court from having any knowledge of the ability or reputation of many of the most noted lawyers or judges, since no one is allowed to practice before the highest court unless he is a resident of the city of its location, and a member of its particular bar, and the rules providing for appeals are very narrow in their limitations. Under these circumstances, the members of those courts are not, like our Justices of the Supreme Court of the United States, or the members of the Privy Council of Great Britain, the best possible advisers with reference to the selection of creditable legal representatives upon the great tribunal, and it was stated that in many cases they were about the last authority to whom the appointing Power would be likely to turn with success for such advice and cooperation. Under these circumstances, the adoption of this feature of our plan was hopeless from the first; but, out of courteous regard for the United States, the *Comite d'Examen* directed the reporter to mention the importance of a complete disregard of political considerations in the choice of members of the court.

It will be seen that nothing in the proposed plan of organization of the permanent tribunal is absolutely contrary to the fundamental ideas set forth in the American proposal, and the code of procedure contains nothing contrary to the principles of equity pleading in English or American courts. In view of the fact that a large majority of the members of the arbitration Court must necessarily be Europeans trained in the principles of the Roman Law, it has been deemed important from the first to secure all possible guarantees against practice or procedure which would put nations having the Common Law as the basis of their jurisprudence at a disadvantage. It is believed that this end has been successfully accomplished.

Attention is called to the fact that the entire plan for the tribunal and its use is voluntary, so far as sovereign States are concerned. The only seeming exceptions to this rule are contained in Article 1, which provides that the Signatory Powers agree to employ their efforts for securing the pacific regulation of international differences; and Article 27, which says that the Signatory Powers consider it to be a duty, in the case where an acute conflict threatens to break out between two or more of them, to remind those latter that the permanent court is open to them. The obligation thus imposed is not legal or diplomatic in its nature. These articles merely express a general moral duty for the performance of which each State is accountable only to itself. In order, however, to make assurance doubly sure and to leave no doubt whatever of the meaning of the Convention, as affecting the United States of America, the Commission made the following declaration in the full session of the Conference, held July 25:

The Delegation of the United States of America, in signing the Convention regulating the peaceful adjustment of international differences, as proposed by the International Peace Conference, make the following declaration:

Nothing contained in this convention shall be so construed as to require the United States of America to depart from its traditional policy of not intruding upon, interfering with, or entangling itself in the political questions or policy or internal administration of any foreign State; nor shall anything contained in the said Convention be construed to imply a relinquishment by the United States of America of its traditional attitude toward purely American questions.

Under the reserve of this declaration the United States delegates signed the Arbitration Convention itself.

Article 8 of the Convention, providing for a special form of Mediation, was proposed individually by Mr. Holls of the United States Commission. It is fully explained in the report of M. Descamps and in the minutes of the meeting of the Committee at which it was unanimously adopted. Being purely voluntary in its character, it is at least certain that it conflicts with no American interest, while, on the contrary, it is hoped that in particular crises, when the other means provided by the Convention of keeping or restoring peace have failed, it may prove to have real and practical value. It is certain that, by the Continental States of Europe, it has been exceedingly well received.

The Convention for the peaceful adjustment of international differences, if ratified by the Senate, will require no special enabling legislation on the part of Congress, beyond the annual appropriation of a sum sufficient to pay the share of the United States of the expenses of the Arbitration Bureau at The Hague. It is provided that these expenses shall be borne by the Signatory Powers in the same proportion as is now prescribed by the World's Postal Convention, so that the share, even of a great Power, will be very small.

All of which is most respectfully submitted.

ANDREW D. WHITE,
SETH LOW,
FREDERICK W. HOLLS.

CONVENTION (I) FOR THE PACIFIC SETTLEMENT OF INTERNATIONAL DISPUTES (HAGUE I) (29 July 1899)

Entry into Force: 4 September 1900

His Majesty the Emperor of Germany, King of Prussia; [etc.]:

Animated by a strong desire to concert for the maintenance of the general peace;

Resolved to second by their best efforts the friendly settlement of international disputes;

Recognizing the solidarity which unites the members of the society of civilized nations;

Desirous of extending the empire of law, and of strengthening the appreciation of international justice;

Convinced that the permanent institution of a Court of Arbitration, accessible to all, in the midst of the independent Powers, will contribute effectively to this result;

Having regard to the advantages attending the general and regular organization of arbitral procedure;

Sharing the opinion of the august Initiator of the International Peace Conference that it is expedient to record in an international Agreement the principles of equity and right on which are based the security of States and the welfare of peoples;

Being desirous of concluding a Convention to this effect, have appointed as their plenipotentiaries, to wit:

[List of plenipotentiaries.]

Who, after communication of their full powers, found in good and due form, have agreed on the following provisions:

Title I. On The Maintenance of the General Peace

Article 1

With a view to obviating, as far as possible, recourse to force in the relations between States, the Signatory Powers agree to use their best efforts to insure the pacific settlement of international differences.

Title II. On Good Offices and Mediation

Article 2

In case of serious disagreement or conflict, before an appeal to arms, the Signatory Powers agree to have recourse, as far as circumstances allow, to the good offices or mediation of one or more friendly Powers.

Article 3

Independently of this recourse, the Signatory Powers recommend that one or more Powers, strangers to the dispute, should, on their own initiative, and as far as circumstances may allow, offer their good offices or mediation to the States at variance.

Powers, strangers to the dispute, have the right to offer good offices or mediation, even during the course of hostilities.

The exercise of this right can never be regarded by one or the other of the parties in conflict as an unfriendly act.

Article 4

The part of the mediator consists in reconciling the opposing claims and appeasing the feelings of resentment which may have arisen between the States at variance.

Article 5

The functions of the mediator are at an end when once it is declared, either by one of the parties to the dispute, or by the mediator himself, that the means of reconciliation proposed by him are not accepted.

Article 6

Good offices and mediation, either at the request of the parties at variance, or on the initiative of Powers strangers to the dispute, have exclusively the character of advice and never have binding force.

Article 7

The acceptance of mediation can not, unless there be an agreement to the contrary, have the effect of interrupting, delaying, or hindering mobilization or other measures of preparation for war.

If mediation, occurs after the commencement of hostilities it causes no interruption to the military operations in progress, unless there be an agreement to the contrary.

Article 8

The Signatory Powers are agreed in recommending the application, when circumstances allow, of special mediation in the following form:

In case of a serious difference endangering the peace, the States at variance choose respectively a Power, to whom they intrust the mission of entering into direct communication with the Power chosen on the other side, with the object of preventing the rupture of pacific relations.

For the period of this mandate, the term of which, unless otherwise stipulated, cannot exceed thirty days, the States in conflict cease from all direct communication on the subject of the dispute, which is regarded as referred exclusively to the mediating Powers, who must use their best efforts to settle it.
In case of a definite rupture of pacific relations, these Powers are charged with the joint task of taking advantage of any opportunity to restore peace.

Title III. On International Commissions of Inquiry

Article 9

In differences of an international nature involving neither honor nor vital interests, and arising from a difference of opinion on points of fact, the Signatory Powers recommend that the parties, who have not been able to come to an agreement by means of diplomacy, should as far as circumstances allow, institute an International Commission of Inquiry, to facilitate a solution of these differences by elucidating the facts by means of an impartial and conscientious investigation.

Article 10

The International Commissions of Inquiry are constituted by special agreement between the parties in conflict.

The Convention for an inquiry defines the facts to be examined and the extent of the Commissioners' powers.

It settles the procedure.

On the inquiry both sides must be heard.

The form and the periods to be observed, if not stated in the inquiry Convention, are decided by the Commission itself.

Article 11

The International Commissions of Inquiry are formed, unless otherwise stipulated, in the manner fixed by Article 32 of the present convention.

Article 12

The powers in dispute engage to supply the International Commission of Inquiry, as fully as they may think possible, with all means and facilities necessary to enable it to be completely acquainted with and to accurately understand the facts in question.

Article 13

The International Commission of Inquiry communicates its Report to the conflicting Powers, signed by all the members of the Commission.

Article 14

The report of the International Commission of Inquiry is limited to a statement of facts, and has in no way the character of an Arbitral Award. It leaves the conflicting Powers entire freedom as to the effect to be given to this statement.

Title IV. On International Arbitration

Chapter I. On the System of Arbitration

Article 15

International arbitration has for its object the settlement of differences between States by judges of their own choice, and on the basis of respect for law.

Article 16

In questions of a legal nature, and especially in the interpretation or application of International Conventions, arbitration is recognized by the Signatory Powers as the most effective, and at the same time the most equitable, means of settling disputes which diplomacy has failed to settle.

Article 17

The Arbitration Convention is concluded for questions already existing or for questions which may arise eventually. It may embrace any dispute or only disputes of a certain category.

Article 18

The Arbitration Convention implies the engagement to submit loyally to the Award.

Article 19

Independently of general or private Treaties expressly stipulating recourse to arbitration as obligatory on the Signatory Powers, these Powers reserve to themselves the right of concluding, either before the ratification of the present Act or later, new Agreements, general or private, with a view to extending obligatory arbitration to all cases which they may consider it possible to submit to it.

Chapter II. On the Permanent Court of Arbitration

Article 20

With the object of facilitating an immediate recourse to arbitration for international differences, which it has not been possible to settle by diplomacy, the Signatory Powers undertake to organize a permanent Court of Arbitration, accessible at all times and operating, unless otherwise stipulated by the parties, in accordance with the Rules of Procedure inserted in the present Convention.

Article 21

The Permanent Court shall be competent for all arbitration cases, unless the parties agree to institute a special Tribunal.

Article 22

An International Bureau, established at The Hague, serves as record office for the Court. This Bureau is the channel for communications relative to the meetings of the Court.

It has the custody of the archives and conducts all the administrative business.

The Signatory Powers undertake to communicate to the International Bureau at The Hague a duly certified copy of any conditions of arbitration arrived at between them, and of any award concerning them delivered by special Tribunals. They undertake also to communicate to the Bureau the Laws, Regulations, and documents eventually showing the execution of the awards given by the Court.

Article 23

Within the three months following its ratification of the present Act, each Signatory Power shall select four persons at the most, of known competency in questions of international law, of the highest moral reputation, and disposed to accept the duties of Arbitrators. The persons thus selected shall be inscribed, as members of the Court, in a list which shall be notified by the Bureau to all the Signatory Powers.

Any alteration in the list of Arbitrators is brought by the Bureau to the knowledge of the Signatory Powers.

Two or more Powers may agree on the selection in common of one or more Members. The same person can be selected by different Powers. The Members of the Court are appointed for a term of six years. Their appointments can be renewed.

In case of the death or retirement of a member of the Court, his place shall be filled in accordance with the method of his appointment.

Article 24

When the Signatory Powers desire to have recourse to the Permanent Court for the settlement of a difference that has arisen between them, the Arbitrators called upon to form the competent Tribunal to decide this difference, must be chosen from the general list of members of the Court.

Failing the direct agreement of the parties on the composition of the Arbitration Tribunal, the following course shall be pursued:

Each party appoints two Arbitrators, and these together choose an Umpire.
If the votes are equal, the choice of the Umpire is intrusted to a third Power, selected by the parties by common accord.

If an agreement is not arrived at on this subject, each party selects a different Power, and the choice of the Umpire is made in concert by the Powers thus selected.

The Tribunal being thus composed, the parties notify to the Bureau their determination to have recourse to the Court and the names of the Arbitrators.

The Tribunal of Arbitration assembles on the date fixed by the parties.

The Members of the Court, in the discharge of their duties and out of their own country, enjoy diplomatic privileges and immunities.

Article 25

The Tribunal of Arbitration has its ordinary seat at The Hague. Except in cases of necessity, the place of session can only be altered by the Tribunal with the assent of the parties.

Article 26

The International Bureau at The Hague is authorized to place its premises and its staff at the disposal of the Signatory Powers for the operations of any special Board of Arbitration.

The jurisdiction of the Permanent Court, may, within the conditions laid down in the Regulations, be extended to disputes between non-Signatory Powers, or between Signatory Powers and non-Signatory Powers, if the parties are agreed on recourse to this Tribunal.

Article 27

The Signatory Powers consider it their duty, if a serious dispute threatens to break out between two or more of them, to remind these latter that the Permanent Court is open to them.

Consequently, they declare that the fact of reminding the conflicting parties of the provisions of the present Convention, and the advice given to them, in the highest interests of peace, to have recourse to the Permanent Court, can only be regarded as friendly actions.

Article 28

A Permanent Administrative Council, composed of the Diplomatic Representatives of the Signatory Powers accredited to The Hague and of the Netherland Minister for Foreign Affairs, who will act as President, shall be instituted in this town as soon as possible after the ratification of the present Act by at least nine Powers.

This Council will be charged with the establishment and organization of the International Bureau, which will be under its direction and control.

It will notify to the Powers the constitution of the Court and will provide for its installation. It will settle its Rules of Procedure and all other necessary Regulations. It will decide all questions of administration which may arise with regard to the operations of the Court. It will have entire control over the appointment, suspension or dismissal of the officials and employ s of the Bureau.
It will fix the payments and salaries, and control the general expenditure.

At meetings duly summoned the presence of five members is sufficient to render valid the discussions of the Council. The decisions are taken by a majority of votes.

The Council communicates to the Signatory Powers without delay the Regulations adopted by it. It furnishes them with an annual Report on the labours of the Court, the working of the administration, and the expenses.

Article 29

The expenses of the Bureau shall be borne by the Signatory Powers in the proportion fixed for the International Bureau of the Universal Postal Union.

Chapter III. On Arbitral Procedure

Article 30

With a view to encourage the development of arbitration, the Signatory Powers have agreed on the following Rules which shall be applicable to arbitral procedure, unless other rules have been agreed on by the parties.

Article 31

The Powers who have recourse to arbitration sign a special Act (compromis), in which the subject of the difference is clearly defined, as well as the extent of the Arbitrators' powers. This Act implies the undertaking of the parties to submit loyally to the award.

Article 32

The duties of Arbitrator may be conferred on one Arbitrator alone or on several Arbitrators selected by the parties as they please, or chosen by them from the members of the permanent Court of Arbitration established by the present Act.

Failing the constitution of the Tribunal by direct agreement between the parties, the following course shall be pursued: Each party appoints two arbitrators, and these latter together choose an Umpire.

In case of equal voting, the choice of the Umpire is instructed to a third Power, selected by the parties by common accord. If no agreement is arrived at on this subject, each party selects a different Power, and the choice of the Umpire is made in concert by the Powers thus selected.

Article 33

When a Sovereign or the Chief of a State is chosen as Arbitrator, the arbitral procedure is settled by him.

Article 34

The Umpire is by right President of the Tribunal.
When the Tribunal does not include an Umpire it appoints its own President.

Article 35

In case of the death, retirement, or disability from any cause of one of the Arbitrators, his place shall be filled in accordance with the method of his appointment.

Article 36

The Tribunal's place of session is selected by the parties. Failing this selection the Tribunal sits at The Hague. The place thus fixed cannot, except in case of necessity, be changed by the Tribunal without the assent of the parties.

Article 37

The parties have the right to appoint delegates or special agents to attend the Tribunal, for the purpose of serving as intermediaries between them and the Tribunal.

They are further authorized to retain, for the defense of their rights and interests before the Tribunal, counsel or advocates appointed by them for this purpose.

Article 38

The Tribunal decides on the choice of languages to be used by itself, and to be authorized for use before it.

Article 39

As a general rule the arbitral procedure comprises two distinct phases: preliminary examination and discussion.

Preliminary examination consists in the communication by the respective agents to the members of the Tribunal and to the opposite party of all printed or written Acts and of all documents containing the arguments invoked in the case. This communication shall be made in the form and within the periods fixed by the Tribunal in accordance with Article 49.

Discussion consists in the oral development before the Tribunal of the arguments of the parties.

Article 40

Every document produced by one party must be communicated to the other party.

Article 41

The discussions are under the direction of the President. They are only public if it be so decided by the Tribunal, with the assent of the parties. They are recorded in the proces-verbaux drawn up by the Secretaries appointed by the President. These proc s-verbaux alone have an authentic character.

Article 42

When the preliminary examination is concluded, the Tribunal has the right to refuse discussion of all fresh Acts or documents which one party may desire to submit to it without the consent of the other party.

Article 43

The Tribunal is free to take into consideration fresh Acts or documents to which its attention may be drawn by the agents or counsel of the parties. In this case, the Tribunal has the right to require the production of these Acts or documents, but is obliged to make them known to the opposite party.

Article 44

The Tribunal can, besides, require from the agents of the parties the production of all Acts, and can demand all necessary explanations. In case of refusal, the Tribunal takes note of it.

Article 45

The agents and counsel of the parties are authorized to present orally to the Tribunal all the arguments they may think expedient in defence of their case.

Article 46

They have the right to raise objections and points. The decisions of the Tribunal on those points are final, and can not form the subject of any subsequent discussion.

Article 47

The members of the Tribunal have the right to put questions to the agents and counsel of the parties, and to demand explanations from them on doubtful points.

Neither the questions put nor the remarks made by members of the Tribunal during the discussions can be regarded as an expression of opinion by the Tribunal in general, or by its members in particular.

Article 48

The Tribunal is authorized to declare its competence in interpreting the compromis as well as the other Treaties which may be invoked in the case, and in applying the principles of international law.

Article 49

The Tribunal has the right to issue Rules of Procedure for the conduct of the case, to decide the forms and periods within which each party must conclude its arguments, and to arrange all the formalities required for dealing with the evidence.

Article 50

When the agents and counsel of the parties have submitted all explanations and evidence in support of their case, the President pronounces the discussion closed.

Article 51

The deliberations of the Tribunal take place in private. Every decision is taken by a majority of members of the Tribunal. The refusal of a member to vote must be recorded in the proces-verbal.

Article 52

The award, given by a majority of votes, is accompanied by a statement of reasons. It is drawn up in writing and signed by each member of the Tribunal. Those members who are in the minority may record their dissent when signing.

Article 53

The award is read out at a public meeting of the Tribunal, the agents and counsel of the parties being present, or duly summoned to attend.

Article 54

The award, duly pronounced and notified to the agents of the parties at variance, puts an end to the dispute definitively and without appeal.

Article 55

The parties can reserve in the compromis the right to demand the revision of the award. In this case, and unless there be an agreement to the contrary, the demand must be addressed to the Tribunal which pronounced the award. It can only be made on the ground of the discovery of some new fact calculated to exercise a decisive influence on the award, and which, at the time the discussion was closed, was unknown to the Tribunal and to the party demanding the revision.

Proceedings for revision can only be instituted by a decision of the Tribunal expressly recording the existence of the new fact, recognizing in it the character described in the foregoing paragraph, and declaring the demand admissible on this ground. The compromis fixes the period within which the demand for revision must be made.

Article 56

The award is only binding on the parties who concluded the compromis. When there is a question of interpreting a Convention to which Powers other than those concerned in the dispute are parties, the latter notify to the former the compromis they have concluded. Each of these Powers has the right to intervene in the case. If one or more of them avail themselves of this right, the interpretation contained in the award is equally binding on them.

Article 57

Each party pays its own expenses and an equal share of those of the Tribunal.

Article 58
General provisions

The present Convention shall be ratified as speedily as possible. The ratifications shall be deposited at The Hague. A proces-verbal shall be drawn up recording the receipt of each ratification, and a copy duly certified shall be sent, through the diplomatic channel, to all the Powers who were represented at the International Peace Conference at The Hague.

Article 59

The non-Signatory Powers who were represented at the International Peace Conference can adhere to the present Convention. For this purpose they must make known their adhesion to the Contracting Powers by a written notification addressed to the Netherlands Government, and communicated by it to all the other Contracting Powers.

Article 60

The conditions on which the Powers who were not represented at the International Peace Conference can adhere to the present Convention shall form the subject of a subsequent Agreement among the Contracting Powers.

Article 61

In the event of one of the High Contracting Parties denouncing the present Convention, this denunciation would not take effect until a year after its notification made in writing to the Netherlands Government, and by it communicated at once to all the other Contracting Powers.

This denunciation shall only affect the notifying Power. In faith of which the Plenipotentiaries have signed the present Convention and affixed their seals to it.
Done at The Hague, the 29th July, 1899, in a single copy, which shall remain in the archives of the Netherlands Government, and copies of it, duly certified, be sent through the diplomatic channel to the Contracting Powers.
[List of Signatories]

Under reservation of the declaration made at the plenary sitting of the Conference on the 25th of July, 1899

Extract from the proces-verbal:

Nothing contained in this convention shall be so construed as to require the United States of America to depart from its traditional policy of not intruding upon, interfering with, or entangling itself in the political questions of policy or internal administration of any foreign state; nor shall anything contained in the said convention be construed to imply a relinquishment by the United States of America of its traditional attitude toward purely American questions.

Roumania
Under the reservations formulated with respect to Articles 16, 17 and 19 of the present Convention (15, 16 and 18 of the project presented by the committee on examination) and recorded in the proces-verbal of the sitting of the Third Commission of July 20, 1899.

Extract from the proces-verbal:
The Royal Government of Roumania, being completely in favor of the principle of facultative arbitration, of which it appreciates the great importance in international relations, nevertheless does not intend to undertake, by Article 15, an engagement to accept arbitration in every case there provided for, and it believes it ought to form express reservations in that respect.

It can not therefore vote for this article, except under that reservation.
The Royal Government of Roumania declares that it can not adhere to Article 16 except with the express reservation, entered in the proces-verbal, that it has decided not to accept, in any case, an international arbitration for disagreements or disputes previous to the conclusion of the present Convention. The Royal Government of Roumania declares that in adhering to Article 18 of the Convention, it makes no engagement in regard to obligatory arbitration.

Serbia
Under the reservation recorded in the proces-verbal of the Third Commission of July 20, 1899. Extract from the proces-verbal:
In the name of the Royal Government of Servia, we have the honor to declare that our adoption of the principle of good offices and mediation does not imply a recognition of the right of third States to use these means except with the extreme reserve which proceedings of this delicate nature require.

We do not admit good offices and mediation except on condition that their character of purely friendly counsel is maintained fully and completely, and we never could accept them in forms and circumstances such as to impress upon them the character of intervention.

Turkey

Under reservation of the declaration made in the plenary sitting of the Conference of July 25, 1899. Extract from the proces-verbal:

The Turkish delegation, considering that the work of this Conference has been a work of high loyalty and humanity, destined solely to assure general peace by safeguarding the interests and the rights of each one, declares, in the name of its Government, that it adheres to the project just adopted, on the following conditions:

It is formally understood that recourse to good offices and mediation, to commissions of inquiry and arbitration is purely facultative and could not in any case assume an obligatory character or degenerate into intervention; The Imperial Government itself will be the judge of the cases where its interests would permit it to admit these methods without its abstention or refusal to have recourse to them being considered by the signatory States as an unfriendly act.

It goes without saying that in no case could the means in question be applied to questions concerning interior regulation.

Hague II - Laws and Customs of War on Land: 29 July 1899
CONVENTION WITH RESPECT TO THE LAWS AND CUSTOMS OF WAR ON LAND (HAGUE, II) (29 July 1899)

Entry into Force: 4 September 1900

His Majesty the Emperor of Germany, King of Prussia; [etc.]:

Considering that, while seeking means to preserve peace and prevent armed conflicts among nations, it is likewise necessary to have regard to cases where an appeal to arms may be caused by events which their solicitude could not avert;

Animated by the desire to serve, even in this extreme hypothesis, the interest of humanity and the ever increasing requirements of civilization;

Thinking it important, with this object, to revise the laws and general customs of war, either with the view of defining them more precisely, or of laying down certain limits for the purpose of modifying their severity as far as possible;

Inspired by these views which are enjoined at the present day, as they were twenty-five years ago at the time of the Brussels Conference in 1874, by a wise and generous foresight;

Have, in this spirit, adopted a great number of provisions, the object of which is to define and govern the usages of war on land.

In view of the High Contracting Parties, these provisions, the wording of which has been inspired by the desire to diminish the evils of war so far as military necessities permit, are destined to serve as general rules of conduct for belligerents in their relations with each other and with populations.

It has not, however, been possible to agree forthwith on provisions embracing all the circumstances which occur in practice.

On the other hand, it could not be intended by the High Contracting Parties that the cases not provided for should, for want of a written provision, be left to the arbitrary judgment of the military Commanders.
Until a more complete code of the laws of war is issued, the High Contracting Parties think it right to declare that in cases not included in the Regulations adopted by them, populations and belligerents remain under the protection and empire of the principles of international law, as they result from the usages established between civilized nations, from the laws of humanity, and the requirements of the public conscience;

They declare that it is in this sense especially that Articles 1 and 2 of the Regulations adopted must be understood;

The High Contracting Parties, desiring to conclude a Convention to this effect, have appointed as their Plenipotentiaries, to wit:

[List of plenipotentiaries.]

Who, after communication of their full powers, found in good and due form, have agreed on the following:

Article 1

The High Contracting Parties shall issue instructions to their armed land forces, which shall be in conformity with the "Regulations respecting the Laws and Customs of War on Land" annexed to the present Convention.

Article 2

The provisions contained in the Regulations mentioned in Article 1 are only binding on the Contracting Powers, in case of war between two or more of them. These provisions shall cease to be binding from the time when, in a war between Contracting Powers, a non-Contracting Power joins one of the belligerents.

Article 3

The present Convention shall be ratified as speedily as possible. The ratifications shall be deposited at the Hague.

A proces-verbal shall be drawn up recording the receipt of each ratification, and a copy, duly certified, shall be sent through the diplomatic channel, to all the Contracting Powers.

Article 4

Non-Signatory Powers are allowed to adhere to the present Convention. For this purpose they must make their adhesion known to the Contracting Powers by means of a written notification, addressed to the Netherland Government, and by it communicated to all the other Contracting Powers.

Article 5

In the event of one of the High Contracting Parties denouncing the present Convention, such denunciation would not take effect until a year after the written notification made to the Netherland Government, and by it at once communicated to all the other Contracting Powers. This denunciation shall affect only the notifying Power.

In faith of which the Plenipotentiaries have signed the present Convention and affixed their seals thereto.

Done at the Hague the 29th July 1899, in a single copy, which shall be kept in the archives of the Netherland Government, and copies of which, duly certified, shall be delivered to the Contracting Powers through the diplomatic channel.

Annex to the Convention
Regulations Respecting the Laws and Customs of War on Land

Section I. On Belligerents
Chapter I.On the Qualifications of Belligerents

Article 1

The laws, rights, and duties of war apply not only to armies, but also to militia and volunteer corps, fulfilling the following conditions:

To be commanded by a person responsible for his subordinates;
To have a fixed distinctive emblem recognizable at a distance;
To carry arms openly; and
To conduct their operations in accordance with the laws and customs of war.
In countries where militia or volunteer corps constitute the army, or form part of it, they are included under the denomination "army."

Article 2

The population of a territory which has not been occupied who, on the enemy's approach, spontaneously take up arms to resist the invading troops without having time to organize themselves in accordance with Article 1, shall be regarded a belligerent, if they respect the laws and customs of war.

Article 3

The armed forces of the belligerent parties may consist of combatants and non-combatants. In case of capture by the enemy both have a right to be treated as prisoners of war.

Chapter II.On Prisoners of War

Article 4

Prisoners of war are in the power of the hostile Government, but not in that of the individuals or corps who captured them.
They must be humanely treated. All their personal belongings, except arms, horses, and military papers remain their property.

Article 5

Prisoners of war may be interned in a town, fortress, camp, or any other locality, and bound not to go beyond certain fixed limits; but they can only be confined as an indispensable measure of safety.

Article 6

The State may utilize the labor of prisoners of war according to their rank and aptitude. Their tasks shall not be excessive, and shall have nothing to do with the military operations. Prisoners may be authorized to work for the Public Service, for private persons, or on their own account. Work done for the State shall be paid for according to the tariffs in force for soldiers of the national army employed on similar tasks. When the work is for other branches of the Public Service or for private persons, the conditions shall be settled in agreement with the military authorities. The wages of the prisoners shall go towards improving their position, and the balance shall be paid them at the time of their release, after deducting the cost of their maintenance.

Article 7

The Government into whose hands prisoners of war have fallen is bound to maintain them. Failing a special agreement between the belligerents, prisoners of war shall be treated as regards food, quarters, and clothing, on the same footing as the troops of the Government which has captured them.

Article 8

Prisoners of war shall be subject to the laws, regulations, and orders in force in the army of the State into whose hands they have fallen. Any act of insubordination warrants the adoption, as regards them, of such measures of severity as may be necessary.

Escaped prisoners, recaptured before they have succeeded in rejoining their army, or before quitting the territory occupied by the army that captured them, are liable to disciplinary punishment. Prisoners who, after succeeding in escaping are again taken prisoners, are not liable to any punishment for the previous flight.

Article 9

Every prisoner of war, if questioned, is bound to declare his true name and rank, and if he disregards this rule, he is liable to a curtailment of the advantages accorded to the prisoners of war of his class.

Article 10

Prisoners of war may be set at liberty on parole if the laws of their country authorize it, and, in such a case, they are bound, on their personal honor, scrupulously to fulfill, both as regards their own Government and the Government by whom they were made prisoners, the engagements they have contracted.

In such cases, their own Government shall not require of nor accept from them any service incompatible with the parole given.

Article 11

A prisoner of war can not be forced to accept his liberty on parole; similarly the hostile Government is not obliged to assent to the prisoner's request to be set at liberty on parole.

Article 12

Any prisoner of war, who is liberated on parole and recaptured, bearing arms against the Government to whom he had pledged his honor, or against the allies of that Government, forfeits his right to be treated as a prisoner of war, and can be brought before the Courts.

Article 13

Individuals who follow an army without directly belonging to it, such as newspaper correspondents and reporters, sutlers, contractors, who fall into the enemy's hands, and whom the latter think fit to detain, have a right to be treated as prisoners of war, provided they can produce a certificate from the military authorities of the army they were accompanying.

Article 14

A Bureau for information relative to prisoners of war is instituted, on the commencement of hostilities, in each of the belligerent States, and, when necessary, in the neutral countries on whose territory belligerents have been received. This Bureau is intended to answer all inquiries about prisoners of war, and is furnished by the various services concerned with all the necessary information to enable it to keep an individual return for each prisoner of war. It is kept informed of interments and changes, as well as of admissions into hospital and deaths.

It is also the duty of the Information Bureau to receive and collect all objects of personal use, valuables, letters, etc., found on the battlefields or left by prisoners who have died in hospital or ambulance, and to transmit them to those interested.

Article 15

Relief Societies for prisoners of war, which are regularly constituted in accordance with the law of the country with the object of serving as the intermediary for charity, shall receive from the belligerents for themselves and their duly accredited agents every facility, within the bounds of military requirements and Administrative Regulations, for the effective accomplishment of their humane task. Delegates of these Societies may be admitted to the places of interment for the distribution of relief, as also to the halting places of repatriated prisoners, if furnished with a personal permit by the military authorities, and on giving an engagement in writing to comply with all their Regulations for order and police.

Article 16

The Information Bureau shall have the privilege of free postage. Letters, money orders, and valuables, as well as postal parcels destined for the prisoners of war or dispatched by them, shall be free of all postal duties both in the countries of origin and destination, as well as in those they pass through. Gifts and relief in kind for prisoners of war shall be admitted free of all duties of entry and others, as well as of payments for carriage by the Government railways.

Article 17

Officers taken prisoners may receive, if necessary, the full pay allowed them in this position by their country's regulations, the amount to be repaid by their Government.

Article 18

Prisoners of war shall enjoy every latitude in the exercise of their religion, including attendance at their own church services, provided only they comply with the regulations for order and police issued by the military authorities.

Article 19

The wills of prisoners of war are received or drawn up on the same conditions as for soldiers of the National Army.

The same rules shall be observed regarding death certificates, as well as for the burial of prisoners of war, due regard being paid to their grade and rank.

Article 20

After the conclusion of peace, the repatriation of prisoners of war shall take place as speedily as possible.

Chapter III. On the Sick and Wounded

Article 21

The obligations of belligerents with regard to the sick and wounded are governed by the Geneva Convention of the 22nd August, 1864, subject to any modifications which may be introduced into it.

Section II. On Hostilities

Chapter I. On means of injuring the Enemy, Sieges, and Bombardments

Article 22

The right of belligerents to adopt means of injuring the enemy is not unlimited.

Article 23

Besides the prohibitions provided by special Conventions, it is especially prohibited:

To employ poison or poisoned arms;
To kill or wound treacherously individuals belonging to the hostile nation or army;
To kill or wound an enemy who, having laid down arms, or having no longer means of defence, has surrendered at discretion;
To declare that no quarter will be given;
To employ arms, projectiles, or material of a nature to cause superfluous injury;
To make improper use of a flag of truce, the national flag, or military ensigns and the enemy's uniform, as well as the distinctive badges of the Geneva Convention;
To destroy or seize the enemy's property, unless such destruction or seizure be imperatively demanded by the necessities of war.

Article 24

Ruses of war and the employment of methods necessary to obtain information about the enemy and the country, are considered allowable.

Article 25

The attack or bombardment of towns, villages, habitations or buildings which are not defended, is prohibited.

Article 26

The Commander of an attacking force, before commencing a bombardment, except in the case of an assault, should do all he can to warn the authorities.

Article 27

In sieges and bombardments all necessary steps should be taken to spare as far as possible edifices devoted to religion, art, science, and charity, hospitals, and places where the sick and wounded are collected, provided they are not used at the same time for military purposes.

The besieged should indicate these buildings or places by some particular and visible signs, which should previously be notified to the assailants.

Article 28

The pillage of a town or place, even when taken by assault, is prohibited.

Chapter II. On Spies

Article 29

An individual can only be considered a spy if, acting clandestinely, or on false pretences, he obtains, or seeks to obtain information in the zone of operations of a belligerent, with the intention of communicating it to the hostile party.

Thus, soldiers not in disguise who have penetrated into the zone of operations of a hostile army to obtain information are not considered spies. Similarly, the following are not considered spies: soldiers or civilians, carrying out their mission openly, charged with the delivery of despatches destined either for their own army or for that of the enemy. To this class belong likewise individuals sent in balloons to deliver despatches, and generally to maintain communication between the various parts of an army or a territory.

Article 30

A spy taken in the act cannot be punished without previous trial.

Article 31

A spy who, after rejoining the army to which he belongs, is subsequently captured by the enemy, is treated as a prisoner of war, and incurs no responsibility for his previous acts of espionage.

Chapter III. On Flags of Truce

Article 32

An individual is considered a parlementaire who is authorized by one of the belligerents to enter into communication with the other, and who carries a white flag. He has a right to inviolability, as well as the trumpeter, bugler, or drummer, the flag-bearer, and the interpreter who may accompany him.

Article 33

The Chief to whom a flag of truce is sent is not obliged to receive it in all circumstances. He can take all steps necessary to prevent the envoy taking advantage of his mission to obtain information. In case of abuse, he has the right to detain the envoy temporarily.

Article 34

The envoy loses his rights of inviolability if it is proved beyond doubt that he has taken advantage of his privileged position to provoke or commit an act of treachery.

Chapter IV. On Capitulations

Article 35

Capitulations agreed on between the Contracting Parties must be in accordance with the rules of military honor.
When once settled, they must be scrupulously observed by both the parties.

Chapter V. On Armistices

Article 36

An armistice suspends military operations by mutual agreement between the belligerent parties. If its duration is not fixed, the belligerent parties can resume operations at any time, provided always the enemy is warned within the time agreed upon, in accordance with the terms of the armistice.

Article 37

An armistice may be general or local. The first suspends all military operations of the belligerent States; the second, only those between certain fractions of the belligerent armies and in a fixed radius.

Article 38

An armistice must be notified officially, and in good time, to the competent authorities and the troops. Hostilities are suspended immediately after the notification, or at a fixed date.

Article 39

It is for the Contracting Parties to settle, in the terms of the armistice, what communications may be held, on the theatre of war, with the population and with each other.

Article 40

Any serious violation of the armistice by one of the parties gives the other party the right to denounce it, and even, in case of urgency, to recommence hostilities at once.

Article 41

A violation of the terms of the armistice by private individuals acting on their own initiative, only confers the right of demanding the punishment of the offenders, and, if necessary, indemnity for the losses sustained.

Section III. On Military Authority Over Hostile Territory

Territory is considered occupied when it is actually placed under the authority of the hostile army. The occupation applies only to the territory where such authority is established, and in a position to assert itself.

Article 43

The authority of the legitimate power having actually passed into the hands of the occupant, the latter shall take all steps in his power to re-establish and insure, as far as possible, public order and safety, while respecting, unless absolutely prevented, the laws in force in the country.

Article 44

Any compulsion of the population of occupied territory to take part in military operations against its own country is prohibited.

Article 45

Any pressure on the population of occupied territory to take the oath to the hostile Power is prohibited.

Article 46

Family honors and rights, individual lives and private property, as well as religious convictions and liberty, must be respected. Private property cannot be confiscated.

Article 47

Pillage is formally prohibited.

Article 48

If, in the territory occupied, the occupant collects the taxes, dues, and tolls imposed for the benefit of the State, he shall do it, as far as possible, in accordance with the rules in existence and the assessment in force, and will in consequence be bound to defray the expenses of the administration of the occupied territory on the same scale as that by which the legitimate Government was bound.

Article 49

If, besides the taxes mentioned in the preceding Article, the occupant levies other money taxes in the occupied territory, this can only be for military necessities or the administration of such territory.

Article 50

No general penalty, pecuniary or otherwise, can be inflicted on the population on account of the acts of individuals for which it cannot be regarded as collectively responsible.

Article 51

No tax shall be collected except under a written order and on the responsibility of a Commander-in-Chief.

This collection shall only take place, as far as possible, in accordance with the rules in existence and the assessment of taxes in force.
For every payment a receipt shall be given to the taxpayer.

Article 52

Neither requisitions in kind nor services can be demanded from communes or inhabitants except for the necessities of the army of occupation. They must be in proportion to the resources of the country, and of such a nature as not to involve the population in the obligation of taking part in military operations against their country.

These requisitions and services shall only be demanded on the authority of the Commander in the locality occupied. The contributions in kind shall, as far as possible, be paid for in ready money; if not, their receipt shall be acknowledged.

Article 53

An army of occupation can only take possession of the cash, funds, and property liable to requisition belonging strictly to the State, depots of arms, means of transport, stores and supplies, and, generally, all movable property of the State which may be used for military operations.

Railway plant, land telegraphs, telephones, steamers, and other ships, apart from cases governed by maritime law, as well as depots of arms and, generally, all kinds of war material, even though belonging to Companies or to private persons, are likewise material which may serve for military operations, but they must be restored at the conclusion of peace, and indemnities paid for them.

Article 54

The plant of railways coming from neutral States, whether the property of those States, or of Companies, or of private persons, shall be sent back to them as soon as possible.

Article 55

The occupying State shall only be regarded as administrator and usufructuary of the public buildings, real property, forests, and agricultural works belonging to the hostile State, and situated in the occupied country. It must protect the capital of these properties, and administer it according to the rules of usufruct.

Article 56

The property of the communes, that of religious, charitable, and educational institutions, and those of arts and science, even when State property, shall be treated as private property.

All seizure of, and destruction, or intentional damage done to such institutions, to historical monuments, works of art or science, is prohibited, and should be made the subject of proceedings.

Section IV. On the Internment of Belligerents and the Care of the Wounded in Neutral Countries

Article 57

A neutral State which receives in its territory troops belonging to the belligerent armies shall intern them, as far as possible, at a distance from the theatre of war.
It can keep them in camps, and even confine them in fortresses or locations assigned for this purpose.

It shall decide whether officers may be left at liberty on giving their parole that they will not leave the neutral territory without authorization.

Article 58

Failing a special Convention, the neutral State shall supply the interned with the food, clothing, and relief required by humanity. At the conclusion of peace, the expenses caused by the internment shall be made good.

Article 59

A neutral State may authorize the passage through its territory of wounded or sick belonging to the belligerent armies, on condition that the trains bringing them shall carry neither combatants nor war material. In such a case, the neutral State is bound to adopt such measures of safety and control as may be necessary for the purpose.

Wounded and sick brought under these conditions into neutral territory by one of the belligerents, and belonging to the hostile party, must be guarded by the neutral State, so as to insure their not taking part again in the military operations. The same duty shall devolve on the neutral State with regard to wounded or sick of the other army who may be committed to its care.

Article 60

The Geneva Convention applies to sick and wounded interned in neutral territory.

Hague III - Adaptation to Maritime Warfare of Principles of Geneva Convention of 1864: July 29, 1899

Convention signed at The Hague July 29,1899; Senate advice and consent to ratification May 4, 1900; Ratified by the President of the United States August 3, 1900; Proces-verbal of first deposit of ratifications (including that of the United States) at The Hague dated September 4, 1900; Entered into force September 4, 1900; Proclaimed by the President of the United States November 1, 1901; Replaced by convention of October 18, 1907, on the same subject, as between contracting parties to the later convention.

CONVENTION FOR THE ADAPTATION TO MARITIME WARFARE OF THE PRINCIPLES OF THE GENEVA CONVENTION OF AUGUST 22, 1864

His Majesty the Emperor of Germany, King of Prussia; His Majesty the Emperor of Austria, King of Bohemia etc., and Apostolic King of Hungary; His Majesty the King of the Belgians; His Majesty the Emperor of China; His Majesty the King of Denmark; His Majesty the King of Spain and in His Name Her Majesty the Queen Regent of the Kingdom; the President of the United States of America; the President of the United Mexican States; the President of the French Republic; Her Majesty the Queen of the United Kingdom of Great Britain and Ireland, Empress of India; His Majesty the King of the Hellenes; His Majesty the King of Italy; His Majesty the Emperor of Japan; His Royal Highness the Grand Duke of Luxemburg, Duke of Nassau; His Highness the Prince of Montenegro; Her Majesty the Queen of the Netherlands; His Imperial Majesty the Shah of Persia; His Majesty the King of Portugal and of the Algarves etc.; His Majesty the King of Roumania; His Majesty the Emperor of all the Russias; His Majesty the King of Servia; His Majesty the King of Siam; His Majesty the King of Sweden and Norway; the Swiss Federal Council; His Majesty the Emperor of the Ottomans and His Royal Highness the Prince of Bulgaria.

Alike animated by the desire to diminish, as far as depends on them the evils inseparable from warfare, and wishing with this object to adapt to maritime warfare the principles of the Geneva Convention of the 22nd August, 1864,2 have decided to conclude a convention to this effect:

They have, in consequence, appointed as their Plenipotentiaries, to wit:
[List of Plenipotentiaries]
Who, after communication of their full powers, found in good and due form, have agreed on the following provisions:

Article 1

Military hospital ships, that is to say, ships constructed or assigned by States specially and solely for the purpose of assisting the wounded, sick or shipwrecked, and the names of which shall have been communicated to the belligerent Powers at the beginning or during the course of hostilities, and in any case before they are employed, shall be respected and cannot be captured while hostilities last.

These ships, moreover, are not on the same footing as men-of-war as regards their stay in a neutral port.

Article 2

Hospital ships, equipped wholly or in part at the cost of private individuals or officially recognized relief Societies, shall likewise be respected and exempt from capture, provided the belligerent Power to whom they belong has given them an official commission and has notified their names to the hostile Power at the commencement of or during hostilities, and in any case before they are employed.

These ships should be furnished with a certificate from the competent authorities, declaring that they had been under their control while fitting out and on final departure.

Article 3

Hospital-ships, equipped wholly or in part at the cost of private individuals or officially recognized Societies of neutral countries, shall be respected and exempt from capture, if the neutral Power to whom they belong has given them an official commission and notified their names to the belligerent powers at the commencement of or during hostilities, and in any case before they are employed.

Article 4

The ships mentioned in Articles 1, 2, and 3 shall afford relief and assistance to the wounded, sick, and shipwrecked of the belligerents independently of their nationality.

The Governments engage not to use these ships for any military purpose. These ships must not in any way hamper the movements of the combatants. During and after an engagement they will act at their own risk and peril. The belligerents will have the right to control and visit them; they can refuse to help them, order them off, make them take a certain course, and put a Commissioner on board; they can even detain them, if important circumstances require it. As far as possible the belligerents shall inscribe in the sailing papers of the hospital-ships the orders they give them.

Article 5

The military hospital-ships shall be distinguished by being painted white outside with a horizontal band of green about a metre and a half in breadth.

The ships mentioned in Articles 2 and 3 shall be distinguished by being painted white outside with a horizontal band of red about a metre and a half in breadth.
The boats of the ships above mentioned, as also small craft which may be used for hospital work, shall be distinguished by similar painting. All hospital ships shall make themselves known by hoisting, together with their national flag, the white flag with a red cross provided by the Geneva Convention.

Article 6

Neutral merchantmen, yachts, or vessels, having, or taking on board, sick, wounded, or shipwrecked of the belligerents, cannot be captured for so doing, but they are liable to capture for any violation of neutrality they may have committed.

Article 7

The religious, medical, or hospital staff of any captured ship is inviolable, and its members cannot be made prisoners of war. On leaving the ship they take with them the objects and surgical instruments which are their own private property.
This staff shall continue to discharge its duties while necessary, and can afterwards leave when the Commander-in-Chief considers it possible.

The belligerents must guarantee to the staff that has fallen into their hands the enjoyment of their salaries intact.

Article 8

Sailors and soldiers who are taken on board when sick or wounded, to whatever nation they belong, shall be protected and looked after by the captors.

Article 9

The shipwrecked, wounded, or sick of one of the belligerents who fall into the hands of the other, are prisoners of war. The captor must decide, according to circumstances, if it is best to keep them or send them to a port of his own country, to a neutral port, or even to a hostile port. In the last case, prisoners thus repatriated cannot serve as long as the war lasts.

Article 10

(Excluded)[11]

Article 11

The rules contained in the above Articles are binding only on the Contracting Powers, in case of war between two or more of them. The said rules shall cease to be binding from the time when, in a war between the Contracting Powers, one of the belligerents is joined by a non-Contracting Power.

Article 12

The present Convention shall be ratified as soon as possible. The ratifications shall be deposited at The Hague. On the receipt of each ratification a proces-verbal shall be drawn up, a copy of which, duly certified, shall be sent through the diplomatic channel to all the Contracting Powers.

Article 13

The non-Signatory Powers who accepted the Geneva Convention of the 22nd August, 1864, are allowed to adhere to the present Convention. For this purpose they must make their adhesion known to the Contracting. Powers by means of a written notification addressed to the Netherlands Government, and by it communicated to all the other Contracting Powers.

Article 14

In the event of one of the High Contracting Parties denouncing the present Convention, such denunciation shall not take effect until a year after the notification made in writing to the Netherlands Government, and forthwith communicated by it to all the other Contracting Powers.

This denunciation shall only affect the notifying Power. In testimony whereof the respective Plenipotentiaries have signed the present Convention and affixed their seals thereto.

Done at The Hague the 29th July, 1899, in single copy, which shall be kept in the archives of the Government of the Netherlands, and copies of which duly certified, shall be sent through the diplomatic channel to the Contracting Powers.
[Signatures of the Plenipotentiaries]

---

[11] In the original French this article was identical with art. 15 of the convention of Oct. 18, 1907 (TS 543), post, p. 705.

Hague IV - Prohibiting Launching of Projectiles and Explosives from Balloons : July 29, 1899

Declaration signed at The Hague July 29, 1899; Senate advice and consent to ratification February 5, 1900; Ratified by the President of the United States April 7, 1900; Proces-verbal of first deposit of ratifications (including that of the United States) at The Hague dated September 4, 1900; Entered into force September 4, 1900; Proclaimed by the President of the United States November 1, 1901; Expired September 4, 1905; a new declaration on the same subject was signed on October 18, 1907.

Declaration

The Undersigned, Plenipotentiaries of the Powers represented at the International Peace Conference at The Hague, duly authorized to that effect by their Governments, inspired by the sentiments which found expression in the Declaration of St. Petersburg of the 29th November (11th December), 1868,

Declare that:
The Contracting Powers agree to prohibit, for a term of five years, the launching of projectiles and explosives from balloons, or by other new methods of similar nature.

The present Declaration is only binding on the Contracting Powers in case of war between two or more of them. It shall cease to be binding from the time when, in a war between the Contracting Powers, one of the belligerents is joined by a non-Contracting Power. The present Declaration shall be ratified as soon as possible. The ratifications shall be deposited at The Hague.

A proces-verbal shall be drawn up on the receipt of each ratification, of which a copy, duly certified, shall be sent through the diplomatic channel to all the Contracting Powers. The non-Signatory Powers may adhere to the present Declaration. For this purpose they must make their adhesion known to the Contracting Powers by means of a written notification addressed to the Netherlands Government, and by it forthwith communicated to all the other Contracting Powers.

In the event of one of the High Contracting Parties denouncing the present Declaration, such denunciation shall not take effect until a year after the notification made in writing to the Netherlands Government, and by it forthwith communicated to all the other Contracting Powers. This denunciation shall only affect the notifying Power.

In faith of which the Plenipotentiaries have signed the present Declaration, and affixed their seals thereto.

Done at The Hague the 29th July, 1899, in a single copy, which shall be kept in the archives of the Netherlands Government, and of which copies, duly certified, shall be sent through the diplomatic channel to the Contracting Powers.
[Signatures of Plenipotentiaries]

Declaration I - on the Launching of Projectiles and Explosives from Balloons; July 29, 1899

The Undersigned, Plenipotentiaries of the Powers represented at the International Peace Conference at The Hague, duly authorized to that effect by their Governments,

Inspired by the sentiments which found expression in the Declaration of St. Petersburg of the 29th November (11th December), 1868,

Declare that:

The Contracting Powers agree to prohibit, for a term of five years, the launching of projectiles and explosives from balloons, or by other new methods of a similar nature.

The present Declaration is only binding on the Contracting Powers in case of war between two or more of them.

It shall cease to be binding from the time when, in a war between the Contracting Powers, one of the belligerents is joined by a non-Contracting Power.

The present Declaration shall be ratified as soon as possible. The ratifications shall be deposited at The Hague.

A proces-verbal shall be drawn up on the receipt of each ratification, of which a copy, duly certified, shall be sent through the diplomatic channel to all the Contracting Powers. The non-Signatory Powers may adhere to the present Declaration. For this purpose they must make their adhesions known to the Contracting Powers by means of a written notification addressed to the Netherlands Government, and communicated by it to all the other Contracting Powers.

In the event of one of the High Contracting Parties denouncing the present Declaration, such denunciation shall not take effect until a year after the notification made in writing to the Netherlands Government, and by it forthwith communicated to all the other Contracting Powers.

Thus denunciation shall only affect the notifying Power.

In faith of which the Plenipotentiaries have signed the present Declaration, and affixed their seals thereto.

Done at The Hague the 29th July, 1899, in a single copy, which shall be kept in the archives of the Netherlands Government, and of which copies, duly certified, shall be sent through the diplomatic channel to the Contracting Powers.

Declaration II - on the Use of Projectiles the Object of Which is the Diffusion of Asphyxiating or Deleterious Gases; July 29, 1899

The Undersigned, Plenipotentiaries of the Powers represented at the International Peace Conference at The Hague, duly authorized to that effect by their Governments,

Inspired by the sentiments which found expression in the Declaration of St. Petersburg of the 29th November (11th December), 1868,

Declare as follows:
The Contracting Powers agree to abstain from the use of projectiles the object of which is the diffusion of asphyxiating or deleterious gases. The present Declaration is only binding on the Contracting Powers in the case of a war between two or more of them.

It shall cease to be binding from the time when, in a war between the Contracting Powers, one of the belligerents shall be joined by a non-Contracting Power. The present Declaration shall be ratified as soon as possible. The ratifications shall be deposited at The Hague.

A proces-verbal shall be drawn up on the receipt of each ratification, a copy of which, duly certified, shall be sent through the diplomatic channel to all the Contracting Powers.

The non-Signatory Powers can adhere to the present Declaration. For this purpose they must make their adhesion known to the Contracting Powers by means of a written notification addressed to the Netherlands Government, and by it communicated to all the other Contracting Powers.

In the event of one of the High Contracting Parties denouncing the present Declaration, such denunciation shall not take effect until a year after the notification made in writing to the Government the Netherlands, and forthwith communicated by it to all the other Contracting Powers. This denunciation shall only affect the notifying Powers.

In faith of which the Plenipotentiaries have signed the present Declaration, and affixed their seals thereto.
Done at The Hague, the 29th July, 1899, in a single copy, which shall be kept in the archives of the Netherlands Government, and copies of which, duly certified, shall be sent by the diplomatic channel to the Contracting Powers.
[Signatures]

Declaration III - on the Use of Bullets Which Expand or Flatten Easily in the Human Body; July 29, 1899

The Undersigned, Plenipotentiaries of the Powers represented at the International Peace Conference at The Hague, duly authorized to that effect by their Governments,

Inspired by the sentiments which found expression in the Declaration of St. Petersburg of the 29th November (11th December), 1868,

Declare as follows:
The Contracting Parties agree to abstain from the use of bullets which expand or flatten easily in the human body, such as bullets with a hard envelope which does not entirely cover the core, or is pierced with incisions.

The present Declaration is only binding for the Contracting Powers in the case of a war between two or more of them. It shall cease to be binding from the time when, in a war between the Contracting Parties, one of the belligerents is joined by a non-Contracting Power. The present Declaration shall be ratified as soon as possible. The ratification shall be deposited at The Hague.

A proces-verbal shall be drawn up on the receipt of each ratification, a copy of which, duly certified, shall be sent through the diplomatic channel to all the Contracting Powers.

The non-Signatory Powers may adhere to the present Declaration. For this purpose they must make their adhesion known to the Contracting Powers by means of a written notification addressed to the Netherlands Government, and by it communicated to all the other Contracting Powers.

In the event of one of the High Contracting Parties denouncing the present Declaration, such denunciation shall not take effect until a year after the notification made in writing to the Netherlands Government, and forthwith communicated by it to all the other Contracting Powers.

This denunciation shall only affect the notifying Power. In faith of which the Plenipotentiaries have signed the present Declaration, and have affixed their seals thereto.
Done at The Hague the 29th July, 1899, in a single copy, which shall be kept in the archives of the Netherlands Government, and of which copies, duly certified, shall be sent through the diplomatic channel to the Contracting Powers.
[Signatures]

Final Act of the International Peace Conference; July 29, 1899

The International Peace Conference, convoked in the best interests of humanity by His Majesty the Emperor of All the Russias, assembled, on the invitation of the Government of Her Majesty the Queen of the Netherlands, in the Royal House in the Wood at The Hague on the 18th May, 1899.

The Powers enumerated in the following list took part in the Conference, to which they appointed the Delegates named below:
[List of Plenipotentiaries]

In a series of meetings, between the 18th May and the 29th July, 1899, in which the constant desire of the Delegates above mentioned has been to realize, in the fullest manner possible, the generous views of the August Initiator of the Conference and the intentions of their Governments, the Conference has agreed, for submission for signature by the Plenipotentiaries, on the text of the Conventions and Declarations enumerated below and annexed to the present Act:

I. Convention for the peaceful adjustment of international differences.
II. Convention regarding the laws and customs of war by land.
III. Convention for the adaptation to maritime warfare of the principles of the Geneva Convention of the 22d August, 1864.
IV. Three Declarations:

1. To prohibit the launching of projectiles and explosives from balloons or by other similar new methods.

2. To prohibit the use of projectiles the only object of which is the diffusion of asphyxiating or deleterious gases.

3. To prohibit the use of bullets which expand or flatten easily in the human body, such as bullets with a hard envelope, of which the envelope does not entirely cover the core, or is pierced with incisions.

These Conventions and Declarations shall form so many separate Acts. These Acts shall be dated this day, and may be signed up to the 31st December, 1899, by the Plenipotentiaries of the Powers represented at the International Peace Conference at The Hague.
Guided by the same sentiments, the Conference has adopted unanimously the following Resolution:

" The Conference is of opinion that the restriction of military charges, which are at present a heavy burden on the world, is extremely desirable for the increase of the material and moral welfare of mankind."

It has, besides, formulated the following wishes:

1. The Conference, taking into consideration the preliminary step taken by the Swiss Federal Government for the revision of the Geneva Convention, expresses the wish that steps may be shortly taken for the assembly of a Special Conference having for its object the revision of that convention.
This wish was voted unanimously.

2. The Conference expresses the wish that the questions of the rights and duties of neutrals may be inserted in the programme of a Conference in the near future.

3. The Conference expresses the wish that the questions with regard to rifles and naval guns, as considered by it, may be studied by the Governments with the object of coming to an agreement respecting the employment of new types and calibers.

4. The Conference expresses the wish that the Governments, taking into consideration the proposals made at the Conference, may examine the possibility of an agreement as to the limitation of armed forces by land and sea, and of war budgets.

5. The Conference expresses the wish that the proposal, which contemplates the declaration of the inviolability of private property in naval warfare, may be referred to a subsequent Conference for consideration.

6. The Conference expresses the wish that the proposal to settle the question of the bombardment of posts, towns, and villages by a naval force may be referred to a subsequent Conference for consideration.

The last five wishes were voted unanimously, saving some abstentions.

In faith of which, the Plenipotentiaries have signed the present Act, and have affixed their seals thereto.

Done at The Hague, 29th July, 1899, in one copy only, which shall be deposited in the Ministry for Foreign Affairs, and of which copies, duly certified, shall be delivered to all the Powers represented at the Conference.
[Signatures.]

1907

In the final Act of the Conference in the Hague of 1899 a proposal was made to hold a subsequent Conference to consider matters on which no agreement had been reached. Russia, the leading state at the first Conference had matters of more urgency (war with Japan).[12] So the second conference was called at the suggestion of USA's President Theodore Roosevelt in 1904, but postponed because of the war between Russia and Japan. The Second Peace Conference was held from June 15 to October 18, 1907, to expand upon the original Hague Convention, modifying some parts and adding others, with an increased focus on naval warfare. The British tried to secure limitation of armaments, but were defeated by the other powers, led by Germany, which feared a British attempt to stop the growth of the German fleet. Germany also rejected proposals for compulsory arbitration.
However, the conference did enlarge the machinery for voluntary arbitration, and established conventions regulating the collection of debts, rules of war, and the rights and obligations of neutrals.
The Convention and the Regulations on land warfare were revised at the Second International Peace Conference in 1907. The two versions of the Convention and the Regulations differ only slightly from each other. Seventeen of the states which ratified the 1899 Convention did not ratify the 1907 version (Argentina, Bulgaria, Chile, Columbia, Ecuador, Greece, Italy, Korea, Montenegro, Paraguay, Persia, Peru, Serbia, Spain, Turkey, Uruguay, Venezuela). These states or their successor states remain formally bound by the 1899 Convention in their relations with the other parties thereto. As between the parties to the 1907 Convention, this Convention has replaced the 1899 Convention (see Article 4 of the 1907 Convention).

The Final Agreement was signed on October 18, 1907, and entered into force on January 26, 1910.[13]

In this conference forty-four countries were officially represented and through their delegates took part in the proceedings, contributing in larger or lesser degree to the results reached by this illustrious assembly. The second conference was seen as a failure, with few major decisions. However, the meeting of major powers did prefigure later 20th-century attempts at international cooperation. In general, at the time some even deemed the Hague Peace Conferences of 1899 and 1907 to be failures the goals of arms limitation and an established system of arbitration replacing war in practice failing to be

[12] *Laws of war and international law*, WLP 2002, p. 88.
[13] < http://en.wikipedia.org/wiki/Hague_Conventions_of_1899_and_1907>.

achieved. However, the outcome of the Conferences actually had significant impact on the regulation of (the use of) weapons technology.[14]

Hague I - Pacific Settlement of International Disputes: 18 October 1907
Convention for the Pacific Settlement of International Disputes

His Majesty the German Emperor, King of Prussia; the President of the United States of America; the President of the Argentine Republic; His Majesty the Emperor of Austria, King of Bohemia, etc., and Apostolic King of Hungary; His Majesty the King of the Belgians; the President of the Republic of Bolivia; the President of the Republic of the United States of Brazil; His Royal Highness the Prince of Bulgaria; the President of the Republic of Chile; His Majesty the Emperor of China; the President of the Republic of Colombia; the Provisional Governor of the Republic of Cuba; His Majesty the King of Denmark; the President of the Dominican Republic; the President of the Republic of Ecuador; His Majesty the King of Spain; the President of the French Republic; His Majesty the King of the United Kingdom of Great Britain and Ireland and of the British Dominions beyond the Seas, Emperor of India; His Majesty the King of the Hellenes; the President of the Republic of Guatemala; the President of the Republic of Haiti; His Majesty the King of Italy; His Majesty the Emperor of Japan; His Royal Highness the Grand Duke of Luxembourg, Duke of Nassau; the President of the United States of Mexico; His Royal Highness the Prince of Montenegro; the President of the Republic of Nicaragua; His Majesty the King of Norway; the President of the Republic of Panama; the President of the Republic of Paraguay; Her Majesty the Queen of the Netherlands; the President of the Republic of Peru; His Imperial Majesty the Shah of Persia; His Majesty the King of Roumania; His Majesty the Emperor of All the Russias; the President of the Republic of Salvador; His Majesty the King of Servia; His Majesty the King of Siam; His Majesty the King of Sweden; the Swiss Federal Council; His Majesty the Emperor of the Ottomans; the President of the Oriental Republic of Uruguay; the President of the United States of Venezuela;

Animated by the sincere desire to work for the maintenance of general peace;

Resolved to promote by all the efforts in their power the friendly settlement of international disputes;

Recognizing the solidarity uniting the members of the society of civilized nations;

Desirous of extending the empire of law and of strengthening the appreciation of international justice;

---

[14] K. Dijkhof, War, *Law and Technology*, WLP 2010, p 28.

Convinced that the permanent institution of a Tribunal of Arbitration accessible to all, in the midst of independent Powers, will contribute effectively to this result;

Having regard to the advantages attending the general and regular organization of the procedure of arbitration;

Sharing the opinion of the august initiator of the International Peace Conference that it is expedient to record in an International Agreement the principles of equity and right on which are based the security of States and the welfare of peoples;

Being desirous, with this object, of insuring the better working in practice of Commissions of Inquiry and Tribunals of Arbitration, and of facilitating recourse to arbitration in cases which allow of a summary procedure;

Have deemed it necessary to revise in certain particulars and to complete the work of the First Peace Conference for the pacific settlement of international disputes;

The High Contracting Parties have resolved to conclude a new Convention for this purpose, and have appointed the following as their Plenipotentiaries:
(List of Plenipotentiaries.)

Who, after deposited their full powers, found in good and due form, have agreed upon the following:

Part I. The maintenance of General Peace

Article 1

With a view to obviating as far as possible recourse to force in the relations between States, the Contracting Powers agree to use their best efforts to ensure the pacific settlement of international differences.

Part II. Good Offices and Mediation

Article 2

In case of serious disagreement or dispute, before an appeal to arms, the Contracting Powers agree to have recourse, as far as circumstances allow, to the good offices or mediation of one or more friendly Powers.

Article 3

Independently of this recourse, the Contracting Powers deem it expedient and desirable that one or more Powers, strangers to the dispute, should, on their own initiative and as far as circumstances may alow, offer their good offices or mediation to the States at variance. Powers strangers to the dispute have the right to offer good offices or mediation even during the course of hostilities. The exercise of this right can never be regarded by either of the parties in dispute as an unfriendly act.

Article 4

The part of the mediator consists in reconciling the opposing claims and appeasing the feelings of resentment which may have arisen between the States at variance.

Article 5

The functions of the mediator are at an end when once it is declared, either by one of the parties to the dispute or by the mediator himself, that the means of reconciliation proposed by him are not accepted.

Article 6

Good offices and mediation undertaken either at the request of the parties in dispute or on the initiative of Powers strangers to the dispute have exclusively the character of advice, and never have binding force.

Article 7

The acceptance of mediation cannot, unless there be an agreement to the contrary, have the effect of interrupting, delaying, or hindering mobilization or other measures of preparation for war. If it takes place after the commencement of hostilities, the military operations in progress are not interrupted in the absence of an agreement to the contrary.

Article 8

The Contracting Powers are agreed in recommending the application, when circumstances allow, of special mediation in the following form:

In case of a serious difference endangering peace, the States at variance choose respectively a Power, to which they intrust the mission of entering into direct communication with the Power chosen on the other side, with the object of preventing the rupture of pacific relations.

For the period of this mandate, the term of which, unless otherwise stipulated, cannot exceed thirty days, the States in dispute cease from all direct communication on the subject of the dispute, which is regarded as referred exclusively to the mediating Powers, which must use their best efforts to settle it.
In case of a definite rupture of pacific relations, these Powers are charged with the joint task of taking advantage of any opportunity to restore peace.

Part III. International Commissions of Inquiry

Article 9

In disputes of an international nature involving neither honour nor vital interests, and arising from a difference of opinion on points of facts, the Contracting Powers deem it expedient and desirable that the parties who have not been able to come to an agreement by means of diplomacy, should, as far as circumstances allow, institute an International Commission of Inquiry, to facilitate a solution of these disputes by elucidating the facts by means of an impartial and conscientious investigation.

Article 10

International Commissions of Inquiry are constituted by special agreement between the parties in dispute. The Inquiry convention defines the facts to be examined; it determines the mode and time in which the Commission is to be formed and the extent of the powers of the Commissioners.

It also determines, if there is need, where the Commission is to sit, and whether it may remove to another place, the language the Commission shall use and the languages the use of which shall be authorized before it, as well as the date on which each party must deposit its statement of facts, and, generally speaking, all the conditions upon which the parties have agreed. If the parties consider it necessary to appoint Assessors, the Convention of Inquiry shall determine the mode of their selection and the extent of their powers.

Article 11

If the Inquiry Convention has not determined where the Commission is to sit, it will sit at The Hague.
The place of meeting, once fixed, cannot be altered by the Commission except with the assent of the parties. If the Inquiry Convention has not determined what languages are to be employed, the question shall be decided by the Commission.

Article 12

Unless an undertaking is made to the contrary, Commissions of Inquiry shall be formed in the manner determined by Articles 45 and 57 of the present Convention.

Article 13

Should one of the Commissioners or one of the Assessors, should there be any, either die, or resign, or be unable for any reason whatever to discharge his functions, the same procedure is followed for filling the vacancy as was followed for appointing him.

Article 14

The parties are entitled to appoint special agents to attend the Commission of Inquiry, whose duty it is to represent them and to act as intermediaries between them and the Commission.

They are further authorized to engage counsel or advocates, appointed by themselves, to state their case and uphold their interests before the Commission.

Article 15

The International Bureau of the Permanent Court of Arbitration acts as registry for the Commissions which sit at The Hague, and shall place its offices and staff at the disposal of the Contracting Powers for the use of the Commission of Inquiry.

Article 16

If the Commission meets elsewhere than at The Hague, it appoints a Secretary-General, whose office serves as registry.

It is the function of the registry, under the control of the President, to make the necessary arrangements for the sittings of the Commission, the preparation of the Minutes, and, while the inquiry lasts, for the charge of the archives, which shall subsequently be transferred to the International Bureau at The Hague.

Article 17

In order to facilitate the constitution and working of Commissions of Inquiry, the Contracting Powers recommend the following rules, which shall be applicable to the inquiry procedure in so far as the parties do not adopt other rules.

Article 18

The Commission shall settle the details of the procedure not covered by the special Inquiry Convention or the present Convention, and shall arrange all the formalities required for dealing with the evidence.

Article 19

On the inquiry both sides must be heard. At the dates fixed, each party communicates to the Commission and to the other party the statements of facts, if any, and, in all cases, the instruments, papers, and documents which it considers useful for ascertaining the truth, as well as the list of witnesses and experts whose evidence it wishes to be heard.

Article 20

The Commission is entitled, with the assent of the Powers, to move temporarily to any place where it considers it may be useful to have recourse to this means of inquiry or to send one or more of its members. Permission must be obtained from the State on whose territory it is proposed to hold the inquiry.

Article 21

Every investigation, and every examination of a locality, must be made in the presence of the agents and counsel of the parties or after they have been duly summoned.

Article 22

The Commission is entitled to ask from either party for such explanations and information as it considers necessary.

Article 23

The parties undertake to supply the Commission of Inquiry, as fully as they may think possible, with all means and facilities necessary to enable it to become completely acquainted with, and to accurately understand, the facts in question.
They undertake to make use of the means at their disposal, under their municipal law, to insure the appearance of the witnesses or experts who are in their territory and have been summoned before the Commission.

If the witnesses or experts are unable to appear before the Commission, the parties will arrange for their evidence to be taken before the qualified officials of their own country.

Article 24

For all notices to be served by the Commission in the territory of a third Contracting Power, the Commission shall apply direct to the Government of the said Power. The same rule applies in the case of steps being taken on the spot to procure evidence.

The requests for this purpose are to be executed so far as the means at the disposal of the Power applied to under its municipal law allow. They cannot be rejected unless the Power in question considers they are calculated to impair its sovereign rights or its safety. The Commission will equally be always entitled to act through the Power on whose territory it sits.

Article 25

The witnesses and experts are summoned on the request of the parties or by the Commission of its own motion, and, in every case, through the Government of the State in whose territory they are.

The witnesses are heard in succession and separately in the presence of the agents and counsel, and in the order fixed by the Commission.

Article 26

The examination of witnesses is conducted by the President. The members of the Commission may however put to each witness questions which they consider likely to throw light on and complete his evidence, or get information on any point concerning the witness within the limits of what is necessary in order to get at the truth.
The agents and counsel of the parties may not interrupt the witness when he is making his statement, nor put any direct question to him, but they may ask the President to put such additional questions to the witness as they think expedient.

Article 27

The witness must give his evidence without being allowed to read any written draft. He may, however, be permitted by the President to consult notes or documents if the nature of the facts referred to necessitates their employment.

Article 28

A Minute of the evidence of the witness is drawn up forthwith and read to the witness. The latter may make such alterations and additions as he thinks necessary, which will be recorded at the end of his statement. When the whole of his statement has been read to the witness, he is asked to sign it.

Article 29

The agents are authorized, in the course of or at the close of the inquiry, to present in writing to the Commission and to the other party such statements, requisitions, or summaries of the facts as they consider useful for ascertaining the truth.

Article 30

The Commission considers its decisions in private and the proceedings are secret. All questions are decided by a majority of the members of the Commission. If a member declines to vote, the fact must be recorded in the Minutes.

Article 31

The sittings of the Commission are not public, nor the Minutes and documents connected with the inquiry published except in virtue of a decision of the Commission taken with the consent of the parties.

Article 32

After the parties have presented all the explanations and evidence, and the witnesses have all been heard, the President declares the inquiry terminated, and the Commission adjourns to deliberate and to draw up its Report.

Article 33

The Report is signed by all the members of the Commission. If one of the members refuses to sign, the fact is mentioned; but the validity of the Report is not affected.

Article 34

The Report of the Commission is read at a public sitting, the agents and counsel of the parties being present or duly summoned. A copy of the Report is given to each party.

Article 35

The Report of the Commission is limited to a statement of facts, and has in no way the character of an Award. It leaves to the parties entire freedom as to the effect to be given to the statement.

Article 36

Each party pays its own expenses and an equal share of the expenses incurred by the Commission.

Part IV. International Arbitration

Chapter I. The System of Arbitration

Article 37

International arbitration has for its object the settlement of disputes between States by Judges of their own choice and on the basis of respect for law. Recourse to arbitration implies an engagement to submit in good faith to the Award.

Article 38

In questions of a legal nature, and especially in the interpretation or application of International Conventions, arbitration is recognized by the Contracting Powers as the most effective, and, at the same time, the most equitable means of settling disputes which diplomacy has failed to settle.

Consequently, it would be desirable that, in disputes about the above-mentioned questions, the Contracting Powers should, if the case arose, have recourse to arbitration, in so far as circumstances permit.

Article 39

The Arbitration Convention is concluded for questions already existing or for questions which may arise eventually. It may embrace any dispute or only disputes of a certain category.

Article 40

Independently of general or private Treaties expressly stipulating recourse to arbitration as obligatory on the Contracting Powers, the said Powers reserve to themselves the right of concluding new Agreements, general or particular, with a view to extending compulsory arbitration to all cases which they may consider it possible to submit to it.

Chapter II. The Permanent Court of Arbitration

Article 41

With the object of facilitating an immediate recourse to arbitration for international differences, which it has not been possible to settle by diplomacy, the Contracting Powers undertake to maintain the Permanent Court of Arbitration, as established by the First Peace Conference, accessible at all times, and operating, unless otherwise stipulated by the parties, in accordance with the rules of procedure inserted in the present Convention.

Article 42

The Permanent Court is competent for all arbitration cases, unless the parties agree to institute a special Tribunal.

Article 43

The Permanent Court sits at The Hague. An International Bureau serves as registry for the Court. It is the channel for communications relative to the meetings of the Court; it has charge of the archives and conducts all the administrative business.

The Contracting Powers undertake to communicate to the Bureau, as soon as possible, a certified copy of any conditions of arbitration arrived at between them and of any Award concerning them delivered by a special Tribunal. They likewise undertake to communicate to the Bureau the laws, regulations, and documents eventually showing the execution of the Awards given by the Court.

Article 44

Each Contracting Power selects four persons at the most, of known competency in questions of international law, of the highest moral reputation, and disposed to accept the duties of Arbitrator. The persons thus elected are inscribed, as Members of the Court, in a list which shall be notified to all the Contracting Powers by the Bureau.

Any alteration in the list of Arbitrators is brought by the Bureau to the knowledge of the Contracting Powers. Two or more Powers may agree on the selection in common of one or more Members.

The same person can be selected by different Powers. The Members of the Court are appointed for a term of six years. These appointments are renewable. Should a Member of the Court die or resign, the same procedure is followed for filling the vacancy as was followed for appointing him. In this case the appointment is made for a fresh period of six years.

Article 45

When the Contracting Powers wish to have recourse to the Permanent Court for the settlement of a difference which has arisen between them, the Arbitrators called upon to form the Tribunal with jurisdiction to decide this difference must be chosen from the general list of Members of the Court.
Failing the direct agreement of the parties on the composition of the Arbitration Tribunal, the following course shall be pursued: Each party appoints two Arbitrators, of whom one only can be its national or chosen from among the persons selected by it as Members of the Permanent Court. These Arbitrators together choose an Umpire.

If the votes are equally divided, the choice of the Umpire is intrusted to a third Power, selected by the parties by common accord. If an agreement is not arrived at on this subject each party selects a different Power, and the choice of the Umpire is made in concert by the Powers thus selected.
If, within two months' time, these two Powers cannot come to an agreement, each of them presents two candidates taken from the list of Members of the Permanent Court, exclusive of the members selected by the parties and not being nationals of either of them. Drawing lots determines which of the candidates thus presented shall be Umpire.

Article 46

The Tribunal being thus composed, the parties notify to the Bureau their determination to have recourse to the Court, the text of their `Compromis', and the names of the Arbitrators.

The Bureau communicates without delay to each Arbitrator the '*Compromis*', and the names of the other members of the Tribunal.

The Tribunal assembles at the date fixed by the parties. The Bureau makes the necessary arrangements for the meeting. The members of the Tribunal, in the exercise of their duties and out of their own country, enjoy diplomatic privileges and immunities.

Article 47

The Bureau is authorized to place its offices and staff at the disposal of the Contracting Powers for the use of any special Board of Arbitration. The jurisdiction of the Permanent Court may, within the conditions laid down in the regulations, be extended to disputes between non- Contracting Powers or between Contracting Powers and non-Contracting Powers, if the parties are agreed on recourse to this Tribunal.

Article 48

The Contracting Powers consider it their duty, if a serious dispute threatens to break out between two or more of them, to remind these latter that the Permanent Court is open to them. Consequently, they declare that the fact of reminding the parties at variance of the provisions of the present Convention, and the advice given to them, in the highest interests of peace, to have recourse to the Permanent Court, can only be regarded as friendly actions.

In case of dispute between two Powers, one of them can always address to the International Bureau a note containing a declaration that it would be ready to submit the dispute to arbitration. The Bureau must at once inform the other Power of the declaration.

Article 49

The Permanent Administrative Council, composed of the Diplomatic Representatives of the Contracting Powers accredited to The Hague and of the Netherland Minister for Foreign Affairs, who will act as President, is charged with the direction and control of the International Bureau.

The Council settles its rules of procedure and all other necessary regulations. It decides all questions of administration which may arise with regard to the operations of the Court.

It has entire control over the appointment, suspension, or dismissal of the officials and employs of the Bureau. It fixes the payments and salaries, and controls the general expenditure. At meetings duly summoned the presence of nine members is sufficient to render valid the discussions of the Council. The decisions are taken by a majority of votes.

The Council communicates to the Contracting Powers without delay the regulations adopted by it. It furnishes them with an annual Report on the labours of the Court, the working of the administration, and the expenditure. The Report likewise contains a resume of what is important in the documents comunicated to the Bureau by the Powers in virtue of Article 43, paragraphs 3 and 4.

Article 50

The expenses of the Bureau shall be borne by the Contracting Powers in the proportion fixed for the International Bureau of the Universal Postal Union. The expenses to be charged to the adhering Powers shall be reckoned from the date on which their adhesion comes into force.

Chapter III. Arbitration Procedure

Article 51

With a view to encouraging the development of arbritation, the Contracting Powers have agreed on the following rules, which are applicable to arbitration procedure, unless other rules have been agreed on by the parties.

Article 52

The Powers which have recourse to arbitration sign a '*Compromis*', in which the subject of the dispute is clearly defined, the time allowed for appointing Arbitrators, the form, order, and time in which the communication referred to in Article 63 must be made, and the amount of the sum which each party must deposit in advance to defray the expenses.

The '*Compromis*' likewise defines, if there is occasion, the manner of appointing Arbitrators, any special powers which may eventually belong to the Tribunal, where it shall meet, the language it shall use, and the languages the employment of which shall be authorized before it, and, generally speaking, all the conditions on which the parties are agreed.

Article 53

The Permanent Court is competent to settle the '*Compromis*', if the parties are agreed to have recourse to it for the purpose. It is similarly competent, even if the request is only made by one of the parties, when all attempts to reach an understanding through the diplomatic channel have failed, in the case of:

1. A dispute covered by a general Treaty of Arbitration concluded or renewed after the present Convention has come into force, and providing for a '*Compromis*' in all disputes and not either explicitly or implicitly excluding the settlement of the '*Compromis*' from the competence of the Court. Recourse cannot, however, be had to the Court if the other party declares that in its opinion the dispute does not belong to the category of disputes which can be submitted to compulsory arbitration, unless the Treaty of Arbitration confers upon the Arbitration Tribunal the power of deciding this preliminary question.

2. A dispute arising from contract debts claimed from one Power by another Power as due to its nationals, and for the settlement of which the offer of arbitration has been accepted. This arrangement is not applicable if acceptance is subject to the condition that the *'Compromis'* should be settled in some other way.

Article 54

In the cases contemplated in the preceding Article, the *'Compromis'* shall be settled by a Commission consisting of five members selected in the manner arranged for in Article 45, paragraphs 3 to 6. The fifth member is President of the Commission *ex officio*.

Article 55

The duties of Arbitrator may be conferred on one Arbitrator alone or on several Arbitrators selected by the parties as they please, or chosen by them from the Members of the Permanent Court of Arbitration established by the present Convention. Failing the constitution of the Tribunal by direct agreement between the parties, the course referred to in Article 45, paragraphs 3 to 6, is followed.

Article 56

When a Sovereign or the Chief of a State is chosen as Arbitrator, the arbitration procedure is settled by him.

Article 57

The Umpire is President of the Tribunal *ex officio*. When the Tribunal does not include an Umpire, it appoints its own President.

Article 58

When the *'Compromis'* is settled by a Commission, as contemplated in Article 54, and in the absence of an agreement to the contrary, the Commission itself shall form the Arbitration Tribunal.

Article 59

Should one of the Arbitrators either die, retire, or be unable for any reason whatever to discharge his functions, the same procedure is followed for filling the vacancy as was followed for appointing him.

Article 60

The Tribunal sits at The Hague, unless some other place is selected by the parties. The Tribunal can only sit in the territory of a third Power with the latter's consent. The place of meeting once fixed cannot be altered by the Tribunal, except with the consent of the parties.

Article 61

If the question as to what languages are to be used has not been settled by the *'Compromis'*, it shall be decided by the Tribunal.

Article 62

The parties are entitled to appoint special agents to attend the Tribunal to act as intermediaries between themselves and the Tribunal. They are further authorized to retain for the defence of their rights and interests before the Tribunal counsel or advocates appointed by themselves for this purpose. The Members of the permanent Court may not act as agents, counsel, or advocates except on behalf of the Power which appointed them Members of the Court.

Article 63

As a general rule, arbitration procedure comprises two distinct phases: pleadings and oral discussions.

The pleadings consist in the communication by the respective agents to the members of the Tribunal and the opposite party of cases, counter- cases, and, if necessary, of replies; the parties annex thereto all papers and documents called for in the case. This communication shall be made either directly or through the intermediary of the International Bureau, in the order and within the time fixed by the *'Compromis'*.

The time fixed by the *'Compromis'* may be extended by mutual agreement by the parties, or by the Tribunal when the latter considers it necessary for the purpose of reaching a just decision.

The discussions consists in the oral development before the Tribunal of the arguments of the parties.

Article 64

A certified copy of every document produced by one party must be communicated to the other party.

Article 65

Unless special circumstances arise, the Tribunal does not meet until the pleadings are closed.

Article 66

The discussions are under the control of the President. They are only public if it be so decided by the Tribunal, with the assent of the parties.

They are recorded in minutes drawn up by the Secretaries appointed by the President. These minutes are signed by the President and by one of the Secretaries and alone have an authentic character.

Article 67

After the close of the pleadings, the Tribunal is entitled to refuse discussion of all new papers or documents which one of the parties may wish to submit to it without the consent of the other party.

Article 68

The Tribunal is free to take into consideration new papers of documents to which its attention may be drawn by the agents or counsel of the parties.

In this case, the Tribunal has the right to require the production of these papers or documents, but is obliged to make them known to the opposite party.

Article 69

The Tribunal can, besides, require from the agents of the parties the production of all papers, and can demand all necessary explanations. In case of refusal the Tribunal takes note of it.

Article 70

The agents and the counsel of the parties are authorized to present orally to the Tribunal all the arguments they may consider expedient in defence of their case.

Article 71

They are entitled to raise objections and points. The decisions of the Tribunal on these points are final and cannot form the subject of any subsequent discussion.

Article 72

The members of the Tribunal are entitled to put questions to the agents and counsel of the parties, and to ask them for explanations on doubtful points.

Neither the questions put, nor the remarks made by members of the Tribunal in the course of the discussions, can be regarded as an expression of opinion by the Tribunal in general or by its members in particular.

Article 73

The Tribunal is authorized to declare its competence in interpreting the *'Compromis'*, as well as the other Treaties which may be invoked, and in applying the principles of law.

Article 74

The Tribunal is entitled to issue rules of procedure for the conduct of the case, to decide the forms, order, and time in which each party must conclude its arguments, and to arrange all the formalities required for dealing with the evidence.

Article 75

The parties undertake to supply the Tribunal, as fully as they consider possible, with all the information required for deciding the case.

Article 76

For all notices which the Tribunal has to serve in the territory of a third Contracting Power, the Tribunal shall apply direct to the Government of that Power. The same rule applies in the case of steps being taken to procure evidence on the spot.

The requests for this purpose are to be executed as far as the means at the disposal of the Power applied to under its municipal law allow. They cannot be rejected unless the Power in question considers them calculated to impair its own sovereign rights or its safety. The Court will equally be always entitled to act through the Power on whose territory it sits.

Article 77

When the agents and counsel of the parties have submitted all the explanations and evidence in support of their case the President shall declare the discussion closed.

Article 78

The Tribunal considers its decisions in private and the proceedings remain secret. All questions are decided by a majority of the members of the Tribunal.

Article 79

The Award must give the reasons on which it is based. It contains the names of the Arbitrators; it is signed by the President and Registrar or by the Secretary acting as Registrar.

Article 80

The Award is read out in public sitting, the agents and counsel of the parties being present or duly summoned to attend.

Article 81

The Award, duly pronounced and notified to the agents of the parties, settles the dispute definitively and without appeal.

Article 82

Any dispute arising between the parties as to the interpretation and execution of the Award shall, in the absence of an Agreement to the contrary, be submitted to the Tribunal which pronounced it.

Article 83

The parties can reserve in the '*Compromis*' the right to demand the revision of the Award. In this case and unless there be an Agreement to the contrary, the demand must be addressed to the Tribunal which pronounced the Award. It can only be made on the ground of the discovery of some new fact calculated to exercise a decisive influence upon the Award and which was unknown to the Tribunal and to the party which demanded the revision at the time the discussion was closed.

Proceedings for revision can only be instituted by a decision of the Tribunal expressly recording the existence of the new fact, recognizing in it the character described in the preceding paragraph, and declaring the demand admissible on this ground. The '*Compromis*' fixes the period within which the demand for revision must be made.

Article 84

The Award is not binding except on the parties in dispute. When it concerns the interpretation of a Convention to which Powers other than those in dispute are parties, they shall inform all the Signatory Powers in good time. Each of these Powers is entitled to intervene in the case. If one or more avail themselves of this right, the interpretation contained in the Award is equally binding on them.

Article 85

Each party pays its own expenses and an equal share of the expenses of the Tribunal.

Chapter IV. Arbitration by Summary Procedure

Article 86

With a view to facilitating the working of the system of arbitration in disputes admitting of a summary procedure, the Contracting Powers adopt the following rules, which shall be observed in the absence of other arrangements and subject to the reservation that the provisions of Chapter III apply so far as may be.

Article 87

Each of the parties in dispute appoints an Arbitrator. The two Arbitrators thus selected choose an Umpire. If they do not agree on this point, each of them proposes two candidates taken from the general list of the Members of the Permanent Court exclusive of the members appointed by either of the parties and not being nationals of either of them; which of the candidates thus proposed shall be the Umpire is determined by lot. The Umpire presides over the Tribunal, which gives its decisions by a majority of votes.

Article 88

In the absence of any previous agreement the Tribunal, as soon as it is formed, settles the time within which the two parties must submit their respective cases to it.

Article 89

Each party is represented before the Tribunal by an agent, who serves as intermediary between the Tribunal and the Government who appointed him.

Article 90

The proceedings are conducted exclusively in writing. Each party, however, is entitled to ask that witnesses and experts should be called. The Tribunal has, for its part, the right to demand oral explanations from the agents of the two parties, as well as from the experts and witnesses whose appearance in Court it may consider useful.

Part V. Final Provisions

Article 91

The present Convention, duly ratified, shall replace, as between the Contracting Powers, the Convention for the Pacific Settlement of International Disputes of the 29th July, 1899.

Article 92

The present Convention shall be ratified as soon as possible. The ratifications shall be deposited at The Hague. The first deposit of ratifications shall be recorded in a proces-verbal signed by the Representatives of the Powers which take part therein and by the Netherland Minister for Foreign Affairs.

The subsequent deposits of ratifications shall be made by means of a written notification, addressed to the Netherland Government and accompanied by the instrument of ratification.

A duly certified copy of the proces-verbal relative to the first deposit of ratifications, of the notifications mentioned in the preceding paragraph, and of the instruments of ratification, shall be immediately sent by the Netherland Government, through the diplomatic channel, to the Powers invited to the Second Peace Conference, as well as to those Powers which have adhered to the Convention. In the cases contemplated in the preceding paragraph, the said Government shall at the same time inform the Powers of the date on which it received the notification.

Article 93

Non-Signatory Powers which have been invited to the Second Peace Conference may adhere to the present Convention.

The Power which desires to adhere notifies its intention in writing to the Netherland Government, forwarding to it the act of adhesion, which shall be deposited in the archives of the said Government.

This Government shall immediately forward to all the other Powers invited to the Second Peace Conference a duly certified copy of the notification as well as of the act of adhesion, mentioning the date on which it received the notification.

Article 94

The conditions on which the Powers which have not been invited to the Second Peace Conference may adhere to the present Convention shall form the subject of a subsequent Agreement between the Contracting Powers.

Article 95

The present Convention shall take effect, in the case of the Powers which were not a party to the first deposit of ratifications, sixty days after the date of the proces-verbal of this deposit, and, in the case of the Powers which ratify subsequently or which adhere, sixty days after the notification of their ratification or of their adhesion has been received by the Netherland Government.

Article 96

In the event of one of the Contracting Parties wishing to denounce the present Convention, the denunciation shall be notified in writing to the Netherland Government, which shall immediately communicate a duly certified copy of the notification to all the other Powers informing them of the date on which it was received.

The denunciation shall only have effect in regard to the notifying Power, and one year after the notification has reached the Netherland Government.

Article 97

A register kept by the Netherland Minister for Foreign Affairs shall give the date of the deposit of ratifications effected in virtue of Article 92, paragraphs 3 and 4, as well as the date on which the notifications of adhesion (Article 93, paragraph 2) or of denunciation (Article 96, paragraph 1) have been received.

Each Contracting Power is entitled to have access to this register and to be supplied with duly certified extracts from it.

In faith whereof the Plenipotentiaries have appended their signatures to the present Convention.

Done at The Hague, the 18th October 1907, in a single copy, which shall remain deposited in the archives of the Netherland Government, and duly certified copies of which shall be sent, through the diplomatic channel, to the Contracting Powers.

Hague II - Limitation of Employment of Force for Recovery of Contract Debts : October 18, 1907

Convention signed at The Hague October 18, 1907; Senate advice and consent to ratification, with an understanding, April 17, 1908; Ratified by the President of the United States, with an understanding, February 23, 1909; Proces-verbal of first deposit of ratifications (including that of the United States) at The Hague dated November 27, 1909; Entered into force January 26, 1910; Proclaimed by the President of the United States February 28, 1910

CONVENTION RESPECTING THE LIMITATION OF THE EMPLOYMENT OF FORCE FOR THE RECOVERY OF CONTRACT DEBTS

Article 1

The Contracting Powers agree not to have recourse to armed force for the recovery of contract debts claimed from the Government of one country by the Government of another country as being due to its nationals.

This undertaking is, however, not applicable when the debtor State refuses or neglects to reply to an offer of arbitration, or, after accepting the offer, prevents any compromis from being agreed on, or, after the arbitration, fails to submit to the award.

Article 2

It is further agreed that the arbitration mentioned in paragraph 2 of the foregoing Article shall be subject to the procedure laid down in Part IV, Chapter III, of The Hague Convention for the Pacific Settlement of International Disputes. The award shall determine, except where otherwise agreed between the parties, the validity of the claim, the amount of the debt, and the time and mode of payment.

Article 3

The present Convention shall be ratified as soon as possible. The ratifications shall be deposited at The Hague.
The first deposit of ratifications shall be recorded in a proces-verbal signed by the Representatives of the Powers taking part therein and by the Netherland Minister for Foreign Affairs.

The subsequent deposits of ratifications shall be made by means of a written notification addressed to the Netherland Government and accompanied by the instrument of ratification.

A duly certified copy of the proces-verbal relative to the first deposit of ratifications, of the notifications mentioned in the preceding paragraph, as well as of the instruments of ratification, shall be sent immediately by the Netherland Government, through the diplomatic channel, to the Powers invited to the Second Peace Conference, as well as to the other Powers which have adhered to the Convention. In the cases contemplated in the preceding paragraph, the said Government shall inform them at the same time of the date on which it received the notification.

Article 4

Non-Signatory Powers may adhere to the present Convention. The Power which desires to adhere notifies its intention in writing to the Netherland Government, forwarding to it the act of adhesion, which shall be deposited in the archives of the said Government.

The said Government shall forward immediately to all the other Powers invited to the Second Peace Conference a duly certified copy of the notification, as well as of the act of adhesion, mentioning the date on which it received the notification.

Article 5

The present Convention shall come into force, in the case of the Powers which were a party to the first deposit of ratifications, sixty days after the date of the proces-verbal of this deposit, in the case of the Powers which ratify subsequently or which adhere, sixty days after the notification of their ratification or of their adhesion has been received by the Netherland Government.

Article 6

In the event of one of the Contracting Powers wishing to denounce the present Convention, the denunciation shall be notified in writing to the Netherland Government, which shall immediately communicate a duly certified copy of the notification to all the other Powers, informing them at the same time of the date on which it was received.

The denunciation shall only have effect in regard to the notifying Power, and one year after the notification has reached the Netherland Government.

Article 7

A register kept by the Netherland Ministry for Foreign Affairs shall give the date of the deposit of ratifications made in virtue of Article 3, paragraphs 3 and 4, as well as the date on which the notifications of adhesion (Article 4, paragraph 2) or of denunciation (Article 6, paragraph 1) were received.

Each Contracting Power is entitled to have access to this register and to be supplied with duly certified extracts from it.

In faith whereof the Plenipotentiaries have appended their signatures to the present Convention. Done at The Hague, the 18th October, 1907, in a single copy, which shall remain deposited in the archives of the Netherland Government, and duly certified copies of which shall be sent to the Contracting Powers through the diplomatic channel.

Hague III - Opening of Hostilities: 18 October 1907
CONVENTION RELATIVE TO THE OPENING OF HOSTILITIES

Entered into Force: 26 January 1910

His Majesty the German Emperor, King of Prussia; [etc.]

Considering that it is important, in order to ensure the maintenance of pacific relations, that hostilities should not commence without previous warning;

That it is equally important that the existence of a state of war should be notified without delay to neutral Powers;

Being desirous of concluding a Convention to this effect, have appointed the following as their Plenipotentiaries:
[List of Plenipotentiaries.]

Who, after depositing their full powers, found in good and due form, have agreed upon the following provisions:

Article 1

The Contracting Powers recognize that hostilities between themselves must not commence without previous and explicit warning, in the form either of a reasoned declaration of war or of an ultimatum with conditional declaration of war.

Article 2

The existence of a state of war must be notified to the neutral Powers without delay, and shall not take effect in regard to them until after the receipt of a notification, which may, however, be given by telegraph. Neutral Powers, nevertheless, cannot rely on the absence of notification if it is clearly established that they were in fact aware of the existence of a state of war.

Article 3

Article 1 of the present Convention shall take effect in case of war between two or more of the Contracting Powers.

Article 2 is binding as between a belligerent Power which is a party to the Convention and neutral Powers which are also parties to the Convention.

Article 4

The present Convention shall be ratified as soon as possible. The ratifications shall be deposited at The Hague. The first deposit of ratification shall be recorded in a proces-verbal signed by the Representatives of the Powers which take part therein and by the Netherland Minister for Foreign Affairs.

The subsequent deposits of ratifications shall be made by means of a written notification addressed to the Netherland Government and accompanied by the instrument of ratification.

A duly certified copy of the proces-verbal relative to the first deposit of ratifications, of the notifications mentioned in the preceding paragraph, as well as of the instruments of ratification, shall be at once sent by the Netherland Government through the diplomatic channel to the Powers invited to the Second Peace Conference, as well as to the other Powers which have adhered to the Convention. In the cases contemplated in the preceding paragraph, the said Government shall at the same time inform them of the date on which it received the notification.

Article 5

Non-Signatory Powers may adhere to the present Convention. The Power which wishes to adhere notifies in writing its intention to the Netherland Government, forwarding to it the act of adhesion, which shall be deposited in the archives of the said Government.

The said Government shall at once forward to all the other Powers a duly certified copy of the notification as well as of the act of adhesion, stating the date on which it received the notification.

Article 6

The present Convention shall come into force, in the case of the Powers which were a party to the first deposit of ratifications, sixty days after the date of the proces-verbal of that deposit, and, in the case of the Powers which ratify subsequently or which adhere, sixty days after the notification of their ratification or of their adhesion has been received by the Netherland Government.

Article 7

In the event of one of the High Contracting Parties wishing to denounce the present Convention, the denunciation shall be notified in writing to the Netherland

Government, which shall at once communicate a duly certified copy of the notification to all the other Powers, informing them of the date on which it was received.

The denunciation shall only have effect in regard to the notifying Power, and one year after the notification has reached the Netherland Government.

Article 8

A register kept by the Netherland Ministry for Foreign Affairs shall give the date of the deposit of ratifications made in virtue of Article 4, paragraphs 3 and 4, as well as the date on which the notifications of adhesion (Article 5, paragraph 2) or of denunciation (Article 7, paragraph 1) have been received.

Each Contracting Power is entitled to have access to this register and to be supplied with duly certified extracts from it.

In faith whereof the Plenipotentiaries have appended their signatures to the present Convention.

Done at The Hague, the 18th October, 1907, in a single copy, which shall remain deposited in the archives of the Netherland Government, and duly certified copies of which shall be sent, through the diplomatic channel, to the Powers which have been invited to the Second Peace Conference.
[List of Signatories.]

Hague IV - Laws and Customs of War on Land : 18 October 1907

entered into force: 26 January 1910

CONVENTION RESPECTING THE LAWS AND CUSTOMS OF WAR ON LAND

Seeing that, while seeking means to preserve peace and prevent armed conflicts between nations, it is likewise necessary to bear in mind the case where the appeal to arms has been brought about by events which their care was unable to avert;

Animated by the desire to serve, even in this extreme case, the interests of humanity and the ever progressive needs of civilization;

Thinking it important, with this object, to revise the general laws and customs of war, either with a view to defining them with greater precision or to confining them within such limits as would mitigate their severity as far as possible;

Have deemed it necessary to complete and explain in certain particulars the work of the First Peace Conference, which, following on the Brussels Conference of 1874, and inspired by the ideas dictated by a wise and generous forethought, adopted provisions intended to define and govern the usages of war on land.

According to the views of the High Contracting Parties, these provisions, the wording of which has been inspired by the desire to diminish the evils of war, as far as military requirements permit, are intended to serve as a general rule of conduct for the belligerents in their mutual relations and in their relations with the inhabitants.

It has not, however, been found possible at present to concert regulations covering all the circumstances which arise in practice;

On the other hand, the High Contracting Parties clearly do not intend that unforeseen cases should, in the absence of a written undertaking, be left to the arbitrary judgment of military commanders.

Until a more complete code of the laws of war has been issued, the High Contracting Parties deem it expedient to declare that, in cases not included in the Regulations adopted by them, the inhabitants and the belligerents remain under the protection and the rule of the principles of the law of nations, as they result from the usages established among civilized peoples, from the laws of humanity, and the dictates of the public conscience.

They declare that it is in this sense especially that Articles 1 and 2 of the Regulations adopted must be understood.

The High Contracting Parties, wishing to conclude afresh Convention to this effect, have appointed the following as their Plenipotentiaries:
(List of Plenipotentiaries)

Who, after having deposited their full powers, found in good and due form, have agreed upon the following:

Article 1

The Contracting Powers shall issue instructions to their armed land forces which shall be in conformity with the Regulations respecting the laws and customs of war on land, annexed to the present Convention.

Article 2

The provisions contained in the Regulations referred to in Article 1, as well as in the present Convention, do not apply except between Contracting Powers, and then only if all the belligerents are parties to the Convention.

Article 3

A belligerent party which violates the provisions of the said Regulations shall, if the case demands, be liable to pay compensation It shall be responsible for all acts committed by persons forming part of its armed forces.

Article 4

The present Convention, duly ratified, shall as between the Contracting Powers, be substituted for the Convention of 29 July 1899, respecting the laws and customs of war on land.

The Convention of 1899 remains in force as between the Powers which signed it, and which do not also ratify the present Convention.

Article 5

The present Convention shall be ratified as soon as possible. The ratifications shall be deposited at The Hague.

The first deposit of ratifications shall be recorded in a proces-verbal signed by the Representatives of the Powers which take part therein and by the Netherlands Minister for Foreign Affairs.

The subsequent deposits of ratifications shall be made by means of a written notification, addressed to the Netherlands Government and accompanied by the instrument of ratification.

A duly certified copy of the proces-verbal relative to the first deposit of ratifications, of the notifications mentioned in the preceding paragraph, as well as of the instruments of ratification, shall be immediately sent by the Netherlands Government, through the diplomatic channel, to the Powers invited to the Second Peace Conference, as well as to the other Powers which have adhered to the Convention. In the cases contemplated in the preceding paragraph the said Government shall at the same time inform them of the date on which it received the notification.

Article 6

Non-Signatory Powers may adhere to the present Convention. The Power which desires to adhere notifies in writing its intention to the Netherlands Government, forwarding to it the act of adhesion, which shall be deposited in the archives of the said Government.
This Government shall at once transmit to all the other Powers a duly certified copy of the notification as well as of the act of adhesion, mentioning the date on which it received the notification.

Article 7

The present Convention shall come into force, in the case of the Powers which were a party to the first deposit of ratifications, sixty days after the date of the proces-verbal of this deposit, and, in the case of the Powers which ratify subsequently or which adhere, sixty days after the notification of their ratification or of their adhesion has been received by the Netherlands Government.

Article 8

In the event of one of the Contracting Powers wishing to denounce the present Convention, the denunciation shall be notified in writing to the Netherlands Government, which shall at once communicate a duly certified copy of the notification to all the other Powers, informing them of the date on which it was received.

The denunciation shall only have effect in regard to the notifying Power, and one year after the notification has reached the Netherlands Government.

Article 9

A register kept by the Netherlands Ministry for Foreign Affairs shall give the date of the deposit of ratifications made in virtue of Article 5, paragraphs 3 and 4, as well as the date on which the notifications of adhesion (Article 6, paragraph 2), or of denunciation (Article 8, paragraph 1) were received.

Each Contracting Power is entitled to have access to this register and to be supplied with duly certified extracts.

In faith whereof the Plenipotentiaries have appended their signatures to the present Convention.

Done at The Hague 18 October 1907, in a single copy, which shall remain deposited in the archives of the Netherlands Government, and duly certified copies of which shall be sent, through the diplomatic channel to the Powers which have been invited to the Second Peace Conference.
(List of Signatories)

Annex to the Convention

Regulations Respecting the Laws and Customs of War on Land

Section I.On Belligerents

Chapter I. The Qualifications of Belligerents

Article 1

The laws, rights, and duties of war apply not only to armies, but also to militia and volunteer corps fulfilling the following conditions:

To be commanded by a person responsible for his subordinates;
To have a fixed distinctive emblem recognizable at a distance;
To carry arms openly; and
To conduct their operations in accordance with the laws and customs of war.
In countries where militia or volunteer corps constitute the army, or form part of it, they are included under the denomination "army."

Article 2

The inhabitants of a territory which has not been occupied, who, on the approach of the enemy, spontaneously take up arms to resist the invading troops without having had time to organize themselves in accordance with Article 1, shall be regarded as belligerents if they carry arms openly and if they respect the laws and customs of war.

Article 3

The armed forces of the belligerent parties may consist of combatants and non-combatants. In the case of capture by the enemy, both have a right to be treated as prisoners of war.

Chapter II. Prisoners of War

Article 4

Prisoners of war are in the power of the hostile Government, but not of the individuals or corps who capture them. They must be humanely treated. All their personal belongings, except arms, horses, and military papers, remain their property.

Article 5

Prisoners of war may be interned in a town, fortress, camp, or other place, and bound not to go beyond certain fixed limits, but they cannot be confined except as in indispensable measure of safety and only while the circumstances which necessitate the measure continue to exist.

Article 6

The State may utilize the labour of prisoners of war according to their rank and aptitude, officers excepted. The tasks shall not be excessive and shall have no connection with the operations of the war.

Prisoners may be authorized to work for the public service, for private persons, or on their own account. Work done for the State is paid for at the rates in force for work of a similar kind done by soldiers of the national army, or, if there are none in force, at a rate according to the work executed.

When the work is for other branches of the public service or for private persons the conditions are settled in agreement with the military authorities.

The wages of the prisoners shall go towards improving their position, and the balance shall be paid them on their release, after deducting the cost of their maintenance.

Article 7

The Government into whose hands prisoners of war have fallen is charged with their maintenance. In the absence of a special agreement between the belligerents, prisoners of war shall be treated as regards board, lodging, and clothing on the same footing as the troops of the Government who captured them.

Article 8

Prisoners of war shall be subject to the laws, regulations, and orders in force in the army of the State in whose power they are. Any act of insubordination justifies the adoption towards them of such measures of severity as may be considered necessary.

Escaped prisoners who are retaken before being able to rejoin their own army or before leaving the territory occupied by the army which captured them are liable to disciplinary punishment. Prisoners who, after succeeding in escaping, are again taken prisoners, are not liable to any punishment on account of the previous flight.

Article 9

Every prisoner of war is bound to give, if he is questioned on the subject, his true name and rank, and if he infringes this rule, he is liable to have the advantages given to prisoners of his class curtailed.

Article 10

Prisoners of war may be set at liberty on parole if the laws of their country allow, and, in such cases, they are bound, on their personal honour, scrupulously to fulfil, both towards their own Government and the Government by whom they were made prisoners, the engagements they have contracted.

In such cases their own Government is bound neither to require of nor accept from them any service incompatible with the parole given.

Article 11

A prisoner of war cannot be compelled to accept his liberty on parole; similarly the hostile Government is not obliged to accede to the request of the prisoner to be set at liberty on parole.

Article 12

Prisoners of war liberated on parole and recaptured bearing arms against the Government to whom they had pledged their honour, or against the allies of that Government, forfeit their right to be treated as prisoners of war, and can be brought before the courts.

Article 13

Individuals who follow an army without directly belonging to it, such as newspaper correspondents and reporters, sutlers and contractors, who fall into the enemy's hands and whom the latter thinks expedient to detain, are entitled to be treated as prisoners of war, provided they are in possession of a certificate from the military authorities of the army which they were accompanying.

Article 14

An inquiry office for prisoners of war is instituted on the commencement of hostilities in each of the belligerent States, and, when necessary, in neutral countries which have received belligerents in their territory. It is the function of this office to reply to all inquiries about the prisoners. It receives from the various services concerned full information respecting internments and transfers. releases on parole, exchanges, escapes, admissions into hospital, deaths, as well as other information necessary to enable it to make out and keep up to date an individual return for each prisoner of war. The office must state in this return the regimental number, name and surname, age, place of origin, rank, unit, wounds, date and place of capture, internment, wounding, and death, as well as any observations of a special character. The individual return shall be sent to the Government of the other belligerent after the conclusion of peace.

It is likewise the function of the inquiry office to receive and collect all objects of personal use, valuables, letters, etc., found on the field of battle or left by prisoners who have been released on parole, or exchanged, or who have escaped, or died in hospitals or ambulances, and to forward them to those concerned.

Article 15

Relief societies for prisoners of war, which are properly constituted in accordance with the laws of their country and with the object of serving as the channel for charitable effort shall receive from the belligerents, for themselves and their duly accredited agents every facility for the efficient performance of their humane task within the bounds imposed by military necessities and administrative regulations. Agents of these societies may be admitted to the places of internment for the purpose of distributing relief, as also to the halting places of repatriated prisoners, if furnished with a personal permit by the military authorities, and on giving an undertaking in writing to comply with all measures of order and police which the latter may issue.

Article 16

Inquiry offices enjoy the privilege of free postage. Letters, money orders, and valuables, as well as parcels by post, intended for prisoners of war, or dispatched by them, shall be exempt from all postal duties in the countries of origin and destination, as well as in the countries they pass through.

Presents and relief in kind for prisoners of war shall be admitted free of all import or other duties, as well as of payments for carriage by the State railways.

Article 17

Officers taken prisoners shall receive the same rate of pay as of officers of corresponding rank in the country where they are detained, the amount to be ultimately refunded by their own Government.

Article 18

Prisoners of war shall enjoy complete liberty in the exercise of their religion, including attendance at the services of whatever church they may belong to, on the sole condition that they comply with the measures of order and police issued by the military authorities.

Article 19

The wills of prisoners of war are received or drawn up in the same way as for soldiers of the national army. The same rules shall be observed regarding death certificates as well as for the burial of prisoners of war, due regard being paid to their grade and rank.

Article 20

After the conclusion of peace, the repatriation of prisoners of war shall be carried out as quickly as possible.

Chapter III.The Sick and Wounded

Article 21

The obligations of belligerents with regard to the sick and wounded are governed by the Geneva Convention.

Section II. Hostilities

Chapter I. Means of Injuring the Enemy, Sieges, and bombardments

Article 22

The right of belligerents to adopt means of injuring the enemy is not unlimited.

Article 23

In addition to the prohibitions provided by special Conventions, it is especially forbidden:

To employ poison or poisoned weapons;
To kill or wound treacherously individuals belonging to the hostile nation or army;
To kill or wound an enemy who, having laid down his arms, or having no longer means of defence, has surrendered at discretion;
To declare that no quarter will be given;

To employ arms, projectiles, or material calculated to cause unnecessary suffering;
To make improper use of a flag of truce, of the national flag or of the military insignia and uniform of the enemy, as well as the distinctive badges of the Geneva Convention;
To destroy or seize the enemy's property, unless such destruction or seizure be imperatively demanded by the necessities of war;
To declare abolished, suspended, or inadmissible in a court of law the rights and actions of the nationals of the hostile party. A belligerent is likewise forbidden to compel the nationals of the hostile party to take part in the operations of war directed against their own country, even if they were in the belligerent's service before the commencement of the war.

Article 24

Ruses of war and the employment of measures necessary for obtaining information about the enemy and the country are considered permissible.

Article 25

The attack or bombardment, by whatever means, of towns, villages, dwellings, or buildings which are undefended is prohibited.

Article 26

The officer in command of an attacking force must, before commencing a bombardment, except in cases of assault, do all in his power to warn the authorities.

Article 27

In sieges and bombardments all necessary steps must be taken to spare, as far as possible, buildings dedicated to religion, art, science, or charitable purposes, historic monuments, hospitals, and places where the sick and wounded are collected, provided they are not being used at the time for military purposes.

It is the duty of the besieged to indicate the presence of such buildings or places by distinctive and visible signs, which shall be notified to the enemy beforehand.

Article 28

The pillage of a town or place, even when taken by assault, is prohibited.

Chapter II. Spies

Article 29

A person can only be considered a spy when, acting clandestinely or on false pretences, he obtains or endeavours to obtain information in the zone of operations of a belligerent, with the intention of communicating it to the hostile party.

Thus, soldiers not wearing a disguise who have penetrated into the zone of operations of the hostile army, for the purpose of obtaining information, are not considered spies. Similarly, the following are not considered spies: Soldiers and civilians, carrying out their mission openly, entrusted with the delivery of despatches intended either for their own army or for the enemy's army. To this class belong likewise persons sent in balloons for the purpose of carrying despatches and, generally, of maintaining communications between the different parts of an army or a territory.

Article 30

A spy taken in the act shall not be punished without previous trial.

Article 31

A spy who, after rejoining the army to which he belongs, is subsequently captured by the enemy, is treated as a prisoner of war, and incurs no responsibility for his previous acts of espionage.

Chapter III. Flags of Truce

Article 32

A person is regarded as a parlementaire who has been authorized by one of the belligerents to enter into communication with the other, and who advances bearing a white flag. He has a right to inviolability, as well as the trumpeter, bugler or drummer, the flag-bearer and interpreter who may accompany him.

Article 33

The commander to whom a parlementaire is sent is not in all cases obliged to receive him.

He may take all the necessary steps to prevent the parlementaire taking advantage of his mission to obtain information. In case of abuse, he has the right to detain the parlementaire temporarily.

Article 34

The parlementaire loses his rights of inviolability if it is proved in a clear and incontestable manner that he has taken advantage of his privileged position to provoke or commit an act of treason.

Chapter IV. Capitulations

Article 35

Capitulations agreed upon between the Contracting Parties must take into account the rules of military honour. Once settled, they must be scrupulously observed by both parties.

Chapter V. Armistices

Article 36

An armistice suspends military operations by mutual agreement between the belligerent parties. If its duration is not defined, the belligerent parties may resume operations at any time, provided always that the enemy is warned within the time agreed upon, in accordance with the terms of the armistice.

Article 37

An armistice may be general or local. The first suspends the military operations of the belligerent States everywhere; the second only between certain fractions of the belligerent armies and within a fixed radius.

Article 38

An armistice must be notified officially and in good time to the competent authorities and to the troops. Hostilities are suspended immediately after the notification, or on the date fixed.

Article 39

It rests with the Contracting Parties to settle, in the terms of the armistice, what communications may be held in the theatre of war with the inhabitants and between the inhabitants of one belligerent State and those of the other.

Article 40

Any serious violation of the armistice by one of the parties gives the other party the right of denouncing it, and even, in cases of urgency, of recommencing hostilities immediately.

Article 41

A violation of the terms of the armistice by private persons acting on their own initiative only entitles the injured party to demand the punishment of the offenders or, if necessary, compensation for the losses sustained.

Section III. Military Authority Over The Territory Of The Hostile State

Article 42

Territory is considered occupied when it is actually placed under the authority of the hostile army.

The occupation extends only to the territory where such authority has been established and can be exercised.

Article 43

The authority of the legitimate power having in fact passed into the hands of the occupant, the latter shall take all the measures in his power to restore, and ensure, as far as possible, public order and safety, while respecting, unless absolutely prevented, the laws in force in the country.

Article 44

A belligerent is forbidden to force the inhabitants of territory occupied by it to furnish information about the army of the other belligerent, or about its means of defense.

Article 45

It is forbidden to compel the inhabitants of occupied territory to swear allegiance to the hostile Power.

Article 46

Family honour and rights, the lives of persons, and private property, as well as religious convictions and practice, must be respected. Private property cannot be confiscated.

Article 47

Pillage is formally forbidden.

Article 48

If, in the territory occupied, the occupant collects the taxes, dues, and tolls imposed for the benefit of the State, he shall do so, as far as is possible, in accordance with the rules of assessment and incidence in force, and shall in consequence be bound to defray the expenses of the administration of the occupied territory to the same extent as the legitimate Government was so bound.

Article 49

If, in addition to the taxes mentioned in the above article, the occupant levies other money contributions in the occupied territory, this shall only be for the needs of the army or of the administration of the territory in question.

Article 50

No general penalty, pecuniary or otherwise, shall be inflicted upon the population on account of the acts of individuals for which they cannot be regarded as jointly and severally responsible.

Article 51

No contribution shall be collected except under a written order, and on the responsibility of a commander-in-chief.

The collection of the said contribution shall only be effected as far as possible in accordance with the rules of assessment and incidence of the taxes in force.
For every contribution a receipt shall be given to the contributors.

Article 52

Requisitions in kind and services shall not be demanded from municipalities or inhabitants except for the needs of the army of occupation. They shall be in proportion to the resources of the country, and of such a nature as not to involve the inhabitants in the obligation of taking part in military operations against their own country.

Such requisitions and services shall only be demanded on the authority of the commander in the locality occupied. Contributions in kind shall as far as possible be paid for in cash; if not, a receipt shall be given and the payment of the amount due shall be made as soon as possible.

Article 53

An army of occupation can only take possession of cash, funds, and realizable securities which are strictly the property of the State, depots of arms, means of transport, stores and supplies, and, generally, all movable property belonging to the State which may be used for military operations.

All appliances, whether on land, at sea, or in the air, adapted for the transmission of news, or for the transport of persons or things, exclusive of cases governed by naval law, depots of arms, and, generally, all kinds of munitions of war, may be seized, even if they belong to private individuals, but must be restored and compensation fixed when peace is made.

Article 54

Submarine cables connecting an occupied territory with a neutral territory shall not be seized or destroyed except in the case of absolute necessity. They must likewise be restored and compensation fixed when peace is made.

Article 55

The occupying State shall be regarded only as administrator and usufructuary of public buildings, real estate, forests, and agricultural estates belonging to the hostile State, and situated in the occupied country. It must safeguard the capital of these properties, and administer them in accordance with the rules of usufruct.

Article 56

The property of municipalities, that of institutions dedicated to religion, charity and education, the arts and sciences, even when State property, shall be treated as private property.

All seizure of, destruction or wilful damage done to institutions of this character, historic monuments, works of art and science, is forbidden, and should be made the subject of legal proceedings.

Hague V - Rights and Duties of Neutral Powers and Persons in Case of War on Land: 18 October 1907

CONVENTION RESPECTING THE RIGHTS AND DUTIES OF NEUTRAL POWERS AND PERSONS IN CASE OF WAR ON LAND

With a view to laying down more clearly the rights and duties of neutral Powers in case of war on land and regulating the position of the belligerents who have taken refuge in neutral territory;

Being likewise desirous of defining the meaning of the term "neutral," pending the possibility of settling, in its entirety, the position of neutral individuals in their relations with the belligerents;

Have resolved to conclude a Convention to this effect, and have, in consequence, appointed the following as their Plenipotentiaries:
(List of Plenipotentiaries.)

Who, after having deposited their full powers, found in good and due form, have agreed upon the following full powers, found in good and due form, have agreed upon the following provisions:

Chapter I. The Rights and Duties of Neutral Powers

Article 1

The territory of neutral Powers is inviolable.

Article 2

Belligerents are forbidden to move troops or convoys of either munitions of war or supplies across the territory of a neutral Power.

Article 3

Belligerents are likewise forbidden to:

(a) Erect on the territory of a neutral Power a wireless telegraphy station or other apparatus for the purpose of communicating with belligerent forces on land or sea;

(b) Use any installation of this kind established by them before the war on the territory of a neutral Power for purely military purposes, and which has not been opened for the service of public messages.

Article 4

Corps of combatants cannot be formed nor recruiting agencies opened on the territory of a neutral Power to assist the belligerents.

Article 5

A neutral Power must not allow any of the acts referred to in Articles 2 to 4 to occur on its territory.

It is not called upon to punish acts in violation of its neutrality unless the said acts have been committed on its own territory.

Article 6

The responsibility of a neutral Power is not engaged by the fact of persons crossing the frontier separately to offer their services to one of the belligerents.

Article 7

A neutral Power is not called upon to prevent the export or transport, on behalf of one or other of the belligerents, of arms, munitions of war, or, in general, of anything which can be of use to an army or a fleet.

Article 8

A neutral Power is not called upon to forbid or restrict the use on behalf of the belligerents of telegraph or telephone cables or of wireless telegraphy apparatus belonging to it or to companies or private individuals.

Article 9

Every measure of restriction or prohibition taken by a neutral Power in regard to the matters referred to in Articles 7 and 8 must be impartially applied by it to both belligerents.

A neutral Power must see to the same obligation being observed by companies or private individuals owning telegraph or telephone cables or wireless telegraphy apparatus.

Article 10

The fact of a neutral Power resisting, even by force, attempts to violate its neutrality cannot be regarded as a hostile act.

Chapter II. Belligerents Interned and Wounded Tended in Neutral Territory

Article 11

A neutral Power which receives on its territory troops belonging to the belligerent armies shall intern them, as far as possible, at a distance from the theatre of war.

It may keep them in camps and even confine them in fortresses or in places set apart for this purpose.

It shall decide whether officers can be left at liberty on giving their parole not to leave the neutral territory without permission.

Article 12

In the absence of a special convention to the contrary, the neutral Power shall supply the interned with the food, clothing, and relief required by humanity. At the conclusion of peace the expenses caused by the internment shall be made good.

Article 13

A neutral Power which receives escaped prisoners of war shall leave them at liberty. If it allows them to remain in its territory it may assign them a place of residence.

The same rule applies to prisoners of war brought by troops taking refuge in the territory of a neutral Power.

Article 14

A neutral Power may authorize the passage over its territory of the sick and wounded belonging to the belligerent armies, on condition that the trains bringing them shall carry neither personnel nor war material. In such a case, the neutral Power is bound to take whatever measures of safety and control are necessary for the purpose.

The sick or wounded brought under the these conditions into neutral territory by one of the belligerents, and belonging to the hostile party, must be guarded by the neutral Power so as to ensure their not taking part again in the military operations. The same duty shall devolve on the neutral State with regard to wounded or sick of the other army who may be committed to its care.

Article 15

The Geneva Convention applies to sick and wounded interned in neutral territory.

Chapter III. Neutral Persons

Article 16

The nationals of a State which is not taking part in the war are considered as neutrals.

Article 17

A neutral cannot avail himself of his neutrality:

(a) If he commits hostile acts against a belligerent;

(b) If he commits acts in favor of a belligerent, particularly if he voluntarily enlists in the ranks of the armed force of one of the parties. In such a case, the neutral shall not be more severely treated by the belligerent as against whom he has abandoned his neutrality than a national of the other belligerent State could be for the same act.

Article 18

The following acts shall not be considered as committed in favour of one belligerent in the sense of Article 17, letter (b):

(a) Supplies furnished or loans made to one of the belligerents, provided that the person who furnishes the supplies or who makes the loans lives neither in the territory of the other party nor in the territory occupied by him, and that the supplies do not come from these territories;

(b) Services rendered in matters of police or civil administration.

Chapter IV. Railway Material

Article 19

Railway material coming from the territory of neutral Powers, whether it be the property of the said Powers or of companies or private persons, and recognizable as such, shall not be requisitioned or utilized by a belligerent except where and to the extent that it is absolutely necessary. It shall be sent back as soon possible to the country of origin.

A neutral Power may likewise, in case of necessity, retain and utilize to an equal extent material coming from the territory of the belligerent Power.

Compensation shall be paid by one Party or the other in proportion to the material used, and to the period of usage.

Chapter V. Final Provisions

Article 20

The provisions of the present Convention do not apply except between Contracting Powers and then only if all the belligerents are Parties to the Convention.

Article 21

The present Convention shall be ratified as soon as possible. The ratifications shall be deposited at The Hague. The first deposit of ratifications shall be recorded in a proces-verbal signed by the representatives of the Powers which take part therein and by the Netherlands Minister for Foreign Affairs.

The subsequent deposits of ratifications shall be made by means of a written notification, addressed to the Netherlands Government and accompanied by the instrument of ratification.

A duly certified copy of the proces-verbal relative to the first deposit of ratifications, of the notifications mentioned in the preceding paragraph, and of the instruments of ratification shall be immediately sent by the Netherlands Government, through the diplomatic channel, to the Powers invited to the Second Peace Conference as well as to the other Powers which have adhered to the Convention. In the cases contemplated in the preceding paragraph, the said Government shall at the same time inform them of the date on which it received the notification.

Article 22

Non-Signatory Powers may adhere to the present Convention. The Power which desires to adhere notifies its intention in writing to the Netherlands Government, forwarding to it the act of adhesion, which shall be deposited in the archives of the said Government.

This Government shall immediately forward to all the other Powers a duly certified copy of the notification as well as of the act of adhesion, mentioning the date on which it received the notification.

Article 23

The present Convention shall come into force, in the case of the Powers which were a Party to the first deposit of ratifications, sixty days after the date of the proces-verbal of this deposit, and, in the case of the Powers which ratify subsequently or which adhere, sixty days after the notification of their ratification or of their adhesion has been received by the Netherlands Government.

Article 24

In the event of one of the Contracting Powers wishing to denounce the present Convention, the denunciation shall be notified in writing to the Netherlands Government, which shall immediately communicate a duly certified copy of the notification to all the other Powers, informing them at the same time of the date on which it was received.

The denunciation shall only have effect in regard to the notifying Power, and one year after the notification has reached the Netherlands Government.

Article 25

A register kept by the Netherlands Ministry of Foreign Affairs shall give the date of the deposit of ratifications made in virtue of Article 21, paragraphs 3 and 4, as well as the date on which the notifications of adhesion (Article 22, paragraph 2) or of denunciation (Article 24, paragraph 1) have been received.

Each Contracting Power is entitled to have access to this register and to be supplied with duly certified extracts from it.

In faith whereof the Plenipotentiaries have appended their signatures to the present Convention.

Done at The Hague, 18 October 1907, in a single copy, which shall remain deposited in the archives of the Netherlands Government and duly certified copies of which shall be sent, through the diplomatic channel, to the Powers which have been invited to the Second Peace Conference.

Hague VI - Status of Enemy Merchant Ships at the Outbreak of Hostilities : 18 October 1907

CONVENTION RELATING TO THE STATUS OF ENEMY MERCHANT SHIPS AT THE OUTBREAK OF HOSTILITIES

Anxious to ensure the security of international commerce against the surprises of war, and wishing, in accordance with modern practice, to protect as far as possible operations undertaken in good faith and in process of being carried out before the outbreak of hostilities, have resolved to conclude a Convention to this effect, and have appointed the following persons as their Plenipotentiaries:
(List of Plenipotentiaries)

Who, after having deposited their full powers, found in good and due form, have agreed upon the following provisions:

Article 1

When a merchant ship belonging to one of the belligerent Powers is at the commencement of hostilities in an enemy port, it is desirable that it should be allowed to depart freely, either immediately, or after a reasonable number of days of grace, and to proceed, after being furnished with a pass, direct to its port of destination or any other port indicated.

The same rule should apply in the case of a ship which has left its last port of departure before the commencement of the war and entered a port belonging to the enemy while still ignorant that hostilities had broken out.

Article 2

A merchant ship unable, owing to circumstances of force majeure, to leave the enemy port within the period contemplated in the above article, or which was not allowed to leave, cannot be confiscated.

The belligerent may only detain it, without payment of compensation, but subject to the obligation of restoring it after the war, or requisition it on payment of compensation.

Article 3

Enemy merchant ships which left their last port of departure before the commencement of the war, and are encountered on the high seas while still ignorant of the outbreak of hostilities cannot be confiscated. They are only liable to detention on the understanding that they shall be restored after the war without compensation, or to be requisitioned, or even destroyed, on payment of compensation, but in such cases provision must be made for the safety of the persons on board as well as the security of the ship's papers.

After touching at a port in their own country or at a neutral port, these ships are subject to the laws and customs of maritime war.

Article 4

Enemy cargo on board the vessels referred to in Articles 1 and 2 is likewise liable to be detained and restored after the termination of the war without payment of compensation, or to be requisitioned on payment of compensation, with or without the ship. The same rule applies in the case of cargo on board the vessels referred to in Article 3.

Article 5

The present Convention does not affect merchant ships whose build shows that they are intended for conversion into war-ships.

Article 6

The provisions of the present Convention do not apply except between Contracting Powers, and then only if all the belligerents are Parties to the Convention.

Article 7

The present Convention shall be ratified as soon as possible. The ratifications shall be deposited at The Hague. The first deposit of ratifications shall be recorded in a proces-verbal signed by the representatives of the Powers which take part therein and by the Netherlands Minister for Foreign Affairs. The subsequent deposits of ratifications shall be made by means of a written notification addressed to the Netherlands Government and accompanied by the instrument of ratification.

A duly certified copy of the proces-verbal relative to the first deposit of ratifications, of the notifications mentioned in the preceding paragraph, as well as of the instruments of ratification, shall be at once sent by the Netherlands Government, through the diplomatic channel, to the Powers invited to the Second Peace Conference, as well as to the other Powers which have adhered to the Convention. In the cases contemplated in the preceding paragraph, the said Government shall at the same time inform them of the date on which it received the notification.

Article 8

Non-Signatory Powers may adhere to the present Convention. The Power which desires to adhere notifies in writing its intention to the Netherlands Government, forwarding to it the act of adhesion, which shall be deposited in the archives of the said Government.

The said Government shall at once transmit to all the other Powers a duly certified copy of the notification as well as of the act of adhesion, stating the date on which it received the notification.

Article 9

The present Convention shall come into force, in the case the of the Powers which were a party to the first deposit of ratifications, I be sixty days after the date of the proces-verbal of that deposit, and, in the case of the Powers which ratify subsequently or which adhere, sixty days after the notification of their ratification or of their adhesion has been received by the Netherlands Government.

Article 10

In the event of one of the Contracting Powers wishing to denounce the present Convention, the denunciation shall be notified in writing to the Netherlands Government, which shall at once communicate a certified copy of the notification to all the other Powers, informing them of the date on which it was received.

The denunciation shall only have effect in regard to the notifying Power, and one year after the notification has reached the Netherlands Government.

Article 11

A register kept by the Ministry of Foreign Affairs shall give the date of the deposit of ratifications made in virtue of Article 7, paragraphs 3 and 4, as well as the date on which the notifications of adhesion (Article 8, paragraph 2) or of denunciation (Article 10, paragraph 1) have been received.

Each Contracting Power is entitled to have access to this register and to be supplied with certified extracts from it.

In faith whereof the Plenipotentiaries have appended to the present Convention their signatures.

Done at The Hague, 18 October 1907, in a single copy, which shall remain deposited in the archives of the Netherlands Government, and duly certified copies of which shall be sent through the diplomatic channel, to the Powers which have been invited to the Second Peace Conference.

Hague VII - Conversion of Merchant Ships into War Ships: 18 October 1907

CONVENTION RELATING TO THE CONVERSION OF MERCHANT SHIPS INTO WAR-SHIPS

Whereas it is desirable, in view of the incorporation in time of war of merchant ships in the fighting fleet, to define the conditions subject to which this operation may be effected;

Whereas, however, the Contracting Powers have been unable to come to an agreement on the question whether the conversion of a merchant ship into a war-ship may take place upon the high seas, it is understood that the question of the place where such conversion is effected remains outside the scope of this agreement and is in no way affected by the following rules;

Being desirous of concluding a Convention to this effect, have appointed the following as their Plenipotentiaries:
(List of Plenipotentiaries)

Who, after having deposited their full powers, found in good and due form, have agreed upon the following provisions:

Article 1

A merchant ship converted into a war-ship cannot have the rights and duties accruing to such vessels unless it is placed under the direct authority, immediate control, and responsibility of the Power whose flag it flies.

Article 2

Merchant ships converted into war-ships must bear the external marks which distinguish the war-ships of their nationality.

Article 3

The commander must be in the service of the State and duly commissioned by the competent authorities. His name must figure on the list of the officers of the fighting fleet.

Article 4

The crew must be subject to military discipline.

Article 5

Every merchant ship converted into a war-ship must observe in its operations the laws and customs of war.

Article 6

A belligerent who converts a merchant ship into a war-ship must, as soon as possible, announce such conversion in the list of war-ships.

Article 7

The provisions of the present Convention do not apply except between Contracting Powers, and then only if all the belligerents are Parties to the Convention.

Article 8

The present Convention shall be ratified as soon as possible. The ratifications shall be deposited at The Hague. The first deposit of ratifications shall be recorded in a proces-verbal signed by the representatives of the Powers who take part therein and by the Netherlands Minister for Foreign Affairs.

The subsequent deposits of ratifications shall be made by means of a written notification, addressed to the Netherlands Government and accompanied by the instrument of ratification.

A duly certified copy of the proces-verbal relative to the first deposit of ratifications, of the notifications mentioned in the to preceding paragraph, as well as of the instruments of ratification, shall be at once sent by the Netherlands Government, through the diplomatic channel, to the Powers invited to the Second Peace Conference, as well as to the other Powers which have adhered to the Convention. In the cases contemplated in the preceding paragraph the said Government shall at the same time inform them of the date on which it received the notification.

Article 9

Non-Signatory Powers may adhere to the present Convention.

The Power which desires to adhere notifies its intention in writing to the Netherlands Government, forwarding to it the act of adhesion, which shall be deposited in the archives of the said Government.

That Government shall at once transmit to all the other Powers a duly certified copy of the notification as well as of the act of adhesion, stating the date on which it received the notification.

Article 10

The present Convention shall come into force, in the case of the Powers which were a party to the first deposit of ratifications, sixty days after the date of the proces-verbal of this deposit, and, in the case of the Powers which ratify subsequently or which adhere, sixty days after the notification of their ratification or of their adhesion has been received by the Netherlands Government.

Article 11

In the event of one of the Contracting Powers wishing to denounce the present Convention, the denunciation shall be notified in writing to the Netherlands Government, which shall at once communicate a duly certified copy of the notification to all the other Powers, informing them of the date on which it was received.

The denunciation shall only have effect in regard to the notifying Power, and one year after the notification has reached the Netherlands Government.

Article 12

A register kept by the Netherlands Ministry for Foreign Affairs shall give the date of the deposit of ratifications made in virtue of Article 8, paragraphs 3 and 4, as well as the date on which the notifications of adhesion (Article 9, paragraph 2) or of denunciation (Article 11, paragraph 1) have been received.

Each Contracting Power is entitled to have access to this register and to be supplied with duly certified extracts from it.

In faith whereof the Plenipotentiaries have appended their signatures to the present Convention.

Done at The Hague, 18 October 1907, in a single copy, which shall remain deposited in the archives of the Netherlands Government, and duly certified copies of which shall be sent, through the diplomatic channel, to the Powers which have been invited to the Second Peace Conference.

Hague VIII - Laying of Automatic Submarine Contact Mines: 18 October 1907

CONVENTION RELATIVE TO THE LAYING OF AUTOMATIC SUBMARINE CONTACT MINES

Inspired by the principle of the freedom of sea routes, the common highway of all nations;

Seeing that, although the existing position of affairs makes it impossible to forbid the employment of automatic submarine contact mines, it is nevertheless desirable to restrict and regulate their employment in order to mitigate the severity of war and to ensure, as far as possible, to peaceful navigation the security to which it is entitled, despite the existence of war;

Until such time as it is found possible to formulate rules on the subject which shall ensure to the interests involved all the guarantees desirable;

Have resolved to conclude a Convention for this purpose, and have appointed the following as their Plenipotentiaries:
(List of Plenipotentiaries)

Who, after having deposited their full powers, found in good and due form, have agreed upon the following provisions:

Article 1

It is forbidden - 1. To lay unanchored automatic contact mines, except when they are so constructed as to become harmless one hour at most after the person who laid them ceases to control them; 2. To lay anchored automatic contact mines which do not become harmless as soon as they have broken loose from their moorings; 3. To use torpedoes which do not become harmless when they have missed their mark.

Article 2

It is forbidden to lay automatic contact mines off the coast and ports of the enemy, with the sole object of intercepting commercial shipping.

Article 3

When anchored automatic contact mines are employed, every possible precaution must be taken for the security of peaceful shipping.

The belligerents undertake to do their utmost to render these mines harmless within a limited time, and, should they cease to be under surveillance, to notify the danger zones as soon as military exigencies permit, by a notice addressed to ship owners, which must also be communicated to the Governments through the diplomatic channel.

Article 4

Neutral Powers which lay automatic contact mines off their coasts must observe the same rules and take the same precautions as are imposed on belligerents.
The neutral Power must inform ship owners, by a notice issued in advance, where automatic contact mines have been laid. This notice must be communicated at once to the Governments through the diplomatic channel.

Article 5

At the close of the war, the Contracting Powers undertake to do their utmost to remove the mines which they have laid, each Power removing its own mines. As regards anchored automatic contact mines laid by one of the belligerents off the coast of the other, their position must be notified to the other party by the Power which laid them, and each Power must proceed with the least possible delay to remove the mines in its own waters.

Article 6

The Contracting Powers which do not at present own perfected mines of the pattern contemplated in the present Convention, and which, consequently, could not at present carry out the rules laid down in Articles 1 and 3, undertake to convert the materiel of their mines as soon as possible, so as to bring it into conformity with the foregoing requirements.

Article 7

The provisions of the present Convention do not apply except between Contracting Powers, and then only if all the belligerents are parties to the Convention.

Article 8

The present Convention shall be ratified as soon as possible.

The ratifications shall be deposited at The Hague.

The first deposit of ratifications shall be recorded in a proces-verbal signed by the representatives of the Powers which take part therein and by the Netherlands Minister for Foreign Affairs.

The subsequent deposits of ratifications shall be made by means of a written notification addressed to the Netherlands Government and accompanied by the instrument of ratification.

A duly certified copy of the proces-verbal relative to the first deposit of ratifications, of the notifications mentioned in the preceding paragraph, as well as of the instruments of ratification, shall be at once sent, by the Netherlands Government, through the diplomatic channel, to the Powers invited to the Second Peace Conference, as well as to the other Powers which have adhered to the Convention. In the cases contemplated in the preceding paragraph, the said Government shall inform them at the same time of the date on which it has received the notification.

Article 9

Non-Signatory Powers may adhere to the present Convention.

The Power which desires to adhere notifies in writing its intention to the Netherlands Government, transmitting to it the act of adhesion, which shall be deposited in the archives of the said Government.

This Government shall at once transmit to all the other Powers a duly certified copy of the notification as well as of the act of adhesion, stating the date on which it received the notification.

Article 10

The present Convention shall come into force, in the case of the Powers which were a party to the first deposit of ratifications, sixty days after the date of the proces-verbal of this deposit, and, in the case of the Powers which ratify subsequently or adhere, sixty days after the notification of their ratification or of their adhesion has been received by the Netherlands Government.

Article 11

The present Convention shall remain in force for seven years, dating from the sixtieth day after the date of the first deposit of ratifications. Unless denounced, it shall continue in force after the expiration of this period.

The denunciation shall be notified in writing to the Netherlands Government, which shall at once communicate a duly certified copy of the notification to all the Powers, informing them of the date on which it was received. The denunciation shall only have effect in regard to the notifying Power, and six months after the notification has reached the Netherlands Government.

Article 12

The Contracting Powers undertake to reopen the question of the employment of automatic contact mines six months before the expiration of the period contemplated in the first paragraph of the preceding article, in the event of the question not having been already reopened and settled by the Third Peace Conference.

If the Contracting Powers conclude a fresh Convention relative to the employment of mines, the present Convention shall cease to be applicable from the moment it comes into force.

Article 13

A register kept by the Netherlands Ministry for Foreign Affairs shall give the date of the deposit of ratifications made in virtue of Article 8, paragraphs 3 and 4, as well as the date on which the notifications of adhesion (Article 9, paragraph 2) or of denunciation (Article 11, paragraph 3) have been received.

Each Contracting Power is entitled to have access to this register and to be supplied with duly certified extracts from it.

In faith whereof the Plenipotentiaries have appended their signatures to the present Convention.

Done at The Hague, 18 October 1907, in a single copy, which shall remain deposited in the archives of the Netherlands Government, and duly certified copies of which shall be sent, through the diplomatic channel, to the Powers which have been invited to the Second Peace Conference.<

Hague IX - Bombardment by Naval Forces in Time of War: 18 October 1907

CONVENTION CONCERNING BOMBARDMENT BY NAVAL FORCES IN TIME OF WAR

Animated by the desire to realize the wish expressed by the First Peace Conference respecting the bombardment by naval forces of undefended ports, towns, and villages;

Whereas it is expedient that bombardments by naval forces should be subject to rules of general application which would safeguard the rights of the inhabitants and assure the preservation of the more important buildings, by applying as far as possible to this operation of war the principles of the Regulation of 1899 respecting the laws and customs of land war;

Actuated, accordingly, by the desire to serve the interests of humanity and to diminish the severity and disasters of war;

Have resolved to conclude a Convention to this effect, and have, for this purpose, appointed the following as their Plenipotentiaries:
(List of Plenipotentiaries)

Who, after depositing their full powers, gound in good and due form, have agreed upon the following provisions:

Chapter I
The Bombardment of Undefended Ports, Towns, Villages, Dwellings, or Buildings

Article 1

The bombardment by naval forces of undefended ports, towns, villages, dwellings, or buildings is forbidden.

A place cannot be bombarded solely because automatic submarine contact mines are anchored off the harbour.

Article 2

Military works, military or naval establishments, depots of arms or war mat riel, workshops or plant which could be utilized for the needs of the hostile fleet or army, and the ships of war in the harbour, are not, however, included in this prohibition. The commander of a naval force may destroy them with artillery, after a summons followed by a reasonable time of waiting, if all other means are impossible, and when the local authorities have not themselves destroyed them within the time fixed.

He incurs no responsibility for any unavoidable damage which may be caused by a bombardment under such circumstances.

If for military reasons immediate action is necessary, and no delay can be allowed the enemy, it is understood that the prohibition to bombard the undefended town holds good, as in the case given in paragraph 1, and that the commander shall take all due measures in order that the town may suffer as little harm as possible.

Article 3

After due notice has been given, the bombardment of undefended ports, towns, villages, dwellings, or buildings may be commenced, if the local authorities, after a formal summons has been made to them, decline to comply with requisitions for provisions or supplies necessary for the immediate use of the naval force before the place in question.

These requisitions shall be in proportion to the resources of the place. They shall only be demanded in the name of the commander of the said naval force, and they shall, as far as possible, be paid for in cash; if not, they shall be evidenced by receipts.

Article 4

Undefended ports, towns, villages, dwellings, or buildings may not be bombarded on account of failure to pay money contributions.

Chapter II. General Provisions

Article 5

In bombardments by naval forces all the necessary measures must be taken by the commander to spare as far as possible sacred edifices, buildings used for artistic, scientific, or charitable purposes, historic monuments, hospitals, and places where the sick or wounded are collected, on the understanding that they are not used at the same time for military purposes.

It is the duty of the inhabitants to indicate such monuments, edifices, or places by visible signs, which shall consist of large, stiff rectangular panels divided diagonally into two coloured triangular portions, the upper portion black, the lower portion white.

Article 6

If the military situation permits, the commander of the attacking naval force, before commencing the bombardment, must do his utmost to warn the authorities.

Article 7

A town or place, even when taken by storm, may not be pillaged.

Chapter III. Final Provisions

Article. 8

The provisions of the present Convention do not apply except between Contracting Powers, and then only if all the belligerents are parties to the Convention.

Article 9

The present Convention shall be ratified as soon as possible. The ratifications shall be deposited at The Hague.
The first deposit of ratifications shall be recorded in a proces-verbal signed by the representatives of the Powers which take part therein and by the Netherlands Minister of Foreign Affairs.

The subsequent deposits of ratifications shall be made by means of a written notification addressed to the Netherlands Government and accompanied by the instrument of ratification.

A duly certified copy of the proces-verbal relative to the first deposit of ratifications, of the notifications mentioned in the preceding paragraph, as well as of the instruments of ratification, shall be at once sent by the Netherlands Government, through the diplomatic channel, to the Powers invited to the Second Peace Conference, as well as to the other Powers which have adhered to the Convention. In the cases contemplated in the preceding paragraph, the said Government shall inform them at the same time of the date on which it received the notification.

Article 10

Non-Signatory Powers may adhere to the present Convention. The Power which desires to adhere shall notify its intention to the Netherlands Government, forwarding to it the act of adhesion, which shall be deposited in the archives of the said Government.

This Government shall immediately forward to all the other Powers a duly certified copy of the notification, as well as of the act of adhesion, mentioning the date on which it received the notification.

Article 11

The present Convention shall come into force, in the case of the Powers which were a party to the first deposit of ratifications, sixty days after the date of the proces-verbal of that deposit, and, in the case of the Powers which ratify subsequently or which adhere, sixty days after the notification of their ratification or of their adhesion has been received by the Netherlands Government.

Article 12

In the event of one of the Contracting Powers wishing to denounce the present Convention, the denunciation shall be notified in writing to the Netherlands Government, which shall at once communicate a duly certified copy of the notification to all the other Powers informing them of the date on which it was received.

The denunciation shall only have effect in regard to the notifying Power, and one year after the notification has reached the Netherlands Government.

Article 13

A register kept by the Netherlands Minister for Foreign Affairs shall give the date of the deposit of ratifications made in virtue of Article 9, paragraphs 3 and 4, as well as the date on which the notifications of adhesion (Article 10, paragraph 2) or of denunciation (Article 12, paragraph 1) have been received.

Each Contracting Power is entitled to have access to this register and to be supplied with duly certified extracts from it.

In faith whereof the Plenipotentiaries have appended their signatures to the present Convention.

Done at The Hague, 18 October 1907, in a single copy, which shall remain deposited in the archives of the Netherlands Government, and duly certified copies of which shall be sent, through the diplomatic channel, to the Powers which have been invited to the Second Peace Conference.
(List of Signatories)

Hague X - Adaptation to Maritime War of the Principles of the Geneva Convention: 18 October 1907

CONVENTION FOR THE ADAPTATION TO MARITIME WAR OF THE PRINCIPLES OF THE GENEVA CONVENTION

His Majesty the German Emperor, King of Prussia,

Animated alike by the desire to diminish, as far as depends on them, the inevitable evils of war; and wishing with this object to adapt to maritime warfare the principles of the Geneva Convention of the 6th July, 1906;

Have resolved to conclude a Convention for the purpose of revising the Convention of the 29th July, 1899, relative to this question, and have appointed the following as their Plenipotentiaries:
[List of Plenipotentiaries]

Who, after having deposited their full powers, found to be in good and due form, have agreed to the following provisions:

Article 1

Military hospital-ships, that is to say, ships constructed or fitted out by States specially and solely with a view to assisting the wounded, sick, and shipwrecked, the names of which shall have been communicated to the belligerent Powers at the commencement or during the course of hostilities, and in any case before they are employed, shall be respected, and cannot be captured while hostilities last.

These ships, moreover, are not on the same footing as ships of war as regards their stay in a neutral port.

Article 2

Hospital-ships, equipped wholly or in part at the expense of private individuals or officially recognized relief societies, shall likewise be respected and exempt from capture, if the belligerent Power to wholly they belong has given them an official commission and has notified their names to the adverse Power at the commencement of or during hostilities, and in any case before they are employed.

These ships must be provided with a certificate from the competent authorities declaring that the ships have been under their control while fitting out and on final departure.

Article 3

Hospital-ships, equipped wholly or ill part at the expense of private individuals or officially recognized societies of neutral countries, shall be respected and exempt from capture, on condition that they are placed under the control of one of the belligerents, with the previous consent of their own Government and with the authorization of the belligerent himself, and that the latter has notified their name to his adversary at the commencement of or during hostilities, and in any case, before they are employed.

Article 4

The ships mentioned in Articles 1, 2, and 3 shall afford relief and assistance to the wounded, sick, and shipwrecked of the belligerents without distinction of nationality.

The Governments undertake not to use these ships for any military purpose. These ships must not in any way hamper the movements of the combatants. During and after an engagement they will act at their own risk and peril.

The belligerents shall have the right to control and search them; they can refuse their assistance, order them off, make them take a certain course, and put a commissioner on board; they can even detain them, if the gravity of the circumstances requires it.

As far as possible, the belligerents shall enter in the log of the hospital-ships the orders which they give them.

Article 5

Military hospital-ships shall be distinguished by being painted white outside with a horizontal band of green about a metre and a half in breadth.

The ships mentioned in Articles 2 and 3 shall be distinguished by being painted white outside with a horizontal band of red about a metre and a half in breadth.

The boats of the ships above mentioned, as also small craft which may be used for hospital work, shall he distinguished by similar painting.

All hospital-ships shall make themselves known by hoisting, with their national flag, the white flag with a red cross provided by the Geneva Convention, and further, if they belong to a neutral State, by flying at the mainmast the national flag of the belligerent under whose control they are placed.

Hospital-ships which, under the terms of Article 4, are detained by the enemy, must haul down the national flag of the belligerent to whom they belong.

The ships and boats above mentioned which wish to ensure by night the freedom from interference to which they are entitled, must, subject to the assent of the belligerent they are accompanying, take the necessary measures to render their special painting sufficiently plain.

Article 6

The distinguishing signs referred to in Article 5 can be used, whether in time of peace or in time of war, only for protecting or indicating the ships therein mentioned.

Article 7

In the case of a light on board a vessel of war, the sick-wards shall be respected and spared as far as possible.

The said sick-wards and the materiel belonging to them remain subject to the laws of war, but cannot be used for any purpose other than that for which they were originally intended, so long as they are required for the sick and wounded.
The commander, however, into whose power they have fallen may apply them to other purposes, in case of urgent military necessity, after seeing that the. sick and wounded on board are properly provided for.

Article 8

Hospital-ships and sick-wards of vessels arc no longer entitled to protection if they are employed for the purpose of injuring the enemy.

Neither the fact of the personnel of the said ships and sickwards being armed for maintaining order and for defending the sick and wounded. nor the presence of wireless telegraph apparatus on board, is a sufficient reason for withdrawing protection.

Article 9

Belligerents may appeal to the charity of the commanders of neutral merchant-ships, yachts, or boats to take on board and care for the sick and wounded.

Vessels responding to this appeal, and also vessels which have of their own accord rescued sick, wounded, or shipwrecked men, shall enjoy special protection and certain immunities. In no case can they be captured for having such persons on board, but, apart from special undertakings that may have been made to them, they remain liable to capture for any violations of neutrality they may have committed.

Article 10

The religious, medical, and hospital staff of any captured ship is inviolable, and its members cannot be made prisoners of war. On leaving the ship they take away with them the objects and surgical instruments which are their own private property.

This staff shall continue to discharge its duties while necessary, and can afterwards leave, when the commander-in-chief considers it possible.

The belligerents must guarantee to the said staff, when it has fallen into their hands, the same allowances and pay as are given to the staff of corresponding rank in their own navy.

Article 11

Sailors and soldiers on board, when sick or wounded, as well as other persons officially attached to fleets or armies, to whatever nation they belong, shall be respected and cared for by the captors.

Article 12

Any vessel of war belonging to a belligerent may demand the delivery of sick, wounded, or shipwrecked men on board military hospital- ships, hospital-ships belonging to relief societies or-to private individuals, merchant-ships, yachts, or boats; whatever the nationality of these vessels.

Article 13

If sick, wounded, or shipwrecked persons are taken on board a neutral vessel of war, every possible precaution must be taken that they can not again take part in the operations of the war.

Article 14

The shipwrecked, wounded, or sick of one of the belligerents who fall into the power of the other are prisoners of war. The captor must decide, according to circumstances, whether to keep them, or to send them to a port of his own country, to a neutral port, or even to an enemy port. In this last case, prisoners thus repatriated cannot serve again while the war lasts.

Article 15

The shipwrecked, sick, or wounded, who are landed at a neutral sort with the consent of the local authorities, must, unless an arrangement is made to the contrary between the neutral State and the belligerent States, be guarded by the neutral State so that they can not again take part in the operations of the war.

The expenses of caring for them in hospital. and interning them shall be borne by the State to which the shipwrecked, sick, or wounded persons belong.

Article 16

After every engagement, the two belligerents, so far as military interests permit, shall take steps to look for the shipwrecked, sick, and wounded, and to protect them, as well as the dead, against pillage and ill treatment.

They shall see that the burial, whether by land or sea, or cremation of the dead shall be preceded by a careful examination of the corpse.

Article 17

Each belligerent shall send, as early as possible, to the authorities of their country, navy, or army the military marks or documents of identity found on the dead and a list of the names of the sick and wounded gathered up by him.

The belligerents shall keep each other informed as to internments and transfers as well as to the admissions into hospital and deaths which have occurred among the sick and wounded in their hands. They shall collect all the objects of personal use, valuables, letters, &c., which are found in the captured ships, or which have been left by the sick or wounded who died in hospital, in order to have them forwarded to the persons concerned by the authorities of their own country.

Article 18

The provisions of the present Convention do not apply except between Contracting Powers, and only if all the belligerents are parties to the Convention.

Article 19

The commanders in chief of the belligerent fleets must arrange for the details of carrying out the preceding articles, as well as for cases not covered thereby, in accordance with the instructions of their respective Governments and in conformity with the general principles of the present Convention.

Article 20

The Signatory Powers shall take the necessary measures to instruct their naval forces, and especially the protected personnel, in the provisions of the present Convention, and to bring them to the knowledge of the population.

Article 21

The Signatory Powers likewise undertake to enact or to propose to their legislatures, if their criminal laws are inadequate, the measures necessary for checking in time of war individual acts of pillage and ill- treatment of the sick and wounded of the Navy as well as for punishing, as an unjustifiable adoption of naval or military marks, the unauthorized use of the distinctive marks mentioned in Article 5 by vessels not protected by the present Convention.

They will communicate to each other, through the Netherlands Government, the enactments for preventing such acts at the latest within five years of the ratification of the present Convention.

Article 22

In the case of operations of war between the land and the sea forces of belligerents, the provisions of the present Convention do not apply except to the forces actually embarked.

Article 23

The present Convention shall be ratified as soon as possible. The ratifications shall be deposited at The Hague. The first deposit of ratifications shall be recorded in a proces-verbal signed by the Representatives of the Powers taking part therein and by the Netherlands Minister for Foreign Affairs.

Subsequent deposits of ratifications shall be made by means of a written notification addressed to the Netherlands Government and accompanied by the instrument of ratification.

A certified copy of the proces-verbal relative to the first deposit of ratifications, of the notifications mentioned in the preceding paragraph, as well as of the instruments of ratification, shall be at once sent by the Netherlands Government through the diplomatic channel to the Powers invited to the Second Peace Conference, as well as to the other

Powers which shall have adhered to the Convention. In the cases contemplated in the preceding paragraph the said Government shall inform them at the same time of the (late on which it received the notification.

Article 24

Non-signatory Powers which have accepted the Geneva Convention of the 6th July, 1906, may adhere to the present Convention.

A Power which desires to adhere notifies its intention to the Netherlands Government in writing, forwarding to it the act of adherence, which shall be deposited in the archives of the said Government.

The said Government shall at once transmit to all the other Powers a duly certified copy of the notification as well as of the act of adherence mentioning the date on which it received the notification.

Article 25

The present Convention, duly ratified, shall replace as between Contracting Powers, the Convention of the 29th July, 1899, for the adaptation to maritime warfare of the principles of the Geneva Convention.

The Convention of 1899 remains in force as between the Powers which signed it but which do not also ratify the present Convention.

Article 26

The present Convention shall take effect in the case of the Powers which were parties to the first deposit of ratifications, sixty days after the date of the proces-verbal of this deposit, and, in the case of the Powers which ratify subsequently or which adhere sixty days after the notification of their ratification or of their adherence has been received by the Netherlands Government.

Article 27

In the event of one of the Contracting 'Powers wishing to denounce the present Convention, the denunciation shall be notified in writing to the Netherlands Government, which shall at once communicate a duly certified copy of the notification to all the other Powers, informing them at the same time of the date on which it was received.

The denunciation shall have effect only in regard to the notifying Power, and one year after the notification has reached the Netherlands Government.

Article 28

A register kept by the Netherlands Ministry for Foreign Affairs shall give the date of the deposit of ratifications made in virtue of Article 23, paragraphs 3 and 4, as well as the date on which the notifications of adherence (Article 24, paragraph 2) or of denunciation (Article 27, paragraph 1) have been received.

Each Contracting Power is entitled to have access to this register and to be supplied with duly certified extracts from it.

In faith whereof the Plenipotentiaries have appended their signatures to the present Convention.

Done at The Hague, the 18th October, 1907, in a single copy, which shall remain deposited m the archives of the Netherlands Government, and duly certified copies of which shall be sent, through the diplomatic channel, to the Powers which have been invited to the Second Peace Conference.

And whereas the said Convention has been duly ratified by the Government of the United States of America, by and with the advice and consent of the Senate thereof, and by the Governments of Germany, Austria-Hungary, China, Denmark, Mexico. the Netherlands, Russia, Bolivia, and Salvador, and the ratifications of the said Governments were, under the provisions of Article 23 of the said Convention, deposited by their respective plenipotentiaries with the Netherlands Government on November 27, 1909;
(Signatures)

Hague XI - Restrictions With Regard to the Exercise of the Right of Capture in Naval War : 18 October 1907

CONVENTION RELATIVE TO CERTAIN RESTRICTIONS WITH REGARD TO THE EXERCISE OF THE RIGHT OF CAPTURE IN NAVAL WAR

Recognizing the necessity of more effectively ensuring than hitherto the equitable application of law to the international relations of maritime Powers in time of war;

Considering that, for this purpose, it is expedient, in giving up or, if necessary, in harmonizing for the common interest certain conflicting practices of long standing, to commence codifying in regulations of general application the guarantees due to peaceful commerce and legitimate business, as well as the conduct of hostilities by sea; that it is expedient to lay down in written mutual engagements the principles which have hitherto remained in the uncertain domain of controversy or have been left to the discretion of Governments;

That, from henceforth, a certain number of rules may be made, without affecting the common law now in force with regard to the matters which that law has left unsettled;

Have appointed the following as their Plenipotentiaries:
(List of Plenipotentiaries)

Who, after having deposited their full powers, found in good and due form, have agreed upon the following provisions:

Chapter I. Postal Correspondence

Article 1

The postal correspondence of neutrals or belligerents, whatever its official or private character may be, found on the high seas on board a neutral or enemy ship, is inviolable. If the ship is detained, the correspondence is forwarded by the captor with the least possible delay.

The provisions of the preceding paragraph do not apply, in case of violation of blockade, to correspondence destined for or proceeding from a blockaded port.

Article 2

The inviolability of postal correspondence does not exempt a neutral mail ship from the laws and customs of maritime war as to neutral merchant ships in general. The ship, however, may not be searched except when absolutely necessary, and then only with as much consideration and expedition as possible.

Chapter II. The Exemption from Capture of Certain Vessels

Article 3

Vessels used exclusively for fishing along the coast or small boats employed in local trade are exempt from capture, as well as their appliances, rigging, tackle, and cargo. They cease to be exempt as soon as they take any part whatever in hostilities.

The Contracting Powers agree not to take advantage of the harmless character of the said vessels in order to use them for military purposes while preserving their peaceful appearance.

Article 4

Vessels charged with religious, scientific, or philanthropic missions are likewise exempt from capture.

Chapter III. Regulations Regarding the Crews of Enemy Merchant Ships Captured by a Belligerent

Article 5

When an enemy merchant ship is captured by a belligerent, such of its crew as are nationals of a neutral State are not made prisoners of war.

The same rule applies in the case of the captain and officers likewise nationals of a neutral State, if they promise formally in writing not to serve on an enemy ship while the war lasts.

Article 6

The captain, officers, and members of the crew, when nationals of the enemy State, are not made prisoners of war, on condition that they make a formal promise in writing, not to undertake, while hostilities last, any service connected with the operations of the war.

Article 7

The names of the persons retaining their liberty under the conditions laid down in Article 5, paragraph 2, and in Article 6, are notified by the belligerent captor to the other belligerent. The latter is forbidden knowingly to employ the said persons.

Article 8

The provisions of the three preceding articles do not apply to ships taking part in the hostilities.

Chapter IV. Final Provisions

Article 9

The provisions of the present Convention do not apply except between Contracting Powers, and then only if all the belligerents are parties to the Convention.

Article 10

The present Convention shall be ratified as soon as possible. The ratifications shall be deposited at The Hague. The first deposit of ratifications shall be recorded in a proces-verbal signed by the representatives of the Powers taking part therein and by the Netherlands Minister for Foreign Affairs.
Subsequent deposits of ratifications shall be made by means of a written notification, addressed to the Netherlands Government and accompanied by the instrument of ratification.

A duly certified copy of the proces-verbal relative to the first deposit of ratifications, of the notifications mentioned in the preceding paragraph, as well as of the instruments of ratification, shall be at once sent by the Netherlands Government, through the diplomatic channel, to the Powers invited to the Second Peace Conference, as well as to the other Powers which have adhered to the Convention. In the cases contemplated in the preceding paragraph, the said Government shall inform them at the same time of the date on which it received the notification.

Article 11

Non-Signatory Powers may adhere to the present Convention.

The Power which desires to adhere notifies its intention in writing to the Netherlands Government, forwarding to it the act of adhesion, which shall be deposited in the archives of the said Government.

This Government shall at once transmit to all the other Powers a duly certified copy of the notification as well as of the act of adhesion, mentioning the date on which it received the notification.

Article 12

The present Convention shall come into force in the case of the Powers which were a party to the first deposit of ratifications, sixty days after the proces-verbal of that deposit, and, in the case of the Powers which ratify subsequently or which adhere, sixty days after the notification of their ratification has been received by the Netherlands Government.

Article 13

In the event of one of the Contracting Powers wishing to denounce the present Convention, the denunciation shall be notified in writing to the Netherlands Government, which shall at once communicate a duly certified copy of the notification lo all the other Powers informing them of the date on which it was received.

The denunciation shall only have effect in regard to the notifying Power, and one year after the notification has reached the Netherlands Government.

Article 14

A register kept by the Netherlands Ministry for Foreign Affairs shall give the date of the deposit of ratifications made in virtue of Article 10, paragraphs 3 and 4, as well as the date on which the notifications of adhesion (Article 11, paragraph 2) or of denunciation (Article 13, paragraph 1) have been received.

Each Contracting Power is entitled to have access to this register and to be supplied with duly certified extracts from it.

In faith whereof the Plenipotentiaries have appended their signatures to the present Convention.

Done at The Hague, 18 October 1907, in a single copy, which shall remain deposited in the archives of the Netherlands Government, and duly certified copies of which shall be sent, through the diplomatic channel, to the Powers invited to the Second Peace Conference.

Hague XIII -Rights and Duties of Neutral Powers in Naval War: 18 October 1907

CONVENTION CONCERNING THE RIGHTS AND DUTIES OF NEUTRAL POWERS IN NAVAL WAR

With a view to harmonizing the divergent views which, in the event of naval war, are still held on the relations between neutral Powers and belligerent Powers, and to anticipating the difficulties to which such divergence of views might give rise;

Seeing that, even if it is not possible at present to concert measures applicable to all circumstances which may in practice occur, it is nevertheless undeniably advantageous to frame, as far as possible, rules of general application to meet the case where war has unfortunately broken out;

Seeing that, in cases not covered by the present Convention, it is expedient to take into consideration the general principles of the law of nations;

Seeing that it is desirable that the Powers should issue detailed enactments to regulate the results of the attitude of neutrality when adopted by them;

Seeing that it is, for neutral Powers, an admitted duty to apply these rules impartially to the several belligerents;

Seeing that, in this category of ideas, these rules should not, in principle, be altered, in the course of the war, by a neutral Power, except in a case where experience has shown the necessity for such change for the protection of the rights of that Power;

Have agreed to observe the following common rules, which cannot however modify provisions laid down in existing general treaties, and have appointed as their Plenipotentiaries, namely:
(List of Plenipotentiaries)

Who, after having deposited their full powers, found in good and due form, have agreed upon the following provisions:

Article 1

Belligerents are bound to respect the sovereign rights of neutral Powers and to abstain, in neutral territory or neutral waters, from any act which would, if knowingly permitted by any Power, constitute a violation of neutrality.

Article 2

Any act of hostility, including capture and the exercise of the right of search, committed by belligerent war-ships in the territorial waters of a neutral Power, constitutes a violation of neutrality and is strictly forbidden.

Article 3

When a ship has been captured in the territorial waters of a neutral Power, this Power must employ, if the prize is still within its jurisdiction, the means at its disposal to release the prize with its officers and crew, and to intern the prize crew.

If the prize is not in the jurisdiction of the neutral Power, the captor Government, on the demand of that Power, must liberate the prize with its officers and crew.

Article 4

A prize court cannot be set up by a belligerent on neutral territory or on a vessel in neutral waters.

Article 5

Belligerents are forbidden to use neutral ports and waters as a base of naval operations against their adversaries, and in particular to erect wireless telegraphy stations or any apparatus for the purpose of communicating with the belligerent forces on land or sea.

Article 6

The supply, in any manner, directly or indirectly, by a neutral Power to a belligerent Power, of war-ships, ammunition, or war material of any kind whatever, is forbidden.

Article 7

A neutral Power is not bound to prevent the export or transit, for the use of either belligerent, of arms, ammunition, or, in general, of anything which could be of use to an army or fleet.

Article 8

A neutral Government is bound to employ the means at its disposal to prevent the fitting out or arming of any vessel within its jurisdiction which it has reason to believe is intended to cruise, or engage in hostile operations, against a Power with which that Government is at peace. It is also bound to display the same vigilance to prevent the departure from its jurisdiction of any vessel intended to cruise, or engage in hostile operations, which had been adapted entirely or partly within the said jurisdiction for use in war.

Article 9

A neutral Power must apply impartially to the two belligerents the conditions, restrictions, or prohibitions made by it in regard to the admission into its ports, roadsteads, or territorial waters, of belligerent war-ships or of their prizes.

Nevertheless, a neutral Power may forbid a belligerent vessel which has failed to conform to the orders and regulations made by it, or which has violated neutrality, to enter its ports or roadsteads.

Article 10

The neutrality of a Power is not affected by the mere passage through its territorial waters of war-ships or prizes belonging to belligerents.

Article 11

A neutral Power may allow belligerent war-ships to employ its licensed pilots.

Article 12

In the absence of special provisions to the contrary in the legislation of a neutral Power, belligerent war-ships are not permitted to remain in the ports, roadsteads, or territorial waters of the said Power for more than twenty-four hours, except in the cases covered by the present Convention.

Article 13

If a Power which has been informed of the outbreak of hostilities learns that a belligerent war-ship is in one of its ports or roadsteads, or in its territorial waters, it must notify the said ship to depart within twenty-four hours or within the time prescribed by local regulations.

Article 14

A belligerent war-ship may not prolong its stay in a neutral port beyond the permissible time except on account of damage or stress of weather. It must depart as soon as the cause of the delay is at an end.

The regulations as to the question of the length of time which these vessels may remain in neutral ports, roadsteads, or waters, do not apply to war-ships devoted exclusively to religious, scientific, or philanthropic purposes.

Article 15

In the absence of special provisions to the contrary in the legislation of a neutral Power, the maximum number of warships belonging to a belligerent which may be in one of the ports or roadsteads of that Power simultaneously shall be three.

Article 16

When war-ships belonging to both belligerents are present simultaneously in a neutral port or roadstead, a period of not less than twenty-four hours must elapse between the departure of the ship belonging to one belligerent and the departure of the ship belonging to the other.

The order of departure is determined by the order of arrival, unless the ship which arrived first is so circumstanced that an extension of its stay is permissible.
A belligerent war-ship may not leave a neutral port or roadstead until twenty-four hours after the departure of a merchant ship flying the flag of its adversary.

Article 17

In neutral ports and roadsteads belligerent war-ships may only carry out such repairs as are absolutely necessary to render them seaworthy, and may not add in any manner whatsoever to their fighting force. The local authorities of the neutral Power shall decide what repairs are necessary, and these must be carried out with the least possible delay.

Article 18

Belligerent war-ships may not make use of neutral ports, roadsteads, or territorial waters for replenishing or increasing their supplies of war material or their armament, or for completing their crews.

Article 19

Belligerent war-ships may only revictual in neutral ports or roadsteads to bring up their supplies to the peace standard.

Similarly these vessels may only ship sufficient fuel to enable them to reach the nearest port in their own country. They may, on the other hand, fill up their bunkers built to carry fuel, when in neutral countries which have adopted this method of determining the amount of fuel to be supplied.

If, in accordance with the law of the neutral Power, the ships are not supplied with coal within twenty-four hours of their arrival, the permissible duration of their stay is extended by twenty-four hours.

Article 20

Belligerent war-ships which have shipped fuel in a port belonging to a neutral Power may not within the succeeding three months replenish their supply in a port of the same Power.

Article 21

A prize may only be brought into a neutral port on account of unseaworthiness, stress of weather, or want of fuel or provisions.

It must leave as soon as the circumstances which justified its entry are at an end. If it does not, the neutral Power must order it to leave at once; should it fail to obey, the neutral Power must employ the means at its disposal to release it with its officers and crew and to intern the prize crew.

Article 22

A neutral Power must, similarly, release a prize brought into one of its ports under circumstances other than those referred to in Article 21.

Article 23

A neutral Power may allow prizes to enter its ports and roadsteads, whether under convoy or not, when they are brought there to be sequestrated pending the decision of a Prize Court. It may have the prize taken to another of its ports.

If the prize is convoyed by a war-ship, the prize crew may go on board the convoying ship. If the prize is not under convoy, the prize crew are left at liberty.

Article 24

If, notwithstanding the notification of the neutral Power, a belligerent ship of war does not leave a port where it is not entitled to remain, the neutral Power is entitled to take such measures as it considers necessary to render the ship incapable of taking the sea during the war, and the commanding officer of the ship must facilitate the execution of

such measures. When a belligerent ship is detained by a neutral Power, the officers and crew are likewise detained.
The officers and crew thus detained may be left in the ship or kept either on another vessel or on land, and may be subjected to the measures of restriction which it may appear necessary to impose upon them. A sufficient number of men for looking after the vessel must, however, be always left on board.

The officers may be left at liberty on giving their word not to quit the neutral territory without permission.

Article 25

A neutral Power is bound to exercise such surveillance as the means at its disposal allow to prevent any violation of the provisions of the above Articles occurring in its ports or roadsteads or in its waters.

Article 26

The exercise by a neutral Power of the rights laid down in the present Convention can under no circumstances be considered as an unfriendly act by one or other belligerent who has accepted the articles relating thereto.

Article 27

The Contracting Powers shall communicate to each other in due course all laws, proclamations, and other enactments regulating in their respective countries the status of belligerent war-ships in their ports and waters, by means of a communication addressed to the Government of the Netherlands, and forwarded immediately by that Government to the other Contracting Powers.

Article 28

The provisions of the present Convention do not apply except between Contracting Powers, and then only if all the belligerents are parties to the Convention.

Article 29

The present Convention shall be ratified as soon as possible. The ratifications shall be deposited at The Hague. The first deposit of ratifications shall be recorded in a proces-verbal signed by the representatives of the Powers which take part therein and by the Netherlands Minister for Foreign Affairs. The subsequent deposits of ratifications shall be made by means of a written notification addressed to the Netherlands Government and accompanied by the instrument of ratification.

A duly certified copy of the proces-verbal relative to the first deposit of ratifications, of the ratifications mentioned in the preceding paragraph, as well as of the instruments of ratification, shall be at once sent by the Netherlands Government, through the diplomatic channel, to the Powers invited to the Second Peace Conference, as well as to the other Powers which have adhered to the Convention. In the cases contemplated in the preceding paragraph, the said Government shall inform them at the same time of the date on which it received the notification.

Article 30

Non-Signatory Powers may adhere to the present Convention. The Power which desires to adhere notifies in writing its intention to the Netherlands Government, forwarding to it the act of adhesion, which shall be deposited in the archives of the said Government.

That Government shall at once transmit to all the other Powers a duly certified copy of the notification as well as of the act of adhesion, mentioning the date on which it received the notification.

Article 31

The present Convention shall come into force in the case of the Powers which were a party to the first deposit of the ratifications, sixty days after the date of the proces-verbal of that deposit, and, in the case of the Powers who ratify subsequently or who adhere, sixty days after the notification of their ratification or of their decision has been received by the Netherlands Government.

Article 32

In the event of one of the Contracting Powers wishing to denounce the present Convention, the denunciation shall be notified in writing to the Netherlands Government, who shall at once communicate a duly certified copy of the notification to all the other Powers, informing them of the date on which it was received.

The denunciation shall only have effect in regard to the notifying Power, and one year after the notification has been made to the Netherlands Government.

Article 33

A register kept by the Netherlands Ministry for Foreign Affairs shall give the date of the deposit of ratifications made by Article 29, paragraphs 3 and 4, as well as the date on which the notifications of adhesion (Article 30, paragraph 2) or of denunciation (Article 32, paragraph 1) have been received.

Each Contracting Power is entitled to have access to this register and to be supplied with duly certified extracts.

In faith whereof the Plenipotentiaries have appended their signatures to the present Convention.

Done at The Hague, 18 October 1907, in a single copy, which shall remain deposited in the archives of the Netherlands Government, and duly certified copies of which shall be sent, through the diplomatic channel, to the Powers which have been invited to the Second Peace Conference.

List of the signatory and Contracting Powers of the Hague Convention of 1899 and 1907 and Dates on which the Convention(s) took effect for each of them

as of June 2007

	1899	1907
Argentina	15-06-1907	
Australia	01-04-1960	21-02-1997
Austria	04-09-1900	26-01-1910
Belarus	04-06-1962	04-04-1962
Belgium	04-09-1900	07-10-1910
Belize		21-01-2003
Benin		16-09-2005
Bolivia	15-06-1907	26-01-1910
Brazil	15-06-1907	06-03-1914
Bulgaria	04-09-1900	10-06-2000
Burkina Faso	30-08-1961	30-08-1961
Cambodia	04-01-1956	04-01-1956
Cameroon	01-08-1961	01-08-1961
Canada	19-08-1960	09-07-1994
Chile	15-06-1907	18-01-1998
People's Republic of China	21-11-1904	26-01-1910
Colombia	15-06-1907	17-03-1997
Democratic Republic of the Congo	25-03-1961	25-03-1961
Costa Rica		20-07-1999
Croatia (Declaration of Succession)	02-10-1998	
Cuba	15-06-1907	22-04-1912
Cyprus		12-11-1993
Czech Republic		01-01-1993
Denmark	04-09-1900	26-01-1910
Dominican Republic	15-06-1907	07-09-1958
Ecuador	03-07-1907	
Egypt	20-06-1907	04-11-1968
El Salvador	20-06-1907	26-01-1910
Eritrea	04-10-1997	
Estonia		01-09-2003
Ethiopia	28-09-2003	
Fiji	02-04-1973	
Finland		09-06-1922
France	04-09-1900	06-12-1910
Germany	04-09-1900	26-01-1910
Greece	04-04-1901	

Guatemala	15-06-1907	14-05-1911
Guyana	25-01-1998	
Haiti	15-06-1907	03-04-1910
Honduras	01-12-1961	30-01-1962
Hungary	04-09-1900	26-01-1910
Iceland	08-12-1955	08-12-1955
India	29-07-1950	
Iran	04-09-1900	
Iraq	31-08-1970	30-10-1970
Ireland		06-07-2002
Israel		17-06-1962
Italy	04-09-1900	
Japan	06-10-1900	11-02-1912
Jordan		27-01-1992

	1899	**1907**
Kenya		11-06-2006
Republic of Korea		21-02-2000
Kuwait		14-09-2003
Kyrgyzstan	04-06-1992	04-06-1992
Lao People's Democratic Republic	18-07-1955	18-07-1955
Latvia		12-08-2001
Lebanon	14-02-1968	14-04-1968
Libyan Arab Jamahiriya		02-09-1996
Liechtenstein		23-09-1994
Lithuania		09-01-2005
Luxembourg	12-07-1901	04-11-1912
Former Yugoslav Republic of Macedonia		17-02-2001
Malaysia		06-05-2002
Malta		07-09-1968
Mauritius	03-08-1970	
Mexico	17-04-1901	26-01-1910
Montenegro	**10-04-1907**	
Morocco		04-06-2001
Netherlands	04-09-1900	26-01-1910
New Zealand	10-02-1959	
Nicaragua	15-06-1907	14-02-1910
Nigeria		16-02-1987
Norway	04-09-1900	18-11-1910
Pakistan	05-08-1950	
Panama	15-06-1907	10-11-1911
Paraguay	15-06-1907	24-06-1933
Peru	15-06-1907	
Poland		26-05-1922
Portugal	04-09-1900	12-06-1911
Qatar		02-12-2005
Romania	04-09-1900	30-04-1912
Russian Federation	07-03-1955	07-03-1955
Saudi Arabia		20-01-2002
Senegal	01-08-1977	30-09-1977
Serbia, Republic of (Declaration of Succession)	04-09-2001	
Singapore		11-09-1993

Slovak Republic		01-01-1993
Slovenia (Declaration of Succession)	05-09-1996	29-03-2004
South Africa		21-12-1998
Spain	04-09-1900	17-05-1913
Sri Lanka	09-02-1955	
Sudan		02-12-1966
Surinam		27-12-1992
Swaziland		25-12-1970
Sweden	04-09-1900	26-01-1910
Switzerland	29-12-1900	11-07-1910
Thailand	04-09-1900	11-05-1910
Togo		17-12-2004
Turkey	12-06-1907	
Uganda		30-04-1966
Ukraine	04-04-1962	04-04-1962
United Kingdom of Great Britain and Northern Ireland	04-09-1900	12-10-1970
United States of America	04-09-1900	26-01-1910
Uruguay	17-06-1907	
Venezuela	15-06-1907	
Zambia		01-01-2000
Zimbabwe	19-09-1984	

The Martens Clause

"Until a more complete code of laws of war has been issued, the high contracting parties deem it expedient to declare that, in cases not included in the regulations adopted by them, the inhabitants and the belligerents remain under the protection and the rule of the principles of the law of nations, as they result from the usages established among civilized peoples, from the laws of humanity, and the dictates of the public conscience."

These famous words, the Martens Clause, are at the core of the laws of war, as well as the centre of a tense debate. Since the framing of the clause at the 1899 Hague Peace Conference
much has been said about its interpretation, its origins, and its meaning in practice for the laws of war.

Martens, a Russian lawyer and diplomat from Estonia, can be seen as the individual with the
single greatest influence on the Hague Peace Conferences and their outcomes. His influence was so great that many contemporaries ascribed him the role of initiator of the Peace Conference itself, although he was unaware of the upcoming convocation before it reached the press and the general public. When Martens got the news he was irritated by it despite being one of the leading legal scholars and authors in the peace movement. As a realistic diplomat he thought the chances of success were slim and that the entire project would do more harm than good.

The Martens clause is highly instructive to the debate and tensions surrounding the laws of war. The dilemma between positive law and moral imperatives become quite clear when analyzing the clause and its interpretations. Although it does not pose a clear rule regarding means and methods of war, it is perceived by some as a regulation enabling the laws of war to deal with. The clause has the potential to be a strong open norm placing a heavy dictate of humanitarian concern on the means and methods of warfare.

Eventually, the efforts of Martens were deemed so great that both the delegates and the general public came to refer to him as '**the soul of the Hague Conference.**[15]

Results and influence of the conferences on International Law

In general, however, the Hague Conventions constitute the starting point for that part of International Humanitarian Law which purports to regulate the methods and means of combat. Further, substantial portions of the Hague Conventions are now regarded as constituting part of customary international law.

Next to the final agreements of 1899 and 1907 the conventions had other outcomes. At both conferences, limitations on armaments and expansion of armed forces were proposed. This did not succeed, but the Conventions did establish various points including a ban on types of war technology, and the adoption of the Convention for the Pacific Settlement of International Disputes, which created the Permanent Court of Arbitration. The two Conventions established a model for multilateral meetings to hash out international law, influencing the formation of the League of Nations in 1919.[16]

Establishing of the permanent court of arbitration (PCA)

The PCA is an intergovernmental organization with over one hundred member states. The PCA was established by the 1899 Convention for the Pacific Settlement of International Disputes, concluded at The Hague during the first Hague Peace Conference. PCA was established to facilitate arbitration and other forms of dispute resolution between states, the PCA has developed into a modern, multi-faceted arbitral institution that is now perfectly situated at the juncture between public and private international law to meet the rapidly evolving dispute resolution needs of the

[15] K. Dijkhof, *War, Law and Technology*, WLP 2010, p 76-78.

[16] <http://www.cfr.org/publication/9597/hague_conventions_1899_1907.html>.

international community. Today the PCA provides services for the resolution of disputes involving various combinations of states, state entities, intergovernmental organizations, and private parties.[17]

[17] <http://www.pca-cpa.org/showpage.asp?pag_id=1027>.

SETTLEMENT OF INTERNATIONAL DISPUTES*

His Majesty the German Emperor, King of Prussia; His Majesty the Emperor of Austria, King of Bohemia, etc. and Apostolic King of Hungary; His Majesty the King of the Belgians; His Majesty the Emperor of China; His Majesty the King of Denmark; His Majesty the King of Spain and in His Name Her Majesty the Queen Regent of the Kingdom; the President of the United States of America; the President of the United Mexican States; the President of the French Republic; Her Majesty the Queen of the United Kingdom of Great Britain and Ireland, Empress of India; His Majesty the King of the Hellenes; His Majesty the King of Italy; His Majesty the Emperor of Japan; His Royal Highness the Grand Duke of Luxembourg, Duke of Nassau; His Highness the Prince of Montenegro; Her Majesty the Queen of the Netherlands; His Imperial Majesty the Shah of Persia; His Majesty the King of Portugal and of the Algarves, etc.; His Majesty the King of Roumania; His Majesty the Emperor of all the Russias; His Majesty the King of Serbia; his Majesty the King of Siam; His Majesty the King of Sweden and Norway; the Swiss Federal Council; His Majesty the Emperor of the Ottomans and His Royal Highness the Prince of Bulgaria;

Animated by a strong desire to work for the maintenance of general peace;

Resolved to promote by their best efforts the friendly settlement of international disputes;

Recognizing the solidarity uniting the members of the society of civilized nations;

Desirous of extending the empire of law, and of strengthening the appreciation of international justice;

Convinced that the permanent institution of a tribunal of arbitration, accessible to all, in the midst of the independent Powers, will contribute effectively to this result;

Having regard to the advantages attending the general and regular organization of the procedure of arbitration;
Sharing the opinion of the august initiator of the International Peace Conference that it is expedient to record in an international agreement the principles of equity and right on which are based the security of States and the welfare of peoples;

Being desirous of concluding a Convention to this effect, have appointed as their plenipotentiaries, to wit:
(Here follow the names of plenipotentiaries.)

---

* The text of the Convention reproduced here is a translation of the French text adopted at the 1899 Peace Conference. The French-language version is authoritative.

Who, after having communicated their full powers, found in good and due form, have agreed on the following provisions:

Title I. On the Maintenance of the General Peace

Article 1

With a view to obviating, as far as possible, recourse to force in the relations between States, the Signatory Powers agree to use their best efforts to insure the pacific settlement of international differences.

Title II. On Good Offices and Mediation

Article 2

In case of serious disagreement or conflict, before an appeal to arms the Signatory Powers agree to have recourse, as far as circumstances allow, to the good offices or mediation of one or more friendly Powers.

Article 3

Independently of this recourse, the Signatory Powers recommend that one or more Powers, strangers to the dispute, should, on their own initiative, and as far as circumstances may allow, offer their good offices or mediation to the States at variance.

Powers, strangers to the dispute, have the right to offer good offices or mediation, even during the course of hostilities.

The exercise of this right can never be regarded by one or the other of the parties in conflict as an unfriendly act.

Article 4

The part of the mediator consists in reconciling the opposing claims and appeasing the feelings of resentment which may have arisen between the States at variance.

Article 5

The functions of the mediator are at an end when once it is declared, either by one of the parties to the dispute, or by the mediator himself, that the means of reconciliation proposed by him are not accepted.

Article 6

Good offices and mediation, either at the request of the parties at variance, or on the initiative of Powers strangers to the dispute, have exclusively the character of advice, and never have binding force.

Article 7

The acceptance of mediation cannot, unless there be an agreement to the contrary, have the effect of interrupting, delaying, or hindering mobilization or other measures of preparation for war.

If mediation occurs after the commencement of hostilities, it causes no interruption to the military operations in progress, unless there be an agreement to the contrary.

Article 8

The Signatory Powers are agreed in recommending the application, when circumstances allow, of special mediation in the following form:

In case of a serious difference endangering the peace, the States at variance choose respectively a Power, to whom they intrust the mission of entering into direct communication with the Power chosen on the other side, with the object of preventing the rupture of pacific relations.

For the period of this mandate, the term of which, unless otherwise stipulated, cannot exceed thirty days, the States in conflict cease from all direct communication on the subject of the dispute, which is regarded as referred exclusively to the mediating Powers, who must use their best efforts to settle it. In case of a definite rupture of pacific relations, these Powers are charged with the joint task of taking advantage of any opportunity to restore peace.

Article 9

In differences of an international nature involving neither honour nor vital interests, and arising from a difference of opinion on points of fact, the Signatory Powers recommend that the parties, who have not been able to come to an agreement by means of diplomacy, should, as far as circumstances allow, institute an International Commission of Inquiry, to facilitate a solution of these differences by elucidating the facts by means of an impartial and conscientious investigation.

Article 10

The International Commissions of Inquiry are constituted by special agreement between the parties in conflict. The Convention for an inquiry defines the facts to be examined and the extent of the Commissioners' powers. It settles the procedure. On the inquiry both sides must be heard. The form and the periods to be observed, if not stated in the Inquiry Convention, are decided by the Commission itself.

Article 11

The International Commissions of Inquiry are formed, unless otherwise stipulated, in the manner fixed by Article 32 of the present Convention.

Article 12

The Powers in dispute engage to supply the International Commission of Inquiry, as fully as they may think possible, with all means and facilities necessary to enable it to be completely acquainted with and to accurately understand the facts in question.

Article 13

The International Commission of Inquiry communicates its Report to the conflicting Powers, signed by all the members of the Commission.

Article 14

The Report of the International Commission of Inquiry is limited to a statement of facts, and has in no way the character of an Arbitral Award. It leaves the conflicting Powers entire freedom as to the effect to be given to this statement.

Title IV. On International Arbitration

Chapter I. On the System of Arbitration

Article 15

International arbitration has for its object the settlement of differences between States by judges of their own choice, and on the basis of respect for law.

Article 16

In questions of a legal nature, and especially in the interpretation or application of International Conventions, arbitration is recognized by the Signatory Powers as the most effective, and at the same time the most equitable, means of settling disputes which diplomacy has failed to settle.

Article 17

The Arbitration Convention is concluded for questions already existing or for questions which may arise eventually. It may embrace any dispute or only disputes of a certain category.

Article 18

The Arbitration Convention implies the engagement to submit loyally to the Award.

Article 19

Independently of general or private Treaties expressly stipulating recourse to arbitration as obligatory on the Signatory Powers, these Powers reserve to themselves the right of concluding, either before the ratification of the present Act or later, new Agreements, general or private, with a view to extending obligatory arbitration to all cases which they may consider it possible to submit to it.

Chapter II. On the Permanent Court of Arbitration

Article 20

With the object of facilitating an immediate recourse to arbitration for international differences, which it has not been possible to settle by diplomacy, the Signatory Powers undertake to organize a Permanent Court of Arbitration, accessible at all times and operating, unless otherwise stipulated by the parties, in accordance with the Rules of Procedure inserted in the present Convention.

Article 21

The Permanent Court shall be competent for all arbitration cases, unless the parties agree to institute a special Tribunal.

Article 22

An International Bureau, established at The Hague, serves as record office for the Court. This Bureau is the channel for communications relative to the meetings of the Court. It has the custody of the archives and conducts all the administrative business. The Signatory Powers undertake to communicate to the International Bureau at The Hague a duly certified copy of any conditions of arbitration arrived at between them, and of any award concerning them delivered by special Tribunals. They undertake also to communicate to the Bureau the Laws, Regulations, and documents eventually showing the execution of the Awards given by the Court.

Article 23

Within the three months following its ratification of the present Act, each Signatory Power shall select four persons at the most, of known competency in questions of international law, of the highest moral reputation, and disposed to accept the duties of Arbitrators.

The persons thus selected shall be inscribed, as Members of the Court, in a list which shall be notified by the Bureau to all the Signatory Powers. Any alteration in the list of Arbitrators is brought by the Bureau to the knowledge of the Signatory Powers. Two or more Powers may agree on the selection in common of one or more Members. The same person can be selected by different Powers. The Members of the Court are appointed for a term of six years. Their appointments can be renewed. In case of the death or retirement of a Member of the Court, his place shall be filled in accordance with the method of this appointment.

Article 24

When the Signatory Powers desire to have recourse to the Permanent Court for the settlement of a difference that has arisen between them, the Arbitrators called upon to form the competent Tribunal to decide this difference, must be chosen from the general list of Members of the Court.

Failing the direct agreement of the parties on the composition of the Arbitration Tribunal, the following course shall be pursued:

Each party appoints two Arbitrators, and these together choose an Umpire.
If the votes are equal, the choice of the Umpire is intrusted to a third Power, selected by the parties by common accord.

If an agreement is not arrived at on this subject, each party selects a different Power, and the choice of the Umpire is made in concert by the Powers thus selected.

The Tribunal being thus composed, the parties notify to the Bureau their determination to have recourse to the Court and the names of the Arbitrators.

The Tribunal of Arbitration assembles on the date fixed by the parties.

The Members of the Court, in the discharge of their duties and out of their own country, enjoy diplomatic privileges and immunities.

Article 25

The Tribunal of Arbitration has its ordinary seat at The Hague. Except in cases of necessity, the place of session can only be altered by the Tribunal with the assent of the parties.

Article 26

The International Bureau at The Hague is authorized to place its premises and its staff at the disposal of the Signatory Powers for the operations of any special Board of Arbitration.

The jurisdiction of the Permanent Court may, within the conditions laid down in the Regulations, be extended to disputes between non-Signatory Powers, or between Signatory Powers and non-Signatory Powers, if the parties are agreed on recourse to this Tribunal.

Article 27

The Signatory Powers consider it their duty, if a serious dispute threatens to break out between two or more of them, to remind these latter that the Permanent Court is open to them.

Consequently, they declare that the fact of reminding the conflicting parties of the provisions of the present Convention, and the advice given to them, in the highest interests of peace, to have recourse to the Permanent Court, can only be regarded as friendly actions.

Article 28

A Permanent Administrative Council composed of the Diplomatic Representatives of the Signatory Powers accredited to The Hague and of the Netherlands Minister for Foreign Affairs, who will act as President, shall be instituted in this town as soon as possible after the ratification of the present Act by at least nine Powers. This Council will be charged with the establishment and organization of the International Bureau, which will be under its direction and control. It will notify to the Powers the constitution of the Court and will provide for its installation. It will settle its Rules of Procedure and all other necessary Regulations. It will decide all questions of administration which may arise with regard to the operations of the Court. It will have entire control over the appointment, suspension or dismissal of the officials and employees of the Bureau. It will fix the payments and salaries, and control the general expenditure. At meetings duly summoned the presence of five members is sufficient to render valid the discussions of the Council. The decisions are taken by a majority of votes. The Council communicates to the Signatory Powers without delay the Regulations adopted by it. It furnished them with an annual Report on the labours of the Court, the working of the administration, and the expenses.

Article 29

The expenses of the Bureau shall be borne by the Signatory Powers in the proportion fixed for the International Bureau of the Universal Postal Union.

Chapter III. On Arbitral Procedure

Article 30

With a view to encourage the development of arbitration, the Signatory Powers have agreed on the following Rules which shall be applicable to arbitral procedure, unless other Rules have been agreed on by the parties.

Article 31

The Powers who have recourse to arbitration sign a special Act ('Compromis'), in which the subject of the difference is clearly defined, as well as the extent of the Arbitrators' powers. This Act implies the undertaking of the parties to submit loyally to the Award.

Article 32

The duties of Arbitrator may be conferred on one Arbitrator alone or on several Arbitrators selected by the parties as they please, or chosen by them from the Members of the Permanent Court of Arbitration established by the present Act.
Failing the constitution of the Tribunal by direct agreement between the parties, the following course shall be pursued:

- Each party appoints two Arbitrators, and these latter together choose an Umpire.

- In case of equal voting, the choice of the Umpire is intrusted to a third Power, selected by the parties by common accord.
- If no agreement is arrived at on this subject, each party selects a different Power, and the choice of the Umpire is made in concert by the Powers thus selected.

Article 33

When a Sovereign or the Chief of a State is chosen as Arbitrator, the arbitral procedure is settled by him.

Article 34

The Umpire is by right President of the Tribunal. When the Tribunal does not include an Umpire, it appoints its own President.

Article 35

In case of the death, retirement, or disability from any cause of one of the Arbitrators, his place shall be filled in accordance with the method of his appointment.

Article 36

The Tribunal's place of session is selected by the parties. Failing this selection the Tribunal sits at The Hague. The place thus fixed cannot, except in case of necessity, be changed by the Tribunal without the assent of the parties.

Article 37

The parties have the right to appoint delegates or special agents to attend the Tribunal, for the purpose of serving as intermediaries between them and the Tribunal. They are further authorized to retain, for the defence of their rights and interests before the Tribunal, counsel or advocates appointed by them for this purpose.

Article 38

The Tribunal decides on the choice of languages to be used by itself, and to be authorized for use before it.

Article 39

As a general rule the arbitral procedure comprises two distinct phases; preliminary examination and discussion. Preliminary examination consists in the communication by the respective agents to the members of the Tribunal and to the opposite party of all printed or written Acts and of all documents containing the arguments invoked in the case. This communication shall be made in the form and within the periods fixed by the Tribunal in accordance with Article 49. Discussion consists in the oral development before the Tribunal of the arguments of the parties.

Article 40

Every document produced by one party must be communicated to the other party.

Article 41

The discussions are under the direction of the President. They are only public if it be so decided by the Tribunal, with the assent of the parties. They are recorded in the *procès-verbaux* drawn up by the Secretaries appointed by the President. These *procès-verbaux* alone have an authentic character.

Article 42

When the preliminary examination is concluded, the Tribunal has the right to refuse discussion of all fresh Acts or documents which one party may desire to submit to it without the consent of the other party.

Article 43

The Tribunal is free to take into consideration fresh Acts or documents to which its attention may be drawn by the agents or counsel of the parties. In this case, the Tribunal has the right to require the production of these Acts or documents, but is obliged to make them known to the opposite party.

Article 44

The Tribunal can, besides, require from the agents of the parties the production of all Acts, and can demand all necessary explanations. In case of refusal, the Tribunal takes note of it.

Article 45

The agents and counsel of the parties are authorized to present orally to the Tribunal all the arguments they may think expedient in defence of their case.

Article 46

They have the right to raise objections and points. The decisions of the Tribunal on those points are final, and cannot form the subject of any subsequent discussion.

Article 47

The members of the Tribunal have the right to put questions to the agents and counsel of the parties, and to demand explanations from them on doubtful points. Neither the questions put nor the remarks made by members of the Tribunal during the discussions can be regarded as an expression of opinion by the Tribunal in general, or by its members in particular.

Article 48

The Tribunal is authorized to declare its competence in interpreting the 'Compromis' as well as the other Treaties which may be invoked in the case, and in applying the principles of international law.

Article 49

The Tribunal has the right to issue Rules of Procedure for the conduct of the case, to decide the forms and periods within which each party must conclude its arguments, and to arrange all the formalities required for dealing with the evidence.

Article 50

When the agents and counsel of the parties have submitted all explanations and evidence in support of their case, the President pronounces the discussion closed.

Article 51

The deliberations of the Tribunal take place in private. Every decision is taken by a majority of members of the Tribunal. The refusal of a member to vote must be recorded in the *procès-verbal.*

Article 52

The Award, given by a majority of votes, is accompanied by a statement of reasons. It is drawn up in writing and signed by each member of the Tribunal. Those members who are in the minority may record their dissent when signing.

Article 53

The Award is read out at a public meeting of the Tribunal, the agents and counsel of the parties being present, or duly summoned to attend.

Article 54

The Award, duly pronounced and notified to the agents of the parties at variance, puts an end to the dispute definitively and without appeal.

Article 55

The parties can reserve in the 'Compromis' the right to demand the revision of the Award. In this case, and unless there be an agreement to the contrary, the demand must be addressed to the Tribunal which pronounced the Award. It can only be made on the ground of the discovery of some new fact calculated to exercise a decisive influence on the Award, and which, at the time the discussion was closed, was unknown to the Tribunal and to the party demanding the revision.

Proceedings for revision can only be instituted by a decision of the Tribunal expressly recording the existence of the new fact, recognizing in it the character described in the foregoing paragraph, and declaring the demand admissible on this ground. The 'Compromis' fixes the period within which the demand for revision must be made.

Article 56

The Award is only binding on the parties who concluded the 'Compromis'. When there is a question of interpreting a Convention to which Powers other than those concerned in the dispute are parties, the latter notify to the former the 'Compromis' they have concluded. Each of these Powers has the right to intervene in the case. If one or more of them avail themselves of this right, the interpretation contained in the Award is equally binding on them.

Article 57

Each party pays its own expenses and an equal share of those of the Tribunal.

Article 58
General Provisions

The present Convention shall be ratified as speedily as possible. The ratifications shall be deposited at The Hague. A *procès-verbal* shall be drawn up recording the receipt of each ratification, and a copy duly certified shall be sent, through the diplomatic channel, to all the Powers who were represented at the International Peace Conference at The Hague.

Article 59

The non-Signatory Powers who were represented at the International Peace Conference can adhere to the present Convention. For this purpose they must make known their adhesion to the Contracting Powers by a written notification addressed to the Netherlands Government, and communicated by it to all the other Contracting Powers.

Article 60

The conditions on which the Powers who were not represented at the International Peace Conference can adhere to the present Convention shall form the subject of a subsequent Agreement among the Contracting Powers.

Article 61

In the event of one of the High Contracting Parties denouncing the present Convention, this denunciation would not take effect until a year after its notification made in writing to the Netherlands Government, and by it communicated at once to all the other Contracting Powers. This denunciation shall only affect the notifying Power.

In faith of which the Plenipotentiaries have signed the present Convention and affixed their seals to it.

Done at The Hague, the 29th July, 1899, in a single copy, which shall remain in the archives of the Netherlands Government, and copies of it, duly certified, be sent through the diplomatic channel to the Contracting Powers.

1907 CONVENTION FOR THE PACIFIC SETTLEMENT OF INTERNATIONAL DISPUTES*

His Majesty the German Emperor, King of Prussia; the President of the United States of America; the President of the Argentine Republic; His Majesty the Emperor of Austria, King of Bohemia, etc., and Apostolic King of Hungary; His Majesty the King of the Belgians; the President of the Republic of Bolivia; the President of the Republic of the United States of Brazil; His Royal Highness the Prince of Bulgaria; the President of the Republic of Chile; His Majesty the Emperor of China; the President of the Republic of Colombia; the Provisional Governor of the Republic of Cuba; His Majesty the King of Denmark; the President of the Dominican Republic; the President of the Republic of Ecuador; His Majesty the King of Spain; the President of the French Republic; His Majesty the King of the United Kingdom of Great Britain and Ireland and of the British Dominions beyond the Seas, Emperor of India; His Majesty the King of the Hellenes; the President of the Republic of Guatemala; the President of the Republic of Haiti; His Majesty the King of Italy; His Majesty the Emperor of Japan; His Royal Highness the Grand Duke of Luxembourg, Duke of Nassau; the President of the United States of Mexico; His Royal Highness the Prince of Montenegro; the President of the Republic of Nicaragua; His Majesty the King of Norway; the President of the Republic of Panama; the President of the Republic of Paraguay; Her Majesty the Queen of the Netherlands; the President of the Republic of Peru; His Imperial Majesty the Shah of Persia; His Majesty the King of Roumania; His Majesty the Emperor of All the Russias; the President of the Republic of Salvador; His Majesty the King of Servia; His Majesty the King of Siam; His Majesty the King of Sweden; the Swiss Federal Council; His Majesty the Emperor of the Ottomans; the President of the Oriental Republic of Uruguay; the President of the United States of Venezuela;

Animated by the sincere desire to work for the maintenance of general peace;

Resolved to promote by all the efforts in their power the friendly settlement of international disputes;

Recognizing the solidarity uniting the members of the society of civilized nations;
Desirous of extending the empire of law and of strengthening the appreciation of international justice;

Convinced that the permanent institution of a Tribunal of Arbitration accessible to all, in the midst of independent Powers, will contribute effectively to this result;

---

* The text of the Convention reproduced here is a translation of the French text adopted at the 1907.

Having regard to the advantages attending the general and regular organization of the procedure of arbitration;

Sharing the opinion of the august initiator of the International Peace Conference that it is expedient to record in an International Agreement the principles of equity and right on which are based the security of States and the welfare of peoples;

Being desirous, with this object, of insuring the better working in practice of Commissions of Inquiry and Tribunals of Arbitration, and of facilitating recourse to arbitration in cases which allow of a summary procedure;

Have deemed it necessary to revise in certain particulars and to complete the work of the First Peace Conference for the pacific settlement of international disputes;

The High Contracting Parties have resolved to conclude a new Convention for this purpose, and have appointed the following as their Plenipotentiaries:
(Here follow the names of Plenipotentiaries.)

Who, after having deposited their full powers, found in good and due form, have agreed upon the following:

Part I. The maintenance of General Peace

Article 1

With a view to obviating as far as possible recourse to force in the relations between States, the Contracting Powers agree to use their best efforts to ensure the pacific settlement of international differences.

Part II. Good Offices and Mediation

Article 2

In case of serious disagreement or dispute, before an appeal to arms, the Contracting Powers agree to have recourse, as far as circumstances allow, to the good offices or mediation of one or more friendly Powers.

Article 3

Independently of this recourse, the Contracting Powers deem it expedient and desirable that one or more Powers, strangers to the dispute, should, on their own initiative and as far as circumstances may allow, offer their good offices or mediation to the States at variance.

Powers strangers to the dispute have the right to offer good offices or mediation even during the course of hostilities. The exercise of this right can never be regarded by either of the parties in dispute as an unfriendly act.

Article 4

The part of the mediator consists in reconciling the opposing claims and appeasing the feelings of resentment which may have arisen between the States at variance.

Article 5

The functions of the mediator are at an end when once it is declared, either by one of the parties to the dispute or by the mediator himself, that the means of reconciliation proposed by him are not accepted.

Article 6

Good offices and mediation undertaken either at the request of the parties in dispute or on the initiative of Powers strangers to the dispute have exclusively the character of advice, and never have binding force.

Article 7

The acceptance of mediation cannot, unless there be an agreement to the contrary, have the effect of interrupting, delaying, or hindering mobilization or other measures of preparation for war. If it takes place after the commencement of hostilities, the military operations in progress are not interrupted in the absence of an agreement to the contrary.

Article 8

The Contracting Powers are agreed in recommending the application, when circumstances allow, of special mediation in the following form: In case of a serious difference endangering peace, the States at variance choose respectively a Power, to which they intrust the mission of entering into direct communication with the Power chosen on the other side, with the object of preventing the rupture of pacific relations.

For the period of this mandate, the term of which, unless otherwise stipulated, cannot exceed thirty days, the States in dispute cease from all direct communication on the subject of the dispute, which is regarded as referred exclusively to the mediating Powers, which must use their best efforts to settle it.

In case of a definite rupture of pacific relations, these Powers are charged with the joint task of taking advantage of any opportunity to restore peace.

Part III. International Commissions of Inquiry

Article 9

In disputes of an international nature involving neither honour nor vital interests, and arising from a difference of opinion on points of facts, the Contracting Powers deem it expedient and desirable that the parties who have not been able to come to an agreement by means of diplomacy, should, as far as circumstances allow, institute an International Commission of Inquiry, to facilitate a solution of these disputes by elucidating the facts by means of an impartial and conscientious investigation.

Article 10

International Commissions of Inquiry are constituted by special agreement between the parties in dispute. The Inquiry Convention defines the facts to be examined; it determines the mode and time in which the Commission is to be formed and the extent of the powers of the Commissioners.

It also determines, if there is need, where the Commission is to sit, and whether it may remove to another place, the language the Commission shall use and the languages the use of which shall be authorized before it, as well as the date on which each party must deposit its statement of facts, and, generally speaking, all the conditions upon which the parties have agreed.

If the parties consider it necessary to appoint Assessors, the Convention of Inquiry shall determine the mode of their selection and the extent of their powers.

Article 11

If the Inquiry Convention has not determined where the Commission is to sit, it will sit at The Hague. The place of meeting, once fixed, cannot be altered by the Commission except with the assent of the parties. If the Inquiry Convention has not determined what languages are to be employed, the question shall be decided by the Commission.

Article 12

Unless an undertaking is made to the contrary, Commissions of Inquiry shall be formed in the manner determined by Articles 45 and 57 of the present Convention.

Article 13

Should one of the Commissioners or one of the Assessors, should there be any, either die, or resign, or be unable for any reason whatever to discharge his functions, the same procedure is followed for filling the vacancy as was followed for appointing him.

Article 14

The parties are entitled to appoint special agents to attend the Commission of Inquiry, whose duty it is to represent them and to act as intermediaries between them and the Commission.

They are further authorized to engage counsel or advocates, appointed by themselves, to state their case and uphold their interests before the Commission.

Article 15

The International Bureau of the Permanent Court of Arbitration acts as registry for the Commissions which sit at The Hague, and shall place its offices and staff at the disposal of the Contracting Powers for the use of the Commission of Inquiry.

Article 16

If the Commission meets elsewhere than at The Hague, it appoints a Secretary-General, whose office serves as registry. It is the function of the registry, under the control of the President, to make the necessary arrangements for the sittings of the Commission, the preparation of the Minutes, and, while the inquiry lasts, for the charge of the archives, which shall subsequently be transferred to the International Bureau at The Hague.

Article 17

In order to facilitate the constitution and working of Commissions of Inquiry, the Contracting Powers recommend the following rules, which shall be applicable to the inquiry procedure in so far as the parties do not adopt other rules.

Article 18

The Commission shall settle the details of the procedure not covered by the special Inquiry Convention or the present Convention, and shall arrange all the formalities required for dealing with the evidence.

Article 19

On the inquiry both sides must be heard. At the dates fixed, each party communicates to the Commission and to the other party the statements of facts, if any, and, in all cases, the instruments, papers, and documents which it considers useful for ascertaining the truth, as well as the list of witnesses and experts whose evidence it wishes to be heard.

Article 20

The Commission is entitled, with the assent of the Powers, to move temporarily to any place where it considers it may be useful to have recourse to this means of inquiry or to send one or more of its members. Permission must be obtained from the State on whose territory it is proposed to hold the inquiry.

Article 21

Every investigation, and every examination of a locality, must be made in the presence of the agents and counsel of the parties or after they have been duly summoned.

Article 22

The Commission is entitled to ask from either party for such explanations and information as it considers necessary.

Article 23

The parties undertake to supply the Commission of Inquiry, as fully as they may think possible, with all means and facilities necessary to enable it to become completely acquainted with, and to accurately understand, the facts in question.

They undertake to make use of the means at their disposal, under their municipal law, to insure the appearance of the witnesses or experts who are in their territory and have been summoned before the Commission. If the witnesses or experts are unable to appear before the Commission, the parties will arrange for their evidence to be taken before the qualified officials of their own country.

Article 24

For all notices to be served by the Commission in the territory of a third Contracting Power, the Commission shall apply direct to the Government of the said Power. The same rule applies in the case of steps being taken on the spot to procure evidence. The requests for this purpose are to be executed so far as the means at the disposal of the Power applied to under its municipal law allow. They cannot be rejected unless the Power in question considers they are calculated to impair its sovereign rights or its safety. The Commission will equally be always entitled to act through the Power on whose territory it sits.

Article 25

The witnesses and experts are summoned on the request of the parties or by the Commission of its own motion, and, in every case, through the Government of the State in whose territory they are.

The witnesses are heard in succession and separately in the presence of the agents and counsel, and in the order fixed by the Commission.

Article 26

The examination of witnesses is conducted by the President. The members of the Commission may however put to each witness questions which they consider likely to throw light on and complete his evidence, or get information on any point concerning the witness within the limits of what is necessary in order to get at the truth.

The agents and counsel of the parties may not interrupt the witness when he is making his statement, nor put any direct question to him, but they may ask the President to put such additional questions to the witness as they think expedient.

Article 27

The witness must give his evidence without being allowed to read any written draft. He may, however, be permitted by the President to consult notes or documents if the nature of the facts referred to necessitates their employment.

Article 28

A Minute of the evidence of the witness is drawn up forthwith and read to the witness. The latter may make such alterations and additions as he thinks necessary, which will be recorded at the end of his statement. When the whole of his statement has been read to the witness, he is asked to sign it.

Article 29

The agents are authorized, in the course of or at the close of the inquiry, to present in writing to the Commission and to the other party such statements, requisitions, or summaries of the facts as they consider useful for ascertaining the truth.

Article 30

The Commission considers its decisions in private and the proceedings are secret. All questions are decided by a majority of the members of the Commission. If a member declines to vote, the fact must be recorded in the Minutes.

Article 31

The sittings of the Commission are not public, nor the Minutes and documents connected with the inquiry published except in virtue of a decision of the Commission taken with the consent of the parties.

Article 32

After the parties have presented all the explanations and evidence, and the witnesses have all been heard, the President declares the inquiry terminated, and the Commission adjourns to deliberate and to draw up its Report.

Article 33

The Report is signed by all the members of the Commission. If one of the members refuses to sign, the fact is mentioned; but the validity of the Report is not affected.

Article 34

The Report of the Commission is read at a public sitting, the agents and counsel of the parties being present or duly summoned. A copy of the Report is given to each party.

Article 35

The Report of the Commission is limited to a statement of facts, and has in no way the character of an Award. It leaves to the parties entire freedom as to the effect to be given to the statement.

Article 36

Each party pays its own expenses and an equal share of the expenses incurred by the Commission.

Part IV. International Arbitration
Chapter I. The System of Arbitration

Article 37

International arbitration has for its object the settlement of disputes between States by Judges of their own choice and on the basis of respect for law. Recourse to arbitration implies an engagement to submit in good faith to the Award.

Article 38

In questions of a legal nature, and especially in the interpretation or application of International Conventions, arbitration is recognized by the Contracting Powers as the most effective, and, at the same time, the most equitable means of settling disputes which diplomacy has failed to settle.

Consequently, it would be desirable that, in disputes about the above-mentioned questions, the Contracting Powers should, if the case arose, have recourse to arbitration, in so far as circumstances permit.

Article 39

The Arbitration Convention is concluded for questions already existing or for questions which may arise eventually. It may embrace any dispute or only disputes of a certain category.

Article 40

Independently of general or private Treaties expressly stipulating recourse to arbitration as obligatory on the Contracting Powers, the said Powers reserve to themselves the right of concluding new Agreements, general or particular, with a view to extending compulsory arbitration to all cases which they may consider it possible to submit to it.

Chapter II. The Permanent Court of Arbitration

Article 41

With the object of facilitating an immediate recourse to arbitration for international differences, which it has not been possible to settle by diplomacy, the Contracting Powers undertake to maintain the Permanent Court of Arbitration, as established by the First Peace Conference, accessible at all times, and operating, unless otherwise stipulated by the parties, in accordance with the rules of procedure inserted in the present Convention.

Article 42

The Permanent Court is competent for all arbitration cases, unless the parties agree to institute a special Tribunal.

Article 43

The Permanent Court sits at The Hague. An International Bureau serves as registry for the Court. It is the channel for communications relative to the meetings of the Court; it has charge of the archives and conducts all the administrative business.

The Contracting Powers undertake to communicate to the Bureau, as soon as possible, a certified copy of any conditions of arbitration arrived at between them and of any Award concerning them delivered by a special Tribunal. They likewise undertake to communicate to the Bureau the laws, regulations, and documents eventually showing the execution of the Awards given by the Court.

Article 44

Each Contracting Power selects four persons at the most, of known competency in questions of international law, of the highest moral reputation, and disposed to accept the duties of Arbitrator.

The persons thus elected are inscribed, as Members of the Court, in a list which shall be notified to all the Contracting Powers by the Bureau. Any alteration in the list of Arbitrators is brought by the Bureau to the knowledge of the Contracting Powers. Two or more Powers may agree on the selection in common of one or more Members. The same person can be selected by different Powers. The Members of the Court are appointed for a term of six years. These appointments are renewable. Should a Member of the Court die or resign, the same procedure is followed for filling the vacancy as was followed for appointing him. In this case the appointment is made for a fresh period of six years.

Article 45

When the Contracting Powers wish to have recourse to the Permanent Court for the settlement of a difference which has arisen between them, the Arbitrators called upon to form the Tribunal with jurisdiction to decide this difference must be chosen from the general list of Members of the Court.

Failing the direct agreement of the parties on the composition of the Arbitration Tribunal, the following course shall be pursued: Each party appoints two Arbitrators, of whom one only can be its national or chosen from among the persons selected by it as Members of the Permanent Court. These Arbitrators together choose an Umpire.

If the votes are equally divided, the choice of the Umpire is intrusted to a third Power, selected by the parties by common accord.

If an agreement is not arrived at on this subject each party selects a different Power, and the choice of the Umpire is made in concert by the Powers thus selected.
If, within two months' time, these two Powers cannot come to an agreement, each of them presents two candidates taken from the list of Members of the Permanent Court, exclusive of the members selected by the parties and not being nationals of either of them. Drawing lots determines which of the candidates thus presented shall be Umpire.

Article 46

The Tribunal being thus composed, the parties notify to the Bureau their determination to have recourse to the Court, the text of their 'Compromis', and the names of the Arbitrators.

The Bureau communicates without delay to each Arbitrator the 'Compromis', and the names of the other members of the Tribunal. The Tribunal assembles at the date fixed by the parties. The Bureau makes the necessary arrangements for the meeting. The members of the Tribunal, in the exercise of their duties and out of their own country, enjoy diplomatic privileges and immunities.

Article 47

The Bureau is authorized to place its offices and staff at the disposal of the Contracting Powers for the use of any special Board of Arbitration. The jurisdiction of the Permanent Court may, within the conditions laid down in the regulations, be extended to disputes between non-Contracting Powers or between Contracting Powers and non-Contracting Powers, if the parties are agreed on recourse to this Tribunal.

Article 48

The Contracting Powers consider it their duty, if a serious dispute threatens to break out between two or more of them, to remind these latter that the Permanent Court is open to them.

Consequently, they declare that the fact of reminding the parties at variance of the provisions of the present Convention, and the advice given to them, in the highest interests of peace, to have recourse to the Permanent Court, can only be regarded as friendly actions.

In case of dispute between two Powers, one of them can always address to the International Bureau a note containing a declaration that it would be ready to submit the dispute to arbitration. The Bureau must at once inform the other Power of the declaration.

Article 49

The Permanent Administrative Council, composed of the Diplomatic Representatives of the Contracting Powers accredited to The Hague and of the Netherlands Minister for Foreign Affairs, who will act as President, is charged with the direction and control of the International Bureau.

The Council settles its rules of procedure and all other necessary regulations. It decides all questions of administration which may arise with regard to the operations of the Court. It has entire control over the appointment, suspension, or dismissal of the officials and employees of the Bureau. It fixes the payments and salaries, and controls the general expenditure. At meetings duly summoned the presence of nine members is sufficient to render valid the discussions of the Council. The decisions are taken by a majority of votes.

The Council communicates to the Contracting Powers without delay the regulations adopted by it. It furnishes them with an annual Report on the labours of the Court, the working of the administration, and the expenditure. The Report likewise contains a résumé of what is important in the documents communicated to the Bureau by the Powers in virtue of Article 43, paragraphs 3 and 4.

Article 50

The expenses of the Bureau shall be borne by the Contracting Powers in the proportion fixed for the International Bureau of the Universal Postal Union. The expenses to be charged to the adhering Powers shall be reckoned from the date on which their adhesion comes into force.

Chapter III. Arbitration Procedure

Article 51

With a view to encouraging the development of arbitration, the Contracting Powers have agreed on the following rules, which are applicable to arbitration procedure, unless other rules have been agreed on by the parties.

Article 52

The Powers which have recourse to arbitration sign a 'Compromis', in which the subject of the dispute is clearly defined, the time allowed for appointing Arbitrators, the form, order, and time in which the communication referred to in Article 63 must be made, and the amount of the sum which each party must deposit in advance to defray the expenses.

The 'Compromis' likewise defines, if there is occasion, the manner of appointing Arbitrators, any special powers which may eventually belong to the Tribunal, where it shall meet, the language it shall use, and the languages the employment of which shall be authorized before it, and, generally speaking, all the conditions on which the parties are agreed.

Article 53

The Permanent Court is competent to settle the 'Compromis', if the parties are agreed to have recourse to it for the purpose. It is similarly competent, even if the request is only made by one of the parties, when all attempts to reach an understanding through the diplomatic channel have failed, in the case of:

1. A dispute covered by a general Treaty of Arbitration concluded or renewed after the present Convention has come into force, and providing for a 'Compromis' in all disputes and not either explicitly or implicitly excluding the settlement of the 'Compromis' from the competence of the Court. Recourse cannot, however, be had to the Court if the other party declares that in its opinion the dispute does not belong to the category of disputes which can be submitted to compulsory arbitration, unless the Treaty of Arbitration confers upon the Arbitration Tribunal the power of deciding this preliminary question.

2. A dispute arising from contract debts claimed from one Power by another Power as due to its nationals, and for the settlement of which the offer of arbitration has been accepted. This arrangement is not applicable if acceptance is subject to the condition that the 'Compromis' should be settled in some other way.

Article 54

In the cases contemplated in the preceding Article, the 'Compromis' shall be settled by a Commission consisting of five members selected in the manner arranged for in Article 45, paragraphs 3 to 6. The fifth member is President of the Commission ex officio.

Article 55

The duties of Arbitrator may be conferred on one Arbitrator alone or on several Arbitrators selected by the parties as they please, or chosen by them from the Members of the Permanent Court of Arbitration established by the present Convention. Failing the constitution of the Tribunal by direct agreement between the parties, the course referred to in Article 45, paragraphs 3 to 6, is followed.

Article 56

When a Sovereign or the Chief of a State is chosen as Arbitrator, the arbitration procedure is settled by him.

Article 57

The Umpire is President of the Tribunal ex officio. When the Tribunal does not include an Umpire, it appoints its own President.

Article 58

When the 'Compromis' is settled by a Commission, as contemplated in Article 54, and in the absence of an agreement to the contrary, the Commission itself shall form the Arbitration Tribunal.

Article 59

Should one of the Arbitrators either die, retire, or be unable for any reason whatever to discharge his functions, the same procedure is followed for filling the vacancy as was followed for appointing him.

Article 60

The Tribunal sits at The Hague, unless some other place is selected by the parties. The Tribunal can only sit in the territory of a third Power with the latter's consent. The place of meeting once fixed cannot be altered by the Tribunal, except with the consent of the parties.

Article 61

If the question as to what languages are to be used has not been settled by the 'Compromis', it shall be decided by the Tribunal.

Article 62

The parties are entitled to appoint special agents to attend the Tribunal to act as intermediaries between themselves and the Tribunal. They are further authorized to retain for the defence of their rights and interests before the Tribunal counsel or advocates appointed by themselves for this purpose. The Members of the Permanent Court may not act as agents, counsel, or advocates except on behalf of the Power which appointed them Members of the Court.

Article 63

As a general rule, arbitration procedure comprises two distinct phases: pleadings and oral discussions. The pleadings consist in the communication by the respective agents to the members of the Tribunal and the opposite party of cases, counter-cases, and, if necessary, of replies; the parties annex thereto all papers and documents called for in the case. This communication shall be made either directly or through the intermediary of the International Bureau, in the order and within the time fixed by the 'Compromis'.

The time fixed by the 'Compromis' may be extended by mutual agreement by the parties, or by the Tribunal when the latter considers it necessary for the purpose of reaching a just decision. The discussions consist in the oral development before the Tribunal of the arguments of the parties.

Article 64

A certified copy of every document produced by one party must be communicated to the other party.

Article 65

Unless special circumstances arise, the Tribunal does not meet until the pleadings are closed.

Article 66

The discussions are under the control of the President. They are only public if it be so decided by the Tribunal, with the assent of the parties. They are recorded in minutes drawn up by the Secretaries appointed by the President. These minutes are signed by the President and by one of the Secretaries and alone have
an authentic character.

Article 67

After the close of the pleadings, the Tribunal is entitled to refuse discussion of all new papers or documents which one of the parties may wish to submit to it without the consent of the other party.

Article 68

The Tribunal is free to take into consideration new papers or documents to which its attention may be drawn by the agents or counsel of the parties. In this case, the Tribunal has the right to require the production of these papers or documents, but is obliged to make them known to the opposite party.

Article 69

The Tribunal can, besides, require from the agents of the parties the production of all papers, and can demand all necessary explanations. In case of refusal the Tribunal takes note of it.

Article 70

The agents and the counsel of the parties are authorized to present orally to the Tribunal all the arguments they may consider expedient in defence of their case.

Article 71

They are entitled to raise objections and points. The decisions of the Tribunal on these points are final and cannot form the subject of any subsequent discussion.

Article 72

The members of the Tribunal are entitled to put questions to the agents and counsel of the parties, and to ask them for explanations on doubtful points. Neither the questions put, nor the remarks made by members of the Tribunal in the course of the discussions, can be regarded as an expression of opinion by the Tribunal in general or by its members in particular.

Article 73

The Tribunal is authorized to declare its competence in interpreting the 'Compromis', as well as the other Treaties which may be invoked, and in applying the principles of law.

Article 74

The Tribunal is entitled to issue rules of procedure for the conduct of the case, to decide the forms, order, and time in which each party must conclude its arguments, and to arrange all the formalities required for dealing with the evidence.

Article 75

The parties undertake to supply the Tribunal, as fully as they consider possible, with all the information required for deciding the case.

Article 76

For all notices which the Tribunal has to serve in the territory of a third Contracting Power, the Tribunal shall apply direct to the Government of that Power. The same rule applies in the case of steps being taken to procure evidence on the spot.

The requests for this purpose are to be executed as far as the means at the disposal of the Power applied to under its municipal law allow. They cannot be rejected unless the Power in question considers them calculated to impair its own sovereign rights or its safety. The Court will equally be always entitled to act through the Power on whose territory it sits.

Article 77

When the agents and counsel of the parties have submitted all the explanations and evidence in support of their case the President shall declare the discussion closed.

Article 78

The Tribunal considers its decisions in private and the proceedings remain secret. All questions are decided by a majority of the members of the Tribunal.

Article 79

The Award must give the reasons on which it is based. It contains the names of the Arbitrators; it is signed by the President and Registrar or by the Secretary acting as Registrar.

Article 80

The Award is read out in public sitting, the agents and counsel of the parties being present or duly summoned to attend.

Article 81

The Award, duly pronounced and notified to the agents of the parties, settles the dispute definitively and without appeal.

Article 82

Any dispute arising between the parties as to the interpretation and execution of the Award shall, in the absence of an Agreement to the contrary, be submitted to the Tribunal which pronounced it.

Article 83

The parties can reserve in the 'Compromis' the right to demand the revision of the Award. In this case and unless there be an Agreement to the contrary, the demand must be addressed to the Tribunal which pronounced the Award. It can only be made on the ground of the discovery of some new fact calculated to exercise a decisive influence upon the Award and which was unknown to the Tribunal and to the party which demanded the revision at the time the discussion was closed. Proceedings for revision can only be instituted by a decision of the Tribunal expressly recording the existence of the new fact, recognizing in it the character described in the preceding paragraph, and declaring the demand admissible on this ground. The 'Compromis' fixes the period within which the demand for revision must be made.

Article 84

The Award is not binding except on the parties in dispute. When it concerns the interpretation of a Convention to which Powers other than those in dispute are parties, they shall inform all the Signatory Powers in good time. Each of these Powers is entitled to intervene in the case. If one or more avail themselves of this right, the interpretation contained in the Award is equally binding on them.

Article 85

Each party pays its own expenses and an equal share of the expenses of the Tribunal.

Chapter IV. Arbitration by Summary Procedure

Article 86

With a view to facilitating the working of the system of arbitration in disputes admitting of a summary procedure, the Contracting Powers adopt the following rules, which shall be observed in the absence of other arrangements and subject to the reservation that the provisions of Chapter III apply so far as may be.

Article 87

Each of the parties in dispute appoints an Arbitrator. The two Arbitrators thus selected choose an Umpire. If they do not agree on this point, each of them proposes two candidates taken from the general list of the Members of the Permanent Court exclusive of the members appointed by either of the parties and not being nationals of either of them; which of the candidates thus proposed shall be the Umpire is determined by lot. The Umpire presides over the Tribunal, which gives its decisions by a majority of votes.

Article 88

In the absence of any previous agreement the Tribunal, as soon as it is formed, settles the time within which the two parties must submit their respective cases to it.

Article 89

Each party is represented before the Tribunal by an agent, who serves as intermediary between the Tribunal and the Government who appointed him.

Article 90

The proceedings are conducted exclusively in writing. Each party, however, is entitled to ask that witnesses and experts should be called. The Tribunal has, for its part, the right to demand oral explanations from the agents of the two parties, as well as from the experts and witnesses whose appearance in Court it may consider useful.

Part V. Final Provisions

Article 91

The present Convention, duly ratified, shall replace, as between the Contracting Powers, the Convention for the Pacific Settlement of International Disputes of the 29th July, 1899.

Article 92

The present Convention shall be ratified as soon as possible. The ratifications shall be deposited at The Hague. The first deposit of ratifications shall be recorded in a *procès-verbal* signed by the Representatives of the Powers which take part therein and by the Netherlands Minister for Foreign Affairs.

The subsequent deposits of ratifications shall be made by means of a written notification, addressed to the Netherlands Government and accompanied by the instrument of ratification.

A duly certified copy of the *procès-verbal* relative to the first deposit of ratifications, of the notifications mentioned in the preceding paragraph, and of the instruments of ratification, shall be immediately sent by the Netherlands Government, through the diplomatic channel, to the Powers invited to the Second Peace Conference, as well as to those Powers which have adhered to the Convention. In the cases contemplated in the preceding paragraph, the said Government shall at the same time inform the Powers of the date on which it received the notification.

Article 93

Non-Signatory Powers which have been invited to the Second Peace Conference may adhere to the present Convention. The Power which desires to adhere notifies its intention in writing to the Netherlands Government, forwarding to it the act of adhesion, which shall be deposited in the archives of the said Government. This Government shall immediately forward to all the other Powers invited to the Second Peace Conference a duly certified copy of the notification as well as of the act of adhesion, mentioning the date on which it received the notification.

Article 94

The conditions on which the Powers which have not been invited to the Second Peace Conference may adhere to the present Convention shall form the subject of a subsequent Agreement between the Contracting Powers.

Article 95

The present Convention shall take effect, in the case of the Powers which were not a party to the first deposit of ratifications, sixty days after the date of the *procès-verbal* of this deposit, and, in the case of the Powers which ratify subsequently or which adhere, sixty days after the notification of their ratification or of their adhesion has been received by the Netherlands Government.

Article 96

In the event of one of the Contracting Parties wishing to denounce the present Convention, the denunciation shall be notified in writing to the Netherlands Government, which shall immediately communicate a duly certified copy of the notification to all the other Powers informing them of the date on which it was received. The denunciation shall only have effect in regard to the notifying Power, and one year after the notification has reached the Netherlands Government.

Article 97

A register kept by the Netherlands Minister for Foreign Affairs shall give the date of the deposit of ratifications effected in virtue of Article 92, paragraphs 3 and 4, as well as the date on which the notifications of adhesion (Article 93, paragraph 2) or of denunciation (Article 96, paragraph 1) have been received. Each Contracting Power is entitled to have access to this register and to be supplied with duly certified extracts from it.

In faith whereof the Plenipotentiaries have appended their signatures to the present Convention.

Done at The Hague, the 18th October, 1907, in a single copy, which shall remain deposited in the archives of the Netherlands Government, and duly certified copies of which shall be sent, through the diplomatic channel, to the Contracting Powers.

Next Conference

The conference scheduled for 1915 failed to meet as World War I broke out, the conference idea strongly influenced the creation of the more highly organized League of Nations and United Nations after the war. Although the Hague Conference of 1899 and 1907, failed to prevent the break out of World War I, the conference itself has great significance. The conference shows international efforts to protect peace from tensions and aggressions of the time. The Hague Conference called for organizations and peace conventions like Geneva Protocol to support humanity even in the midst of the war. The Conventions did not apply as a matter of treaty law during the two World Wars. The interbellum (between Wars) (1925-1945) was a difficult time for the laws of war. On the one hand, the horrible events of the First World War and the remaining tension in global politics made it very clear that progress in the laws of war was highly desirable. On the other hand, the same factors, unresolved bitterness from the First World War and continuing fragility of international relations, made it all the more difficult for States to accept limitations to their means and methods of warfare. Such limitations are only acceptable when one trusts potential adversaries to also comply with them, and trust was scarce at the time.

This is not to say that nothing happened. Numerous international meetings in various places were held on the subject. Treaties were drafted and Declarations were solemnly pledged to. The Versailles Treaty even presented limitation of armaments as 'punishment' for the Germans. Nonetheless, it proved quite difficult to regulate much further than the agreements of the Hague Peace Conferences.[18]

Some of the Conventions and declarations of the peace conferences of 1899 and 1907 have been superseded, inspired by the World Wars, in whole or in part by more recent treaties. For example the Geneva convention of 1929 revised parts of the Hague Conventions concerning prisoners of war.

[18] K. Dijkhof, War, Law and Technology, WLP 2010, p 53.

CONVENTION BETWEEN THE UNITED STATES OF AMERICA AND OTHER POWERS, RELATING TO PRISONERS OF WAR

Signed at Geneva, July 27, 1929; ratification advised by the Senate, January 7, 1932; ratified by the President, January 16, 1932, ratification of the United States of America deposited with the Government of Switzerland, February 4, 1932; proclaimed, August 4, 1932.

BY THE PRESIDENT OF THE UNITED STATES OF AMERICA

A PROCLAMATION

WHEREAS, a Convention Relating to the Treatment of Prisoners of War was signed by the respective Plenipotentiaries of the United States of America and forty-six other countries, at Geneva on July 27, 1929 the original of which Convention in the French language is word for word as follows:

CONVENTION OF JULY 27, 1929, RELATIVE TO THE TREATMENT OF PRISONERS OF WAR

The President of the German Reich, the President of the United States of America, the Federal President of the Republic of Austria, His Majesty the King of the Belgians, the President of the Republic of Bolivia, the President of the Republic of the United States of Brazil, His Majesty the King of Great Britain, Ireland, and the British Dominions beyond the Seas, Emperor of India, His Majesty the King of the Bulgarians, the President of the Republic of Chile, the President of the Republic of China, the President of the Republic of Colombia, the President of the Republic of Cuba, His Majesty the King of Denmark and Iceland, the President of the Dominican Republic, His Majesty the King of Egypt, His Majesty the King of Spain, the President of the Republic of Estonia, the President of the Republic of Finland, the President of the French Republic, the President of the Hellenic Republic, His Serene Highness the Regent of Hungary, His Majesty the King of Italy, His Majesty the Emperor of Japan, the President of the Republic of Latvia, Her Royal Highness the Grand Duchess of Luxembourg, the President of the United States of Mexico, the President of the Republic of Nicaragua, His Majesty the King of Norway, Her Majesty the Queen of the Netherlands, His Imperial Majesty the Shah of Persia the President of the Republic of Poland, the President of the Portuguese Republic, His Majesty the King of Rumania, His Majesty the King of the Serbs, Croats and Slovenes, His Majesty the King of Siam, His Majesty the King of Sweden, the Swiss Federal Council, the President of the Czechoslovak Republic, the President of the Turkish Republic, the President of the Oriental Republic of Uruguay, [and] the President of the Republic of the United States of Venezuela,

Recognizing that, in the extreme case of a war, it will be the duty of every Power to diminish, so far as possible the unavoidable rigors thereof an to mitigate the fate of prisoners of war;

Desirous of developing the principles which inspired the international conventions of The Hague, in particular the Convention relative to the laws and customs of war and the Regulations annexed thereto;

Have decided to conclude a Convention to that end, and have appointed. the following as their plenipotentiaries, namely:
[Here follows a list of Participants]

Title I. General Provisions

Article 1

The present Convention shall apply, without prejudice to the stipulations of Title VII:

To all persons mentioned in Articles 1, 2 and 3 of the Regulations annexed to the Hague Convention respecting the laws and customs of war on land, of October 18, 1907, and captured by the enemy.

2) To all persons belonging to the armed forces of belligerent parties, captured by the enemy in the course of military operations at sea or in the air, except for such derogations as might be rendered inevitable by the conditions of capture. However, such derogations shall not infringe upon the fundamental principles of the present Convention; they shall cease from the moment when the persons captured have rejoined a prisoners-of-war camp.

Article 2

Prisoners of war are in the power of the hostile Power, but not of the individuals or corps who have captured them. They must at all times be humanely treated and protected, particularly against acts of violence, insults and public curiosity. Measures of reprisal against them are prohibited.

Article 3

Prisoners of war have the right to have their person and their honor respected. Women shall be treated with all the regard due to their sex. Prisoners retain their full civil status.

Article 4

The Power detaining prisoners of war is bound to provide for their maintenance. Difference in treatment among prisoners is lawful only when it is based on the military rank, state of physical or mental health, professional qualifications or sex of those who profit thereby.

Title II. Capture

Article 5

Every prisoner of war is bound to give, if he is questioned on the subject, his true name and rank, or else his regimental number. If he infringes this rule, he is liable to have the advantages given to prisoners of his class curtailed.

No coercion may be used on prisoners to secure information to the condition of their army or country. Prisoners who refuse to answer may not be threatened, insulted, or exposed to unpleasant or disadvantageous treatment of any kind whatever.

If, because of his physical or mental condition, a prisoner is unable to identify himself, he shall be turned over to the medical corps.

Article 6

All effects and objects of personal use except arms, horses, military equipment and military papers shall remain in the possession of prisoners of war, as well as metal helmets and gas masks.

Money in the possession of prisoners may not be taken away from them except by order of an officer and after the amount is determined. A receipt shall be given. Money thus taken away shall be entered to the amount of each prisoner. Identification documents, insignia of rank, decorations and objects of value may not be taken from prisoners.

Title III. Captivity

Section I. Evacuation of prisoners of war.

Article 7

Prisoners of war shall be evacuated within the shortest possible period after their capture, to spots located in a region far enough from the zone of combat for them to be out of danger.

Only prisoners who, because of wounds or sickness would run greater risks by being evacuated than by remaining where they are may be temporarily kept in a dangerous zone.

Prisoners shall not be needlessly exposed to danger while awaiting their evacuation from the combat zone.

Evacuation of prisoners on foot may normally be effected only by stages of 20 kilometers a day, unless the necessity of reaching water and food depots requires longer stages.

Article 8

Belligerents axe bound mutually to notify each other of their capture of prisoners within the shortest period possible, through the intermediary of the information bureaus, such as are organized according to Article 77. They are likewise bound to inform each other of the official addresses to which the correspondence of their families may be sent to prisoners of war.

As soon as possible, every prisoner must be enabled to correspond with his family himself, under the conditions provided in Articles 36 et seq.

As regards prisoners captured at sea, the provisions of the present article shall be observed as soon as possible after arrival at port.

Section II. Prisoners-of-War Camps

Article 9

Prisoners of war may be interned in a town, fortress, or other place, and bound not to go beyond certain fixed limits. They may also be interned in enclosed camps; they may not be confined or imprisoned except as an indispensable measure of safety or sanitation, and only while the circumtances which necessitate the measure continue to exist.

Prisoners captured in unhealthful regions or where the climate is injurious for persons coming from temperate regions, shall be transported, as soon as possible, to a more favorable climate.

Belligerents shall, so far as possible, avoid assembling in a single camp prisoners of different races or nationalities.

No prisoner may, at any time, be sent into a region where he might be exposed to the fire of the combat zone, nor used to give protection from bombardment to certain points or certain regions by his presence.

Chapter 1. Installation of Camps

Article 10

Prisoners of war shall be lodged in buildings or in barracks affording all possible guarantees of hygiene and healthfulness. The quarters must be fully protected from. dampness, sufficiently heated and lighted. All precautions must be taken against danger of fire.

With regard to dormitories the total surface, minimum cubic amount of air, arrangement and material of bedding-the conditions shall be the same as for the troops at base camps of the detaining Power.

Chapter 2. Food and Clothing of Prisoners of War

Article 11

The food ration of prisoners of war shall be equal in quantity and quality to that of troops at base camps. Furthermore, prisoners shall receive facilities for preparing, themselves, additional food which thy might have.

Sufficiency of potable water shall be furnished them. The use of tobacco shall be permitted. Prisoners may be employed in the kitchens. All collective disciplinary measures affecting the food are prohibited.

Article 12

Clothing, linen and footwear shall be furnished prisoners of war by the detaining Power. Replacement and repairing of these effects must be assured regularly. In addition, laborers must receive work clothes wherever the nature of the work requires it. Canteens shall be installed in all camps where prisoners may obtain, at the local market price, food products and ordinary objects. Profits made by the canteens for camp administrations shall be used for the benefit of prisoners.

Chapter 3. Sanitary Service in Camps

Article 13

Belligerents shall. be bound to take all sanitary measures necessary to assure the cleanliness and healthfulness of camps and to prevent epidemics. Prisoners of war shall have at their disposal, day and night, installations conforming to sanitary rules and constantly maintained in a state of cleanliness.

Furthermore, and without Prejudice to baths and showers of which the camp shall be as well provided as possible, prisoners shall be furnished a sufficient quantity of water for the care of their own bodily cleanliness. It shall be possible for them to take physical exercise and enjoy the open air.

Article 14

Every camp shall have an infirmary, where prisoners of war shall receive every kind of attention they need. If necessary, isolated quarters shall be reserved for the sick affected with contagious diseases.

Expenses of treatment, including therein those of temporary prosthetic equipment, shall become by the detaining Power. Upon request, belligerents shall be bound to deliver to every prisoner treated an official statement showing the nature and duration of his illness as well as the attention received.

It shall be lawful for belligerents reciprocally to authorize, by means of private arrangements the retention in the camps of physicians and attendants to care for prisoners of their own country. Prisoners affected. with a serious illness or whose condition necessitates an important surgical operation, must be admitted, at the expense of the detaining Power, to any military or civil medical unit qualified to treat them.

Article 15

Medical inspections of prisoners of war shall be arranged at least once a month. Their purpose shall be the supervision of the general state of health and cleanliness, and the detection of contagious diseases, particularly tuberculosis and venereal diseases.

Chapter 4. Intellectual and Moral Needs of Prisoners of War

Article 16

Prisoners of war shall enjoy complete liberty in the exercise of their religion, including attendance at the services of their faith, on the sole condition that they comply with the measures of order and police issued by the military authorities.
Ministers of a religion, prisoners of war, whatever their denomination, shall be allowed to minister fully to members of the same religion.

Article 17

So far as possible belligerents shall encourage intellectual diversions and sports organized by prisoners of war.

Chapter 5. Internal Discipline of Camps.

Article 18

Every camp of prisoners of war shall be placed under the command of a responsible officer. Besides the external marks of respect provided by the regulations in force in their armies with regard to their nationals prisoners of war must salute all officers of the detaining Power. Officers who are prisoners of war are bound to salute only officers of a higher or equal rank of that Power.

Article 19

The wearing of insignia of rank and of decorations shall be permitted.

Article 20

Regulations, orders, notices and proclamations of every kind must be communicated to prisoners of war in a language which they understand. The same principle shall be applied in examinations.

Chapter 6. Special Provisions Regarding Officers and Persons of Equivalent status

Article 21

Upon the beginning of hostilities, belligerents shall be bound to communicate to one another the titles and ranks in use in their respective armies, with a view to assuring equality of treatment between corresponding ranks of officers and persons of equivalent status. Officers and persons of equivalent status who are prisoners of war shall be treated with the regard due their rank and age.

Article 22

In order to assure service in officers' camps, soldiers of the same army who are prisoners of war and, wherever possible, who speak the same language, shall be assigned thereto, in sufficient numbers, considering the rank of the officers and persons of equivalent status.

The latter shall secure their food and clothing from the pay which shall be granted them by the detaining Power. Administration of the mess-fund by the officers themselves must be facilitated in every way.

Chapter 7. Financial Resources of Prisoners of War

Article 23

Subject to private arrangements between belligerent Powers, and particularly those provided in Article 24, officers and persons of equivalent status who are prisoners of war shall receive from the detaining Power the same pay as officers of corresponding rank in the armies of that Power, on the condition, however, that this pay does not exceed that to which they are entitled in the armies of the country which they have Served. This pay shall be granted them in full, once a month if possible, and without being liable to any deduction for expenses incumbent on the detaining Power, even when they are in favor of the prisoners. An agreement between the belligerents shall fix the rate of exchange applicable to this payment; in the absence of such an agreement, the rate adopted shall. be that in force at the opening of hostilities. All payments made to prisoners of war as pay must be reimbursed, at the end of hostilities, by the Power which they have served.

Article 24

Upon the outbreak of hostilities, the belligerents shall, by common agreement, fix the maximum amount of ready money which prisoners of war of various ranks and classes shall be allowed to keep in their possession. Any surplus taken or withheld from a prisoner shall be entered to his account, the same as any deposit of money effected by him, and may not be converted into another currency without his consent.

Pay to the credit of their accounts shall be given to prisoner., of war at the end of their captivity. During their imprisonment, facilities shall be granted them for the transfer of these amounts, in whole or in part, to banks or private persons in their country of origin.

Chapter 8. Transfer of Prisoners of War

Article 25

Unless the conduct of military operation so requires, sick and wounded prisoners of war shall, not be transferred as long as their recovery might be endangered by the trip.

Article 26

In case of transfer, prisoners of war shall be officially notified of their new destination in advance; they shall, be allowed to take with them their personal effects, their correspondence and - packages which have arrived for them. All due measures shall be taken that Correspondence and packages addressed to their former camp may be forwarded to them without delay. Money deposited to the account Of transferred prisoners shall be transmitted to the competent authority of their new place of residence. The expenses occasioned by the transfer shall be charged to the detaining Power.

Section III. Labor Of Prisoners of War

Chapter 1. Generalities

Article 27

Belligerents May Utilize the labor of able prisoners of war, according to their rank and aptitude, officers and persons of equivalent status excepted. However, if officers or persons of equivalent status request suitable work, it shall be secured for them so far as is possible. Noncommissioned officers who are prisoners of war shall only be required to do supervisory work, unless they expressly request a remunerative occupation.

Belligerents shall be bound, during the whole period of captivity, to allow to prisoners of war who are victims of accidents in connection' with their work the enjoyment of the benefit of the provisions applicable to laborers of the same class according to the legislation of the detaining Power. With regard to prisoners of war to whom these legal provisions might not be applied by reason of the legislation of that Power, the latter undertakes to recommend to its legislative body all proper measures equitably to indemnify the victims.

Chapter 2. Organization of the labor

Article 28

The detaining Power shall assume entire responsibility for the maintenance, care, treatment and payment of wages of prisoners of war working for the account of private persons.

Article 29

No prisoner of war may be employed at labors for which he is physically unfit.

Article 30

The length of the day's work of prisoners of war, including therein the trip going and returning, shall not be excessive and must not, in any case, exceed that allowed for the civil workers in the region employed at the same work. Every prisoner shall be allowed a rest of twenty-four consecutive hours every week, preferably on Sunday.

Chapter 3. Prohibited labor

Article 31

Labor furnished by prisoners of war shall have no direct relation with war operations. It is especially prohibited to use prisoners for manufacturing and transporting arms or munitions of any kind or for transporting material intended for combatant units.

In case of violation of the provisions of the preceding paragraph, prisoners, after executing or beginning to execute the order, shall be free to have their protests presented through the mediation of the agents whose functions are set forth in Articles 43 and 44, or, in the absence of an agent, through the mediation of representatives of the protecting Power.

Article 32

It is forbidden to use prisoners of war at unhealthful or dangerous work.
Any aggravation of the conditions of labor by disciplinary measures is forbidden.

Chapter 4. Labor Detachments

Article 33

The system of labor detachments must be similar to that of prisoners-of-war camps, particularly; with regard to sanitary conditions, food, attention in case of accident or sickness, correspondence and the receipt of packages.

Every labor detachment shall be dependent on a prisoners' camp. The commander of this camp shall be responsible for the observation, in the labor detachment, of the provisions of the present Convention.

Chapter 5. Wages

Article 34

Prisoners of war shall not receive wages for work connected with the administration, management and maintenance of the camps. Prisoners utilized for other work shall be entitled to wages to be fixed by agreements between the belligerents.

These agreements shall also specify the part which the camp administration may retain, the amount which shall belong to the prisoner of war and the manner in that amount shall be put at his disposal during the period of his captivity.

While awaiting the conclusion of the said agreements, payment for labor of prisoners shall be settled according to the rules given below:

(a) Work done for the State shall be paid for in accordance with the rates in force for soldiers. of the national army doing the same work, or, if none exists, ac cording to a rate in harmony with the work performed.

(b) When the work is done for the account of other public administrations or for private persons, conditions shall be regulated by agreement with the military authority.

The pay remaining to the credit of the prisoner shall be delivered to him at the end of his captivity. In case of death,- it shall be forwarded through the diplomatic channel to the heirs of the deceased.

Section IV. External Relations of Prisoners of War

Article 35

Upon the outbreak of hostilities, belligerents shall publish the measures provided for the execution of the provisions of this section.

Article 36

Each of the belligerents shall periodically determine the number of letters and postal cards per month which prisoners of war of the various classes shall be allowed to send, and shall inform the other belligerent of this number. These letters and cards shall be transmitted by post by the shortest route. They may not be delayed or retained for disciplinary reasons.

Within a period of not more than one week after his arrival at the camp, and likewise in case of sickness, every prisoner shall be enabled to write his family a postal card informing it of his capture and of the state of his health. The said postal cards shall be forwarded as rapidly as possible and may not be delayed in any manner. As a general rule, correspondence of prisoners shall be written in their native language. Belligerents may allow correspondence in other languages.

Article 37

Prisoners of war shall be allowed individually to receive parcels by mail, containing foods and other articles intended to supply them with food or clothing. Packages shall be delivered to the addressees and a receipt given.

Article 38

Letters and consignments of money or valuables, as well as parcels by post intended for prisoners of war or dispatched by them, either directly, or by the mediation of the information bureaus provided for in Article 77, shall be exempt from all postal duties in the countries of origin and destination, as well as in the countries they pass through.
Presents and relief in kind for prisoners shall be likewise exempt from all import and other duties, its well as of payments for carriage by the State railways. Prisoners may, in cases of acknowledged urgency, be allowed to send telegrams, paying the usual charges.

Article 39

Prisoners of war shall be allowed to receive shipments of books individually, which may be subject to censorship. Representatives of the protecting Powers and duly recognized and authorized aid societies may send books and collections of books to the libraries of prisoners' camps. The transmission of these shipments to libraries may not be delayed under the pretext of censorship difficulties.

Article 40

Censorship of correspondence must be effected within the shortest possible time. Furthermore, inspection of parcels post must be effected under proper conditions to guarantee the preservation of the products which they may contain and, if possible, in the presence of the addressee or an agent duly recognized by him. Prohibitions of correspondence promulgated by the belligerents for military or political reasons, must be transient in character and as short as possible.

Article 41

Belligerents shall assure all facilities for the transmission of instruments, papers or documents intended for prisoners of war or signed by them, particularly of powers of attorney and wills. They shall take the necessary measures to assure, in case of necessity, the authentication of signatures made by prisoners.

Section V. Prisoners' Relations with the Authorities

Chapter 1. Complaints of Prisoners of War because of the Conditions of Captivity

Article 42

Prisoners of war shall have the right to inform the military authorities in whose power they are of their requests with regard to the conditions of captivity to which they are subjected. They shall also have the right to address themselves to representatives of the protecting Powers to indicate to them the points on which they have complaints to formulate with regard to the conditions of captivity. These requests and complaints must be transmitted immediately. Even if they am recognized to be unfounded, they may not occasion any punishment.

Chapter 2. Representatives of Prisoners of War

Article 43

In every place where there are prisoners of war, they shall be a allowed to appoint agents entrusted with representing them directly with military authorities and protecting Powers. This appointment shall be subject to the approval of the military authority. The agents shall be entrusted with the reception and distribution of collective shipments. Likewise, in case the prisoners should decide to organize a mutual assistance system among themselves, this organization would be in the sphere of the agents. Further, they may lend their offices to prisoners to facilitate their relations with the aid societies mentioned in Article 78.

In camps of officers and persons of equivalent status, the senior officer prisoner of the highest rank shall be recognized as intermediary between the camp authorities and the officers and persons of equivalent status who are prisoners. For this purpose, he shall have the power to appoint a prisoner officer to assist him as an interpreter during the conferences with the camp authorities.

Article 44

When the agents are employed as laborers, their activity as representatives of prisoners of war must be counted m the compulsory period of labor. All facilities shall be accorded the agents for their intercourse with the military authorities and with the protecting Power. This intercourse shall not be limited.

No representative of the prisoners may be transferred without the necessary time being allowed him to inform his successors about affairs under consideration.

Chapter 3. Penalties Applicable to Prisoners of War

1. General Provisions

Article 45

Prisoners of war shall be subject to the laws, regulations, and orders in force in the armies of the detaining Power. An act of insubordination shall justify the adoption towards them of the measures provided by such laws, regulations and orders. The provisions of the present chapter, however, are reserved.

Article 46

Punishments other than those provided for the same acts for soldiers of the national armies may not be imposed upon prisoners of war by the military authorities and courts of the detaining Power. Rank being identical, officers, noncommissioned officers or soldiers who are prisoners of war undergoing a disciplinary punishment, shall not be subject to less favorable treatment than that provided in the armies of the detaining Power with regard to the same punishment.

Any corporal punishment, any imprisonment in quarters without daylight and, in general, any form of cruelty, is forbidden. Collective punishment for individual acts is also forbidden.

Article 47

Acts constituting an offense against discipline, and particularly attempted escape, shall be verified immediately; for all prisoners of war, commissioned or not, preventive arrest shall be reduced to the absolute minimum. Judicial proceedings against prisoners of war shall be conducted as rapidly as the circumstances permit; preventive imprisonment shall be limited as much as possible. In all cases, the duration of preventive imprisonment shall be deducted from the disciplinary or judicial punishment inflicted, provided that this deduction is allowed for national soldiers.

Article 48

Prisoners of war may not be treated differently from other prisoners after having suffered the judicial or disciplinary punishment which has been imposed on them. However, prisoners punished as a result of attempted escape may be subjected to special surveillance, which, however, may not entail the suppression of the guarantees granted prisoners by the present Convention.

Article 49

No prisoner of war may be deprived of his rank by the detaining Power. Prisoners given disciplinary punishment may not be deprived of the prerogatives attached to their rank. In particular, officers and persons of equivalent status who suffer punishment involving deprivation of liberty shall not be placed in. the same quarters as noncommissioned officers or privates being punished.

Article 50

Escaped prisoners of war who are retaken before being able to rejoin their own army or to leave the territory occupied by the army which captured them shall be liable only to disciplinary punishment. Prisoners who, after having succeeded in rejoining their army or in leaving the territory occupied by the army which captured them, may again be taken prisoners, shall not be liable to any punishment on account of their previous flight.

Article 51

Attempted escape, even if it is a repetition of the offense, shall not be considered as an aggravating circumstance in case the prisoner of war should be given over to the courts on account of crimes or offenses against persons or property committed in the course of that attempt. After an attempted or accomplished escape, the comrades of the person escaping who assisted in the escape, may incur only disciplinary punishment on this account.

Article 52

Belligerents shall see that the competent authorities exercise the greatest leniency in deciding the question of whether an infraction committed by a prisoner of war should be punished by disciplinary or judicial measures. This shall be the case especially when it is a question of deciding on acts in connection with escape or attempted escape. A prisoner may not be punished more than once because of the same act or the same count.

Article 53

No prisoner of war on whom a disciplinary punishment has been imposed, who might be eligible for repatriation, maybe kept back because he has not undergone the punishment. Prisoners to be repatriated who might be threatened with a penal prosecution may be excluded from repatriation. until the end of the proceedings and, if necessary, until the completion of the punishment; those who might already be imprisoned by reason of a sentence may be detained until the end of their imprisonment. Belligerents shall communicate to each other the lists of those who may not be repatriated for the reasons given in the preceding paragraph.

2. Disciplinary Punishments

Article 54

Arrest is the most severe disciplinary punishment which may be imposed on a prisoner of war. The duration of a single punishment may not exceed thirty days. This maximum of thirty days may not, further, be exceeded in the case of several acts for which the prisoner has to undergo discipline at the time when it is ordered for him, whether or not these acts are connected. When, during or after the end of a period of arrest, a prisoner shall have a. new disciplinary punishment imposed upon him, a space of at least three days shall separate each of the periods of arrest, if one of them is ten days or more.

Article 55

Subject to the provisions given in the last paragraph of Article 11, food restrictions allowed in the armies of the detaining Power are applicable, as an increase in punishment, to prisoners of war given disciplinary punishment. However, these restrictions may be ordered only. if the state of health of the prisoners punished permits it.

Article 56

In no case may prisoners of war be transferred to penitentiary establishments (prisons, penitentiaries, convict prisons, etc.) there to undergo disciplinary punishment. The quarters in which they undergo disciplinary punishment shall conform to sanitary requirements. Prisoners punished shall be enabled to keep themselves in a state of cleanliness. These prisoners shall every dg be allowed to exercise or to stay m the open air at least two hours.

Article 57

Prisoners of war given disciplinary punishment shall be allowed to read and write, as well as to send and receive letters. On the other hand, packages and money sent may be not delivered to the addressees until the expiration of the punishment. If the packages not distributed contain perishable products, these shall be turned over to the camp infirmary or kitchen.

Article 58

Prisoners of war given disciplinary punishment shall be allowed, on their request, to be present at the daily medical inspection. They shall receive the care considered necessary by the doctors and, if necessary, shall be removed to the camp infirmary or to hospitals.

Article 59

Excepting the competence of courts and higher military authorities, disciplinary punishment may be ordered only by an officer provided with disciplinary powers in his capacity as commander of a camp or detachment, or by the responsible officer replacing him.

3. Judicial Suits

Article 60

At the opening of a judicial proceeding directed against a prisoner of war, the detaining Power shall advise the representative of the protecting Power thereof as soon as possible, and always before the date set for the opening of the trial.

This advice shall contain the. following information:

(a) Civil state and rank of prisoner;

(b) Place of sojourn or imprisonment;

(c) Specification of the [count] or counts of the indictment, giving the legal provisions applicable.

If it is not possible to mention in that advice the court which will pass upon the matter, the date of opening the trial and the place where it will take place this information must be furnished to the representative of the protecting Power later, as soon as possible, and at all. events, at least three weeks before the opening of the trial.

Article 61

No prisoner of war may be sentenced without having had an opportunity to defend himself. No prisoner may be obliged to admit himself guilty of the act of which he is accused.

Article 62

The prisoner of war shall be entitled to assistance by a qualified counsel of his choice, and, if necessary, to have recourse to the services of a competent interpreter. He shall be advised of his right by the detaining Power, in due time before the trial. In default of a choice by the prisoner, the protecting Power may obtain a counsel for him. The detaining Power shall deliver to the protecting Power, on its request, a list of persons qualified to present the defense. Representatives of the protecting Power shall be entitled to attend the trial of the case. The only exception to this rule is the case where the trial of the case must be secret in the interest of the safety of the State. The detaining Power should so advise the protecting Power.

Article 63

Sentence may be pronounced against a prisoner of war only by the same courts and according to the same procedure as in the case of persons belonging to the armed forces of the detaining Power.

Article 64

Every prisoner of war shall have tile right of appeal against any sentence rendered with regard to him, in the same way as individuals belonging to the armed forces of the detaining Power.

Article 65

Sentences pronounced against prisoners of war shall be communicated to the protecting Power immediately.

Article 66

If the death penalty is pronounced against a prisoner of war, a communication setting forth in detail the nature and circumstances of the offense shall be sent as soon as possible to the representative of the protecting Power, for transmission to the Power in whose armies the prisoner served. The sentence shall not be executed before the expiration of a period of at least three months after this communication.

Article 67

No prisoner of war may be deprived of the benefit of the provisions of Article 42 of the present Convention as a result of a sentence or otherwise.

Title IV. Termination of Captivity

Section 1. Direct Repatriation and Hospitalization in a Neutral Country

Article 68

Belligerents are bound to send, back to their own country, regardless of rank or number, seriously sick and seriously injured prisoners of war, after having brought them to a condition where they can be transported. Agreements between belligerents shall accordingly settle as soon as possible the cases of invalidity or of sickness, entailing direct repatriation, as well as the cases entailing possible hospitalization in a neutral country. While awaiting the conclusion of these agreements, belligerents may have reference to the model agreement annexed, for documentary purposes, to the present Convention.

Article 69

Upon the outbreak of hostilities, belligerents shall come to an agreement to name mixed medical commissions. These commissions shall be composed of three members, two of them belonging to a neutral country and one appointed by the detaining Power; one of the physicians of the neutral country shall preside. These mixed medical commissions shall proceed to the examination of sick or wounded prisoners and shall make all due decisions regarding them. Decisions of these commissions shall he by majority and carried out with the least possible delay.

Article 70

Besides those who are designated by the camp physician, the following prisoners of war shall be inspected by the mixed medical Commission mentioned in Article 69, with a view to their direct repatriation or their hospitalization in a neutral country:

(a) Prisoners who make such a request directly of the camp physician;

(b) Prisoners who are presented by the agents provided for in Article 43, acting on their own initiative or at the request of the prisoners themselves;

(c) Prisoners who have been proposed by the Power in whose armies they have served or by an aid society duly recognized and authorized by that Power.

Article 71

Prisoners of war who are victims of accidents in connection with work, except those voluntarily injured, shall enjoy. the benefit of the same provisions, as far as repatriation or possible hospitalization in a neutral country are concerned.

Article 72

Throughout the duration of hostilities and for humane considerations, belligerents may conclude agreements with a view to the direct repatriation or hospitalization in a neutral country of able-bodied prisoners of war who have undergone a long period of captivity.

Article 73

The expenses of repatriation or of transportation to a neutral country of prisoners of war shall be borne, from the frontiers of the detaining Power, by the Power in whose armies the prisoners. have served.

Article 74

No repatriated person may be utilized in active military service.

Section II. Release and Repatriation Upon Cessation of Hostilities

Article 75

When belligerents conclude a t convention of armistice, they h must, in principle, have appear therein stipulations regarding the repatriation of prisoners of war. If it has not been possible to insert stipulations in this regard in such convention, belligerents shall nevertheless come to an agreement in this regard as soon as possible. In any case, repatriation of prisoners shall be effected with the least possible delay after the conclusion of peace.

Prisoners of war against whom a penal prosecution might be pending for a crime or an offense t of municipal law may, however, be detained until the end of the proceedings and, if necessary, until the expiration of the punishment. The same shall be true of those sentenced for a crime or offense of municipal law.

On agreement between the belligerents, commissions may be established for the purpose of searching for dispersed prisoners and assuring their repatriation.

Title V. Death OF prisoners of war

Article 76

Wills of prisoners of war shall be received and drawn up in the same way as for soldiers of the national army. The same rules shall be observed regarding death certificates. Belligerents shall see that prisoners of war dying in captivity are honorably buried and that the graves bear all due information, are respected and properly maintained.

Title VI. Bureaus of Relief and Information Concerning Prisoners of War

Article 77

Upon the outbreak of hostilities, each of the belligerent Powers, as well as the neutral Powers which have received belligerents, shall institute an official information bureau for prisoners of war who are within their territory.
Within the shortest possible period, each of the belligerent Powers shall inform its information bureau of every capture of prisoners effected by its armies, giving it all the information regarding identity which it has, allowing it quickly to advise the families concerned, and informing it of the official addresses to which families may write to prisoners.

The information bureau shall immediately forward all this information to the interested Powers, through the intervention, on one hand, of the protecting Powers and, on the other, of the central agency provided for in Article 79. The information bureau, being charged with replying to all inquiries about of war, shall receive from the various services concerned full information respecting interments, and transfers, releases on parole, repatriations, escapes, stays in hospitals, deaths, as well as other information necessary to enable it to make out and keep up to date an individual return for each prisoner of war.

The bureau shall state in this return, in so far as is possible and subject to the provisions of Article 5: the regimental number, given names and surname, date and place of birth, rank and unit of the interested party, the given name of the father and the name of the mother, the address of the person to be advised in case of accident, wounds, date and place of capture, internment, wounding, and death, as well as any other important information. Weekly lists containing all new information likely to facilitate the identification o each prisoner shall be transmitted to the interested Powers.

At the conclusion of peace the individual return of the prisoner of war shall be delivered to the Power which he served. The information bureau shall t further be bound to receive all objects of personal use, valuables, letters, pay vouchers, identification marks, etc., which are left by prisoners of war who have been repatriated, released on parole, escaped or died, and to transmit them to the countries interested.

Article 78

Relief societies for prisoners of war, which are properly constituted in accordance with the laws of their country and with the object of serving as the channel for charitable effort, shall receive from the belligerents, for themselves and their duly accredited agents, every facility for the efficient performance of their humane task within the bounds imposed by military necessities. Agents of these societies may be admitted to the camps for the purpose of distributing relief, as also to the halting places of repatriated prisoners, if furnished with a personal permit by the military authorities, and on giving an undertaking in writing to comply with all measures of order and police which the latter may issue.

Article 79

A central information agency for prisoners of war shall be created in a neutral country. The International Committee of the Red Cross shall propose the organization of such an agency to the interested Powers, if it considers it necessary.

The function of that agency shall be to centralize all information respecting prisoners, which it may obtain through official or private channels; it shall transmit it as quickly as possible to the country of origin of the prisoners or to the Power which they have served.

These provisions must not be interpreted as restricting the humanitarian activity of the International Committee of the Red Cross.

Article 80

Information bureaus shall enjoy the privilege of free postage on postal matter, as well as all exemptions provided in Article 38.

Title VII. Application of the Convention to Certain Classes of Civilians

Article 81

Individuals who follow armed forces without directly belonging thereto, such as newspaper correspondents and reporters, sutlers, contractors, who fall into the enemy's hands and whom the latter think expedient to detain, shall be entitled to be treated as prisoners of war, provided they are in possession of a certificate from the military authorities of the armed forces which they were accompanying.

Title VIII. Execution of the Convention

Section I. General Provisions

Article 82

The provisions of the present Convention must be respected by the High Contracting Parties under all circumstances. In case, in time of war, one of the belligerents is not a party to the Convention, its provisions shall nevertheless remain in force as between the belligerents who are parties thereto.

Article 83

The High Contracting Parties reserve the right to conclude special convention-, on all questions relative to prisoners of war, on which it seems to them expedient to have particular regulations. Prisoners of war shall receive the benefit of these agreements until the completion of repatriation, except in the case of express stipulations to the contrary contained in the above-mentioned agreements or in later agreements, or also except in the case of more favorable measures taken by one or the other of the belligerent Powers respecting the prisoners which they hold.

In order to assure the reciprocal application of the stipulations of the present Convention, and to facilitate the conclusion of the special conventions provided for above, belligerents may, upon the commencement of hostilities, authorize meetings of representatives of the respective authorities charged with the administration of prisoners of war.

Article 84

The text of the present Convention and of the special conventions provided for in the foregoing article, shall be posted, wherever possible in the native language of the prisoners of war, in places where it may be consulted by all the prisoners. The text of these conventions shall be communicated to prisoners who find it impossible to get the information from the posted text, upon their request.

Article 85

The High Contracting Parties shall communicate to one another through the Swiss Federal Council, the official translations of the present Convention as well as of the laws and regulations which they may come to adopt to assure the application of the present Convention.

Section II. Organization of Control

Article 86

The High Contracting Parties recognize that the regular application of the present Convention will find a guaranty in the possibility of collaboration of the protecting Powers charged with safeguarding the interests of belligerents; in this respect, the protecting Powers may, besides their diplomatic personnel, appoint delegates from among their own nationals or from among the nationals of other neutral Powers. These delegates must be subject to the approval of the belligerent near which they exercise their mission.

Representatives of the protecting Power or its accepted delegates shall be permitted to go to any place, without exception, where prisoners of war are interned. They shall have access to all places occupied by prisoners and may interview them, as a general rule without witnesses, personally or through interpreters.

Belligerents shall so far as possible facilitate the task of representatives or accepted delegates of the protecting Power. The military authorities shall be informed of their visit.

Belligerents may come to an agreement to allow persons of the same nationality as the prisoners to be permitted to take part in inspection trips.

Article 87

In case of disagreement between the belligerents as to the application of the provisions of the present Convention, the protecting Powers must, in so far as possible, lend their good offices for the purpose of settling the difference. For this purpose, each of the protecting Powers may, in particular, suggest to the interested belligerents a meeting of representatives thereof, possibly upon a neutral territory suitably chosen. Belligerents shall be bound to accede U proposals in this sense which are made to them. The protecting Power may, if occasion arises, submit for the approval of the Powers concerned a person belonging to a neutral Power or a person delegated by the International Committee of the Red Cross, who shall be summoned to take part in this meeting.

Article 88

The foregoing provisions are not an obstacle to the humanitarian activity which the International Committee of the Red Cross may use for the protection of prisoners of war, with the consent of the interested belligerents.

Section III. Final Provisions

Article 89

In the relations between Powers bound by the Hague Convention respecting the Laws and Customs of War on Land, whether it is a question of that of July 29, 1899, or that of October 18, 1907, and who participate in the present Convention, this latter shall complete Chapter 11 of the Regulations annexed to the said Hague Conventions.

Article 90

The present Convention, which will bear this day's date, may be signed up to February 1, 1930, on behalf of all the countries represented at the Conference which opened at Geneva July 1, 1929.

Article 91

The present Convention shall be ratified as soon as possible. The ratifications shall be deposited at Berne. A record of the deposit of each instrument of ratification shall be prepared, a duly certified copy of which shall be forwarded by the Swiss Federal Council to the Governments of all the countries on whose behalf the Convention has been signed or notification of adherence made.

Article 92

The present Convention shall become effective six months after the deposit of at least two instruments of ratification. Subsequently, it shall become effective for each High Contracting Party six months after the deposit of its instrument of ratification.

Article 93

From the date on which it becomes effective, the present Convention shall be open for adherences given on behalf of any country in whose name this Convention was not signed.

Article 94

Adherence shall be given by written notification addressed to the Swiss Federal Council and shall take effect six months after the date of their receipt. The Swiss Federal Council shall communicate adherences to the Government of all the countries on whose behalf the Convention was signed or notification of adherence made.

Article 95

A state of war shall give immediate effect to ratifications deposited and to adherences; notified by belligerent Powers prior to or after the outbreak of hostilities. The communication of ratifications or adherences received from Powers at war shall be made by the Swiss Federal Council by the most rapid method.

Article 96

Each of the High Contracting Parties shall have the right to denounce the present Convention. The denunciation shall not take effect until one year after notification has been made in writing to the Swiss Federal Council. The latter shall communicate such notification to the Governments of all the High Contracting Parties.

The denunciation shall have effect only with respect to the High Contracting Party which gave notification thereof. Moreover, such denunciation shall not take effect during a war in which the denouncing Power is involved. In this case, the present Convention shall continue, in effect, beyond the period of one year, until the conclusion of peace, and, in any event, until the processes of repatriation axe completed.

Article 97

A duly certified copy of the present Convention shall be deposited in the archives of the League of Nations by the Swiss Federal Council. Likewise, ratifications, adherences, and denunciations of which the Swiss Federal Council shall be notified, shall be communicated by it to the League of Nations.

IN FAITH WHEREOF, the Plenipotentiaries named above have signed the present Convention.

DONE at Geneva, the twenty-seventh of July, one thousand nine hundred and twenty-nine, in a single copy, which shall remain in the archives of the Swiss Confederation and duly certified copies of which shall be forwarded to the Governments of all the countries invited to the Conference.
[Here follows a long list of signatories]

Annex to the Convention of May 27 1929 Relative to the Treatment of Prisoners of War

Model Agreement Concerning Direct Repatriation And Hospitalization In A Neutral Country Of Prisoners Of War For Reasons Of Health

I. Governing Principles for Direct Repatriation and Hospitalization in a Neutral Country

A. Direct Repatriation

There shall be repatriated directly:

1. Sick and wounded who, according to medical opinion, are not likely to recover in one year, their condition requiring treatment and their mental or physical fitness appearing to have suffered considerable diminution;

2. Incurable sick and wounded whose mental or physical fitness appears to have suffered considerable diminution;

3. Cured sick and wounded whose mental or physical fitness appears to have suffered considerable diminution.

B. Hospitalization in a Neutral Country

There shall be placed in hospitals:

1. Sick and wounded -whose cure within a period of one year is to be expected, such cure appearing certain and more rapid if the sick and wounded are given the benefit of the resources offered by the neutral country than if their captivity properly so-called is prolonged;

2. Prisoners of war whose mental or physical health appears, according to medical opinion, to be seriously menaced by continuance in captivity, while hospitalization in a neutral country would probably remove this danger.

C. Repatriation Of Those Hospitalized In A Neutral Country

There shall be repatriated the prisoners of war hospitalized in a neutral country who belong to the following categories:

1. Those whose state of health appears to be or to be becoming such that they fall within the categories of persons eligible to repatriation for reasons of health;

2. The recovered whose mental or physical fitness seems to have suffered a considerable diminution.

II. Special Principles for Direct Repatriation or Hospitalization in a Neutral Country

A. Repatriation

There shall be repatriated:

1. All prisoners of war who, as the result of organic injuries, have the following impairments, actual or functional: loss of a member, paralysis, articular or other defects, provided that the loss is at least a foot or a hand, or is equivalent to the loss of a foot or a hand;

2. All wounded or injured prisoners of war whose condition is such that it renders them invalids whose cure, within a period of one year, can not be anticipated from a medical standpoint;

3. All the sick whose condition is such that it renders them invalids whose cure, within a period of one year, can not be anticipated from a medical standpoint;
The following, in particular, belong to this category:

(a) Progressive tuberculosis of any organs which, according to medical opinion, can no longer be cured or at least considerably improved by a course of treatmnent in a neutral country.

(b) Nontubercular affections of the respiratory organs presumed incurable (such as, above all, strongly developed pulmonary emphysema, with or without bronchitis, bronchiectasis, serious asthma, gas poisoning, etc.);
(c) Serious chronic affections of the organs of circulation (for example: valvular affections with tendencies to disorders of compensation, relatively serious affections of the myocardium, pericardium of the vessels, especially inoperable aneurisms of the large vessels, etc.);

(d) Serious chronic affections of the digestive organs;

(e) Serious chronic affections of the 'urinary and sexual organs (particularly, for example; all cases of confirmed chronic nephritis with complete semeiology, and most especially when cardiac and vascular impairments already exist; likewise, pyelites and chronic cystitis, etc.);

(f) Serious chronic diseases of the central and peripheral nervous system (such as, particularly, serious neurasthenia and hysteria, all unquestionable cases of epilepsy, serious cases of Basedow's disease, etc.);

(g) Blindness in both eyes, or m one eye when the vision of the other remains below in spite of the use of corrective glasses; reduction in acuteness of vision in case it is impossible to restore it by correction to the acuteness of 1/2 for one eye at least; other ocular affections coming in the present class (glaucoma, iritis, choroiditis, etc.);

(h) Total deafness in both ears, as well as total deafness in one ear in case the partially deaf ear does not discern the ordinary spoken voice at a distance of one meter:

(i) All unquestionable cases of mental affections;

(k) All serious cases of chronic poisoning by metals or other causes (lead poisoning, mercury poisoning, morphinism, cocainism, alcoholism, gas poisoning, etc.);

(l) Chronic affections of the organs of locomotion (arthritis deformans, gout, rheumatism with impairments clinically discoverable), provided they are serious;

(m) All malignant growths, if they are not amenable to relatively minor operations without endangering the life of the patient;
(n) All cases of malaria with noticeable organic changes. (important chronic increase in size of the liver, of the spleen, cachexia, etc.);

(o) Serious chronic cutaneous affections, in so far as their nature does not constitute a medical indication for hospitalization in a neutral country;

(p) Serious avitaminoses (beriberi, pellagra, chronic scurvy).

B. Hospitalization

Prisoners of war must be hospitalized if they have the following affections:

1. All forms of tuberculosis of any organs whatever if, according to present medical knowledge, they may be cured, or at least considerably improved by methods applicable in a neutral country (altitude, treatment in sanatoria, etc.);

2. All forms-necessitating treatment-of affections of the respiratory, circulatory, digestive, genito-urinary, and nervous organs, of organs of the senses, of the locomotor and cutaneous apparatus; provided, however, that the forms of these affections do not belong to the categories requiring direct repatriation, or are not acute diseases properly so-called susceptible to a complete cure. The affections contemplated in this paragraph are those which offer really better chances of cure for the patient by the application of means of treatment available in a neutral country than if he were treated in captivity.

Nervous troubles, the efficient or determinant causes of which are the events of the war or even of the captivity itself, such as the psychasthenia of prisoners of war and other analogous cases, should be given special consideration.

All duly verified cases of this kind should be hospitalized, provided that the seriousness or constitutional character thereof does not make them cases for direct repatriation.

Cases of psychasthenia of prisoners of war which are not cured after three months of hospitalization in a neutral country or which, after this period has expired, are not obviously on the road to final recovery, should be repatriated.

3. All cases of wounds or lesions and their consequences which offer better chances of cure in a neutral country than in captivity, provided that these cases axe not either eligible for direct repatriation or else are insignificant.

4. All cases of malaria, duly verified and not presenting organic changes clinically discoverable (chronic enlargement of the liver, of the spleen, cachexia, etc.), if the stay in a neutral country offers particularly favorable prospects of final cure;

5. All cases of poisoning (particularly by gases, metals, alkaloids) for which the prospects of cure in a neutral country are especially favorable.

There shall be excluded from hospitalization:

1. All duly verified cases of mental affections.

2. All organic, or functional nervous affections reputed to be incurable; (These two categories belong to those giving a right to direct repatriation.)

3. Serious chronic alcoholism;

4. All contagious affections during the period in which they are transmissible (acute infectious diseases, primaxy and secondary syphilis, trachoma, leprosy, etc.).

III. General Observations

The conditions given above should, generally speaking, be interpreted and applied in as broad a spirit as possible.

This breadth of interpretation should be especially applied to the neuropathic or psychopathic conditions caused or brought to a head by the events of the war or even of the captivity itself (psychasthenia of prisoners of war), and also to cases of tuberculosis in all degrees.

It is needless to state that camp physicians and the mixed medical commissions may find themselves confronted with a great number of cases not mentioned among the examples given under Section 11, or cases not fitting in with these examples. The examples mentioned above axe given only as typical examples; an analogous list of examples of surgical alterations has not been drawn up because, with the exception of cases incontestable by their very nature (amputations), it is difficult to make a list of particular type; experience has shown that a recital of these particular cases was not without disadvantages in practice.

All cases not fitting exactly into the examples cited shall be decided by invoking the spirit of the above governing principles.

AND WHEREAS, the said Convention has been duly ratified on the part of the United States of America and the instrument of ratification of the United States of America was deposited with the Government of Switzerland on February 4, 1932;

AND WHEREAS, in accordance with Article 92 thereof, the said Convention became effective in respect of the United States of America six months after the deposit of its instrument of ratification, namely, on August 4, 1932;

Now, THEREFORE, be it known that I, Herbert Hoover, President of the United States of America, have caused the said Convention to be made public to the end that the same and every article and clause thereof may be observed and fulfilled with good faith by the United States of America and the citizens thereof.

IN TESTIMONY WHEREOF, I have hereunto set my hand and caused the seal of the United States of America to be affixed.

DONE at the city of Washington this fourth day of August in the year of our Lord one thousand nine hundred and thirty- two, and of the Independence of the United States of America the one hundred and fifty-seventh.

HERBERT HOOVER
By the President:
W. R. CASTLE, Jr
Acting Secretary of State.

(1) Annexed Regulations:

ART. 1. The laws, -rights, and duties of war apply not only to armies, but also to militia and volunteer corps fulfilling the following conditions:

To be commanded by a person responsible for his subordinates;
To have a fixed distinctive emblem recognizable at a distance;
To carry arms openly; and
To conduct their operations in accordance with the laws and customs of war.

In countries where militia or volunteer corps constitute the army, or form part of it, they are included under the denomination "army."

ART. 2. The inhabitants of a territory which has not been occupied, who, on the approach of the enemy, spontaneously take up arms to resist the invading troops without having had time to organize themselves in accordance with Article 1, shall be regarded as belligerents if they carry arms openly and if they respect the laws and customs of war.

ART. 3. The armed forces of the belligerent parties may consist of combatants and noncombatants. In the case of capture by the enemy, both have a right to be treated as prisoners of war.

Geneva Conventions 1949

An other example, the conventions III of 1899 and X of 1907 have been superseded by the 1949 GC (Geneva Conference in 1949) II.[19] The Geneva Conference of 1949 also revised the convention of 1929 related to prisoners of War in GC 1949 III.

Convention (I) for the Amelioration of the Condition of the Wounded and Sick in Armed Forces in the Field, August 1

Entry Into Force: 21 October 1950

The undersigned Plenipotentiaries of the Governments represented at the Diplomatic Conference held at Geneva from 21 April to 12 August 1949, for the purpose of revising the Geneva Convention for the Relief of the Wounded and Sick in Armies in the Field of 27 July 1929, have agreed as follows:

Chapter I. General Provisions

Article 1

The High Contracting Parties undertake to respect and to ensure respect for the present Convention in all circumstances.

Article 2

In addition to the provisions which shall be implemented in peacetime, the present Convention shall apply to all cases of declared war or of any other armed conflict which may arise between two or more of the High Contracting Parties, even if the state of war is not recognized by one of them. The Convention shall also apply to all cases of partial or total occupation of the territory of a High Contracting Party, even if the said occupation meets with no armed resistance.

Although one of the Powers in conflict may not be a party to the present Convention, the Powers who are parties thereto shall remain bound by it in their mutual relations. They shall furthermore be bound by the Convention in relation to the said Power, if the latter accepts and applies the provisions thereof.

---

[19] A. Cassese, *The oxford companion to; International criminal justice*, Oxford University Press 2009, p. 340.

Article 3

In the case of armed conflict not of an international character occurring in the territory of one of the High Contracting Parties, each Party to the conflict shall be bound to apply, as a minimum, the following provisions:

(1) Persons taking no active part in the hostilities, including members of armed forces who have laid down their arms and those placed hors de combat by sickness, wounds, detention, or any other cause, shall in all circumstances be treated humanely,without any adverse distinction founded on race, colour, religion or faith, sex, birth or wealth, or any other similar criteria. To this end, the following acts are and shall remain prohibited at any time and in any place whatsoever with respect to the above-mentioned persons: (a) violence to life and person, in particular murder of all kinds, mutilation, cruel treatment and torture; (b) taking of hostages; (c) outrages upon personal dignity, in particular humiliating and degrading treatment; (d) the passing of sentences and the carrying out of executions without previous judgment pronounced by a regularly constituted court, affording all the judicial guarantees which are recognized as indispensable by civilized peoples.

(2) The wounded and sick shall be collected and cared for.

An impartial humanitarian body, such as the International Committee of the Red Cross, may offer its services to the Parties to the conflict.

The Parties to the conflict should further endeavour to bring into force, by means of special agreements, all or part of the other provisions of the present Convention. The application of the preceding provisions shall not affect the legal status of the Parties to the conflict.

Article 4

Neutral Powers shall apply by analogy the provisions of the present Convention to the wounded and sick, and to members of the medical personnel and to chaplains of the armed forces of the Parties to the conflict, received or interned in their territory, as well as to dead persons found.

Article 5

For the protected persons who have fallen into the hands of the enemy, the present Convention shall apply until their final repatriation.

Article 6

In addition to the agreements expressly provided for in Articles 10, 15, 23, 28, 31, 36, 37 and 52, the High Contracting Parties may conclude other special agreements for all matters concerning which they may deem it suitable to make separate provision. No special agreement shall adversely affect the situation of the wounded and sick, of members of the medical personnel or of chaplains, as defined by the present Convention, nor restrict the rights which it confers upon them.

Wounded and sick, as well as medical personnel and chaplains, shall continue to have the benefit of such agreements as long as the Convention is applicable to them, except where express provisions to the contrary are contained in the aforesaid or in subsequent agreements, or where more favourable measures have been taken j with regard to them by one or other of the Parties to the conflict.

Article 7

Wounded and sick, as well as members of the medical personnel and chaplains, may in no circumstances renounce in part or in entirety the rights secured to them by the present Convention, and by the special agreements referred to in the foregoing Article, if such there be.

Article 8

The present Convention shall be applied with the cooperation and under the scrutiny of the Protecting Powers whose duty it is to safeguard the interests of the Parties to the conflict. For this purpose, the Protecting Powers may appoint, apart from their diplomatic or consular staff, delegates from amongst their own nationals or the nationals of other neutral Powers. The said delegates shall be subject to the approval of the Power with which they are to carry out their duties.
The Parties to the conflict shall facilitate to the greatest extent possible, the task of the representatives or delegates of the Protecting Powers.

The representatives or delegates of the Protecting Powers shall not in any case exceed their mission under the present Convention. They shall, in particular, take account of the imperative necessities of security of the State wherein they carry out their duties. Their activities shall only be restricted as an exceptional and temporary measure when this is rendered necessary by imperative military necessities.

Article 9

The provisions of the present Convention constitute no obstacle to the humanitarian activities which the International Committee of the Red Cross or any other impartial humanitarian organization may, subject to the consent of the Parties to the conflict concerned, undertake for the protection of wounded and sick, medical personnel and chaplains, and for their relief.

Article 10

The High Contracting Parties may at any time agree to entrust to an organization which offers all guarantees of impartiality and efficacy the duties incumbent on the Protecting Powers by virtue of the present Convention.

When wounded and sick, or medical personnel and chaplains do not benefit or cease to benefit, no matter for what reason, by the activities of a Protecting Power or of an organization provided for in the first paragraph above, the Detaining Power shall request a neutral State, or such an organization, to undertake the functions performed under the present Convention by a Protecting Power designated by the Parties to a conflict.

If protection cannot be arranged accordingly, the Detaining Power shall request or shall accept, subject to the provisions of this Article, the offer of the services of a humanitarian organization, such as the International Committee of the Red Cross, to assume the humanitarian functions performed by Protecting Powers under the present Convention.

Any neutral Power, or any organization invited by the Power concerned or offering itself for these purposes, shall be required to act with a sense of responsibility towards the Party to the conflict on which persons protected by the present Convention depend, and shall be required to furnish sufficient assurances that it is in a position to undertake the appropriate functions and to discharge them impartially.

No derogation from the preceding provisions shall be made by special agreements between Powers one of which is restricted, even temporarily, in its freedom to negotiate with the other Power or its allies by reason of military events, more particularly where the whole, or a substantial part, of the territory of the said Power is occupied.

Whenever, in the present Convention, mention is made of a Protecting Power, such mention also applies to substitute organizations in the sense of the present Article.

Article 11

In cases where they deem it advisable in the interest of protected persons, particularly in cases of disagreement between the Parties to the conflict as to the application or interpretation of the provisions of the present Convention, the Protecting Powers shall lend their good offices with a view to settling the disagreement.

For this purpose, each of the Protecting Powers may, either at the invitation of one Party or on its own initiative, propose to the Parties to the conflict a meeting of their representatives, in particular of the authorities responsible for the wounded and sick, members of medical personnel and chaplains, possibly on neutral territory suitably chosen. The Parties to the conflict shall be bound to give effect to the proposals made to them for this purpose. The Protecting Powers may, if necessary, propose for approval by the Parties to the conflict, a person belonging to a neutral Power or delegated by the International Committee of the Red Cross, who shall be invited to take part in such a meeting

Chapter II. Wounded and Sick

Article 12

Members of the armed forces and other persons mentioned in the following Article, who are wounded or sick, shall be respected and protected in all circumstances. They shall be treated humanely and cared for by the Party to the conflict in whose power they may be, without any adverse distinction founded on sex, race, nationality, religion, political opinions, or any other similar criteria. Any attempts upon their lives, or violence to their persons, shall be strictly prohibited; in particular, they shall not be murdered or exterminated, subjected to torture or to biological experiments; they shall not wilfully be left without medical assistance and care, nor shall conditions exposing them to contagion or infection be created.

Only urgent medical reasons will authorize priority in the order of treatment to be administered. Women shall be treated with all consideration due to their sex. The Party to the conflict which is compelled to abandon wounded or sick to the enemy shall, as far as military considerations permit, leave with them a part of its medical personnel and material to assist in their care.

Article 13

The present Convention shall apply to the wounded and sick belonging to the following categories:

(1) Members of the armed forces of a Party to the conflict, as well as members of militias or volunteer corps forming part of such armed forces.

(2) Members of other militias and members of other volunteer corps, including those of organized resistance movements, belonging to a Party to the conflict and operating in or

outside their own territory, even if this territory is occupied, provided that such militias or volunteer corps, including such organized resistance movements, fulfil the following conditions: (a) that of being commanded by a person responsible for his subordinates; (b)that of having a fixed distinctive sign recognizable at a distance; (c) that of carrying arms openly; (d)that of conducting their operations in accordance with the laws and customs of war.

(3) Members of regular armed forces who profess allegiance to a Government or an authority not recognized by the Detaining Power.

(4) Persons who accompany the armed forces without actually being members thereof, such as civil members of military aircraft crews, war correspondents, supply contractors, members of labour units or of services responsible for the welfare of the armed forces, provided that they have received authorization from the armed forces which they accompany.

(5) Members of crews, including masters, pilots and apprentices, of the merchant marine and the crews of civil aircraft of the Parties to the conflict, who do not benefit by more favourable treatment under any other provisions in international law.

(6) Inhabitants of a non-occupied territory, who on the approach of the enemy, spontaneously take up arms to resist the invading forces, without having had time to form themselves into regular armed units, provided they carry arms openly and respect the laws and customs of war.

Article 14

Subject to the provisions of Article 12, the wounded and sick of a belligerent who fall into enemy hands shall be prisoners of war, and the provisions of international law concerning prisoners of war shall apply to them.

Article 15

At all times, and particularly after an engagement, Parties to the conflict shall, without delay, take all possible measures to search for and collect the wounded and sick, to protect them against pillage and ill-treatment, to ensure their adequate care, and to search for the dead and prevent their being despoiled.

Whenever circumstances permit, an armistice or a suspension of fire shall be arranged, or local arrangements made, to permit the removal, exchange and transport of the wounded left on the battlefield.

Likewise, local arrangements may be concluded between Parties to the conflict for the removal or exchange of wounded and sick from a besieged or encircled area, and for the passage of medical and religious personnel and equipment on their way to that area.

Article 16

Parties to the conflict shall record as soon as possible, in respect of each wounded, sick or dead person of the adverse Party falling into their hands, any particulars which may assist in his identification. These records should if possible include: (a) designation of the Power on which he depends; (b) army, regimental, personal or serial number; (c) surname; (d) first name or names; (e) date of birth; (f) any other particulars shown on his identity card or disc; (g) date and place of capture or death; (h) particulars concerning wounds or illness, or cause of death.

As soon as possible the above mentioned information shall be forwarded to the Information Bureau described in Article 122 of the Geneva Convention relative to the Treatment of Prisoners of War of 12 August 1949, which shall transmit this information to the Power on which these persons depend through the intermediary of the Protecting Power and of the Central Prisoners of War Agency.

Parties to the conflict shall prepare and forward to each other through the same bureau, certificates of death or duly authenticated lists of the dead. They shall likewise collect and forward through the same bureau one half of a double identity disc, last wills or other documents of importance to the next of kin, money and in general all articles of an intrinsic or sentimental value, which are found on the dead. These articles, together with unidentified articles, shall be sent in sealed packets, accompanied by statements giving all particulars necessary for the identification of the deceased owners, as well as by a complete list of the contents of the parcel.

Article 17

Parties to the conflict shall ensure that burial or cremation of the dead, carried out individually as far as circumstances permit, is preceded by a careful examination, if possible by a medical examination, of the bodies, with a view to confirming death, establishing identity and enabling a report to be made. One half of the double identity disc, or the identity disc itself if it is a single disc, should remain on the body.

Bodies shall not be cremated except for imperative reasons of hygiene or for motives based on the religion of the deceased. In case of cremation, the circumstances and reasons for cremation shall be stated in detail in the death certificate or on the authenticated list of the dead.

They shall further ensure that the dead are honourably interred, if possible according to the rites of the religion to which they belonged, that their graves are respected, grouped if possible according to the nationality of the deceased, properly maintained and marked so that they may always be found. For this purpose, they shall organize at the commencement of hostilities an Official Graves Registration Service, to allow subsequent exhumations and to ensure the identification of bodies, whatever the site of the graves, and the possible transportation to the home country. These provisions shall likewise apply to the ashes, which shall be kept by the Graves Registration Service until proper disposal thereof in accordance with the wishes of the home country.

As soon as circumstances permit, and at latest at the end of hostilities, these Services shall exchange, through the Information Bureau mentioned in the second paragraph of Article 16, lists showing the exact location and markings of the graves, together with particulars of the dead interred therein.

Article 18

The military authorities may appeal to the charity of the inhabitants voluntarily to collect and care for, under their direction, the wounded and sick, granting persons who have responded to this appeal the necessary protection and facilities. Should the adverse Party take or retake control of the area, he shall likewise grant these persons the same protection and the same facilities.

The military authorities shall permit the inhabitants and relief societies, even in invaded or occupied areas, spontaneously to collect and care for wounded or sick of whatever nationality. The civilian population shall respect these wounded and sick, and in particular abstain from offering them violence. No one may ever be molested or convicted for having nursed the wounded or sick. The provisions of the present Article do not relieve the occupying Power of its obligation to give both physical and moral care to the wounded and sick.

Chapter III. Medical Units and Establishments

Article 19

Fixed establishments and mobile medical units of the Medical Service may in no circumstances be attacked, but shall at all times be respected and protected by the Parties to the conflict. Should they fall into the hands of the adverse Party, their personnel shall be free to pursue their duties, as long as the capturing Power has not itself ensured the necessary care of the wounded and sick found in such establishments and units.

The responsible authorities shall ensure that the said medical establishments and units are, as far as possible, situated in such a manner that attacks against military objectives cannot imperil their safety.

Article 20

Hospital ships entitled to the protection of the Geneva Convention for the Amelioration of the Condition of Wounded, Sick and Shipwrecked Members of Armed Forces at Sea of 12 August 1949, shall not be attacked from the land.

Article 21

The protection to which fixed establishments and mobile medical units of the Medical Service are entitled shall not cease unless they are used to commit, outside their humanitarian duties, acts harmful to the enemy. Protection may, however, cease only after a due warning has been given, naming, in all appropriate cases, a reasonable time limit, and after such warning has remained unheeded.

Article 22

The following conditions shall not be considered as depriving a medical unit or establishment of the protection guaranteed by Article 19:

(1) That the personnel of the unit or establishment are armed, and that they use the arms in their own defence, or in that of the wounded and sick in their charge.

(2) That in the absence of armed orderlies, the unit or establishment is protected by a picket or by sentries or by an escort.

(3) That small arms and ammunition taken from the wounded and sick and not yet handed to the proper service, are found in the unit or establishment.

(4) That personnel and material of the veterinary service are found in the unit or establishment, without forming an integral part thereof.

(5) That the humanitarian activities of medical units and establishments or of their personnel extend to the care of civilian wounded or sick.

Article 23

In time of peace, the High Contracting Parties and, after the outbreak of hostilities, the Parties thereto, may establish in their own territory and, if the need arises, in occupied areas, hospital zones and localities so organized as to protect the wounded and sick from the effects of war, as well as the personnel entrusted with the organization and administration of these zones and localities and with the care of the persons therein assembled.

Upon the outbreak and during the course of hostilities, the Parties concerned may conclude agreements on mutual recognition of the hospital zones and localities they have created. They may for this purpose implement the provisions of the Draft Agreement annexed to the present Convention, with such amendments as they may consider necessary.

The Protecting Powers and the International Committee of the Red Cross are invited to lend their good offices in order to facilitate the institution and recognition of these hospital zones and localities.

Chapter IV. Personnel

Article 24

Medical personnel exclusively engaged in the search for, or the collection, transport or treatment of the wounded or sick, or in the prevention of disease, staff exclusively engaged in the administration of medical units and establishments, as well as chaplains attached to the armed forces, shall be respected and protected in all circumstances.

Article 25

Members of the armed forces specially trained for employment, should the need arise, as hospital orderlies, nurses or auxiliary stretcher-bearers, in the search for or the collection, transport or treatment of the wounded and sick shall likewise be respected and protected if they are carrying out these duties at the time when they come into contact with the enemy or fall into his hands.

Article 26

The staff of National Red Cross Societies and that of other Voluntary Aid Societies, duly recognized and authorized by their Governments, who may be employed on the same duties as the personnel named in Article 24, are placed on the same footing as the personnel named in the said Article, provided that the staff of such societies are subject to military laws and regulations.

Each High Contracting Party shall notify to the other, either in time of peace or at the commencement of or during hostilities, but in any case before actually employing them, the names of the societies which it has authorized, under its responsibility, to render assistance to the regular medical service of its armed forces.

Article 27

A recognized Society of a neutral country can only lend the assistance of its medical personnel and units to a Party to the conflict with the previous consent of its own Government and the authorization of the Party to the conflict concerned. That personnel and those units shall be placed under the control of that Party to the conflict.

The neutral Government shall notify this consent to the adversary of the State which accepts such assistance. The Party to the conflict who accepts such assistance is bound to notify the adverse Party thereof before making any use of it.

In no circumstances shall this assistance be considered as interference in the conflict. The members of the personnel named in the first paragraph shall be duly furnished with the identity cards provided for in Article 40 before leaving the neutral country to which they belong.

Article 28

Personnel designated in Articles 24 and 26 who fall into the hands of the adverse Party, shall be retained only in so far as the state of health, the spiritual needs and the number of prisoners of war require. Personnel thus retained shall not be deemed prisoners of war. Nevertheless they shall at least benefit by all the provisions of the Geneva Convention relative to the Treatment of Prisoners of War of 12 August 1949. Within the framework of the military laws and regulations of the Detaining Power, and under the authority of its competent service, they shall continue to carry out, in accordance with their professional ethics, their medical and spiritual duties on behalf of prisoners of war, preferably those of the armed forces to which they themselves belong. They shall further enjoy the following facilities for carrying out their medical or spiritual duties:

(a) They shall be authorized to visit periodically the prisoners of war in labour units or hospitals outside the camp. The Detaining Power shall put at their disposal the means of transport required.

(b) In each camp the senior medical officer of the highest rank shall be responsible to the military authorities of the camp for the professional activity of the retained medical personnel. For this purpose, from the outbreak of hostilities, the Parties to the conflict shall agree regarding the corresponding seniority of the ranks of their medical personnel, including those of the societies designated in Article 26. In all questions arising out of their duties, this medical officer, and the chaplains, shall have direct access to the military and medical authorities of the camp who shall grant them the facilities they may require for correspondence relating to these questions.

(c) Although retained personnel in a camp shall be subject to its internal discipline, they shall not, however, be required to perform any work outside their medical or religious duties.

During hostilities the Parties to the conflict shall make arrangements for relieving where possible retained personnel, and shall settle the procedure of such relief. None of the preceding provisions shall relieve the Detaining Power of the obligations imposed upon it with regard to the medical and spiritual welfare of the prisoners of war.

Article 29

Members of the personnel designated in Article 25 who have fallen into the hands of the enemy, shall be prisoners of war, but shall be employed on their medical duties in so far as the need arises.

Article 30

Personnel whose retention is not indispensable by virtue of the provisions of Article 28 shall be returned to the Party to the conflict to whom they belong, as soon as a road is open for their return and military requirements permit. Pending their return, they shall not be deemed prisoners of war. Nevertheless they shall at least benefit by all the provisions of the Geneva Convention relative to the Treatment of Prisoners of War of 12 August 1949. They shall continue to fulfil their duties under the orders of the adverse Party and shall preferably be engaged in the care of the wounded and sick of the Party to the conflict to which they themselves belong. On their departure, they shall take with them the effects, personal belongings, valuables and instruments belonging to them.

Article 31

The selection of personnel for return under Article 30 shall be made irrespective of any consideration of race, religion or political opinion, but preferably according to the chronological order of their capture and their state of health.

As from the outbreak of hostilities, Parties to the conflict may determine by special agreement the percentage of personnel to be retained, in proportion to the number of prisoners and the distribution of the said personnel in the camps.

Article 32

Persons designated in Article 27 who have fallen into the hands of the adverse Party may not be detained. Unless otherwise agreed, they shall have permission to return to their country, or if this is not possible, to the territory of the Party to the conflict in whose service they were, as soon as a route for their return is open and military considerations permit.

Pending their release, they shall continue their work under the direction of the adverse Party; they shall preferably be engaged in the care of the wounded and sick of the Party to the conflict in whose service they were. On their departure, they shall take with them their effects personal articles and valuables and the instruments, arms and if possible the means of transport belonging to them.

The Parties to the conflict shall secure to this personnel, while in their power, the same food, lodging, allowances and pay as are granted to the corresponding personnel of their armed forces. The food shall in any case be sufficient as regards quantity, quality and variety to keep the said personnel in a normal state of health.

Chapter V. Buildings and Material

Article 33

The material of mobile medical units of the armed forces which fall into the hands of the enemy, shall be reserved for the care of wounded and sick. The buildings, material and stores of fixed medical establishments of the armed forces shall remain subject to the laws of war, but may not be diverted from that purpose as long as they are required for the care of wounded and sick.

Nevertheless, the commanders of forces in the field may make use of them, in case of urgent military necessity, provided that they make previous arrangements for the welfare of the wounded and sick who are nursed in them. The material and stores defined in the present Article shall not be intentionally destroyed.

Article 34

The real and personal property of aid societies which are admitted to the privileges of the Convention shall be regarded as private property.

The right of requisition recognized for belligerents by the laws and customs of war shall not be exercised except in case of urgent necessity, and only after the welfare of the wounded and sick has been ensured.

Chapter VI. Medical Transports

Article 35

Transports of wounded and sick or of medical equipment shall be respected and protected in the same way as mobile medical units. Should such transports or vehicles fall into the hands of the adverse Party, they shall be subject to the laws of war, on condition that the Party to the conflict who captures them shall in all cases ensure the care of the wounded and sick they contain. The civilian personnel and all means of transport obtained by requisition shall be subject to the general rules of international law.

Article 36

Medical aircraft, that is to say, aircraft exclusively employed for the removal of wounded and sick and for the transport of medical personnel and equipment, shall not be attacked, but shall be respected by the belligerents, while flying at heights, times and on routes specifically agreed upon between the belligerents concerned.

They shall bear, clearly marked, the distinctive emblem prescribed in Article 38, together with their national colours on their lower, upper and lateral surfaces. They shall be provided with any other markings or means of identification that may be agreed upon between the belligerents upon the outbreak or during the course of hostilities. Unless agreed otherwise, flights over enemy or enemy-occupied territory are prohibited.

Medical aircraft shall obey every summons to land. In the event of a landing thus imposed, the aircraft with its occupants may continue its flight after examination, if any. In the event of an involuntary landing in enemy or enemy-occupied territory, the wounded and sick, as well as the crew of the aircraft shall be prisoners of war. The medical personnel shall be treated according to Article 24 and the Articles following.

Article 37

Subject to the provisions of the second paragraph, medical aircraft of Parties to the conflict may fly over the territory of neutral Powers, land on it in case of necessity, or use it as a port of call. They shall give the neutral Powers previous notice of their passage over the said territory and obey all summons to alight, on land or water. They will be immune from attack only when flying on routes, at heights and at times specifically agreed upon between the Parties to the conflict and the neutral Power concerned.

The neutral Powers may, however, place conditions or restrictions on the passage or landing of medical aircraft on their territory. Such possible conditions or restrictions shall be applied equally to all Parties to the conflict. Unless agreed otherwise between the neutral Power and the Parties to the conflict, the wounded and sick who are disembarked, with the consent of the local authorities, on neutral territory by medical aircraft, shall be detained by the neutral Power, where so required by international law, in such a manner that they cannot again take part in operations of war. The cost of their accommodation and internment shall be borne by the Power on which they depend.

Chapter VII.The Distinctive Emblem

Article 38

As a compliment to Switzerland, the heraldic emblem of the red cross on a white ground, formed by reversing the Federal colours, is retained as the emblem and distinctive sign of the Medical Service of armed forces. Nevertheless, in the case of countries which already use as emblem, in place of the red cross, the red crescent or the red lion and sun on a white ground, those emblems are also recognized by the terms of the present Convention.

Article 39

Under the direction of the competent military authority, the emblem shall be displayed on the flags, armlets and on all equipment employed in the Medical Service.

Article 40

The personnel designated in Article 24 and in Articles 26 and 27 shall wear, affixed to the left arm, a water-resistant armlet bearing the distinctive emblem, issued and stamped by the military authority. Such personnel, in addition to wearing the identity disc mentioned in Article 16, shall also carry a special identity card bearing the distinctive emblem. This card shall be water-resistant and of such size that it can be carried in the pocket. It shall be worded in the national language, and shall mention at least the surname and first names, the date of birth, the rank and the service number of the bearer, and shall state in what capacity he is entitled to the protection of the present Convention. The card shall bear the photograph of the owner and also either his signature or his finger-prints or both. It shall be embossed with the stamp of the military authority.

The identity card shall be uniform throughout the same armed forces and, as far as possible, of a similar type in the armed forces of the High Contracting Parties. The Parties to the conflict may be guided by the model which is annexed, by way of example, to the present Convention. They shall inform each other, at the outbreak of hostilities, of the model they are using. Identity cards should be made out, if possible, at least in duplicate, one copy being kept by the home country.

In no circumstances may the said personnel be deprived of their insignia or identity cards nor of the right to wear the armlet. In case of loss, they shall be entitled to receive duplicates of the cards and to have the insignia replaced.

Article 41

The personnel designated in Article 25 shall wear, but only while carrying out medical duties, a white armlet bearing in its centre the distinctive sign in miniature; the armlet shall be issued and stamped by the military authority. Military identity documents to be carried by this type of personnel shall specify what special training they have received, the temporary character of the duties they are engaged upon, and their authority for wearing the armlet.

Article 42

The distinctive flag of the Convention shall be hoisted only over such medical units and establishments as are entitled to be respected under the Convention, and only with the consent of the military authorities. In mobile units, as in fixed establishments, it may be accompanied by the national flag of the Party to the conflict to which the unit or establishment belongs.

Nevertheless, medical units which have fallen into the hands of the enemy shall not fly any flag other than that of the Convention. Parties to the conflict shall take the necessary steps, in so far as military considerations permit, to make the distinctive emblems indicating medical units and establishments clearly visible to the enemy land, air or naval forces, in order to obviate the possibility of any hostile action.

Article 43

The medical units belonging to neutral countries, which may have been authorized to lend their services to a belligerent under the conditions laid down in Article 27, shall fly, along with the flag of the Convention, the national flag of that belligerent, wherever the latter makes use of the faculty conferred on him by Article 42. Subject to orders to the contrary by the responsible military authorities, they may on all occasions fly their national flag, even if they fall into the hands of the adverse Party.

Article 44

With the exception of the cases mentioned in the following paragraphs of the present Article, the emblem of the red cross on a white ground and the words " Red Cross" or " Geneva Cross " may not be employed, either in time of peace or in time of war, except to indicate or to protect the medical units and establishments, the personnel and material protected by the present Convention and other Conventions dealing with similar matters. The same shall apply to the emblems mentioned in Article 38, second paragraph, in respect of the countries which use them. The National Red Cross Societies and other societies designated in Article 26 shall have the right to use the distinctive emblem conferring the protection of the Convention only within the framework of the present paragraph.

Furthermore, National Red Cross (Red Crescent, Red Lion and Sun) Societies may, in time of peace, in accordance with their rational legislation, make use of the name and emblem of the Red Cross for their other activities which are in conformity with the principles laid down by the International Red Cross Conferences. When those activities are carried out in time of war, the conditions for the use of the emblem shall be such that it cannot be considered as conferring the protection of the Convention; the emblem shall be comparatively small in size and may not be placed on armlets or on the roofs of buildings. The international Red Cross organizations and their duly authorized personnel shall be permitted to make use, at all times, of the emblem of the red cross on a white ground.

As an exceptional measure, in conformity with national legislation and with the express permission of one of the National Red Cross (Red Crescent, Red Lion and Sun) Societies, the emblem of the Convention may be employed in time of peace to identify vehicles used as ambulances and to mark the position of aid stations exclusively assigned to the purpose of giving free treatment to the wounded or sick.

Chapter VIII. Execution of the Convention

Article 45

Each Party to the conflict, acting through its Commanders-in-Chief, shall ensure the detailed execution of the preceding Articles, and provide for unforeseen cases, in conformity with the general principles of the present Convention.

Article 46

Reprisals against the wounded, sick, personnel, buildings or equipment protected by the Convention are prohibited.

Article 47

The High Contracting Parties undertake, in time of peace as in time of war, to disseminate the text of the present Convention as widely as possible in their respective countries, and, in particular, to include the study thereof in their programmes of military and, if possible, civil instruction, so that the principles thereof may become known to the entire population, in particular to the armed fighting forces, the medical personnel and the chaplains.

Article 48

The High Contracting Parties shall communicate to one another through the Swiss Federal Council and, during hostilities, through the Protecting Powers, the official translations of the present Convention, as well as the laws and regulations which they may adopt to ensure the application thereof.

Chapter IX. Repression of Abuses and Infractions

Article 49

The High Contracting Parties undertake to enact any legislation necessary to provide effective penal sanctions for persons committing, or ordering to be committed, any of the grave breaches of the present Convention defined in the following Article.

Each High Contracting Party shall be under the obligation to search for persons alleged to have committed, or to have ordered to be committed, such grave breaches, arid shall bring such persons, regardless of their nationality, before its own courts. It may also, if it prefers, and in accordance with the provisions of its own legislation, hand such persons over for trial to another High Contracting Party concerned, provided such High Contracting Party has made out a prima facie case.

Each High Contracting Party shall take measures necessary for the suppression of all acts contrary to the provisions of the present Convention other than the grave breaches defined in the following Article.

In all circumstances, the accused persons shall benefit by safeguards of proper trial and defence, which shall not be less favourable than those provided by Article 105 and those following, of the Geneva Convention relative to the Treatment of Prisoners of War of 12 August 1949.

Article 50

Grave breaches to which the preceding Article relates shall be those involving any of the following acts, if committed against persons or property protected by the Convention: wilful killing, torture or inhuman treatment, including biological experiments, wilfully causing great suffering or serious injury to body or health, and extensive destruction and appropriation of property, not justified by military necessity and carried out unlawfully and wantonly.

Article 51

No High Contracting Party shall be allowed to absolve itself or any other High Contracting Party of any liability incurred by itself or by another High Contracting Party in respect of breaches referred to in the preceding Article.

Article 52

At the request of a Party to the conflict, an enquiry shall be instituted, in a manner to be decided between the interested Parties, concerning any alleged violation of the Convention.

If agreement has not been reached concerning the procedure for the enquiry, the Parties should agree on the choice of an umpire who will decide upon the procedure to be followed. Once the violation has been established, the Parties to the conflict shall put an end to it and shall repress it with the least possible delay.

Article 53

The use by individuals, societies, firms or companies either public or private, other than those entitled thereto under the present Convention, of the emblem or the designation " Red Cross " or " Geneva Cross " or any sign or designation constituting an imitation thereof, whatever the object of such use, and irrespective of the date of its adoption, shall be prohibited at all times. By reason of the tribute paid to Switzerland by the adoption of the reversed Federal colours, and of the confusion which may arise between the arms of Switzerland and the distinctive emblem of the Convention, the use by private individuals, societies or firms, of the arms of the Swiss Confederation, or of marks constituting an imitation thereof, whether as trademarks or commercial marks, or as parts of such marks, or for a purpose contrary to commercial honesty, or in circumstances capable of wounding Swiss national sentiment, shall be prohibited at all times.

Nevertheless, such High Contracting Parties as were not party to the Geneva Convention of 27 July 1929, may grant to prior users of the emblems, designations, signs or marks designated in the first paragraph, a time limit not to exceed three years from the coming into force of the present Convention to discontinue such use provided that the said use shall not be such as would appear, in time of war, to confer the protection of the Convention. The prohibition laid down in the first paragraph of the present Article shall also apply, without effect on any rights acquired through prior use, to the emblems and marks mentioned in the second paragraph of Article 38.

Article 54

The High Contracting Parties shall, if their legislation is not already adequate, take measures necessary for the prevention and repression, at all times, of the abuses referred to under Article 53.

Article 55
Final Provisions

The present Convention is established in English and in French. Both texts are equally authentic. The Swiss Federal Council shall arrange for official translations of the Convention to be made in the Russian and Spanish languages.

Article 55

The present Convention, which bears the date of this day, is open to signature until 12 February 1950, in the name of the Powers represented at the Conference which opened at Geneva on 21 April 1949; furthermore, by Powers not represented at that Conference but which are Parties to the Geneva Conventions of 1864, 1906 or 1929 for the Relief of the Wounded and Sick in Armies in the Field.

Article 57

The present Convention shall be ratified as soon as possible and the ratifications shall be deposited at Berne. A record shall be drawn up of the deposit of each instrument of ratification and certified copies of this record shall be transmitted by the Swiss Federal Council to all the Powers in whose name the Convention has been signed, or whose accession has been notified.

Article 58

The present Convention shall come into force six months after not less than two instruments of ratification have been deposited. Thereafter, it shall come into force for each High Contracting Party six months after the deposit of the instrument of ratification.

Article 59

The present Convention replaces the Conventions of 22 August 1864, 6 July 1906, and 27 July 1929, in relations between the High Contracting Parties.

Article 60

From the date of its coming into force, it shall be open to any Power in whose name the present Convention has not been signed, to accede to this Convention.
Art. 61. Accessions shall be notified in writing to the Swiss Federal Council, and shall take effect six months after the date on which they are received. The Swiss Federal Council shall communicate the accessions to all the Powers in whose name the Convention has been signed, or whose accession has been notified.

Article 62

The situations provided for in Articles 2 and 3 shall give immediate effect to ratifications deposited and accessions notified by the Parties to the conflict before or after the beginning of hostilities or occupation. The Swiss Federal Council shall communicate by the quickest method any ratifications or accessions received from Parties to the conflict.

Article 63

Each of the High Contracting Parties shall be at liberty to denounce the present Convention. The denunciation shall be notified in writing to the Swiss Federal Council, which shall transmit it to the Governments of all the High Contracting Parties. The denunciation shall take effect one year after the notification thereof has been made to the Swiss Federal Council. However, a denunciation of which notification has been made at a time when the denouncing Power is involved in a conflict shall not take effect until peace has been concluded, and until after operations connected with release and repatriation of the persons protected by the present Convention have been terminated.

The denunciation shall have effect only in respect of the denouncing Power. It shall in no way impair the obligations which the Parties to the conflict shall remain bound to fulfil by virtue of the principles of the law of nations, as they result from the usages established among civilized peoples, from the laws of humanity and the dictates of the public conscience.

Article 64

The Swiss Federal Council shall register the present Convention with the Secretariat of the United Nations. The Swiss Federal Council shall also inform the Secretariat of the United Nations of all ratifications, accessions and denunciations received by it with respect to the present Convention.

In witness whereof the undersigned, having deposited their respective full powers, have signed the present Convention.

Done at Geneva this twelfth day of August 1949, in the English and French languages. The original shall be deposited in the archives of the Swiss Confederation. The Swiss Federal Council shall transmit certified copies thereof to each of the Signatory and Acceding States.
(Here follow signatures)

Annex I
Draft Agreement Relating to Hospital Zones and Localities

Article 1

Hospital zones shall be strictly observed for the persons named in Article 23 of the Geneva Convention for the Amelioration of the Condition of the Wounded and Sick in the Armed Forces in the Field of 12 August 1949, and for the personnel entrusted with the organization and administration of these zones and localities, and with the care of the persons therein assembled. Nevertheless, persons whose permanent residence is within such zones shall have the right to stay there.

Article 2

No persons residing, in whatever capacity, in a hospital zone shall perform any work, either within or without the zone, directly connected with military operations or the production of war material.

Article 3

The Power establishing a hospital zone shall take all necessary measures to prohibit access to all persons who have no right of residence or entry therein.

Article 4

Hospital zones shall fulfil the following conditions:

(a) They shall comprise only a small part of the territory governed by the Power which has established them.

(b) They shall be thinly populated in relation to the possibilities of accommodation.

(c) They shall be far removed and free from all military objectives, or large industrial or administrative establishments. (d) They shall not be situated in areas which, according to every probability, may become important for the conduct of the war.

Article 5

Hospital zones shall be subject to the following obligations:

(a) The lines of communication and means of transport which they possess shall not be used for the transport of military personnel or material, even in transit.

(b) They shall in no case be defended by military means.

Article 6

Hospital zones shall be marked by means of red crosses (red crescents, red lions and suns) on a white background placed on the outer precincts and on the buildings. They may be similarly marked at night by means of appropriate illumination.

Article 7

The Powers shall communicate to all High Contracting Parties in peacetime or on the outbreak of hostilities, a list of the hospital zones in the territories governed by them. They shall also give notice of any new zones set up during hostilities.

As soon as the adverse Party has receive the above-mentioned notification, the zone shall be regularly constituted. If, however, the adverse Party considers that the conditions of the present agreement have not been fulfilled, it may refuse to recognize the zone by giving immediate notice thereof to the Party responsible for the said Zone, or may make its recognition of such zone dependent upon the institution of the control provided for in Article 8.

Article 8

Any Power having recognized one of several hospital zones instituted by the adverse Party shall be entitled to demand control by one or more Special Commissioners, for the purpose of ascertaining if the zones fulfil the conditions and obligations stipulated in the present agreement.

For this purpose, the members of the Special Commissions shall at all times have free access to the various zones and may even reside there permanently. They shall be given all facilities for their duties of inspection.

Article 9

Should the Special Commissions note any facts which they consider contrary to the stipulations of the present agreement, they shall at once draw the attention of the Power governing the said zone to these facts, and shall fix a time limit of five days within which the matter should be rectified. They shall duly notify the Power who has recognized the zone.

If, when the time limit has expired, the Power governing the zone has not complied with the warning, the adverse Party may declare that it is no longer bound by the present agreement in respect of the said zone.

Article 10

Any Power setting up one or more hospital zones and localities, and the adverse Parties to whom their existence has been notified, shall nominate or have nominated by neutral Powers, the persons who shall be members of the Special Commissions mentioned in Articles 8 and 9,

Article 11

In no circumstances may hospital zones be the object of attack. They shall be protected and respected at all times by the Parties to the conflict.

Article 12

In the case of occupation of a territory, the hospital zones therein shall continue to be respected and utilized as such.

Their purpose may, however, be modified by the Occupying Power, on condition that all measures are taken to ensure the safety of the persons accomodated.

Article 13

The present agreement shall also apply to localities which the Powers may utilize for the same purposes as hospital zones.

Convention (II) for the Amelioration of the Condition of Wounded, Sick and Shipwrecked Members of Armed Forces at Sea, August 12

Entry into Force: 21 October 1950

The undersigned Plenipotentiaries of the Governments represented at the Diplomatic Conference held at Geneva from April 21 to August 12, 1949, for the purpose of revising the Xth Hague Convention of October 18, 1907, for the Adaptation to Maritime Warfare of the Principles of the Geneva Convention of 1906, have agreed as follows:

Chapter I. General Provisions

Article 1

The High Contracting Parties undertake to respect and to ensure respect for the present Convention in all circumstances.

Article 2

In addition to the provisions which shall be implemented in peacetime, the present Convention shall apply to all cases of declared war or of any other armed conflict which may arise between two or more of the High Contracting Parties, even if the state of war is not recognized by one of them. The Convention shall also apply to all cases of partial or total occupation of the territory of a High Contracting Party, even if the said occupation meets with no armed resistance. Although one of the Powers in conflict may not be a party to the present Convention, the Powers who are parties thereto shall remain bound by it in their mutual relations. They shall furthermore be bound by the Convention in relation to the said Power, if the latter accepts and applies the provisions thereof.

Article 3

In the case of armed conflict not of an international character occurring in the territory of one of the High Contracting Parties, each Party to the conflict shall be bound to apply, as a minimum, the following provisions:

(1) Persons taking no active part in the hostilities, including members of armed forces who have laid down their arms and those placed hors de combat by sickness, wounds, detention, or any other cause, shall in all circumstances be treated humanely, without any adverse distinction founded on race, colour, religion or faith, sex, birth or wealth, or any other similar criteria.

To this end, the following acts are and shall remain prohibited at any time and in any place whatsoever with respect to the above-mentioned persons:

(a) violence to life and person, in particular murder of all kinds, mutilation, cruel treatment and torture;

(b) taking of hostages;

(c) outrages upon personal dignity, in particular, humiliating and degrading treatment;

(d) the passing of sentences and the carrying out of executions without previous judgment pronounced by a regularly constituted court, affording all the judicial guarantees which are recognized as indispensable by civilized peoples.

(2) The wounded, sick and shipwrecked shall be collected and cared for.

An impartial humanitarian body, such as the International Committee of the Red Cross, may offer its services to the Parties to the conflict. The Parties to the conflict should further endeavour to bring into force, by means of special agreements, all or part of the other provisions of the present Convention. The application of the preceding provisions shall not affect the legal status of the Parties to the conflict.

Article 4

In case of hostilities between land and naval forces of Parties to the conflict, the provisions of the present Convention shall apply only to forces on board ship.
Forces put ashore shall immediately become subject to the provisions of the Geneva Convention for the Amelioration of the Condition of the Wounded and Sick in Armed Forces in the Field of August 12, 1949.

Article 5

Neutral Powers shall apply by analogy the provisions of the present Convention to the wounded, sick and shipwrecked, and to members of the medical personnel and to chaplains of the armed forces of the Parties to the conflict received or interned in their territory, as well as to dead persons found.

Article 6

In addition to the agreements expressly provided for in Articles 10, 18, 31, 38, 39, 40, 43 and 53, the High Contracting Parties may conclude other special agreements for all matters concerning which they may deem it suitable to make separate provision. No special agreement shall adversely affect the situation of wounded, sick and shipwrecked persons, of members of the medical personnel or of chaplains, as defined by the present Convention, nor restrict the rights which it confers upon them.

Wounded, sick and shipwrecked persons, as well as medical personnel and chaplains, shall continue to have the benefit of such agreements as long as the Convention is applicable to them, except where express provisions to the contrary are contained in the aforesaid or in subsequent agreements, or where more favourable measures have been taken with regard to them by one or other of the Parties to the conflict.

Article 7

Wounded, sick and shipwrecked persons, as well as members of the medical personnel and chaplains, may in no circumstances renounce in part or in entirety the rights secured to them by the present Convention, and by the special agreements referred to in the foregoing Article, if such there be.

Article 8

The present Convention shall be applied with the cooperation and under the scrutiny of the Protecting Powers whose duty it is to safeguard the interests of the Parties to the conflict. For this purpose, the Protecting Powers may appoint, apart from their diplomatic or consular staff, delegates from amongst their own nationals or the nationals of other neutral Powers. The said delegates shall be subject to the approval of the Power with which they are to carry out their duties.
The Parties to the conflict shall facilitate to the greatest extent possible the task of the representatives or delegates of the Protecting Powers.

The representatives or delegates of the Protecting Powers shall not in any case exceed their mission under the present Convention. They shall, in particular, take account of the imperative necessities of security of the State wherein they carry out their duties. Their activities shall only be restricted as an exceptional and temporary measure when this is rendered necessary by imperative military necessities.

Article 9

The provisions of the present Convention constitute no obstacle to the humanitarian activities which the International Committee of the Red Cross or any other impartial humanitarian organization may, subject to the consent of the Parties to the conflict concerned, undertake for the protection of wounded, sick and shipwrecked persons, medical personnel and chaplains, and for their relief.

Article 10

The High Contracting Parties may at any time agree to entrust to an organization which offers all guarantees of impartiality and efficacy the duties incumbent on the Protecting Powers by virtue of the present Convention. When wounded, sick and shipwrecked, or medical personnel and chaplains do not benefit or cease to benefit, no matter for what reason, by the activities of a Protecting Power or of an organization provided for in the first paragraph above, the Detaining Power shall request a neutral State, or such an organization, to undertake the functions performed under the present Convention by a Protecting Power designated by the Parties to a conflict.

If protection cannot be arranged accordingly, the Detaining Power shall request or shall accept, subject to the provisions of this Article, the offer of the services of a humanitarian organization, such as the International Committee of the Red Cross, to assume the humanitarian functions performed by Protecting Powers under the present Convention.

Any neutral Power, or any organization invited by the Power concerned or offering itself for these purposes, shall be required to act with a sense of responsibility towards the Party to the conflict on which persons protected by the present Convention depend, and shall be required to furnish sufficient assurances that it is in a position to undertake the appropriate functions and to discharge them impartially.

No derogation from the preceding provisions shall be made by special agreements between Powers one of which is restricted, even temporarily, in its freedom to negotiate with the other Power or its allies by reason of military events, more particularly where the whole, or a substantial part, of the territory of the said Power is occupied. Whenever, in the present Convention, mention is made of a Protecting Power, such mention also applies to substitute organizations in the sense of the present Article.

Article 11

In cases where they deem it advisable in the interest of protected persons, particularly in cases of disagreement between the Parties to the conflict as to the application or interpretation of the provisions of the present Convention, the Protecting Powers shall lend their good offices with a view to settling the disagreement.

For this purpose, each of the Protecting Powers may, either at the invitation of one Party or on its own initiative, propose to the Parties to the conflict a meeting of their representatives, in particular of the authorities responsible for the wounded, sick and shipwrecked, medical personnel and chaplains, possibly on neutral territory suitably chosen. The Parties to the conflict shall be bound to give effect to the proposals made to them for this purpose. The Protecting Powers may, if necessary, propose for approval by the Parties to the conflict, a person belonging to a neutral Power or delegated by the International Committee of the Red Cross, who shall be invited to take part in such a meeting.

Chapter II. Wounded, Sick and Shipwrecked

Article 12

Members of the armed forces and other persons mentioned in the following Article, who are at sea and who are wounded, sick or shipwrecked, shall be respected and protected in all circumstances, it being understood that the term "shipwreck" means shipwreck from any cause and includes forced landings at sea by or from aircraft.
Such persons shall be treated humanely and cared for by the Parties to the conflict in whose power they may be, without any adverse distinction founded on sex, race, nationality, religion, political opinions, or any other similar criteria. Any attempts upon their lives, or violence to their persons, shall be strictly prohibited; in particular, they shall not be murdered or exterminated, subjected to torture or to biological experiments; they shall not wilfully be left without medical assistance and care, nor shall conditions exposing them to contagion or infection be created. Only urgent medical reasons will authorize priority in the order of treatment to be administered. Women shall be treated with all consideration due to their sex.

Article 13

The present Convention shall apply to the wounded, sick and shipwrecked at sea belonging to the following categories:

(1) Members of the armed forces of a Party to the conflict, as well as members of militias or volunteer corps forming part of such armed forces.

(2) Members of other militias and members of other volunteer corps, including those of organized resistance movements, belonging to a Party to the conflict and operating in or outside their own territory, even if this territory is occupied, provided that such militias or volunteer corps, including such organized resistance movements, fulfil the following conditions:

(a) that of being commanded by a person responsible for his subordinates;
(b) that of having a fixed distinctive sign recognizable at a distance;
(c) that of carrying arms openly;
(d) that of conducting their operations in accordance with the laws and customs of war.

(3) Members of regular armed forces who profess allegiance to a Government or an authority not recognized by the Detaining Power.
(4) Persons who accompany the armed forces without actually being members thereof, such as civilian members of military aircraft crews, war correspondents, supply contractors, members of labour units or of services responsible for the welfare of the armed forces, provided that they have received authorization from the armed forces which they accompany.
(5) Members of crews, including masters, pilots and apprentices, of the merchant marine and the crews of civil aircraft of the Parties to the conflict, who do not benefit by more favourable treatment under any other provisions of international law.

(6) Inhabitants of a non-occupied territory who, on the approach of the enemy, spontaneously take up arms to resist the invading forces, without having had time to form themselves into regular armed units, provided they carry arms openly and respect the laws and customs of war.

Article 14

All warships of a belligerent Party shall have the right to demand that the wounded, sick or shipwrecked on board military hospital ships, and hospital ships belonging to relief societies or to private individuals, as well as merchant vessels, yachts and other craft shall be surrendered, whatever their nationality, provided that the wounded and sick are in a fit state to be moved and that the warship can provide adequate facilities for necessary medical treatment.

Article 15

If wounded, sick or shipwrecked persons are taken on board a neutral warship or a neutral military aircraft, it shall be ensured, where so required by international law, that they can take no further part in operations of war.

Article 16

Subject to the provisions of Article 12, the wounded, sick and shipwrecked of a belligerent who fall into enemy hands shall be prisoners of war, and the provisions of international law concerning prisoners of war shall apply to them. The captor may decide, according to circumstances, whether it is expedient to hold them, or to convey them to a port in the captor's own country, to a neutral port or even to a port in enemy territory. In the last case, prisoners of war thus returned to their home country may not serve for the duration of the war.

Article 17

Wounded, sick or shipwrecked persons who are landed in neutral ports with the consent of the local authorities, shall, failing arrangements to the contrary between the neutral and the belligerent Powers, be so guarded by the neutral Power, where so required by international law, that the said persons cannot again take part in operations of war.

The costs of hospital accommodation and internment shall be borne by the Power on whom the wounded, sick or shipwrecked persons depend.

Article 18

After each engagement, Parties to the conflict shall, without delay, take all possible measures to search for and collect the shipwrecked, wounded and sick, to protect them against pillage and ill-treatment, to ensure their adequate care, and to search for the dead and prevent their being despoiled.

Whenever circumstances permit, the Parties to the conflict shall conclude local arrangements for the removal of the wounded and sick by sea from a besieged or encircled area and for the passage of medical and religious personnel and equipment on their way to that area.

Article 19

The Parties to the conflict shall record as soon as possible, in respect of each shipwrecked, wounded, sick or dead person of the adverse Party falling into their hands, any particulars which may assist in his identification. These records should if possible include:

(a) designation of the Power on which he depends;
(b) army, regimental, personal or serial number;
(c) surname;
(d) first name or names;
(e) date of birth;
(f) any other particulars shown on his identity card or disc;
(g) date and place of capture or death;
(h) particulars concerning wounds or illness, or cause of death.

As soon as possible the above-mentioned information shall be forwarded to the information bureau described in Article 122 of the Geneva Convention relative to the Treatment of Prisoners of War of August 12, 1949, which shall transmit this information to the Power on which these persons depend through the intermediary of the Protecting Power and of the Central Prisoners of War Agency.

Parties to the conflict shall prepare and forward to each other through the same bureau, certificates of death or duly authenticated lists of the dead. They shall likewise collect and forward through the same bureau one half of the double identity disc, or the identity disc itself if it is a single disc, last wills or other documents of importance to the next of kin, money and in general all Articles of an intrinsic or sentimental value, which are found on the dead. These Articles, together with unidentified Articles, shall be sent in sealed packets, accompanied by statements giving all particulars necessary for the identification of the deceased owners, as well as by a complete list of the contents of the parcel.

Article 20

Parties to the conflict shall ensure that burial at sea of the dead, carried out individually as far as circumstances permit, is preceded by a careful examination, if possible by a medical examination, of the bodies, with a view to confirming death, establishing identity and enabling a report to be made. Where a double identity disc is used, one half of the disc should remain on the body.

If dead persons are landed, the provisions of the Geneva Convention for the Amelioration of the Condition of the Wounded and Sick in Armed Forces in the Field of August 12, 1949 shall be applicable.

Article 21

The Parties to the conflict may appeal to the charity of commanders of neutral merchant vessels, yachts or other craft, to take on board and care for wounded, sick or shipwrecked persons, and to collect the dead.

Vessels of any kind responding to this appeal, and those having of their own accord collected wounded, sick or shipwrecked persons, shall enjoy special protection and facilities to carry out such assistance.

They may, in no case, be captured on account of any such transport; but, in the absence of any promise to the contrary, they shall remain liable to capture for any violations of neutrality they may have committed.

Chapter III. Hospital Ships

Article 22

Military hospital ships, that is to say, ships built or equipped by the Powers specially and solely with a view to assisting the wounded, sick and shipwrecked, to treating them and to transporting them, may in no circumstances be attacked or captured, but shall at all times be respected and protected, on condition that their names and descriptions have been notified to the Parties to the conflict ten days before those ships are employed. The characteristics which must appear in the notification shall include registered gross tonnage, the length from stem to stern and the number of masts and funnels.

Article 23

Establishments ashore entitled to the protection of the Geneva Convention for the Amelioration of the Condition of the Wounded and Sick in Armed Forces in the Field of August 12, 1949 shall be protected from bombardment or attack from the sea.

Article 24

Hospital ships utilized by National Red Cross Societies, by officially recognized relief societies or by private persons shall have the same protection as military hospital ships and shall be exempt from capture, if the Party to the conflict on which they depend has given them an official commission and in so far as the provisions of Article 22 concerning notification have been complied with.

These ships must be provided with certificates from the responsible authorities, stating that the vessels have been under their control while fitting out and on departure.

Article 25

Hospital ships utilized by National Red Cross Societies, officially recognized relief societies, or private persons of neutral countries shall have the same protection as military hospital ships and shall be exempt from capture, on condition that they have placed themselves under the control of one of the Parties to the conflict, with the previous consent of their own governments and with the authorization of the Party to the conflict concerned, in so far as the provisions of Article 22 concerning notification have been complied with.

Article 26

The protection mentioned in Articles 22, 24 and 25 shall apply to hospital ships of any tonnage and to their lifeboats, wherever they are operating. Nevertheless, to ensure the maximum comfort and security, the Parties to the conflict shall endeavour to utilize, for the transport of wounded, sick and shipwrecked over long distances and on the high seas, only hospital ships of over 2,000 tons gross.

Article 27

Under the same conditions as those provided for in Articles 22 and 24, small craft employed by the State or by the officially recognized lifeboat institutions for coastal rescue operations, shall also be respected and protected, so far as operational requirements permit. The same shall apply so far as possible to fixed coastal installations used exclusively by these craft for their humanitarian missions.

Article 28

Should fighting occur on board a warship, the sick-bays shall be respected and spared as far as possible. Sick-bays and their equipment shall remain subject to the laws of warfare, but may not be diverted from their purpose so long as they are required for the wounded and sick. Nevertheless, the commander into whose power they have fallen may, after ensuring the proper care of the wounded and sick who are accommodated therein, apply them to other purposes in case of urgent military necessity.

Article 29

Any hospital ship in a port which falls into the hands of the enemy shall be authorized to leave the said port.

Article 30

The vessels described in Articles 22, 24, 25 and 27 shall afford relief and assistance to the wounded, sick and shipwrecked without distinction of nationality. The High Contracting Parties undertake not to use these vessels for any military purpose. Such vessels shall in no wise hamper the movements of the combatants. During and after an engagement, they will act at their own risk.

Article 31

The Parties to the conflict shall have the right to control and search the vessels mentioned in Articles 22, 24, 25 and 27. They can refuse assistance from these vessels, order them off, make them take a certain course, control the use of their wireless and other means of communication, and even detain them for a period not exceeding seven days from the time of interception, if the gravity of the circumstances so requires. They may put a commissioner temporarily on board whose sole task shall be to see that orders given in virtue of the provisions of the preceding paragraph are carried out.

As far as possible, the Parties to the conflict shall enter in the log of the hospital ship in a language he can understand, the orders they have given the captain of the vessel.

Parties to the conflict may, either unilaterally or by particular agreements, put on board their ships neutral observers who shall verify the strict observation of the provisions contained in the present Convention.

Article 32

Vessels described in Articles 22, 24, 25 and 27 are not classed as warships as regards their stay in a neutral port.

Article 33

Merchant vessels which have been transformed into hospital ships cannot be put to any other use throughout the duration of hostilities.

Article 34

The protection to which hospital ships and sick-bays are entitled shall not cease unless they are used to commit, outside their humanitarian duties, acts harmful to the enemy. Protection may, however, cease only after due warning has been given, naming in all appropriate cases a reasonable time limit, and after such warning has remained unheeded. In particular, hospital ships may not possess or use a secret code for their wireless or other means of communication.

Article 35

The following conditions shall not be considered as depriving hospital ships or sick-bays of vessels of the protection due to them:

(1) The fact that the crews of ships or sick-bays are armed for the maintenance of order, for their own defence or that of the sick and wounded.

(2) The presence on board of apparatus exclusively intended to facilitate navigation or communication.

(3) The discovery on board hospital ships or in sick-bays of portable arms and ammunition taken from the wounded, sick and shipwrecked and not yet handed to the proper service.

(4) The fact that the humanitarian activities of hospital ships and sick-bays of vessels or of the crews extend to the care of wounded, sick or shipwrecked civilians.

(5) The transport of equipment and of personnel intended exclusively for medical duties, over and above the normal requirements.

Chapter IV. Personnel

Article 36

The religious, medical and hospital personnel of hospital ships and their crews shall be respected and protected; they may not be captured during the time they are in the service of the hospital ship, whether or not there are wounded and sick on board.

Article 37

The religious, medical and hospital personnel assigned to the medical or spiritual care of the persons designated in Articles 12 and 13 shall, if they fall into the hands of the enemy, be respected and protected; they may continue to carry out their duties as long as this is necessary for the care of the wounded and sick. They shall afterwards be sent back as soon as the Commander-in-Chief, under whose authority they are, considers it practicable. They may take with them, on leaving the ship, their personal property.

If, however, it prove necessary to retain some of this personnel owing to the medical or spiritual needs of prisoners of war, everything possible shall be done for their earliest possible landing.

Retained personnel shall be subject, on landing, to the provisions of the Geneva Convention for the Amelioration of the Condition of the Wounded and Sick in Armed Forces in the Field of August 12, 1949.

Chapter V. Medical Transports

Article 38

Ships chartered for that purpose shall be authorized to transport equipment exclusively intended for the treatment of wounded and sick members of armed forces or for the prevention of disease, provided that the particulars regarding their voyage have been notified to the adverse Power and approved by the latter. The adverse Power shall preserve the right to board the carrier ships, but not to capture them or seize the equipment carried.

By agreement amongst the Parties to the conflict, neutral observers may be placed on board such ships to verify the equipment carried. For this purpose, free access to the equipment shall be given.

Article 39

Medical aircraft, that is to say, aircraft exclusively employed for the removal of the wounded, sick and shipwrecked, and for the transport of medical personnel and equipment, may not be the object of attack, but shall be respected by the Parties to the conflict, while flying at heights, at times and on routes specifically agreed upon between the Parties to the conflict concerned.

They shall be clearly marked with the distinctive emblem prescribed in Article 41, together with their national colours, on their lower, upper and lateral surfaces. They shall be provided with any other markings or means of identification which may be agreed upon between the Parties to the conflict upon the outbreak or during the course of hostilities. Unless agreed otherwise, flights over enemy or enemy-occupied territory are prohibited. Medical aircraft shall obey every summons to alight on land or water. In the event of having thus to alight, the aircraft with its occupants may continue its flight after examination, if any.

In the event of alighting involuntarily on land or water in enemy or enemy-occupied territory, the wounded, sick and shipwrecked, as well as the crew of the aircraft shall be prisoners of war. The medical personnel shall be treated according to Articles 36 and 37.

Article 40

Subject to the provisions of the second paragraph, medical aircraft of Parties to the conflict may fly over the territory of neutral Powers, land thereon in case of necessity, or use it as a port of call. They shall give neutral Powers prior notice of their passage over the said territory, and obey every summons to alight, on land or water. They will be immune from attack only when flying on routes, at heights and at times specifically agreed upon between the Parties to the conflict and the neutral Power concerned.

The neutral Powers may, however, place conditions or restrictions on the passage or landing of medical aircraft on their territory. Such possible conditions or restrictions shall be applied equally to all Parties to the conflict. Unless otherwise agreed between the neutral Powers and the Parties to the conflict, the wounded, sick or shipwrecked who are disembarked with the consent of the local authorities on neutral territory by medical aircraft shall be detained by the neutral Power, where so required by international law, in such a manner that they cannot again take part in operations of war. The cost of their accommodation and internment shall be borne by the Power on which they depend.

Chapter VI. The Distinctive Emblem

Article 41

Under the direction of the competent military authority, the emblem of the red cross on a white ground shall be displayed on the flags, armlets and on all equipment employed in the Medical Service.

Nevertheless, in the case of countries which already use as emblem, in place of the red cross, the red crescent or the red lion and sun on a white ground, these emblems are also recognized by the terms of the present Convention.

Article 42

The personnel designated in Articles 36 and 37 shall wear, affixed to the left arm, a water-resistant armlet bearing the distinctive emblem, issued and stamped by the military authority. Such personnel, in addition to wearing the identity disc mentioned in Article 19, shall also carry a special identity card bearing the distinctive emblem. This card shall be water-resistant and of such size that it can be carried in the pocket. It shall be worded in the national language, shall mention at least the surname and first names, the date of birth, the rank and the service number of the bearer, and shall state in what capacity he is entitled to the protection of the present Convention. The card shall bear the photograph of the owner and also either his signature or his fingerprints or both. It shall be embossed with the stamp of the military authority.

The identity card shall be uniform throughout the same armed forces and, as far as possible, of a similar type in the armed forces of the High Contracting Parties. The Parties to the conflict may be guided by the model which is annexed, by way of example, to the present Convention. They shall inform each other, at the outbreak of hostilities, of the model they are using. Identity cards should be made out, if possible, at least in duplicate, one copy being kept by the home country.

In no circumstances may the said personnel be deprived of their insignia or identity cards nor of the right to wear the armlet. In case of loss they shall be entitled to receive duplicates of the cards and to have the insignia replaced.

Article 43

The ships designated in Articles 22, 24, 25 and 27 shall be distinctively marked as follows:

(a) All exterior surfaces shall be white.

(b) One or more dark red crosses, as large as possible, shall be painted and displayed on each side of the hull and on the horizontal surfaces, so placed as to afford the greatest possible visibility from the sea and from the air.

All hospital ships shall make themselves known by hoisting their national flag and further, if they belong to a neutral state, the flag of the Party to the conflict whose direction they have accepted. A white flag with a red cross shall be flown at the mainmast as high as possible.

Lifeboats of hospital ships, coastal lifeboats and au small craft used by the Medical Service shall be painted white with dark red crosses prominently displayed and shall, in general, comply with the identification system prescribed above for hospital ships.

The above-mentioned ships and craft, which may wish to ensure by night and in times of reduced visibility the protection to which they are entitled, must, subject to the assent of the Party to the conflict under whose power they are, take the necessary measures to render their painting and distinctive emblems sufficiently apparent.

Hospital ships which, in accordance with Article 31, are provisionally detained by the enemy, must haul down the flag of the Party to the conflict in whose service they are or whose direction they have accepted.

Coastal lifeboats, if they continue to operate with the consent of the Occupying Power from a base which is occupied, may be allowed, when away from their base, to continue to fly their own national colours along with a flag carrying a red cross on a white ground, subject to prior notification to all the Parties to the conflict concerned. All the provisions in this Article relating to the red cross shall apply equally to the other emblems mentioned in Article 41. Parties to the conflict shall at all times endeavour to conclude mutual agreements in order to use the most modern methods available to facilitate the identification of hospital ships.

Article 44

The distinguishing signs referred to in Article 43 can only be used, whether in time of peace or war, for indicating or protecting the ships therein mentioned, except as may be provided in any other international Convention or by agreement between all the Parties to the conflict concerned.

Article 45

The High Contracting Parties shall, if their legislation is not already adequate, take the measures necessary for the prevention and repression, at all times, of any abuse of the distinctive signs provided for under Article 43.

Chapter VII. Execution of the Convention

Article 46

Each Party to the conflict, acting through its Commanders-in-Chief, shall ensure the detailed execution of the preceding Articles and provide for unforeseen cases, in conformity with the general principles of the present Convention.

Article 47

Reprisals against the wounded, sick and shipwrecked persons, the personnel, the vessels or the equipment protected by the Convention are prohibited.

Article 48

The High Contracting Parties undertake, in time of peace as in time of war, to disseminate the text of the present Convention as widely as possible in their respective countries, and, in particular, to include the study thereof in their programmes of military and, if possible, civil instruction, so that the principles thereof may become known to the entire population, in particular to the armed fighting forces, the medical personnel and the chaplains.

Article 49

The High Contracting Parties shall communicate to one another through the Swiss Federal Council and, during hostilities, through the Protecting Powers, the official translations of the present Convention, as well as the laws and regulations which they may adopt to ensure the application thereof.

Chapter VIII. Repression of Abuses and Infractions

Article 50

The High Contracting Parties undertake to enact any legislation necessary to provide effective penal sanctions for persons committing, or ordering to be committed, any of the grave breaches of the present Convention defined in the following Article.

Each High Contracting Party shall be under the obligation to search for persons alleged to have committed, or to have ordered to be committed, such grave breaches, and shall bring such persons, regardless of their nationality, before its own courts. It may also, if it prefers, and in accordance with the provisions of its own legislation, hand such persons over for trial to another High Contracting Party concerned, provided such High Contracting Party has made out a prima facie case.

Each High Contracting Party shall take measures necessary for the suppression of all acts contrary to the provisions of the present Convention other than the grave breaches defined in the following Article.

In all circumstances, the accused persons shall benefit by safeguards of proper trial and defence, which shall not be less favourable than those provided by Article 105 and those following of the Geneva Convention relative to the Treatment of Prisoners of War of August 12, 1949.

Article 51

Grave breaches to which the preceding Article relates shall be those involving any of the following acts, if committed against persons or property protected by the Convention: wilful killing, torture or inhuman treatment, including biological experiments, wilfully causing great suffering or serious injury to body or health, and extensive destruction and appropriation of property, not justified by military necessity and carried out unlawfully and wantonly.

Article 52

No High Contracting Party shall be allowed to absolve itself or any other High Contracting Party of any liability incurred by itself or by another High Contracting Party in respect of breaches referred to in the preceding Article.

Article 53

At the request of a Party to the conflict, an enquiry shall be instituted, in a manner to be decided between the interested Parties, concerning any alleged violation of the Convention. If agreement has not been reached concerning the procedure for the enquiry, the Parties should agree on the choice of an umpire, who will decide upon the procedure to be followed. Once the violation has been established, the Parties to the conflict shall put an end to it and shall repress it with the least possible delay.

Final Provisions
Article 54

The present Convention is established in English and in French. Both texts are equally authentic. The Swiss Federal Council shall arrange for official translations of the Convention to be made in the Russian and Spanish languages.

Article 55

The present Convention, which bears the date of this day, is open to signature until February 12, 1950, in the name of the Powers represented at the Conference which opened at Geneva on April 21, 1949; furthermore, by Powers not represented at that Conference, but which are parties to the Xth Hague Convention of October 13, 1907 for the adaptation to Maritime Warfare of the Principles of the Geneva Convention of 1906, or to the Geneva Conventions of 1864, 1906 or 1929 for the Relief of the Wounded and Sick in Armies in the Field.

Article 56

The present Convention shall be ratified as soon as possible and the ratifications shall be deposited at Berne. A record shall be drawn up of the deposit of each instrument of ratification and certified copies of this record shall be transmitted by the Swiss Federal Council to all the Powers in whose name the Convention has been signed, or whose accession has been notified.

Article 57

The present Convention shall come into force six months after not less than two instruments of ratification have been deposited. Thereafter, it shall come into force for each High Contracting Party six months after the deposit of the instrument of ratification.

Article 58

The present Convention replaces the Xth Hague Convention of October 18, 1907, for the adaptation to Maritime Warfare of the principles of the Geneva Convention of 1906, in relations between the High Contracting Parties.

Article 59

From the date of its coming into force, it shall be open to any Power in whose name the present Convention has not been signed, to accede to this Convention.

Article 60

Accessions shall be notified in writing to the Swiss Federal Council, and shall take effect six months after the date on which they are received. The Swiss Federal Council shall communicate the accessions to all the Powers in whose name the Convention has been signed, or whose accession has been notified.

Article 61

The situations provided for in Articles 2 and 3 shall give immediate effect to ratifications deposited and accessions notified by the Parties to the conflict before or after the beginning of hostilities or occupation. The Swiss Federal Council shall communicate by the quickest method any ratifications or accessions received from Parties to the conflict.

Article 62

Each of the High Contracting Parties shall be at liberty to denounce the present Convention.

The denunciation shall be notified in writing to the Swiss Federal Council, which shall transmit it to the Governments of all the High Contracting Parties.

The denunciation shall take effect one year after the notification thereof has been made to the Swiss Federal Council. However, a denunciation of which notification has been made at a time when the denouncing Power is involved in a conflict shall not take effect until peace has been concluded, and until after operations connected with the release and repatriation of the persons protected by the present Convention have been terminated.

The denunciation shall have effect only in respect of the denouncing Power. It shall in no way impair the obligations which the Parties to the conflict shall remain bound to fulfil by virtue of the principles of the law of nations, as they result from the usages established among civilized peoples, from the laws of humanity and the dictates of the public conscience.

Article 63

The Swiss Federal Council shall register the present Convention with the Secretariat of the United Nations. The Swiss Federal Council shall also inform the Secretariat of the United Nations of all ratifications, accessions and denunciations received by it with respect to the present Convention.

IN WITNESS WHEREOF the undersigned, having deposited their respective full powers, have signed the present Convention.

DONE at Geneva this twelfth day of August 1949, in the English and French languages. The original shall be deposited in the Archives of the Swiss Confederation. The Swiss Federal Council shall transmit certified copies thereof to each of the signatory and acceding States.

Convention (III) Relative to the Treatment of Prisoners of War; August 12

Entry into Force: 21 October 1950

The undersigned Plenipotentiaries of the Governments represented at the Diplomatic Conference held at Geneva from April 21 to August 12, 1949, for the purpose of revising the Convention concluded at Geneva on July 27, 1929 relative to the Treatment of Prisoners of War, have agreed as follows:

Part I. General Provisions

Article 1

The High Contracting Parties undertake to respect and to ensure respect for the present Convention in all circumstances.

Article 2

In addition to the provisions which shall be implemented in peace time, the present Convention shall apply to all cases of declared war or of any other armed conflict which may arise between two or more of the High Contracting Parties, even if the state of war is not recognized by one of them.

The Convention shall also apply to all cases of partial or total occupation of the territory of a High Contracting Party, even if the said occupation meets with no armed resistance.

Although one of the Powers in conflict may not be a party to the present Convention, the Powers who are parties thereto shall remain bound by it in their mutual relations. They shall furthermore be bound by the Convention in relation to the said Power, if the latter accepts and applies the provisions thereof.

Article 3

In the case of armed conflict not of an international character occurring in the territory of one of the High Contracting Parties, each Party to the conflict shall be bound to apply, as a minimum, the following provisions:

(1) Persons taking no active part in the hostilities, including members of armed forces who have laid down their arms and those placed hors de combat by sickness, wounds, detention, or any other cause, shall in all circumstances be treated humanely, without any adverse distinction founded on race, colour, religion or faith, sex, birth or wealth, or any other similar criteria. To this end the following acts are and shall remain prohibited at any time and in any place whatsoever with respect to the above-mentioned persons:

(a) violence to life and person, in particular murder of all kinds, mutilation, cruel treatment and torture;
(b) taking of hostages;
(c) outrages upon personal dignity, in particular, humiliating and degrading treatment;
(d) the passing of sentences and the carrying out of executions without previous judgment pronounced by a regularly constituted court affording all the judicial guarantees which are recognized as indispensable by civilized peoples.

(2) The wounded and sick shall be collected and cared for.

An impartial humanitarian body, such as the International Committee of the Red Cross, may offer its services to the Parties to the conflict.
The Parties to the conflict should further endeavour to bring into force, by means of special agreements, all or part of the other provisions of the present Convention. The application of the preceding provisions shall not affect the legal status of the Parties to the conflict.

Article 4

A. Prisoners of war, in the sense of the present Convention, are persons belonging to one of the following categories, who have fallen into the power of the enemy:

(1) Members of the armed forces of a Party to the conflict, as well as members of militias or volunteer corps forming part of such armed forces.

(2) Members of other militias and members of other volunteer corps, including those of organized resistance movements, belonging to a Party to the conflict and operating in or outside their own territory, even if this territory is occupied, provided that such militias or volunteer corps, including such organized resistance movements, fulfil the following conditions: (a) that of being commanded by a person responsible for his subordinates; (b) that of having a fixed distinctive sign recognizable at a distance; (c) that of carrying

arms openly; (d) that of conducting their operations in accordance with the laws and customs of war.

(3) Members of regular armed forces who profess allegiance to a government or an authority not recognized by the Detaining Power.

(4) Persons who accompany the armed forces without actually being members thereof, such as civilian members of military aircraft crews, war correspondents, supply contractors, members of labour units or of services responsible for the welfare of the armed forces, provided that they have received authorization, from the armed forces which they accompany, who shall provide them for that purpose with an identity card similar to the annexed model.

(5) Members of crews, including masters, pilots and apprentices, of the merchant marine and the crews of civil aircraft of the Parties to the conflict, who do not benefit by more favourable treatment under any other provisions of international law.

(6) Inhabitants of a non-occupied territory, who on the approach of the enemy spontaneously take up arms to resist the invading forces, without having had time to form themselves into regular armed units, provided they carry arms openly and respect the laws and customs of war.

B. The following shall likewise be treated as prisoners of war under the present Convention:

(1) Persons belonging, or having belonged, to the armed forces of the occupied country, if the occupying Power considers it necessary by reason of such allegiance to intern them, even though it has originally liberated them while hostilities were going on outside the territory it occupies, in particular where such persons have made an unsuccessful attempt to rejoin the armed forces to which they belong and which are engaged in combat, or where they fail to comply with a summons made to them with a view to internment.

(2) The persons belonging to one of the categories enumerated in the present Article, who have been received by neutral or non-belligerent Powers on their territory and whom these Powers are required to intern under international law, without prejudice to any more favourable treatment which these Powers may choose to give and with the exception of Articles 8, 10, 15, 30, fifth paragraph, 58-67, 92, 126 and, where diplomatic relations exist between the Parties to the conflict and the neutral or non-belligerent Power concerned, those Articles concerning the Protecting Power. Where such diplomatic relations exist, the Parties to a conflict on whom these persons depend shall be allowed to perform towards them the functions of a Protecting Power as provided in

the present Convention, without prejudice to the functions which these Parties normally exercise in conformity with diplomatic and consular usage and treaties.

C. This Article shall in no way affect the status of medical personnel and chaplains as provided for in Article 33 of the present Convention.

Article 5

The present Convention shall apply to the persons referred to in Article 4 from the time they fall into the power of the enemy and until their final release and repatriation.

Should any doubt arise as to whether persons, having committed a belligerent act and having fallen into the hands of the enemy, belong to any of the categories enumerated in Article 4, such persons shall enjoy the protection of the present Convention until such time as their status has been determined by a competent tribunal.

Article 6

In addition to the agreements expressly provided for in Articles 10, 23, 28, 33, 60, 65, 66, 67, 72, 73, 75, 109, 110, 118, 119, 122 and 132, the High Contracting Parties may conclude other special agreements for all matters concerning which they may deem it suitable to make separate provision. No special agreement shall adversely affect the situation of prisoners of war, as defined by the present Convention, nor restrict the rights which it confers upon them. Prisoners of war shall continue to have the benefit of such agreements as long as the Convention is applicable to them, except where express provisions to the contrary are contained in the aforesaid or in subsequent agreements, or where more favourable measures have been taken with regard to them by one or other of the Parties to the conflict.

Article 7

Prisoners of war may in no circumstances renounce in part or in entirety the rights secured to them by the present Convention, and by the special agreements referred to in the foregoing Article, if such there be.

Article 8

The present Convention shall be applied with the cooperation and under the scrutiny of the Protecting Powers whose duty it is to safeguard the interests of the Parties to the conflict. For this purpose, the Protecting Powers may appoint, apart from their diplomatic or consular staff, delegates from amongst their own nationals or the nationals of other neutral Powers. The said delegates shall be subject to the approval of the Power with which they are to carry out their duties.

The Parties to the conflict shall facilitate to the greatest extent possible the task of the representatives or delegates of the Protecting Powers. The representatives or delegates of the Protecting Powers shall not in any case exceed their mission under the present Convention. They shall, in particular, take account of the imperative necessities of security of the State wherein they carry out their duties.

Article 9

The provisions of the present Convention constitute no obstacle to the humanitarian activities which the International Committee of the Red Cross or any other impartial humanitarian organization may, subject to the consent of the Parties to the conflict concerned, undertake for the protection of prisoners of war and for their relief.

Article 10

The High Contracting Parties may at any time agree to entrust to an organization which offers all guarantees of impartiality and efficacy the duties incumbent on the Protecting Powers by virtue of the present Convention. When prisoners of war do not benefit or cease to benefit, no matter for what reason, by the activities of a Protecting Power or of an organization provided for in the first paragraph above, the Detaining Power shall request a neutral State, or such an organization, to undertake the functions performed under the present Convention by a Protecting Power designated by the Parties to a conflict.

If protection cannot be arranged accordingly, the Detaining Power shall request or shall accept, subject to the provisions of this Article, the offer of the services of a humanitarian organization, such as the International Committee of the Red Cross to assume the humanitarian functions performed by Protecting Powers under the present Convention.

Any neutral Power or any organization invited by the Power concerned or offering itself for these purposes, shall be required to act with a sense of responsibility towards the Party to the conflict on which persons protected by the present Convention depend, and shall be required to furnish sufficient assurances that it is in a position to undertake the appropriate functions and to discharge them impartially.

No derogation from the preceding provisions shall be made by special agreements between Powers one of which is restricted, even temporarily, in its freedom to negotiate with the other Power or its allies by reason of military events, more particularly where the whole, or a substantial part, of the territory of the said Power is occupied. Whenever in the present Convention mention is made of a Protecting Power, such mention applies to substitute organizations in the sense of the present Article.

Article 11

In cases where they deem it advisable in the interest of protected persons, particularly in cases of disagreement between the Parties to the conflict as to the application or interpretation of the provisions of the present Convention, the Protecting Powers shall lend their good offices with a view to settling the disagreement.

For this purpose, each of the Protecting Powers may, either at the invitation of one Party or on its own initiative, propose to the Parties to the conflict a meeting of their representatives, and in particular of the authorities responsible for prisoners of war, possibly on neutral territory suitably chosen. The Parties to the conflict shall be bound to give effect to the proposals made to them for this purpose. The Protecting Powers may, if necessary, propose for approval by the Parties to the conflict a person belonging to a neutral Power, or delegated by the International Committee of the Red Cross, who shall be invited to take part in such a meeting.

Part II. General Protection of Prisoners of War

Article 12

Prisoners of war are in the hands of the enemy Power, but not of the individuals or military units who have captured them. Irrespective of the individual responsibilities that may exist, the Detaining Power is responsible for the treatment given them.

Prisoners of war may only be transferred by the Detaining Power to a Power which is a party to the Convention and after the Detaining Power has satisfied itself of the willingness and ability of such transferee Power to apply the Convention. When prisoners of war are transferred under such circumstances, responsibility for the application of the Convention rests on the Power accepting them while they are in its custody.

Nevertheless, if that Power fails to carry out the provisions of the Convention in any important respect, the Power by whom the prisoners of war were transferred shall, upon being notified by the Protecting Power, take effective measures to correct the situation or shall request the return of the prisoners of war. Such requests must be complied with.

Article 13

Prisoners of war must at all times be humanely treated. Any unlawful act or omission by the Detaining Power causing death or seriously endangering the health of a prisoner of war in its custody is prohibited, and will be regarded as a serious breach of the present Convention. In particular, no prisoner of war may be subjected to physical mutilation or to medical or scientific experiments of any kind which are not justified by the medical, dental or hospital treatment of the prisoner concerned and carried out in his interest. Likewise, prisoners of war must at all times be protected, particularly against acts of violence or intimidation and against insults and public curiosity. Measures of reprisal against prisoners of war are prohibited.

Article 14

Prisoners of war are entitled in all circumstances to respect for their persons and their honour. Women shall be treated with all the regard due to their sex and shall in all cases benefit by treatment as favourable as that granted to men. Prisoners of war shall retain the full civil capacity which they enjoyed at the time of their capture. The Detaining Power may not restrict the exercise, either within or without its own territory, of the rights such capacity confers except in so far as the captivity requires.

Article 15

The Power detaining prisoners of war shall be bound to provide free of charge for their maintenance and for the medical attention required by their state of health.

Article 16

Taking into consideration the provisions of the present Convention relating to rank and sex, and subject to any privileged treatment which may be accorded to them by reason of their state of health, age or professional qualifications, all prisoners of war shall be treated alike by the Detaining Power, without any adverse distinction based on race, nationality, religious belief or political opinions, or any other distinction founded on similar criteria.

Part III. Captivity

Section I. Beginning of Captivity

Article 17

Every prisoner of war, when questioned on the subject, is bound to give only his surname, first names and rank, date of birth, and army, regimental, personal or serial number, or failing this, equivalent information. If he wilfully infringes this rule, he may render himself liable to a restriction of the privileges accorded to his rank or status.

Each Party to a conflict is required to furnish the persons under its jurisdiction who are liable to become prisoners of war, with an identity card showing the owner's surname, first names, rank, army, regimental, personal or serial number or equivalent information, and date of birth. The identity card may, furthermore, bear the signature or the fingerprints, or both, of the owner, and may bear, as well, any other information the Party to the conflict may wish to add concerning persons belonging to its armed forces. As far as possible the card shall measure 6.5 x 10 cm. and shall be issued in duplicate. The identity card shall be shown by the prisoner of war upon demand, but may in no case be taken away from him.

No physical or mental torture, nor any other form of coercion, may be inflicted on prisoners of war to secure from them information of any kind whatever. Prisoners of war who refuse to answer may not be threatened, insulted, or exposed to unpleasant or disadvantageous treatment of any kind. Prisoners of war who, owing to their physical or mental condition, are unable to state their identity, shall be handed over to the medical service. The identity of such prisoners shall be established by all possible means, subject to the provisions of the preceding paragraph. The questioning of prisoners of war shall be carried out in a language which they understand.

Article 18

All effects and articles of personal use, except arms, horses, military equipment and military documents, shall remain in the possession of prisoners of war, likewise their metal helmets and gas masks and like articles issued for personal protection. Effects and articles used for their clothing or feeding shall likewise remain in their possession, even if such effects and articles belong to their regulation military equipment. At no time should prisoners of war be without identity documents. The Detaining Power shall supply such documents to prisoners of war who possess none.

Badges of rank and nationality, decorations and articles having above all a personal or sentimental value may not be taken from prisoners of war. Sums of money carried by prisoners of war may not be taken away from them except by order of an officer, and after the amount and particulars of the owner have been recorded in a special register and an itemized receipt has been given, legibly inscribed with the name, rank and unit of the person issuing the said receipt. Sums in the currency of the Detaining Power, or which are changed into such currency at the prisoner's request, shall be placed to the credit of the prisoner's account as provided in Article 64.

The Detaining Power may withdraw articles of value from prisoners of war only for reasons of security; when such articles are withdrawn, the procedure laid down for sums of money impounded shall apply. Such objects, likewise sums taken away in any currency other than that of the Detaining Power and the conversion of which has not been asked for by the owners, shall be kept in the custody of the Detaining Power and shall be returned in their initial shape to prisoners of war at the end of their captivity.

Article 19

Prisoners of war shall be evacuated, as soon as possible after their capture, to camps situated in an area far enough from the combat zone for them to be out of danger. Only those prisoners of war who, owing to wounds or sickness, would run greater risks by being evacuated than by remaining where they are, may be temporarily kept back in a danger zone. Prisoners of war shall not be unnecessarily exposed to danger while awaiting evacuation from a fighting zone.

Article 20

The evacuation of prisoners of war shall always be effected humanely and in conditions similar to those for the forces of the Detaining Power in their changes of station.

The Detaining Power shall supply prisoners of war who are being evacuated with sufficient food and potable water, and with the necessary clothing and medical attention. The Detaining Power shall take all suitable precautions to ensure their safety during evacuation, and shall establish as soon as possible a list of the prisoners of war who are evacuated. If prisoners of war must, during evacuation, pass through transit camps, their stay in such camps shall be as brief as possible.

Section II. Internment of Prisoners of War

Chapter I. General Observations

Article 21

The Detaining Power may subject prisoners of war to internment. It may impose on them the obligation of not leaving, beyond certain limits, the camp where they are interned, or if the said camp is fenced in, of not going outside its perimeter. Subject to the provisions of the present Convention relative to penal and disciplinary sanctions, prisoners of war may not be held in close confinement except where necessary to safeguard their health and then only during the continuation of the circumstances which make such confinement necessary.

Prisoners of war may be partially or wholly released on parole or promise, in so far as is allowed by the laws of the Power on which they depend. Such measures shall be taken particularly in cases where this may contribute to the improvement of their state of health. No prisoner of war shall be compelled to accept liberty on parole or promise.

Upon the outbreak of hostilities, each Party to the conflict shall notify the adverse Party of the laws and regulations allowing or forbidding its own nationals to accept liberty on parole or promise. Prisoners of war who are paroled or who have given their promise in conformity with the laws and regulations so notified, are bound on their personal honour scrupulously to fulfil, both towards the Power on which they depend and towards the Power which has captured them, the engagements of their paroles or promises. In such cases, the Power on which they depend is bound neither to require nor to accept from them any service incompatible with the parole or promise given.

Article 22

Prisoners of war may be interned only in premises located on land and affording every guarantee of hygiene and healthfulness. Except in particular cases which are justified by the interest of the prisoners themselves, they shall not be interned in penitentiaries.

Prisoners of war interned in unhealthy areas, or where the climate is injurious for them, shall be removed as soon as possible to a more favourable climate. The Detaining Power shall assemble prisoners of war in camps or camp compounds according to their nationality, language and customs, provided that such prisoners shall not be separated from prisoners of war belonging to the armed forces with which they were serving at the time of their capture, except with their consent.

Article 23

No prisoner of war may at any time be sent to, or detained in areas where he may be exposed to the fire of the combat zone, nor may his presence be used to render certain points or areas immune from military operations. Prisoners of war shall have shelters against air bombardment and other hazards of war, to the same extent as the local civilian population. With the exception of those engaged in the protection of their quarters against the aforesaid hazards, they may enter such shelters as soon as possible after the giving of the alarm. Any other protective measure taken in favour of the population shall also apply to them. Detaining Powers shall give the Powers concerned, through the intermediary of the Protecting Powers, all useful information regarding the geographical location of prisoner of war camps.

Whenever military considerations permit, prisoner of war camps shall be indicated in the day-time by the letters PW or PG, placed so as to be clearly visible from the air. The Powers concerned may, however, agree upon any other system of marking. Only prisoner of war camps shall be marked as such.

Article 24

Transit or screening camps of a permanent kind shall be fitted out under conditions similar to those described in the present Section, and the prisoners therein shall have the same treatment as in other camps.

Chapter II. Quarters, Food and Clothing of Prisoners of War

Article 25

Prisoners of war shall be quartered under conditions as favourable as those for the forces of the Detaining Power who are billeted in the same area. The said conditions shall make allowance for the habits and customs of the prisoners and shall in no case be prejudicial to their health.

The foregoing provisions shall apply in particular to the dormitories of prisoners of war as regards both total surface and minimum cubic space, and the general installations, bedding and blankets. The premises provided for the use of prisoners of war individually or collectively, shall be entirely protected from dampness and adequately heated and lighted, in particular between dusk and lights out. All precautions must be taken against the danger of fire. In any camps in which women prisoners of war, as well as men, are accommodated, separate dormitories shall be provided for them.

Article 26

The basic daily food rations shall be sufficient in quantity, quality and variety to keep prisoners of war in good health and to prevent loss of weight or the development of nutritional deficiencies. Account shall also be taken of the habitual diet of the prisoners.

The Detaining Power shall supply prisoners of war who work with such additional rations as are necessary for the labour on which they are employed. Sufficient drinking water shall be supplied to prisoners of war. The use of tobacco shall be permitted. Prisoners of war shall, as far as possible, be associated with the preparation of their meals; they may be employed for that purpose in the kitchens. Furthermore, they shall be given the means of preparing, themselves, the additional food in their possession.

Adequate premises shall be provided for messing. Collective disciplinary measures affecting food are prohibited.

Article 27

Clothing, underwear and footwear shall be supplied to prisoners of war in sufficient quantities by the Detaining Power, which shall make allowance for the climate of the region where the prisoners are detained. Uniforms of enemy armed forces captured by the Detaining Power should, if suitable for the climate, be made available to clothe prisoners of war. The regular replacement and repair of the above articles shall be assured by the Detaining Power. In addition, prisoners of war who work shall receive appropriate clothing, wherever the nature of the work demands.

Article 28

Canteens shall be installed in all camps, where prisoners of war may procure foodstuffs, soap and tobacco and ordinary articles in daily use. The tariff shall never be in excess of local market prices. The profits made by camp canteens shall be used for the benefit of the prisoners; a special fund shall be created for this purpose. The prisoners' representative shall have the right to collaborate in the management of the canteen and of this fund.

When a camp is closed down, the credit balance of the special fund shall be handed to an international welfare organization, to be employed for the benefit of prisoners of war of the same nationality as those who have contributed to the fund. In case of a general repatriation, such profits shall be kept by the Detaining Power, subject to any agreement to the contrary between the Powers concerned.

Chapter III. Hygiene and Medical Attention

Article 29

The Detaining Power shall be bound to take all sanitary measures necessary to ensure the cleanliness and healthfulness of camps and to prevent epidemics.
Prisoners of war shall have for their use, day and night, conveniences which conform to the rules of hygiene and are maintained in a constant state of cleanliness. In any camps in which women prisoners of war are accommodated, separate conveniences shall be provided for them. Also, apart from the baths and showers with which the camps shall be furnished prisoners of war shall be provided with sufficient water and soap for their personal toilet and for washing their personal laundry; the necessary installations, facilities and time shall be granted them for that purpose.

Article 30

Every camp shall have an adequate infirmary where prisoners of war may have the attention they require, as well as appropriate diet. Isolation wards shall, if necessary, be set aside for cases of contagious or mental disease. Prisoners of war suffering from serious disease, or whose condition necessitates special treatment, a surgical operation or hospital care, must be admitted to any military or civilian medical unit where such treatment can be given, even if their repatriation is contemplated in the near future. Special facilities shall be afforded for the care to be given to the disabled, in particular to the blind, and for their. rehabilitation, pending repatriation.

Prisoners of war shall have the attention, preferably, of medical personnel of the Power on which they depend and, if possible, of their nationality.

Prisoners of war may not be prevented from presenting themselves to the medical authorities for examination. The detaining authorities shall, upon request, issue to every prisoner who has undergone treatment, an official certificate indicating the nature of his illness or injury, and the duration and kind of treatment received. A duplicate of this certificate shall be forwarded to the Central Prisoners of War Agency. The costs of treatment, including those of any apparatus necessary for the maintenance of prisoners of war in good health, particularly dentures and other artificial appliances, and spectacles, shall be borne by the Detaining Power.

Article 31

Medical inspections of prisoners of war shall be held at least once a month. They shall include the checking and the recording of the weight of each prisoner of war. Their purpose shall be, in particular, to supervise the general state of health, nutrition and cleanliness of prisoners and to detect contagious diseases, especially tuberculosis, malaria and venereal disease. For this purpose the most efficient methods available shall be employed, e.g. periodic mass miniature radiography for the early detection of tuberculosis

Article 32

Prisoners of war who, though not attached to the medical service of their armed forces, are physicians, surgeons, dentists, nurses or medical orderlies, may be required by the Detaining Power to exercise their medical functions in the interests of prisoners of war dependent on the same Power. In that case they shall continue to be prisoners of war, but shall receive the same treatment as corresponding medical personnel retained by the Detaining Power. They shall be exempted from any other work under Article 49.

Chapter IV. Medical Personnel and Chaplains Retained to Assist Prisoners of War

Article 33

Members of the medical personnel and chaplains while retained by the Detaining Power with a view to assisting prisoners of war, shall not be considered as prisoners of war. They shall, however, receive as a minimum the benefits and protection of the present Convention, and shall also be granted all facilities necessary to provide for the medical care of, and religious ministration to prisoners of war.

They shall continue to exercise their medical and spiritual functions for the benefit of prisoners of war, preferably those belonging to the armed forces upon which they depend, within the scope of the military laws and regulations of the Detaining Power and under the control of its competent services, in accordance with their professional etiquette. They shall also benefit by the following facilities in the exercise of their medical or spiritual functions:

(a) They shall be authorized to visit periodically prisoners of war situated in working detachments or in hospitals outside the camp. For this purpose, the Detaining Power shall place at their disposal the necessary means of transport.

(b) The senior medical officer in each camp shall be responsible to the camp military authorities for everything connected with the activities of retained medical personnel. For this purpose, Parties to the conflict shall agree at the outbreak of hostilities on the subject of the corresponding ranks of the medical personnel, including that of societies mentioned in Article 26 of the Geneva Convention for the Amelioration of the Condition of the Wounded and Sick in Armed Forces in the Field of August 12, 1949. This senior medical officer, as well as chaplains, shall have the right to deal with the competent authorities of the camp on all questions relating to their duties. Such authorities shall afford them all necessary facilities for correspondence relating to these questions.

(c) Although they shall be subject to the internal discipline of the camp in which they are retained, such personnel may not be compelled to carry out any work other than that concerned with their medical or religious duties.

During hostilities, the Parties to the conflict shall agree concerning the possible relief of retained personnel and shall settle the procedure to be followed.

None of the preceding provisions shall relieve the Detaining Power of its obligations with regard to prisoners of war from the medical or spiritual point of view.

Chapter V. Religious, Intellectual and Physical Activities

Article 34

Prisoners of war shall enjoy complete latitude in the exercise of their religious duties, including attendance at the service of their faith, on condition that they comply with the disciplinary routine prescribed by the military authorities.
Adequate premises shall be provided where religious services may be held.

Article 35

Chaplains who fall into the hands of the enemy Power and who remain or are retained with a view to assisting prisoners of war, shall be allowed to minister to them and to exercise freely their ministry amongst prisoners of war of the same religion, in accordance with their religious conscience. They shall be allocated among the various camps and labour detachments containing prisoners of war belonging to the same forces, speaking the same language or practising the same religion. They shall enjoy the necessary facilities, including the means of transport provided for in Article 33, for visiting the prisoners of war outside their camp. They shall be free to correspond, subject to censorship, on matters concerning their religious duties with the ecclesiastical authorities in the country of detention and with international religious organizations. Letters and cards which they may send for this purpose shall be in addition to the quota provided for in Article 71.

Article 36

Prisoners of war who are ministers of religion, without having officiated as chaplains to their own forces, shall be at liberty, whatever their denomination, to minister freely to the members of their community. For this purpose, they shall receive the same treatment as the chaplains retained by the Detaining Power. They shall not be obliged to do any other work.

Article 37

When prisoners of war have not the assistance of a retained chaplain or of a prisoner of war minister of their faith, a minister belonging to the prisoners' or a similar denomination, or in his absence a qualified layman, if such a course is feasible from a confessional point of view, shall be appointed, at the request of the prisoners concerned, to fill this office. This appointment, subject to the approval of the Detaining Power, shall take place with the agreement of the community of prisoners concerned and, wherever necessary, with the approval of the local religious authorities of the same faith. The person thus appointed shall comply with all regulations established by the Detaining Power in the interests of discipline and military security.

Article 38

While respecting the individual preferences of every prisoner, the Detaining Power shall encourage the practice of intellectual, educational, and recreational pursuits, sports and games amongst prisoners, and shall take the measures necessary to ensure the exercise thereof by providing them with adequate premises and necessary equipment. Prisoners shall have opportunities for taking physical exercise, including sports and games, and for being out of doors. Sufficient open spaces shall be provided for this purpose in all camps.

Chapter VI. Discipline

Article 39

Every prisoner of war camp shall be put under the immediate authority of a responsible commissioned officer belonging to the regular armed forces of the Detaining Power. Such officer shall have in his possession a copy of the present Convention; he shall ensure that its provisions are known to the camp staff and the guard and shall be responsible, under the direction of his government, for its application.

Prisoners of war, with the exception of officers, must salute and show to all officers of the Detaining Power the external marks of respect provided for by the regulations applying in their own forces. Officer prisoners of war are bound to salute only officers of a higher rank of the Detaining Power; they must, however, salute the camp commander regardless of his rank.

Article 40

The wearing of badges of rank and nationality, as well as of decorations, shall be permitted.

Article 41

In every camp the text of the present Convention and its Annexes and the contents of any special agreement provided for in Article 6, shall be posted, in the prisoners' own language, in places where all may read them. Copies shall be supplied, on request, to the prisoners who cannot have access to the copy which has been posted. Regulations, orders, notices and publications of every kind relating to the conduct of prisoners of war shall be issued to them in a language which they understand. Such regulations, orders and publications shall be posted in the manner described above and copies shall be handed to the prisoners' representative. Every order and command addressed to prisoners of war individually must likewise be given in a language which they understand.

Article 42

The use of weapons against prisoners of war, especially against those who are escaping or attempting to escape, shall constitute an extreme measure, which shall always be preceded by warnings appropriate to the circumstances.

Chapter VII. Rank of Prisoners of War

Article 43

Upon the outbreak of hostilities, the Parties to the conflict shall communicate to one another the titles and ranks of all the persons mentioned in Article 4 of the present Convention, in order to ensure equality of treatment between prisoners of equivalent rank. Titles and ranks which are subsequently created shall form the subject of similar communications.

The Detaining Power shall recognize promotions in rank which have been accorded to prisoners of war and which have been duly notified by the Power on which these prisoners depend.

Article 44

Officers and prisoners of equivalent status shall be treated with the regard due to their rank and age. In order to ensure service in officers' camps, other ranks of the same armed forces who, as far as possible, speak the same language, shall be assigned in sufficient numbers, account being taken of the rank of officers and prisoners of equivalent status. Such orderlies shall not be required to perform any other work. Supervision of the mess by the officers themselves shall be facilitated in every way.

Article 45

Prisoners of war other than officers and prisoners of equivalent status shall be treated with the regard due to their rank and age. Supervision of the mess by the prisoners themselves shall be facilitated in every way.

Chapter VIII. Transfer of Prisoners of War after their Arrival in Camp

Article 46

The Detaining Power, when deciding upon the transfer of prisoners of war, shall take into account the interests of the prisoners themselves, more especially so as not to increase the difficulty of their repatriation. The transfer of prisoners of war shall always be effected humanely and in conditions not less favourable than those under which the forces of the Detaining Power are transferred. Account shall always be taken of the climatic conditions to which the prisoners of war are accustomed and the conditions of transfer shall in no case be prejudicial to their health.

The Detaining Power shall supply prisoners of war during transfer with sufficient food and drinking water to keep them in good health, likewise with the necessary clothing, shelter and medical attention. The Detaining Power shall take adequate precautions especially in case of transport by sea or by air, to ensure their safety during transfer, and shall draw up a complete list of all transferred prisoners before their departure.

Article 47

Sick or wounded prisoners of war shall not be transferred as long as their recovery may be endangered by the journey, unless their safety imperatively demands it. If the combat zone draws closer to a camp, the prisoners of war in the said camp shall not be transferred unless their transfer can be carried out in adequate conditions of safety, or unless they are exposed to greater risks by remaining on the spot than by being transferred.

Article 48

In the event of transfer, prisoners of war shall be officially advised of their departure and of their new postal address. Such notifications shall be given in time for them to pack their luggage and inform their next of kin. They shall be allowed to take with them their personal effects, and the correspondence and parcels which have arrived for them. The weight of such baggage may be limited, if the conditions of transfer so require, to what each prisoner can reasonably carry, which shall in no case be more than twenty-five kilograms per head.

Mail and parcels addressed to their former camp shall be forwarded to them without delay. The camp commander shall take, in agreement with the prisoners' representative, any measures needed to ensure the transport of the prisoners' community property and of the luggage they are unable to take with them in consequence of restrictions imposed by virtue of the second paragraph of this Article. The costs of transfers shall be borne by the Detaining Power.

Section III. Labour of Prisoners of War

Article 49

The Detaining Power may utilize the labour of prisoners of war who are physically fit, taking into account their age, sex, rank and physical aptitude, and with a view particularly to maintaining them in a good state of physical and mental health.

Non-commissioned officers who are prisoners of war shall only be required to do supervisory work. Those not so required may ask for other suitable work which shall, so far as possible, be found for them. If officers or persons of equivalent status ask for suitable work, it shall be found for them, so far as possible, but they may in no circumstances be compelled to work.

Article 50

Besides work connected with camp administration, installation or maintenance, prisoners of war may be compelled to do only such work as is included in the following classes:

(a) agriculture;
(b) industries connected with the production or the extraction of raw materials, and manufacturing industries, with the exception of metallurgical, machinery and chemical industries; public works and building operations which have no military character or purpose;
(c) transport and handling of stores which are not military in character or purpose;
(d) commercial business, and arts and crafts;
(e) domestic service;
(f) public utility services having no military character or purpose.

Should the above provisions be infringed, prisoners of war shall be allowed to exercise their right of complaint, in conformity with Article 78.

Article 51

Prisoners of war must be granted suitable working conditions, especially as regards accommodation, food, clothing and equipment; such conditions shall not be inferior to those enjoyed by nationals of the Detaining Power employed in similar work; account shall also be taken of climatic conditions. The Detaining Power, in utilizing the labour of prisoners of war, shall ensure that in areas in which such prisoners are employed, the national legislation concerning the protection of labour, and, more particularly, the regulations for the safety of workers, are duly applied.

Prisoners of war shall receive training and be provided with the means of protection suitable to the work they will have to do and similar to those accorded to the nationals of the Detaining Power. Subject to the provisions of Article 52, prisoners may be submitted to the normal risks run by these civilian workers.
Conditions of labour shall in no case be rendered more arduous by disciplinary measures.

Article 52

Unless he be a volunteer, no prisoner of war may be employed on labour which is of an unhealthy or dangerous nature. No prisoner of war shall be assigned to labour which would be looked upon as humiliating for a member of the Detaining Power's own forces. The removal of mines or similar devices shall be considered as dangerous labour.

Article 53

The duration of the daily labour of prisoners of war, including the time of the journey to and fro, shall not be excessive, and must in no case exceed that permitted for civilian workers in the district, who are nationals of the Detaining Power and employed on the same work. Prisoners of war must be allowed, in the middle of the day's work, a rest of not less than one hour. This rest will be the same as that to which workers of the Detaining Power are entitled, if the latter is of longer duration. They shall be allowed in addition a rest of twenty-four consecutive hours every week, preferably on Sunday or the day of rest in their country of origin. Furthermore, every prisoner who has worked for one year shall be granted a rest of eight consecutive days, during which his working pay shall be paid him. If methods of labour such as piece work are employed, the length of the working period shall not be rendered excessive thereby.

Article 54

The working pay due to prisoners of war shall be fixed in accordance with the provisions of Article 62 of the present Convention. Prisoners of war who sustain accidents in connection with work, or who contract a disease in the course, or in consequence of their work, shall receive all the care their condition may require. The Detaining Power shall furthermore deliver to such prisoners of war a medical certificate enabling them to submit their claims to the Power on which they depend, and shall send a duplicate to the Central Prisoners of War Agency provided for in Article 123.

Article 55

The fitness of prisoners of war for work shall be periodically verified by medical examinations at least once a month. The examinations shall have particular regard to the nature of the work which prisoners of war are required to do. If any prisoner of war considers himself incapable of working, he shall be permitted to appear before the medical authorities of his camp. Physicians or surgeons may recommend that the prisoners who are, in their opinion, unfit for work, be exempted therefrom.

Article 56

The organization and administration of labour detachments shall be similar to those of prisoner of war camps. Every labour detachment shall remain under the control of and administratively part of a prisoner of war camp. The military authorities and the commander of the said camp shall be responsible, under the direction of their government, for the observance of the provisions of the present Convention in labour detachments. The camp commander shall keep an up-to-date record of the labour detachments dependent on his camp, and shall communicate it to the delegates of the Protecting Power, of the International Committee of the Red Cross, or of other agencies giving relief to prisoners of war, who may visit the camp.

Article 57

The treatment of prisoners of war who work for private persons, even if the latter are responsible for guarding and protecting them, shall not be inferior to that which is provided for by the present Convention. The Detaining Power, the military authorities and the commander of the camp to which such prisoners belong shall be entirely responsible for the maintenance, care, treatment, and payment of the working pay of such prisoners of war. Such prisoners of war shall have the right to remain in communication with the prisoners' representatives in the camps on which they depend.

Section IV. Financial Resources of Prisoners of War

Article 58

Upon the outbreak of hostilities, and pending an arrangement on this matter with the Protecting Power, the Detaining Power may determine the maximum amount of money in cash or in any similar form, that prisoners may have in their possession. Any amount in excess, which was properly in their possession and which has been taken or withheld from them, shall be placed to their account, together with any monies deposited by them, and shall not be converted into any other currency without their consent.

If prisoners of war are permitted to purchase services or commodities outside the camp against payment in cash, such payments shall be made by the prisoner himself or by the camp administration who will charge them to the accounts of the prisoners concerned. The Detaining Power will establish the necessary rules in this respect.

Article 59

Cash which was taken from prisoners of war, in accordance with Article 18, at the time of their capture, and which is in the currency of the Detaining Power, shall be placed to their separate accounts, in accordance with the provisions of Article 64 of the present Section. The amounts, in the currency of the Detaining Power, due to the conversion of sums in other currencies that are taken from the prisoners of war at the same time, shall also be credited to their separate accounts.

Article 60

The Detaining Power shall grant all prisoners of war a monthly advance of pay, the amount of which shall be fixed by conversion, into the currency of the said Power, of the following amounts:

Category I : Prisoners ranking below sergeants: eight Swiss francs.
Category II : Sergeants and other non-commissioned officers, or prisoners of equivalent rank: twelve Swiss francs.
Category III: Warrant officers and commissioned officers below the rank of major or prisoners of equivalent rank: fifty Swiss francs.
Category IV : Majors, lieutenant-colonels, colonels or prisoners of equivalent rank: sixty Swiss francs.
Category V : General officers or prisoners of war of equivalent rank: seventy-five Swiss francs.

However, the Parties to the conflict concerned may by special agreement modify the amount of advances of pay due to prisoners of the preceding categories.

Furthermore, if the amounts indicated in the first paragraph above would be unduly high compared with the pay of the Detaining Power's armed forces or would, for any reason, seriously embarrass the Detaining Power, then, pending the conclusion of a special agreement with the Power on which the prisoners depend to vary the amounts indicated above, the Detaining Power:

(a) shall continue to credit the accounts of the prisoners with the amounts indicated in the first paragraph above;
(b) may temporarily limit the amount made available from these advances of pay to prisoners of war for their own use, to sums which are reasonable, but which, for Category I, shall never be inferior to the amount that the Detaining Power gives to the members of its own armed forces.

The reasons for any limitations will be given without delay to the Protecting Power.

Article 61

The Detaining Power shall accept for distribution as supplementary pay to prisoners of war sums which the Power on which the prisoners depend may forward to them, on condition that the sums to be paid shall be the same for each prisoner of the same category, shall be payable to all prisoners of that category depending on that Power, and shall be placed in their separate accounts, at the earliest opportunity, in accordance with the provisions of Article 64. Such supplementary pay shall not relieve the Detaining Power of any obligation under this Convention.

Article 62

Prisoners of war shall be paid a fair working rate of pay by the detaining authorities direct. The rate shall be fixed by the said authorities, but shall at no time be less than one-fourth of one Swiss franc for a full working day. The Detaining Power shall inform prisoners of war, as well as the Power on which they depend, through the intermediary of the Protecting Power, of the rate of daily working pay that it has fixed.

Working pay shall likewise be paid by the detaining authorities to prisoners of war permanently detailed to duties or to a skilled or semi-skilled occupation in connection with the administration, installation or maintenance of camps, and to the prisoners who are required to carry out spiritual or medical duties on behalf of their comrades.

The working pay of the prisoners' representative, of his advisers, if any, and of his assistants, shall be paid out of the fund maintained by canteen profits. The scale of this working pay shall be fixed by the prisoners' representative and approved by the camp commander. If there is no such fund, the detaining authorities shall pay these prisoners a fair working rate of pay.

Article 63

Prisoners of war shall be permitted to receive remittances of money addressed to them individually or collectively. Every prisoner of war shall have at his disposal the credit balance of his account as provided for in the following Article, within the limits fixed by the Detaining Power, which shall make such payments as are requested. Subject to financial or monetary restrictions which the Detaining Power regards as essential, prisoners of war may also have payments made abroad. In this case payments addressed by prisoners of war to dependents shall be given priority. In any event, and subject to the consent of the Power on which they depend, prisoners may have payments made in their own country, as follows: the Detaining Power shall send to the aforesaid Power through the Protecting Power, a notification giving all the necessary particulars concerning the prisoners of war, the beneficiaries of the payments, and the amount of the sums to be paid, expressed in the Detaining Power's currency. The said notification shall be signed by the prisoners and countersigned by the camp commander. The Detaining Power shall debit the prisoners' account by a corresponding amount; the sums thus debited shall be placed by it to the credit of the Power on which the prisoners depend. To apply the foregoing provisions, the Detaining Power may usefully consult the Model Regulations in Annex V of the present Convention.

Article 64

The Detaining Power shall hold an account for each prisoner of war, showing at least the following:

(1) The amounts due to the prisoner or received by him as advances of pay, as working pay or derived from any other source; the sums in the currency of the Detaining Power which were taken from him; the sums taken from him and converted at his request into the currency of the said Power.

(2) The payments made to the prisoner in cash, or in any other similar form; the payments made on his behalf and at his request; the sums transferred under Article 63, third paragraph.

Article 65

Every item entered in the account of a prisoner of war shall be countersigned or initialled by him, or by the prisoners' representative acting on his behalf. Prisoners of war shall at all times be afforded reasonable facilities for consulting and obtaining copies of their accounts, which may likewise be inspected by the representatives of the Protecting Powers at the time of visits to the camp. When prisoners of war are transferred from one camp to another, their personal accounts will follow them. In case of transfer from one Detaining Power to another, the monies which are their property and are not in the currency of the Detaining Power will follow them. They shall be given certificates for any other monies standing to the credit of their accounts. The Parties to the conflict concerned may agree to notify to each other at specific intervals through the Protecting Power, the amount of the accounts of the prisoners of war.

Article 66

On the termination of captivity, through the release of a prisoner of war or his repatriation, the Detaining Power shall give him a statement, signed by an authorized officer of that Power, showing the credit balance then due to him. The Detaining Power shall also send through the Protecting Power to the government upon which the prisoner of war depends, lists giving all appropriate particulars of all prisoners of war whose captivity has been terminated by repatriation, release, escape, death or any other means, and showing the amount of their credit balances. Such lists shall be certified on each sheet by an authorized representative of the Detaining Power. Any of the above provisions of this Article may be varied by mutual agreement between any two Parties to the conflict. The Power on which the prisoner of war depends shall be responsible for settling with him any credit balance due to him from the Detaining Power on the termination of his captivity.

Article 67

Advances of pay, issued to prisoners of war in conformity with Article 60, shall be considered as made on behalf of the Power on which they depend. Such advances of pay, as well as all payments made by the said Power under Article 63, third paragraph, and Article 68, shall form the subject of arrangements between the Powers concerned, at the close of hostilities.

Article 68

Any claim by a prisoner of war for compensation in respect of any injury or other disability arising out of work shall be referred to the Power on which he depends, through the Protecting Power. In accordance with Article 54, the Detaining Power will, in all cases, provide the prisoner of war concerned with a statement showing the nature of the injury or disability, the circumstances in which it arose and particulars of medical or hospital treatment given for it. This statement will be signed by a responsible officer of the Detaining Power and the medical particulars certified by a medical officer. Any claim by a prisoner of war for compensation in respect of personal effects monies or valuables impounded by the Detaining Power under Article 18 and not forthcoming on his repatriation, or in respect of loss alleged to be due to the fault of the Detaining Power or any of its servants, shall likewise be referred to the Power on which he depends. Nevertheless, any such personal effects required for use by the prisoners of war whilst in captivity shall be replaced at the expense of the Detaining Power. The Detaining Power will, in all cases, provide the prisoner of war with a statement, signed by a responsible officer, showing all available information regarding the reasons why such effects, monies or valuables have not been restored to him. A copy of this statement will be forwarded to the Power on which he depends through the Central Prisoners of War Agency provided for in Article 123.

Section V. Relations of Prisoners of War with the Exterior

Article 69

Immediately upon prisoners of war falling into its power, the Detaining Power shall inform them and the Powers on which they depend, through the Protecting Power, of the measures taken to carry out the provisions of the present Section. They shall likewise inform the parties concerned of any subsequent modifications of such measures.

Article 70

Immediately upon capture, or not more than one week after arrival at a camp, even if it is a transit camp, likewise in case of sickness or transfer to hospital or to another camp, every prisoner of war shall be enabled to write direct to his family, on the one hand, and to the Central Prisoners of War Agency provided for in Article 123, on the other hand, a card similar, if possible, to the model annexed to the present Convention, informing his relatives of his capture, address and state of health. The said cards shall be forwarded as rapidly as possible and may not be delayed in any manner.

Article 71

Prisoners of war shall be allowed to send and receive letters and cards. If the Detaining Power deems it necessary to limit the number of letters and cards sent by each prisoner of war, the said number shall not be less than two letters and four cards monthly, exclusive of the capture cards provided for in Article 70, and conforming as closely as possible to the models annexed to the present Convention. Further limitations may be imposed only if the Protecting Power is satisfied that it would be in the interests of the prisoners of war concerned to do so owing to difficulties of translation caused by the Detaining Power's inability to find sufficient qualified linguists to carry out the necessary censorship. If limitations must be placed on the correspondence addressed to prisoners of war, they may be ordered only by the Power on which the prisoners depend, possibly at the request of the Detaining Power. Such letters and cards must be conveyed by the most rapid method at the disposal of the Detaining Power; they may not be delayed or retained for disciplinary reasons.

Prisoners of war who have been without news for a long period, or who are unable to receive news from their next of kin or to give them news by the ordinary postal route, as well as those who are at a great distance from their homes, shall be permitted to send telegrams, the fees being charged against the prisoners of war's accounts with the Detaining Power or paid in the currency at their disposal. They shall likewise benefit by this measure in cases of urgency. As a general rule, the correspondence of prisoners of war shall be written in their native language. The Parties to the conflict may allow correspondence in other languages. Sacks containing prisoner of war mail must be securely sealed and labelled so as clearly to indicate their contents, and must be addressed to offices of destination.

Article 72

Prisoners of war shall be allowed to receive by post or by any other means individual parcels or collective shipments containing, in particular, foodstuffs, clothing, medical supplies and articles of a religious, educational or recreational character which may meet their needs, including books, devotional articles, scientific equipment, examination papers, musical instruments, sports outfits and materials allowing prisoners of war to pursue their studies or their cultural activities.

Such shipments shall in no way free the Detaining Power from the obligations imposed upon it by virtue of the present Convention. The only limits which may be placed on these shipments shall be those proposed by the Protecting Power in the interest of the prisoners themselves, or by the International Committee of the Red Cross or any other organization giving assistance to the prisoners, in respect of their own shipments only, on account of exceptional strain on transport or communications. The conditions for the sending of individual parcels and collective relief shall, if necessary, be the subject of special agreements between the Powers concerned, which may in no case delay the receipt by the prisoners of relief supplies. Books may not be included in parcels of clothing and foodstuffs. Medical supplies shall, as a rule, be sent in collective parcels.

Article 73

In the absence of special agreements between the Powers concerned on the conditions for the receipt and distribution of collective relief shipments, the rules and regulations concerning collective shipments, which are annexed to the present Convention, shall be applied.

The special agreements referred to above shall in no case restrict the right of prisoners' representatives to take possession of collective relief shipments intended for prisoners of war, to proceed to their distribution or to dispose of them in the interest of the prisoners. Nor shall such agreements restrict the right of representatives of the Protecting Power, the International Committee of the Red Cross or any other organization giving assistance to prisoners of war and responsible for the forwarding of collective shipments, to supervise their distribution to the recipients.

Article 74

All relief shipments for prisoners of war shall be exempt from import, customs and other dues. Correspondence, relief shipments and authorized remittances of money addressed to prisoners of war or despatched by them through the post office, either direct or through the Information Bureaux provided for in Article 122 and the Central Prisoners of War Agency provided for in Article 123, shall be exempt from any postal dues, both in the countries of origin and destination, and in intermediate countries. If relief shipments intended for prisoners of war cannot be sent through the post office by reason of weight or for any other cause, the cost of transportation shall be borne by the Detaining Power in all the territories under its control. The other Powers party to the Convention shall bear the cost of transport in their respective territories. In the absence of special agreements between the Parties concerned, the costs connected with transport of such shipments, other than costs covered by the above exemption, shall be charged to the senders. The High Contracting Parties shall endeavour to reduce, so far as possible, the rates charged for telegrams sent by prisoners of war, or addressed to them.

Article 75

Should military operations prevent the Powers concerned from fulfilling their obligation to assure the transport of the shipments referred to in Articles 70, 71, 72 and 77, the Protecting Powers concerned, the International Committee of the Red Cross or any other organization duly approved by the Parties to the conflict may undertake to ensure the conveyance of such shipments by suitable means (railway wagons, motor vehicles, vessels or aircraft, etc.). For this purpose, the High Contracting Parties shall endeavour to supply them with such transport and to allow its circulation, especially by granting the necessary safe-conducts.
Such transport may also be used to convey:

(a) correspondence, lists and reports exchanged between the Central Information Agency referred to in Article 123 and the National Bureaux referred to in Article 122;

(b) correspondence and reports relating to prisoners of war which the Protecting Powers, the International Committee of the Red Cross or any other body assisting the prisoners, exchange either with their own delegates or with the Parties to the conflict.

These provisions in no way detract from the right of any Party to the conflict to arrange other means of transport, if it should so prefer, nor preclude the granting of safe-conducts, under mutually agreed conditions, to such means of transport. In the absence of special agreements, the costs occasioned by the use of such means of transport shall be borne proportionally by the Parties to the conflict whose nationals are benefited thereby.

Article 76

The censoring of correspondence addressed to prisoners of war or despatched by them shall be done as quickly as possible. Mail shall be censored only by the despatching State and the receiving State, and once only by each. The examination of consignments intended for prisoners of war shall not be carried out under conditions that will expose the goods contained in them to deterioration; except in the case of written or printed matter, it shall be done in the presence of the addressee, or of a fellow-prisoner duly delegated by him. The delivery to prisoners of individual or collective consignments shall not be delayed under the pretext of difficulties of censorship. Any prohibition of correspondence ordered by Parties to the conflict, either for military or political reasons, shall be only temporary and its duration shall be as short as possible.

Article 77

The Detaining Powers shall provide all facilities for the transmission, through the Protecting Power or the Central Prisoners of War Agency provided for in Article 123 of instruments, papers or documents intended for prisoners of war or despatched by them, especially powers of attorney and wills. In all cases they shall facilitate the preparation and execution of such documents on behalf of prisoners of war; in particular, they shall allow them to consult a lawyer and shall take what measures are necessary for the authentication of their signatures.

Section VI. Relations Between Prisoners of War and the Authorities

Chapter I. Complaints of Prisoners of War Respecting the conditions of Captivity

Article 78

Prisoners of war shall have the right to make known to the military authorities in whose power they are, their requests regarding the conditions of captivity to which they are subjected. They shall also have the unrestricted right to apply to the representatives of the Protecting Powers either through their prisoners' representative or, if they consider it necessary, direct, in order to draw their attention to any points on which they may have complaints to make regarding their conditions of captivity.

These requests and complaints shall not be limited nor considered to be a part of the correspondence quota referred to in Article 71. They must be transmitted immediately.

Even if they are recognized to be unfounded, they may not give rise to any punishment. Prisoners' representatives may send periodic reports on the situation in the camps and the needs of the prisoners of war to the representatives of the Protecting Powers.

Chapter II. Prisoner of War Representatives

Article 79

In all places where there are prisoners of war, except in those where there are officers, the prisoners shall freely elect by secret ballot, every six months, and also in case of vacancies, prisoners' representatives entrusted with representing them before the military authorities, the Protecting Powers, the International Committee of the Red Cross and any other organization which may assist them. These prisoners' representatives shall be eligible for re-election. In camps for officers and persons of equivalent status or in mixed camps, the senior officer among the prisoners of war shall be recognized as the camp prisoners' representative. In camps for officers, he shall be assisted by one or more advisers chosen by the officers; in mixed camps, his assistants shall be chosen from among the prisoners of war who are not officers and shall be elected by them.

Officer prisoners of war of the same nationality shall be stationed in labour camps for prisoners of war, for the purpose of carrying out the camp administration duties for which the prisoners of war are responsible. These officers may be elected as prisoners' representatives under the first paragraph of this Article. In such a case the assistants to the prisoners' representatives shall be chosen from among those prisoners of war who are not officers. Every representative elected must be approved by the Detaining Power before he has the right to commence his duties. Where the Detaining Power refuses to approve a prisoner of war elected by his fellow prisoners of war, it must inform the Protecting Power of the reason for such refusal. In all cases the prisoners' representative must have the same nationality, language and customs as the prisoners of war whom he represents. Thus, prisoners of war distributed in different sections of a camp, according to their nationality, language or customs, shall have for each section their own prisoners' representative, in accordance with the foregoing paragraphs.

Article 80

Prisoners' representatives shall further the physical, spiritual and intellectual well-being of prisoners of war. In particular, where the prisoners decide to organize amongst themselves a system of mutual assistance, this organization will be within the province of the prisoners' representative, in addition to the special duties entrusted to him by other provisions of the present Convention.
Prisoners' representatives shall not be held responsible, simply by reason of their duties, for any offences committed by prisoners of war.

Article 81

Prisoners' representatives shall not be required to perform any other work, if the accomplishment of their duties is thereby made more difficult. Prisoners' representatives may appoint from amongst the prisoners such assistants as they may require. All material facilities shall be granted them, particularly a certain freedom of movement necessary for the accomplishment of their duties (inspection of labour detachments, receipt of supplies, etc.). Prisoners' representatives shall be permitted to visit premises where prisoners of war are detained, and every prisoner of war shall have the right to consult freely his prisoners' representative.

All facilities shall likewise be accorded to the prisoners' representatives for communication by post and telegraph with the detaining authorities, the Protecting Powers, the International Committee of the Red Cross and their delegates, the Mixed Medical Commissions and the bodies which give assistance to prisoners of war. Prisoners' representatives of labour detachments shall enjoy the same facilities for communication with the prisoners' representatives of the principal camp. Such communications shall not be restricted, nor considered as forming a part of the quota mentioned in Article 71. Prisoners' representatives who are transferred shall be allowed a reasonable time to acquaint their successors with current affairs. In case of dismissal, the reasons therefor shall be communicated to the Protecting Power.

Chapter III. Penal and Disciplinary Sanctions

I. General Provisions

Article 82

A prisoner of war shall be subject to the laws, regulations and orders in force in the armed forces of the Detaining Power; the Detaining Power shall be justified in taking judicial or disciplinary measures in respect of any offence committed by a prisoner of war against such laws, regulations or orders. However, no proceedings or punishments contrary to the provisions of this Chapter shall be allowed. If any law, regulation or order of the Detaining Power shall declare acts committed by a prisoner of war to be punishable, whereas the same acts would not be punishable if committed by a member of the forces of the Detaining Power, such acts shall entail disciplinary punishments only.

Article 83

In deciding whether proceedings in respect of an offence alleged to have been committed by a prisoner of war shall be judicial or disciplinary, the Detaining Power shall ensure that the competent authorities exercise the greatest leniency and adopt, wherever possible, disciplinary rather than judicial measures.

Article 84

A prisoner of war shall be tried only by a military court, unless the existing laws of the Detaining Power expressly permit the civil courts to try a member of the armed forces of the Detaining Power in respect of the particular offence alleged to have been committed by the prisoner of war. In no circumstances whatever shall a prisoner of war be tried by a court of any kind which does not offer the essential guarantees of independence and impartiality as generally recognized, and, in particular, the procedure of which does not afford the accused the rights and means of defence provided for in Article 105.

Article 85

Prisoners of war prosecuted under the laws of the Detaining Power for acts committed prior to capture shall retain, even if convicted, the benefits of the present Convention.

Article 86

No prisoner of war may be punished more than once for the same act or on the same charge.

Article 87

Prisoners of war may not be sentenced by the military authorities and courts of the Detaining Power to any penalties except those provided for in respect of members of the armed forces of the said Power who have committed the same acts. When fixing the penalty, the courts or authorities of the Detaining Power shall take into consideration, to the widest extent possible, the fact that the accused, not being a national of the Detaining Power, is not bound to it by any duty of allegiance, and that he is in its power as the result of circumstances independent of his own will. The said courts or authorities shall be at liberty to reduce the penalty provided for the violation of which the prisoner of war is accused, and shall therefore not be bound to apply the minimum penalty prescribed.

Collective punishment for individual acts, corporal punishment, imprisonment in premises without daylight and, in general, any form of torture or cruelty, are forbidden. No prisoner of war may be deprived of his rank by the Detaining Power, or prevented from wearing his badges.

Article 88

Officers, non-commissioned officers and men who are prisoners of war undergoing a disciplinary or judicial punishment, shall not be subjected to more severe treatment than that applied in respect of the same punishment to members of the armed forces of the Detaining Power of equivalent rank.

A woman prisoner of war shall not be awarded or sentenced to a punishment more severe, or treated whilst undergoing punishment more severely, than a woman member of the armed forces of the Detaining Power dealt with for a similar offence. In no case may a woman prisoner of war be awarded or sentenced to a punishment more severe, or treated whilst undergoing punishment more severely, than a male member of the armed forces of the Detaining Power dealt with for a similar offence. Prisoners of war who have served disciplinary or judicial sentences may not be treated differently from other prisoners of war.

II. Disciplinary Sanctions

Article 89

The disciplinary punishments applicable to prisoners of war are the following:

(1) A fine which shall not exceed 50 per cent of the advances of pay and working pay which the prisoner of war would otherwise receive under the provisions of Articles 60 and 62 during a period of not more than thirty days.
(2) Discontinuance of privileges granted over and above the treatment provided for by the present Convention.
(3) Fatigue duties not exceeding two hours daily.
(4) Confinement.

The punishment referred to under (3) shall not be applied to officers.
In no case shall disciplinary punishments be inhuman, brutal or dangerous to the health of prisoners of war.

Article 90

The duration of any single punishment shall in no case exceed thirty days. Any period of confinement awaiting the hearing of a disciplinary offence or the award of disciplinary punishment shall be deducted from an award pronounced against a prisoner of war. The maximum of thirty days provided above may not be exceeded, even if the prisoner of war is answerable for several acts at the same time when he is awarded punishment, whether such acts are related or not.

The period between the pronouncing of an award of disciplinary punishment and its execution shall not exceed one month. When a prisoner of war is awarded a further disciplinary punishment, a period of at least three days shall elapse between the execution of any two of the punishments, if the duration of one of these is ten days or more.

Article 91

The escape of a prisoner of war shall be deemed to have succeeded when:

(1) he has joined the armed forces of the Power on which he depends, or those of an allied Power;
(2) he has left the territory under the control of the Detaining Power, or of an ally of the said Power;
(3) he has joined a ship flying the flag of the Power on which he depends, or of an allied Power, in the territorial waters of the Detaining Power, the said ship not being under the control of the last named Power.

Prisoners of war who have made good their escape in the sense of this Article and who are recaptured, shall not be liable to any punishment in respect of their previous escape.

Article 92

A prisoner of war who attempts to escape and is recaptured before having made good his escape in the sense of Article 91 shall be liable only to a disciplinary punishment in respect of this act, even if it is a repeated offence. A prisoner of war who is recaptured shall be handed over without delay to the competent military authority. Article 88, fourth paragraph, notwithstanding, prisoners of war punished as a result of an unsuccessful escape may be subjected to special surveillance. Such surveillance must not affect the state of their health, must be undergone in a prisoner of war camp, and must not entail the suppression of any of the safeguards granted them by the present Convention.

Article 93

Escape or attempt to escape, even if it is a repeated offence, shall not be deemed an aggravating circumstance if the prisoner of war is subjected to trial by judicial proceedings in respect of an offence committed during his escape or attempt to escape. In conformity with the principle stated in Article 83, offences committed by prisoners of war with the sole intention of facilitating their escape and which do not entail any violence against life or limb, such as offences against public property, theft without intention of self-enrichment, the drawing up or use of false papers, or the wearing of civilian clothing, shall occasion disciplinary punishment only. Prisoners of war who aid or abet an escape or an attempt to escape shall be liable on this count to disciplinary punishment only.

Article 94

If an escaped prisoner of war is recaptured, the Power on which he depends shall be notified thereof in the manner defined in Article 122, provided notification of his escape has been made.

Article 95

A prisoner of war accused of an offence against discipline shall not be kept in confinement pending the hearing unless a member of the armed forces of the Detaining Power would be so kept if he were accused of a similar offence, or if it is essential in the interests of camp order and discipline. Any period spent by a prisoner of war in confinement awaiting the disposal of an offence against discipline shall be reduced to an absolute minimum and shall not exceed fourteen days. The provisions of Articles 97 and 98 of this Chapter shall apply to prisoners of war who are in confinement awaiting the disposal of offences against discipline.

Article 96

Acts which constitute offences against discipline shall be investigated immediately. Without prejudice to the competence of courts and superior military authorities, disciplinary punishment may be ordered only by an officer having disciplinary powers in his capacity as camp commander, or by a responsible officer who replaces him or to whom he has delegated his disciplinary powers.

In no case may such powers be delegated to a prisoner of war or be exercised by a prisoner of war. Before any disciplinary award is pronounced, the accused shall be given precise information regarding the offences of which he is accused, and given an opportunity of explaining his conduct and of defending himself. He shall be permitted, in particular, to call witnesses and to have recourse, if necessary, to the services of a qualified interpreter. The decision shall be announced to the accused prisoner of war and to the prisoners' representative. A record of disciplinary punishments shall be maintained by the camp commander and shall be open to inspection by representatives of the Protecting Power.

Article 97

Prisoners of war shall not in any case be transferred to penitentiary establishments (prisons, penitentiaries, convict prisons, etc.) to undergo disciplinary punishment therein. All premises in which disciplinary punishments are undergone shall conform to the sanitary requirements set forth in Article 25. A prisoner of war undergoing punishment shall be enabled to keep himself in a state of cleanliness, in conformity with Article 29.

Officers and persons of equivalent status shall not be lodged in the same quarters as non-commissioned officers or men. Women prisoners of war undergoing disciplinary punishment shall be confined in separate quarters from male prisoners of war and shall be under the immediate supervision of women.

Article 98

A prisoner of war undergoing confinement as a disciplinary punishment, shall continue to enjoy the benefits of.the provisions of this Convention except in so far as these are necessarily rendered inapplicable by the mere fact that he is confined. In no case may he be deprived of the benefits of the provisions of Articles 78 and 126.

A prisoner of war awarded disciplinary punishment may not be deprived of the prerogatives attached to his rank. Prisoners of war awarded disciplinary punishment shall be allowed to exercise and to stay in the open air at least two hours daily. They shall be allowed, on their request, to be present at the daily medical inspections. They shall receive the attention which their state of health requires and, if necessary, shall be removed to the camp infirmary or to a hospital. They shall have permission to read and write, likewise to send and receive lettersParcels and remittances of money however, may be withheld from them until the completion of the punishment; they shall meanwhile be entrusted to the prisoners' representative, who-will hand over to the infirmary the perishable goods contained in such parcels.

III. Judicial Proceedings

Article 99

No prisoner of war may be tried or sentenced for an act which is not forbidden by the law of the Detaining Power or by international law, in force at the time the said act was committed. No moral or physical coercion may be exerted on a prisoner of war in order to induce him to admit himself guilty of the act of which he is accused. No prisoner of war may be convicted without having had an opportunity to present his defence and the assistance of a qualified advocate or counsel.

Article 100

Prisoners of war and the Protecting Powers shall be informed as soon as possible of the offences which are punishable by the death sentence under the laws of the Detaining Power. Other offences shall not thereafter be made punishable by the death penalty without the concurrence of the Power on which the prisoners of war depend. The death sentence cannot be pronounced on a prisoner of war unless the attention of the court has, in accordance with Article 87, second paragraph, been particularly called to the fact that since the accused is not a national of the Detaining Power, he is not bound to it by any duty of allegiance, and that he is in its power as the result of circumstances independent of his own will.

Article 101

If the death penalty is pronounced on a prisoner of war, the sentence shall not be executed before the expiration of a period of at least six months from the date when the Protecting Power receives, at an indicated address, the detailed communication provided for in Article 107.

Article 102

A prisoner of war can be validly sentenced only if the sentence has been pronounced by the same courts according to the same procedure as in the case of members of the armed forces of the Detaining Power, and if, furthermore, the provisions of the present Chapter have been observed.

Article 103

Judicial investigations relating to a prisoner of war shall be conducted as rapidly as circumstances permit and so that his trial shall take place as soon as possible. A prisoner of war shall not be confined while awaiting trial unless a member of the armed forces of the Detaining Power would be so confined if he were accused of a similar offence, or if it is essential to do so in the interests of national security. In no circumstances shall this confinement exceed three months. Any period spent by a prisoner of war in confinement awaiting trial shall be deducted from any sentence of imprisonment passed upon him and taken into account in fixing any penalty. The provisions of Articles 97 and 98 of this Chapter shall apply to a prisoner of war whilst in confinement awaiting trial.

Article 104

In any case in which the Detaining Power has decided to institute judicial proceedings against a prisoner of war, it shall notify the Protecting Power as soon as possible and at least three weeks before the opening of the trial. This period of three weeks shall run as from the day on which such notification reaches the Protecting Power at the address previously indicated by the latter to the Detaining Power. The said notification shall contain the following information:

(1) Surname and first names of the prisoner of war, his rank, his army, regimental, personal or serial number, his date of birth, and his profession or trade, if any;
(2) Place of internment or confinement;
(3) Specification of the charge or charges on which the prisoner of war is to be arraigned, giving the legal provisions applicable;
(4) Designation of the court which will try the case, likewise the date and place fixed for the opening of the trial.

The same communication shall be made by the Detaining Power to the prisoners' representative. If no evidence is submitted, at the opening of a trial, that the notification referred to above was received by the Protecting Power, by the prisoner of war and by the prisoners' representative concerned, at least three weeks before the opening of the trial, then the latter cannot take place and must be adjourned.

Article 105

The prisoner of war shall be entitled to assistance by one of his prisoner comrades, to defence by a qualified advocate or counsel of his own choice, to the calling of witnesses and, if he deems necessary, to the services of a competent interpreter. He shall be advised of these rights by the Detaining Power in due time before the trial. Failing a choice by the prisoner of war, the Protecting Power shall find him an advocate or counsel, and shall have at least one week at its disposal for the purpose. The Detaining Power shall deliver to the said Power, on request, a list of persons qualified to present the defence. Failing a choice of an advocate or counsel by the prisoner of war or the Protecting Power, the Detaining Power shall appoint a competent advocate or counsel to conduct the defence.

The advocate or counsel conducting the defence on behalf of the prisoner of war shall have at his disposal a period of two weeks at least before the opening of the trial, as well as the necessary facilities to prepare the defence of the accused. He may, in particular, freely visit the accused and interview him in private. He may also confer with any witnesses for the defence, including prisoners of war. He shall have the benefit of these facilities until the term of appeal or petition has expired.

Particulars of the charge or charges on which the prisoner of war is to be arraigned, as well as the documents which are generally communicated to the accused by virtue of the laws in force in the armed forces of the Detaining Power, shall be communicated to the accused prisoner of war in a language which he understands, and in good time before the opening of the trial. The same communication in the same circumstances shall be made to the advocate or counsel conducting the defence on behalf of the prisoner of war.

The representatives of the Protecting Power shall be entitled to attend the trial of the case, unless, exceptionally, this is held in camera in the interest of State security. In such a case the Detaining Power shall advise the Protecting Power accordingly.

Article 106

Every prisoner of war shall have, in the same manner as the members of the armed forces of the Detaining Power, the right of appeal or petition from any sentence pronounced upon him, with a view to the quashing or revising of the sentence or the reopening of the trial. He shall be fully informed of his right to appeal or petition and of the time limit within which he may do so.

Article 107

Any judgment and sentence pronounced upon a prisoner of war shall be immediately reported to the Protecting Power in the form of a summary communication, which shall also indicate whether he has the right of appeal with a view to the quashing of the sentence or the reopening of the trial. This communication shall likewise be sent to the prisoners' representative concerned. It shall also be sent to the accused prisoner of war in a language he understands, if the sentence was not pronounced in his presence. The Detaining Power shall also immediately communicate to the Protecting Power the decision of the prisoner of war to use or to waive his right of appeal.

Furthermore, if a prisoner of war is finally convicted or if a sentence pronounced on a prisoner of war in the first instance is a death sentence, the Detaining Power shall as soon as possible address to the Protecting Power a detailed communication containing:

(1) the precise wording of the finding and sentence;
(2) a summarized report of any preliminary investigation and of the trial, emphasizing in particular the elements of the prosecution and the defence;
(3) notification, where applicable, of the establishment where the sentence will be served.

The communications provided for in the foregoing sub-paragraphs shall be sent to the Protecting Power at the address previously made known to the Detaining Power.

Article 108

Sentences pronounced on prisoners of war after a conviction has become duly enforceable, shall be served in the same establishments and under the same conditions as in the case of members of the armed forces of the Detaining Power. These conditions shall in all cases conform to the requirements of health and humanity.

A woman prisoner of war on whom such a sentence has been pronounced shall be confined in separate quarters and shall be under the supervision of women. In any case, prisoners of war sentenced to a penalty depriving them of their liberty shall retain the benefit of the provisions of Articles 78 and 126 of the present Convention. Furthermore, they shall be entitled to receive and despatch correspondence, to receive at least one relief parcel monthly, to take regular exercise in the open air, to have the medical care required by their state of health, and the spiritual assistance they may desire. Penalties to which they may be subjected shall be in accordance with the provisions of Article 87, third paragraph.

Part IV. Termination of Captivity

Section I. Direct Repatriation And Accommodation In Neutral Countries

Article 109

Subject to the provisions of the third paragraph of this Article, Parties to the conflict are bound to send back to their own country, regardless of number or rank, seriously wounded and seriously sick prisoners of war, after having cared for them until they are fit to travel, in accordance with the first paragraph of the following Article. Throughout the duration of hostilities, Parties to the conflict shall endeavour, with the cooperation of the neutral Powers concerned, to make arrangements for the accommodation in neutral countries of the sick and wounded prisoners of war referred to in the second paragraph of the following Article. They may, in addition, conclude agreements with a view to the direct repatriation or internment in a neutral country of able-bodied prisoners of war who have undergone a long period of captivity. No sick or injured prisoner of war who is eligible for repatriation under the first paragraph of this Article, may be repatriated against his will during hostilities.

Article 110

The following shall be repatriated direct:

(1) Incurably wounded and sick whose mental or physical fitness seems to have been gravely diminished.
(2) Wounded and sick who, according to medical opinion, are not likely to recover within one year, whose condition requires treatment and whose mental or physical fitness seems to have been gravely diminished.

(3) Wounded and sick who have recovered, but whose mental or physical fitness seems to have been gravely and permanently diminished.

The following may be accommodated in a neutral country:

(1) Wounded and sick whose recovery may be expected within one year of the date of the wound or the beginning of the illness, if treatment in a neutral country might increase the prospects of a more certain and speedy recovery.
(2) Prisoners of war whose mental or physical health, according to medical opinion, is seriously threatened by continued captivity, but whose accommodation in a neutral country might remove such a threat.

The conditions which prisoners of war accommodated in a neutral country must fulfil in order to permit their repatriation shall be fixed, as shall likewise their status, by agreement between the Powers concerned. In general, prisoners of war who have been accommodated in a neutral country, and who belong to the following categories, should be repatriated:

(1) Those whose state of health has deteriorated so as to fulfil the condition laid down for direct repatriation;
(2) Those whose mental or physical powers remain, even after treatment, considerably impaired.

If no special agreements are concluded between the Parties to the conflict concerned, to determine the cases of disablement or sickness entailing direct repatriation or accommodation in a neutral country, such cases shall be settled in accordance with the principles laid down in the Model Agreement concerning direct repatriation and accommodation in neutral countries of wounded and sick prisoners of war and in the Regulations concerning Mixed Medical Commissions annexed to the present Convention.

Article 111

The Detaining Power, the Power on which the prisoners of war depend, and a neutral Power agreed upon by these two Powers, shall endeavour to conclude agreements which will enable prisoners of war to be interned in the territory of the said neutral Power until the close of hostilities.

Article 112

Upon the outbreak of hostilities, Mixed Medical Commissions shall be appointed to examine sick and wounded prisoners of war, and to make all appropriate decisions regarding them. The appointment, duties and functioning of these Commissions shall be in conformity with the provisions of the Regulations annexed to the present Convention. However, prisoners of war who, in the opinion of the medical authorities of the Detaining Power, are manifestly seriously injured or seriously sick, may be repatriated without having to be examined by a Mixed Medical Commission.

Article 113

Besides those who are designated by the medical authorities of the Detaining Power, wounded or sick prisoners of war belonging to the categories listed below shall be entitled to present themselves for examination by the Mixed Medical Commissions provided for in the foregoing Article:

(1) Wounded and sick proposed by a physician or surgeon who is of the same nationality, or a national of a Party to the conflict allied with the Power on which the said prisoners depend, and who exercises his functions in the camp.
(2) Wounded and sick proposed by their prisoners' representative.
(3) Wounded and sick proposed by the Power on which they depend, or by an organization duly recognized by the said Power and giving assistance to the prisoners.

Prisoners of war who do not belong to one of the three foregoing categories may nevertheless present themselves for examination by Mixed Medical Commissions, but shall be examined only after those belonging to the said categories.

The physician or surgeon of the same nationality as the prisoners who present themselves for examination by the Mixed Medical Commission, likewise the prisoners' representative of the said prisoners, shall have permission to be present at the examination.

Article 114

Prisoners of war who meet with accidents shall, unless the injury is self-inflicted, have the benefit of the provisions of this Convention as regards repatriation or accommodation in a neutral country.

Article 115

No prisoner of war on whom a disciplinary punishment has been imposed and who is eligible for repatriation or for accommodation in a neutral country, may be kept back on the plea that he has not undergone his punishment. Prisoners of war detained in connection with a judicial prosecution or conviction, and who are designated for repatriation or accommodation in a neutral country, may benefit by such measures before the end of the proceedings or the completion of the punishment, if the Detaining Power consents. Parties to the conflict shall communicate to each other the names of those who will be detained until the end of the proceedings or the completion of the punishment.

Article 116

The cost of repatriating prisoners of war or of transporting them to a neutral country shall be borne, from the frontiers of the Detaining Power, by the Power on which the said prisoners depend.

Article 117

No repatriated person may be employed on active military service.

Section II. Release And Repatriation Of Prisoners Of War At The Close Of Hostilities

Article 118

Prisoners of war shall be released and repatriated without delay after the cessation of active hostilities. In the absence of stipulations to the above effect in any agreement concluded between the Parties to the conflict with a view to the cessation of hostilities, or failing any such agreement, each of the Detaining Powers shall itself establish and execute without delay a plan of repatriation in conformity with the principle laid down in the foregoing paragraph. In either case, the measures adopted shall be brought to the knowledge of the prisoners of war.

The costs of repatriation of prisoners of war shall in all cases be equitably apportioned between the Detaining Power and the Power on which the prisoners depend. This apportionment shall be carried out on the following basis:

(a) If the two Powers are contiguous, the Power on which the prisoners of war depend shall bear the costs of repatriation from the frontiers of the Detaining Power.
(b) If the two Powers are not contiguous, the Detaining Power shall bear the costs of transport of prisoners of war over its own territory as far as its frontier or its port of embarkation nearest to the territory of the Power on which the prisoners of war

depend. The Parties concerned shall agree between themselves as to the equitable apportionment of the remaining costs of the repatriation. The conclusion of this agreement shall in no circumstances justify any delay in the repatriation of the prisoners of war.

Article 119

Repatriation shall be effected in conditions similar to those laid down in Articles 46 to 48 inclusive of the present Convention for the transfer of prisoners of war, having regard to the provisions of Article 118 and to those of the following paragraphs. On repatriation, any articles of value impounded from prisoners of war under Article 18, and any foreign currency which has not been converted into the currency of the Detaining Power, shall be restored to them. Articles of value and foreign currency which, for any reason whatever, are not restored to prisoners of war on repatriation, shall be despatched to the Information Bureau set up under Article 122.

Prisoners of war shall be allowed to take with them their personal effects, and any correspondence and parcels which have arrived for them. The weight of such baggage may be limited, if the conditions of repatriation so require, to what each prisoner can reasonably carry. Each prisoner shall in all cases be authorized to carry at least twenty-five kilograms. The other personal effects of the repatriated prisoner shall be left in the charge of the Detaining Power which shall have them forwarded to him as soon as it has concluded an agreement to this effect, regulating the conditions of transport and the payment of the costs involved, with the Power on which the prisoner depends.

Prisoners of war against whom criminal proceedings for an indictable offence are pending may be detained until the end of such proceedings, and, if necessary, until the completion of the punishment. The same shall apply to prisoners of war already convicted for an indictable offence. Parties to the conflict shall communicate to each other the names of any prisoners of war who are detained until the end of the proceedings or until punishment has been completed. By agreement between the Parties to the conflict, commissions shall be established for the purpose of searching for dispersed prisoners of war and of assuring their repatriation with the least possible delay.

Section III. Death of Prisoners of War

Article 120

Wills of prisoners of war shall be drawn up so as to satisfy the conditions of validity required by the legislation of their country of origin, which will take steps to inform the Detaining Power of its requirements in this respect. At the request of the prisoner of war and, in all cases, after death, the will shall be transmitted without delay to the Protecting

Power; a certified copy shall be sent to the Central Agency. Death certificates, in the form annexed to the present Convention, or lists certified by a responsible officer, of all persons who die as prisoners of war shall be forwarded as rapidly as possible to the Prisoner of War Information Bureau established in accordance with Article 122. The death certificates or certified lists shall show particulars of identity as set out in the third paragraph of Article 17, and also the date and place of death, the cause of death, the date and place of burial and all particulars necessary to identify the graves.

The burial or cremation of a prisoner of war shall be preceded by a medical examination of the body with a view to confirming death and enabling a report to be made and, where necessary, establishing identity. The detaining authorities shall ensure that prisoners of war who have died in captivity are honourably buried, if possible according to the rites of the religion to which they belonged, and that their graves are respected, suitably maintained and marked so as to be found at any time. Wherever possible, deceased prisoners of war who depended on the same Power shall be interred in the same place. Deceased prisoners of war shall be buried in individual graves unless unavoidable circumstances require the use of collective graves. Bodies may be cremated only for imperative reasons of hygiene, on account of the religion of the deceased or in accordance with his express wish to this effect. In case of cremation, the fact shall be stated and the reasons given in the death certificate of the deceased.

In order that graves may always be found, all particulars of burials and graves shall be recorded with a Graves Registration Service established by the Detaining Power. Lists of graves and particulars of the prisoners of war interred in cemeteries and elsewhere shall be transmitted to the Power on which such prisoners of war depended. Responsibility for the care of these graves and for records of any subsequent moves of the bodies shall rest on the Power controlling the territory, if a Party to the present Convention. These provisions shall also apply to the ashes, which shall be kept by the Graves Registration Service until proper disposal thereof in accordance with the wishes of the home country.

Article 121

Every death or serious injury of a prisoner of war caused or suspected to have been caused by a sentry, another prisoner of war, or any other person, as well as any death the cause of which is unknown, shall be immediately followed by an official enquiry by the Detaining Power. A communication on this subject shall be sent immediately to the Protecting Power. Statements shall be taken from witnesses, especially from those who are prisoners of war, and a report including such statements shall be forwarded to the Protecting Power. If the enquiry indicates the guilt of one or more persons, the Detaining Power shall take all measures for the prosecution of the person or persons responsible.

Part V. Information Bureaux and Relief Societies for Prisoners of War

Article 122

Upon the outbreak of a conflict and in all cases of occupation, each of the Parties to the conflict shall institute an official Information Bureau for prisoners of war who are in its power. Neutral or non-belligerent Powers who may have received within their territory persons belonging to one of the categories referred to in Article 4, shall take the same action with respect to such persons. The Power concerned shall ensure that the Prisoners of War Information Bureau is provided with the necessary accommodation, equipment and staff to ensure its efficient working. It shall be at liberty to employ prisoners of war in such a Bureau under the conditions laid down in the Section of the present Convention dealing with work by prisoners of war. Within the shortest possible period, each of the Parties to the conflict shall give its Bureau the information referred to in the fourth, fifth and sixth paragraphs of this Article regarding any enemy person belonging to one of the categories referred to in Article 4, who has fallen into its power. Neutral or non-belligerent Powers shall take the same action with regard to persons belonging to such categories whom they have received within their territory.

The Bureau shall immediately forward such information by the most rapid means to the Powers concerned, through the intermediary of the Protecting Powers and likewise of the Central Agency provided for in Article 123. This information shall make it possible quickly to advise the next of kin concerned. Subject to the provisions of Article 17, the information shall include, in so far as available to the Information Bureau, in respect of each prisoner of war, his surname, first names, rank, army, regimental, personal or serial number, place and full date of birth, indication of the Power on which he depends, first name of the father and maiden name of the mother, name and address of the person to be informed and the address to which correspondence for the prisoner may be sent.

The Information Bureau shall receive from the various departments concerned information regarding transfers, releases, repatriations, escapes, admissions to hospital, and deaths, and shall transmit such information in the manner described in the third paragraph above. Likewise, information regarding the state of health of prisoners of war who are seriously ill or seriously wounded shall be supplied regularly, every week if possible. The Information Bureau shall also be responsible for replying to all enquiries sent to it concerning prisoners of war, including those who have died in captivity; it will make any enquiries necessary to obtain the information which is asked for if this is not in its possession. All written communications made by the Bureau shall be authenticated by a signature or a seal.

The Information Bureau shall furthermore be charged with collecting all personal valuables, including sums in currencies other than that of the Detaining Power and documents of importance to the next of kin, left by prisoners of war who have been repatriated or released, or who have escaped or died, and shall forward the said valuables to the Powers concerned. Such articles shall be sent by the Bureau in sealed packets which shall be accompanied by statements giving clear and full particulars of the identity of the person to whom the articles belonged, and by a complete list of the contents of the parcel. Other personal effects of such prisoners of war shall be transmitted under arrangements agreed upon between the Parties to the conflict concerned.

Article 123

A Central Prisoners of War Information Agency shall be created in a neutral country. The International Committee of the Red Cross shall, if it deems necessary, propose to the Powers concerned the organization of such an Agency.
The function of the Agency shall be to collect all the information it may obtain through official or private channels respecting prisoners of war, and to transmit it as rapidly as possible to the country of origin of the prisoners of war or to the Power on which they depend. It shall receive from the Parties to the conflict all facilities for effecting such transmissions.

The High Contracting Parties, and in particular those whose nationals benefit by the services of the Central Agency, are requested to give the said Agency the financial aid it may require. The foregoing provisions shall in no way be interpreted as restricting the humanitarian activities of the International Committee of the Red Cross, or of the relief societies provided for in Article 125.

Article 124

The national Information Bureaux and the Central Information Agency shall enjoy free postage for mail, likewise all the exemptions provided for in Article 74, and further, so far as possible, exemption from telegraphic charges or, at least, greatly reduced rates.

Article 125

Subject to the measures which the Detaining Powers may consider essential to ensure their security or to meet any other reasonable need, the representatives of religious organizations, relief societies, or any other organization assisting prisoners of war, shall receive from the said Powers, for themselves and their duly accredited agents, all necessary facilities for visiting the prisoners, for distributing relief supplies and material, from any source, intended for religious, educational or recreative purposes, and for assisting them in organizing their leisure time within the camps. Such societies or organizations may be constituted in the territory of the Detaining Power or in any other country, or they may have an international character.

The Detaining Power may limit the number of societies and organizations whose delegates are allowed to carry out their activities in its territory and under its supervision, on condition, however, that such limitation shall not hinder the effective operation of adequate relief to all prisoners of war. The special position of the International Committee of the Red Cross in this field shall be recognized and respected at all times. As soon as relief supplies or material intended for the above-mentioned purposes are handed over to prisoners of war, or very shortly afterwards, receipts for each consignment, signed by the prisoners' representative, shall be forwarded to the relief society or organization making the shipment. At the same time, receipts for these consignments shall be supplied by the administrative authorities responsible for guarding the prisoners.

Part VI. Execution of the Convention

Section I. General Provisions

Article 126

Representatives or delegates of the Protecting Powers shall have permission to go to all places where prisoners of war may be, particularly to places of internment, imprisonment and labour, and shall have access to all premises occupied by prisoners of war; they shall also be allowed to go to the places of departure, passage and arrival of prisoners who are being transferred. They shall be able to interview the prisoners, and in particular the prisoners' representatives, without witnesses, either personally or through an interpreter.

Representatives and delegates of the Protecting Powers shall have full liberty to select the places they wish to visit. The duration and frequency of these visits shall not be restricted. Visits may not be prohibited except for reasons of imperative military necessity, and then only as an exceptional and temporary measure. The Detaining Power and the Power on which the said prisoners of war depend may agree, if necessary, that compatriots of these prisoners of war be permitted to participate in the visits. The delegates of the International Committee of the Red Cross shall enjoy the same prerogatives. The appointment of such delegates shall be submitted to the approval of the Power detaining the prisoners of war to be visited.

Article 127

The High Contracting Parties undertake, in time of peace as in time of war, to disseminate the text of the present Convention as widely as possible in their respective countries, and, in particular, to include the study thereof in their programmes of military and, if possible, civil instruction, so that the principles thereof may become known to all their armed forces and to the entire population.

Any military or other authorities, who in time of war assume responsibilities in respect of prisoners of war, must possess the text of the Convention and be specially instructed as to its provisions.

Article 128

The High Contracting Parties shall communicate to one another through the Swiss Federal Council and, during hostilities, through the Protecting Powers, the official translations of the present Convention, as well as the laws and regulations which they may adopt to ensure the application thereof.

Article 129

The High Contracting Parties undertake to enact any legislation necessary to provide effective penal sanctions for persons committing, or ordering to be committed, any of the grave breaches of the present Convention defined in the following Article.

Each High Contracting Party shall be under the obligation to search for persons alleged to have committed. or to have ordered to be committed, such grave breaches, and shall bring such persons, regardless of their nationality, before its own courts. It may also, if it prefers, and in accordance with the provisions of its own legislation, hand such persons over for trial to another High Contracting Party concerned, provided such High Contracting Party has made out a prima facie case.

Each High Contracting Party shall take measures necessary for the suppression of all acts contrary to the provisions of the present Convention other than the grave breaches defined in the following Article. In all circumstances, the accused persons shall benefit by safeguards of proper trial and defence, which shall not be less favourable than those provided by Article 105 and those following of the present Convention.

Article 130

Grave breaches to which the preceding Article relates shall be those involving any of the following acts, if committed against persons or property protected by the Convention: wilful killing, torture or inhuman treatment, including biological experiments, wilfully causing great suffering or serious injury to body or health, compelling a prisoner of war to serve in the forces of the hostile Power, or wilfully depriving a prisoner of war of the rights of fair and regular trial prescribed in this Convention.

Article 131

No High Contracting Party shall be allowed to absolve itself or any other High Contracting Party of any liability incurred by itself or by another High Contracting Party in respect of breaches referred to in the preceding Article.

Article 132

At the request of a Party to the conflict, an enquiry shall be instituted, in a manner to be decided between the interested Parties, concerning any alleged violation of the Convention. If agreement has not been reached concerning the procedure for the enquiry, the Parties should agree on the choice of an umpire who will decide upon the procedure to be followed. Once the violation has been established, the Parties to the conflict shall put an end to it and shall repress it with the least possible delay.

Section II. Final Provisions

Article 133

The present Convention is established in English and in French. Both texts are equally authentic.
The Swiss Federal Council shall arrange for official translations of the Convention to be made in the Russian and Spanish languages.

Article 134

The present Convention replaces the Convention of July 27, 1929, in relations between the High Contracting Parties.

Article 135

In the relations between the Powers which are bound by the Hague Convention respecting the Laws and Customs of War on Land, whether that of July 29, 1899, or that of October 18, 1907, and which are parties to the present Convention, this last Convention shall be complementary to Chapter II of the Regulations annexed to the above-mentioned Conventions of the Hague.

Article 136

The present Convention, which bears the date of this day, is open to signature until February 12, 1950, in the name of the Powers represented at the Conference which opened at Geneva on April 21, 1949; furthermore, by Powers not represented at that Conference, but which are parties to the Convention of July 27, 1929.

Article 137

The present Convention shall be ratified as soon as possible and the ratifications shall be deposited at Berne. A record shall be drawn up of the deposit of each instrument of ratification and certified copies of this record shall be transmitted by the Swiss Federal Council to all the Powers in whose name the Convention has been signed, or whose accession has been notified.

Article 138

The present Convention shall come into force six months after not less than two instruments of ratification have been deposited. Thereafter, it shall come into force for each High Contracting Party six months after the deposit of the instrument of ratification.

Article 139

From the date of its coming into force, it shall be open to any Power in whose name the present Convention has not been signed, to accede to this Convention.

Article 140

Accessions shall be notified in writing to the Swiss Federal Council, and shall take effect six months after the date on which they are received. The Swiss Federal Council shall communicate the accessions to all the Powers in whose name the Convention has been signed, or whose accession has been notified.

Article 141

The situations provided for in Articles 2 and 3 shall give immediate effect to ratifications deposited and accessions notified by the Parties to the conflict before or after the beginning of hostilities or occupation. The Swiss Federal Council shall communicate by the quickest method any ratifications or accessions received from Parties to the conflict.

Article 142

Each of the High Contracting Parties shall be at liberty to denounce the present Convention. The denunciation shall be notified in writing to the Swiss Federal Council, which shall transmit it to the Governments of all the High Contracting Parties. The denunciation shall take effect one year after the notification thereof has been made to the Swiss Federal Council. However, a denunciation of which notification has been made at a time when the denouncing Power is involved in a conflict shall not take effect until peace has been concluded, and until after operations connected with release and repatriation of the persons protected by the present Convention have been terminated. The denunciation shall have effect only in respect of the denouncing Power. It shall in no way impair the obligations which the Parties to the conflict shall remain bound to fulfil by virtue of the principles of the law of nations, as they result from the usages established among civilized peoples, from the laws of humanity and the dictates of the public conscience.

Article 143

The Swiss Federal Council shall register the present Convention with the Secretariat of the United Nations. The Swiss Federal Council shall also inform the Secretariat of the United Nations of all ratifications, accessions and denunciations received by it with respect to the present Convention.

IN WITNESS WHEREOF the undersigned, having deposited their respective full powers, have signed the present Convention.

DONE at Geneva this twelfth day of August 1949, in the English and French languages. The original shall be deposited in the Archives of the Swiss Confederation. The Swiss Federal Council shall transmit certified copies thereof to each of the signatory and acceding States.

Annex I
Model Agreement Concerning Direct Repatriation And Accommodation In Neutral Countries Of Wounded And Sick Prisoners Of War (see Article 110)

I. Principles For Direct Repatriation And Accommodation In Neutral Countries

A. Direct Repatriation

The following shall be repatriated direct:

(1) All prisoners of war suffering from the following disabilities as the result of trauma: loss of a limb, paralysis, articular or other disabilities, when this disability is at least the loss of a hand or a foot, or the equivalent of the loss of a hand or a foot. Without prejudice to a more generous interpretation, the following shall be considered as equivalent to the loss of a hand or a foot:

(a) Loss of a hand or of all the fingers, or of the thumb and forefinger of one hand; loss of a foot, or of all the toes and metatarsals of one foot.
(b) Ankylosis, loss of osseous tissue, cicatricial contracture preventing the functioning of one of the large articulations or of all the digital joints of one hand.
(c) Pseudarthrosis of the long bones.
(d) Deformities due to fracture or other injury which seriously interfere with function and weight-bearing power.

(2) All wounded prisoners of war whose condition has become chronic, to the extent that prognosis appears to exclude recovery--in spite of treatment--within one year from the date of the injury, as, for example, in case of:

(a) Projectile in the heart, even if the Mixed Medical Commission should fail, at the time of their examination, to detect any serious disorders.
(b) Metallic splinter in the brain or the lungs, even if the Mixed Medical Commission cannot, at the time of examination, detect any local or general reaction.
(c) Osteomyelitis, when recovery cannot be foreseen in the course of the year following the injury, and which seems likely to result in ankylosis of a joint, or other impairments equivalent to the loss of a hand or a foot.
(d) Perforating and suppurating injury to the large joints.
(e) Injury to the skull, with loss or shifting of bony tissue.
(f) Injury or burning of the face with loss of tissue and functional lesions.
(g) Injury to the spinal cord.
(h) Lesion of the peripheral nerves, the sequelae of which are equivalent to the loss of a hand or foot, and the cure of which requires more than a year from the date of injury, for.example: injury to the brachial or lumbosacral plexus median or sciatic nerves, likewise combined injury to the radial and cubital nerves or to the lateral popliteal nerve (N. peroneous communis) and medial popliteal nerve (N. tibialis); etc. The separate injury of the radial (musculo-spiral), cubital, lateral or medial

popliteal nerves shall not, however, warrant repatriation except in case of contractures or of serious neurotrophic disturbance.
(i) Injury to the urinary system, with incapacitating results.

(3) All sick prisoners of war whose condition has become chronic to the extent that prognosis seems to exclude recovery--in, spite of treatment-- within one year from the inception of the disease, as, for example, in case of:

(a) Progressive tuberculosis of any organ which, according to medical prognosis, cannot be cured or at least considerably improved by treatment in a neutral country.
(b) Exudate pleurisy.
(c) Serious diseases of the respiratory organs of non-tubercular etiology, presumed incurable, for example: serious pulmonary emphysema, with or without bronchitis; chronic asthma *; chronic bronchitis * lasting more than one year in captivity; bronchiectasis *; etc.
(d) Serious chronic affections of the circulatory system, for example: valvular lesions and myocarditis *, which have shown signs of circulatory failure during captivity, even though the Mixed Medical Commission cannot detect any such signs at the time of examination; affections of the pericardium and the vessels (Buerger's disease, aneurisms of the large vessels); etc.
(e) Serious chronic affections of the digestive organs, for example: gastric or duodenal ulcer; sequelae of gastric operations performed in captivity; chronic gastritis, enteritis or colitis, having lasted more than one year and seriously affecting the general condition; cirrhosis of the liver; chronic cholecystopathy[20]; etc.
(f) Serious chronic affections of the genito-urinary organs, for example: chronic diseases of the kidney with consequent disorders; nephrectomy because of a tubercular kidney; chronic pyelitis or chronic cystitis; hydronephrosis or pyonephrosis; chronic grave gynaecological conditions; normal pregnancy and obstetrical disorder, where it is impossible to accommodate in a neutral country; etc.
(g) Serious chronic diseases of the central and peripheral nervous system, for example: all obvious psychoses and psychoneuroses, such as serious hysteria, serious captivity psychoneurosis, etc., duly verified by a specialist *; any epilepsy duly verified by the camp physician *; cerebral arteriosclerosis; chronic neuritis lasting more than one year; etc.
(h) Serious chronic diseases of the neuro-vegetative system, with considerable diminution of mental or physical fitness, noticeable loss of weight and general asthenia.
(i) Blindness of both eyes, or of one eye when the vision of the other is less than 1 in spite of the use of corrective glasses; diminution of visual acuity in cases where it is

[20] The decision of the Mixed Medical Commission shall be based to a great extent on the records kept by camp physicians and surgeons of the same nationality as the prisoners of war, or on an examination by medical specialists of the Detaining Power.

impossible to restore it by correction to an acuity of 1/2 in at least one eye *; other grave ocular affections, for example: glaucoma, iritis, choroiditis; trachoma; etc.
(k) Auditive disorders, such as total unilateral deafness, if the other ear does not discern the ordinary spoken word at a distance of one metre *; etc.
(l) Serious affections of metabolism, for example: diabetes mellitus requiring insulin treatment; etc.
(m) Serious disorders of the endocrine glands, for example: thyrotoxicosis; hypothyrosis; Addison's disease; Simmonds' cachexia; tetany; etc.
(n) Grave and chronic disorders of the blood-forming organs.
(o) Serious cases of chronic intoxication, for example: lead poisoning, mercury poisoning, morphinism, cocainism, alcoholism; gas or radiation poisoning; etc.
(p) Chronic affections of locomotion, with obvious functional disorders, for example: arthritis deformans; primary and secondary progressive chronic polyarthritis; rheumatism with serious clinical symptoms; etc.
(q) Serious chronic skin diseases, not amenable to treatment.
(r) Any malignant growth.
(s) Serious chronic infectious diseases, persisting for one year after their inception, for example: malaria with decided organic impairment, amoebic or bacillary dysentery with grave disorders; tertiary visceral syphilis resistant to treatment; leprosy; etc.
(t) Serious avitaminosis or serious inanition.

B. Accommodation In Neutral Countries

The following shall be eligible for accommodation in a neutral country:

(1) All wounded prisoners of war who are not likely to recover in captivity, but who might be cured or whose condition might be considerably improved by accommodation in a neutral country.

(2) Prisoners of war suffering from any form of tuberculosis, of whatever organ, and whose treatment in a neutral country would be likely to lead to recovery or at least to considerable improvement, with the exception of primary tuberculosis cured before captivity.

(3) Prisoners of war suffering from affections requiring treatment of the respiratory, circulatory, digestive, nervous, sensory, genito-urinary, cutaneous, locomotive organs, etc., if such treatment would clearly have better results in a neutral country than in captivity.

(4) Prisoners of war who have undergone a nephrectomy in captivity for a non-tubercular renal affection; cases of osteomyelitis, on the way to recovery or latent; diabetes mellitus not requiring insulin treatment; etc.

(5) Prisoners of war suffering from war or captivity neuroses. Cases of captivity neurosis which are not cured after three months of accommodation in a neutral country, or which after that length of time are not clearly on the way to complete cure, shall be repatriated.

(6) All prisoners of war suffering from chronic intoxication (gases, metals, alkaloids, etc.), for whom the prospects of cure in a neutral country are especially favourable.

(7) All women prisoners of war who are pregnant or mothers with infants and small children.

The following cases shall not be eligible for accommodation in a neutral country:

(1) All duly verified chronic psychoses.
(2) All organic or functional nervous affections considered to be incurable.
(3) All contagious diseases during the period in which they are transmissible, with the exception of tuberculosis.

II. General Observations

(1) The conditions given shall, in a general way, be interpreted and applied in as broad a spirit as possible. Neuropathic and psychopathic conditions caused by war or captivity, as well as cases of tuberculosis in all stages, shall above all benefit by such liberal interpretation. Prisoners of war who have sustained several wounds, none of which, considered by itself, justifies repatriation, shall be examined in the same spirit, with due regard for the psychic traumatism due to the number of their wounds.

(2) All unquestionable cases giving the right to direct repatriation (amputation, total blindness or deafness, open pulmonary tuberculosis, mental disorder, malignant growth, etc.) shall be examined and repatriated as soon as possible by the camp physicians or by military medical commissions appointed by the Detaining Power.

(3) Injuries and diseases which existed before the war and which have not become worse, as well as war injuries which have not prevented subsequent military service, shall not entitle to direct repatriation.

(4) The provisions of this Annex shall be interpreted and applied in a similar manner in all countries party to the conflict. The Powers and authorities concerned shall grant to Mixed Medical Commissions all the facilities necessary for the accomplishment of their task.

(5) The examples quoted under (1) above represent only typical cases. Cases which do not correspond exactly to these provisions shall be judged in the spirit of the provisions

of Article 110 of the present Convention, and of the principles embodied in the present Agreement.

Annex II
Regulations Concerning Mixed Medical Commissions
(see Article 112)

Article 1

The Mixed Medical Commissions provided for in Article 112 of the Convention shall be composed of three members, two of whom shall belong to a neutral country, the third being appointed by the Detaining Power. One of the neutral members shall take the chair.

Article 2

The two neutral members shall be appointed by the International Committee of the Red Cross, acting in agreement with the Protecting Power, at the request of the Detaining Power. They may be domiciled either in their country of origin, in any other neutral country, or in the territory of the Detaining Power.

Article 3

The neutral members shall be approved by the Parties to the conflict concerned, who shall notify their approval to the International Committee of the Red Cross and to the Protecting Power. Upon such notification, the neutral members shall be considered as effectively appointed.

Article 4

Deputy members shall also be appointed in sufficient number to replace the regular members in case of need. They shall be appointed at the same time as the regular members or, at least, as soon as possible.

Article 5

If for any reason the International Committee of the Red Cross cannot arrange for the appointment of the neutral members, this shall be done by the Power protecting the interests of the prisoners of war to be examined.

Article 6

So far as possible, one of the two neutral members shall be a surgeon and the other a physician.

Article 7

The neutral members shall be entirely independent of the Parties to the conflict, which shall grant them all facilities in the accomplishment of their duties.

Article 8

By agreement with the Detaining Power, the International Committee of the Red Cross, when making the appointments provided for in Articles 2 and 4 of the present Regulations, shall settle the terms of serv ice of the nominees.

Article 9

The Mixed Medical Commissions shall begin their work as soon as possible after the neutral members have been approved, and in any case within a period of three months from the date of such approval.

Article 10

The Mixed Medical Commissions shall examine all the prisoners designated in Article 113 of the Convention. They shall propose repatriation, rejection, or reference to a later examination. Their decisions shall be made by a majority vote.

Article 11

The decisions made by the Mixed Medical Commissions in each specific case shall be communicated, during the month following their visit, to the Detaining Power, the Protecting Power and the International Committee of the Red Cross. The Mixed Medical Commissions shall also inform each prisoner of war examined of the decision made, and shall issue to those whose repatriation has been proposed, certificates similar to the model appended to the present Convention.

Article 12

The Detaining Power shall be required to carry out the decisions of the Mixed Medical Commissions within three months of the time when it receives due notification of such decisions.

Article 13

If there is no neutral physician in a country where the services of a Mixed Medical Commission seem to be required, and if it is for any reason impossible to appoint neutral doctors who are resident in another country, the Detaining Power, acting in agreement with the Protecting Power, shall set up a Medical Commission which shall undertake the same duties as a Mixed Medical Commission, subject to the provisions of Articles 1, 2, 3, 4, 5 and 8 of the present Regulations.

Article 14

Mixed Medical Commissions shall function permanently and shall visit each camp at intervals of not more than six months.

Annex III
Regulations Concerning Collective Relief
(see Article 73)

Article 1

Prisoners' representatives shall be allowed to distribute collective relief shipments for which they are responsible, to all prisoners of war administered by their camp, including those who are in hospitals, or in prisons or other penal establishments.

Article 2

The distribution of collective relief shipments shall be effected in accordance with the instructions of the donors and with a plan drawn up by the prisoners' representatives. The issue of medical stores shall, however, be made for preference in agreement with the senior medical officers, and the latter may, in hospitals and infirmaries, waive the said instructions, if the needs of their patients so demand. Within the limits thus defined, the distribution shall always be carried out equitably.

Article 3

The said prisoners' representatives or their assistants shall be allowed to go to the points of arrival of relief supplies near their camps, so as to enable the prisoners' representatives or their assistants to verify the quality as well as the quantity of the goods received, and to make out detailed reports thereon for the donors.

Article 4

Prisoners' representatives shall be given the facilities necessary for verifying whether the distribution of collective relief in all subdivisions and annexes of their camps has been carried out in accordance with their instructions.

Article 5

Prisoners' representatives shall be allowed to fill up, and cause to be filled up by the prisoners' representatives of labour detachments or by the senior medical officers of infirmaries and hospitals, forms or questionnaires intended for the donors, relating to collective relief supplies (distribution, requirements, quantities, etc.). Such forms and questionnaires, duly completed, shall be forwarded to the donors without delay.

Article 6

In order to secure the regular issue of collective relief to the prisoners of war in their camp, and to meet any needs that may arise from the arrival of new contingents of prisoners, prisoners' representatives shall be allowed to build up and maintain adequate reserve stocks of collective relief. For this purpose, they shall have suitable warehouses at their disposal; each warehouse shall be provided with two locks, the prisoners' representative holding the keys of one lock and the camp commander the keys of the other.

Article 7

When collective consignments of clothing are available, each prisoner of war shall retain in his possession at least one complete set of clothes. If a prisoner has more than one set of clothes, the prisoners' representative shall be permitted to withdraw excess clothing from those with the largest number of sets, or particular articles in excess of one, if this is necessary in order to supply prisoners who are less well provided. He shall not, however, withdraw second sets of underclothing, socks or footwear, unless this is the only means of providing for prisoners of war with none.

Article 8

The High Contracting Parties, and the Detaining Powers in particular, shall authorize, as far as possible and subject to the regulations governing the supply of the population, all purchases of goods made in their territories for the distribution of collective relief to prisoners of war. They shall similarly facilitate the transfer of funds and other financial measures of a technical or administrative nature taken for the purpose of making such purchases.

Article 9

The foregoing provisions shall not constitute an obstacle to the right of prisoners of war to receive collective relief before their arrival in a camp or in the course of transfer, nor to the possibility of representatives of the Protecting Power, the International Committee of the Red Cross, or any other body giving assistance to prisoners which may be responsible for the forwarding of such supplies, ensuring the distribution thereof to the addressees by any other means that they may deem useful.

[Annex IV -- not included]

Annex V

Model Regulations Concerning Payments Sent By Prisoners To Their Own Country (see Article 63)

(1) The notification referred to in the third paragraph of Article 63 will show:

(a) number as specified in Article 17, rank, surname and first names of the prisoner of war who is the payer;
(b) the name and address of the payee in the country of origin;
(c) the amount to be so paid in the currency of the country in which he is detained.

(2) The notification will be signed by the prisoner of war, or his witnessed mark made upon it if he cannot write, and shall be countersigned by the prisoners' representative.

(3) The camp commander will add to this notification a certificate that the prisoner of war concerned has a credit balance of not less than the amount registered as payable.

(4) The notification may be made up in lists, each sheet of such lists being witnessed by the prisoners' representative and certified by the camp commander.

Convention (IV) Relative to the Protection of Civilian Persons in Time of War, August 12 1949

The undersigned Plenipotentiaries of the Governments represented at the Diplomatic Conference held at Geneva from 21 April to 12 August 1949, for the purpose of establishing a Convention for the Protection of Civilians in Time of War, have agreed as follows:

Part I. General Provisions

Article 1

The High Contracting Parties undertake to respect and to ensure respect for the present Convention in all circumstances.

Article 2

In addition to the provisions which shall be implemented in peace-time, the present Convention shall apply to all cases of declared war or of any other armed conflict which may arise between two or more of the High Contracting Parties, even if the state of war is not recognized by one of them. The Convention shall also apply to all cases of partial or total occupation of the territory of a High Contracting Party, even if the said occupation meets with no armed resistance. Although one of the Powers in conflict may not be a party to the present Convention, the Powers who are parties thereto shall remain bound by it in their mutual relations. They shall furthermore be bound by the Convention in relation to the said Power, if the latter accepts and applies the provisions thereof.

Article 3

In the case of armed conflict not of an international character occurring in the territory of one of the High Contracting Parties, each Party to the conflict shall be bound to apply, as a minimum, the following provisions:

(1) Persons taking no active part in the hostilities, including members of armed forces who have laid down their arms and those placed hors de combat by sickness, wounds, detention, or any other cause, shall in all circumstances be treated humanely, without any adverse distinction founded on race, colour, religion or faith, sex, birth or wealth, or any other similar criteria. To this end the following acts are and shall remain prohibited at any time and in any place whatsoever with respect to the above-mentioned persons: (a) violence to life and person, in particular murder of all kinds, mutilation, cruel treatment and torture; (b) taking of hostages; (c) outrages upon personal dignity, in particular humiliating and degrading treatment; (d) the passing of sentences and the carrying out of executions without previous judgment pronounced by a regularly

constituted court, affording all the judicial guarantees which are recognized as indispensable by civilized peoples. (2) The wounded and sick shall be collected and cared for.

An impartial humanitarian body, such as the International Committee of the Red Cross, may offer its services to the Parties to the conflict. The Parties to the conflict should further endeavour to bring into force, by means of special agreements, all or part of the other provisions of the present Convention. The application of the preceding provisions shall not affect the legal status of the Parties to the conflict.

Article 4

Persons protected by the Convention are those who, at a given moment and in any manner whatsoever, find themselves, in case of a conflict or occupation, in the hands of a Party to the conflict or Occupying Power of which they are not nationals. Nationals of a State which is not bound by the Convention are not protected by it. Nationals of a neutral State who find themselves in the territory of a belligerent State, and nationals of a co-belligerent State, shall not be regarded as protected persons while the State of which they are nationals has normal diplomatic representation in the State in whose hands they are. The provisions of Part II are, however, wider in application, as defined in Article 13. Persons protected by the Geneva Convention for the Amelioration of the Condition of the Wounded and Sick in Armed Forces in the Field of 12 August 1949, or by the Geneva Convention for the Amelioration of the Condition of Wounded, Sick and Shipwrecked Members of Armed Forces at Sea of 12 August 1949, or by the Geneva Convention relative to the Treatment of Prisoners of War of 12 August 1949, shall not be considered as protected persons within the meaning of the present Convention.

Article 5

Where in the territory of a Party to the conflict, the latter is satisfied that an individual protected person is definitely suspected of or engaged in activities hostile to the security of the State, such individual person shall not be entitled to claim such rights and privileges under the present Convention as would, if exercised in the favour of such individual person, be prejudicial to the security of such State. Where in occupied territory an individual protected person is detained as a spy or saboteur, or as a person under definite suspicion of activity hostile to the security of the Occupying Power, such person shall, in those cases where absolute military security so requires, be regarded as having forfeited rights of communication under the present Convention.

In each case, such persons shall nevertheless be treated with humanity and, in case of trial, shall not be deprived of the rights of fair and regular trial prescribed by the present Convention. They shall also be granted the full rights and privileges of a protected person under the present Convention at the earliest date consistent with the security of the State or Occupying Power, as the case may be.

Article 6

The present Convention shall apply from the outset of any conflict or occupation mentioned in Article 2. In the territory of Parties to the conflict, the application of the present Convention shall cease on the general close of military operations. In the case of occupied territory, the application of the present Convention shall cease one year after the general close of military operations; however, the Occupying Power shall be bound, for the duration of the occupation, to the extent that such Power exercises the functions of government in such territory, by the provisions of the following Articles of the present Convention: 1 to 12, 27, 29 to 34, 47, 49, 51, 52, 53, 59, 61 to 77, 143.

Protected persons whose release, repatriation or re-establishment may take place after such dates shall meanwhile continue to benefit by the present Convention.

Article 7

In addition to the agreements expressly provided for in Articles 11, 14, 15, 17, 36, 108, 109, 132, 133 and 149, the High Contracting Parties may conclude other special agreements for all matters concerning which they may deem it suitable to make separate provision. No special agreement shall adversely affect the situation of protected persons, as defined by the present Convention, not restrict the rights which it confers upon them.

Protected persons shall continue to have the benefit of such agreements as long as the Convention is applicable to them, except where express provisions to the contrary are contained in the aforesaid or in subsequent agreements, or where more favourable measures have been taken with regard to them by one or other of the Parties to the conflict.

Article 8

Protected persons may in no circumstances renounce in part or in entirety the rights secured to them by the present Convention, and by the special agreements referred to in the foregoing Article, if such there be.

Article 9

The present Convention shall be applied with the cooperation and under the scrutiny of the Protecting Powers whose duty it is to safeguard the interests of the Parties to the conflict. For this purpose, the Protecting Powers may appoint, apart from their diplomatic or consular staff, delegates from amongst their own nationals or the nationals of other neutral Powers. The said delegates shall be subject to the approval of the Power with which they are to carry out their duties. The Parties to the conflict shall facilitate to the greatest extent possible the task of the representatives or delegates of the Protecting Powers. The representatives or delegates of the Protecting Powers shall not in any case exceed their mission under the present Convention. They shall, in particular, take account of the imperative necessities of security of the State wherein they carry out their duties.

Article 10

The provisions of the present Convention constitute no obstacle to the humanitarian activities which the International Committee of the Red Cross or any other impartial humanitarian organization may, subject to the consent of the Parties to the conflict concerned, undertake for the protection of civilian persons and for their relief.

Article 11

The High Contracting Parties may at any time agree to entrust to an international organization which offers all guarantees of impartiality and efficacy the duties incumbent on the Protecting Powers by virtue of the present Convention. When persons protected by the present Convention do not benefit or cease to benefit, no matter for what reason, by the activities of a Protecting Power or of an organization provided for in the first paragraph above, the Detaining Power shall request a neutral State, or such an organization, to undertake the functions performed under the present Convention by a Protecting Power designated by the Parties to a conflict.

If protection cannot be arranged accordingly, the Detaining Power shall request or shall accept, subject to the provisions of this Article, the offer of the services of a humanitarian organization, such as the International Committee of the Red Cross, to assume the humanitarian functions performed by Protecting Powers under the present Convention. Any neutral Power or any organization invited by the Power concerned or offering itself for these purposes, shall be required to act with a sense of responsibility towards the Party to the conflict on which persons protected by the present Convention depend, and shall be required to furnish sufficient assurances that it is in a position to undertake the appropriate functions and to discharge them impartially.

No derogation from the preceding provisions shall be made by special agreements between Powers one of which is restricted, even temporarily, in its freedom to negotiate with the other Power or its allies by reason of military events, more particularly where the whole, or a substantial part, of the territory of the said Power is occupied.

Whenever in the present Convention mention is made of a Protecting Power, such mention applies to substitute organizations in the sense of the present Article. The provisions of this Article shall extend and be adapted to cases of nationals of a neutral State who are in occupied territory or who find themselves in the territory of a belligerent State in which the State of which they are nationals has not normal diplomatic representation.

Article 12

In cases where they deem it advisable in the interest of protected persons, particularly in cases of disagreement between the Parties to the conflict as to the application or interpretation of the provisions of the present Convention, the Protecting Powers shall lend their good offices with a view to settling the disagreement.

For this purpose, each of the Protecting Powers may, either at the invitation of one Party or on its own initiative, propose to the Parties to the conflict a meeting of their representatives, and in particular of the authorities responsible for protected persons, possibly on neutral territory suitably chosen. The Parties to the conflict shall be bound to give effect to the proposals made to them for this purpose. The Protecting Powers may, if necessary, propose for approval by the Parties to the conflict a person belonging to a neutral Power, or delegated by the International Committee of the Red Cross, who shall be invited to take part in such a meeting.

Part II. General Protection of Populations against Certain Consequences of War

Article 13

The provisions of Part II cover the whole of the populations of the countries in conflict, without any adverse distinction based, in particular, on race, nationality, religion or political opinion, and are intended to alleviate the sufferings caused by war.

Article 14

In time of peace, the High Contracting Parties and, after the outbreak of hostilities, the Parties thereto, may establish in their own territory and, if the need arises, in occupied areas, hospital and safety zones and localities so organized as to protect from the effects of war, wounded, sick and aged persons, children under fifteen, expectant mothers and mothers of children under seven.
Upon the outbreak and during the course of hostilities, the Parties concerned may conclude agreements on mutual recognition of the zones and localities they have created. They may for this purpose implement the provisions of the Draft Agreement annexed to the present Convention, with such amendments as they may consider necessary.

The Protecting Powers and the International Committee of the Red Cross are invited to lend their good offices in order to facilitate the institution and recognition of these hospital and safety zones and localities.

Article 15

Any Party to the conflict may, either direct or through a neutral State or some humanitarian organization, propose to the adverse Party to establish, in the regions where fighting is taking place, neutralized zones intended to shelter from the effects of war the following persons, without distinction: (a) wounded and sick combatants or non-combatants; (b) civilian persons who take no part in hostilities, and who, while they reside in the zones, perform no work of a military character.

When the Parties concerned have agreed upon the geographical position, administration, food supply and supervision of the proposed neutralized zone, a written agreement shall be concluded and signed by the representatives of the Parties to the conflict. The agreement shall fix the beginning and the duration of the neutralization of the zone.

Article 16

The wounded and sick, as well as the infirm, and expectant mothers, shall be the object of particular protection and respect. As far as military considerations allow, each Party to the conflict shall facilitate the steps taken to search for the killed and wounded, to assist the shipwrecked and other persons exposed to grave danger, and to protect them against pillage and ill-treatment.

Article 17

The Parties to the conflict shall endeavour to conclude local agreements for the removal from besieged or encircled areas, of wounded, sick, infirm, and aged persons, children and maternity cases, and for the passage of ministers of all religions, medical personnel and medical equipment on their way to such areas.
Art. 18. Civilian hospitals organized to give care to the wounded and sick, the infirm and maternity cases, may in no circumstances be the object of attack but shall at all times be respected and protected by the Parties to the conflict. States which are Parties to a conflict shall provide all civilian hospitals with certificates showing that they are civilian hospitals and that the buildings which they occupy are not used for any purpose which would deprive these hospitals of protection in accordance with Article 19. Civilian hospitals shall be marked by means of the emblem provided for in Article 38 of the Geneva Convention for the Amelioration of the Condition of the Wounded and Sick in Armed Forces in the Field of 12 August 1949, but only if so authorized by the State.

The Parties to the conflict shall, in so far as military considerations permit, take the necessary steps to make the distinctive emblems indicating civilian hospitals clearly visible to the enemy land, air and naval forces in order to obviate the possibility of any hostile action. In view of the dangers to which hospitals may be exposed by being close to military objectives, it is recommended that such hospitals be situated as far as possible from such objectives.

Article 19

The protection to which civilian hospitals are entitled shall not cease unless they are used to commit, outside their humanitarian duties, acts harmful to the enemy. Protection may, however, cease only after due warning has been given, naming, in all appropriate cases, a reasonable time limit and after such warning has remained unheeded. The fact that sick or wounded members of the armed forces are nursed in these hospitals, or the presence of small arms and ammunition taken from such combatants which have not yet been handed to the proper service, shall not be considered to be acts harmful to the enemy.

Article 20

Persons regularly and solely engaged in the operation and administration of civilian hospitals, including the personnel engaged in the search for, removal and transporting of and caring for wounded and sick civilians, the infirm and maternity cases shall be respected and protected. In occupied territory and in zones of military operations, the above personnel shall be recognizable by means of an identity card certifying their status, bearing the photograph of the holder and embossed with the stamp of the responsible authority, and also by means of a stamped, water-resistant armlet which they shall wear on the left arm while carrying out their duties. This armlet shall be issued by the State and shall bear the emblem provided for in Article 38 of the Geneva Convention for the Amelioration of the Condition of the Wounded and Sick in Armed Forces in the Field of 12 August 1949.

Other personnel who are engaged in the operation and administration of civilian hospitals shall be entitled to respect and protection and to wear the armlet, as provided in and under the conditions prescribed in this Article, while they are employed on such duties. The identity card shall state the duties on which they are employed. The management of each hospital shall at all times hold at the disposal of the competent national or occupying authorities an up-to-date list of such personnel.

Article 21

Convoys of vehicles or hospital trains on land or specially provided vessels on sea, conveying wounded and sick civilians, the infirm and maternity cases, shall be respected and protected in the same manner as the hospitals provided for in Article 18, and shall be marked, with the consent of the State, by the display of the distinctive emblem provided for in Article 38 of the Geneva Convention for the Amelioration of the Condition of the Wounded and Sick in Armed Forces in the Field of 12 August 1949.

Article 22

Aircraft exclusively employed for the removal of wounded and sick civilians, the infirm and maternity cases or for the transport of medical personnel and equipment, shall not be attacked, but shall be respected while flying at heights, times and on routes specifically agreed upon between all the Parties to the conflict concerned.

They may be marked with the distinctive emblem provided for in Article 38 of the Geneva Convention for the Amelioration of the Condition of the Wounded and Sick in Armed Forces in the Field of 12 August 1949. Unless agreed otherwise, flights over enemy or enemy occupied territory are prohibited. Such aircraft shall obey every summons to land. In the event of a landing thus imposed, the aircraft with its occupants may continue its flight after examination, if any.

Article 23

Each High Contracting Party shall allow the free passage of all consignments of medical and hospital stores and objects necessary for religious worship intended only for civilians of another High Contracting Party, even if the latter is its adversary. It shall likewise permit the free passage of all consignments of essential foodstuffs, clothing and tonics intended for children under fifteen, expectant mothers and maternity cases.

The obligation of a High Contracting Party to allow the free passage of the consignments indicated in the preceding paragraph is subject to the condition that this Party is satisfied that there are no serious reasons for fearing: (a) that the consignments may be diverted from their destination, (b) that the control may not be effective, or (c) that a definite advantage may accrue to the military efforts or economy of the enemy through the substitution of the above-mentioned consignments for goods which would otherwise be provided or produced by the enemy or through the release of such material, services or facilities as would otherwise be required for the production of such goods. The Power which allows the passage of the consignments indicated in the first paragraph of this Article may make such permission conditional on the distribution to the persons benefited thereby being made under the local supervision of the Protecting Powers.

Such consignments shall be forwarded as rapidly as possible, and the Power which permits their free passage shall have the right to prescribe the technical arrangements under which such passage is allowed.

Article 24

The Parties to the conflict shall take the necessary measures to ensure that children under fifteen, who are orphaned or are separated from their families as a result of the war, are not left to their own resources, and that their maintenance, the exercise of their religion and their education are facilitated in all circumstances. Their education shall, as far as possible, be entrusted to persons of a similar cultural tradition. The Parties to the conflict shall facilitate the reception of such children in a neutral country for the duration of the conflict with the consent of the Protecting Power, if any, and under due safeguards for the observance of the principles stated in the first paragraph. They shall, furthermore, endeavour to arrange for all children under twelve to be identified by the wearing of identity discs, or by some other means.

Article 25

All persons in the territory of a Party to the conflict, or in a territory occupied by it, shall be enabled to give news of a strictly personal nature to members of their families, wherever they may be, and to receive news from them. This correspondence shall be forwarded speedily and without undue delay. If, as a result of circumstances, it becomes difficult or impossible to exchange family correspondence by the ordinary post, the Parties to the conflict concerned shall apply to a neutral intermediary, such as the Central Agency provided for in Article 140, and shall decide in consultation with it how to ensure the fulfilment of their obligations under the best possible conditions, in particular with the cooperation of the National Red Cross (Red Crescent, Red Lion and Sun) Societies.

If the Parties to the conflict deem it necessary to restrict family correspondence, such restrictions shall be confined to the compulsory use of standard forms containing twenty-five freely chosen words, and to the limitation of the number of these forms despatched to one each month.

Article 26

Each Party to the conflict shall facilitate enquiries made by members of families dispersed owing to the war, with the object of renewing contact with one another and of meeting, if possible. It shall encourage, in particular, the work of organizations engaged on this task provided they are acceptable to it and conform to its security regulations.

Part III. Status and Treatment of Protected Persons

Section I. Provisions Common to the Territories of the Parties to the Conflict and to Occupied Territories

Article 27

Protected persons are entitled, in all circumstances, to respect for their persons, their honour, their family rights, their religious convictions and practices, and their manners and customs. They shall at all times be humanely treated, and shall be protected especially against all acts of violence or threats thereof and against insults and public curiosity. Women shall be especially protected against any attack on their honour, in particular against rape, enforced prostitutiOn, or any form of indecent assault.

Without prejudice to the provisions relating to their state of health, age and sex, all protected persons shall be treated with the same consideration by the Party to the conflict in whose power they are, without any adverse distinction based, in particular, on race, religion or political opinion. However, the Parties to the conflict may take such measures of control and security in regard to protected persons as may be necessary as a result of the war.

Article 28

The presence of a protected person may not be used to render certain points or areas immune from military operations.

Article 29

The Party to the conflict in whose hands protected persons may be, is responsible for the treatment accorded to them by its agents, irrespective of any individual responsibility which may be incurred.

Article 30

Protected persons shall have every facility for making application to the Protecting Powers, the International Committee of the Red Cross, the National Red Cross (Red Crescent, Red Lion and Sun) Society of the country where they may be, as well as to any organization that might assist them. These several organizations shall be granted all facilities for that purpose by the authorities, within the bounds set by military or security considerations. Apart from the visits of the delegates of the Protecting Powers and of the International Committee of the Red Cross, provided for by Article 143, the Detaining or

Occupying Powers shall facilitate, as much as possible, visits to protected persons by the representatives of other organizations whose object is to give spiritual aid or material relief to such persons.

Article 31

No physical or moral coercion shall be exercised against protected persons, in particular to obtain information from them or from third parties.

Article 32

The High Contracting Parties specifically agree that each of them is prohibited from taking any measure of such a character as to cause the physical suffering or extermination of protected persons in their hands. This prohibition applies not only to murder, torture, corporal punishments, mutilation and medical or scientific experiments not necessitated by the medical treatment of a protected person, but also to any other measures of brutality whether applied by civilian or military agents.

Article 33

No protected person may be punished for an offence he or she has not personally committed. Collective penalties and likewise all measures of intimidation or of terrorism are prohibited. Pillage is prohibited. Reprisals against protected persons and their property are prohibited.

Article 34

The taking of hostages is prohibited.

Section II. Aliens in the Territory of a Party to the Conflict

Article 35

All protected persons who may desire to leave the territory at the outset of, or during a conflict, shall be entitled to do so, unless their departure is contrary to the national interests of the State. The applications of such persons to leave shall be decided in accordance with regularly established procedures and the decision shall be taken as rapidly as possible. Those persons permitted to leave may provide themselves with the necessary funds for their journey and take with them a reasonable amount of their effects and articles of personal use. If any such person is refused permission to leave the territory, he shall be entitled to have refusal reconsidered, as soon as possible by an appropriate court or administrative board designated by the Detaining Power for that purpose. Upon request, representatives of the Protecting Power shall, unless reasons of security prevent it, or the persons concerned object, be furnished with the reasons for refusal of any request for permission to leave the territory and be given, as expeditiously as possible, the names of all persons who have been denied permission to leave.

Article 36

Departures permitted under the foregoing Article shall be carried out in satisfactory conditions as regards safety, hygiene, sanitation and food. All costs in connection therewith, from the point of exit in the territory of the Detaining Power, shall be borne by the country of destination, or, in the case of accommodation in a neutral country, by the Power whose nationals are benefited. The practical details of such movements may, if necessary, be settled by special agreements between the Powers concerned. The foregoing shall not prejudice such special agreements as may be concluded between Parties to the conflict concerning the exchange and repatriation of their nationals in enemy hands.

Article 37

Protected persons who are confined pending proceedings or subject to a sentence involving loss of liberty, shall during their confinement be humanely treated. As soon as they are released, they may ask to leave the territory in conformity with the foregoing Articles.

Article 38

With the exception of special measures authorized by the present Convention, in particularly by Article 27 and 41 thereof, the situation of protected persons shall continue to be regulated, in principle, by the provisions concerning aliens in time of peace. In any case, the following rights shall be granted to them: (1) they shall be enabled to receive the individual or collective relief that may be sent to them. (2) they shall, if their state of health so requires, receive medical attention and hospital treatment to the same extent as the nationals of the State concerned. (3) they shall be allowed to practise their religion and to receive spiritual assistance from ministers of their faith. (4) if they reside in an area particularly exposed to the dangers of war, they shall be authorized to move from that area to the same extent as the nationals of the State concerned. (5) children under fifteen years, pregnant women and mothers of children under seven years shall benefit by any preferential treatment to the same extent as the nationals of the State concerned.

Article 39

Protected persons who, as a result of the war, have lost their gainful employment, shall be granted the opportunity to find paid employment. That opportunity shall, subject to security considerations and to the provisions of Article 40, be equal to that enjoyed by the nationals of the Power in whose territory they are. Where a Party to the conflict applies to a protected person methods of control which result in his being unable to support himself, and especially if such a person is prevented for reasons of security from finding paid employment on reasonable conditions, the said Party shall ensure his support and that of his dependents. Protected persons may in any case receive allowances from their home country, the Protecting Power, or the relief societies referred to in Article 30.

Article 40

Protected persons may be compelled to work only to the same extent as nationals of the Party to the conflict in whose territory they are. If protected persons are of enemy nationality, they may only be compelled to do work which is normally necessary to ensure the feeding, sheltering, clothing, transport and health of human beings and which is not directly related to the conduct of military operations. In the cases mentioned in the two preceding paragraphs, protected persons compelled to work shall have the benefit of the same working conditions and of the same safeguards as national workers in particular as regards wages, hours of labour, clothing and equipment, previous training and compensation for occupational accidents and diseases. If the above provisions are infringed, protected persons shall be allowed to exercise their right of complaint in accordance with Article 30.

Article 41

Should the Power, in whose hands protected persons may be, consider the measures of control mentioned in the present Convention to be inadequate, it may not have recourse to any other measure of control more severe than that of assigned residence or internment, in accordance with the provisions of Articles 42 and 43. In applying the provisions of Article 39, second paragraph, to the cases of persons required to leave their usual places of residence by virtue of a decision placing them in assigned residence, by virtue of a decision placing them in assigned residence, elsewhere, the Detaining Power shall be guided as closely as possible by the standards of welfare set forth in Part III, Section IV of this Convention.

Article 42

The internment or placing in assigned residence of protected persons may be ordered only if the security of the Detaining Power makes it absolutely necessary. If any person, acting through the representatives of the Protecting Power, voluntarily demands internment, and if his situation renders this step necessary, he shall be interned by the Power in whose hands he may be.

Article 43

Any protected person who has been interned or placed in assigned residence shall be entitled to have such action reconsidered as soon as possible by an appropriate court or administrative board designated by the Detaining Power for that purpose. If the internment or placing in assigned residence is maintained, the court or administrative board shall periodically, and at least twice yearly, give consideration to his or her case, with a view to the favourable amendment of the initial decision, if circumstances permit. Unless the protected persons concerned object, the Detaining Power shall, as rapidly as possible, give the Protecting Power the names of any protected persons who have been interned or subjected to assigned residence, or who have been released from internment or assigned residence. The decisions of the courts or boards mentioned in the first paragraph of the present Article shall also, subject to the same conditions, be notified as rapidly as possible to the Protecting Power.

Article 44

In applying the measures of control mentioned in the present Convention, the Detaining Power shall not treat as enemy aliens exclusively on the basis of their nationality de jure of an enemy State, refugees who do not, in fact, enjoy the protection of any government.

Article 45

Protected persons shall not be transferred to a Power which is not a party to the Convention. This provision shall in no way constitute an obstacle to the repatriation of protected persons, or to their return to their country of residence after the cessation of hostilities.

Protected persons may be transferred by the Detaining Power only to a Power which is a party to the present Convention and after the Detaining Power has satisfied itself of the willingness and ability of such transferee Power to apply the present Convention. If protected persons are transferred under such circumstances, responsibility for the application of the present Convention rests on the Power accepting them, while they are in its custody. Nevertheless, if that Power fails to carry out the provisions of the present Convention in any important respect, the Power by which the protected persons were transferred shall, upon being so notified by the Protecting Power, take effective measures to correct the situation or shall request the return of the protected persons. Such request must be complied with.

In no circumstances shall a protected person be transferred to a country where he or she may have reason to fear persecution for his or her political opinions or religious beliefs.

The provisions of this Article do not constitute an obstacle to the extradition, in pursuance of extradition treaties concluded before the outbreak of hostilities, of protected persons accused of offences against ordinary criminal law.

Article 46

In so far as they have not been previously withdrawn, restrictive measures taken regarding protected persons shall be cancelled as soon as possible after the close of hostilities. Restrictive measures affecting their property shall be cancelled, in accordance with the law of the Detaining Power, as soon as possible after the close of hostilities.

Section III. Occupied Territories

Article 47

Protected persons who are in occupied territory shall not be deprived, in any case or in any manner whatsoever, of the benefits of the present Convention by any change introduced, as the result of the occupation of a territory, into the institutions or government of the said territory, nor by any agreement concluded between the authorities of the occupied territories and the Occupying Power, nor by any annexation by the latter of the whole or part of the occupied territory.

Article 48

Protected persons who are not nationals of the Power whose territory is occupied, may avail themselves of the right to leave the territory subject to the provisions of Article 35, and decisions thereon shall be taken in accordance with the procedure which the Occupying Power shall establish in accordance with the said Article.

Article 49

Individual or mass forcible transfers, as well as deportations of protected persons from occupied territory to the territory of the Occupying Power or to that of any other country, occupied or not, are prohibited, regardless of their motive. Nevertheless, the Occupying Power may undertake total or partial evacuation of a given area if the security of the population or imperative military reasons so demand. Such evacuations may not involve the displacement of protected persons outside the bounds of the occupied territory except when for material reasons it is impossible to avoid such displacement. Persons thus evacuated shall be transferred back to their homes as soon as hostilities in the area in question have ceased.

The Occupying Power undertaking such transfers or evacuations shall ensure, to the greatest practicable extent, that proper accommodation is provided to receive the protected persons, that the removals are effected in satisfactory conditions of hygiene, health, safety and nutrition, and that members of the same family are not separated. The Protecting Power shall be informed of any transfers and evacuations as soon as they have taken place. The Occupying Power shall not detain protected persons in an area particularly exposed to the dangers of war unless the security of the population or imperative military reasons so demand.
The Occupying Power shall not deport or transfer parts of its own civilian population into the territory it occupies.

Article 50

The Occupying Power shall, with the cooperation of the national and local authorities, facilitate the proper working of all institutions devoted to the care and education of children. The Occupying Power shall take all necessary steps to facilitate the identification of children and the registration of their parentage. It may not, in any case, change their personal status, nor enlist them in formations or organizations subordinate to it. Should the local institutions be inadequate for the purpose, the Occupying Power shall make arrangements for the maintenance and education, if possible by persons of their own nationality, language and religion, of children who are orphaned or separated from their parents as a result of the war and who cannot be adequately cared for by a near relative or friend. A special section of the Bureau set up in accordance with Article 136 shall be responsible for taking all necessary steps to identify children whose identity is in doubt. Particulars of their parents or other near relatives should always be recorded if available. The Occupying Power shall not hinder the application of any preferential measures in regard to food, medical care and protection against the effects of war which may have been adopted prior to the occupation in favour of children under fifteen years, expectant mothers, and mothers of children under seven years.

Article 51

The Occupying Power may not compel protected persons to serve in its armed or auxiliary forces. No pressure or propaganda which aims at securing voluntary enlistment is permitted. The Occupying Power may not compel protected persons to work unless they are over eighteen years of age, and then only on work which is necessary either for the needs of the army of occupation, or for the public utility services, or for the feeding, sheltering, clothing, transportation or health of the population of the occupied country. Protected persons may not be compelled to undertake any work which would involve them in the obligation of taking part in military operations. The Occupying Power may not compel protected persons to employ forcible means to ensure the security of the installations where they are performing compulsory labour.

The work shall be carried out only in the occupied territory where the persons whose services have been requisitioned are. Every such person shall, so far as possible, be kept in his usual place of employment. Workers shall be paid a fair wage and the work shall be proportionate to their physical and intellectual capacities. The legislation in force in the occupied country concerning working conditions, and safeguards as regards, in particular, such matters as wages, hours of work, equipment, preliminary training and compensation for occupational accidents and diseases, shall be applicable to the protected persons assigned to the work referred to in this Article. In no case shall requisition of labour lead to a mobilization of workers in an organization of a military or semi-military character.

Article 52

No contract, agreement or regulation shall impair the right of any worker, whether voluntary or not and wherever he may be, to apply to the representatives of the Protecting Power in order to request the said Power's intervention. All measures aiming at creating unemployment or at restricting the opportunities offered to workers in an occupied territory, in order to induce them to work for the Occupying Power, are prohibited.

Article 53

Any destruction by the Occupying Power of real or personal property belonging individually or collectively to private persons, or to the State, or to other public authorities, or to social or cooperative organizations, is prohibited, except where such destruction is rendered absolutely necessary by military operations.

Article 54

The Occupying Power may not alter the status of public officials or judges in the occupied territories, or in any way apply sanctions to or take any measures of coercion or discrimination against them, should they abstain from fulfilling their functions for reasons of conscience. This prohibition does not prejudice the application of the second paragraph of Article 51. It does not affect the right of the Occupying Power to remove public officials from their posts.

Article 55

To the fullest extent of the means available to it, the Occupying Power has the duty of ensuring the food and medical supplies of the population; it should, in particular, bring in the necessary foodstuffs, medical stores and other articles if the resources of the occupied territory are inadequate. The Occupying Power may not requisition foodstuffs, articles or medical supplies available in the occupied territory, except for use by the occupation forces and administration personnel, and then only if the requirements of the civilian population have been taken into account. Subject to the provisions of other international Conventions, the Occupying Power shall make arrangements to ensure that fair value is paid for any requisitioned goods. The Protecting Power shall, at any time, be at liberty to verify the state of the food and medical supplies in occupied territories, except where temporary restrictions are made necessary by imperative military requirements.

Article 56

To the fullest extent of the means available to it, the public Occupying Power has the duty of ensuring and maintaining, with the cooperation of national and local authorities, the medical and hospital establishments and services, public health and hygiene in the occupied territory, with particular reference to the adoption and application of the prophylactic and preventive measures necessary to combat the spread of contagious diseases and epidemics. Medical personnel of all categories shall be allowed to carry out their duties.

If new hospitals are set up in occupied territory and if the competent organs of the occupied State are not operating there, the occupying authorities shall, if necessary, grant them the recognition provided for in Article 18. In similar circumstances, the occupying authorities shall also grant recognition to hospital personnel and transport vehicles under the provisions of Articles 20 and 21. In adopting measures of health and hygiene and in their implementation, the Occupying Power shall take into consideration the moral and ethical susceptibilities of the population of the occupied territory.

Article 57

The Occupying Power may requisition civilian hospitals of hospitals only temporarily and only in cases of urgent necessity for the care of military wounded and sick, and then on condition that suitable arrangements are made in due time for the care and treatment of the patients and for the needs of the civilian population for hospital accommodation. The material and stores of civilian hospitals cannot be requisitioned so long as they are necessary for the needs of the civilian population.

Article 58

The Occupying Power shall permit ministers of religion to give spiritual assistance to the members of their religious communities. The Occupying Power shall also accept consignments of books and articles required for religious needs and shall facilitate their distribution in occupied territory.

Article 59

If the whole or part of the population of an occupied territory is inadequately supplied, the Occupying Power shall agree to relief schemes on behalf of the said population, and shall facilitate them by all the means at its disposal. Such schemes, which may be undertaken either by States or by impartial humanitarian organizations such as the International Committee of the Red Cross, shall consist, in particular, of the provision of consignments of foodstuffs, medical supplies and clothing. All Contracting Parties shall permit the free passage of these consignments and shall guarantee their protection. A Power granting free passage to consignments on their way to territory occupied by an adverse Party to the conflict shall, however, have the right to search the consignments, to regulate their passage according to prescribed times and routes, and to be reasonably satisfied through the Protecting Power that these consignments are to be used for the relief of the needy population and are not to be used for the benefit of the Occupying Power.

Article 60

Relief consignments shall in no way relieve the Occupying Power of any of its responsibilities under Articles 55, 56 and 59. The Occupying Power shall in no way whatsoever divert relief consignments from the purpose for which they are intended, except in cases of urgent necessity, in the interests of the population of the occupied territory and with the consent of the Protecting Power.

Article 61

The distribution of the relief consignments referred to in the foregoing Articles shall be carried out with the cooperation and under the supervision of the Protecting Power. This duty may also be delegated, by agreement between the Occupying Power and the Protecting Power, to a neutral Power, to the International Committee of the Red Cross or to any other impartial humanitarian body. Such consignments shall be exempt in occupied territory from all charges, taxes or customs duties unless these are necessary in the interests of the economy of the territory. The Occupying Power shall facilitate the rapid distribution of these consignments. All Contracting Parties shall endeavour to permit the transit and transport, free of charge, of such relief consignments on their way to occupied territories.

Article 62

Subject to imperative reasons of security, protected persons in occupied territories shall be permitted to receive the individual relief consignments sent to them.

Article 63

Subject to temporary and exceptional measures imposed for urgent reasons of security by the Occupying Power:

(a) recognized National Red Cross (Red Crescent, Red Lion and Sun) Societies shall be able to pursue their activities in accordance with Red Cross principles, as defined by the International Red Cross Conferences. Other relief societies shall be permitted to continue their humanitarian activities under similar conditions;

(b) the Occupying Power may not require any changes in the personnel or structure of these societies, which would prejudice the aforesaid activities.

The same principles shall apply to the activities and personnel of special organizations of a non-military character, which already exist or which may be established, for the purpose of ensuring the living conditions of the civilian population by the maintenance of the essential public utility services, by the distribution of relief and by the organization of rescues.

Article 64

The penal laws of the occupied territory shall remain in force, with the exception that they may be repealed or suspended by the Occupying Power in cases where they constitute a threat to its security or an obstacle to the application of the present Convention. Subject to the latter consideration and to the necessity for ensuring the effective administration of justice, the tribunals of the occupied territory shall continue to function in respect of all offences covered by the said laws.

The Occupying Power may, however, subject the population of the occupied territory to provisions which are essential to enable the Occupying Power to fulfil its obligations under the present Convention, to maintain the orderly government of the territory, and to ensure the security of the Occupying Power, of the members and property of the occupying forces or administration, and likewise of the establishments and lines of communication used by them.

Article 65

The penal provisions enacted by the Occupying Power shall not come into force before they have been published and brought to the knowledge of the inhabitants in their own language. The effect of these penal provisions shall not be retroactive.

Article 66

In case of a breach of the penal provisions promulgated by it by virtue of the second paragraph of Article 64 the Occupying Power may hand over the accused to its properly constituted, non-political military courts, on condition that the said courts sit in the occupied country. Courts of appeal shall preferably sit in the occupied country.

Article 67

The courts shall apply only those provisions of law which were applicable prior to the offence, and which are in accordance with general principles of law, in particular the principle that the penalty shall be proportionate to the offence. They shall take into consideration the fact the accused is not a national of the Occupying Power.

Article 68

Protected persons who commit an offence which is solely intended to harm the Occupying Power, but which does not constitute an attempt on the life or limb of members of the occupying forces or administration, nor a grave collective danger, nor seriously damage the property of the occupying forces or administration or the installations used by them, shall be liable to internment or simple imprisonment, provided the duration of such internment or imprisonment is proportionate to the offence committed. Furthermore, internment or imprisonment shall, for such offences, be the only measure adopted for depriving protected persons of liberty. The courts provided for under Article 66 of the present Convention may at their discretion convert a sentence of imprisonment to one of internment for the same period.

The penal provisions promulgated by the Occupying Power in accordance with Articles 64 and 65 may impose the death penalty on a protected person only in cases where the person is guilty of espionage, of serious acts of sabotage against the military installations of the Occupying Power or of intentional offences which have caused the death of one or more persons, provided that such offences were punishable by death under the law of the occupied territory in force before the occupation began. The death penalty may not be pronounced on a protected person unless the attention of the court has been particularly called to the fact that since the accused is not a national of the Occupying Power, he is not bound to it by any duty of allegiance. In any case, the death penalty may not be pronounced on a protected person who was under eighteen years of age at the time of the offence.

Article 69

In all cases the duration of the period during which a protected person accused of an offence is under arrest awaiting trial or punishment shall be deducted from any period of imprisonment of awarded.

Article 70

Protected persons shall not be arrested, prosecuted or convicted by the Occupying Power for acts committed or for opinions expressed before the occupation, or during a temporary interruption thereof, with the exception of breaches of the laws and customs of war. Nationals of the occupying Power who, before the outbreak of hostilities, have sought refuge in the territory of the occupied State, shall not be arrested, prosecuted, convicted or deported from the occupied territory, except for offences committed after the outbreak of hostilities, or for offences under common law committed before the outbreak of hostilities which, according to the law of the occupied State, would have justified extradition in time of peace.

Article 71

No sentence shall be pronounced by the competent courts of the Occupying Power except after a regular trial. Accused persons who are prosecuted by the Occupying Power shall be promptly informed, in writing, in a language which they understand, of the particulars of the charges preferred against them, and shall be brought to trial as rapidly as possible. The Protecting Power shall be informed of all proceedings instituted by the Occupying Power against protected persons in respect of charges involving the death penalty or imprisonment for two years or more; it shall be enabled, at any time, to obtain information regarding the state of such proceedings. Furthermore, the Protecting Power shall be entitled, on request, to be furnished with all particulars of these and of any other proceedings instituted by the Occupying Power against protected persons.
The notification to the Protecting Power, as provided for in the second paragraph above, shall be sent immediately, and shall in any case reach the Protecting Power three weeks before the date of the first hearing. Unless, at the opening of the trial, evidence is submitted that the provisions of this Article are fully complied with, the trial shall not proceed. The notification shall include the following particulars: (a) description of the accused; (b) place of residence or detention; (c) specification of the charge or charges (with mention of the penal provisions under which it is brought); (d) designation of the court which will hear the case; (e) place and date of the first hearing.

Article 72

Accused persons shall have the right to present evidence necessary to their defence and may, in particular, call witnesses. They shall have the right to be assisted by a qualified advocate or counsel of their own choice, who shall be able to visit them freely and shall enjoy the necessary facilities for preparing the defence. Failing a choice by the accused, the Protecting Power may provide him with an advocate or counsel. When an accused person has to meet a serious charge and the Protecting Power is not functioning, the Occupying Power, subject to the consent of the accused, shall provide an advocate or counsel. Accused persons shall, unless they freely waive such assistance, be aided by an interpreter, both during preliminary investigation and during the hearing in court. They shall have at any time the right to object to the interpreter and to ask for his replacement.

Article 73

A convicted person shall have the right of appeal provided for by the laws applied by the court. He shall be fully informed of his right to appeal or petition and of the time limit within which he may do so. The penal procedure provided in the present Section shall apply, as far as it is applicable, to appeals. Where the laws applied by the Court make no provision for appeals, the convicted person shall have the right to petition against the finding and sentence to the competent authority of the Occupying Power.

Article 74

Representatives of the Protecting Power shall have the right to attend the trial of any protected person, unless the hearing has, as an exceptional measure, to be held in camera in the interests of the security of the Occupying Power, which shall then notify the Protecting Power. A notification in respect of the date and place of trial shall be sent to the Protecting Power. Any judgement involving a sentence of death, or imprisonment for two years or more, shall be communicated, with the relevant grounds, as rapidly as possible to the Protecting Power. The notification shall contain a reference to the notification made under Article 71 and, in the case of sentences of imprisonment, the name of the place where the sentence is to be served. A record of judgements other than those referred to above shall be kept by the court and shall be open to inspection by representatives of the Protecting Power. Any period allowed for appeal in the case of sentences involving the death penalty, or imprisonment of two years or more, shall not run until notification of judgement has been received by the Protecting Power.

Article 75

In no case shall persons condemned to death be deprived of the right of petition for pardon or reprieve. No death sentence shall be carried out before the expiration of a period of a least six months from the date of receipt by the Protecting Power of the notification of the final judgment confirming such death sentence, or of an order denying pardon or reprieve. The six months period of suspension of the death sentence herein prescribed may be reduced in individual cases in circumstances of grave emergency involving an organized threat to the security of the Occupying Power or its forces, provided always that the Protecting Power is notified of such reduction and is given reasonable time and opportunity to make representations to the competent occupying authorities in respect of such death sentences.

Article 76

Protected persons accused of offences shall be detained in the occupied country, and if convicted they shall serve their sentences therein. They shall, if possible, be separated from other detainees and shall enjoy conditions of food and hygiene which will be sufficient to keep them in good health, and which will be at least equal to those obtaining in prisons in the occupied country. They shall receive the medical attention required by their state of health. They shall also have the right to receive any spiritual assistance which they may require. Women shall be confined in separate quarters and shall be under the direct supervision of women. Proper regard shall be paid to the special treatment due to minors. Protected persons who are detained shall have the right to be visited by delegates of the Protecting Power and of the International Committee of the Red Cross, in accordance with the provisions of Article 143. Such persons shall have the right to receive at least one relief parcel monthly.

Article77

Protected persons who have been accused of offences or convicted by the courts in occupied territory, shall be handed over at the close of occupation, with the relevant records, to the authorities of the liberated territory.

Article 78

If the Occupying Power considers it necessary, for imperative reasons of security, to take safety measures concerning protected persons, it may, at the most, subject them to assigned residence or to internment. Decisions regarding such assigned residence or internment shall be made according to a regular procedure to be prescribed by the Occupying Power in accordance with the provisions of the present Convention. This procedure shall include the right of appeal for the parties concerned. Appeals shall be decided with the least possible delay. In the event of the decision being upheld, it shall be subject to periodical review, if possible every six months, by a competent body set up by the said Power. Protected persons made subject to assigned residence and thus required to leave their homes shall enjoy the full benefit of Article 39 of the present Convention.

Section IV. Regulations for the Treatment of Internees

Chapter I. General Provisions

Article 79

The Parties to the conflict shall not intern protected persons, except in accordance with the provisions of Articles 41, 42, 43, 68 and 78.

Article 80

Internees shall retain their full civil capacity and shall exercise such attendant rights as may be compatible with their status.

Article 81

Parties to the conflict who intern protected persons shall be bound to provide free of charge for their maintenance, and to grant them also the medical attention required by their state of health. No deduction from the allowances, salaries or credits due to the internees shall be made for the repayment of these costs. The Detaining Power shall provide for the support of those dependent on the internees, if such dependents are without adequate means of support or are unable to earn a living.

Article82

The Detaining Power shall, as far as possible, accommodate the internees according to their nationality, language and customs. Internees who are nationals of the same country shall not be separated merely because they have different languages. Throughout the duration of their internment, members of the same family, and in particular parents and children, shall be lodged together in the same place of internment, except when separation of a temporary nature is necessitated for reasons of employment or health or for the purposes of enforcement of the provisions of Chapter IX of the present Section. Internees may request that their children who are left at liberty without parental care shall be interned with them. Wherever possible, interned members of the same family shall be housed in the same premises and given separate accommodation from other internees, together with facilities for leading a proper family life.

Chapter II. Places of Internment

Article 83

The Detaining Power shall not set up places of internment in areas particularly exposed to the dangers of war. The Detaining Power shall give the enemy Powers, through the intermediary of the Protecting Powers, all useful information regarding the geographical location of places of internment. Whenever military considerations permit, internment camps shall be indicated by the letters IC, placed so as to be clearly visible in the daytime from the air. The Powers concerned may, however, agree upon any other system of marking. No place other than an internment camp shall be marked as such.

Article 84

Internees shall be accommodated and administered separately from prisoners of war and from persons deprived of liberty for any other reason.

Article 85

The Detaining Power is bound to take all necessary and possible measures to ensure that protected persons shall, from the outset of their internment, be accommodated in buildings or quarters which afford every possible safeguard as regards hygiene and health, and provide efficient protection against the rigours of the climate and the effects of the war. In no case shall permanent places of internment be situated in unhealthy areas or in districts, the climate of which is injurious to the internees. In all cases where the district, in which a protected person is temporarily interned, is an unhealthy area or has a climate which is harmful to his health, he shall be removed to a more suitable place of internment as rapidly as circumstances permit.

The premises shall be fully protected from dampness, adequately heated and lighted, in particular between dusk and lights out. The sleeping quarters shall be sufficiently spacious and well ventilated, and the internees shall have suitable bedding and sufficient blankets, account being taken of the climate, and the age, sex, and state of health of the internees.

Internees shall have for their use, day and night, sanitary conveniences which conform to the rules of hygiene, and are constantly maintained in a state of cleanliness. They shall be provided with sufficient water and soap for their daily personal toilet and for washing their personal laundry; installations and facilities necessary for this purpose shall be granted to them. Showers or baths shall also be available. The necessary time shall be set aside for washing and for cleaning. Whenever it is necessary, as an exceptional and temporary measure, to accommodate women internees who are not members of a family unit in the same place of internment as men, the provision of separate sleeping quarters and sanitary conveniences for the use of such women internees shall be obligatory.

Article 86

The Detaining Power shall place at the disposal of interned persons, of whatever denomination, premises suitable for the holding of their religious services.

Article 87

Canteens shall be installed in every place of internment, except where other suitable facilities are available. Their purpose shall be to enable internees to make purchases, at prices not higher than local market prices, of foodstuffs and articles of everyday use, including soap and tobacco, such as would increase their personal well-being and comfort. Profits made by canteens shall be credited to a welfare fund to be set up for each place of internment, and administered for the benefit of the internees attached to such place of internment. The Internee Committee provided for in Article 102 shall have the right to check the management of the canteen and of the said fund.

When a place of internment is closed down, the balance of the welfare fund shall be transferred to the welfare fund of a place of internment for internees of the same nationality, or, if such a place does not exist, to a central welfare fund which shall be administered for the benefit of all internees remaining in the custody of the Detaining Power. In case of a general release, the said profits shall be kept by the Detaining Power, subject to any agreement to the contrary between the Powers concerned.

Article 88

In all places of internment exposed to air raids and other hazards of war, shelters adequate in number and structure to ensure the necessary protection shall be installed. In case of alarms, the measures internees shall be free to enter such shelters as quickly as possible, excepting those who remain for the protection of their quarters against the aforesaid hazards. Any protective measures taken in favour of the population shall also apply to them. All due precautions must be taken in places of internment against the danger of fire.

Chapter III. Food and Clothing

Article 89

Daily food rations for internees shall be sufficient in quantity, quality and variety to keep internees in a good state of health and prevent the development of nutritional deficiencies. Account shall also be taken of the customary diet of the internees. Internees shall also be given the means by which they can prepare for themselves any additional food in their possession. Sufficient drinking water shall be supplied to internees. The use of tobacco shall be permitted. Internees who work shall receive additional rations in proportion to the kind of labour which they perform. Expectant and nursing mothers and children under fifteen years of age, shall be given additional food, in proportion to their physiological needs.

Article 90

When taken into custody, internees shall be given all facilities to provide themselves with the necessary clothing, footwear and change of underwear, and later on, to procure further supplies if required. Should any internees not have sufficient clothing, account being taken of the climate, and be unable to procure any, it shall be provided free of charge to them by the Detaining Power. The clothing supplied by the Detaining Power to internees and the outward markings placed on their own clothes shall not be ignominious nor expose them to ridicule. Workers shall receive suitable working outfits, including protective clothing, whenever the nature of their work so requires.

Chapter IV. Hygiene and Medical Attention

Article 91

Every place of internment shall have an adequate infirmary, under the direction of a qualified doctor, where internees may have the attention they require, as well as appropriate diet. Isolation wards shall be set aside for cases of contagious or mental diseases. Maternity cases and internees suffering from serious diseases, or whose condition requires special treatment, a surgical operation or hospital care, must be admitted to any institution where adequate treatment can be given and shall receive care not inferior to that provided for the general population. Internees shall, for preference, have the attention of medical personnel of their own nationality. Internees may not be prevented from presenting themselves to the medical authorities for examination. The medical authorities of the Detaining Power shall, upon request, issue to every internee who has undergone treatment an official certificate showing the nature of his illness or injury, and the duration and nature of the treatment given. A duplicate of this certificate shall be forwarded to the Central Agency provided for in Article 140. Treatment, including the provision of any apparatus necessary for the maintenance of internees in good health, particularly dentures and other artificial appliances and spectacles, shall be free of charge to the internee.

Article 92

Medical inspections of internees shall be made at least once a month. Their purpose shall be, in particular, to supervise the general state of health, nutrition and cleanliness of internees, and to detect contagious diseases, especially tuberculosis, malaria, and venereal diseases. Such inspections shall include, in particular, the checking of weight of each internee and, at least once a year, radioscopic examination.

Chapter V. Religious, Intellectual and Physical Activities

Article 93

Internees shall enjoy complete latitude in the exercise of their religious duties, including attendance at the services of their faith, on condition that they comply with the disciplinary routine prescribed by the detaining authorities. Ministers of religion who are interned shall be allowed to minister freely to the members of their community. For this purpose the Detaining Power shall ensure their equitable allocation amongst the various places of internment in which there are internees speaking the same language and belonging to the same religion. Should such ministers be too few in number, the Detaining Power shall provide them with the necessary facilities, including means of transport, for moving from one place to another, and they shall be authorized to visit any internees who are in hospital. Ministers of religion shall be at liberty to correspond on matters concerning their ministry with the religious authorities in the country of detention and, as far as possible, with the international religious organizations of their faith. Such correspondence shall not be considered as forming a part of the quota mentioned in Article 107. It shall, however, be subject to the provisions of Article 112.

When internees do not have at their disposal the assistance of ministers of their faith, or should these latter be too few in number, the local religious authorities of the same faith may appoint, in agreement with the Detaining Power, a minister of the internees' faith or, if such a course is feasible from a denominational point of view, a minister of similar religion or a qualified layman. The latter shall enjoy the facilities granted to the ministry he has assumed. Persons so appointed shall comply with all regulations laid down by the Detaining Power in the interests of discipline and security.

Article 94

The Detaining Power shall encourage intellectual, educational and recreational pursuits, sports and games amongst internees, whilst leaving them free to take part in them or not. It shall take all practicable measures to ensure the exercice thereof, in particular by providing suitable premises. All possible facilities shall be granted to internees to continue their studies or to take up new subjects. The education of children and young people shall be ensured; they shall be allowed to attend schools either within the place of internment or outside. Internees shall be given opportunities for physical exercise, sports and outdoor games. For this purpose, sufficient open spaces shall be set aside in all places of internment. Special playgrounds shall be reserved for children and young people.

Article 95

The Detaining Power shall not employ internees as workers, unless they so desire. Employment which, if undertaken under compulsion by a protected person not in internment, would involve a breach of Articles 40 or 51 of the present Convention, and employment on work which is of a degrading or humiliating character are in any case prohibited. After a working period of six weeks, internees shall be free to give up work at any moment, subject to eight days' notice. These provisions constitute no obstacle to the right of the Detaining Power to employ interned doctors, dentists and other medical personnel in their professional capacity on behalf of their fellow internees, or to employ internees for administrative and maintenance work in places of internment and to detail such persons for work in the kitchens or for other domestic tasks, or to require such persons to undertake duties connected with the protection of internees against aerial bombardment or other war risks. No internee may, however, be required to perform tasks for which he is, in the opinion of a medical officer, physically unsuited.

The Detaining Power shall take entire responsibility for all working conditions, for medical attention, for the payment of wages, and for ensuring that all employed internees receive compensation for occupational accidents and diseases. The standards prescribed for the said working conditions and for compensation shall be in accordance with the national laws and regulations, and with the existing practice; they shall in no case be inferior to those obtaining for work of the same nature in the same district. Wages for work done shall be determined on an equitable basis by special agreements between the internees, the Detaining Power, and, if the case arises, employers other than the Detaining Power to provide for free maintenance of internees and for the medical attention which their state of health may require. Internees permanently detailed for categories of work mentioned in the third paragraph of this Article, shall be paid fair wages by the Detaining Power. The working conditions and the scale of compensation for occupational accidents and diseases to internees, thus detailed, shall not be inferior to those applicable to work of the same nature in the same district.

Article 96

All labour detachments shall remain part of and dependent upon a place of internment. The competent authorities of the Detaining Power and the commandant of a place of internment shall be responsible for the observance in a labour detachment of the provisions of the present Convention. The commandant shall keep an up-to-date list of the labour detachments subordinate to him and shall communicate it to the delegates of the Protecting Power, of the International Committee of the Red Cross and of other humanitarian organizations who may visit the places of internment.

Chapter VI. Personal Property and Financial Resources

Article 97

Internees shall be permitted to retain articles of personal use. Monies, cheques, bonds, etc., and valuables in their possession may not be taken from them except in accordance with established procedure. Detailed receipts shall be given therefor. The amounts shall be paid into the account of every internee as provided for in Article 98. Such amounts may not be converted into any other currency unless legislation in force in the territory in which the owner is interned so requires or the internee gives his consent. Articles which have above all a personal or sentimental value may not be taken away. A woman internee shall not be searched except by a woman.

On release or repatriation, internees shall be given all articles, monies or other valuables taken from them during internment and shall receive in currency the balance of any credit to their accounts kept in accordance with Article 98, with the exception of any articles or amounts withheld by the Detaining Power by virtue of its legislation in force. If the property of an internee is so withheld, the owner shall receive a detailed receipt. Family or identity documents in the possession of internees may not be taken away without a receipt being given. At no time shall internees be left without identity documents. If they have none, they shall be issued with special documents drawn up by the detaining authorities, which will serve as their identity papers until the end of their internment. Internees may keep on their persons a certain amount of money, in cash or in the shape of purchase coupons, to enable them to make purchases.

Article 98

All internees shall receive regular allowances, sufficient to enable them to purchase goods and articles, such as tobacco, toilet requisites, etc. Such allowances may take the form of credits or purchase coupons. Furthermore, internees may receive allowances from the Power to which they owe allegiance, the Protecting Powers, the organizations which may assist them, or their families, as well as the income on their property in accordance with the law of the Detaining Power. The amount of allowances granted by the Power to which they o~e allegiance shall be the same for each category of internees (infirm, sick, pregnant women, etc.) but may not be allocated by that Power or distributed by the Detaining Power on the basis of discriminations between internees which are prohibited by Article 27 of the present Convention.

The Detaining Power shall open a regular account for every internee, to which shall be credited the allowances named in the present Article, the wages earned and the remittances received, together with such sums taken from him as may be available under the legislation in force in the territory in which he is interned. Internees shall be granted all facilities consistent with the legislation in force in such territory to make remittances to their families and to other dependants. They may draw from their accounts the amounts necessary for their personal expenses, within the limits fixed by the Detaining Power. They shall at all times be afforded reasonable facilities for consulting and obtaining copies of their accounts. A statement of accounts shall be furnished to the Protecting Power, on request, and shall accompany the internee in case of transfer.

Chapter VII. Administration and Discipline

Article 99

Every place of internment shall be put under the authority of a responsible officer, chosen from the regular military forces or the regular civil administration of the

Detaining Power. The officer in charge of the place of internment must have in his possession a copy of the present Convention in the official language, or one of the official languages, of his country and shall be responsible for its application. The staff in control of internees shall be instructed in the provisions of the present Convention and of the administrative measures adopted to ensure its application.

The text of the present Convention and the texts of special agreements concluded under the said Convention shall be posted inside the place of internment, in a language which the internees understand, or shall be in the possession of the Internee Committee. Regulations, orders, notices and publications of every kind shall be communicated to the internees and posted inside the places of internment, in a language which they understand. Every order and command addressed to internees individually must, likewise, be given in a language which they understand.

Article 100

The disciplinary regime in places of internment shall be consistent with humanitarian principles, and shall in no circumstances include regulations imposing on internees any physical exertion dangerous to their health or involving physical or moral victimization. Identification by tattooing or imprinting signs or markings on the body, is prohibited. In particular, prolonged standing and roll-calls, punishment drill, military drill and manoeuvres, or the reduction of food rations, are prohibited.

Article 101

Internees shall have the right to present to the authorities in whose power they are, any petition with regard to the conditions of internment to which they are subjected. They shall also have the right to apply without restriction through the Internee Committee or, if they consider it necessary, direct to the representatives of the Protecting Power, in order to indicate to them any points on which they may have complaints to make with regard to the conditions of internment. Such petitions and complaints shall be transmitted forthwith and without alteration, and even if the latter are recognized to be unfounded, they may not occasion any punishment. Periodic reports on the situation in places of internment and as to the needs of the internees may be sent by the Internee Committees to the representatives of the Protecting Powers.

Article 102

In every place of internment, the internees shall freely elect by secret ballot every six months, the members of a Committee empowered to represent them before the Detaining and the Protecting Powers, the International Committee of the Red Cross and any other organization which may assist them. The members of the Committee shall be eligible for re-election. Internees so elected shall enter upon their duties after their election has been approved by the detaining authorities. The reasons for any refusals or dismissals shall be communicated to the Protecting Powers concerned.

Article 103

The Internee Committees shall further the physical, spiritual and intellectual well-being of the internees. In case the internees decide, in particular, to organize a system of mutual assistance amongst themselves, this organization would be within the competence of the Committees in addition to the special duties entrusted to them under other provisions of the present Convention.

Article 104

Members of Internee Committees shall not be required to perform any other work, if the accomplishment of their duties is rendered more difficult thereby. Members of Internee Committees may appoint from amongst the internees such assistants as they may require. All material facilities shall be granted to them, particularly a certain freedom of movement necessary for the accomplishment of their duties (visits to labour detachments, receipt of supplies, etc.). All facilities shall likewise be accorded to members of Internee Committees for communication by post and telegraph with the detaining authorities, the Protecting Powers, the International Committee of the Red Cross and their delegates, and with the organizations which give assistance to internees. Committee members in labour detachments shall enjoy similar facilities for communication with their Internee Committee in the principal place of internment. Such communications shall not be limited, nor considered as forming a part of the quota mentioned in Article 107. Members of Internee Committees who are transferred shall be allowed a reasonable time to acquaint their successors with current affairs.

Chapter VIII. Relations with the Exterior

Article 105

Immediately upon interning protected persons, the Detaining Powers shall inform them, the Power to which they owe allegiance and their Protecting Power of the measures taken for executing the provisions of the present Chapter. The Detaining Powers shall likewise inform the Parties concerned of any subsequent modifications of such measures.

Article 106

As soon as he is interned, or at the latest not more than one week after his arrival in a place of internment, and likewise in cases of sickness or transfer to another place of internment or to a hospital, every internee shall be enabled to send direct to his family, on the one hand, and to the Central Agency provided for by Article 140, on the other, an internment card similar, if possible, to the model annexed to the present Convention, informing his relatives of his detention, address and state of health. The said cards shall be forwarded as rapidly as possible and may not be delayed in any way.

Article 107

Internees shall be allowed to send and receive letters and cards. If the Detaining Power deems it necessary to limit the number of letters and cards sent by each internee, the said number shall not be less than two letters and four cards monthly; these shall be drawn up so as to conform as closely as possible to the models annexed to the present Convention. If limitations must be placed on the correspondence addressed to internees, they may be ordered only by the Power to which such internees owe allegiance, possibly at the request of the Detaining Power. Such letters and cards must be conveyed with reasonable despatch; they may not be delayed or retained for disciplinary reasons.

Internees who have been a long time without news, or who find it impossible to receive news from their relatives, or to give them news by the ordinary postal route, as well as those who are at a considerable distance from their homes, shall be allowed to send telegrams, the charges being paid by them in the currency at their disposal. They shall likewise benefit by this provision in cases which are recognized to be urgent. As a rule, internees' mail shall be written in their own language. The Parties to the conflict may authorize correspondence in other languages.

Article 108

Internees shall be allowed to receive, by post or by any other means, individual parcels or collective shipments containing in particular foodstuffs, clothing, medical supplies, as well as books and objects of a devotional, educational or recreational character which may meet their needs. Such shipments shall in no way free the Detaining Power from the obligations imposed upon it by virtue of the present Convention.

Should military necessity require the quantity of such shipments to be limited, due notice thereof shall be given to the Protecting Power and to the International Committee of the Red Cross, or to any other organization giving assistance to the internees and responsible for the forwarding of such shipments. The conditions for the sending of individual parcels and collective shipments shall, if necessary, be the subject of special agreements between the Powers concerned, which may in no case delay the receipt by the internees of relief supplies. Parcels of clothing and foodstuffs may not include books. Medical relief supplies shall, as a rule, be sent in collective parcels.

Article 109

In the absence of special agreements between Parties to the conflict regarding the conditions for the receipt and distribution of collective relief shipments, the regulations concerning collective relief which are annexed to the present Convention shall be applied. The special agreements provided for above shall in no case restrict the right of Internee Committees to take possession of collective relief shipments intended for internees, to undertake their distribution and to dispose of them in the interests of the recipients. Nor shall such agreements restrict the right of representatives of the Protecting Powers, the International Committee of the Red Cross, or any other organization giving assistance to internees and responsible for the forwarding of collective shipments, to supervise their distribution to the recipients.

Article 110

An relief shipments for internees shall be exempt from import, customs and other dues. All matter sent by mail, including relief parcels sent by parcel post and remittances of money, addressed from other countries to internees or despatched by them through the post office, either direct or through the Information Bureaux provided for in Article 136 and the Central Information Agency provided for in Article 140, shall be exempt from all postal dues both in the countries of origin and destination and in intermediate countries. To this effect, in particular, the exemption provided by the Universal Postal Convention of 1947 and by the agreements of the Universal Postal Union in favour of civilians of enemy nationality detained in camps or civilian prisons, shall be extended to the other interned persons protected by the present Convention. The countries not signatory to the above-mentioned agreements shall be bound to grant freedom from charges in the same circumstances.

The cost of transporting relief shipments which are intended for internees and which, by reason of their weight or any other cause, cannot be sent through the post office, shall be borne by the Detaining Power in all the territories under its control. Other Powers which are Parties to the present Convention shall bear the cost of transport in their respective territories. Costs connected with the transport of such shipments, which are not covered by the above paragraphs, shall be charged to the senders. The High Contracting Parties shall endeavour to reduce, so far as possible, the charges for telegrams sent by internees, or addressed to them.

Article 111

Should military operations prevent the Powers concerned from fulfilling their obligation to ensure the conveyance of the mail and relief shipments provided for in Articles 106, 107, 108 and 113, the Protecting Powers concerned, the International Committee of the Red Cross or any other organization duly approved by the Parties to the conflict may undertake to ensure the conveyance of such shipments by suitable means (rail, motor vehicles, vessels or aircraft, etc.). For this purpose, the High Contracting Parties shall endeavour to supply them with such transport, and to allow its circulation, especially by granting the necessary safe-conducts.

Such transport may also be used to convey: (a) correspondence, lists and reports exchanged between the Central Information Agency referred to in Article 140 and the National Bureaux referred to in Article 136; (b) correspondence and reports relating to internees which the Protecting Powers, the International Committee of the Red Cross or any other organization assisting the internees exchange either with their own delegates or with the Parties to the conflict. These provisions in no way detract from the right of any Party to the conflict to arrange other means of transport if it should so prefer, nor preclude the granting of safe-conducts, under mutually agreed conditions, to such means of transport.
The costs occasioned by the use of such means of transport shall be borne, in proportion to the importance of the shipments, by the Parties to the conflict whose nationals are benefited thereby.

Article 112

The censoring of correspondence addressed to internees or despatched by them shall be done as quickly as possible. The examination of consignments intended for internees shall not be carried out under conditions that will expose the goods contained in them to deterioration. It shall be done in the presence of the addressee, or of a fellow-internee duly delegated by him. The delivery to internees of individual or collective consignments shall not be delayed under the pretext of difficulties of censorship. Any prohibition of correspondence ordered by the Parties to the conflict either for military or political reasons, shall be only temporary and its duration shall be as short as possible.

Article 113

The Detaining Powers shall provide all reasonable execution facilities for the transmission, through the Protecting Power or the Central Agency provided for in Article 140, or as otherwise required, of wills, powers of attorney, letters of authority, or any other documents intended for internees or despatched by them.
In all cases the Detaining Powers shall facilitate the execution and authentication in due legal form of such documents on behalf of internees, in particular by allowing them to consult a lawyer.

Article 114

The Detaining Power shall afford internees all facilities to enable them to manage their property, provided this is not incompatible with the conditions of internment and the law which is applicable. For this purpose, the said Power may give them permission to leave the place of internment in urgent cases and if circumstances allow.

Article 115

In all cases where an internee is a party to proceedings in any court, the Detaining Power shall, if he so requests, cause the court to be informed of his detention and shall, within legal limits, ensure that all necessary steps are taken to prevent him from being in any way prejudiced, by reason of his internment, as regards the preparation and conduct of his case or as regards the execution of any judgment of the court.

Article 116

Every internee shall be allowed to receive visitors, especially near relatives, at regular intervals and as frequently as possible. As far as is possible, internees shall be permitted to visit their homes in urgent cases, particularly in cases of death or serious illness of relatives.

Chapter IX. Penal and Disciplinary Sanctions

Article 117

Subject to the provisions of the present Chapter, the laws in force in the territory in which they are detained will continue to apply to internees who commit offences during internment. If general laws, regulations or orders declare acts committed by internees to be punishable, whereas the same acts are not punishable when committed by persons who are not internees, such acts shall entail disciplinary punishments only. No internee may be punished more than once for the same act, or on the same count.

Article 118

The courts or authorities shall in passing sentence take as far as possible into account the fact that the defendant is not a national of the Detaining Power. They shall be free to reduce the penalty prescribed for the offence with which the internee is charged and shall not be obliged, to this end, to apply the minimum sentence prescribed. Imprisonment in premises without daylight, and, in general, all forms of cruelty without exception are forbidden.

Internees who have served disciplinary or judicial sentences shall not be treated differently from other internees. The duration of preventive detention undergone by an internee shall be deducted from any disciplinary or judicial penalty involving confinement to which he may be sentenced. Internee Committees shall be informed of all judicial proceedings instituted against internees whom they represent, and of their result.

Article 119

The disciplinary punishments applicable to internees shall be the following: (1) a fine which shall not exceed 50 per cent of the wages which the internee would otherwise receive under the provisions of Article 95 during a period of not more than thirty days. (2) discontinuance of privileges granted over and above the treatment provided for by the present Convention (3) fatigue duties, not exceeding two hours daily, in connection with the maintenance of the place of internment. (4) confinement.

In no case shall disciplinary penalties be inhuman, brutal or dangerous for the health of internees. Account shall be taken of the internee's age, sex and state of health. The duration of any single punishment shall in no case exceed a maximum of thirty consecutive days, even if the internee is answerable for several breaches of discipline when his case is dealt with, whether such breaches are connected or not.

Article 120

Internees who are recaptured after having escaped or when attempting to escape, shall be liable only to disciplinary punishment in respect of this act, even if it is a repeated offence. Article 118, paragraph 3, notwithstanding, internees punished as a result of escape or attempt to escape, may be subjected to special surveillance, on condition that such surveillance does not affect the state of their health, that it is exercised in a place of internment and that it does not entail the abolition of any of the safeguards granted by the present Convention. Internees who aid and abet an escape or attempt to escape, shall be liable on this count to disciplinary punishment only.

Article 121

Escape, or attempt to escape, even if it is a repeated offence, shall not be deemed an aggravating circumstance in cases where an internee is prosecuted for offences committed during his escape. The Parties to the conflict shall ensure that the competent authorities exercise leniency in deciding whether punishment inflicted for an offence shall be of a disciplinary or judicial nature, especially in respect of acts committed in connection with an escape, whether successful or not.

Article 122

Acts which constitute offences against discipline shall be investigated immediately. This rule shall be applied, in particular, in cases of escape or attempt to escape. Recaptured internees shall be handed over to the competent authorities as soon as possible. In cases of offences against discipline, confinement awaiting trial shall be reduced to an absolute minimum for all internees, and shall not exceed fourteen days. Its duration shall in any case be deducted from any sentence of confinement. The provisions of Articles 124 and

125 shall apply to internees who are in confinement awaiting trial for offences against discipline.

Article 123

Without prejudice to the competence of courts and higher authorities, disciplinary punishment may be ordered only by the commandant of the place of internment, or by a responsible officer or official who replaces him, or to whom he has delegated his disciplinary powers. Before any disciplinary punishment is awarded, the accused internee shall be given precise information regarding the offences of which he is accused, and given an opportunity of explaining his conduct and of defending himself. He shall be permitted, in particular, to call witnesses and to have recourse, if necessary, to the services of a qualified interpreter. The decision shall be announced in the presence of the accused and of a member of the Internee Committee. The period elapsing between the time of award of a disciplinary punishment and its execution shall not exceed one month.

When an internee is awarded a further disciplinary punishment, a period of at least three days shall elapse between the execution of any two of the punishments, if the duration of one of these is ten days or more. A record of disciplinary punishments shall be maintained by the commandant of the place of internment and shall be open to inspection by representatives of the Protecting Power.

Article 124

Internees shall not in any case be transferred to penitentiary establishments (prisons, penitentiaries, convict prisons, etc.) to undergo disciplinary punishment therein. The premises in which disciplinary punishments are undergone shall conform to sanitary requirements: they shall in particular be provided with adequate bedding. Internees undergoing punishment shall beenabled to keep themselves in a state of cleanliness. Women internees undergoing disciplinary punishment shall be confined in separate quarters from male internees and shall be under the immediate supervision of women.

Article 125

Internees awarded disciplinary punishment shall be allowed to exercise and to stay in the open air at least two hours daily. They shall be allowed, if they so request, to be present at the daily medical inspections. They shall receive the attention which their state of health requires and, if necessary, shall be removed to the infirmary of the place of internment or to a hospital.

They shall have permission to read and write, likewise to send and receive letters. Parcels and remittances of money, however, may be withheld from them until the completion of their punishment; such consignments shall meanwhile be entrusted to the Internee Committee, who will hand over to the infirmary the perishable goods contained in the parcels. No internee given a disciplinary punishment may be deprived of the benefit of the provisions of Articles 107 and 143 of the present Convention.

Article 126

The provisions of Articles 71 to 76 inclusive shall apply, by analogy, to proceedings against internees who are in the national territory of the Detaining Power.

Chapter X. Transfers of Internees

Article 127

The transfer of internees shall always be effected humanely. As a general rule, it shall be carried out by rail or other means of transport, and under conditions at least equal to those obtaining for the forces of the Detaining Power in their changes of station. If, as an exceptional measure, such removals have to be effected on foot, they may not take place unless the internees are in a fit state of health, and may not in any case expose them to excessive fatigue.

The Detaining Power shall supply internees during transfer with drinking water and food sufficient in quantity, quality and variety to maintain them in good health, and also with the necessary clothing, adequate shelter and the necessary medical attention. The Detaining Power shall take all suitable precautions to ensure their safety during transfer, and shall establish before their departure a complete list of all internees transferred.

Sick, wounded or infirm internees and maternity cases shall not be transferred if the journey would be seriously detrimental to them, unless their safety imperatively so demands. If the combat zone draws close to a place of internment, the internees in the said place shall not be transferred unless their removal can be carried out in adequate conditions of safety, or unless they are exposed to greater risks by remaining on the spot than by being transferred. When making decisions regarding the transfer of internees, the Detaining Power shall take their interests into account and, in particular, shall not do anything to increase the difficulties of repatriating them or returning them to their own homes.

Article 128

In the event of transfer, internees shall be officially advised of their departure and of their new postal address. Such notification shall be given in time for them to pack their luggage and inform their next of kin. They shall be allowed to take with them their personal effects, and the correspondence and parcels which have arrived for them. The

weight of such baggage may be limited if the conditions of transfer so require, but in no case to less than twenty-five kilograms per internee.
Mail and parcels addressed to their former place of internment shall be forwarded to them without delay. The commandant of the place of internment shall take, in agreement with the Internee Committee, any measures needed to ensure the transport of the internees' community property and of the luggage the internees are unable to take with them in consequence of restrictions imposed by virtue of the second paragraph.

Chapter XI. Deaths

Article 129

The wills of internees shall be received for safe-keeping by the responsible authorities; and if the event of the death of an internee his will shall be transmitted without delay to a person whom he has previously designated. Deaths of internees shall be certified in every case by a doctor, and a death certificate shall be made out, showing the causes of death and the conditions under which it occurred.

An official record of the death, duly registered, shall be drawn up in accordance with the procedure relating thereto in force in the territory where the place of internment is situated, and a duly certified copy of such record shall be transmitted without delay to the Protecting Power as well as to the Central Agency referred to in Article 140.

Article 130

The detaining authorities shall ensure that internees who die while interned are honourably buried, if possible according to the rites of the religion to which they belonged and that their graves are respected, properly maintained, and marked in such a way that they can always be recognized.

Deceased internees shall be buried in individual graves unless unavoidable circumstances require the use of collective graves. Bodies may be cremated only for imperative reasons of hygiene, on account of the religion of the deceased or in accordance with his expressed wish to this effect. In case of cremation, the fact shall be stated and the reasons given in the death certificate of the deceased. The ashes shall be retained for safe-keeping by the detaining authorities and shall be transferred as soon as possible to the next of kin on their request.

As soon as circumstances permit, and not later than the close of hostilities, the Detaining Power shall forward lists of graves of deceased internees to the Powers on whom deceased internees depended, through the Information Bureaux provided for in Article 136. Such lists shall include all particulars necessary for the identification of the deceased internees, as well as the exact location of their graves.

Article 131

Every death or serious injury of an internee, caused or suspected to have been caused by a sentry, another internee or any other person, as well as any death the cause of which is unknown, shall be immediately followed by an official enquiry by the Detaining Power.

A communication on this subject shall be sent immediately to the Protecting Power. The evidence of any witnesses shall be taken, and a report including such evidence shall be prepared and forwarded to the said Protecting Power. If the enquiry indicates the guilt of one or more persons, the Detaining Power shall take all necessary steps to ensure the prosecution of the person or persons responsible.

Chapter XII. Release, Repatriation and Accommodation in Neutral Countries

Article 132

Each interned person shall be released by the Detaining Power as soon as the reasons which necessitated his internment no longer exist. The Parties to the conflict shall, moreover, endeavour during the course of hostilities, to conclude agreements for the release, the repatriation, the return to places of residence or the accommodation in a neutral country of certain classes of internees, in particular children, pregnant women and mothers with infants and young children, wounded and sick, and internees who have been detained for a long time.

Article 133

Internment shall cease as soon as possible after the close of hostilities. Internees in the territory of a Party to the conflict against whom penal proceedings are pending for offences not exclusively subject to disciplinary penalties, may be detained until the close of such proceedings and, if circumstances require, until the completion of the penalty. The same shall apply to internees who have been previously sentenced to a punishment depriving them of liberty. By agreement between the Detaining Power and the Powers concerned, committees may be set up after the close of hostilities, or of the occupation of territories, to search for dispersed internees.

Article 134

The High Contracting Parties shall endeavour, upon the Repatriation close of hostilities or occupation, to ensure the return of all internees to their last place of residence, or to facilitate their residence repatriation.

Article 135

The Detaining Power shall bear the expense of returning released internees to the places where they were residing when interned, or, if it took them into custody while they were in transit or on the high seas, the cost of completing their journey or of their return to their point of departure.
Where a Detaining Power refuses permission to reside in its territory to a released internee who previously had his permanent domicile therein, such Detaining Power shall pay the cost of the said internee's repatriation. If, however, the internee elects to return to his country on his own responsibility or in obedience to the Government of the Power to which he owes allegiance, the Detaining Power need not pay the expenses of his journey beyond the point of his departure from its territory. The Detaining Power need not pay the cost of repatriation of an internee who was interned at his own request. If internees are transferred in accordance with Article 45, the transferring and receiving Powers shall agree on the portion of the above costs to be borne by each. The foregoing shall not prejudice such special agreements as may be concluded between Parties to the conflict concerning the exchange and repatriation of their nationals in enemy hands.

Section V. Information Bureaux and Central Agency

Article 136

Upon the outbreak of a conflict and in all cases of occupation, each of the Parties to the conflict shall establish an official Information Bureau responsible for receiving and transmitting information in respect of the protected persons who are in its power.

Each of the Parties to the conflict shall, within the shortest possible period, give its Bureau information of any measure taken by it concerning any protected persons who are kept in custody for more than two weeks, who are subjected to assigned residence or who are interned. It shall, furthermore, require its various departments concerned with such matters to provide the aforesaid Bureau promptly with information concerning all changes pertaining to these protected persons, as, for example, transfers, releases, repatriations, escapes, admittances to hospitals, births and deaths.

Article 137

Each national Bureau shall immediately forward information concerning protected persons by the most rapid means to the Powers in whose territory they resided, through the intermediary of the Protecting Powers and likewise through the Central Agency provided for in Article 140. The Bureaux shall also reply to all enquiries which may be received regarding protected persons. Information Bureaux shall transmit information concerning a protected person unless its transmission might be detrimental to the person concerned or to his or her relatives. Even in such a case, the information may not be withheld from the Central Agency which, upon being notified of the circumstances, will take the necessary precautions indicated in Article 140. All communications in writing made by any Bureau shall be authenticated by a signature or a seal.

Article 138

The information received by the national Bureau and transmitted by it shall be of such a character as to make it possible to identify the protected person exactly and to advise his next of kin quickly. The information in respect of each person shall include at least his surname, first names, place and date of birth, nationality last residence and distinguishing characteristics, the first name of the father and the maiden name of the mother, the date, place and nature of the action taken with regard to the individual, the address at which correspondence may be sent to him and the name and address of the person to be informed.

Likewise, information regarding the state of health of internees who are seriously ill or seriously wounded shall be supplied regularly and if possible every week.

Article 139

Each national Information Bureau shall, furthermore, be responsible for collecting all personal valuables left by protected persons mentioned in Article 136, in particular those who have been repatriated or released, or who have escaped or died; it shall forward the said valuables to those concerned, either direct, or, if necessary, through the Central Agency. Such articles shall be sent by the Bureau in sealed packets which shall be accompanied by statements giving clear and full identity particulars of the person to whom the articles belonged, and by a complete list of the contents of the parcel. Detailed records shall be maintained of the receipt and despatch of all such valuables.

Article 140

A Central Information Agency for protected persons, in particular for internees, shall be created in a neutral country. The International Committee of the Red Cross shall, if it deems necessary, propose to the Powers concerned the organization of such an Agency, which may be the same as that provided for in Article 123 of the Geneva Convention relative to the Treatment of Prisoners of War of 12 August 1949.

The function of the Agency shall be to collect all information of the type set forth in Article 136 which it may obtain through official or private channels and to transmit it as rapidly as possible to the countries of origin or of residence of the persons concerned, except in cases where such transmissions might be detrimental to the persons whom the said information concerns, or to their relatives. It shall receive from the Parties to the conflict all reasonable facilities for effecting such transmissions. The High Contracting Parties, and in particular those whose nationals benefit by the services of the Central Agency, are requested to give the said Agency the financial aid it may require. The foregoing provisions shall in no way be interpreted as restricting the humanitarian activities of the International Committee of the Red Cross and of the relief Societies described in Article 142.

Article 141

The national Information Bureaux and the Central Information Agency shall enjoy free postage for all mail, likewise the exemptions provided for in Article 110, and further, so far as possible, exemption from telegraphic charges or, at least, greatly reduced rates.

Part IV. Execution of the Convention

Section I. General Provisions

Article 142

Subject to the measures which the Detaining Powers may consider essential to ensure their security or to meet any other reasonable need, the representatives of religious organizations, relief societies, or any other organizations assisting the protected persons, shall receive from these Powers, for themselves or their duly accredited agents, all facilities for visiting the protected persons, for distributing relief supplies and material from any source, intended for educational, recreational or religious purposes, or for assisting them in organizing their leisure time within the places of internment. Such societies or organizations may be constituted in the territory of the Detaining Power, or in any other country, or they may have an international character.
The Detaining Power may limit the number of societies and organizations whose delegates are allowed to carry out their activities in its territory and under its supervision, on condition, however, that such limitation shall not hinder the supply of effective and adequate relief to all protected persons. The special position of the International Committee of the Red Cross in this field shall be recognized and respected at all times.

Article 143

Representatives or delegates of the Protecting Powers shall have permission to go to all places where protected persons are, particularly to places of internment, detention and work. They shall have access to all premises occupied by protected persons and shall be able to interview the latter without witnesses, personally or through an interpreter. Such visits may not be prohibited except for reasons of imperative military necessity, and then only as an exceptional and temporary measure. Their duration and frequency shall not be restricted.

Such representatives and delegates shall have full liberty to select the places they wish to visit. The Detaining or Occupying Power, the Protecting Power and when occasion arises the Power of origin of the persons to be visited, may agree that compatriots of the internees shall be permitted to participate in the visits. The delegates of the International Committee of the Red Cross shall also enjoy the above prerogatives. The appointment of such delegates shall be submitted to the approval of the Power governing the territories where they will carry out their duties.

Article 144

The High Contracting Parties undertake, in time of peace as in time of war, to disseminate the text of the present Convention as widely as possible in their respective countries, and, in particular, to include the study thereof in their programmes of military and, if possible, civil instruction, so that the principles thereof may become known to the entire population. Any civilian, military, police or other authorities, who in time of war assume responsibilities in respect of protected persons, must possess the text of the Convention and be specially instructed as to its provisions.

Article 145

The High Contracting Parties shall communicate to one another through the Swiss Federal Council and, during hostilities, through the Protecting Powers, the official translations of the present Convention, as well as the laws and regulations which they may adopt to ensure the application thereof.

Article 146

The High Contracting Parties undertake to enact any legislation necessary to provide effective penal sanctions for persons committing, or ordering to be committed, any of the grave breaches of the present Convention defined in the following Article. Each High Contracting Party shall be under the obligation to search for persons alleged to have committed, or to have ordered to be committed, such grave breaches, and shall bring such persons, regardless of their nationality, before its own courts. It may also, if it prefers, and in accordance with the provisions of its own legislation, hand such persons over for trial to another High Contracting Party concerned, provided such High Contracting Party has made out a prima facie case.

Each High Contracting Party shall take measures necessary for the suppression of all acts contrary to the provisions of the present Convention other than the grave breaches defined in the following Article.

In all circumstances, the accused persons shall benefit by safeguards of proper trial and defence, which shall not be less favourable than those provided by Article 105 and those following of the Geneva Convention relative to the Treatment of Prisoners of War of 12 August 1949.

Article 147

Grave breaches to which the preceding Article relates shall be those involving any of the following acts, if committed against persons or property protected by the present Convention: wilful killing, torture or inhuman treatment, including biological experiments, wilfully causing great suffering or serious injury to body or health, unlawful deportation or transfer or unlawful confinement of a protected person, compelling a protected person to serve in the forces of a hostile Power, or wilfully depriving a protected person of the rights of fair and regular trial prescribed in the present Convention, taking of hostages and extensive destruction and appropriation of property, not justified by military necessity and carried out unlawfully and wantonly.

Article 148

No High Contracting Party shall be allowed to absolve itself or any other High Contracting Party of any liability incurred by itself or by another High Contracting Party in respect of breaches referred to in the preceding Article.

Article 149

At the request of a Party to the conflict, an enquiry shall be instituted, in a manner to be decided between the interested Parties, concerning any alleged violation of the Convention. If agreement has not been reached concerning the procedure for the enquiry, the Parties should agree on the choice of an umpire who will decide upon the procedure to be followed. Once the violation has been established, the Parties to the conflict shall put an end to it and shall repress it with the least possible delay.

Section II. Final Provisions

Article 150

The present Convention is established in English and in French. Both texts are equally authentic. The Swiss Federal Council shall arrange for official translations of the Convention to be made in the Russian and Spanish languages.

Article 151

The present Convention, which bears the date of this day, is open to signature until 12 February 1950, in the name of the Powers represented at the Conference which opened at Geneva on 21 April 1949.

Article 152

The present Convention shall be ratified as soon as possible and the ratifications shall be deposited at Berne. A record shall be drawn up of the deposit of each instrument of ratification and certified copies of this record shall be transmitted by the Swiss Federal Council to all the Powers in whose name the Convention has been signed, or whose accession has been notified.

Article 153

The present Convention shall come into force six months after not less than two instruments of ratification have been deposited. Thereafter, it shall come into force for each High Contracting Party six months after the deposit of the instrument of ratification.

Article 154

In the relations between the Powers who are bound by the Hague Conventions respecting the Laws and Customs of War on Land, whether that of 29 July 1899, or that of 18 October 1907, and who are parties to the present Convention, this last Convention shall be supplementary to Sections II and III of the Regulations annexed to the above-mentioned Conventions of The Hague.

Article 155

From the date of its coming into force, it shall be open to any Power in whose name the present Convention has not been signed, to accede to this Convention.

Article 156

Accessions shall be notified in writing to the Swiss Federal Council, and shall take effect six months after the date on which they are received. The Swiss Federal Council shall communicate the accessions to all the Powers in whose name the Convention has been signed, or whose accession has been notified.

Article 157

The situations provided for in Articles 2 and 3 shall effective immediate effect to ratifications deposited and accessions notified by the Parties to the conflict before or after the beginning of hostilities or occupation. The Swiss Federal Council shall communicate by the quickest method any ratifications or accessions received from Parties to the conflict.

Article 158

Each of the High Contracting Parties shall be at liberty to denounce the present Convention. The denunciation shall be notified in writing to the Swiss Federal Council, which shall transmit it to the Governments of all the High Contracting Parties. The denunciation shall take effect one year after the notification thereof has been made to the Swiss Federal Council. However, a denunciation of which notification has been made at a time when the denouncing Power is involved in a conflict shall not take effect until peace has been concluded, and until after operations connected with release, repatriation and re-establishment of the persons protected by the present Convention have been terminated.

The denunciation shall have effect only in respect of the denouncing Power. It shall in no way impair the obligations which the Parties to the conflict shall remain bound to fulfil by virtue of the principles of the law of nations, as they result from the usages established among civilized peoples, from the laws of humanity and the dictates of the public conscience.

Article 159

The Swiss Federal Council shall register the present Convention with the Secretariat of the United Nations. The Swiss Federal Council shall also inform the Secretariat of the United Nations of all ratifications, accessions and denunciations received by it with respect to the present Convention.

In witness whereof the undersigned, having deposited their respective full powers, have signed the present Convention.

Done at Geneva this twelfth day of August 1949, in the English and French languages. The original shall be deposited in the Archives of the Swiss Confederation. The Swiss Federal Council shall transmit certified copies thereof to each of the signatory and acceding States.

Annex I
Draft Agreement Relating to Hospital and Safety Zones and Localities

Article 1

Hospital and safety zones shall be strictly reserved for the persons mentioned in Article 23 of the Geneva Convention for the Amelioration of the Condition of the Wounded and Sick in Armed Forces in the Field of 12 August 1949, and in Article 14 of the Geneva Convention relative to the Protection of Civilian Persons in Time of War of 12 August 1949, and for the personnel entrusted with the organization and administration of these zones and localities, and with the care of the persons therein assembled. Nevertheless, persons whose permanent residence is within such zones shall have the right to stay there.

Article 2

No persons residing, in whatever capacity, in a hospital and safety zone shall perform any work, either within or without the zone, directly connected with military operations or the production of war material.

Article 3

The Power establishing a hospital and safety zone shall take all necessary measures to prohibit access to all persons who have no right of residence or entry therein.

Article 4

Hospital and safety zones shall fulfil the following conditions: (a) they shall comprise only a small part of the territory governed by the Power which has established them (b) they shall be thinly populated in relation to the possibilities of accommodation (c) they shall be far removed and free from all military objectives, or large industrial or administrative establishments (d) they shall not be situated in areas which, according to every probability, may become important for the conduct of the war.

Article 5

Hospital and safety zones shall be subject to the following obligations: (a) the lines of communication and means of transport which they possess shall not be used for the transport of military personnel or material, even in transit (b) they shall in no case be defended by military means.

Article 6

Hospital and safety zones shall be marked by means of oblique red bands on a white ground, placed on the buildings and outer precincts. Zones reserved exclusively for the wounded and sick may be marked by means of the Red Cross (Red Crescent, Red Lion and Sun) emblem on a white ground.

They may be similarly marked at night by means of appropriate illumination.

Article 7

The Powers shall communicate to all the High Contracting Parties in peacetime or on the outbreak of hostilities, a list of the hospital and safety zones in the territories governed by them. They shall also give notice of any new zones set up during hostilities. As soon as the adverse party has received the above-mentioned notification, the zone shall be regularly established. If, however, the adverse party considers that the conditions of the present agreement have not been fulfilled, it may refuse to recognize the zone by giving immediate notice thereof to the Party responsible for the said zone, or may make its recognition of such zone dependent upon the institution of the control provided for in Article 8.

Article 8

Any Power having recognized one or several hospital and safety zones instituted by the adverse Party shall be entitled to demand control by one or more Special Commissions, for the purpose of ascertaining if the zones fulfil the conditions and obligations stipulated in the present agreement. For this purpose, members of the Special Commissions shall at all times have free access to the various zones and may even reside there permanently. They shall be given all facilities for their duties of inspection.

Article 9

Should the Special Commissions note any facts which they consider contrary to the stipulations of the present agreement, they shall at once draw the attention of the Power governing the said zone to these facts, and shall fix a time limit of five days within which the matter should be rectified. They shall duly notify the Power which has recognized the zone. If, when the time limit has expired, the Power governing the zone has not complied with the warning, the adverse Party may declare that it is no longer bound by the present agreement in respect of the said zone.

Article 10

Any Power setting up one or more hospital and safety zones, and the adverse Parties to whom their existence has been notified, shall nominate or have nominated by the Protecting Powers or by other neutral Powers, persons eligible to be members of the Special Commissions mentioned in Articles 8 and 9.

Article 11

In no circumstances may hospital and safety zones be the object of attack. They shall be protected and respected at all times by the Parties to the conflict.

Article 12

In the case of occupation of a territory, the hospital and safety zones therein shall continue to be respected and utilized as such. Their purpose may, however, be modified by the Occupying Power, on condition that all measures are taken to ensure the safety of the persons accommodated.

Article 13

The present agreement shall also apply to localities which the Powers may utilize for the same purposes as hospital and safety zones.

Annex II
Draft Regulations concerning Collective Relief

Article 1

The Internee Committees shall be allowed to distribute collective relief shipments for which they are responsible to all internees who are dependent for administration on the said Committee's place of internment, including those internees who are in hospitals, or in prison or other penitentiary establishments.

Article 2

The distribution of collective relief shipments shall be effected in accordance with the instructions of the donors and with a plan drawn up by the Internee Committees. The issue of medical stores shall, however, be made for preference in agreement with the senior medical officers, and the latter may, in hospitals and infirmaries, waive the said instructions, if the needs of their patients so demand. Within the limits thus defined, the distribution shall always be carried out equitably.

Article 3

Members of Internee Committees shall be allowed to go to the railway stations or other points of arrival of relief supplies near their places of internment so as to enable them to verify the quantity as well as the quality of the goods received and to make out detailed reports thereon for the donors.

Article 4

Internee Committees shall be given the facilities necessary for verifying whether the distribution of collective relief in all subdivisions and annexes of their places of internment has been carried out in accordance with their instructions.

Article 5

Internee Committees shall be allowed to complete, and to cause to be completed by members of the Internee Committees in labour detachments or by the senior medical officers of infirmaries and hospitals, forms or questionnaires intended for the donors, relating to collective relief supplies (distribution, requirements, quantities, etc.). Such forms and questionnaires, duly completed, shall be forwarded to the donors without delay.

Article 6

In order to secure the regular distribution of collective relief supplies to the internees in their place of internment, and to meet any needs that may arise through the arrival of fresh parties of internees, the Internee Committees shall be allowed to create and maintain sufficient reserve stocks of collective relief. For this purpose, they shall have suitable warehouses at their disposal; each warehouse shall be provided with two locks, the Internee Committee holding the keys of one lock, and the commandant of the place of internment the keys of the other.

Article 7

The High Contracting Parties, and the Detaining Powers in particular, shall, so far as is in any way possible and subject to the regulations governing the food supply of the population, authorize purchases of goods to be made in their territories for the distribution of collective relief to the internees. They shall likewise facilitate the transfer of funds and other financial measures of a technical or administrative nature taken for the purpose of making such purchases.

Article 8

The foregoing provisions shall not constitute an obstacle to the right of internees to receive collective relief before their arrival in a place of internment or in the course of their transfer, nor to the possibility of representatives of the Protecting Power, or of the International Committee of the Red Cross or any other humanitarian organization giving assistance to internees and responsible for forwarding such supplies, ensuring the distribution thereof to the recipients by any other means they may deem suitable.

Cont'd

However, we should clearly remember and see the original purpose of the Hague conference: to keep peace around world. The assembly of nations did not help much to put a stop to increase of armaments nor tensions, showing the limitations of international treaties and warns of nominal conferences.[21]

The importance of the Peace Conferences also turns out in the fact, as said before, the provisions of the two Peace Conventions on land warfare formed a body of customary international law. As such they are also binding on states which are not formally parties to them. In 1946 the Nüremberg International Military Tribunal stated with regard to the Hague Convention on land warfare of 1907: "The rules of land warfare expressed in the Convention undoubtedly represented an advance over existing International Law at the time of their adoption ... but by 1939 these rules were recognized by all civilized nations and were regarded as being declaratory of the laws and customs of war" The International Military Tribunal for the Far East expressed, in 1948, an identical view. The rules embodied in the Regulations were partly reaffirmed and developed by the two Protocols Additional to the Geneva Conventions of 1949 adopted in 1977.[22]

---

[21] <http://www.zum.de/whkmla/sp/0910/pillow/pillow1.html#VI2>.

[22] K. Dijkhof, War, *Law and Technology*, WLP 2010, p 44.

Protocol Additional to the Geneva Conventions of 12 August 1949, and relating to the Protection of Victims of International Armed Conflicts (Protocol I), 8 June 1977

Preamble

The High Contracting Parties,

Proclaiming their earnest wish to see peace prevail among peoples,

Recalling that every State has the duty, in conformity with the Charter of the United Nations, to refrain in its international relations from the threat or use of force against the sovereignty, territorial integrity or political independence of any State, or in any other manner inconsistent with the purposes of the United Nations,

Believing it necessary nevertheless to reaffirm and develop the provisions protecting the victims of armed conflicts and to supplement measures intended to reinforce their application,

Expressing their conviction that nothing in this Protocol or in the Geneva Conventions of 12 August 1949 can be construed as legitimizing or authorizing any act of aggression or any other use of force inconsistent with the Charter of the United Nations,

Reaffirming further that the provisions of the Geneva Conventions of 12 August 1949 and of this Protocol must be fully applied in all circumstances to all persons who are protected by those instruments, without any adverse distinction based on the nature or origin of the armed conflict or on the causes espoused by or attributed to the Parties to the conflict,

Have agreed on the following:

Part I. General Provisions

Article 1
General principles and scope of application

1. The High Contracting Parties undertake to respect and to ensure respect for this Protocol in all circumstances.

2. In cases not covered by this Protocol or by other international agreements, civilians and combatants remain under the protection and authority of the principles of international law derived from established custom, from the principles of humanity and from dictates of public conscience.

3. This Protocol, which supplements the Geneva Conventions of 12 August 1949 for the protection of war victims, shall apply in the situations referred to in Article 2 common to those Conventions.

4. The situations referred to in the preceding paragraph include armed conflicts in which peoples are fighting against colonial domination and alien occupation and against racist regimes in the exercise of their right of self-determination, as enshrined in the Charter of the United Nations and the Declaration on Principles of International Law concerning Friendly Relations and Co-operation among States in accordance with the Charter of the United Nations.

Article 2
Definitions

For the purposes of this Protocol

(a) "First Convention", "Second Convention", "Third Convention" and "Fourth Convention" mean, respectively, the Geneva Convention for the Amelioration of the Condition of the Wounded and Sick in Armed Forces in the Field of 12 August 1949; the Geneva Convention for the Amelioration of the Condition of Wounded, Sick and Ship-wrecked Members of Armed Forces at Sea of 12 August 1949; the Geneva Convention relative to the Treatment of Prisoners of War of 12 August 1949; the Geneva Convention relative to the Protection of Civilian Persons in Time of War of 12 August 1949; "the Conventions" means the four Geneva Conventions of 12 August 1949 for the protection of war victims;
(b) "Rules of international law applicable in armed conflict" means the rules applicable in armed conflict set forth in international agreements to which the Parties to the conflict are Parties and the generally recognized principles and rules of international law which are applicable to armed conflict;

(c) "Protecting Power" means a neutral or other State not a Party to the conflict which has been designated by a Party to the conflict and accepted by the adverse Party and has agreed to carry out the functions assigned to a Protecting Power under the Conventions and this Protocol;

(d) "Substitute" means an organization acting in place of a Protecting Power in accordance with Article 5.

Article 3
Beginning and end of application

Without prejudice to the provisions which are applicable at all times:

(a) the Conventions and this Protocol shall apply from the beginning of any situation referred to in Article 1 of this Protocol.

(b) the application of the Conventions and of this Protocol shall cease, in the territory of Parties to the conflict, on the general close of military operations and, in the case of occupied territories, on the termination of the occupation, except, in either circumstance, for those persons whose final release, repatriation or re-establishment takes place thereafter. These persons shall continue to benefit from the relevant provisions of the Conventions and of this Protocol until their final release repatriation or re-establishment.

Article 4
Legal status of the Parties to the conflict

The application of the Conventions and of this Protocol, as well as the conclusion of the agreements provided for therein, shall not affect the legal status of the Parties to the conflict. Neither the occupation of a territory nor the application of the Conventions and this Protocol shall affect the legal status of the territory in question.

Article 5
Appointment of Protecting Powers and of their substitute

1. It is the duty of the Parties to a conflict from the beginning of that conflict to secure the supervision and implementation of the Conventions and of this Protocol by the application of the system of Protecting Powers, including inter alia the designation and acceptance of those Powers, in accordance with the following paragraphs. Protecting Powers shall have the duty of safeguarding the interests of the Parties to the conflict.

2. From the beginning of a situation referred to in Article 1, each Party to the conflict shall without delay designate a Protecting Power for the purpose of applying the Conventions and this Protocol and shall, likewise without delay and for the same purpose, permit the activities or a Protecting Power which has been accepted by it as such after designation by the adverse Party.

3. If a Protecting Power has not been designated or accepted from the beginning of a situation referred to in Article 1, the International Committee of the Red Cross, without prejudice to the right of any other impartial humanitarian organization to do likewise, shall offer its good offices to the Parties to the conflict with a view to the designation without delay of a Protecting Power to which the Parties to the conflict consent. For that purpose it may inter alia ask each Party to provide it with a list of at least five States which that Party considers acceptable to act as Protecting Power on its behalf in relation to an adverse Party and ask each adverse Party to provide a list or at least five States which it would accept as the Protecting Power of the first Party; these lists shall be communicated to the Committee within two weeks after the receipt or the request; it shall compare them and seek the agreement of any proposed State named on both lists.

4. If, despite the foregoing, there is no Protecting Power, the Parties to the conflict shall accept without delay an offer which may be made by the International Committee of the Red Cross or by any other organization which offers all guarantees of impartiality and efficacy, after due consultations with the said Parties and taking into account the result of these consultations, to act as a substitute. The functioning of such a substitute is subject to the consent of the Parties to the conflict; every effort shall be made by the Parties to the conflict to facilitate the operations of the substitute in the performance of its tasks under the Conventions and this Protocol.

5. In accordance with Article 4, the designation and acceptance of Protecting Powers for the purpose of applying the Conventions and this Protocol shall not affect the legal status of the Parties to the conflict or of any territory, including occupied territory.

6. The maintenance of diplomatic relations between Parties to the conflict or the entrusting of the protection of a Party's interests and those of its nationals to a third State in accordance with the rules of international law relating to diplomatic relations is no obstacle to the designation of Protecting Powers for the purpose of applying the Conventions and this Protocol.

7. Any subsequent mention in this Protocol of a Protecting Power includes also a substitute.

Article 6
Qualified persons

1. The High Contracting Parties shall, also in peacetime, endeavour, with the assistance of the national Red Cross (Red Crescent, Red Lion and Sun) Societies, to train qualified personnel to facilitate the application of the Conventions and of this Protocol, and in particular the activities of the Protecting Powers.

2. The recruitment and training of such personnel are within domestic jurisdiction.

3. The International Committee of the Red Cross shall hold at the disposal of the High Contracting Parties the lists of persons so trained which the High Contracting Parties may have established and may have transmitted to it for that purpose.

4. The conditions governing the employment of such personnel outside the national territory shall, in each case, be the subject of special agreements between the Parties concerned.

Article 7
Meetings

The depositary of this Protocol shall convene a meeting of the High Contracting Parties, at the request of one or more of the said Parties and upon, the approval of the majority of the said Parties, to consider general problems concerning the application of the Conventions and of the Protocol.

Part II.Wounded, Sick and Shipwrecked

Section I.General Protection

Article 8
Terminology

For the purposes of this Protocol:

(a) "Wounded" and "sick" mean persons, whether military or civilian, who, because of trauma, disease or other physical or mental disorder or disability, are in need of medical assistance or care and who refrain from any act of hostility. These terms also cover maternity cases, new-born babies and other persons who may be in need of immediate medical assistance or care, such as the infirm or expectant mothers, and who refrain from any act of hostility;

(b) "Shipwrecked" means persons, whether military or civilian, who are in peril at sea or in other waters as a result of misfortune affecting them or the vessel or aircraft carrying them and who refrain from any act of hostility. These persons, provided that they continue to refrain from any act of hostility, shall continue to be considered shipwrecked during their rescue until they acquire another status under the Conventions or this Protocol;

(c) "Medical personnel" means those persons assigned, by a Party to the conflict, exclusively to the medical purposes enumerated under e) or to the administration of medical units or to the operation or administration of medical transports. Such assignments may be either permanent ortemporary. The term includes:

(i) medical personnel of a Party to the conflict, whether military or civilian, including those described in the First and Second Conventions, and those assigned to civil defence organizations;
(ii) medical personnel of national Red Cross (Red Crescent, Red Lion and Sun) Societies and other national voluntary aid societies duly recognized and authorized by a Party to the conflict;
(iii) medical personnel or medical units or medical transports described in Article 9, paragraph 2.

(d) "Religious personnel" means military or civilian persons, such as chaplains, who are exclusively engaged in the work of their ministry and attached:

(i) to the armed forces of a Party to the conflict;
(ii) to medical units or medical transports of a Party to the conflict;
(iii) to medical units or medical transports described in Article 9, Paragraph 2; or
(iv) to civil defence organizations of a Party to the conflict.

The attachment of religious personnel may be either permanent or temporary, and the relevant provisions mentioned under k) apply to them;

(e) "Medical units" means establishments and other units, whether military or civilian, organized for medical purposes, namely the search for, collection, transportation, diagnosis or treatment - including first-aid treatment - of the wounded, sick and shipwrecked, or for the prevention of disease. The term includes for example, hospitals and other similar units, blood transfusion centres, preventive medicine centres and institutes, medical depots and the medical and pharmaceutical stores of such units. Medical units may be fixed or mobile, permanent or temporary;

(f) "Medical transportation" means the conveyance by land, water or air of the wounded, sick, shipwrecked, medical personnel, religious personnel, medical equipment or medical supplies protected by the Conventions and by this Protocol;

(g) "Medical transports" means any means of transportation, whether military or civilian, permanent or temporary, assigned exclusively to medical transportation and under the control of a competent authority of a Party to the conflict;

(h) "Medical vehicles" means any medical transports by land;

(i) "Medical ships and craft" means any medical transports by water;

(j) "Medical aircraft" means any medical transports by air;

(k) "Permanent medical personnel", "permanent medical units" and "permanent medical transports" mean those assigned exclusively to medical purposes for an indeterminate period. "Temporary medical personnel" "temporary medical-units" and "temporary medical transports" mean those devoted exclusively to medical purposes for limited periods during the whole of such periods. Unless otherwise specified, the terms "medical personnel", "medical units" and "medical transports" cover both permanent and temporary categories;

(l) "Distinctive emblem" means the distinctive emblem of the red cross, red crescent or red lion and sun on a white ground when used for the protection of medical units and transports, or medical and religious personnel, equipment or supplies;

(m) "Distinctive signal" means any signal or message specified for the identification exclusively of medical units or transports in Chapter III of Annex I to this Protocol.

Article 9
Field of application

1. This Part, the provisions of which are intended to ameliorate the condition of the wounded, sick and shipwrecked, shall apply to all those affected by a situation referred to in Article 1, without any adverse distinction founded on race, colour, sex, language, religion or belief political or other opinion, national or social origin, wealth, birth or other status, or on any other similar criteria.

2. The relevant provisions of Articles 27 and 32 of the First Convention shall apply to permanent medical units and transports (other than hospital ships, to which Article 25 of the Second Convention applies) and their personnel made available to a Party to the conflict for humanitarian purposes:

(a) by a neutral or other State which is not a Party to that conflict;
(b) by a recognized and authorized aid society of such a State;
(c) by an impartial international humanitarian organization.

Article 10
Protection and care

1. All the wounded, sick and shipwrecked, to whichever Party they belong, shall be respected and protected.

2. In all circumstances they shall be treated humanely and shall receive, to the fullest extent practicable and with the least possible delay, the medical care and attention required by their condition. There shall be no distinction among them founded on any grounds other than medical ones.

Article 11
Protection of persons

1. The physical or mental health and integrity of persons who are in the power of the adverse Party or who are interned, detained or otherwise deprived of liberty as a result of a situation referred to in Article 1 shall not be endangered by any unjustified act or omission. Accordingly, it is prohibited to subject the persons described in this Article to any medical procedure which is not indicated by the state of health of the person concerned and which is not consistent with generally accepted medical standards which would be applied under similar medical circumstances to persons who are nationals of the Party conducting the procedure and who are in no way deprived of liberty.

2. It is, in particular, prohibited to carry out on such persons, even with their consent:

(a) physical mutilations;
(b) medical or scientific experiments;
(c) removal of tissue or organs for transplantation, except where these acts are justified in conformity with the conditions provided for in paragraph 1.

3. Exceptions to the prohibition in paragraph 2 (c) may be made only in the case of donations of blood for transfusion or of skin for grafting, provided that they are given voluntarily and without any coercion or inducement, and then only for therapeutic purposes, under conditions consistent with generally accepted medical standards and controls designed for the benefit of both the donor and the recipient.
4. Any wilful act or omission which seriously endangers the physical or mental health or integrity of any person who is in the power of a Party other than the one on which he

depends and which either violates any of the prohibitions in paragraphs 1 and 2 or fails to comply with the requirements of paragraph 3 shall be a grave breach of this Protocol.

5. The persons described in paragraph 1 have the right to refuse any surgical operation. In case of refusal, medical personnel shall endeavour to obtain a written statement to that effect, signed or acknowledged by the patient.

6. Each Party to the conflict shall keep a medical record for every donation of blood for transfusion or skin for grafting by persons referred to in paragraph 1, if that donation is made under the responsibility of that Party. In addition, each Party to the conflict shall endeavour to keep a record of all medical procedures undertaken with respect to any person who is interned, detained or otherwise deprived of liberty as a result of a situation referred to in Article 1. These records shall be available at all times for inspection by the Protecting Power.

Article 12
Protection of medical units

1. Medical units shall be respected and protected at all times and shall not be the object of attack.

2. Paragraph 1 shall apply to civilian medical units, provided that they:

(a) belong to one of the Parties to the conflict;
(b) are recognized and authorized by the competent authority of one of the Parties to the conflict; or
(c) are authorized in conformity with Article 9, paragraph 2, of this Protocol or Article 27 of the First Convention.

3. The Parties to the conflict are invited to notify each other of the location of their fixed medical units. The absence of such notification shall not exempt any of the Parties from the obligation to comply with the provisions of paragraph 1.

4. Under no circumstances shall medical units be used in an attempt to shield military objectives from attack. Whenever possible, the Parties to the conflict shall ensure that medical units are so sited that attacks against military objectives do not imperil their safety.

Article 13
Discontinuance of protection of civilian medical units

1. The protection to which civilian medical units are entitled shall not cease unless they are used to commit, outside their humanitarian function, acts harmful to the enemy.

Protection may, however, cease only after a warning has been given setting, whenever appropriate, a reasonable time-limit, and after such warning has remained unheeded.

2. The following shall not be considered as acts harmful to the enemy:

(a) that the personnel of the unit are equipped with light individual weapons for their own defence or for that of the wounded and sick in their charge;
(b) that the unit is guarded by a picket or by sentries or by an escort;
(c) that small arms and ammunition taken from the wounded and sick, and not yet handed to the proper service, are found in the units;
(d) that members of the armed forces or other combatants are in the unit for medical reasons.

Article 14
Limitations on requisition of civilian medical units

1. The Occupying Power has the duty to ensure that the medical needs of the civilian population in occupied territory continue to be satisfied.

2. The Occupying Power shall not, therefore, requisition civilian medical units, their equipment, their materiel or the services of their personnel, so long as these resources are necessary for the provision of adequate medical services for the civilian population and for the continuing medical care of any wounded and sick already under treatment.

3. Provided that the general rule in paragraph 2 continues to be observed, the Occupying Power may requisition the said resources, subject to the following particular conditions:

(a) that the resources are necessary for the adequate and immediate medical treatment of the wounded and sick members of the armed forces of the Occupying Power or of prisoners of war;
(b) that the requisition continues only while such necessity exists; and
(c) that immediate arrangements are made to ensure that the medical needs of the civilian population, as well as those of any wounded and sick under treatment who are affected by the requisition, continue to be satisfied.

Article 15
Protection of civilian medical and religious personnel

1. Civilian medical personnel shall be respected and protected.

2. If needed, all available help shall be afforded to civilian medical personnel in an area where civilian medical services are disrupted by reason of combat activity.

3. The Occupying Power shall afford civilian medical personnel in occupied territories every assistance to enable them to perform, to the best of their ability, their humanitarian functions. The Occupying Power may not require that, in the performance of those functions, such personnel shall give priority to the treatment of any person except on medical grounds. They shall not be compelled to carry out tasks which are not compatible with their humanitarian mission.

4. Civilian medical personnel shall have access to any place where their services are essential, subject to such supervisory and safety measures as the relevant Party to the conflict may deem necessary.

5. Civilian religious personnel shall be respected and protected. The provisions of the Conventions and of this Protocol concerning the protection and identification of medical personnel shall apply equally to such persons.

Article 16
General protection of medical duties

1. Under no circumstances shall any person be punished for carrying out medical activities compatible with medical ethics, regardless of the person benefiting therefrom.

2. Persons engaged in medical activities shall not be compelled to perform acts or to carry out work contrary to the rules of medical ethics or to other medical rules designed for the benefit of the wounded and sick or to the provisions of the Conventions or of this Protocol, or to refrain from performing acts or from carrying out work required by those rules and provisions.

3. No person engaged in medical activities shall be compelled to give to anyone belonging either to an adverse Party, or to his own Party except as required by the law of the latter Party, any information concerning the wounded and sick who are, or who have been, under his care, if such information would, in his opinion, prove harmful to the patients concerned or to their families. Regulations for the compulsory notification of communicable diseases shall, however, be respected.

Article 17
Role of the civilian population and of aid societies

1. The civilian population shall respect the wounded, sick and shipwrecked, even if they belong to the adverse Party, and shall commit no act of violence against them. The civilian population and aid societies, such as national Red Cross (Red Crescent, Red Lion and Sun) Societies, shall be permitted, even on their own initiative, to collect and care for the wounded, sick and shipwrecked, even in invaded or occupied areas. No one shall be harmed, prosecuted, convicted or punished for such humanitarian acts.

2. The Parties to the conflict may appeal to the civilian population and the aid societies referred to in paragraph 1 to collect and care for the wounded, sick and shipwrecked, and to search for the dead and report their location; they shall grant both protection and the necessary facilities to those who respond to this appeal. If the adverse Party gains or regains control of the area, that Party also shall afford the same protection and facilities for as long as they are needed.

Article 18
Identification

1. Each Party to the conflict shall endeavour to ensure that medical and religious personnel and medical units and transports are identifiable.
2. Each Party to the conflict shall also endeavour to adopt and to implement methods and procedures which will make it possible to recognize medical units and transports which use the distinctive emblem and distinctive signals.

3. In occupied territory and in areas where fighting is taking place or is likely to take place, civilian medical personnel and civilian religious personnel should be recognizable by the distinctive emblem and an identity card certifying their status.

4. With the consent of the competent authority, medical units and transports shall be marked by the distinctive emblem. The ships and craft referred to in Article 22 of this Protocol shall be marked in accordance with the provisions of the Second Convention.

5. In addition to the distinctive emblem, a Party to the conflict may, as provided in Chapter III of Annex I to this Protocol, authorize the use of distinctive signals to identify medical units and transports. Exceptionally, in the special cases covered in that Chapter, medical transports may use distinctive signals without displaying the distinctive emblem.

6. The application of the provisions of paragraphs 1 to 5 of this article is governed by Chapters I to III of Annex I to this Protocol. Signals designated in Chapter III of the Annex for the exclusive use of medical units and transports shall not, except as provided therein, be used for any purpose other than to identify the medical units and transports specified in that Chapter.

7. This article does not authorize any wider use of the distinctive emblem in peacetime than is prescribed in Article 44 of the First Convention.

8. The provisions of the Conventions and of this Protocol relating to supervision of the use of the distinctive emblem and to the prevention and repression of any misuse thereof shall be applicable to distinctive signals.

Article 19
Neutral and other States not Parties to the conflict

Neutral and other States not Parties to the conflict shall apply the relevant provisions of this Protocol to persons protected by this Part who may be received or interned within their territory, and to any dead of the Parties to that conflict whom they may find.

Article 20
Prohibition of reprisals

Reprisals against the persons and objects protected by this Part are prohibited.

Section II. Medical Transportation

Article 21
Medical vehicles

Medical vehicles shall be respected and protected in the same way as mobile medical units under the Conventions and this Protocol.

Article 22
Hospital ships and coastal rescue craft

1. The provisions of the Conventions relating to:

(a) vessels described in Articles 22, 24, 25 and 27 of the Second Convention,
(b) their lifeboats and small craft,
(c) their personnel and crews, and
(d) the wounded; sick and shipwrecked on board.

shall also apply where these vessels carry civilian wounded, sick and shipwrecked who do not belong to any of the categories mentioned in Article 13 of the Second Convention. Such civilians shall not, however, be subject to surrender to any Party which is not their own, or to capture at sea. If they find themselves in the power of a Party to the conflict other than their own they shall be covered by the Fourth Convention and by this Protocol.

2. The protection provided by the Conventions to vessels described in Article 25 of the Second Convention shall extend to hospital ships made available for humanitarian purposes to a Party to the conflict:

(a) by a neutral or other State which is not a Party to that conflict; or
(b) by an impartial international humanitarian organization,provided that, in either case, the requirements set out in that Article are complied with.

3. Small craft described in Article 27 of the Second Convention shall be protected, even if the notification envisaged by that Article has not been made. The Parties to the conflict are, nevertheless, invited to inform each other of any details of such craft which will facilitate their identification and recognition.

Article 23
Other medical ships and craft

1. Medical ships and craft other than those referred to in Article 22 of this Protocol and Article 38 of the Second Convention shall, whether at sea or in other waters, be respected and protected in the same way as mobile medical units under the Conventions and this Protocol. Since this protection can only be effective if they can be identified and recognized as medical ships or craft, such vessels should be marked with the distinctive emblem and as far as possible comply with the second paragraph of Article 43 of the Second Convention.

2. The ships and craft referred to in paragraph 1 shall remain subject to the laws of war. Any warship on the surface able immediately to enforce its command may order them to stop, order them off, or make them take a certain course, and they shall obey every such command. Such ships and craft may not in any other way be diverted from their medical mission so long as they are needed for the wounded, sick and shipwrecked on board.

3. The protection provided in paragraph 1 shall cease only under the conditions set out in Articles 34 and 35 of the Second Convention. A clear refusal to obey a command given in accordance with paragraph 2 shall be an act harmful to the enemy under Article 34 of the Second Convention.

4. A Party to the conflict may notify any adverse Party as far in advance of sailing as possible of the name, description, expected time of sailing, course and estimated speed of the medical ship or craft, particularly in the case of ships of over 2,000 gross tons, and may provide any other information which would facilitate identification and recognition. The adverse Party shall acknowledge receipt of such information.

5. The provisions of Article 37 of the Second Convention shall apply to medical and religious personnel in such ships and craft.

6. The provisions of the Second Convention shall apply to the wounded, sick and shipwrecked belonging to the categories referred to in Article 13 of the Second Convention and in Article 44 of this Protocol who may be on board such medical ships

and craft. Wounded, sick and shipwrecked civilians who do not belong to any or the categories mentioned in Article 13 of the Second Convention shall not be subject, at sea, either to surrender to any Party which is not their own, or to removal from such ships or craft; if they find themselves in the power of a Party to the conflict other than their own, they shall be covered by the Fourth Convention and by this Protocol.

Article 24
Protection of medical Aircraft

Medical aircraft shall be respected and protected, subject to the provisions of this Part.

Article 25
Medical aircraft in areas not controlled by an adverse Party

In and over land areas physically controlled by friendly forces, or in and over sea areas not physically controlled by an adverse Party, the respect and protection of medical aircraft of a Party to the conflict is not dependent on any agreement with an adverse Party. For greater safety, however, a Party to the conflict operating its medical aircraft in these areas may notify the adverse Party, as provided in Article 29, in particular when such aircraft are making flights bringing them within range of surface-to-air weapons systems of the adverse Party.

Article 26
Medical aircraft in contact or similar zones

1. ln and over those parts of the contact zone which are physically controlled by friendly forces and in and over those areas the physical control of which is not clearly established, protection for medical aircraft can be fully effective only by prior agreement between the competent military authorities of the Parties to the conflict, as provided for in Article 29. Although, in the absence of such an agreement, medical aircraft operate at their own risk, they shall nevertheless be respected after they have been recognized as such.

2. "Contact zone" means any area on land where the forward elements of opposing forces are in contact with each other, especially where they are exposed to direct fire from the ground.

Article 27
Medical aircraft in areas controlled by an adverse Party

1. The medical aircraft of a Party to the conflict shall continue to be protected while flying over land or sea areas physically controlled by an adverse Party, provided that

prior agreement to such flights has been obtained from the competent authority of that adverse Party.

2. A medical aircraft which flies over an area physically controlled by an adverse Party without, or in deviation from the terms of, an agreement provided for in paragraph 1, either through navigational error or because of an emergency affecting the safety of the flight, shall make every effort to identify itself and to inform the adverse Party of the circumstances. As soon as such medical aircraft has been recognized by the adverse Party, that Party shall make all reasonable efforts to give the order to land or to alight on water, referred to in Article 30, paragraph 1, or to take other measures to safeguard its own interests, and, in either case, to allow the aircraft time for compliance, before resorting to an attack against the aircraft.

Article 28
Restrictions on operations of medical aircraft

1. The Parties to the conflict are prohibited from using their medical aircraft to attempt to acquire any military advantage over an adverse Party. The presence of medical aircraft shall not be used in an attempt to render military objectives immune from attack.

2. Medical aircraft shall not be used to collect or transmit intelligence data and shall not carry any equipment intended for such purposes. They are prohibited from carrying any persons or cargo not included within the definition in Article 8 (6). The carrying on board of the personal effects of the occupants or of equipment intended solely to facilitate navigation, communication or identification shall not be considered as prohibited.

3. Medical aircraft shall not carry any armament except small arms and ammunition taken from the wounded, sick and shipwrecked on board and not yet handed to the proper service, and such light individual weapons as may be necessary to enable the medical personnel on board to defend themselves and the wounded, sick and shipwrecked in their charge.

4. While carrying out the flights referred to in Articles 26 and 27, medical aircraft shall not, except by prior agreement with the adverse Party, be used to search for the wounded, sick and shipwrecked.

Article 29
Notifications and agreements concerning medical aircraft

1. Notifications under Article 25, or requests for prior agreement under Articles 26, 27, 28, paragraph 4, or 31 shall state the proposed number of medical aircraft, their flight

plans and means of identification, and shall be understood to mean that every flight will be carried out in compliance with Article 28.

2. A Party which receives a notification given under Article 25 shall at once acknowledge receipt of such notification. 3. A Party which receives a request for prior agreement under Articles 25, 27, 28, paragraph 4, or 31 shall, as rapidly as possible, notify the requesting Party:

(a) that the request is agreed to;
(b) that the request is denied; or
(c) of reasonable alternative proposals to the request. It may also propose prohibition or restriction of other flights in the area during the time involved.

If the Party which submitted the request accepts the alternative proposals, it shall notify the other Party of such acceptance.

4. The Parties shall take the necessary measures to ensure that notifications and agreements can be made rapidly.

5. The Parties shall also take the necessary measures to disseminate rapidly the substance of any such notifications and agreements to the military units concerned and shall instruct those units regarding the means of identification that will be used by the medical aircraft in question.

Article 30
Landing and inspection of medical aircraft

1. Medical aircraft flying over areas which are physically controlled by an adverse Party, or over areas the physical control of which is not clearly established, may be ordered to land or to alight on water, as appropriate, to permit inspection in accordance with the following paragraphs. Medical aircraft shall obey any such order.

2. If such an aircraft lands or alights on water, whether ordered to do so or for other reasons, it may be subjected to inspection solely to determine the matters referred to in paragraphs 3 and 4. Any such inspection shall be commenced without delay and shall be conducted expeditiously. The inspecting Party shall not require the wounded and sick to be removed from the aircraft unless their removal is essential for the inspection. That Party shall in any event ensure that the condition of the wounded and sick is not adversely affected by the inspection or by the removal.

3. If the inspection discloses that the aircraft:

(a) is a medical aircraft within the meaning of Article 8, sub-paragraph j),

(b) is not in violation of the conditions prescribed in Article 28, and
(c) has not flown without or in breach of a prior agreement where such agreement is required,

the aircraft and those of its occupants who belong to the adverse Party or to a neutral or other State not a Party to the conflict shall be authorized to continue the flight without delay.

4. If the inspection discloses that the aircraft:

(a) is not a medical aircraft within the meaning of Article 8, sub-paragraph j),
(b) is in violation or the conditions prescribed in Article 28, or
(c) has flown without or in breach of a prior agreement where such agreement is required,

the aircraft may be seized. Its occupants shall be treated in conformity with the relevant provisions of the Conventions and of this Protocol. Any aircraft seized which had been assigned as a permanent medical aircraft may be used thereafter only as a medical aircraft.

Article 31
Neutral or other States not Parties to the conflict

1. Except by prior agreement, medical aircraft shall not fly over or land in the territory of a neutral or other State not a Party to the conflict. However, with such an agreement, they shall be respected throughout their flight and also for the duration of any calls in the territory. Nevertheless they shall obey any summons to land or to alight on water, as appropriate.

2. Should a medical aircraft, in the absence of an agreement or in deviation from the terms of an agreement, fly over the territory of a neutral or other State not a Party to the conflict, either through navigational error or because of an emergency affecting the safety of the flight, it shall make every effort to give notice of the flight and to identify itself. As soon as such medical aircraft is recognized, that State shall make all reasonable efforts to give the order to land or to alight on water referred to in Article 30, paragraph 1, or to take other measures to safeguard its own interests, and, in either case, to allow the aircraft time for compliance, before resorting to an attack against the aircraft.

3. If a medical aircraft, either by agreement or in the circumstances mentioned in paragraph 2, lands or alights on water in the territory of a neutral or other State not Party to the conflict, whether ordered to do so or for other reasons, the aircraft shall be subject to inspection for the purposes of determining whether it is in fact a medical aircraft. The inspection shall be commenced without delay and shall be conducted expeditiously. The inspecting Party shall not require the wounded and sick of the Party operating the

aircraft to be removed from it unless their removal is essential for the inspection. The inspecting Party shall in any event ensure that the condition of the wounded and sick is not adversely affected by the inspection or the removal. If the inspection discloses that the aircraft is in fact a medical aircraft, the aircraft with its occupants, other than those who must be detained in accordance with the rules of international law applicable in armed conflict, shall be allowed to resume its flight, and reasonable facilities shall be given for the continuation of the flight. If the inspection discloses that the aircraft is not a medical aircraft, it shall be seized and the occupants treated in accordance with paragraph 4.

4. The wounded, sick and shipwrecked disembarked, otherwise than temporarily, from a medical aircraft with the consent of the local authorities in the territory of a neutral or other State not a Party to the conflict shall, unless agreed otherwise between that State and the Parties to the conflict, be detained by that State where so required by the rules of international law applicable in armed conflict, in such a manner that they cannot again take part in the hostilities. The cost of hospital treatment and internment shall be borne by the State to which those persons belong.

5. Neutral or other States not Parties to the conflict shall apply any conditions and restrictions on the passage of medical aircraft over, or on the landing of medical aircraft in, their territory equally to all Parties to the conflict.

Section III. Missing and Dead Persons

Article 32
General principle

In the implementation of this Section, the activities of the High Contracting Parties, of the Parties to the conflict and of the international humanitarian organizations mentioned in the Conventions and in this Protocol shall be prompted mainly by the right of families to know the fate of their relatives.

Article 33
Missing persons

1. As soon as circumstances permit, and at the latest from the end of active hostilities, each Party to the conflict shall search for the persons who have been reported missing by an adverse Party. Such adverse Party shall transmit all relevant information concerning such persons in order to facilitate such searches.

2. In order to facilitate the gathering of information pursuant to the preceding paragraph, each Party to the conflict shall, with respect to persons who would not receive more favourable consideration under the Conventions and this Protocol:

(a) record the information specified in Article 138 of the Fourth Convention in respect of such persons who have been detained, imprisoned or otherwise held in captivity for more than two weeks as a result of hostilities or occupation, or who have died during any period of detention;

(b) to the fullest extent possible, facilitate and, if need be, carry out the search for and the recording of information concerning such persons if they have died in other circumstances as a result of hostilities or occupation.

3. Information concerning persons reported missing pursuant to paragraph 1 and requests for such information shall be transmitted either directly or through the Protecting Power or the Central Tracing Agency of the International Committee of the Red Cross or national Red Cross (Red Crescent, Red Lion and Sun) Societies. Where the information is not transmitted through the International Committee of the Red Cross and its Central Tracing Agency, each Party to the conflict shall ensure that such information is also supplied to the Central Tracing Agency.

4. The Parties to the conflict shall endeavour to agree on arrangements for teams to search for, identify and recover the dead from battlefield areas, including arrangements, if appropriate, for such teams to be accompanied by personnel of the adverse Party while carrying out these missions in areas controlled by the adverse Party. Personnel of such teams shall be respected and protected while exclusively carrying out these duties.

Article 34
Remains of deceased

1. The remains of persons who have died for reasons related to occupation or in detention resulting from occupation or hostilities and those or persons not nationals of the country in which they have died as a result of hostilities shall be respected, and the gravesites of all such persons shall be respected, maintained and marked as provided for in Article 130 of the Fourth Convention, where their remains or gravesites would not receive more favourable consideration under the Conventions and this Protocol.

2. As soon as circumstances and the relations between the adverse Parties permit, the High Contracting Parties in whose territories graves and, as the case may be, other locations of the remains of persons who have died as a result of hostilities or during occupation or in detention are situated, shall conclude agreements in order:

(a) to facilitate access to the gravesites by relatives of the deceased and by representatives of official graves registration services and to regulate the practical arrangements for such access;
(b) to protect and maintain such gravesites permanently;

(c) to facilitate the return of the remains of the deceased and of personal effects to the home country upon its request or, unless that country objects, upon the request of the next of kin.

3. In the absence of the agreements provided for in paragraph 2 (b) or (c) and if the home country or such deceased is not willing to arrange at its expense for the maintenance of such gravesites, the High Contracting Party in whose territory the gravesites are situated may offer to facilitate the return of the remains of the deceased to the home country. Where such an offer has not been accepted the High Contracting Party may, after the expiry of five years from the date of the offer and upon due notice to the home country, adopt the arrangements laid down in its own laws relating to cemeteries and graves.

4. A High Contracting Party in whose territory the grave sites referred to in this Article are situated shall be permitted to exhume the remains only:

(a) in accordance with paragraphs 2 (c) and 3, or
(b) where exhumation is a matter or overriding public necessity, including cases of medical and investigative necessity, in which case the High Contracting Party shall at all times respect the remains, and shall give notice to the home country or its intention to exhume the remains together with details of the intended place of reinterment.

Part III. Methods and Means of Warfare Combatant and Prisoners-Of-War

Section I. Methods and Means of Warfare

Article 35
Basic rules

1. In any armed conflict, the right of the Parties to the conflict to choose methods or means of warfare is not unlimited.
2. It is prohibited to employ weapons, projectiles and material and methods of warfare of a nature to cause superfluous injury or unnecessary suffering.

3. It is prohibited to employ methods or means of warfare which are intended, or may be expected, to cause widespread, long-term and severe damage to the natural environment.

Article 36
New weapons

In the study, development, acquisition or adoption of a new weapon, means or method of warfare, a High Contracting Party is under an obligation to determine whether its employment would, in some or all circumstances, be prohibited by this Protocol or by any other rule of international law applicable to the High Contracting Party.

Article 37
Prohibition of Perfidy

1. It is prohibited to kill, injure or capture an adversary by resort to perfidy. Acts inviting the confidence of an adversary to lead him to believe that he is entitled to, or is obliged to accord, protection under the rules of international law applicable in armed conflict, with intent to betray that confidence, shall constitute perfidy. The following acts are examples of perfidy:

(a) the feigning of an intent to negotiate under a flag of truce or of a surrender;
(b) the feigning of an incapacitation by wounds or sickness;
(c) the feigning of civilian, non-combatant status; and
(d) the feigning of protected status by the use of signs, emblems or uniforms of the United Nations or of neutral or other States not Parties to the conflict.

2. Ruses of war are not prohibited. Such ruses are acts which are intended to mislead an adversary or to induce him to act recklessly but which infringe no rule of international law applicable in armed conflict and which are not perfidious because they do not invite the confidence of an adversary with respect to protection under that law. The following are examples of such ruses: the use of camouflage, decoys, mock operations and misinformation.

Article 38
Recognized emblems

1. It is prohibited to make improper use of the distinctive emblem of the red cross, red crescent or red lion and sun or of other emblems, signs or signals provided for by the Conventions or by this Protocol. It is also prohibited to misuse deliberately in an armed conflict other internationally recognized protective emblems, signs or signals, including the flag of truce, and the protective emblem of cultural property.

2. It is prohibited to make use of the distinctive emblem of the United Nations, except as authorized by that Organization.

Article 39
Emblems of nationality

1. It is prohibited to make use in an armed conflict of the flags or military emblems, insignia or uniforms of neutral or other States not Parties to the conflict.

2. It is prohibited to make use of the flags or military emblems, insignia or uniforms of adverse Parties while engaging in attacks or in order to shield, favour, protect or impede military operations.

3. Nothing in this Article or in Article 37, paragraph 1 (d), shall affect the existing generally recognized rules of international law applicable to espionage or to the use of flags in the conduct of armed conflict at sea.

Article 40
Quarter

It is prohibited to order that there shall be no survivors, to threaten an adversary therewith or to conduct hostilities on this basis.

Article 41
Safeguard of an enemy hors de combat

1. A person who is recognized or who, in the circumstances, should be recognized to be hors de combat shall not be made the object of attack.
2. A person is hors de combat if:

(a) he is in the power of an adverse Party;
(b) he clearly expresses an intention to surrender; or
(c) he has been rendered unconscious or is otherwise incapacitated by wounds or sickness, and therefore is incapable of defending himself;

provided that in any of these cases he abstains from any hostile act and does not attempt to escape.

3. When persons entitled to protection as prisoners of war have fallen into the power of an adverse Party under unusual conditions of combat which prevent their evacuation as provided for in Part III, Section I, of the Third Convention, they shall be released and all feasible precautions shall be taken to ensure their safety.

Article 42
Occupants of aircraft

1. No person parachuting from an aircraft in distress shall be made the object of attack during his descent.

2. Upon reaching the ground in territory controlled by an adverse Party, a person who has parachuted from an aircraft in distress shall be given an opportunity to surrender before being made the object of attack, unless it is apparent that he is engaging in a hostile act.

3. Airborne troops are not protected by this Article.

Section II. Combatants and Prisoners of War

Article 43
Armed forces

1. The armed forces of a Party to a conflict consist of all organized armed forces, groups and units which are under a command responsible to that Party for the conduct of its subordinates, even if that Party is represented by a government or an authority not recognized by an adverse Party. Such armed forces shall be subject to an internal disciplinary system which, inter alia, shall enforce compliance with the rules of international law applicable in armed conflict.

2. Members of the armed forces of a Party to a conflict (other than medical personnel and chaplains covered by Article 33 of the Third Convention) are combatants, that is to say, they have the right to participate directly in hostilities.

3. Whenever a Party to a conflict incorporates a paramilitary or armed law enforcement agency into its armed forces it shall so notify the other Parties to the conflict.

Article 44
Combatants and prisoners of war

1. Any combatant, as defined in Article 43, who falls into the power of an adverse Party shall be a prisoner of war.

2. While all combatants are obliged to comply with the rules of international law applicable in armed conflict, violations of these rules shall not deprive a combatant of his right to be a combatant or, if he falls into the power of an adverse Party, of his right to be a prisoner of war, except as provided in paragraphs 3 and 4.

3. In order to promote the protection of the civilian population from the effects of hostilities, combatants are obliged to distinguish themselves from the civilian population

while they are engaged in an attack or in a military operation preparatory to an attack. Recognizing, however, that there are situations in armed conflicts where, owing to the nature of the hostilities an armed combatant cannot so distinguish himself, he shall retain his status as a combatant, provided that, in such situations, hecarries his arms openly:

(a) during each military engagement, and
(b) during such time as he is visible to the adversary while he is engaged in a military deployment preceding the launching of an attack in which he is to participate.

Acts which comply with the requirements of this paragraph shall not be considered as perfidious within the meaning of Article 37, paragraph 1 (c).

4. A combatant who falls into the power of an adverse Party while failing to meet the requirements set forth in the second sentence of paragraph 3 shall forfeit his right to be a prisoner of war, but he shall, nevertheless, be given protections equivalent in all respects to those accorded to prisoners of war by the Third Convention and by this Protocol. This protection includes protections equivalent to those accorded to prisoners of war by the Third Convention in the case where such a person is tried and punished for any offences he has committed.

5. Any combatant who falls into the power of an adverse Party while not engaged in an attack or in a military operation preparatory to an attack shall not forfeit his rights to be a combatant and a prisoner of war by virtue of his prior activities.

6. This Article is without prejudice to the right of any person to be a prisoner of war pursuant to Article 4 of the Third Convention.

7. This Article is not intended to change the generally accepted practice of States with respect to the wearing of the uniform by combatants assigned to the regular, uniformed armed units of a Party to the conflict.

8. In addition to the categories of persons mentioned in Article 13 of the First and Second Conventions, all members of the armed forces of a Party to the conflict, as defined in Article 43 of this Protocol, shall be entitled to protection under those Conventions if they are wounded or sick or, in the case of the Second Convention, shipwrecked at sea or in other waters.

Article 45
Protection of persons who have taken part in hostilities

1. A person who takes part in hostilities and falls into the power of an adverse Party shall be presumed to be a prisoner of war, and therefore shall be protected by the Third

Convention, if he claims the status of prisoner of war, or if he appears to be entitled to such status, or if the Party on which he depends claims such status on his behalf by notification to the detaining Power or to the Protecting Power. Should any doubt arise as to whether any such person is entitled to the status of prisoner of war, he shall continue to have such status and, therefore, to be protected by the Third Convention and this Protocol until such time as his status has been determined by a competent tribunal.
2. If a person who has fallen into the power of an adverse Party is not held as a prisoner of war and is to be tried by that Party for an offence arising out of the hostilities, he shall have the right to assert his entitlement to prisoner-of-war status before a judicial tribunal and to have that question adjudicated. Whenever possible under the applicable procedure, this adjudication shall occur before the trial for the offence. The representatives of the Protecting Power shall be entitled to attend the proceedings in which that question is adjudicated, unless, exceptionally, the proceedings are held in camera in the interest of State security. In such a case the detaining Power shall advise the Protecting Power accordingly.

3. Any person who has taken part in hostilities, who is not entitled to prisoner-of-war status and who does not benefit from more favourable treatment in accordance with the Fourth Convention shall have the right at all times to the protection of Article 75 of this Protocol. In occupied territory, any such person, unless he is held as a spy, shall also be entitled, notwithstanding Article 5 of the Fourth Convention, to his rights of communication under that Convention.

Article 46
Spies

1. Notwithstanding any other provision of the Conventions or of this Protocol, any member of the armed forces of a Party to the conflict who falls into the power of an adverse Party while engaging in espionage shall not have the right to the status of prisoner of war and may be treated as a spy.

2. A member of the armed forces of a Party to the conflict who, on behalf of that Party and in territory controlled by an adverse Party, gathers or attempts to gather information shall not be considered as engaging in espionage if, while so acting, he is in the uniform of his armed forces.

3. A member of the armed forces of a Party to the conflict who is a resident of territory occupied by an adverse Party and who, on behalf of the Party on which he depends, gathers or attempts to gather information of military value within that territory shall not be considered as engaging in espionage unless he does so through an act of false pretences or deliberately in a clandestine manner. Moreover, such a resident shall not lose his right to the status of prisoner of war and may not be treated as a spy unless he is captured while engaging in espionage.

4. A member of the armed forces of a Party to the conflict who is not a resident of territory occupied by an adverse Party and who has engaged in espionage in that territory shall not lose his right to the status of prisoner of war and may not be treated as a spy unless he is captured before he has rejoined the armed forces to which he belongs.

Article 47
Mercenaries

1. A mercenary shall not have the right to be a combatant or a prisoner of war.

2. A mercenary is any person who:

(a) is specially recruited locally or abroad in order to fight in an armed conflict;
(b) does, in fact, take a direct part in the hostilities;
(c) is motivated to take part in the hostilities essentially by the desire for private gain and, in fact, is promised, by or on behalf of a Party to the conflict, material compensation substantially in excess of that promised or paid to combatants of similar ranks and functions in the armed forces of that Party;
(d) is neither a national of a Party to the conflict nor a resident of territory controlled by a Party to the conflict;
(e) is not a member of the armed forces of a Party to the conflict; and
(f) has not been sent by a State which is not a Party to the conflict on official duty as a member of its armed forces.

Part IV. Civilian Population

Section I. General Protection Against Effects of Hostilities

Chapter I. Basic rule and field of application

Article 48
Basic rule

In order to ensure respect for and protection of the civilian population and civilian objects, the Parties to the conflict shall at all times distinguish between the civilian population and combatants and between civilian objects and military objectives and accordingly shall direct their operations only against military objectives.

Article 49
Definition of attacks and scope of application

1. "Attacks" means acts of violence against the adversary, whether in offence or in

defence.

2. The provisions of this Protocol with respect to attacks apply to all attacks in whatever territory conducted, including the national territory belonging to a Party to the conflict but under the control of an adverse Party.

3. The provisions of this section apply to any land, air or sea warfare which may affect the civilian population, individual civilians or civilian objects on land. They further apply to all attacks from the sea or from the air against objectives on land but do not otherwise affect the rules of international law applicable in armed conflict at sea or in the air.

4. The provisions of this section are additional to the rules concerning humanitarian protection contained in the Fourth Convention, particularly in part II thereof, and in other international agreements binding upon the High Contracting Parties, as well as to other rules of international law relating to the protection of civilians and civilian objects on land, at sea or in the air against the effects of hostilities.

Chapter II. Civilians and civilian population

Article 50
Definition of civilians and civilian population

1. A civilian is any person who does not belong to one of the categories of persons referred to in Article 4 (A) (1), (2), (3) and (6) of the Third Convention and in Article 43 of this Protocol. In case of doubt whether a person is a civilian, that person shall be considered to be a civilian.

2. The civilian population comprises all persons who are civilians.

3. The presence within the civilian population of individuals who do not come within the definition of civilians does not deprive the population of its civilian character.

Article 51
Protection of the civilian population

1. The civilian population and individual civilians shall enjoy general protection against dangers arising from military operations. To give effect to this protection, the following rules, which are additional to other applicable rules of international law, shall be observed in all circumstances.

2. The civilian population as such, as well as individual civilians, shall not be the object of attack. Acts or threats of violence the primary purpose of which is to spread terror among the civilian population are prohibited.

3. Civilians shall enjoy the protection afforded by this section, unless and for such time as they take a direct part in hostilities.

4. Indiscriminate attacks are prohibited. Indiscriminate attacks are:

(a) those which are not directed at a specific military objective;
(b) those which employ a method or means of combat which cannot be directed at a specific military objective; or
(c) those which employ a method or means of combat the effects of which cannot be limited as required by this Protocol;

and consequently, in each such case, are of a nature to strike military objectives and civilians or civilian objects without distinction.

5. Among others, the following types of attacks are to be considered as indiscriminate:

(a) an attack by bombardment by any methods or means which treats as a single military objective a number of clearly separated and distinct military objectives located in a city, town, village or other area containing a similar concentration of civilians or civilian objects; and

(b) an attack which may be expected to cause incidental loss of civilian life, injury to civilians, damage to civilian objects, or a combination thereof, which would be excessive in relation to the concrete and direct military advantage anticipated.

6. Attacks against the civilian population or civilians by way of reprisals are prohibited.

7. The presence or movements of the civilian population or individual civilians shall not be used to render certain points or areas immune from military operations, in particular in attempts to shield military objectives from attacks or to shield, favour or impede military operations. The Parties to the conflict shall not direct the movement of the civilian population or individual civilians in order to attempt to shield military objectives from attacks or to shield military operations.

8. Any violation of these prohibitions shall not release the Parties to the conflict from their legal obligations with respect to the civilian population and civilians, including the obligation to take the precautionary measures provided for in Article 57.

Chapter III. Civilian objects

Article 52
General Protection of civilian objects

1. Civilian objects shall not be the object of attack or of reprisals. Civilian objects are all objects which are not military objectives as defined in paragraph 2.

2. Attacks shall be limited strictly to military objectives. In so far as objects are concerned, military objectives are limited to those objects which by their nature, location, purpose or use make an effective contribution to military action and whose total or partial destruction, capture or neutralization, in the circumstances ruling at the time, offers a definite military advantage.

3. In case of doubt whether an object which is normally dedicated to civilian purposes, such as a place of worship, a house or other dwelling or a school, is being used to make an effective contribution to military action, it shall be presumed not to be so used.

Article 53
Protection of cultural objects and of places of worship

Without prejudice to the provisions of the Hague Convention for the Protection of Cultural Property in the Event of Armed Conflict of 14 May 1954, and of other relevant international instruments, it is prohibited:

(a) to commit any acts of hostility directed against the historic monuments, works of art or places of worship which constitute the cultural or spiritual heritage of peoples;
(b) to use such objects in support of the military effort;
(c) to make such objects the object of reprisals.

Article 54
Protection of objects indispensable to the survival of the civilian population

1. Starvation of civilians as a method of warfare is prohibited.

2. It is prohibited to attack, destroy, remove or render useless objects indispensable to the survival of the civilian population, such as food-stuffs, agricultural areas for the production of food-stuffs, crops, livestock, drinking water installations and supplies and irrigation works, for the specific purpose of denying them for their sustenance value to the civilian population or to the adverse Party, whatever the motive, whether in order to starve out civilians, to cause them to move away, or for any other motive.

3. The prohibitions in paragraph 2 shall not apply to such of the objects covered by it as are used by an adverse Party:

(a) as sustenance solely for the members of its armed forces; or

(b) if not as sustenance, then in direct support of military action, provided, however, that in no event shall actions against these objects be taken which may be expected to leave the civilian population with such inadequate food or water as to cause its starvation or force its movement.

4. These objects shall not be made the object of reprisals.

5. In recognition of the vital requirements of any Party to the conflict in the defence of its national territory against invasion, derogation from the prohibitions contained in paragraph 2 may be made by a Party to the conflict within such territory under its own control where required by imperative military necessity.

Article 55
Protection of the natural environment

1. Care shall be taken in warfare to protect the natural environment against widespread, long-term and severe damage. This protection includes a prohibition of the use of methods or means of warfare which are intended or may be expected to cause such damage to the natural environment and thereby to prejudice the health or survival of the population.

2. Attacks against the natural environment by way of reprisals are prohibited.

Article 56
Protection of works and installations containing dangerous forces

1. Works or installations containing dangerous forces, namely dams, dykes and nuclear electrical generating stations, shall not be made the object of attack, even where these objects are military objectives, if such attack may cause the release of dangerous forces and consequent severe losses among the civilian population. Other military objectives located at or in the vicinity of these works or installations shall not be made the object of attack if such attack may cause the release of dangerous forces from the works or installations and consequent severe losses among the civilian population.

2. The special protection against attack provided by paragraph 1 shall cease:

(a) for a dam or a dyke only if it is used for other than its normal function and in regular, significant and direct support of military operations and if such attack is the only feasible way to terminate such support;
(b) for a nuclear electrical generating station only if it provides electric power in regular, significant and direct support of military operations and if such attack is the only feasible way to terminate such support;

(c) for other military objectives located at or in the vicinity of these works or installations only if they are used in regular, significant and direct support of military operations and if such attack is the only feasible way to terminate such support.

3. In all cases, the civilian population and individual civilians shall remain entitled to all the protection accorded them by international law, including the protection of the precautionary measures provided for in Article 57. If the protection Ceases and any of the works, installations or military objectives mentioned in paragraph 1 is attacked, all practical precautions shall be taken to avoid the release of the dangerous forces.

4. It is prohibited to make any of the works, installations or military objectives mentioned in paragraph 1 the object of reprisals.

5. The Parties to the conflict shall endeavour to avoid locating any military objectives in the vicinity of the works or installations mentioned in paragraph 1. Nevertheless, installations erected for the sole purpose of defending the protected works or installations from attack are permissible and shall not themselves be made the object of attack, provided that they are not used in hostilities except for defensive actions necessary to respond to attacks against the protected works or installations and that their armament is limited to weapons capable only of repelling hostile action against the protected works or installations.

6. The High Contracting Parties and the Parties to the conflict are urged to conclude further agreements among themselves to provide additional protection for objects containing dangerous forces.

7. In order to facilitate the identification of the objects protected by this article, the Parties to the conflict may mark them with a special sign consisting of a group of three bright orange circles placed on the same axis, as specified in Article 16 of Annex I to this Protocol [Article 17 of Amended Annex]. The absence of such marking in no way relieves any Party to the conflict of its obligations under this Article.

Chapter IV. Precautionary measures

Article 57
Precautions in attack

1. In the conduct of military operations, constant care shall be taken to spare the civilian population, civilians and civilian objects.

2. With respect to attacks, the following precautions shall be taken:

(a) those who plan or decide upon an attack shall:

(i) do everything feasible to verify that the objectives to be attacked are neither civilians nor civilian objects and are not subject to special protection but are military objectives within the meaning of paragraph 2 of Article 52 and that it is not prohibited by the provisions of this Protocol to attack them;
(ii) take all feasible precautions in the choice of means and methods of attack with a view to avoiding, and in any event to minimizing, incidental loss or civilian life, injury to civilians and damage to civilian objects;
(iii) refrain from deciding to launch any attack which may be expected to cause incidental loss of civilian life, injury to civilians, damage to civilian objects, or a combination thereof, which would be excessive in relation to the concrete and direct military advantage anticipated;

(b) an attack shall be cancelled or suspended if it becomes apparent that the objective is not a military one or is subject to special protection or that the attack may be expected to cause incidental loss of civilian life, injury to civilians, damage to civilian objects, or a combination thereof, which would be excessive in relation to the concrete and direct military advantage anticipated;

(c) effective advance warning shall be given of attacks which may affect the civilian population, unless circumstances do not permit.

3. When a choice is possible between several military objectives for obtaining a similar military advantage, the objective to be selected shall be that the attack on which may be expected to cause the least danger to civilian lives and to civilian objects.

4. In the conduct of military operations at sea or in the air, each Party to the conflict shall, in conformity with its rights and duties under the rules of international law applicable in armed conflict, take all reasonable precautions to avoid losses of civilian lives and damage to civilian objects.

5. No provision of this article may be construed as authorizing any attacks against the civilian population, civilians or civilian objects.

Article 58
Precautions against the effects of attacks

The Parties to the conflict shall, to the maximum extent feasible:
(a) without prejudice to Article 49 of the Fourth Convention, endeavour to remove the civilian population, individual civilians and civilian objects under their control from the vicinity of military objectives;
(b) avoid locating military objectives within or near densely populated areas;

(c) take the other necessary precautions to protect the civilian population, individual civilians and civilian objects under their control against the dangers resulting from military operations.

Chapter V. Localities and zones under special protection

Article 59
Non-defended localities

1. It is prohibited for the Parties to the conflict to attack, by any means whatsoever, non-defended localities.

2. The appropriate authorities of a Party to the conflict may declare as a non-defended locality any inhabited place near or in a zone where armed forces are in contact which is open for occupation by an adverse Party. Such a locality shall fulfil the following conditions:

(a) all combatants, as well as mobile weapons and mobile military equipment must have been evacuated;
(b) no hostile use shall be made of fixed military installations or establishments;
(c) no acts of hostility shall be committed by the authorities or by the population; and
(d) no activities in support of military operations shall be undertaken.

3. The presence, in this locality, of persons specially protected under the Conventions and this Protocol, and of police forces retained for the sole purpose of maintaining law and order, is not contrary to the conditions laid down in paragraph 2.

4. The declaration made under paragraph 2 shall be addressed to the adverse Party and shall define and describe, as precisely as possible, the limits of the non-defended locality. The Party to the conflict to which the declaration is addressed shall acknowledge its receipt and shall treat the locality as a non-defended locality unless the conditions laid down in paragraph 2 are not in fact fulfilled, in which event it shall immediately so inform the Party making the declaration. Even if the conditions laid down in paragraph 2 are not fulfilled, the locality shall continue to enjoy the protection provided by the other provisions of this Protocol and the other rules of international law applicable in armed conflict.

5. The Parties to the conflict may agree on the establishment of non-defended localities even if such localities do not fulfil the conditions laid down in paragraph 2. The agreement should define and describe, as precisely as possible, the limits of the non-defended locality; if necessary, it may lay down the methods of supervision.

6. The Party which is in control of a locality governed by such an agreement shall mark

it, so far as possible, by such signs as may be agreed upon with the other Party, which shall be displayed where they are clearly visible, especially on its perimeter and limits and on highways.

7. A locality loses its status as a non-defended locality when its ceases to fulfil the conditions laid down in paragraph 2 or in the agreement referred to in paragraph 5. In such an eventuality, the locality shall continue to enjoy the protection provided by the other provisions of this Protocol and the other rules of international law applicable in armed conflict.

Article 60
Demilitarized zones

1. It is prohibited for the Parties to the conflict to extend their military operations to zones on which they have conferred by agreement the status of demilitarized zone, if such extension is contrary to the terms of this agreement.

2. The agreement shall be an express agreement, may be concluded verbally or in writing, either directly or through a Protecting Power or any impartial humanitarian organization, and may consist of reciprocal and concordant declarations. The agreement may be concluded in peacetime, as well as after the outbreak of hostilities, and should define and describe, as precisely as possible, the limits of the demilitarized zone and, if necessary, lay down the methods of supervision.

3. The subject of such an agreement shall normally be any zone which fulfils the following conditions:

(a) all combatants, as well as mobile weapons and mobile military equipment, must have been evacuated;
(b) no hostile use shall be made of fixed military installations or establishments;
(c) no acts of hostility shall be committed by the authorities or by the population; And
(d) any activity linked to the military effort must have ceased.

The Parties to the conflict shall agree upon the interpretation to be given to the condition laid down in subparagraph (d) and upon persons to be admitted to the demilitarized zone other than those mentioned in paragraph 4.

4. The presence, in this zone, of persons specially protected under the Conventions and this Protocol, and of police forces retained for the sole purpose of maintaining law and order, is not contrary to the conditions laid down in paragraph 3.

5. The Party which is in control of such a zone shall mark it, so far as possible, by such

signs as may be agreed upon with the other Party, which shall be displayed where they are clearly visible, especially on its perimeter and limits and on highways.

6. If the fighting draws near to a demilitarized zone, and if the Parties to the conflict have so agreed, none of them may use the zone for purposes related to the conduct of military operations or unilaterally revoke its status.

7. If one of the Parties to the conflict commits a material breach of the provisions of paragraphs 3 or 6, the other Party shall be released from its obligations under the agreement conferring upon the zone the status of demilitarized zone. In such an eventuality, the zone loses its status but shall continue to enjoy the protection provided by the other provisions of this Protocol and the other rules of international law applicable in armed conflict.

Chapter VI. Civil defence
Article 61
Definitions and scope

For the purpose of this Protocol:

(1) "Civil defence" means the performance of some or all of the undermentioned humanitarian tasks intended to protect the civilian population against the dangers, and to help it to recover from the immediate effects, of hostilities or disasters and also to provide the conditions necessary for its survival. These tasks are:

(a) warning;
(b) evacuation;
(c) management of shelters;
(d) management of blackout measures;
(e) rescue;
(f) medical services, including first aid, and religious assistance;
(g) fire-fighting;
(h) detection and marking of danger areas;
(i) decontamination and similar protective measures;
(j) provision of emergency accommodation and supplies;
(k) emergency assistance in the restoration and maintenance of order in distressed areas;
(l) emergency repair of indispensable public utilities;
(m) emergency disposal of the dead;
(n) assistance in the preservation of objects essential for survival;

(o) complementary activities necessary to carry out any of the tasks mentioned above, including, but not limited to, planning and organization;

(2) "Civil defence organizations" means those establishments and other units which are organized or authorized by the competent authorities of a Party to the conflict to perform any of the tasks mentioned under (1), and which are assigned and devoted exclusively to such tasks;

(3) "Personnel" of civil defence organizations means those persons assigned by a Party to the conflict exclusively to the performance of the tasks mentioned under (1), including personnel assigned by the competent authority of that Party exclusively to the administration of these organizations;

(4) "Matériel" of civil defence organizations means equipment, supplies and transports used by these organizations for the performance of the tasks mentioned under (1).

Article 62
General protection

1. Civilian civil defence organizations and their personnel shall be respected and protected, subject to the provisions of this Protocol, particularly the provisions of this section. They shall be entitled to perform their civil defence tasks except in case of imperative military necessity.

2. The provisions of paragraph 1 shall also apply to civilians who, although not members of civilian civil defence organizations, respond to an appeal from the competent authorities and perform civil defence tasks under their control.

3. Buildings and matériel used for civil defence purposes and shelters provided for the civilian population are covered by Article 52. Objects used for civil defence purposes may not be destroyed or diverted from their proper use except by the Party to which they belong.

Article 63
Civil defence in occupied territories

1. In occupied territories, civilian civil defence organizations shall receive from the authorities the facilities necessary for the performance of their tasks. In no Circumstances shall their personnel be compelled to perform activities which would interfere with the proper performance of these tasks. The Occupying Power shall not change the structure or personnel of such organizations in any way which might

jeopardize the efficient performance of their mission. These organizations shall not be required to give priority to the nationals or interests of that Power.

2. The Occupying Power shall not compel, coerce or induce civilian civil defence organizations to perform their tasks in any manner prejudicial to the interests of the civilian population.
3. The Occupying Power may disarm civil defence personnel for reasons of security.

4. The Occupying Power shall neither divert from their proper use nor requisition buildings or matériel belonging to or used by civil defence organizations if such diversion or requisition would be harmful to the civilian population.

5. Provided that the general rule in paragraph 4 continues to be observed, the Occupying Power may requisition or divert these resources, subject to the following particular conditions:

(a) that the buildings or matériel are necessary for other needs of the civilian population; and
(b) that the requisition or diversion continues only while such necessity exists.

6. The Occupying Power shall neither divert nor requisition shelters provided for the use of the civilian population or needed by such population.

Article 64
Civilian civil defence organizations of neutral or other States not Parties to the conflict and international co-ordinating organizations

1. Articles 62, 63, 65 and 66 shall also apply to the personnel and matériel of civilian civil defence organizations of neutral or other States not Parties to the conflict which perform civil defence tasks mentioned in Article 61 in the territory of a Party to the conflict, with the consent and under the control of that Party. Notification of such assistance shall be given as soon as possible to any adverse Party concerned. In no circumstances shall this activity be deemed to be an interference in the conflict. This activity should, however, be performed with due regard to the security interests of the Parties to the conflict concerned.

2. The Parties to the conflict receiving the assistance referred to in paragraph 1 and the High Contracting Parties granting it should facilitate international co-ordination of such civil defence actions when appropriate. In such cases the relevant international organizations are covered by the provisions of this Chapter.
3. In occupied territories, the Occupying Power may only exclude or restrict the activities of civilian civil defence organizations of neutral or other States not Parties to the conflict and of international co-ordinating organizations if it can ensure the adequate

performance of civil defence tasks from its own resources or those of the occupied territory.

Article 65
Cessation of protection

1. The protection to which civilian civil defence organizations, their personnel, buildings, shelters and matériel are entitled shall not cease unless they commit or are used to commit, outside their proper tasks, acts harmful to the enemy. Protection may, however, cease only after a warning has been given setting, whenever appropriate, a reasonable time-limit, and after such warning has remained unheeded.

2. The following shall not be considered as acts harmful to the enemy:

(a) that civil defence tasks are carried out under the direction or control of military authorities;
(b) that civilian civil defence personnel co-operate with military personnel in the performance of civil defence tasks, or that some military personnel are attached to civilian civil defence organizations;
(c) that the performance of civil defence tasks may incidentally benefit military victims, particularly those who are hors de combat.

3. It shall also not be considered as an act harmful to the enemy that civilian civil defence personnel bear light individual weapons for the purpose of maintaining order or for self-defence. However, in areas where land fighting is taking place or is likely to take place, the Parties to the conflict shall undertake the appropriate measures to limit these weapons to handguns, such as pistols or revolvers, in order to assist in distinguishing between civil defence personnel and combatants. Although civil defence personnel bear other light individual weapons in such areas, they shall nevertheless be respected and protected as soon as they have been recognized as such.

4. The formation of civilian civil defence organizations along military lines, and compulsory service in them, shall also not deprive them of the protection conferred by this Chapter.

Article 66
Identification

1. Each Party to the conflict shall endeavour to ensure that its civil defence organizations, their personnel, buildings and matériel are identifiable while they are exclusively devoted to the performance of civil defence tasks. Shelters provided for the civilian population should be similarly identifiable.

2. Each Party to the conflict shall also endeavour to adopt and implement methods and

procedures which will make it possible to recognize civilian shelters as well as civil defence personnel, buildings and matériel on which the international distinctive sign of civil defence is displayed.

3. In occupied territories and in areas where fighting is taking place or is likely to take place, civilian civil defence personnel should be recognizable by the international distinctive sign of civil defence and by an identity card certifying their status.

4. The international distinctive sign of civil defence is an equilateral blue triangle on an orange ground when used for the protection of civil defence organizations, their personnel, buildings and matériel and for civilian shelters.

5. In addition to the distinctive sign, Parties to the conflict may agree upon the use of distinctive signals for civil defence identification purposes.

6. The application of the provisions of paragraphs 1 to 4 is governed by Chapter V of Annex I to this Protocol.

7. In time of peace, the sign described in paragraph 4 may, with the consent of the competent national authorities, be used for civil defence identification purposes.

8. The High Contracting Parties and the Parties to the conflict shall take the measures necessary to supervise the display of the international distinctive sign of civil defence and to prevent and repress any misuse thereof.

9. The identification of civil defence medical and religious personnel, medical units and medical transports is also governed by Article 18.

Article 67
Members of the armed forces and military units assigned to civil defence organizations

1. Members of the armed forces and military units assigned to civil defence organizations shall be respected and protected, provided that:

(a) such personnel and such units are permanently assigned and exclusively devoted to the performance of any of the tasks mentioned in Article 61;
(b) if so assigned, such personnel do not perform any other military duties during the conflict;
(c) such personnel are clearly distinguishable from the other members of the armed forces by prominently displaying the international distinctive sign of civil defence, which shall be as large as appropriate, and such personnel are provided with the

identity card referred to in Chapter V of Annex I to this Protocol certifying their status;
(d) such personnel and such units are equipped only with light individual weapons for the purpose of maintaining order or for self-defence. The provisions of Article 65, paragraph 3 shall also apply in this case;
(e) such personnel do not participate directly in hostilities, and do not commit, or are not used to commit, outside their civil defence tasks, acts harmful to the adverse Party
(f) such personnel and such units perform their civil defence tasks only within the national territory of their Party.

The non-observance of the conditions stated in (e) above by any member of the armed forces who is bound by the conditions prescribed in (a) and (b) above is prohibited.

2. Military personnel serving within civil defence organizations shall, if they fall into the power of an adverse Party, be prisoners of war. In occupied territory they may, but only in the interest of the civilian population of that territory, be employed on civil defence tasks in so far as the need arises, provided however that, if such work is dangerous, they volunteer for such tasks.

3. The buildings and major items of equipment and transports of military units assigned to civil defence organizations shall be clearly marked with the international distinctive sign of civil defence. This distinctive sign shall be as large as appropriate.
4. The matériel and buildings of military units permanently assigned to civil defence organizations and exclusively devoted to the performance of civil defence tasks shall, if they fall into the hands of an adverse Party, remain subject to the laws of war. They may not be diverted from their civil defence purpose so long as they are required for the performance of civil defence tasks, except in case of imperative military necessity, unless previous arrangements have been made for adequate provision for the needs of the civilian population.

Section II. Relief in Favour of the Civilian Population

Article 68
Field of application

The provisions of this Section apply to the civilian population as defined in this Protocol and are supplementary to Articles 23, 55, 59, 60, 61 and 62 and other relevant provisions of the Fourth Convention.

Article 69
Basic needs in occupied territories

1. In addition to the duties specified in Article 55 of the Fourth Convention concerning food and medical supplies, the Occupying Power shall, to the fullest extent of the means available to it and without any adverse distinction, also ensure the provision of clothing, bedding, means of shelter, other supplies essential to the survival of the civilian population of the occupied territory and objects necessary for religious worship.

2. Relief actions for the benefit of the civilian population of occupied territories are governed by Articles 59, 60, 61, 62, 108, 109, 110 and 111 of the Fourth Convention, and by Article 71 of this Protocol, and shall be implemented without delay.

Article 70
Relief actions

1. If the civilian population of any territory under the control of a Party to the conflict, other than occupied territory, is not adequately provided with the supplies mentioned in Article 69, relief actions which are humanitarian and impartial in character and conducted without any adverse distinction shall be undertaken, subject to the agreement of the Parties concerned in such relief actions. Offers of such relief shall not be regarded as interference in the armed conflict or as unfriendly acts. In the distribution of relief consignments, priority shall be given to those persons, such as children, expectant mothers, maternity cases and nursing mothers, who, under the Fourth Convention or under this Protocol, are to be accorded privileged treatment or special protection.

2. The Parties to the conflict and each High Contracting Party shall allow and facilitate rapid and unimpeded passage of all relief consignments, equipment and personnel provided in accordance with this Section, even if such assistance is destined for the civilian population of the adverse Party.

3. The Parties to the conflict and each High Contracting Party which allow the passage of relief consignments, equipment and personnel in accordance with paragraph 2:

(a) shall have the right to prescribe the technical arrangements, including search, under which such passage is permitted;
(b) may make such permission conditional on the distribution of this assistance being made under the local supervision of a Protecting Power;
(c) shall, in no way whatsoever, divert relief consignments from the purpose for which they are intended nor delay their forwarding, except in cases of urgent necessity in the interest of the civilian population concerned.

4. The Parties to the conflict shall protect relief consignments and facilitate their rapid distribution.

5. The Parties to the conflict and each High Contracting Party concerned shall encourage and facilitate effective international co-ordination of the relief actions referred to in paragraph 1.

Article 71
Personnel participating in relief actions

1. Where necessary, relief personnel may form part of the assistance provided in any relief action, in particular for the transportation and distribution of relief consignments; the participation of such personnel shall be subject to the approval of the Party in whose territory they will carry out their duties.

2. Such personnel shall be respected and protected.

3. Each Party in receipt of relief consignments shall, to the fullest extent practicable, assist the relief personnel referred to in paragraph 1 in carrying out their relief mission. Only in case of imperative military necessity may the activities of the relief personnel be limited or their movements temporarily restricted.

4. Under no circumstances may relief personnel exceed the terms of their mission under this Protocol. In particular they shall take account of the security requirements of the Party in whose territory they are carrying out their duties. The mission of any of the personnel who do not respect these conditions may be terminated.

Section III. Treatment of Persons in the Power of a Party to the Conflict
Chapter I. Field of application and protection of persons and objects

Article 72
Field of application

The provisions of this Section are additional to the rules concerning humanitarian protection of civilians and civilian objects in the power of a Party to the conflict contained in the Fourth Convention, particularly Parts I and III thereof, as well as to other applicable rules of international law relating to the protection of fundamental human rights during international armed conflict.

Article 73
Refugees and stateless persons

Persons who, before the beginning of hostilities, were considered as stateless persons or refugees under the relevant international instruments accepted by the Parties concerned or under the national legislation of the State of refuge or State of residence shall be protected persons within the meaning of Parts I and III of the Fourth Convention, in all circumstances and without any adverse distinction.

Article 74
Reunion of dispersed families

The High Contracting Parties and the Parties to the conflict shall facilitate in every possible way the reunion of families dispersed as a result of armed conflicts and shall encourage in particular the work of the humanitarian organizations engaged in this task in accordance with the provisions of the Conventions and of this Protocol and in conformity with their respective security regulations.

Article 75
Fundamental guarantees

1. In so far as they are affected by a situation referred to in Article 1 of this Protocol, persons who are in the power of a Party to the conflict and who do not benefit from more favourable treatment under the Conventions or under this Protocol shall be treated humanely in all circumstances and shall enjoy, as a minimum, the protection provided by this Article without any adverse distinction based upon race, colour, sex, language, religion or belief, political or other opinion, national or social origin, wealth, birth or other status, or on any other similar criteria. Each Party shall respect the person, honour, convictions and religious practices of all such persons.

2. The following acts are and shall remain prohibited at any time and in any place whatsoever, whether committed by civilian or by military agents:

(a) violence to the life, health, or physical or mental well-being of persons, in particular:

(i) murder;
(ii) torture of all kinds, whether physical or mental;
(iii) corporal punishment; and
(iv) mutilation;

(b) outrages upon personal dignity, in particular humiliating and degrading treatment, enforced prostitution and any form of indecent assault;

(c) the taking of hostages;
(d) collective punishments; and
(e) threats to commit any of the foregoing acts.

3. Any person arrested, detained or interned for actions related to the armed conflict shall be informed promptly, in a language he understands, of the reasons why these measures have been taken. Except in cases of arrest or detention for penal offences, such persons shall be released with the minimum delay possible and in any event as soon as the circumstances justifying the arrest, detention or internment have ceased to exist.

4. No sentence may be passed and no penalty may be executed on a person found guilty of a penal offence related to the armed conflict except pursuant to a conviction pronounced by an impartial and regularly constituted court respecting the generally recognized principles of regular judicial procedure, which include the following:

(a) the procedure shall provide for an accused to be informed without delay of the particulars of the offence alleged against him and shall afford the accused before and during his trial all necessary rights and means of defence;
(b) no one shall be convicted of an offence except on the basis of individual penal responsibility;
(c) no one shall be accused or convicted of a criminal offence on account or any act or omission which did not constitute a criminal offence under the national or international law to which he was subject at the time when it was committed; nor shall a heavier penalty be imposed than that which was applicable at the time when the criminal offence was committed; if, after the commission of the offence, provision is made by law for the imposition of a lighter penalty, the offender shall benefit thereby;
(d) anyone charged with an offence is presumed innocent until proved guilty according to law;
(e) anyone charged with an offence shall have the right to be tried in his presence;
(f) no one shall be compelled to testify against himself or to confess guilt;
(g) anyone charged with an offence shall have the right to examine, or have examined, the witnesses against him and to obtain the attendance and examination of witnesses on his behalf under the same conditions as witnesses against him;
(h) no one shall be prosecuted or punished by the same Party for an offence in respect of which a final judgement acquitting or convicting that person has been previously pronounced under the same law and judicial procedure;
(i) anyone prosecuted for an offence shall have the right to have the judgement pronounced publicly; and
(j) a convicted person shall be advised on conviction or his judicial and other remedies and of the time-limits within which they may be exercised.

5. Women whose liberty has been restricted for reasons related to the armed conflict shall be held in quarters separated from men's quarters. They shall be under the

immediate supervision of women. Nevertheless, in cases where families are detained or interned, they shall, whenever possible, be held in the same place and accommodated as family units.

6. Persons who are arrested, detained or interned for reasons related to the armed conflict shall enjoy the protection provided by this Article until their final release, repatriation or re-establishment, even after the end of the armed conflict.

7. In order to avoid any doubt concerning the prosecution and trial of persons accused of war crimes or crimes against humanity, the following principles shall apply:

(a) persons who are accused of such crimes should be submitted for the purpose of prosecution and trial in accordance with the applicable rules of international law; and
(b) any such persons who do not benefit from more favourable treatment under the Conventions or this Protocol shall be accorded the treatment provided by this Article, whether or not the crimes of which they are accused constitute grave breaches of the Conventions or of this Protocol.

8. No provision of this Article may be construed as limiting or infringing any other more favourable provision granting greater protection, under any applicable rules of international law, to persons covered by paragraph 1.

Chapter II. Measures in favour of women and children

Article 76
Protection of women

1. Women shall be the object of special respect and shall be protected in particular against rape, forced prostitution and any other form of indecent assault.

2. Pregnant women and mothers having dependent infants who are arrested, detained or interned for reasons related to the armed conflict, shall have their cases considered with the utmost priority.

3. To the maximum extent feasible, the Parties to the conflict shall endeavour to avoid the pronouncement of the death penalty on pregnant women or mothers having dependent infants, for an offence related to the armed conflict. The death penalty for such offences shall not be executed on such women.

Article 77
Protection of children

1. Children shall be the object of special respect and shall be protected against any form of indecent assault. The Parties to the conflict shall provide them with the care and aid they require, whether because of their age or for any other reason.

2. The Parties to the conflict shall take all feasible measures in order that children who have not attained the age of fifteen years do not take a direct part in hostilities and, in particular, they shall refrain from recruiting them into their armed forces. In recruiting among those persons who have attained the age of fifteen years but who have not attained the age of eighteen years the Parties to the conflict shall endeavour to give priority to those who are oldest.

3. If, in exceptional cases, despite the provisions of paragraph 2, children who have not attained the age of fifteen years take a direct part in hostilities and fall into the power of an adverse Party, they shall continue to benefit from the special protection accorded by this Article, whether or not they are prisoners of war.

4. If arrested, detained or interned for reasons related to the armed conflict, children shall be held in quarters separate from the quarters of adults, except where families are accommodated as family units as provided in Article 75, paragraph 5.

5 . The death penalty for an offence related to the armed conflict shall not be executed on persons who had not attained the age of eighteen years at the time the offence was committed.

Article 78
Evacuation of children

1. No Party to the conflict shall arrange for the evacuation of children, other than its own nationals, to a foreign country except for a temporary evacuation where compelling reasons of the health or medical treatment of the children or, except in occupied territory, their safety, so require. Where the parents or legal guardians can be found, their written consent to such evacuation is required. If these persons cannot be found, the written consent to such evacuation of the persons who by law or custom are primarily responsible for the care of the children is required. Any such evacuation shall be supervised by the Protecting Power in agreement with the Parties concerned, namely, the Party arranging for the evacuation, the Party receiving the children and any Parties whose nationals are being evacuated. In each case, all Parties to the conflict shall take all feasible precautions to avoid endangering the evacuation.

2. Whenever an evacuation occurs pursuant to paragraph 1, each child's education, including his religious and moral education as his parents desire, shall be provided while he is away with the greatest possible continuity.

3. With a view to facilitating the return to their families and country of children evacuated pursuant to this Article, the authorities of the Party arranging for the evacuation and, as appropriate, the authorities of the receiving country shall establish for each child a card with photographs, which they shall send to the Central Tracing Agency of the International Committee of the Red Cross. Each card shall bear, whenever possible, and whenever it involves no risk of harm to the child, the following information:

(a) surname(s) of the child;
(b) the child's first name(s);
(c) the child's sex;
(d) the place and date of birth (or, if that date is not known, the approximate age);
(e) the father's full name;
(f) the mother's full name and her maiden name;
(g) the child's next-of-kin;
(h) the child's nationality;
(i) the child's native language, and any other languages he speaks;
(j) the address of the child's family;
(k) any identification number for the child;
(l) the child's state of health;
(m) the child's blood group;
(n) any distinguishing features;
(o) the date on which and the place where the child was found;
(p) the date on which and the place from which the child left the country;
(q) the child's religion, if any;
(r) the child's present address in the receiving country;
(s) should the child die before his return, the date, place and circumstances of death and place of interment.

Chapter III. Journalists

Article 79
Measures or protection for journalists

1. Journalists engaged in dangerous professional missions in areas of armed conflict shall be considered as civilians within the meaning of Article 50, paragraph 1.

2. They shall be protected as such under the Conventions and this Protocol, provided that they take no action adversely affecting their status as civilians, and without prejudice to the right of war correspondents accredited to the armed forces to the status provided for in Article 4 (A) (4) of the Third Convention.

3. They may obtain an identity card similar to the model in Annex II of this Protocol. This card, which shall be issued by the government of the State of which the Journalist is a national or in whose territory he resides or in which the news medium employing him is located, shall attest to his status as a journalist.

Part V. Execution of the Conventions and of its Protocols

Section I. General Provisions

Article 80
Measures for execution

1. The High Contracting Parties and the Parties to the conflict shall without delay take all necessary measures for the execution of their obligations under the Conventions and this Protocol.

2. The High Contracting Parties and the Parties to the conflict shall give orders and instructions to ensure observance of the Conventions and this Protocol, and shall supervise their execution.

Article 81
Activities of the Red Cross and other humanitarian organizations

1. The Parties to the conflict shall grant to the International Committee of the Red Cross all facilities, within their power so as to enable it to carry out the humanitarian functions assigned to it by the Conventions and this Protocol in order to ensure protection and assistance to the victims of conflicts; the International Committee of the Red Cross may also carry out any other humanitarian activities in favour of these victims, subject to the consent of the Parties to the conflict concerned.

2. The Parties to the conflict shall grant to their respective Red Cross (Red Crescent, Red Lion and Sun) organizations the facilities necessary for carrying out their humanitarian activities in favour of the victims of the conflict, in accordance with the provisions of the Conventions and this Protocol and the fundamental principles of the Red Cross as formulated by the International Conferences of the Red Cross.

3. The High Contracting Parties and the Parties to the conflict shall facilitate in every possible way the assistance which Red Cross (Red Crescent, Red Lion and Sun) organizations and the League of Red Cross Societies extend to the victims of conflicts in accordance with the provisions of the Conventions and this Protocol and with the

fundamental principles of the red Cross as formulated by the International Conferences of the Red Cross.

4. The High Contracting Parties and the Parties to the conflict shall, as far as possible, make facilities similar to those mentioned in paragraphs 2 and 3 available to the other humanitarian organizations referred to in the Conventions and this Protocol which are duly authorized by the respective Parties to the conflict and which perform their humanitarian activities in accordance with the provisions of the Conventions and this Protocol.

Article 82
Legal advisers in armed forces

The High Contracting Parties at all times, and the Parties to the conflict in time of armed conflict, shall ensure that legal advisers are available, when necessary, to advise military commanders at the appropriate level on the application of the Conventions and this Protocol and on the appropriate instruction to be given to the armed forces on this subject.

Article 83
Dissemination

1. The High Contracting Parties undertake, in time of peace as in time of armed conflict, to disseminate the Conventions and this Protocol as widely as possible in their respective countries and, in particular, to include the study thereof in their programmes of military instruction and to encourage the study thereof by the civilian population, so that those instruments may become known to the armed forces and to the civilian population.

2. Any military or civilian authorities who, in time of armed conflict, assume responsibilities in respect of the application of the Conventions and this Protocol shall be fully acquainted with the text thereof.

Article 84
Rules of application

The High Contracting Parties shall communicate to one another, as soon as possible, through the depositary and, as appropriate, through the Protecting Powers, their official translations of this Protocol, as well as the laws and regulations which they may adopt to ensure its application.

Section II. Repression of Breaches of the Conventions and of this Protocol

Article 85
Repression of breaches of this Protocol

1. The provisions of the Conventions relating to the repression of breaches and grave breaches, supplemented by this Section, shall apply to the repression of breaches and grave breaches of this Protocol.
2. Acts described as grave breaches in the Conventions are grave breaches of this Protocol if committed against persons in the power of an adverse Party protected by Articles 44, 45 and 73 of this Protocol, or against the wounded, sick and shipwrecked of the adverse Party who are protected by this Protocol, or against those medical or religious personnel, medical units or medical transports which are under the control of the adverse Party and are protected by this Protocol.

3. In addition to the grave breaches defined in Article 11, the following acts shall be regarded as grave breaches of this Protocol, when committed wilfully, in violation of the relevant provisions of this Protocol, and causing death or serious injury to body or health:

(a) making the civilian population or individual civilians the object of attack;
(b) launching an indiscriminate attack affecting the civilian population or civilian objects in the knowledge that such attack will cause excessive loss of life, injury to civilians or damage to civilian objects, as defined in Article 57, paragraph 2 (a)(iii);
(c) launching an attack against works or installations containing dangerous forces in the knowledge that such attack will cause excessive loss of life, injury to civilians or damage to civilian objects, as defined in Article 57, paragraph 2 (a)(iii);
(d) making non-defended localities and demilitarized zones the object of attack;
(e) making a person the object of attack in the knowledge that he is hors de combat;
(f) the perfidious use, in violation of Article 37, of the distinctive emblem of the red cross, red crescent or red lion and sun or of other protective signs recognized by the Conventions or this Protocol.

4. In addition to the grave breaches defined in the preceding paragraphs and in the Conventions, the following shall be regarded as grave breaches of this Protocol, when committed wilfully and in violation of the Conventions or the Protocol:

(a) the transfer by the occupying Power of parts of its own civilian population into the territory it occupies, or the deportation or transfer of all or parts of the population of the occupied territory within or outside this territory, in violation of Article 49 of the Fourth Convention;
(b) unjustifiable delay in the repatriation of prisoners of war or civilians;
(c) practices of apartheid and other inhuman and degrading practices involving outrages upon personal dignity, based on racial discrimination;

(d) making the clearly-recognized historic monuments, works of art or places of worship which constitute the cultural or spiritual heritage of peoples and to which special protection has been given by special arrangement, for example, within the framework of a competent international organization, the object of attack, causing as a result extensive destruction thereof, where there is no evidence of the violation by the adverse Party of Article 53, subparagraph (b), and when such historic monuments, works of art and places of worship are not located in the immediate proximity of military objectives;
(e) depriving a person protected by the Conventions or referred to in paragraph 2 of this Article of the rights of fair and regular trial.

5. Without prejudice to the application of the Conventions and of this Protocol, grave breaches of these instruments shall be regarded as war crimes.

Article 86
Failure to act

1. The High Contracting Parties and the Parties to the conflict shall repress grave breaches, and take measures necessary to suppress all other breaches, of the Conventions or of this Protocol which result from a failure to act when under a duty to do so.

2. The fact that a breach of the Conventions or of this Protocol was committed by a subordinate does not absolve his superiors from penal or disciplinary responsibility, as the case may be, if they knew, or had information which should have enabled them to conclude in the circumstances at the time, that he was committing or was going to commit such a breach and if they did not take all feasible measures within their power to prevent or repress the breach.

Article 87
Duty of commanders

1. The High Contracting Parties and the Parties to the conflict shall require military commanders, with respect to members of the armed forces under their command and other persons under their control, to prevent and, where necessary, to suppress and to report to competent authorities breaches of the Conventions and of this Protocol.

2. In order to prevent and suppress breaches, High Contracting Parties and Parties to the conflict shall require that, commensurate with their level of responsibility, commanders ensure that members of the armed forces under their command are aware of their obligations under the Conventions and this Protocol.

3. The High Contracting Parties and Parties to the conflict shall require any commander who is aware that subordinates or other persons under his control are going to commit

or have committed a breach of the Conventions or of this Protocol, to initiate such steps as are necessary to prevent such violations of the Conventions or this Protocol, and, where appropriate, to initiate disciplinary or penal action against violators thereof.

Article 88
Mutual assistance in criminal matters

1. The High Contracting Parties shall afford one another the greatest measure of assistance in connexion with criminal proceedings brought in respect of grave breaches of the Conventions or of this Protocol.

2. Subject to the rights and obligations established in the Conventions and in Article 85, paragraph 1 of this Protocol, and when circumstances permit, the High Contracting Parties shall co-operate in the matter of extradition. They shall give due consideration to the request of the State in whose territory the alleged offence has occurred.

3. The law of the High Contracting Party requested shall apply in all cases. The provisions of the preceding paragraphs shall not, however, affect the obligations arising from the provisions of any other treaty of a bilateral or multilateral nature which governs or will govern the whole or part of the subject of mutual assistance in criminal matters.

Article 89
Co-operation

In situations of serious violations of the Conventions or of this Protocol, the High Contracting Parties undertake to act jointly or individually, in co-operation with the United Nations and in conformity with the United Nations Charter.

Article 90
International Fact-Finding Commission

1.

(a) An International Fact-Finding Commission (hereinafter referred to as "the Commission") consisting of 15 members of high moral standing and acknowledged impartiality shall be established;

(b) When not less than 20 High Contracting Parties have agreed to accept the competence of the Commission pursuant to paragraph 2, the depositary shall then, and at intervals of five years thereafter, convene a meeting of representatives of those High Contracting Parties for the purpose of electing the members of the Commission. At the meeting, the representatives shall elect the members of the Commission by secret ballot from a list of persons to which each of those High Contracting Parties may nominate one person;

(c) The members of the Commission shall serve in their personal capacity and shall hold office until the election of new members at the ensuing meeting;
(d) At the election, the High Contracting Parties shall ensure that the persons to be elected to the Commission individually possess the qualifications required and that, in the Commission as a whole, equitable geographical representation is assured;
(e) In the case of a casual vacancy, the Commission itself shall fill the vacancy, having due regard to the provisions of the preceding subparagraphs;
(f) The depositary shall make available to the Commission the necessary administrative facilities for the performance of its functions.

2.

(a) The High Contracting Parties may at the time of signing, ratifying or acceding to the Protocol, or at any other subsequent time, declare that they recognize ipso facto and without special agreement, in relation to any other High Contracting Party accepting the same obligation, the competence of the Commission to inquire into allegations by such other Party, as authorized by this Article;
(b) The declarations referred to above shall be deposited with the depositary, which shall transmit copies thereof to the High Contracting Parties;
(c) The Commission shall be competent to:
  (i) inquire into any facts alleged to be a grave breach as defined in the Conventions and this Protocol or other serious violation of the Conventions or of this Protocol;
  (ii) facilitate, through its good offices, the restoration of an attitude of respect for the Conventions and this Protocol;

(d) In other situations, the Commission shall institute an inquiry at the request of a Party to the conflict only with the consent of the other Party or Parties concerned;
(e) Subject to the foregoing provisions or this paragraph, the provisions of Article 52 of the First Convention, Article 53 of the Second Convention, Article 132 or the Third Convention and Article 149 of the Fourth Convention shall continue to apply to any alleged violation of the Conventions and shall extend to any alleged violation of this Protocol.

3.

(a) Unless otherwise agreed by the Parties concerned, all inquiries shall be undertaken by a Chamber consisting of seven members appointed as follows:

  (i) five members of the Commission, not nationals of any Party to the conflict, appointed by the President of the Commission on the basis of equitable representation of the geographical areas, after consultation with the Parties to the conflict;
  (ii) two ad hoc members, not nationals of any Party to the conflict, one to be appointed by each side;

(b) Upon receipt of the request for an inquiry, the President of the Commission shall specify an appropriate time-limit for setting up a Chamber. If any ad hoc member has not been appointed within the time-limit, the President shall immediately appoint such additional member or members of the Commission as may be necessary to complete the membership of the Chamber.

4.

(a) The Chamber set up under paragraph 3 to undertake an inquiry shall invite the Parties to the conflict to assist it and to present evidence. The Chamber may also seek such other evidence as it deems appropriate and may carry out an investigation of the situation in loco;
(b) All evidence shall be fully disclosed to the Parties, which shall have the right to comment on it to the Commission;
(c) Each Party shall have the right to challenge such evidence.

5.

(a) The Commission shall submit to the Parties a report on the findings of fact of the Chamber, with such recommendations as it may deem appropriate;
(b) If the Chamber is unable to secure sufficient evidence for factual and impartial findings, the Commission shall state the reasons for that inability;
(c) The Commission shall not report its findings publicly, unless all the Parties to the conflict have requested the Commission to do so.

6. The Commission shall establish its own rules, including rules for the presidency or the Commission and the presidency of the Chamber. Those rules shall ensure that the functions of the President of the Commission are exercised at all times and that, in the case of an inquiry, they are exercised by a person who is not a national of a Party to the conflict.

7. The administrative expenses of the Commission shall be met by contributions from the High Contracting Parties which made declarations under paragraph 2, and by voluntary contributions. The Party or Parties to the conflict requesting an inquiry shall advance the necessary funds for expenses incurred by a Chamber and shall be reimbursed by the Party or Parties against which the allegations are made to the extent of 50 per cent of the costs of the Chamber. Where there are counter-allegations before the Chamber each side shall advance 50 per cent of the necessary funds.

Article 91
Responsibility

A Party to the conflict which violates the provisions of the Conventions or of this

Protocol shall, if the case demands, be liable to pay compensation. It shall be responsible for all acts committed by persons forming part of its armed forces.

Part IV. Final Resolutions

Article 92
Signature

This Protocol shall be open for signature by the Parties to the Conventions six months after the signing of the Final Act and will remain open for a period or twelve months.

Article 93
Ratification

This Protocol shall be ratified as soon as possible. The instruments of ratification shall be deposited with the Swiss Federal Council, depositary of the Conventions.

Article 94
Accession

This Protocol shall be open for accession by any Party to the Conventions which has not signed it. The instruments of accession shall be deposited with the depositary.

Article 95
Entry into force

1. This Protocol shall enter into force six months after two instruments of ratification or accession have been deposited.

2. For each Party to the Conventions thereafter ratifying or acceding to this Protocol, it shall enter into force six months after the deposit by such Party of its instrument of ratification or accession.

Article 96
Treaty relations upon entry into force or this Protocol

1. When the Parties to the Conventions are also Parties to this Protocol, the Conventions shall apply as supplemented by this Protocol.

2. When one of the Parties to the conflict is not bound by this Protocol, the Parties to the Protocol shall remain bound by it in their mutual relations. They shall furthermore be bound by this Protocol in relation to each of the Parties which are not bound by it, if the latter accepts and applies the provisions thereof.

3. The authority representing a people engaged against a High Contracting Party in an armed conflict of the type referred to in Article 1, paragraph 4, may undertake to apply the Conventions and this Protocol in relation to that conflict by means of a unilateral declaration addressed to the depositary. Such declaration shall, upon its receipt by the depositary, have in relation to that conflict the following effects:

(a) the Conventions and this Protocol are brought into force for the said authority as a Party to the conflict with immediate effect;
(b) the said authority assumes the same rights and obligations as those which have been assumed by a High Contracting Party to the Conventions and this Protocol; and
(c) the Conventions and this Protocol are equally binding upon all Parties to the conflict.

Article 97
Amendment

1. Any High Contracting Party may propose amendments to this Protocol. The text of any proposed amendment shall be communicated to the depositary, which shall decide, after consultation with all the High Contracting Parties and the International Committee of the Red Cross, whether a conference should be convened to consider the proposed amendment.

2. The depositary shall invite to that conference all the High Contracting Parties as well as the Parties to the Conventions, whether or not they are signatories or this Protocol.

Article 98
Revision of Annex I

1. Not later than four years after the entry into force of this Protocol and thereafter at intervals of not less than four years, the International Committee of the Red Cross shall consult the High Contracting Parties concerning Annex I to this Protocol and, if it considers it necessary, may propose a meeting of technical experts to review Annex I and to propose such amendments to it as may appear to be desirable. Unless, within six months of the communication of a proposal for such a meeting to the High Contracting Parties, one third of them object, the International Committee of the Red Cross shall convene the meeting, inviting also observers of appropriate international organizations. Such a meeting shall also be convened by the International Committee of the Red Cross at any time at the request of one third of the High Contracting Parties.

2. The depositary shall convene a conference of the High Contracting Parties and the Parties to the Conventions to consider amendments proposed by the meeting of

technical experts if, after that meeting, the International Committee of the Red Cross or one third of the High Contracting Parties so request.

3. Amendments to Annex I may be adopted at such a conference by a two-thirds majority of the High Contracting Parties present and voting.

4. The depositary shall communicate any amendment so adopted to the High Contracting Parties and to the Parties to the Conventions. The amendment shall be considered to have been accepted at the end of a period of one year after it has been so communicated, unless within that period a declaration of non-acceptance of the amendment has been communicated to the depositary by not less than one third of the High Contracting Parties.

5. An amendment considered to have been accepted in accordance with paragraph 4 shall enter into force three months after its acceptance for all High Contracting Parties other than those which have made a declaration of non-acceptance in accordance with that paragraph. Any Party making such a declaration may at any time withdraw it and the amendment shall then enter into force for that Party three months thereafter.

6. The depositary shall notify the High Contracting Parties and the Parties to the Conventions of the entry into force of any amendment, of the Parties bound thereby, of the date of its entry into force in relation to each Party, of declarations of non-acceptance made in accordance with paragraph 4, and of withdrawals of such declarations.

Article 99
Denunciation

1. In case a High Contracting Party should denounce this Protocol, the denunciation shall only take effect one year after receipt of the instrument of denunciation. If, however, on the expiry of that year the denouncing Party is engaged in one of the situations referred to in Article I, the denunciation shall not take effect before the end of the armed conflict or occupation and not, in any case, before operations connected with the final release, repatriation or re-establishment of the persons protected by the Convention or this Protocol have been terminated.

2. The denunciation shall be notified in writing to the depositary, which shall transmit it to all the High Contracting Parties.

3. The denunciation shall have effect only in respect of the denouncing Party.

4. Any denunciation under paragraph 1 shall not affect the obligations already incurred, by reason of the armed conflict, under this Protocol by such denouncing Party in respect of any act committed before this denunciation becomes effective.

Article 100
Notifications

The depositary shall inform the High Contracting Parties as well as the Parties to the Conventions, whether or not they are signatories of this Protocol, of:

(a) signatures affixed to this Protocol and the deposit of instruments of ratification and accession under Articles 93 and 94;
(b) the date of entry into force of this Protocol under Article 95;
(c) communications and declarations received under Articles 84, 90 and 97;
(d) declarations received under Article 96, paragraph 3, which shall be communicated by the quickest methods; and
(e) denunciations under Article 99.

Article 101
Registration

1. After its entry into force, this Protocol shall be transmitted by the depositary to the Secretariat of the United Nations for registration and publication, in accordance with Article 102 of the Charter of the United Nations.

2. The depositary shall also inform the Secretariat of the United Nations of all ratifications, accessions and denunciations received by it with respect to this Protocol.

Article 102
Authentic texts

The original of this Protocol, of which the Arabic, Chinese, English, French, Russian and Spanish texts are equally authentic, shall be deposited with the depositary, which shall transmit certified true copies thereof to all the Parties to the Conventions.

Protocol Additional to the Geneva Conventions of 12 August 1949, and relating to the Protection of Victims of Non-International Armed Conflicts (Protocol II), 8 June 1977

The High Contracting Parties, Recalling that the humanitarian principles enshrined in Article 3 common to the Geneva Conventions of 12 August 1949, constitute the foundation of respect for the human person in cases of armed conflict not of an international character,

Recalling furthermore that international instruments relating to human rights offer a basic protection to the human person,

Emphasizing the need to ensure a better protection for the victims of those armed conflicts,

Recalling that, in cases not covered by the law in force, the human person remains under the protection of the principles of humanity and the dictates of the public conscience,

Have agreed on the following:

Part I. Scope of this Protocol

Article 1
Material field of application

1. This Protocol, which develops and supplements Article 3 common to the Geneva Conventions of 12 August 1949 without modifying its existing conditions of application, shall apply to all armed conflicts which are not covered by Article 1 of the Protocol Additional to the Geneva Conventions of 12 August 1949, and relating to the Protection of Victims of International Armed Conflicts (Protocol I) and which take place in the territory of a High Contracting Party between its armed forces and dissident armed forces or other organized armed groups which, under responsible command, exercise such control over a part of its territory as to enable them to carry out sustained and concerted military operations and to implement this Protocol.

2. This Protocol shall not apply to situations of internal disturbances and tensions, such as riots, isolated and sporadic acts of violence and other acts of a similar nature, as not being armed conflicts.

Article 2
Personal field of application

1. This Protocol shall be applied without any adverse distinction founded on race, colour, sex, language, religion or belief, political or other opinion, national or social origin, wealth, birth or other status, or on any other similar criteria (hereinafter referred to as "adverse distinction") to all persons affected by an armed conflict as defined in Article 1.

2. At the end of the armed conflict, all the persons who have been deprived of their liberty or whose liberty has been restricted for reasons related to such conflict, as well as those deprived of their liberty or whose liberty is restricted after the conflict for the same reasons, shall enjoy the protection of Articles 5 and 6 until the end of such deprivation or restriction of liberty.

Article 3
Non-intervention

1. Nothing in this Protocol shall be invoked for the purpose of affecting the sovereignty of a State or the responsibility of the government, by all legitimate means, to maintain or re-establish law and order in the State or to defend the national unity and territorial integrity of the State.

2. Nothing in this Protocol shall be invoked as a justification for intervening, directly or indirectly, for any reason whatever, in the armed conflict or in the internal or external affairs of the High Contracting Party in the territory of which that conflict occurs.

Part II. Humane Treatment

Article 4
Fundamental guarantees

1. All persons who do not take a direct part or who have ceased to take part in hostilities, whether or not their liberty has been restricted, are entitled to respect for their person, honour and convictions and religious practices. They shall in all circumstances be treated humanely, without any adverse distinction. It is prohibited to order that there shall be no survivors.

2. Without prejudice to the generality of the foregoing, the following acts against the persons referred to in paragraph I are and shall remain prohibited at any time and in any place whatsoever:

(a) violence to the life, health and physical or mental well-being of persons, in particular murder as well as cruel treatment such as torture, mutilation or any form of corporal punishment;
(b) collective punishments;

(c) taking of hostages;
(d) acts of terrorism;
(e) outrages upon personal dignity, in particular humiliating and degrading treatment, rape, enforced prostitution and any form or indecent assault;
(f) slavery and the slave trade in all their forms;
(g) pillage;
(h) threats to commit any or the foregoing acts.

3. Children shall be provided with the care and aid they require, and in particular:

(a) they shall receive an education, including religious and moral education, in keeping with the wishes of their parents, or in the absence of parents, of those responsible for their care;
(b) all appropriate steps shall be taken to facilitate the reunion of families temporarily separated;
(c) children who have not attained the age of fifteen years shall neither be recruited in the armed forces or groups nor allowed to take part in hostilities;
(d) the special protection provided by this Article to children who have not attained the age of fifteen years shall remain applicable to them if they take a direct part in hostilities despite the provisions of subparagraph (c) and are captured;
(e) measures shall be taken, if necessary, and whenever possible with the consent of their parents or persons who by law or custom are primarily responsible for their care, to remove children temporarily from the area in which hostilities are taking place to a safer area within the country and ensure that they are accompanied by persons responsible for their safety and well-being.

Article 5
Persons whose liberty has been restricted

1. In addition to the provisions of Article 4 the following provisions shall be respected as a minimum with regard to persons deprived of their liberty for reasons related to the armed conflict, whether they are interned or detained;

(a) the wounded and the sick shall be treated in accordance with Article 7;
(b) the persons referred to in this paragraph shall, to the same extent as the local civilian population, be provided with food and drinking water and be afforded safeguards as regards health and hygiene and protection against the rigours of the climate and the dangers of the armed conflict;
(c) they shall be allowed to receive individual or collective relief;
(d) they shall be allowed to practise their religion and, if requested and appropriate, to receive spiritual assistance from persons, such as chaplains, performing religious functions;

(e) they shall, if made to work, have the benefit of working conditions and safeguards similar to those enjoyed by the local civilian population.

2. Those who are responsible for the internment or detention of the persons referred to in paragraph 1 shall also, within the limits of their capabilities, respect the following provisions relating to such persons:

(a) except when men and women of a family are accommodated together, women shall be held in quarters separated from those of men and shall be under the immediate supervision of women;
(b) they shall be allowed to send and receive letters and cards, the number of which may be limited by competent authority if it deems necessary;
(c) places of internment and detention shall not be located close to the combat zone. The persons referred to in paragraph 1 shall be evacuated when the places where they are interned or detained become particularly exposed to danger arising out of the armed conflict, if their evacuation can be carried out under adequate conditions of safety;
(d) they shall have the benefit of medical examinations;
(e) their physical or mental health and integrity shall not be endangered by any unjustified act or omission. Accordingly, it is prohibited to subject the persons described in this Article to any medical procedure which is not indicated by the state of health of the person concerned, and which is not consistent with the generally accepted medical standards applied to free persons under similar medical circumstances.

3. Persons who are not covered by paragraph 1 but whose liberty has been restricted in any way whatsoever for reasons related to the armed conflict shall be treated humanely in accordance with Article 4 and with paragraphs 1 (a), (c) and (d), and 2 (b) of this Article.

4. If it is decided to release persons deprived of their liberty, necessary measures to ensure their safety shall be taken by those so deciding.

Article 6
Penal prosecutions

1. This Article applies to the prosecution and punishment of criminal offences related to the armed conflict.

2. No sentence shall be passed and no penalty shall be executed on a person found guilty of an offence except pursuant to a conviction pronounced by a court offering the essential guarantees of independence and impartiality.
In particular:

(a) the procedure shall provide for an accused to be informed without delay of the particulars of the offence alleged against him and shall afford the accused before and during his trial all necessary rights and means of defence;
(b) no one shall be convicted of an offence except on the basis of individual penal responsibility;
(c) no one shall be held guilty of any criminal offence on account of any act or omission which did not constitute a criminal offence, under the law, at the time when it was committed; nor shall a heavier penalty be imposed than that which was applicable at the time when the criminal offence was committed; if, after the commission of the offence, provision is made by law for the imposition of a lighter penalty, the offender shall benefit thereby;
(d) anyone charged with an offence is presumed innocent until proved guilty according to law;
(e) anyone charged with an offence shall have the right to be tried in his presence;
(f) no one shall be compelled to testify against himself or to confess guilt.

3. A convicted person shall be advised on conviction of his judicial and other remedies and of the time-limits within which they may be exercised.

4. The death penalty shall not be pronounced on persons who were under the age of eighteen years at the time of the offence and shall not be carried out on pregnant women or mothers of young children.

5. At the end of hostilities, the authorities in power shall endeavour to grant the broadest possible amnesty to persons who have participated in the armed conflict, or those deprived of their liberty for reasons related to the armed conflict, whether they are interned or detained.

Part III. Wounded, Sick and Shipwrecked

Article 7
Protection and care

1. All the wounded, sick and shipwrecked, whether or not they have taken part in the armed conflict, shall be respected and protected.

2. In all circumstances they shall be treated humanely and shall receive to the fullest extent practicable and with the least possible delay, the medical care and attention required by their condition. There shall be no distinction among them founded on any grounds other than medical ones.

Article 8
Search

Whenever circumstances permit and particularly after an engagement, all possible measures shall be taken, without delay, to search for and collect the wounded, sick and shipwrecked, to protect them against pillage and ill-treatment, to ensure their adequate care, and to search for the dead, prevent their being despoiled, and decently dispose of them.

Article 9
Protection of medical and religious personnel

1. Medical and religious personnel shall be respected and protected and shall be granted all available help for the performance of their duties. They shall not be compelled to carry out tasks which are not compatible with their humanitarian mission.

2. In the performance of their duties medical personnel may not be required to give priority to any person except on medical grounds.

Article 10
General protection of medical duties

1. Under no circumstances shall any person be punished for having carried out medical activities compatible with medical ethics, regardless of the person benefiting therefrom.

2. Persons engaged in medical activities shall neither be compelled to perform acts or to carry out work contrary to, nor be compelled to refrain from acts required by, the rules of medical ethics or other rules designed for the benefit of the wounded and sick, or this Protocol.

3. The professional obligations of persons engaged in medical activities regarding information which they may acquire concerning the wounded and sick under their care shall, subject to national law, be respected.

4. Subject to national law, no person engaged in medical activities may be penalized in any way for refusing or failing to give information concerning the wounded and sick who are, or who have been, under his care.

Article 11
Protection of medical units and transports

1. Medical units and transports shall be respected and protected at all times and shall not be the object of attack.
2. The protection to which medical units and transports are entitled shall not cease unless they are used to commit hostile acts, outside their humanitarian function. Protection may, however, cease only after a warning has been given, setting, whenever appropriate, a reasonable time-limit, and after such warning has remained unheeded.

Article 12
The distinctive emblem

Under the direction of the competent authority concerned, the distinctive emblem of the red cross, red crescent or red lion and sun on a white ground shall be displayed by medical and religious personnel and medical units, and on medical transports. It shall be respected in all circumstances. It shall not be used improperly.

Part IV. Civilian Population

Article 13
Protection of the civilian population

1. The civilian population and individual civilians shall enjoy general protection against the dangers arising from military operations. To give effect to this protection, the following rules shall be observed in all circumstances.

2. The civilian population as such, as well as individual civilians, shall not be the object of attack. Acts or threats of violence the primary purpose of which is to spread terror among the civilian population are prohibited.

3. Civilians shall enjoy the protection afforded by this part, unless and for such time as they take a direct part in hostilities.

Article 14
Protection of objects indispensable to the survival of the civilian population

Starvation of civilians as a method of combat is prohibited. It is therefore prohibited to attack, destroy, remove or render useless for that purpose, objects indispensable to the survival of the civilian population such as food-stuffs, agricultural areas for the production of food-stuffs, crops, livestock, drinking water installations and supplies and irrigation works.

Article 15
Protection of works and installations containing dangerous forces

Works or installations containing dangerous forces, namely dams, dykes and nuclear electrical generating stations, shall not be made the object of attack, even where these objects are military objectives, if such attack may cause the release of dangerous forces and consequent severe losses among the civilian population.

Article 16
Protection of cultural objects and of places of worship

Without prejudice to the provisions of the Hague Convention for the Protection of Cultural Property in the Event of Armed Conflict of 14 May 1954, it is prohibited to commit any acts of hostility directed against historic monuments, works of art or places of worship which constitute the cultural or spiritual heritage of peoples, and to use them in support of the military effort.

Article 17
Prohibition of forced movement of civilians

1. The displacement of the civilian population shall not be ordered for reasons related to the conflict unless the security of the civilians involved or imperative military reasons so demand. Should such displacements have to be carried out, all possible measures shall be taken in order that the civilian population may be received under satisfactory conditions of shelter, hygiene, health, safety and nutrition.

2. Civilians shall not be compelled to leave their own territory for reasons connected with the conflict.

Article 18
Relief societies and relief actions

1. Relief societies located in the territory of the High Contracting Party, such as Red Cross (Red Crescent, Red Lion and Sun) organizations may offer their services for the performance of their traditional functions in relation to the victims of the armed conflict. The civilian population may, even on its own initiative, offer to collect and care for the wounded, sick and shipwrecked.

2. If the civilian population is suffering undue hardship owing to a lack of the supplies essential for its survival, such as food-stuffs and medical supplies, relief actions for the civilian population which are of an exclusively humanitarian and impartial nature and which are conducted without any adverse distinction shall be undertaken subject to the consent of the High Contracting Party concerned.

Part V. Final Provisions
Article 19
Dissemination

This Protocol shall be disseminated as widely as possible.

Article 20
Signature

This Protocol shall be open for signature by the Parties to the Conventions six months after the signing of the Final Act and will remain open for a period of twelve months.

Article 21
Ratification

This Protocol shall be ratified as soon as possible. The instruments of ratification shall be deposited with the Swiss Federal Council, depositary of the Conventions.

Article 22
Accession

This Protocol shall be open for accession by any Party to the Conventions which has not signed it. The instruments of accession shall be deposited with the depositary.

Article 23
Entry into force

1. This Protocol shall enter into force six months after two instruments of ratification or accession have been deposited.
2. For each Party to the Conventions thereafter ratifying or acceding to this Protocol, it shall enter into force six months after the deposit by such Party of its instrument of ratification or accession.

Article 24
Amendment

1. Any High Contracting Party may propose amendments to this Protocol. The text of any proposed amendment shall be communicated to the depositary which shall decide, after consultation with all the High Contracting Parties and the International Committee of the Red Cross, whether a conference should be convened to consider the proposed amendment.

2. The depositary shall invite to that conference all the High Contracting Parties as well as the Parties to the Conventions, whether or not they are signatories of this Protocol.

Article 25
Denunciation

1. In case a High Contracting Party should denounce this Protocol, the denunciation shall only take effect six months after receipt of the instrument of denunciation. If, however, on the expiry of six months, the denouncing Party is engaged in the situation referred to in Article 1, the denunciation shall not take effect before the end of the armed conflict. Persons who have been deprived of liberty, or whose liberty has been restricted, for reasons related to the conflict shall nevertheless continue to benefit from the provisions of this Protocol until their final release.

2. The denunciation shall be notified in writing to the depositary, which shall transmit it to all the High Contracting Parties.

Article 26
Notifications

The depositary shall inform the High Contracting Parties as well as the Parties to the Conventions, whether or not they are signatories of this Protocol, of:

(a) signatures affixed to this Protocol and the deposit of instruments of ratification and accession under Articles 21 and 22;
(b) the date of entry into force of this Protocol under Article 23; and
(c) communications and declarations received under Article 24.

Article 27
Registration

1. After its entry into force, this Protocol shall be transmitted by the depositary to the Secretariat of the United Nations for registration and publication, in accordance with Article 102 of the Charter of the United Nations.

2. The depositary shall also inform the Secretariat of the United Nations of all ratifications, accessions and denunciations received by it with respect to this Protocol.

Article 28
Authentic texts

The original of this Protocol, of which the Arabic, Chinese, English, French, Russian and

Spanish texts are equally authentic, shall be deposited with the depositary, which shall transmit certified true copies thereof to all the Parties to the Conventions.

Cont'd

The Third Conference envisioned by Secretary Root was held in The Hague in May 1999, at the initiative of the Russian and Dutch governments. It was not a treaty-making conference like the first two, but a centennial commemoration on the theme, "The Peaceful Settlement of Disputes: Prospects for the Twenty-First Century."[23]

Conclusion

As a conclusion the Hague Conferences of 1899 and 1907 didn't immediately seemed and turned out to be a success. However, we viewed the history and historical documents of both conferences to see and understand today's view on the laws of war. The Hague Conferences can be characterized as the fountain-head of international codification (of laws) by the convention method as an effective means of developing international law.[24]

The results of both final Conventions are still important in International Law nowadays. This can be pointed out when we look at the three core areas of the (first) Hague Conference, noticed earlier in this publication, namely: dispute regulation, reduction of armament and the development of Humanitarian War Law.

Dispute regulation

As noticed before the permanent court of arbitration (PCA) was established by the 1899 Convention for the Pacific Settlement of International Disputes. This Court is the first International organization within Dutch boundaries.[25] Between 1900 and 1932 there were approximately twenty disputes settled in front of this Court. The next years this amount decreased enormously. Partly, this was because of the political developments in Europe (first and second World War) but mostly because of the establishing of the Permanent Court of International Justice (1920) which was Court in traditional way. The

---

[23]<http://www.haguepeace.org/index.php?action=history&subAction=conf&selection=when>.

[24] R.P. Dhokolia, 'Reflections on International Law-Making and Its Progressive Development in the Contemporary Era of Transition, in: International law in transition', p. 217.

[25] E.P.J. Myjer, 'Honderd jaar Haagse vredesconferentie: Heeft Den Haag eindelijk een profiel?', *NJB* 1999/852.

PCA on the other hand is exclusively an infrastructure and a list with names of potential arbiters.

The Manifest of the United Nation about peaceful dispute leaves space to the PCA, but there are other forms of dispute regulation developed. A difference of the PCA is it's flexibility compared to the Permanent Court of International Justice (only States could offer a dispute to the court). In 1992 new Secretary General mr. P.J.H. Jonkman renews the PCA (for example new Model Clauses and Submission Agreements). The new rules seems to be more honest and effective to peaceful dispute regulation. Whether or not the new rules will increase the number of treated cases remains to be seen.
However, the PCA offers parties in dispute flexibility and that's what gave a new impulse to the existence of the PCA. The PCA also carried out other jobs like to be registry for complains of States who would violate trustful data by the Organization for the Prohibition of Chemical Weapons (OPCW) and who are directed to the Confidentiality Commission. This points out the confidence international organizations have in the PCA.
Concluded, the PCA contributes in a concrete way to the development of International Law.[26]

Currently, the following documents obtain as the rules of procedure of the PCA.

---

[26] E.P.J. Myjer, 'Honderd jaar Haagse vredesconferentie: Heeft Den Haag eindelijk een profiel?', *NJB* 1999/852..

Permanent Court of Arbitration - Optional Rules for Arbitrating Disputes Between Two States

Effective October 20, 1992

Introduction

These Rules have been elaborated for use in arbitrating disputes arising under treaties or other agreements between two States; they can be modified for use in connection with multilateral treaties. The Rules are based on the UNCITRAL Arbitration Rules with changes in order to:

(i) reflect the public international law character of disputes between States, and diplomatic practice appropriate to such disputes;
(ii) indicate the role of the Secretary-General and the International Bureau of the Permanent Court of Arbitration at The Hague, and the relation of these Rules with the 1899 and 1907 Hague Conventions for the Pacific Settlement of International Disputes; and
(iii) provide freedom for the parties to choose to have an arbitral tribunal of one, three or five persons.

Experience in arbitrations since 1981 suggests that the UNCITRAL Arbitration Rules provide fair and effective procedures for peaceful resolution of disputes between States concerning the interpretation, application and performance of treaties and other agreements, although they were originally designed for commercial arbitration. The Rules are optional and emphasize flexibility and party autonomy. For example:

(i) the Rules, and the services of the Secretary-General and the International Bureau of the Permanent Court of Arbitration, are available for use by *all* States, and are not restricted to disputes in which both States are parties to either The Hague Convention for the Pacific Settlement of International Disputes of 1899 or that of 1907;
(ii) the choice of arbitrators is not limited to persons who are listed as Members of the Permanent Court of Arbitration;
(iii) States have complete freedom to agree upon any individual or institution asappointing authority. In order to provide a failsafe mechanism to preventfrustration of the arbitration, the Rules provide that the SecretaryGeneral will

designate an appointing authority if the parties do not agree upon the authority, or if the authority they choose does not act.

A model clause that States may consider inserting in treaties or other agreements to provide for arbitration of future disputes and a model clause for arbitration of existing disputes are set forth at pages 231-232. These Rules are also appropriate for use in connection with multilateral treaties, provided that appropriate changes are made in the procedures for choosing arbitrators and sharing costs.

Section I. Introductory Rules

Article 1
Scope of Application

1. Where the parties to a treaty or other agreement have agreed in writing that disputes shall be referred to arbitration under the Permanent Court of Arbitration Optional Rules for Arbitrating Disputes between Two States, then such disputes shall be settled in accordance with these Rules subject to such modification as the parties may agree in writing.

2. The International Bureau of the Permanent Court of Arbitration (the 'International Bureau') shall take charge of the archives of the arbitration proceeding. In addition, upon written request of all the parties or of the arbitral tribunal, the International Bureau shall act as a channel of communication between the parties and the arbitral tribunal, provide secretariat services and/or serve as registry.

3. If on the date the arbitration commences either The Hague Convention for the Pacific Settlement of International Disputes of 1899 or The Hague Convention for the Pacific Settlement of International Disputes of 1907 is in force between the parties, the applicable Convention shall remain in force, and the parties, in the exercise of their rights under the Convention, agree that the procedures set forth in these Rules shall govern the arbitration as provided for in the parties' agreement.

Article 2
Notice, Calculation of Periods of Time

1. For the purposes of these Rules, any notice, including a notification, communication or proposal, is deemed to have been received when it has been delivered to the addressee through diplomatic channels. Notice shall be deemed to have been received on the day it is so delivered.

2. For the purposes of calculating a period of time under these Rules, such period shall begin to run on the day following the day when a notice, notification, communication or proposal is received. If the last day of such period is an official holiday or a non-work day in the State of the addressee, the period is extended until the first work day which follows. Official holidays or non-work days occurring during the running of the period of time are included in calculating the period.

Article 3
Notice of Arbitration

1. The party initiating recourse to arbitration (hereinafter called the 'claimant') shall give to the other party (hereinafter called the 'respondent') a notice of arbitration.

2. Arbitral proceedings shall be deemed to commence on the date on which the notice of arbitration is received by the respondent.

3. The notice of arbitration shall include the following:

(a) A demand that the dispute be referred to arbitration;
(b) The names and addresses of the parties;
(c) A reference to the arbitration clause or the separate arbitration agreement that is invoked;
(d) A reference to the treaty or other agreement out of or in relation to which the dispute arises;
(e) The general nature of the claim and an indication of the amount involved, if any;
(f) The relief or remedy sought;
(g) A proposal as to the number of arbitrators (i.e., one, three or five), if the parties have not previously agreed thereon.

4. The notice of arbitration may also include the statement of claim referred to in article 18.

Article 4
Representation and Assistance

Each party shall appoint an agent. The parties may also be assisted by persons of their choice. The name and address of the agent must be communicated in writing to the other party, to the International Bureau and to the arbitral tribunal after it has been appointed.

Section II. Composition of the Arbitral Tribunal

Article 5
Number of Arbitrators

If the parties have not previously agreed on the number of arbitrators (i.e., one, three, or five), and if within thirty days after the receipt by the respondent of the notice of arbitration the parties have not agreed on the number of arbitrators, three arbitrators shall be appointed.

Article 6
Appointment of Arbitrators (Articles 6 to 8)

1. If a sole arbitrator is to be appointed, either party may propose to the other:

(a) The names of one or more persons, one of whom would serve as the sole arbitrator; and
(b) If no appointing authority has been agreed upon by the parties, the name or names of one or more institutions or persons, one of whom would serve as appointing authority.

2. If within sixty days after receipt by a party of a proposal made in accordance with paragraph 1 the parties have not reached agreement on the choice of a sole arbitrator, the sole arbitrator shall be appointed by the appointing authority agreed upon by the parties. If no appointing authority has been agreed upon by the parties, or if the appointing authority agreed upon refuses to act or fails to appoint the arbitrator within sixty days of the receipt of a party's request therefor, either party may request the Secretary-General of the Permanent Court of Arbitration at The Hague (the 'Secretary-General') to designate an appointing authority.

3. The appointing authority shall, at the request of one of the parties, appoint the sole arbitrator as promptly as possible. In making the appointment the appointing authority shall use the following list-procedure, unless both parties agree that the list procedure should not be used or unless the appointing authority determines in its discretion that the use of the list-procedure is not appropriate for the case:

(a) At the request of one of the parties the appointing authority shall communicate to both parties an identical list containing at least three names;
(b) Within thirty days after the receipt of this list, each party may return the list to the appointing authority after having deleted the name or names to which it objects and numbered the remaining names on the list in the order of its preference;
(c) After the expiration of the above period of time the appointing authority shall appoint the sole arbitrator from among the names approved on the lists returned to it and in accordance with the order of preference indicated by the parties;

(d) If for any reason the appointment cannot be made according to this procedure, the appointing authority may exercise its discretion in appointing the sole arbitrator.

4. In making the appointment, the appointing authority shall have regard to such considerations as are likely to secure the appointment of an independent and impartial arbitrator and shall take into account as well the advisability of appointing an arbitrator of a nationality other than the nationalities of the parties.

Article 7

1. If three arbitrators are to be appointed, each party shall appoint one arbitrator. The two arbitrators thus appointed shall choose the third arbitrator who will act as the presiding arbitrator of the tribunal. If five arbitrators are to be appointed, the two party-appointed arbitrators shall choose the remaining three arbitrators and designate one of those three as the presiding arbitrator of the tribunal.

2. If within thirty days after the receipt of a party's notification of the appointment of an arbitrator the other party has not notified the first party of the arbitrator it has appointed:

(a) The first party may request the appointing authority previously designated by the parties to appoint the second arbitrator; or
(b) If no such authority has been previously designated by the parties, or if the appointing authority previously designated refuses to act or fails to appoint the arbitrator within sixty days after receipt of a party's request therefor, the first party may request the Secretary-General of the Permanent Court of Arbitration at The Hague to designate the appointing authority. The first party may then request the appointing authority so designated to appoint the second arbitrator. In either case, the appointing authority may exercise its discretion in appointing the arbitrator.

3. If within sixty days after the appointment of the second arbitrator the two arbitrators have not agreed on the choice of the remaining arbitrators and/or presiding arbitrator, the remaining arbitrators and/or presiding arbitrator shall be appointed by an appointing authority in the same way as a sole arbitrator would be appointed under article 6.

Article 8

1. When an appointing authority is requested to appoint an arbitrator pursuant to article 6 or article 7, the party which makes the request shall send to the appointing authority a copy of the notice of arbitration, a copy of the treaty or other agreement out of or in relation to which the dispute has arisen and a copy of the arbitration agreement if it is

not contained in the treaty or other agreement. The appointing authority may request from either party such information as it deems necessary to fulfil its function.

2. Where the names of one or more persons are proposed for appointment as arbitrators, their full names, addresses and nationalities shall be indicated, together with a description of their qualifications.

3. In appointing arbitrators pursuant to these Rules, the parties and the appointing authority are free to designate persons who are not Members of the Permanent Court of Arbitration at The Hague.

Article 9
Challenge of Arbitrators (Articles 9 to 12)

A prospective arbitrator shall disclose to those who approach him/her in connection with his/her possible appointment any circumstances likely to give rise to justifiable doubts as to his/her impartiality or independence. An arbitrator, once appointed or chosen, shall disclose such circumstances to the parties unless they have already been informed by him/her of these circumstances.

Article 10

1. Any arbitrator may be challenged if circumstances exist that give rise to justifiable doubts as to the arbitrator's impartiality or independence.

2. A party may challenge the arbitrator appointed by him/her only for reasons of which he/she becomes aware after the appointment has been made.

Article 11

1. A party who intends to challenge an arbitrator shall send notice of its challenge within thirty days after the appointment of the challenged arbitrator has been notified to the challenging party or within thirty days after the circumstances mentioned in articles 9 and 10 became known to that party.

2. The challenge shall be notified to the other party, to the arbitrator who is challenged and to the other members of the arbitral tribunal. The notification shall be in writing and shall state the reasons for the challenge.

3. When an arbitrator has been challenged by one party, the other party may agree to the challenge. The arbitrator may also, after the challenge, withdraw from his/her office. In neither case does this imply acceptance of the validity of the grounds for the challenge. In both cases the procedure provided in article 6 or 7 shall be used in full for the

appointment of the substitute arbitrator, even if during the process of appointing the challenged arbitrator a party had failed to exercise his/her right to appoint or to participate in the appointment.

Article 12

1. If the other party does not agree to the challenge and the challenged arbitrator does not withdraw, the decision on the challenge will be made:

(a) When the initial appointment was made by an appointing authority, by that authority;
(b) When the initial appointment was not made by an appointing authority, but an appointing authority has been previously designated, by that authority;
(c) In all other cases, by the appointing authority to be designated in accordance with the procedure for designating an appointing authority as provided for in article 6.

2. If the appointing authority sustains the challenge, a substitute arbitrator shall be appointed or chosen pursuant to the procedure applicable to the appointment or choice of an arbitrator as provided in articles 6 to 9 except that, when this procedure would call for the designation of an appointing authority, the appointment of the arbitrator shall be made by the appointing authority which decided on the challenge.

Article 13
Replacement of an Arbitrator

1. In the event of the death or resignation of an arbitrator during the course of the arbitral proceedings, a substitute arbitrator shall be appointed or chosen pursuant to the procedure provided for in articles 6 to 9 that was applicable to the appointment or choice of the arbitrator being replaced. Any resignation by an arbitrator shall be addressed to the arbitral tribunal and shall not be effective unless the arbitral tribunal determines that there are sufficient reasons to accept the resignation, and if the arbitral tribunal so determines the resignation shall become effective on the date designated by the arbitral tribunal. In the event that an arbitrator whose resignation is not accepted by the tribunal nevertheless fails to participate in the arbitration, the provisions of paragraph 3 of this article shall apply.

2. In the event that an arbitrator fails to act or in the event of the *de jure* or *de facto* impossibility of his/her performing his/her functions, the procedure in respect of the challenge and replacement of an arbitrator as provided in the preceding articles shall apply, subject to the provisions of paragraph 3 of this article.

3. If an arbitrator on a three- or five-person tribunal fails to participate in the arbitration, the other arbitrators shall, unless the parties agree otherwise, have the power in their sole discretion to continue the arbitration and to make any decision, ruling or award, notwithstanding the failure of one arbitrator to participate. In determining whether to continue the arbitration or to render any decision, ruling, or award without the participation of an arbitrator, the other arbitrators shall take into account the stage of the

arbitration, the reason, if any, expressed by the arbitrator for such non-participation, and such other matters as they consider appropriate in the circumstances of the case. In the event that the other arbitrators determine not to continue the arbitration without the nonparticipating arbitrator, the arbitral tribunal shall declare the office vacant, and a substitute arbitrator shall be appointed pursuant to the provisions of articles 6 to 9, unless the parties agree on a different method of appointment.

Article 14
Repetition of Hearings in the Event of the Replacement of an Arbitrator

If under articles 11 to 13 the sole arbitrator or presiding arbitrator is replaced, any hearings held previously shall be repeated; if any other arbitrator is replaced, such prior hearings may be repeated at the discretion of the arbitral tribunal.

Section III. Arbitral Proceedings

Article 15
General Provisions

1. Subject to these Rules, the arbitral tribunal may conduct the arbitration in such manner as it considers appropriate, provided that the parties are treated with equality and that at any stage of the proceedings each party is given a full opportunity of presenting its case.

2. If either party so requests at any appropriate stage of the proceedings, the arbitral tribunal shall hold hearings for the presentation of evidence by witnesses, including expert witnesses, or for oral argument. In the absence of such a request, the arbitral tribunal shall decide whether to hold such hearings or whether the proceedings shall be conducted on the basis of documents and other materials.

3. All documents or information supplied to the arbitral tribunal by one party shall at the same time be communicated by that party to the other party and a copy shall be filed with the International Bureau.

Article 16
Place of Arbitration

1. Unless the parties have agreed otherwise, the place where the arbitration is to be held shall be The Hague, The Netherlands. If the parties agree that the arbitration shall be held at a place other than The Hague, the International Bureau of the Permanent Court of Arbitration shall inform the parties and the arbitral tribunal whether it is willing to

provide the secretariat and registrar services referred to in article 1, paragraph 1, and the services referred to in article 25, paragraph 3.

2. The arbitral tribunal may determine the locale of the arbitration within the country agreed upon by the parties. It may hear witnesses and hold meetings for consultation among its members at any place it deems appropriate, having regard to the circumstances of the arbitration.

3. After inviting the views of the parties, the arbitral tribunal may meet at any place it deems appropriate for the inspection of property or documents. The parties shall be given sufficient notice to enable them to be present at such inspection.

4. The award shall be made at the place of arbitration.

Article 17
Language

1. Subject to an agreement by the parties, the arbitral tribunal shall, promptly after its appointment, determine the language or languages to be used in the proceedings. This determination shall apply to the statement of claim, the statement of defence, and any further written statements and, if oral hearings take place, to the language or languages to be used in such hearings.

2. The arbitral tribunal may order that any documents annexed to the statement of claim or statement of defence, and any supplementary documents or exhibits submitted in the course of the proceedings, delivered in their original language, shall be accompanied by a translation into the language or languages agreed upon by the parties or determined by the arbitral tribunal.

Article 18
Statement of Claim

1. Unless the statement of claim was contained in the notice of arbitration, within a period of time to be determined by the arbitral tribunal, the claimant shall communicate its statement of claim in writing to the respondent and to each of the arbitrators. A copy of the treaty or other agreement and of the arbitration agreement if not contained in the treaty or agreement, shall be annexed thereto.

2. The statement of claim shall include a precise statement of the following particulars:

(a) The names and addresses of the parties;
(b) A statement of the facts supporting the claim;
(c) The points at issue;

(d) The relief or remedy sought.

The claimant may annex to its statement of claim all documents it deems relevant or may add a reference to the documents or other evidence it will submit.

Article 19
Statement of Defence

1. Within a period of time to be determined by the arbitral tribunal, the respondent shall communicate its statement of defence in writing to the claimant and to each of the arbitrators.

2. The statement of defence shall reply to the particulars (b), (c) and (d) of the statement of claim (art. 18, para. 2). The respondent may annex to its statement the documents on which it relies for its defence or may add a reference to the documents or other evidence it will submit.

3. In its statement of defence, or at a later stage in the arbitral proceedings if the arbitral tribunal decides that the delay was justified under the circumstances, the respondent may make a counter-claim arising out of the same treaty or other agreement or rely on a claim arising out of the same treaty or other agreement for the purpose of a set-off.

4. The provisions of article 18, paragraph 2, shall apply to a counter-claim and a claim relied on for the purpose of a set-off.

Article 20
Amendments to the Claim or Defence

During the course of the arbitral proceedings either party may amend or supplement its claim or defence unless the arbitral tribunal considers it inappropriate to allow such amendment having regard to the delay in making it or prejudice to the other party or any other circumstances. However, a claim may not be amended in such a manner that the amended claim falls outside the scope of the arbitration clause or separate arbitration agreement.

Article 21
Pleas as to the Jurisdiction of the Arbitral Tribunal

1. The arbitral tribunal shall have the power to rule on objections that it has no jurisdiction, including any objections with respect to the existence or validity of the arbitration clause or of the separate arbitration agreement.

2. The arbitral tribunal shall have the power to determine the existence or the validity of the treaty or other agreement of which an arbitration clause forms a part. For the purposes of article 21, an arbitration clause which forms part of the treaty or agreement and which provides for arbitration under these Rules shall be treated as an agreement independent of the other terms of the treaty or agreement. A decision by the arbitral tribunal that the treaty or agreement is null and void shall not entail *ipso jure* the invalidity of the arbitration clause.

3. A plea that the arbitral tribunal does not have jurisdiction shall be raised not later than in the statement of defence or, with respect to a counter-claim, in the reply to the counter-claim.

4. In general, the arbitral tribunal should rule on a plea concerning its jurisdiction as a preliminary question. However, the arbitral tribunal may proceed with the arbitration and rule on such a plea in its final award.

Article 22
Further Written Statements

The arbitral tribunal shall, after inviting the views of the parties, decide which further written statements, in addition to the statement of claim and the statement of defence, shall be required from the parties or may be presented by them and shall fix the period of time for communicating such statements.

Article 23
Periods of Time

The periods of time fixed by the arbitral tribunal for the communication of written statements (including the statement of claim and statement of defence) should not exceed ninety days. However, the arbitral tribunal may set longer time limits, if it concludes that an extension is justified.

Article 24
Evidence and Hearings (Articles 24 and 25)

1. Each party shall have the burden of proving the facts relied on to support its claim or defence.

2. The arbitral tribunal may, if it considers it appropriate, require a party to deliver to the tribunal and to the other party, within such a period of time as the arbitral tribunal shall decide, a summary of the documents and other evidence which that party intends to

present in support of the facts in issue set out in its statement of claim or statement of defence.

3. At any time during the arbitral proceedings the arbitral tribunal may call upon the parties to produce documents, exhibits or other evidence within such a period of time as the tribunal shall determine. The tribunal shall take note of any refusal to do so as well as any reasons given for such refusal.

Article 25

1. In the event of an oral hearing, the arbitral tribunal shall give the parties adequate advance notice of the date, time and place thereof.

2. If witnesses are to be heard, at least thirty days before the hearing each party shall communicate to the arbitral tribunal and to the other party the names and addresses of the witnesses it intends to present, the subject upon and the languages in which such witnesses will give their testimony.

3. The International Bureau shall make arrangements for the translation of oral statements made at a hearing and for a record of the hearing if either is deemed necessary by the tribunal under the circumstances of the case, or if the parties have agreed thereto and have communicated such agreement to the tribunal and the International Bureau at least thirty days before the hearing or such longer period before the hearing as the arbitral tribunal may determine.

4. Hearings shall be held *in camera* unless the parties agree otherwise. The arbitral tribunal may require the retirement of any witness or witnesses during the testimony of other witnesses. The arbitral tribunal is free to determine the manner in which witnesses are examined.

5. Evidence of witnesses may also be presented in the form of written statements signed by them.

6. The arbitral tribunal shall determine the admissibility, relevance, materiality and weight of the evidence offered.

Article 26
Interim Measures of Protection

1. Unless the parties otherwise agree, the arbitral tribunal may, at the request of either party, take any interim measures it deems necessary to preserve the respective rights of either party.

2. Such interim measures may be established in the form of an interim award. The arbitral tribunal shall be entitled to require security for the costs of such measures.

3. A request for interim measures addressed by any party to a judicial authority shall not be deemed incompatible with the agreement to arbitrate, or as a waiver of that agreement.

Article 27
Experts

1. The arbitral tribunal may appoint one or more experts to report to it, in writing, on specific issues to be determined by the tribunal. A copy of the expert's terms of reference, established by the arbitral tribunal, shall be communicated to the parties.

2. The parties shall give the expert any relevant information or produce for his/her inspection any relevant documents or goods that he/she may request of them. Any dispute between a party and such expert as to the relevance and appropriateness of the required information or production shall be referred to the arbitral tribunal for decision.

3. Upon receipt of the expert's report, the arbitral tribunal shall communicate a copy of the report to the parties who shall be given the opportunity to express, in writing, their opinion on the report. A party shall be entitled to examine any document on which the expert has relied in his/her report.

4. At the request of either party the expert, after delivery of the report, may be heard at a hearing where the parties shall have the opportunity to be present and to interrogate the expert. At this hearing either party may present expert witnesses in order to testify on the points at issue. The provisions of article 25 shall be applicable to such proceedings.

Article 28
Failure to Appear or to Make Submissions

1. If, within the period of time fixed by the arbitral tribunal, the claimant has failed to communicate its claim without showing sufficient cause for such failure, the arbitral tribunal shall issue an order for the termination of the arbitral proceedings. If, within the period of time fixed by the arbitral tribunal, the respondent has failed to communicate its statement of defence without showing sufficient cause for such failure, the arbitral tribunal shall order that the proceedings continue.
2. If one of the parties, duly notified under these Rules, fails to appear at a hearing, without showing sufficient cause for such failure, the arbitral tribunal may proceed with the arbitration.

3. If one of the parties, duly invited to produce documentary evidence, fails to do so within the established period of time, without showing sufficient cause for such failure, the arbitral tribunal may make the award on the evidence before it.

Article 29
Closure of Hearings

1. The arbitral tribunal may inquire of the parties if they have any further proof to offer or witnesses to be heard or submissions to make and, if there are none, it may declare the hearings closed.

2. The arbitral tribunal may, if it considers it necessary owing to exceptional circumstances, decide, on its own motion or upon application of a party, to reopen the hearings at any time before the award is made.

Article 30
Waiver of Rules

A party who knows that any provision of, or requirement under, these Rules has not been complied with and yet proceeds with the arbitration without promptly stating its objection to such non-compliance, shall be deemed to have waived its right to object.

Section IV. The Award

Article 31
Decisions

1. When there are three or five arbitrators, any award or other decision of the arbitral tribunal shall be made by a majority of the arbitrators.

2. In the case of questions of procedure, when there is no majority or when the arbitral tribunal so authorizes, the presiding arbitrator may decide on his/her own, subject to revision, if any, by the arbitral tribunal.

Article 32
Form and Effect of the Award

1. In addition to making a final award, the arbitral tribunal shall be entitled to make interim, interlocutory, or partial awards.

2. The award shall be made in writing and shall be final and binding on the parties. The parties undertake to carry out the award without delay.

3. The arbitral tribunal shall state the reasons upon which the award is based, unless the parties have agreed that no reasons are to be given.

4. An award shall be signed by the arbitrators and it shall contain the date on which and the place where the award was made. Where there are three or five arbitrators and any one of them fails to sign, the award shall state the reason for the absence of the signature(s).

5. The award may be made public only with the consent of both parties.

6. Copies of the award signed by the arbitrators shall be communicated to the parties by the International Bureau.

Article 33
Applicable Law

1. The arbitral tribunal shall apply the law chosen by the parties, or in the absence of an agreement, shall decide such disputes in accordance with international law by applying:

(a) International conventions, whether general or particular, establishing rules expressly recognized by the contesting States;
(b) International custom, as evidence of a general practice accepted as law;
(c) The general principles of law recognized by civilized nations;
(d) Judicial and arbitral decisions and the teachings of the most highly qualified publicists of the various nations, as subsidiary means for the determination of rules of law.

2. This provision shall not prejudice the power of the arbitral tribunal to decide a case *ex aequo et bono*, if the parties agree thereto.

Article 34
Settlement or Other Grounds for Termination

1. If, before the award is made, the parties agree on a settlement of the dispute, the arbitral tribunal shall either issue an order for the termination of the arbitral proceedings or, if requested by both parties and accepted by the tribunal, record the settlement in the form of an arbitral award on agreed terms. The arbitral tribunal is not obliged to give reasons for such an award.

2. If, before the award is made, the continuation of the arbitral proceedings becomes unnecessary or impossible for any reason not mentioned in paragraph 1, the arbitral tribunal shall inform the parties of its intention to issue an order for the termination of

the proceedings. The arbitral tribunal shall have the power to issue such an order unless a party raises justifiable grounds for objection.

3. Copies of the order for termination of the arbitral proceedings or of the arbitral award on agreed terms, signed by the arbitrators, shall be communicated to the parties by the International Bureau. Where an arbitral award on agreed terms is made, the provisions of article 32, paragraphs 2 and 4 to 6, shall apply.

Article 35
Interpretation of the Award

1. Within sixty days after the receipt of the award, either party, with notice to the other party, may request that the arbitral tribunal give an interpretation of the award.

2. The interpretation shall be given in writing within forty-five days after the receipt of the request. The interpretation shall form part of the award and the provisions of article 32, paragraphs 2 to 6, shall apply.

Article 36
Correction of the Award

1. Within sixty days after the receipt of the award, either party, with notice to the other party, may request the arbitral tribunal to correct in the award any errors in computation, any clerical or typographical errors, or any errors of similar nature. The arbitral tribunal may within thirty days after the communication of the award make such corrections on its own initiative.
2. Such corrections shall be in writing, and the provisions of article 32, paragraphs 2 to 6, shall apply.

Article 37
Additional Award

1. Within sixty days after the receipt of the award, either party, with notice to the other party, may request the arbitral tribunal to make an additional award as to claims presented in the arbitral proceedings but omitted from the award.

2. If the arbitral tribunal considers the request for an additional award to be justified and considers that the omission can be rectified without any further hearings or evidence, it shall complete its award within sixty days after the receipt of the request.

3. When an additional award is made, the provisions of article 32, paragraphs 2 to 6, shall apply.

Article 38
Costs (Articles 38 to 40)

The arbitral tribunal shall fix the costs of arbitration in its award. The term 'costs' includes only:

(a) The fees of the arbitral tribunal;
(b) The travel and other expenses incurred by the arbitrators;
(c) The costs of expert advice and of other assistance required by the arbitral tribunal;
(d) The travel and other expenses of witnesses to the extent such expenses are approved by the arbitral tribunal;
(e) Any fees and expenses of the appointing authority as well as the expenses of the Secretary-General of the Permanent Court of Arbitration at The Hague and the International Bureau.

Article 39

1. The fees of the arbitral tribunal shall be reasonable in amount, taking into account the complexity of the subject-matter, the time spent by the arbitrators, the amount in dispute, if any, and any other relevant circumstances of the case.
2. When a party so requests, the arbitral tribunal shall fix its fees only after consultation with the Secretary-General of the Permanent Court of Arbitration who may make any comment he/she deems appropriate to the arbitral tribunal concerning the fees.

Article 40

1. Each party shall bear its own costs of arbitration. However, the arbitral tribunal may apportion each of such costs between the parties if it determines that apportionment is reasonable, taking into account the circumstances of the case.

2. When the arbitral tribunal issues an order for the termination of the arbitral proceedings or makes an award on agreed terms, it shall fix the costs of arbitration referred to in article 38 and article 39, paragraph 1, in the text of that order or award.

3. No additional fees may be charged by an arbitral tribunal for interpretation or correction or completion of its award under articles 35 to 37.

Article 41
Deposit of Costs

1. The International Bureau following the commencement of the arbitration, may request each party to deposit an equal amount as an advance for the costs referred to in article 38, paragraphs (a), (b), (c) and (e). All amounts deposited by the parties pursuant to this paragraph and paragraph 2 of this article shall be directed to the International Bureau, and disbursed by it for such costs, including, *inter alia*, fees to the arbitrators, the Secretary-General and the International Bureau.

2. During the course of the arbitral proceedings the arbitral tribunal may request supplementary deposits from the parties.

3. If the requested deposits are not paid in full within sixty days after the receipt of the request, the arbitral tribunal shall so inform the parties in order that one or another of them may make the required payment. If such payment is not made, the arbitral tribunal may order the suspension or termination of the arbitral proceedings.

4. After the award has been made, the International Bureau shall render an accounting to the parties of the deposits received and return any unexpended balance to the parties.

Permanent Court of Arbitration - Optional Rules for Arbitrating Disputes Between Two Parties, Of Which Only One is a State

Effective July 6, 1993

Section I. Introductory Rules

Article 1
Scope of Application

1. Where the parties to a contract have agreed in writing that disputes in relation to that contract shall be referred to arbitration under the Permanent Court of Arbitration Optional Rules for Arbitrating Disputes between Two Parties of Which Only One Is a State, then such disputes shall be referred to arbitration in accordance with these Rules subject to such modification as the parties may agree in writing.

2. Agreement by a party to arbitration under these Rules constitutes a waiver of any right of sovereign immunity from jurisdiction, in respect of the dispute in question, to which such party might otherwise be entitled. A waiver of immunity relating to the execution of an arbitral award must be explicitly expressed.

3. These Rules shall govern the arbitration except that where any of these Rules is in conflict with a provision of the law applicable to the arbitration from which the parties cannot derogate, that provision shall prevail.

4. The International Bureau of the Permanent Court of Arbitration at The Hague (the 'International Bureau') shall have charge of the archives of the arbitration proceeding. In addition, the International Bureau shall, upon written request of all the parties or of the arbitral tribunal, act as a channel of communications between the parties and the arbitral tribunal, and provide secretariat services including, *inter alia*, arranging for hearing rooms, interpretation, and stenographic or electronic records of hearings.

Article 2
Notice, Calculation of Periods of Time

1. For the purposes of these Rules, any notice, including a notification, communication or proposal, is deemed to have been received if it is physically delivered to the addressee or if it is delivered at the addressee's habitual residence, place of business or mailing address, or, if none of these can be found after making reasonable inquiry, then at the addressee's last-known residence or place of business or mailing address. Notice shall be deemed to have been received on the day it is so delivered.

2. For the purposes of calculating a period of time under these Rules, such period shall begin to run on the day following the day when a notice, notification, communication or proposal is received. If the last day of such period is an official holiday or a non-business day at the residence or place of business of the addressee, the period is extended until the first business day which follows. Official holidays or non-business days occurring during the running of the period of time are included in calculating the period.

Article 3
Notice of Arbitration

1. The party initiating recourse to arbitration (hereinafter called the 'claimant') shall give to the other party (hereinafter called the 'respondent') a notice of arbitration.

2. Arbitral proceedings shall be deemed to commence on the date on which the notice of arbitration is received by the respondent.

3. The notice of arbitration shall include the following:

(a) A demand that the dispute be referred to arbitration;
(b) The names and addresses of the parties;
(c) A reference to the arbitration clause or the separate arbitration agreement that is invoked;
(d) A reference to the contract out of or in relation to which the dispute arises;
(e) The general nature of the claim and an indication of the amount involved, if any;
(f) The relief or remedy sought;
(g) A proposal as to the number of arbitrators (i.e., one or three), if the parties have not previously agreed thereon.

4. The notice of arbitration may also include:
(a) The proposals for the appointments of a sole arbitrator and an appointing authority referred to in article 6, paragraph 1;
(b) The notification of the appointment of an arbitrator referred to in article 7;
(c) The statement of claim referred to in article 18.

Article 4
Representation and Assistance

The parties may be represented or assisted by persons of their choice. The names and addresses of such persons must be communicated in writing to the other party, to the International Bureau, and to the arbitral tribunal after it has been appointed; such communication must specify whether the appointment is being made for purposes of representation or assistance.

Section II. Composition of the Arbitral Tribunal

Article 5
Number of Arbitrators

If the parties have not previously agreed on the number of arbitrators (i.e., one or three), and if within thirty days after the receipt by the respondent of the notice of arbitration the parties have not agreed that there shall be only one arbitrator, three arbitrators shall be appointed.

Article 6
Appointment of Arbitrators (Articles 6 to 8)

1. If a sole arbitrator is to be appointed, either party may propose to the other:
   (a) The names of one or more persons, one of whom would serve as the sole arbitrator; and
   (b) If no appointing authority has been agreed upon by the parties, the name or names of one or more institutions or persons, one of whom would serve as appointing authority.

2. If within thirty days after receipt by a party of a proposal made in accordance with paragraph 1 the parties have not reached agreement on the choice of a sole arbitrator, the sole arbitrator shall be appointed by the appointing authority agreed upon by the parties. If no appointing authority has been agreed upon by the parties, or if the appointing authority agreed upon refuses to act or fails to appoint the arbitrator within sixty days of the receipt of a party's request therefor, either party may request the Secretary-General of the Permanent Court of Arbitration at The Hague (the 'Secretary-General') to designate an appointing authority.

3. The appointing authority shall, at the request of one of the parties, appoint the sole arbitrator as promptly as possible. In making the appointment the appointing authority shall use the following list-procedure, unless both parties agree that the list-procedure should not be used or unless the appointing authority determines in its discretion that the use of the list-procedure is not appropriate for the case:

   (a) At the request of one of the parties the appointing authority shall communicate to both parties an identical list containing at least three names;
   (b) Within thirty days after the receipt of this list, each party may return the list to the appointing authority after having deleted the name or names to which he objects and numbered the remaining names on the list in the order of its preference;

(c) After the expiration of the above period of time the appointing authority shall appoint the sole arbitrator from among the names approved on the lists returned to it and in accordance with the order of preference indicated by the parties;
(d) If for any reason the appointment cannot be made according to this procedure, the appointing authority may exercise its discretion in appointing the sole arbitrator.

4. In making the appointment, the appointing authority shall have regard to such considerations as are likely to secure the appointment of an independent and impartial arbitrator and shall take into account as well the advisability of appointing an arbitrator of a nationality other than the nationalities of the parties.

Article 7

1. If three arbitrators are to be appointed, each party shall appoint one arbitrator. The two arbitrators thus appointed shall choose the third arbitrator who will act as the presiding arbitrator of the tribunal.

2. If within thirty days after the receipt of a party's notification of the appointment of an arbitrator the other party has not notified the first party of the arbitrator it has appointed:

(a) The first party may request the appointing authority previously designated by the parties to appoint the second arbitrator; or
(b) If no such authority has been previously designated by the parties, or if the appointing authority previously designated refuses to act or fails to appoint the arbitrator within thirty days after receipt of a party's request therefor, the first party may request the Secretary-General to designate the appointing authority.

The first party may then request the appointing authority so designated to appoint the second arbitrator. In either case, the appointing authority may exercise its discretion in appointing the arbitrator.

3. If within thirty days after the appointment of the second arbitrator the two arbitrators have not agreed on the choice of the presiding arbitrator, the presiding arbitrator shall be appointed by an appointing authority in the same way as a sole arbitrator would be appointed under article 6.

Article 8

1. When an appointing authority is requested to appoint an arbitrator pursuant to article 6 or article 7, the party which makes the request shall send to the appointing authority a copy of the notice of arbitration, a copy of the contract out of or in relation to which the dispute has arisen and a copy of the arbitration agreement if it is not contained in the

contract. The appointing authority may require from either party such information as it deems necessary to fulfil its function.

2. Where the names of one or more persons are proposed for appointment as arbitrators, their full names, addresses and nationalities shall be indicated, together with a description of their qualifications.

3. In appointing arbitrators pursuant to these Rules, the parties and the appointing authority are free to designate persons who are not Members of the Permanent Court of Arbitration at The Hague.

Article 9
Challenge of Arbitrators (Articles 9 to 12)

A prospective arbitrator shall disclose to those who approach him/her in connection with his/her possible appointment any circumstances likely to give rise to justifiable doubts as to his/her impartiality or independence. An arbitrator, once appointed or chosen, shall disclose such circumstances to the parties unless they have already been informed by him/her of these circumstances.

Article 10

1. Any arbitrator may be challenged if circumstances exist that give rise to justifiable doubts as to the arbitrator's impartiality or independence.

2. A party may challenge the arbitrator appointed by it only for reasons of which it becomes aware after the appointment has been made.

Article 11

1. A party which intends to challenge an arbitrator shall send notice of its challenge within thirty days after the appointment of the challenged arbitrator has been notified to the challenging party or within thirty days after the circumstances mentioned in articles 9 and 10 became known to that party.

2. The challenge shall be notified to the other party, to the arbitrator who is challenged and to the other members of the arbitral tribunal. The notification shall be in writing and shall state the reasons for the challenge.

3. When an arbitrator has been challenged by one party, the other party may agree to the challenge. The arbitrator may also, after the challenge, withdraw from his/her office. In neither case does this imply acceptance of the validity of the grounds for the challenge. In both cases the procedure provided in article 6 or 7 shall be used in full for the

appointment of the substitute arbitrator, even if during the process of appointing the challenged arbitrator a party had failed to exercise its right to appoint or to participate in the appointment.

Article 12

1. If the other party does not agree to the challenge and the challenged arbitrator does not withdraw, the decision on the challenge will be made:

(a) When the initial appointment was made by an appointing authority, by that authority;
(b) When the initial appointment was not made by an appointing authority, but an appointing authority has been previously designated, by that authority;
(c) In all other cases, by the appointing authority to be designated in accordance with the procedure for designating an appointing authority as provided for in article 6.

2. If the appointing authority sustains the challenge, a substitute arbitrator shall be appointed or chosen pursuant to the procedure applicable to the appointment or choice of an arbitrator as provided in articles 6 to 9 except that, when this procedure would call for the designation of an appointing authority, the appointment of the arbitrator shall be made by the appointing authority which decided on the challenge.

Article 13
Replacement of an Arbitrator

1. In the event of the death or resignation of an arbitrator during the course of the arbitral proceedings, a substitute arbitrator shall be appointed or chosen pursuant to the procedure provided for in articles 6 to 9 that was applicable to the appointment or choice of the arbitrator being replaced. Any resignation by an arbitrator shall be addressed to the arbitral tribunal and shall not be effective unless the arbitral tribunal determines that there are sufficient reasons to accept the resignation, and if the arbitral tribunal so determines the resignation shall become effective on the date designated by the arbitral tribunal. In the event that an arbitrator whose resignation is not accepted by the tribunal nevertheless fails to participate in the arbitration, the provisions of paragraph 3 of this article shall apply.

2. In the event that an arbitrator fails to act or in the event of the *de jure* or *de facto* impossibility of his/her performing his/her functions, the procedure in respect of the challenge and replacement of an arbitrator as provided in the preceding articles shall apply, subject to the provisions of paragraph 3 of this article.

3. If an arbitrator on a three-person tribunal fails to participate in the arbitration, the other arbitrators shall, unless the parties agree otherwise, have the power in their sole

discretion to continue the arbitration and to make any decision, ruling or award, notwithstanding the failure of one arbitrator to participate. In determining whether to continue the arbitration or to render any decision, ruling, or award without the participation of an arbitrator, the other arbitrators shall take into account the stage of the arbitration, the reason, if any, expressed by the arbitrator for such non-participation, and such other matters as they consider appropriate in the circumstances of the case. In the event that the other arbitrators determine not to continue the arbitration without the non participating arbitrator, the arbitral tribunal shall declare the office vacant, and a substitute arbitrator shall be appointed pursuant to the provisions of articles 6 to 9, unless the parties otherwise agree on a different method of appointment.

Article 14
Repetition of Hearings in the Event of the Replacement of an Arbitrator

If under articles 11 to 13 the sole or presiding arbitrator is replaced, any hearings held previously shall be repeated; if any other arbitrator is replaced, such prior hearings may be repeated at the discretion of the arbitral tribunal.

Section III. Abitral Proceedings

Article 15
General Provisions

1. Subject to these Rules, the arbitral tribunal may conduct the arbitration in such manner as it considers appropriate, provided that the parties are treated with equality and that at any stage of the proceedings each party is given a full opportunity of presenting its case.

2. If either party so requests at any appropriate stage of the proceedings, the arbitral tribunal shall hold hearings for the presentation of evidence by witnesses, including expert witnesses, or for oral argument. In the absence of such a request, the arbitral tribunal shall decide whether to hold such hearings or whether the proceedings shall be conducted on the basis of documents and other materials.

3. All documents or information supplied to the arbitral tribunal by one party shall at the same time be communicated by that party to the other party and a copy shall be filed with the International Bureau.

Article 16
Place of Arbitration

1. Unless the parties have agreed upon the place where the arbitration is to be held, such place shall be The Hague, The Netherlands. If the parties agree that the arbitration shall be held at a place other than The Hague, the International Bureau shall inform the parties and the arbitral tribunal whether it is willing to provide the secretariat and registrar services referred to in article 1, paragraph 4, and the services referred to in article 25, paragraph 3.

2. The arbitral tribunal may determine the locale of the arbitration within the country agreed upon by the parties. It may hear witnesses and hold meetings for consultation among its members at any place it deems appropriate, having regard to the circumstances of the arbitration.

3. After inviting the views of the parties, the arbitral tribunal may meet at any place it deems appropriate for the inspection of goods, other property or documents. The parties shall be given sufficient notice to enable them to be present at such inspection.

4. The award shall be made at the place of arbitration.

Article 17
Language

1. Subject to an agreement by the parties, the arbitral tribunal shall, promptly after its appointment, determine the language or languages to be used in the proceedings. This determination shall apply to the statement of claim, the statement of defence, and any further written statements and, if oral hearings take place, to the language or languages to be used in such hearings.

2. The arbitral tribunal may order that any documents annexed to the statement of claim or statement of defence, and any supplementary documents or exhibits submitted in the course of the proceedings, delivered in their original language, shall be accompanied by a translation into the language or languages agreed upon by the parties or determined by the arbitral tribunal.

Article 18
Statement of Claim

1. Unless the statement of claim was contained in the notice of arbitration, within a period of time to be determined by the arbitral tribunal, the claimant shall communicate its statement of claim in writing to the respondent and to each of the arbitrators. A copy of the contract, and of the arbitration agreement if not contained in the contract, shall be annexed thereto.

2. The statement of claim shall include the following particulars:

(a) The names and addresses of the parties;
(b) A statement of the facts supporting the claim;
(c) The points at issue;
(d) The relief or remedy sought.

The claimant may annex to its statement of claim all documents it deems relevant or may add a reference to the documents or other evidence it will submit.

Article 19
Statement of Defence

1. Within a period of time to be determined by the arbitral tribunal, the respondent shall communicate its statement of defence in writing to the claimant and to each of the arbitrators.

2. The statement of defence shall reply to the particulars (b), (c) and (d) of the statement of claim (art. 18, para. 2). The respondent may annex to its statement the documents on which it relies for its defence or may add a reference to the documents or other evidence it will submit.

3. In its statement of defence, or at a later stage in the arbitral proceedings if the arbitral tribunal decides that the delay was justified under the circumstances, the respondent may make a counter-claim arising out of the same contract or rely on a claim arising out of the same contract for the purpose of a set-off.

4. The provisions of article 18, paragraph 2, shall apply to a counter-claim and a claim relied on for the purpose of a set-off.

Article 20
Amendments to the Claim or Defence

During the course of the arbitral proceedings either party may amend or supplement its claim or defence unless the arbitral tribunal considers it inappropriate to allow such amendment having regard to the delay in making it or prejudice to the other party or any other circumstances. However, a claim may not be amended in such a manner that the amended claim falls outside the scope of the arbitration clause or separate arbitration agreement.

Article 21
Pleas as to the Jurisdiction of the Arbitral Tribunal

1. The arbitral tribunal shall have the power to rule on objections that it has no

jurisdiction, including any objections with respect to the existence or validity of the arbitration clause or of the separate arbitration agreement.

2. The arbitral tribunal shall have the power to determine the existence or the validity of the contract of which an arbitration clause forms a part. For the purposes of this article, an arbitration clause which forms part of a contract and which provides for arbitration under these Rules shall be treated as an agreement independent of the other terms of the contract. A decision by the arbitral tribunal that the contract is null and void shall not entail *ipso jure* the invalidity of the arbitration clause.

3. A plea that the arbitral tribunal does not have jurisdiction shall be raised not later than in the statement of defence or, with respect to a counter-claim, in the reply to the counterclaim.

4. In general, the arbitral tribunal should rule on a plea concerning its jurisdiction as a preliminary question. However, the arbitral tribunal may proceed with the arbitration and rule on such a plea in their final award.

Article 22
Further Written Statements

The arbitral tribunal shall decide which further written statements, in addition to the statement of claim and the statement of defence, shall be required from the parties or may be presented by them and shall fix the periods of time for communicating such statements.

Article 23
Periods of Time

The periods of time fixed by the arbitral tribunal for the communication of written statements (including the statement of claim and statement of defence) should not exceed forty-five days. However, the arbitral tribunal may set longer time limits, or extend the time limits, if it concludes that either is justified.

Article 24
Evidence and Hearings (Articles 24 and 25)

1. Each party shall have the burden of proving the facts relied on to support its claim or defence.

2. The arbitral tribunal may, if it considers it appropriate, require a party to deliver to the tribunal and to the other party, within such a period of time as the arbitral tribunal shall

decide, a summary of the documents and other evidence which that party intends to present in support of the facts in issue set out in its statement of claim or statement of defence.

3. At any time during the arbitral proceedings the arbitral tribunal may call upon the parties to produce documents, exhibits or other evidence within such a period of time as the tribunal shall determine. The tribunal shall take formal note of any refusal to do so, as well as any reasons given for such refusal.

Article 25

1. In the event of an oral hearing, the arbitral tribunal shall give the parties adequate advance notice of the date, time and place thereof.

2. If witnesses are to be heard, at least thirty days before the hearing each party shall communicate to the arbitral tribunal and to the other party the names and addresses of the witnesses it intends to present, the subject upon and the languages in which such witnesses will give their testimony.

3. The International Bureau shall make arrangements for the translation of oral statements made at a hearing and for a record of the hearing if either is deemed necessary by the tribunal under the circumstances of the case, or if the parties have agreed thereto and have communicated such agreement to the tribunal and the International Bureau at least thirty days before the hearing, or such longer period before the hearing as the arbitral tribunal may determine.

4. Hearings shall be held *in camera* unless the parties agree otherwise. The arbitral tribunal may require the retirement of any witness or witnesses during the testimony of other witnesses. The arbitral tribunal is free to determine the manner in which witnesses are examined.

5. Evidence of witnesses may also be presented in the form of written statements signed by them.

6. The arbitral tribunal shall determine the admissibility, relevance, materiality and weight of the evidence offered.

Article 26
Interim Measures of Protection

1. Unless the parties agree otherwise, the arbitral tribunal may, at the request of either party, take any interim measures it deems necessary to preserve the respective rights of either party or in respect of the subject-matter of the dispute, including measures for

conservation of the goods forming the subject-matter in dispute, such as ordering their deposit with a third person or the sale of perishable goods.

2. Such interim measures may be established in the form of an interim award. The arbitral tribunal shall be entitled to require security for the costs of such measures.

3. A request for interim measures addressed by any party to a judicial authority shall not be deemed incompatible with the agreement to arbitrate, or as a waiver of that agreement.

Article 27
Experts

1. The arbitral tribunal may appoint one or more experts to report to it, in writing, on specific issues to be determined by the tribunal. A copy of the expert's terms of reference, established by the arbitral tribunal, shall be communicated to the parties.

2. The parties shall give the expert any relevant information or produce for his/her inspection any relevant documents or goods that he/she may require of them. Any dispute between a party and such expert as to the relevance of the required information or production shall be referred to the arbitral tribunal for decision.

3. Upon receipt of the expert's report, the arbitral tribunal shall communicate a copy of the report to the parties which shall be given the opportunity to express, in writing, their opinion on the report. A party shall be entitled to examine any document on which the expert has relied in his/her report.

4. At the request of either party the expert, after delivery of the report, may be heard at a hearing where the parties shall have the opportunity to be present and to interrogate the expert. At this hearing either party may present expert witnesses in order to testify on the points at issue. The provisions of article 25 shall be applicable to such proceedings.

Article 28
Failure to Appear or to Make Submissions

1. If, within the period of time fixed by the arbitral tribunal, the claimant has failed to communicate its claim without showing sufficient cause for such failure, the arbitral tribunal shall issue an order for the termination of the arbitral proceedings. If, within the period of time fixed by the arbitral tribunal, the respondent has failed to communicate its statement of defence without showing sufficient cause for such failure, the arbitral tribunal shall order that the proceedings continue.

2. If one of the parties, duly notified under these Rules, fails to appear at a hearing, without showing sufficient cause for such failure, the arbitral tribunal may proceed with the arbitration.

3. If one of the parties, duly invited to produce documentary evidence, fails to do so within the established period of time, without showing sufficient cause for such failure, the arbitral tribunal may make the award on the evidence before it.

Article 29
Closure of Hearings

1. The arbitral tribunal may inquire of the parties if they have any further proof to offer or witnesses to be heard or submissions to make and, if there are none, it may declare the hearings closed.

2. The arbitral tribunal may, if it considers it necessary owing to exceptional circumstances, decide, on its own motion or upon application of a party, to reopen the hearings at any time before the award is made.

Article 30
Waiver of Rules

A party which knows that any provision of, or requirement under, these Rules has not been complied with and yet proceeds with the arbitration without promptly stating its objection to such non-compliance, shall be deemed to have waived its right to object.

Section IV. The Award

Article 31
Decisions

1. When there are three arbitrators, any award or other decision of the arbitral tribunal shall be made by a majority of the arbitrators.

2. In the case of questions of procedure, when there is no majority or when the arbitral tribunal so authorizes, the presiding arbitrator may decide on his/her own, subject to revision, if any, by the arbitral tribunal.

Article 32
Form and Effect of the Award

1. In addition to making a final award, the arbitral tribunal shall be entitled to make interim, interlocutory, or partial awards.

2. The award shall be made in writing and shall be final and binding on the parties. The parties undertake to carry out the award without delay.

3. The arbitral tribunal shall state the reasons upon which the award is based, unless the parties have agreed that no reasons are to be given.

4. An award shall be signed by the arbitrators and it shall contain the date on which and the place where the award was made. Where there are three arbitrators and one of them fails to sign, the award shall state the reason for the absence of the signature.

5. The award may be made public only with the consent of both parties.

6. Copies of the award signed by the arbitrators shall be communicated to the parties by the International Bureau. The International Bureau may withhold communicating the award to the parties until all costs of the arbitration have been paid.

7. If the arbitration law of the country where the award is made requires that the award be filed or registered by the arbitral tribunal, the tribunal shall comply with this requirement within the period of time required by law.

Article 33
Applicable Law, Amiable Compositeur

1. The arbitral tribunal shall apply the law designated by the parties as applicable to the substance of the dispute. Failing such designation by the parties, the arbitral tribunal shall apply the law determined by the conflict of laws rules which it considers applicable.

2. The arbitral tribunal shall decide as *amiable compositeur* or *ex aequo et bono* only if the parties have expressly authorized the arbitral tribunal to do so and if the law applicable to the arbitral procedure permits such arbitration.
3. In all cases, the arbitral tribunal shall decide in accordance with the terms of the contract and shall take into account the usages of the trade applicable to the transaction.

Article 34
Settlement or Other Grounds for Termination

1. If, before the award is made, the parties agree on a settlement of the dispute, the arbitral tribunal shall either issue an order for the termination of the arbitral proceedings or, if requested by both parties and accepted by the tribunal, record the settlement in the

form of an arbitral award on agreed terms. The arbitral tribunal is not obliged to give reasons for such an award.

2. If, before the award is made, the continuation of the arbitral proceedings becomes unnecessary or impossible for any reason not mentioned in paragraph 1, the arbitral tribunal shall inform the parties of its intention to issue an order for the termination of the proceedings. The arbitral tribunal shall have the power to issue such an order unless a party raises justifiable grounds for objection.

3. Copies of the order for termination of the arbitral proceedings or of the arbitral award on agreed terms, signed by the arbitrators, shall be communicated to the parties by the International Bureau. Where an arbitral award on agreed terms is made, the provisions of article 32, paragraphs 2 and 4 to 7, shall apply.

Article 35
Interpretation of the Award

1. Within thirty days after the receipt of the award, either party, with notice to the other party, may request that the arbitral tribunal give an interpretation of the award.

2. The interpretation shall be given in writing within forty-five days after the receipt of the request. The interpretation shall form part of the award and the provisions of article 32, paragraphs 2 to 7, shall apply.

Article 36
Correction of the Award

1. Within thirty days after the receipt of the award, either party, with notice to the other party, may request the arbitral tribunal to correct in the award any errors in computation, any clerical or typographical errors, or any errors of similar nature. The arbitral tribunal may within thirty days after the communication of the award make such corrections on its own initiative.

2. Such corrections shall be in writing, and the provisions of article 32, paragraphs 2 to 7, shall apply.

Article 37
Additional Award

1. Within sixty days after the receipt of the award, either party, with notice to the other party, may request the arbitral tribunal to make an additional award as to claims presented in the arbitral proceedings but omitted from the award.

2. If the arbitral tribunal considers the request for an additional award to be justified and considers that the omission can be rectified without any further hearings or evidence, it shall complete its award within sixty days after the receipt of the request.

3. When an additional award is made, the provisions of article 32, paragraphs 2 to 7, shall apply.

Article 38
Costs (Articles 38 to 40)

The arbitral tribunal shall fix the costs of arbitration in its award. The term 'costs' includes only:

(a) The fees of the arbitral tribunal to be stated separately as to each arbitrator and to be fixed by the tribunal itself in accordance with article 39;
(b) The travel and other expenses incurred by the arbitrators;
(c) The costs of expert advice and of other assistance required by the arbitral tribunal;
(d) The travel and other expenses of witnesses to the extent such expenses are approved by the arbitral tribunal;
(e) The costs for legal representation and assistance of the successful party if such costs were claimed during the arbitral proceedings, and only to the extent that the arbitral tribunal determines that the amount of such costs is reasonable;
(f) Any fees and expenses of the appointing authority as well as the expenses of the Secretary-General and the International Bureau.

Article 39

1. The fees of the arbitral tribunal shall be reasonable in amount, taking into account the amount in dispute, the complexity of the subject-matter, the time spent by the arbitrators and any other relevant circumstances of the case.

2. If an appointing authority has been agreed upon by the parties or designated by the Secretary-General of the Permanent Court of Arbitration at The Hague, and if that authority has issued a schedule of fees for arbitrators in international cases which it administers, the arbitral tribunal in fixing its fees shall take that schedule of fees into account to the extent that it considers appropriate in the circumstances of the case.

3. If such appointing authority has not issued a schedule of fees for arbitrators in international cases, any party may at any time request the appointing authority to furnish a statement setting forth the basis for establishing fees which is customarily

followed in international cases in which the authority appoints arbitrators. If the appointing authority consents to provide such a statement, the arbitral tribunal in fixing its fees shall take such information into account to the extent that it considers appropriate in the circumstances of the case.

4. In cases referred to in paragraphs 2 and 3, when a party so requests and the appointing authority consents to perform the function, the arbitral tribunal shall fix its fees only after consultation with the appointing authority which may make any comment it deems appropriate to the arbitral tribunal concerning the fees.

Article 40

1. Except as provided in paragraph 2, the costs of arbitration shall in principle be borne by the unsuccessful party. However, the arbitral tribunal may apportion each of such costs between the parties if it determines that apportionment is reasonable, taking into account the circumstances of the case.

2. With respect to the costs of legal representation and assistance referred to in article 38, paragraph (e), the arbitral tribunal, taking into account the circumstances of the case, shall be free to determine which party shall bear such costs or may apportion such costs between the parties if it determines that apportionment is reasonable.

3. When the arbitral tribunal issues an order for the termination of the arbitral proceedings or makes an award on agreed terms, it shall fix the costs of arbitration referred to in articles 38 and 39, paragraph 1, in the text of that order or award.

4. No additional fees may be charged by an arbitral tribunal for interpretation or correction or completion of its award under articles 35 to 37.

Article 41
Deposit of Costs

1. The arbitral tribunal, on its establishment, may request each party to deposit an equal amount as an advance for the costs referred to in article 38, paragraphs (a), (b), (c) and (f). All amounts deposited by the parties pursuant to this paragraph and paragraph 2 of this article shall be paid to the International Bureau, and shall be disbursed by it for such costs, including, *inter alia*, fees to the arbitrators, the Secretary-General and the International Bureau.

2. During the course of the arbitral proceedings the arbitral tribunal may request supplementary deposits from the parties.

3. If an appointing authority has been agreed upon by the parties or designated by the Secretary-General of the Permanent Court of Arbitration at The Hague, and when a party so requests and the appointing authority consents to perform the function, the arbitral tribunal shall fix the amounts of any deposits or supplementary deposits only after consultation with the appointing authority which may make any comments to the arbitral tribunal which it deems appropriate concerning the amount of such deposits and supplementary deposits.

4. If the required deposits are not paid in full within thirty days after the receipt of the request, the arbitral tribunal shall so inform the parties in order that one or another of them may make the required payment. If such payment is not made, the arbitral tribunal may order the suspension or termination of the arbitral proceedings.

5. After the award has been made, the International Bureau shall render an accounting to the parties of the deposits received and return any unexpended balance to the parties.

Permanent Court of Arbitration Optional Rules For Arbitration Involving International Organizations and States

Effective July 1, 1996

Section I. Introductory Rules

Article 1
Scope of Application

1. Where an international organization, on the one hand, and a State or an international organization, on the other hand, have agreed in writing that disputes that may arise or that have arisen between them shall be referred to arbitration under the Permanent Court of Arbitration Optional Rules for Arbitration Involving International Organizations and States, such disputes shall be settled in accordance with these Rules subject to such modification as the parties may agree in writing.

2. For the purpose of the preceding paragraph:

(a) 'International organization' means an intergovernmental organization;
(b) 'State' means any State, whether or not it is a member of the international organization concerned;
(c) The expression 'any agreement' includes the constituent instrument of the organization.

3. The International Bureau of the Permanent Court of Arbitration (the 'International Bureau') shall take charge of the archives of the arbitration proceeding. In addition, upon written request of all the parties or of the arbitral tribunal, the International Bureau shall act as a channel of communication between the parties and the arbitral tribunal, provide secretariat services and/or serve as registry.

Article 2
Notice, Calculation of Periods of Time

1. For the purposes of these Rules, any notice, including a notification, communication or proposal, is deemed to have been received when it has been delivered to the addressee through diplomatic channels, in the case of a State, or by any other means by which it can be ascertained that the notification has reached its destination. Notice shall be deemed to have been received on the day it is so delivered.

2. For the purposes of calculating a period of time under these Rules, such period shall begin to run on the day following the day when a notice, notification, communication or proposal is received. If the last day of such period is an official holiday or a non-work day in the State of the addressee, the period is extended until the first work day which follows. Official holidays or non-work days occurring during the running of the period of time are included in calculating the period.

Article 3
Notice of Arbitration

1. The party initiating recourse to arbitration (hereinafter called the 'claimant') shall give to the other party (hereinafter called the 'respondent') a notice of arbitration.

2. Arbitral proceedings shall be deemed to commence on the date on which the notice of arbitration is received by the respondent.

3. The notice of arbitration shall include the following:

(a) A demand that the dispute be referred to arbitration;
(b) The names and addresses of the parties;
(c) A reference to the constituent instrument of the organization and to any rule, decision, agreement or relationship out of or in relation to which the dispute arises;
(d) Any pertinent arbitration clause or separate arbitration agreement;
(e) The general nature of the claim and an indication of the amount involved, if any;
(f) The relief or remedy sought;
(g) A proposal as to the number of arbitrators (i.e., one, three or five), if the parties have not previously agreed thereon.

4. The notice of arbitration may also include the statement of claim referred to in article 18.

Article 4
Representation and Assistance

Each party shall appoint an agent. The parties may also be assisted by persons of their choice. The name and address of the agent must be communicated in writing to the other party, to the International Bureau and to the arbitral tribunal after it has been appointed.

Section II. Composition of the Arbitral Tribunal

Article 5
Number of Arbitrators

If the parties have not previously agreed on the number of arbitrators (i.e., one, three, or five), and if within thirty days after the receipt by the respondent of the notice of arbitration the parties have not agreed on the number of arbitrators, three arbitrators shall be appointed.

Article 6
Appointment of Arbitrators (Articles 6 to 8)

1. If a sole arbitrator is to be appointed, either party may propose to the other:

(a) The names of one or more persons, one of whom would serve as the sole arbitrator; and
(b) If no appointing authority has been agreed upon by the parties, the name or names of one or more institutions or persons, one of whom would serve as appointing authority.

2. If within sixty days after receipt by a party of a proposal made in accordance with paragraph 1 the parties have not reached agreement on the choice of a sole arbitrator, the sole arbitrator shall be appointed by the appointing authority agreed upon by the parties. If no appointing authority has been agreed upon by the parties, or if the appointing authority agreed upon refuses to act or fails to appoint the arbitrator within sixty days of the receipt of a party's request therefor, either party may request the Secretary-General of the Permanent Court of Arbitration at The Hague (the 'Secretary-General') to designate an appointing authority.

3. The appointing authority shall, at the request of one of the parties, appoint the sole arbitrator as promptly as possible. In making the appointment the appointing authority shall use the following list-procedure, unless both parties agree that the list-procedure should not be used or unless the appointing authority determines in its discretion that the use of the list-procedure is not appropriate for the case:

(a) At the request of one of the parties the appointing authority shall communicate to both parties an identical list containing at least three names;
(b) Within thirty days after the receipt of this list, each party may return the list to the appointing authority after having deleted the name or names to which it objects and numbered the remaining names on the list in the order of its preference;

(c) After the expiration of the above period of time the appointing authority shall appoint the sole arbitrator from among the names approved on the lists returned to it and in accordance with the order of preference indicated by the parties;
(d) If for any reason the appointment cannot be made according to this procedure, the appointing authority may exercise its discretion in appointing the sole arbitrator.

4. In making the appointment, the appointing authority shall have regard to such considerations as are likely to secure the appointment of independent and impartial arbitrators.

Article 7

1. If three arbitrators are to be appointed, each party shall appoint one arbitrator. The two arbitrators thus appointed shall choose the third arbitrator who will act as the presiding arbitrator of the tribunal. If five arbitrators are to be appointed, the two party-appointed arbitrators shall choose the remaining three arbitrators and designate one of those three as the presiding arbitrator of the tribunal.

2. If within thirty days after the receipt of a party's notification of the appointment of an arbitrator the other party has not notified the first party of the arbitrator it has appointed:

(a) The first party may request the appointing authority previously designated by the parties to appoint the second arbitrator; or
(b) If no such authority has been previously designated by the parties, or if the appointing authority previously designated refuses to act or fails to appoint the arbitrator within sixty days after receipt of a party's request therefor, the first party may request the Secretary-General to designate the appointing authority.

The first party may then request the appointing authority so designated to appoint the second arbitrator. In either case, the appointing authority may exercise its discretion in appointing the arbitrator.

3. If within sixty days after the appointment of the second arbitrator the two arbitrators have not agreed on the choice of the remaining arbitrators and/or presiding arbitrator, the remaining arbitrators and/or presiding arbitrator shall be appointed by an appointing authority in the same way as a sole arbitrator would be appointed under article 6.

Article 8

1. When an appointing authority is requested to appoint an arbitrator pursuant to article 6 or article 7, the party which makes the request shall send to the appointing authority a

copy of the notice of arbitration and a copy of the pertinent documents among those mentioned in article 3, paragraph 3(c) and (d). The appointing authority may request from either party such information as it deems necessary to fulfil its function.

2. Where the names of one or more persons are proposed for appointment as arbitrators, their full names, addresses and nationalities shall be indicated, together with a description of their qualifications.

3. In appointing arbitrators pursuant to these Rules, the parties and the appointing authority are free to designate persons who are not Members of the Permanent Court of Arbitration at The Hague.

Article 9
Challenge of Arbitrators (Articles 9 to 12)

A prospective arbitrator shall disclose to those who approach him/her in connection with his/her possible appointment any circumstances likely to give rise to justifiable doubts as to his/her impartiality or independence. An arbitrator, once appointed or chosen, shall disclose such circumstances to the parties unless they have already been informed by him/her of these circumstances.

Article 10

1. Any arbitrator may be challenged if circumstances exist that give rise to justifiable doubts as to the arbitrator's impartiality or independence.

2. A party may challenge the arbitrator appointed by him/her only for reasons of which he/she becomes aware after the appointment has been made.

Article 11

1. A party who intends to challenge an arbitrator shall send notice of its challenge within thirty days after the appointment of the challenged arbitrator has been notified to the challenging party or within thirty days after the circumstances mentioned in articles 9 and 10 became known to that party.

2. The challenge shall be notified to the other party, to the arbitrator who is challenged and to the other members of the arbitral tribunal. The notification shall be in writing and shall state the reasons for the challenge.

3. When an arbitrator has been challenged by one party, the other party may agree to the challenge. The arbitrator may also, after the challenge, withdraw from his/her office. In neither case does this imply acceptance of the validity of the grounds for the challenge. In

both cases the procedure provided in article 6 or 7 shall be used in full for the appointment of the substitute arbitrator, even if during the process of appointing the challenged arbitrator a party had failed to exercise his/her right to appoint or to participate in the appointment.

Article 12

1. If the other party does not agree to the challenge and the challenged arbitrator does not withdraw, the decision on the challenge will be made:

(a) When the initial appointment was made by an appointing authority, by that authority;
(b) When the initial appointment was not made by an appointing authority, but an appointing authority has been previously designated, by that authority;
(c) In all other cases, by the appointing authority to be designated in accordance with the procedure for designating an appointing authority as provided for in article 6.

2. If the appointing authority sustains the challenge, a substitute arbitrator shall be appointed or chosen pursuant to the procedure applicable to the appointment or choice of an arbitrator as provided in articles 6 to 9 except that, when this procedure would call for the designation of an appointing authority, the appointment of the arbitrator shall be made by the appointing authority which decided on the challenge.

Article 13
Replacement of an Arbitrator

1. In the event of the death or resignation of an arbitrator during the course of the arbitral proceedings, a substitute arbitrator shall be appointed or chosen pursuant to the procedure provided for in articles 6 to 9 that was applicable to the appointment or choice of the arbitrator being replaced. Any resignation by an arbitrator shall be addressed to the arbitral tribunal and shall not be effective unless the arbitral tribunal determines that there are sufficient reasons to accept the resignation, and if the arbitral tribunal so determines the resignation shall become effective on the date designated by the arbitral tribunal. In the event that an arbitrator whose resignation is not accepted by the tribunal nevertheless fails to participate in the arbitration, the provisions of paragraph 3 of this article shall apply.

2. In the event that an arbitrator fails to act or in the event of the *de jure* or *de facto* impossibility of his/her performing his/her functions, the procedure in respect of the challenge and replacement of an arbitrator as provided in the preceding articles shall apply, subject to the provisions of paragraph 3 of this article.

3. If an arbitrator on a three- or five-person tribunal fails to participate in the arbitration, the other arbitrators shall, unless the parties agree otherwise, have the power in their sole discretion to continue the arbitration and to make any decision, ruling or award, notwithstanding the failure of one arbitrator to participate. In determining whether to continue the arbitration or to render any decision, ruling, or award without the participation of an arbitrator, the other arbitrators shall take into account the stage of the arbitration, the reason, if any, expressed by the arbitrator for such non-participation, and such other matters as they consider appropriate in the circumstances of the case. In the event that the other arbitrators determine not to continue the arbitration without the nonparticipating arbitrator, the arbitral tribunal shall declare the office vacant, and a substitute arbitrator shall be appointed pursuant to the provisions of articles 6 to 9, unless the parties agree on a different method of appointment.

Article 14
Repetition of Hearings in the Event of the Replacement of an Arbitrator

If under articles 11 to 13 the sole arbitrator or presiding arbitrator is replaced, any hearings held previously shall be repeated; if any other arbitrator is replaced, such prior hearings may be repeated at the discretion of the arbitral tribunal.

Section III. Abitral Proceedings

Article 15
General Provisions

1. Subject to these Rules, the arbitral tribunal may conduct the arbitration in such manner as it considers appropriate, provided that the parties are treated with equality and that at any stage of the proceedings each party is given a full opportunity of presenting its case.

2. If either party so requests at any appropriate stage of the proceedings, the arbitral tribunal shall hold hearings for the presentation of evidence by witnesses, including expert witnesses, or for oral argument. In the absence of such a request, the arbitral tribunal shall decide whether to hold such hearings or whether the proceedings shall be conducted on the basis of documents and other materials.

3. All documents or information supplied to the arbitral tribunal by one party shall at the same time be communicated by that party to the other party and a copy shall be filed with the International Bureau.

Article 16
Place of Arbitration

1. Unless the parties have agreed otherwise, the place where the arbitration is to be held shall be The Hague, The Netherlands. If the parties agree that the arbitration shall be held at a place other than The Hague, the International Bureau shall inform the parties and the arbitral tribunal whether it is willing to provide the secretariat and registrar services referred to in article 1, paragraph 3, and the services referred to in article 25, paragraph 3.

2. The arbitral tribunal may determine the locale of the arbitration within the country agreed upon by the parties. It may hear witnesses and hold meetings for consultation among its members at any place it deems appropriate, having regard to the circumstances of the arbitration.

3. After inviting the views of the parties, the arbitral tribunal may meet at any place it deems appropriate for the inspection of property or documents. The parties shall be given sufficient notice to enable them to be present at such inspection.

4. The award shall be made at the place of arbitration.

Article 17
Language

1. Subject to an agreement by the parties, the arbitral tribunal shall, promptly after its appointment, determine the language or languages to be used in the proceedings. This determination shall apply to the statement of claim, the statement of defence, and any further written statements and, if oral hearings take place, to the language or languages to be used in such hearings.

2. The arbitral tribunal may order that any documents annexed to the statement of claim or statement of defence, and any supplementary documents or exhibits submitted in the course of the proceedings, delivered in their original language, shall be accompanied by a translation into the language or languages agreed upon by the parties or determined by the arbitral tribunal.

Article 18
Statement of Claim

1. Unless the statement of claim was contained in the notice of arbitration, within a period of time to be determined by the arbitral tribunal, the claimant shall communicate its statement of claim in writing to the respondent and to each of the arbitrators. A copy of the documents mentioned in article 8 shall be annexed thereto.

2. The statement of claim shall include a precise statement of the following particulars:

(a) The names and addresses of the parties;
(b) A statement of the facts supporting the claim;
(c) The points at issue;
(d) The relief or remedy sought.

The claimant may annex to its statement of claim all documents it deems relevant or may add a reference to the documents or other evidence it will submit.

Article 19
Statement of Defence

1. Within a period of time to be determined by the arbitral tribunal, the respondent shall communicate its statement of defence in writing to the claimant and to each of the arbitrators.

2. The statement of defence shall reply to the particulars (b), (c) and (d) of the statement of claim (art. 18, para. 2). The respondent may annex to its statement the documents on which it relies for its defence or may add a reference to the documents or other evidence it will submit.

3. In its statement of defence, or at a later stage in the arbitral proceedings if the arbitral tribunal decides that the delay was justified under the circumstances, the respondent may make a counter-claim, or a claim for a set-off, arising out of any of the items mentioned in article 3, paragraph 3(c).

4. The provisions of article 18, paragraph 2, shall apply to a counter-claim and a claim relied on for the purpose of a set-off.

Article 20
Amendments to the Claim or Defence

During the course of the arbitral proceedings either party may amend or supplement its claim or defence unless the arbitral tribunal considers it inappropriate to allow such amendment having regard to the delay in making it or prejudice to the other party or any other circumstances. However, a claim may not be amended in such a manner that the amended claim falls outside the scope of the arbitration clause or separate arbitration agreement.

Article 21
Pleas as to the Jurisdiction of the Arbitral Tribunal

1. The arbitral tribunal shall have the power to rule on objections that it has no jurisdiction, including any objections with respect to the existence or validity of the arbitration clause or of the separate arbitration agreement.

2. The arbitral tribunal shall have the power to determine the existence or the validity of any legal instrument of which an arbitration clause forms a part. For the purposes ofarticle 21, an arbitration clause which forms part of such instrument and which provides for arbitration under these Rules shall be treated as an agreement independent of theother terms of such instrument. A decision by the arbitral tribunal that the instrument isnull and void shall not entail *ipso jure* the invalidity of the arbitration clause.

3. A plea that the arbitral tribunal does not have jurisdiction shall be raised not later than in the statement of defence or, with respect to a counter-claim, in the reply to the counter-claim.

4. In general, the arbitral tribunal should rule on a plea concerning its jurisdiction as a preliminary question. However, the arbitral tribunal may proceed with the arbitration and rule on such a plea in its final award.

Article 22
Further Written Statements

The arbitral tribunal shall, after inviting the views of the parties, decide which further written statements, in addition to the statement of claim and the statement of defence, shall be required from the parties or may be presented by them and shall fix the period of time for communicating such statements.

Article 23
Periods of Time

The periods of time fixed by the arbitral tribunal for the communication of written statements (including the statement of claim and statement of defence) should not exceed ninety days. However, the arbitral tribunal may set longer time limits, if it concludes that an extension is justified.

Article 24

Evidence and Hearings (Articles 24 and 25)

1. Each party shall have the burden of proving the facts relied on to support its claim or defence.

2. The arbitral tribunal may, if it considers it appropriate, require a party to deliver to the tribunal and to the other party, within such a period of time as the arbitral tribunal shall decide, a summary of the documents and other evidence which that party intends to present in support of the facts in issue set out in its statement of claim or statement of defence.

3. At any time during the arbitral proceedings the arbitral tribunal may call upon the parties to produce documents, exhibits or other evidence within such a period of time as the tribunal shall determine. The tribunal shall take note of any refusal to do so as well as any reasons given for such refusal.

Article 25

1. In the event of an oral hearing, the arbitral tribunal shall give the parties adequate advance notice of the date, time and place thereof.

2. If witnesses are to be heard, at least thirty days before the hearing each party shall communicate to the arbitral tribunal and to the other party the names and addresses of the witnesses it intends to present, the subject upon and the languages in which such witnesses will give their testimony.

3. The International Bureau shall make arrangements for the translation of oral statements made at a hearing and for a record of the hearing if either is deemed necessary by the tribunal under the circumstances of the case, or if the parties have agreed thereto and have communicated such agreement to the tribunal and the International Bureau at least thirty days before the hearing or such longer period before the hearing as the arbitral tribunal may determine.

4. Hearings shall be held *in camera* unless the parties agree otherwise. The arbitral tribunal may require the retirement of any witness or witnesses during the testimony of other witnesses. The arbitral tribunal is free to determine the manner in which witnesses are examined.

5. Evidence of witnesses may also be presented in the form of written statements signed by them.

6. The arbitral tribunal shall determine the admissibility, relevance, materiality and weight of the evidence offered.

Article 26
Interim Measures of Protection

1. Unless the parties otherwise agree, the arbitral tribunal may, at the request of either party, take any interim measures it deems necessary to preserve the respective rights of either party.

2. Such interim measures may be established in the form of an interim award. The arbitral tribunal shall be entitled to require security for the costs of such measures.

3. A request for interim measures addressed by any party to a judicial authority shall not be deemed incompatible with the agreement to arbitrate, or as a waiver of that agreement.

Article 27
Experts

1. The arbitral tribunal may appoint one or more experts to report to it, in writing, on specific issues to be determined by the tribunal. A copy of the expert's terms of reference, established by the arbitral tribunal, shall be communicated to the parties.

2. The parties shall give the expert any relevant information or produce for his/her inspection any relevant documents or goods that he/she may request of them. Any dispute between a party and such expert as to the relevance and appropriateness of the required information or production shall be referred to the arbitral tribunal for decision.

3. Upon receipt of the expert's report, the arbitral tribunal shall communicate a copy of the report to the parties who shall be given the opportunity to express, in writing, their opinion on the report. A party shall be entitled to examine any document on which the expert has relied in his/her report.

4. At the request of either party the expert, after delivery of the report, may be heard at a hearing where the parties shall have the opportunity to be present and to interrogate the expert. At this hearing either party may present expert witnesses in order to testify on the points at issue. The provisions of article 25 shall be applicable to such proceedings.

Article 28
Failure to Appear or to Make Submissions

1. If, within the period of time fixed by the arbitral tribunal, the claimant has failed to communicate its claim without showing sufficient cause for such failure, the arbitral tribunal shall issue an order for the termination of the arbitral proceedings. If, within the period of time fixed by the arbitral tribunal, the respondent has failed to communicate its statement of defence without showing sufficient cause for such failure, the arbitral tribunal shall order that the proceedings continue.

2. If one of the parties, duly notified under these Rules, fails to appear at a hearing, without showing sufficient cause for such failure, the arbitral tribunal may proceed with the arbitration.
3. If one of the parties, duly invited to produce documentary evidence, fails to do so within the established period of time, without showing sufficient cause for such failure, the arbitral tribunal may make the award on the evidence before it.

Article 29
Closure of Hearings

1. The arbitral tribunal may inquire of the parties if they have any further proof to offer or witnesses to be heard or submissions to make and, if there are none, it may declare the hearings closed.

2. The arbitral tribunal may, if it considers it necessary owing to exceptional circumstances, decide, on its own motion or upon application of a party, to reopen the hearings at any time before the award is made.

Article 30
Waiver of Rules

A party who knows that any provision of, or requirement under, these Rules has not been complied with and yet proceeds with the arbitration without promptly stating its objection to such non-compliance, shall be deemed to have waived its right to object.

Section IV. The Award

Article 31
Decisions

1. When there are three or five arbitrators, any award or other decision of the arbitral tribunal shall be made by a majority of the arbitrators.

2. In the case of questions of procedure, when there is no majority or when the arbitral tribunal so authorizes, the presiding arbitrator may decide on his/her own, subject to revision, if any, by the arbitral tribunal.

Article 32
Form and Effect of the Award

1. In addition to making a final award, the arbitral tribunal shall be entitled to make interim, interlocutory, or partial awards.

2. The award shall be made in writing and shall be final and binding on the parties. The parties undertake to carry out the award without delay.

3. The arbitral tribunal shall state the reasons upon which the award is based, unless the parties have agreed that no reasons are to be given.

4. An award shall be signed by the arbitrators and it shall contain the date on which and the place where the award was made. Where there are three or five arbitrators and any one of them fails to sign, the award shall state the reason for the absence of the signature(s).

5. The award may be made public only with the consent of both parties.

6. Copies of the award signed by the arbitrators shall be communicated to the parties by the International Bureau.

Article 33
Applicable Law

1. In resolving the dispute, the arbitral tribunal shall apply the rules of the organization concerned and the law applicable to any agreement or relationship between the parties, and, where appropriate, the general principles governing the law of international organizations and the rules of general international law.

2. This provision shall not prejudice the power of the arbitral tribunal to decide a case *ex aequo et bono*, if the parties agree thereto.

Article 34

Settlement or Other Grounds for Termination

1. If, before the award is made, the parties agree on a settlement of the dispute, the arbitral tribunal shall either issue an order for the termination of the arbitral proceedings or, if requested by both parties and accepted by the tribunal, record the settlement in the form of an arbitral award on agreed terms. The arbitral tribunal is not obliged to give reasons for such an award.

2. If, before the award is made, the continuation of the arbitral proceedings becomes unnecessary or impossible for any reason not mentioned in paragraph 1, the arbitral tribunal shall inform the parties of its intention to issue an order for the termination of the proceedings. The arbitral tribunal shall have the power to issue such an order unless a party raises justifiable grounds for objection.

3. Copies of the order for termination of the arbitral proceedings or of the arbitral award on agreed terms, signed by the arbitrators, shall be communicated to the parties by the International Bureau. Where an arbitral award on agreed terms is made, the provisions of article 32, paragraphs 2 and 4 to 6, shall apply.

Article 35
Interpretation of the Award

1. Within sixty days after the receipt of the award, either party, with notice to the other party, may request that the arbitral tribunal give an interpretation of the award.

2. The interpretation shall be given in writing within forty-five days after the receipt of the request. The interpretation shall form part of the award and the provisions of article 32, paragraphs 2 to 6, shall apply.

Article 36
Correction of the Award

1. Within sixty days after the receipt of the award, either party, with notice to the other party, may request the arbitral tribunal to correct in the award any errors in computation, any clerical or typographical errors, or any errors of similar nature. The arbitral tribunal may within thirty days after the communication of the award make such corrections on its own initiative.

2. Such corrections shall be in writing, and the provisions of article 32, paragraphs 2 to 6, shall apply.

Article 37

Additional Award

1. Within sixty days after the receipt of the award, either party, with notice to the other party, may request the arbitral tribunal to make an additional award as to claims presented in the arbitral proceedings but omitted from the award.

2. If the arbitral tribunal considers the request for an additional award to be justified and considers that the omission can be rectified without any further hearings or evidence, it shall complete its award within sixty days after the receipt of the request.

3. When an additional award is made, the provisions of article 32, paragraphs 2 to 6, shall apply.

Article 38
Costs (Articles 38 to 40)

The arbitral tribunal shall fix the costs of arbitration in its award. The term 'costs' includes only:

(a) The fees of the arbitral tribunal;
(b) The travel and other expenses incurred by the arbitrators;
(c) The costs of expert advice and of other assistance required by the arbitral tribunal;
(d) The travel and other expenses of witnesses to the extent such expenses are approved by the arbitral tribunal;
(e) Any fees and expenses of the appointing authority as well as the expenses of the Secretary-General and the International Bureau.

Article 39

1. The fees of the arbitral tribunal shall be reasonable in amount, taking into account the complexity of the subject-matter, the time spent by the arbitrators, the amount in dispute, if any, and any other relevant circumstances of the case.

2. When a party so requests, the arbitral tribunal shall fix its fees only after consultation with the Secretary-General who may make any comment he/she deems appropriate to the arbitral tribunal concerning the fees.

Article 40

1. Each party shall bear its own costs of arbitration. However, the arbitral tribunal may apportion each of such costs between the parties if it determines that apportionment is reasonable, taking into account the circumstances of the case.

2. When the arbitral tribunal issues an order for the termination of the arbitral proceedings or makes an award on agreed terms, it shall fix the costs of arbitration referred to in article 38 and article 39, paragraph 1, in the text of that order or award.

3. No additional fees may be charged by an arbitral tribunal for interpretation or correction or completion of its award under articles 35 to 37.

Article 41
Deposit of Costs

1. The International Bureau following the commencement of the arbitration, may request each party to deposit an equal amount as an advance for the costs referred to in article 38, paragraphs (a), (b), (c) and (e). All amounts deposited by the parties pursuant to this paragraph and paragraph 2 of this article shall be directed to the International Bureau, and disbursed by it for such costs, including, *inter alia*, fees to the arbitrators, the Secretary-General and the International Bureau.

2. During the course of the arbitral proceedings the arbitral tribunal may request supplementary deposits from the parties.

3. If the requested deposits are not paid in full within sixty days after the receipt of the request, the arbitral tribunal shall so inform the parties in order that one or another of them may make the required payment. If such payment is not made, the arbitral tribunal may order the suspension or termination of the arbitral proceedings.

4. After the award has been made, the International Bureau shall render an accounting to the parties of the deposits received and return any unexpended balance to the parties.

Permanent Court of Arbitration Optional Rules For Arbitration Between International Organizations and Private Parties

Effective July 1, 1996

Section I. Introductory Rules

Article 1
Scope of Application

1. Where an international organization and a party that is neither a State nor an international organization have agreed in writing that disputes that may arise or that have arisen between them shall be referred to arbitration under the Permanent Court of Arbitration Optional Rules for Arbitration between International Organizations and Private Parties, such disputes shall be referred to arbitration in accordance with these Rules subject to such modification as the parties may agree in writing. For the purpose of this provision, the term 'international organization' shall mean an intergovernmental organization.

2. Agreement by a party to arbitration under these Rules constitutes a waiver of any right of immunity from jurisdiction, in respect of the dispute in question, to which such party might otherwise be entitled. A waiver of immunity relating to the execution of an arbitral award must be explicitly expressed.

3. These Rules shall govern the arbitration except that where any of these Rules is inconflict with a provision of the law applicable to the arbitration from which the parties cannot derogate, that provision shall prevail.

4. The International Bureau of the Permanent Court of Arbitration at The Hague (the 'International Bureau') shall have charge of the archives of the arbitration proceeding. In addition, the International Bureau shall, upon written request of all the parties or of the arbitral tribunal, act as a channel of communications between the parties and the arbitral tribunal, and provide secretariat services including, *inter alia*, arranging for hearing rooms, interpretation, and stenographic or electronic records of hearings.

Article 2
Notice, Calculation of Periods of Time

1. For the purposes of these Rules, any notice, including a notification, communication or proposal, is deemed to have been received if it is delivered at the seat of the organization and, as far as the other party is concerned, at that party's habitual residence, place of business or mailing address, or, if none of these can be found after making reasonable inquiry, then at the party's last-known residence or place of business or mailing address. Notice shall be deemed to have been received on the day it is so delivered.

2. For the purposes of calculating a period of time under these Rules, such period shall begin to run on the day following the day when a notice, notification, communication or proposal is received. If the last day of such period is an official holiday or a non-business day at the residence or place of business of the addressee, the period is extended until the first business day which follows. Official holidays or non-business days occurring during the running of the period of time are included in calculating the period.

Article 3
Notice of Arbitration

1. The party initiating recourse to arbitration (hereinafter called the 'claimant') shall give to the other party (hereinafter called the 'respondent') a notice of arbitration.

2. Arbitral proceedings shall be deemed to commence on the date on which the notice of arbitration is received by the respondent.

3. The notice of arbitration shall include the following:

(a) A demand that the dispute be referred to arbitration;
(b) The names and addresses of the parties;
(c) A reference to the arbitration clause or the separate arbitration agreement that is invoked;
(d) A reference to the agreement or relationship out of or in relation to which the dispute arises;
(e) The general nature of the claim and an indication of the amount involved, if any;
(f) The relief or remedy sought;
(g) A proposal as to the number of arbitrators (i.e., one or three), if the parties have not previously agreed thereon.

4. The notice of arbitration may also include:

(a) The proposals for the appointments of a sole arbitrator and an appointing authority referred to in article 6, paragraph 1;
(b) The notification of the appointment of an arbitrator referred to in article 7;
(c) The statement of claim referred to in article 18.

Article 4
Representation and Assistance

The parties may be represented or assisted by persons of their choice. The names and addresses of such persons must be communicated in writing to the other party, to the International Bureau, and to the arbitral tribunal after it has been appointed; such communication must specify whether the appointment is being made for purposes of representation or assistance.

Section II. Composition of the Arbitral Tribunal

Article 5
Number of Arbitrators

If the parties have not previously agreed on the number of arbitrators (i.e., one or three), and if within thirty days after the receipt by the respondent of the notice of arbitration the parties have not agreed that there shall be only one arbitrator, three arbitrators shall be appointed.

Article 6
Appointment of Arbitrators (Articles 6 to 8)

1. If a sole arbitrator is to be appointed, either party may propose to the other:

(a) The names of one or more persons, one of whom would serve as the sole arbitrator; and
(b) If no appointing authority has been agreed upon by the parties, the name or names of one or more institutions or persons, one of whom would serve as appointing authority.

2. If within sixty days after receipt by a party of a proposal made in accordance with paragraph 1 the parties have not reached agreement on the choice of a sole arbitrator, the sole arbitrator shall be appointed by the appointing authority agreed upon by the parties. If no appointing authority has been agreed upon by the parties, or if the appointing authority agreed upon refuses to act or fails to appoint the arbitrator within sixty days of the receipt of a party's request therefor, either party may request the Secretary-General of

the Permanent Court of Arbitration at The Hague (the 'Secretary-General') to designate an appointing authority.

3. The appointing authority shall, at the request of one of the parties, appoint the sole arbitrator as promptly as possible. In making the appointment the appointing authority shall use the following list-procedure, unless both parties agree that the list-procedure should not be used or unless the appointing authority determines in its discretion that the use of the list-procedure is not appropriate for the case:

(a) At the request of one of the parties the appointing authority shall communicate to both parties an identical list containing at least three names;
(b) Within thirty days after the receipt of this list, each party may return the list to the appointing authority after having deleted the name or names to which it objects and numbered the remaining names on the list in the order of its preference;
(c) After the expiration of the above period of time the appointing authority shall appoint the sole arbitrator from among the names approved on the lists returned to it and in accordance with the order of preference indicated by the parties;
(d) If for any reason the appointment cannot be made according to this procedure, the appointing authority may exercise its discretion in appointing the sole arbitrator.

4. In making the appointment, the appointing authority shall have regard to such considerations as are likely to secure the appointment of independent and impartial arbitrators.

Article 7

1. If three arbitrators are to be appointed, each party shall appoint one arbitrator. The two arbitrators thus appointed shall choose the third arbitrator who will act as the presiding arbitrator of the tribunal.

2. If within thirty days after the receipt of a party's notification of the appointment of an arbitrator the other party has not notified the first party of the arbitrator it has appointed:

(a) The first party may request the appointing authority previously designated by the parties to appoint the second arbitrator; or
(b) If no such authority has been previously designated by the parties, or if the appointing authority previously designated refuses to act or fails to appoint the arbitrator within sixty days after receipt of a party's request therefor, the first party may request the Secretary-General to designate the appointing authority.

The first party may then request the appointing authority so designated to appoint the second arbitrator. In either case, the appointing authority may exercise its discretion in appointing the arbitrator.

3. If within sixty days after the appointment of the second arbitrator the two arbitrators have not agreed on the choice of the presiding arbitrator, the presiding arbitrator shall be appointed by an appointing authority in the same way as a sole arbitrator would be appointed under article 6.

Article 8

1. When an appointing authority is requested to appoint an arbitrator pursuant to article 6 or article 7, the party which makes the request shall send to the appointing authority a copy of the notice of arbitration, and a copy of the pertinent documents among those mentioned in article 3, paragraph 3(c) and (d). The appointing authority may request from either party such information as
it deems necessary to fulfil its function.

2. Where the names of one or more persons are proposed for appointment as arbitrators, their full names, addresses and nationalities shall be indicated, together with a description of their qualifications.
3. In appointing arbitrators pursuant to these Rules, the parties and the appointing authority are free to designate persons who are not Members of the Permanent Court of Arbitration at The Hague.

Article 9
Challenge of Arbitrators (Articles 9 to 12)

A prospective arbitrator shall disclose to those who approach him/her in connection with his/her possible appointment any circumstances likely to give rise to justifiable doubts as to his/her impartiality or independence. An arbitrator, once appointed or chosen, shall disclose such circumstances to the parties unless they have already been informed by him/her of these circumstances.

Article 10

1. Any arbitrator may be challenged if circumstances exist that give rise to justifiable doubts as to the arbitrator's impartiality or independence.

2. A party may challenge the arbitrator appointed by him/her only for reasons of which he/she becomes aware after the appointment has been made.

Article 11

1. A party who intends to challenge an arbitrator shall send notice of its challenge within thirty days after the appointment of the challenged arbitrator has been notified to the challenging party or within thirty days after the circumstances mentioned in articles 9 and 10 became known to that party.

2. The challenge shall be notified to the other party, to the arbitrator who is challenged and to the other members of the arbitral tribunal. The notification shall be in writing and shall state the reasons for the challenge.

3. When an arbitrator has been challenged by one party, the other party may agree to the challenge. The arbitrator may also, after the challenge, withdraw from his/her office. In neither case does this imply acceptance of the validity of the grounds for the challenge. In both cases the procedure provided in article 6 or 7 shall be used in full for the appointment of the substitute arbitrator, even if during the process of appointing the challenged arbitrator a party had failed to exercise his/her right to appoint or to participate in the appointment.

Article 12

1. If the other party does not agree to the challenge and the challenged arbitrator does not withdraw, the decision on the challenge will be made:

(a) When the initial appointment was made by an appointing authority, by that authority;
(b) When the initial appointment was not made by an appointing authority, but an appointing authority has been previously designated, by that authority;
(c) In all other cases, by the appointing authority to be designated in accordance with the procedure for designating an appointing authority as provided for in article 6.

2. If the appointing authority sustains the challenge, a substitute arbitrator shall be appointed or chosen pursuant to the procedure applicable to the appointment or choice of an arbitrator as provided in articles 6 to 9 except that, when this procedure would call for the designation of an appointing authority, the appointment of the arbitrator shall be made by the appointing authority which decided on the challenge.

Article 13
Replacement of an Arbitrator

1. In the event of the death or resignation of an arbitrator during the course of the arbitral proceedings, a substitute arbitrator shall be appointed or chosen pursuant to the procedure provided for in articles 6 to 9 that was applicable to the appointment or choice of the arbitrator being replaced. Any resignation by an arbitrator shall be addressed to the arbitral tribunal and shall not be effective unless the arbitral tribunal determines that

there are sufficient reasons to accept the resignation, and if the arbitral tribunal so determines the resignation shall become effective on the date designated by the arbitral tribunal. In the event that an arbitrator whose resignation is not accepted by the tribunal nevertheless fails to participate in the arbitration, the provisions of paragraph 3 of this article shall apply.

2. In the event that an arbitrator fails to act or in the event of the *de jure* or *de facto* impossibility of his/her performing his/her functions, the procedure in respect of the challenge and replacement of an arbitrator as provided in the preceding articles shall apply, subject to the provisions of paragraph 3 of this article.

3. If an arbitrator on a three-person tribunal fails to participate in the arbitration, the other arbitrators shall, unless the parties agree otherwise, have the power in their sole discretion to continue the arbitration and to make any decision, ruling or award, notwithstanding the failure of one arbitrator to participate. In determining whether to continue the arbitration or to render any decision, ruling, or award without the participation of an arbitrator, the other arbitrators shall take into account the stage of the arbitration, the reason, if any, expressed by the arbitrator for such non-participation, and such other matters as they consider appropriate in the circumstances of the case. In the event that the other arbitrators determine not to continue the arbitration without the nonparticipating arbitrator, the arbitral tribunal shall declare the office vacant, and a substitute arbitrator shall be appointed pursuant to the provisions of articles 6 to 9, unless the parties agree on a different method of appointment.

Article 14
Repetition of Hearings in the Event of the Replacement of an Arbitrator

If under articles 11 to 13 the sole arbitrator or presiding arbitrator is replaced, any hearings held previously shall be repeated; if any other arbitrator is replaced, such prior hearings may be repeated at the discretion of the arbitral tribunal.

Section III. Abitral Proceedings

Article 15
General Provisions

1. Subject to these Rules, the arbitral tribunal may conduct the arbitration in such manner as it considers appropriate, provided that the parties are treated with equality and that at any stage of the proceedings each party is given a full opportunity of presenting its case.

2. If either party so requests at any appropriate stage of the proceedings, the arbitral tribunal shall hold hearings for the presentation of evidence by witnesses, including expert witnesses, or for oral argument. In the absence of such a request, the arbitral tribunal shall decide whether to hold such hearings or whether the proceedings shall be conducted on the basis of documents and other materials.

3. All documents or information supplied to the arbitral tribunal by one party shall at the same time be communicated by that party to the other party and a copy shall be filed with the International Bureau.

Article 16
Place of Arbitration

1. Unless the parties have agreed otherwise, the place where the arbitration is to be held shall be The Hague, The Netherlands. If the parties agree that the arbitration shall be held at a place other than The Hague, the International Bureau shall inform the parties and the arbitral tribunal whether it is willing to provide the secretariat and registrar services referred to in article 1, paragraph 4, and the services referred to in article 25, paragraph 3.

2. The arbitral tribunal may determine the locale of the arbitration within the country agreed upon by the parties. It may hear witnesses and hold meetings for consultation among its members at any place it deems appropriate, having regard to the circumstances of the arbitration.

3. After inviting the views of the parties, the arbitral tribunal may meet at any place it deems appropriate for the inspection of property or documents. The parties shall be given sufficient notice to enable them to be present at such inspection.

4. The award shall be made at the place of arbitration.

Article 17
Language

1. Subject to an agreement by the parties, the arbitral tribunal shall, promptly after its appointment, determine the language or languages to be used in the proceedings. This determination shall apply to the statement of claim, the statement of defence, and any further written statements and, if oral hearings take place, to the language or languages to be used in such hearings.
2. The arbitral tribunal may order that any documents annexed to the statement of claim or statement of defence, and any supplementary documents or exhibits submitted in the course of the proceedings, delivered in their original language, shall be accompanied by a

translation into the language or languages agreed upon by the parties or determined by the arbitral tribunal.

Article 18
Statement of Claim

1. Unless the statement of claim was contained in the notice of arbitration, within a period of time to be determined by the arbitral tribunal, the claimant shall communicate its statement of claim in writing to the respondent and to each of the arbitrators. A copy of the documents mentioned in article 8 shall be annexed thereto.

2. The statement of claim shall include a precise statement of the following particulars:

(a) The names and addresses of the parties;
(b) A statement of the facts supporting the claim;
(c) The points at issue;
(d) The relief or remedy sought.

The claimant may annex to its statement of claim all documents it deems relevant or may add a reference to the documents or other evidence it will submit.

Article 19
Statement of Defence

1. Within a period of time to be determined by the arbitral tribunal, the respondent shall communicate its statement of defence in writing to the claimant and to each of the arbitrators.

2. The statement of defence shall reply to the particulars (b), (c) and (d) of the statement of claim (art. 18, para. 2). The respondent may annex to its statement the documents on which it relies for its defence or may add a reference to the documents or other evidence it will submit.

3. In its statement of defence, or at a later stage in the arbitral proceedings if the arbitral tribunal decides that the delay was justified under the circumstances, the respondent may make a counter-claim, or a claim for a set-off, arising out of any of the items mentioned in article 3, paragraph 3(c).

4. The provisions of article 18, paragraph 2, shall apply to a counter-claim and a claim relied on for the purpose of a set-off.

Article 20
Amendments to the Claim or Defence

During the course of the arbitral proceedings either party may amend or supplement its claim or defence unless the arbitral tribunal considers it inappropriate to allow such amendment having regard to the delay in making it or prejudice to the other party or any other circumstances. However, a claim may not be amended in such a manner that the amended claim falls outside the scope of the arbitration clause or separate arbitration agreement.

Article 21
Pleas as to the Jurisdiction of the Arbitral Tribunal

1. The arbitral tribunal shall have the power to rule on objections that it has no jurisdiction, including any objections with respect to the existence or validity of the arbitration clause or of the separate arbitration agreement.

2. The arbitral tribunal shall have the power to determine the existence or the validity of any legal instrument of which an arbitration clause forms a part. For the purposes of article 21, an arbitration clause which forms part of such instrument and which provides for arbitration under these Rules shall be treated as an agreement independent of the other terms of such instrument. A decision by the arbitral tribunal that the instrument is null and void shall not entail *ipso jure* the invalidity of the arbitration clause.

3. A plea that the arbitral tribunal does not have jurisdiction shall be raised not later than in the statement of defence or, with respect to a counter-claim, in the reply to the counter-claim.

4. In general, the arbitral tribunal should rule on a plea concerning its jurisdiction as a preliminary question. However, the arbitral tribunal may proceed with the arbitration and rule on such a plea in its final award.

Article 22
Further Written Statements

The arbitral tribunal shall, after inviting the views of the parties, decide which further written statements, in addition to the statement of claim and the statement of defence, shall be required from the parties or may be presented by them and shall fix the period of time for communicating such statements.

Article 23

Periods of Time

The periods of time fixed by the arbitral tribunal for the communication of written statements (including the statement of claim and statement of defence) should not exceed ninety days. However, the arbitral tribunal may set longer time limits, if it concludes that an extension is justified.

Article 24
Evidence and Hearings (Articles 24 and 25)

1. Each party shall have the burden of proving the facts relied on to support its claim or defence.

2. The arbitral tribunal may, if it considers it appropriate, require a party to deliver to the tribunal and to the other party, within such a period of time as the arbitral tribunal shall decide, a summary of the documents and other evidence which that party intends to present in support of the facts in issue set out in its statement of claim or statement of defence.

3. At any time during the arbitral proceedings the arbitral tribunal may call upon the parties to produce documents, exhibits or other evidence within such a period of time as the tribunal shall determine. The tribunal shall take note of any refusal to do so as well as any reasons given for such refusal.

Article 25

1. In the event of an oral hearing, the arbitral tribunal shall give the parties adequate advance notice of the date, time and place thereof.

2. If witnesses are to be heard, at least thirty days before the hearing each party shall communicate to the arbitral tribunal and to the other party the names and addresses of the witnesses it intends to present, the subject upon and the languages in which such witnesses will give their testimony.

3. The International Bureau shall make arrangements for the translation of oral statements made at a hearing and for a record of the hearing if either is deemed necessary by the tribunal under the circumstances of the case, or if the parties have agreed thereto and have communicated such agreement to the tribunal and the International Bureau at least thirty days before the hearing or such longer period before the hearing as the arbitral tribunal may determine.

4. Hearings shall be held *in camera* unless the parties agree otherwise. The arbitral tribunal may require the retirement of any witness or witnesses during the testimony of

other witnesses. The arbitral tribunal is free to determine the manner in which witnesses are examined.

5. Evidence of witnesses may also be presented in the form of written statements signed by them.

6. The arbitral tribunal shall determine the admissibility, relevance, materiality and weight of the evidence offered.

Article 26
Interim Measures of Protection

1. Unless the parties otherwise agree, the arbitral tribunal may, at the request of either party, take any interim measures it deems necessary to preserve the respective rights of either party.

2. Such interim measures may be established in the form of an interim award. The arbitral tribunal shall be entitled to require security for the costs of such measures.

3. A request for interim measures addressed by any party to a judicial authority shall not be deemed incompatible with the agreement to arbitrate, or as a waiver of that agreement

Article 27
Experts

1. The arbitral tribunal may appoint one or more experts to report to it, in writing, on specific issues to be determined by the tribunal. A copy of the expert's terms of reference, established by the arbitral tribunal, shall be communicated to the parties.

2. The parties shall give the expert any relevant information or produce for his/her inspection any relevant documents or goods that he/she may request of them. Any dispute between a party and such expert as to the relevance and appropriateness of the required information or production shall be referred to the arbitral tribunal for decision.

3. Upon receipt of the expert's report, the arbitral tribunal shall communicate a copy of the report to the parties who shall be given the opportunity to express, in writing, their opinion on the report. A party shall be entitled to examine any document on which the expert has relied in his/her report.

4. At the request of either party the expert, after delivery of the report, may be heard at a hearing where the parties shall have the opportunity to be present and to interrogate the expert. At this hearing either party may present expert witnesses in order to testify on the points at issue. The provisions of article 25 shall be applicable to such pro-ceedings.

Article 28
Failure to Appear or to Make Submissions

1. If, within the period of time fixed by the arbitral tribunal, the claimant has failed to communicate its claim without showing sufficient cause for such failure, the arbitral tribunal shall issue an order for the termination of the arbitral proceedings. If, within the period of time fixed by the arbitral tribunal, the respondent has failed to communicate its statement of defence without showing sufficient cause for such failure, the arbitral tribunal shall order that the proceedings continue.
2. If one of the parties, duly notified under these Rules, fails to appear at a hearing, without showing sufficient cause for such failure, the arbitral tribunal may proceed with the arbitration.

3. If one of the parties, duly invited to produce documentary evidence, fails to do so within the established period of time, without showing sufficient cause for such failure, the arbitral tribunal may make the award on the evidence before it.

Article 29
Closure of Hearings

1. The arbitral tribunal may inquire of the parties if they have any further proof to offer or witnesses to be heard or submissions to make and, if there are none, it may declare the hearings closed.

2. The arbitral tribunal may, if it considers it necessary owing to exceptional circumstances, decide, on its own motion or upon application of a party, to reopen the hearings at any time before the award is made.

Article 30
Waiver of Rules

A party who knows that any provision of, or requirement under, these Rules has not been complied with and yet proceeds with the arbitration without promptly stating its objection to such non-compliance, shall be deemed to have waived its right to object.

Section IV. The Award

Article 31
Decisions

1. When there are three arbitrators, any award or other decision of the arbitral tribunal shall be made by a majority of the arbitrators.

2. In the case of questions of procedure, when there is no majority or when the arbitral tribunal so authorizes, the presiding arbitrator may decide on his/her own, subject to revision, if any, by the arbitral tribunal.

Article 32
Form and Effect of the Award

1. In addition to making a final award, the arbitral tribunal shall be entitled to make interim, interlocutory, or partial awards.

2. The award shall be made in writing and shall be final and binding on the parties. The parties undertake to carry out the award without delay.

3. The arbitral tribunal shall state the reasons upon which the award is based, unless the parties have agreed that no reasons are to be given.

4. An award shall be signed by the arbitrators and it shall contain the date on which and the place where the award was made. Where there are three arbitrators and any one of them fails to sign, the award shall state the reason for the absence of the signature(s).

5. The award may be made public only with the consent of both parties.

6. Copies of the award signed by the arbitrators shall be communicated to the parties by the International Bureau.

7. If the arbitration law of the country where the award is made requires that the award be filed or registered by the arbitral tribunal, the tribunal shall comply with this requirement within the period of time required by law.

Article 33
Applicable Law, *Amiable Compositeur*

1. In resolving the dispute, the arbitral tribunal shall have regard both to the rules of the organization concerned and to the law applicable to the agreement or relationship out of

or in relation to which the dispute arises and, where appropriate, to the general principles governing the law of international organizations and to the rules of general international law.

2. The arbitral tribunal shall decide as *amiable compositeur* or *ex aequo et bono* only if the parties have expressly authorized the arbitral tribunal to do so and if the law applicable to the arbitral procedure permits such arbitration.

3. In all cases, the arbitral tribunal shall decide in accordance with the terms of the agreement and shall take into account the usages of the trade applicable to the transaction or relationship.

Article 34
Settlement or Other Grounds for Termination

1. If, before the award is made, the parties agree on a settlement of the dispute, the arbitral tribunal shall either issue an order for the termination of the arbitral proceedings or, if requested by both parties and accepted by the tribunal, record the settlement in the form of an arbitral award on agreed terms. The arbitral tribunal is not obliged to give reasons for such an award.

2. If, before the award is made, the continuation of the arbitral proceedings becomes unnecessary or impossible for any reason not mentioned in paragraph 1, the arbitral tribunal shall inform the parties of its intention to issue an order for the termination of the proceedings. The arbitral tribunal shall have the power to issue such an order unless a party raises justifiable grounds for objection.

3. Copies of the order for termination of the arbitral proceedings or of the arbitral award on agreed terms, signed by the arbitrators, shall be communicated to the parties by the International Bureau. Where an arbitral award on agreed terms is made, the provisions of article 32, paragraphs 2 and 4 to 7, shall apply.

Article 35
Interpretation of the Award

1. Within sixty days after the receipt of the award, either party, with notice to the other party, may request that the arbitral tribunal give an interpretation of the award.

2. The interpretation shall be given in writing within forty-five days after the receipt of the request. The interpretation shall form part of the award and the provisions of article 32, paragraphs 2 to 7, shall apply.

Article 36
Correction of the Award

1. Within sixty days after the receipt of the award, either party, with notice to the other party, may request the arbitral tribunal to correct in the award any errors in computation, any clerical or typographical errors, or any errors of similar nature. The arbitral tribunal may within thirty days after the communication of the award make such corrections on its own initiative.

2. Such corrections shall be in writing, and the provisions of article 32, paragraphs 2 to 7, shall apply.

Article 37
Additional Award

1. Within sixty days after the receipt of the award, either party, with notice to the other party, may request the arbitral tribunal to make an additional award as to claims presented in the arbitral proceedings but omitted from the award.

2. If the arbitral tribunal considers the request for an additional award to be justified and considers that the omission can be rectified without any further hearings or evidence, it shall complete its award within sixty days after the receipt of the request.

3. When an additional award is made, the provisions of article 32, paragraphs 2 to 7, shall apply.

Article 38
Costs (Articles 38 to 40)

The arbitral tribunal shall fix the costs of arbitration in its award. The term 'costs' includes only:

(a) The fees of the arbitral tribunal to be stated separately as to each arbitrator and to be fixed by the tribunal itself in accordance with article 39;
(b) The travel and other expenses incurred by the arbitrators;
(c) The costs of expert advice and of other assistance required by the arbitral tribunal;
(d) The travel and other expenses of witnesses to the extent such expenses are approved by the arbitral tribunal;
(e) The costs for legal representation and assistance of the successful party if such costs were claimed during the arbitral proceedings, and only to the extent that the arbitral tribunal determines that the amount of such costs is reasonable;

(f) Any fees and expenses of the appointing authority as well as the expenses of the Secretary-General and the International Bureau.

Article 39

1. The fees of the arbitral tribunal shall be reasonable in amount, taking into account the complexity of the subject-matter, the time spent by the arbitrators, the amount in dispute, if any, and any other relevant circumstances of the case.

2. When a party so requests, the arbitral tribunal shall fix its fees only after consultation with the Secretary-General who may make any comment he/she deems appropriate to the arbitral tribunal concerning the fees.

Article 40

1. Except as provided in paragraph 2, the costs of arbitration shall in principle be borne by the unsuccessful party. However, the arbitral tribunal may apportion each of such costs between the parties if it determines that apportionment is reasonable, taking into account the circumstances of the case.

2. With respect to the costs of legal representation and assistance referred to in article 38, paragraph (e), the arbitral tribunal, taking into account the circumstances of the case, shall be free to determine which party shall bear such costs or may apportion such costs between the parties if it determines that apportionment is reasonable.

3. When the arbitral tribunal issues an order for the termination of the arbitral proceedings or makes an award on agreed terms, it shall fix the costs of arbitration referred to in article 38 and article 39, paragraph 1, in the text of that order or award.

4. No additional fees may be charged by an arbitral tribunal for interpretation or correction or completion of its award under articles 35 to 37.

Article 41
Deposit of Costs

1. The International Bureau following the commencement of the arbitration, may request each party to deposit an equal amount as an advance for the costs referred to in article 38, paragraphs (a), (b), (c) and (f). All amounts deposited by the parties pursuant to this paragraph and paragraph 2 of this article shall be directed to the International Bureau, and disbursed by it for such costs, including, *inter alia*, fees to the arbitrators, the Secretary-General and the International Bureau.

2. During the course of the arbitral proceedings the arbitral tribunal may request supplementary deposits from the parties.

3. If the requested deposits are not paid in full within sixty days after the receipt of the request, the arbitral tribunal shall so inform the parties in order that one or another of them may make the required payment. If such payment is not made, the arbitral tribunal may order the suspension or termination of the arbitral proceedings.

4. After the award has been made, the International Bureau shall render an accounting to the parties of the deposits received and return any unexpended balance to the parties.

Permanent Court of Arbitration
Optional Conciliation Rules

Effective July 1, 1996

Article 1
Application of the Rules

1. These Rules apply to conciliation of disputes arising out of or relating to a contractual legal relationship or other circumstances where the parties seeking an amicable settlement of their disputes have agreed that the Permanent Court of Arbitration Optional Conciliation Rules apply.

2. The parties may agree to exclude or vary any of these Rules at any time.

3. Where any of these Rules is in conflict with a provision of law from which the parties cannot derogate, that provision prevails.

Article 2
Commencement of Conciliation Proceedings

1. The party initiating conciliation sends to the other party a written invitation to conciliate under these Rules, briefly identifying the subject of the dispute.

2. Conciliation proceedings commence when the other party accepts the invitation to conciliate. If the acceptance is made orally, it is advisable that it be confirmed in writing.

3. If the other party rejects the invitation, there will be no conciliation proceedings.

4. If the party initiating conciliation does not receive a reply within thirty days from the date on which it sends the invitation, or within such other period of time as specified in the invitation, it may elect to treat this as a rejection of the invitation to conciliate. If it so elects, it informs the other party accordingly.

Article 3
Number of Conciliators

There shall be one conciliator unless the parties agree that there shall be two or three conciliators. Where there is more than one conciliator, they ought, as a general rule, to act jointly.

Article 4
Appointment of Conciliators

1.
(a) In conciliation proceedings with one conciliator, the parties shall endeavour to reach agreement on the name of a sole conciliator;
(b) In conciliation proceedings with two conciliators, each party appoints one conciliator;
(c) In conciliation proceedings with three conciliators, each party appoints one conciliator. The parties shall endeavour to reach agreement on the name of the third conciliator.

2. Parties may enlist the assistance of an appropriate institution or person in connection with the appointment of conciliators. In particular,

(a) A party may request such an institution or person to recommend the names of suitable individuals to act as conciliator; or
(b) The parties may agree that the appointment of one or more conciliators be made directly by such an institution or person.

3. Parties may also enlist the assistance of the Secretary-General of the Permanent Court of Arbitration in connection with the appointment of conciliators. In particular,

(a) A party may request the Secretary-General of the Permanent Court of Arbitration to designate an institution or person to perform the function set forth in paragraph 2(a) of this article 4;
(b) The parties may request the Secretary-General of the Permanent Court of Arbitration to designate an institution or person to perform the function set forth in paragraph 2(b) of this article 4; or
(c) The Secretary-General may be the 'person' performing the functions set forth in paragraphs 2(a) and (b) of this article 4, pursuant to a request or agreement.

Article 5
Submission of Statements to Conciliator

1. The conciliator,* upon his appointment requests each party to submit to him a brief written statement describing the general nature of the dispute and the points at issue. Each party sends a copy of its statement to the other party.

2. The conciliator may request each party to submit to him a further written statement of its position and the facts and grounds in support thereof, supplemented by any

documents and other evidence that such party deems appropriate. The party sends a copy of its statement to the other party.

3. At any stage of the conciliation proceedings the conciliator may request a party to submit to him such additional information as he deems appropriate.

Article 6
Representation and Assistance

The parties may be represented or assisted by persons of their choice. The names and addresses of such persons are to be communicated in writing to the other party and to the conciliator; such communication is to specify whether the appointment is made for purposes of representation or of assistance.

Article 7
Role of Conciliator

1. The conciliator assists the parties in an independent and impartial manner in their attempt to reach an amicable settlement of their dispute.

2. The conciliator will be guided by principles of objectivity, fairness and justice, giving consideration to, among other things, the rights and obligations of the parties and the circumstances surrounding the dispute, including any previous practices between the parties.

3. The conciliator may conduct the conciliation proceedings in such a manner as he considers appropriate, taking into account the circumstances of the case, the wishes the parties may express, including any request by a party that the conciliator hear oral statements, and any special need for a speedy settlement of the dispute.

4. The conciliator may, at any stage of the conciliation proceedings, make proposals for a settlement of the dispute. Such proposals need not be in writing and need not be accompanied by a statement of the reasons therefor.

Article 8
Administrative Assistance

In order to facilitate the conduct of the conciliation proceedings, the parties, or the conciliator with the consent of the parties, may arrange for administrative assistance by a suitable institution or person. The parties, or the conciliator with the consent of the parties, may request the International Bureau of the Permanent Court of Arbitration to provide such administrative assistance.

Article 9
Communication between Conciliator and Parties

1. The conciliator may invite the parties to meet with him or may communicate with them orally or in writing. He may meet or communicate with the parties together or with each of them separately.

2. Unless the parties have agreed upon the place where meetings with the conciliator are to be held, such place will be determined by the conciliator, after consultation with the parties, having regard to the circumstances of the conciliation proceedings. The conciliator may request the International Bureau of the Permanent Court of Arbitration to arrange for the place where such meetings will be held.

Article 10
Disclosure of Information

When the conciliator receives factual information concerning the dispute from a party, he discloses the substance of that information to the other party in order that the other party may have the opportunity to present any explanation which he considers appropriate. However, when a party gives any information to the conciliator subject to a specific condition that it be kept confidential, the conciliator does not disclose that information to the other party.

Article 11
Co-operation of Parties with Conciliator

The parties will in good faith co-operate with the conciliator and, in particular, will endeavour to comply with requests by the conciliator to submit written materials, provide evidence and attend meetings.

Article 12
Suggestions by Parties for Settlement of Dispute

Each party may, on its own initiative or at the invitation of the conciliator, submit to the conciliator suggestions for the settlement of the dispute.

Article 13
Settlement Agreement

1. When it appears to the conciliator that there exist elements of a settlement which would be acceptable to the parties, he formulates the terms of a possible settlement and submits them to the parties for their observations. After receiving the parties, the conciliator may reformulate the terms of a possible settlement in the light of such observations.

2. If the parties reach agreement on a settlement of the dispute, they draw up and sign a written settlement agreement. If requested by the parties, the conciliator draws up, or assists the parties in drawing up, the settlement agreement.

3. The parties by signing the settlement agreement put an end to the dispute and are bound by the agreement.

Article 14
Confidentiality

Unless the parties agree otherwise, or the disclosure is required in connection with judicial proceedings pursuant to article 16 hereof, the conciliator and the parties shall keep confidential all matters relating to the conciliation proceedings. Confidentiality extends also to the settlement agreement, except where its disclosure is necessary for purposes of implementation and enforcement.

Article 15
Termination of Conciliation Proceedings

The conciliation proceedings are terminated:

(a) By the signing of the settlement agreement by the parties, on the date of the agreement; or
(b) By a written declaration of the conciliator, after consultation with the parties, to the effect that further efforts at conciliation are no longer justified, on the date of the declaration; or
(c) By a written declaration of the parties addressed to the conciliator to the effect that the conciliation proceedings are terminated, on the date of the declaration; or
(d) By a written declaration of a party to the other party and the conciliator, if appointed, to the effect that the conciliation proceedings are terminated, on the date of the declaration.

Article 16
Resort to Arbitral or Judicial Proceedings

The parties undertake not to initiate, during the conciliation proceedings, any arbitral or judicial proceedings in respect of a dispute that is the subject of the conciliation proceedings, except that a party may initiate arbitral or judicial proceedings where, in its opinion, such proceedings are necessary for preserving its rights.

Article 17
Costs

1. Upon termination of the conciliation proceedings, the conciliator fixes the costs of the conciliation and gives written notice thereof to the parties. The term 'costs' includes only:

(a) The fee of the conciliator which shall be reasonable in amount;
(b) The travel and other expenses of the conciliator;
(c) The travel and other expenses of witnesses requested by the conciliator with the consent of the parties;
(d) The costs of any expert advice requested by the conciliator with the consent of the parties;
(e) The cost of any assistance provided pursuant to articles 4, paragraph (2) and 8 of these Rules;
(f) The costs of any services of the Secretary-General and the International Bureau of the Permanent Court of Arbitration.

2. The costs, as defined above, are borne equally by the parties unless the settlement agreement provides for a different apportionment. All other expenses incurred by a party are borne by that party.

Article 18
Deposits

1. The conciliator, upon his appointment, may request each party to deposit an equal amount as an advance for the costs referred to in article 17, paragraph 1 which he expects will be incurred.

2. During the course of the conciliation proceedings the conciliator may request supplementary deposits in an equal amount from each party.

3. If the required deposits under paragraphs 1 and 2 of this article are not paid in full by both parties within thirty days, the conciliator may suspend the proceedings or may make a written declaration of termination to the parties, effective on the date of that declaration.

4. Upon termination of the conciliation proceedings, the conciliator renders an

accounting to the parties of the deposits received and returns any unexpended balance to the parties.

Article 19
Role of Conciliator in Other Proceedings

The parties and the conciliator undertake that, unless the parties agree otherwise, the conciliator will not act as an arbitrator or as a representative or counsel of a party in any arbitral or judicial proceedings in respect of a dispute that is the subject of the conciliation proceedings. The parties also undertake that they will not present the conciliator as a witness in any such proceedings.

Article 20
Admissibility of Evidence in Other Proceedings

The parties undertake not to rely on or introduce as evidence in arbitral or judicial proceedings, whether or not such proceedings relate to the dispute that is the subject of the conciliation proceedings:

(a) Views expressed or suggestions made by the other party in respect of a possible settlement of the dispute;
(b) Admissions made by the other party in the course of the conciliation proceedings;
(c) Proposals made by the conciliator;
(d) The fact that the other party had indicated its willingness to accept a proposal for settlement made by the conciliator.

Permanent Court Of Arbitration
Optional Rules For Fact-Finding - Commissions Of Inquiry

Effective December 15, 1997

Article 1
Application of the Rules

1. These Rules shall apply when the parties have agreed to have recourse to a Factfinding Commission of Inquiry ('Commission') pursuant to the Permanent Court of Arbitration ('PCA') Optional Rules for Fact-finding Commissions of Inquiry, to establish, by means of an impartial and independent investigation, facts with respect to which there is a difference of opinion between them.

2. The parties may agree to exclude or vary any of these Rules at any time.

Article 2
Initiation of Fact-finding Proceedings

1. The party initiating fact-finding shall send to the other party a written invitation to engage in fact-finding under these Rules, briefly identifying the facts to be established. A copy of the invitation shall also be sent to the International Bureau of the PCA ('International Bureau').

2. If the other party rejects the invitation, there will be no fact-finding proceedings under these Rules.

3. If the party initiating fact-finding does not receive a reply within sixty days from the date on which the invitation was sent, or within such other period of time as specified in the invitation, it may elect to treat this as a rejection of the invitation to engage in factfinding. If it so elects, it shall inform the other party accordingly.

4. The parties may also jointly request in writing, addressed to the Secretary-General of the Permanent Court of Arbitration (the 'Secretary-General'), that a Commission be established. The request shall, to the extent possible, specify the facts to be established, without excluding any relevant new facts that may come up in the course of the factfinding.

Article 3
Number of Commissioners

The Commission may consist of one, three, or five commissioners.* Unless the parties agree otherwise there shall be one commissioner.

Article 4
Appointment of Commissioners

1.

(a) In fact-finding proceedings with one commissioner, the parties shall endeavour to reach agreement on the name of a sole commissioner;
(b) In fact-finding proceedings with three or five commissioners, each party shall appoint one or two commissioners, as the case may be. Within two months of the last appointment, the party-appointed commissioners shall designate a third or fifth commissioner, as the case may be, who will act as President of the Commission.

2. The parties may enlist the assistance of an appropriate institution or person in connection with the appointment of commissioners. In particular,

(a) A party may request such an institution or person to recommend the names of suitable individuals to act as commissioner; or
(b) The parties may agree that the appointment of one or more commissioners be made directly by such an institution or person.

3. The parties may also enlist the assistance of the Secretary-General in connection with the appointment of commissioners. In particular,

(a) A party may request the Secretary-General to designate an institution or person to perform the function set forth in paragraph 2(a) of this article;
(b) The parties may request the Secretary-General to designate an institution or person to perform the function set forth in paragraph 2(b) of this article; or
(c) The Secretary-General may be the 'person' performing the functions set forth in paragraphs 2(a) and (b) of this article, pursuant to a request or agreement.

4. In recommending or appointing individuals to act as commissioners, the institution or person shall have regard to such considerations as are likely to secure the appointment of an independent and impartial commissioner, and, with respect to a sole, third or fifth commissioner, shall take into account the advisability of appointing a commissioner of a nationality other than the nationalities of the parties.

5. Any vacancy on the Commission shall be filled in the manner in which the original appointment of the commissioner being replaced was made.

Article 5
Independence of Commissioners

Commissioners shall act in strict conformity with their mandate and perform their task in an impartial manner. Upon accepting appointment, each commissioner shall submit to the International Bureau a declaration confirming his or her independence from the parties.

Article 6
Place of Meeting of the Commission

1. Unless the parties have agreed otherwise, the Commission shall meet in The Hague. The International Bureau shall act as Registry, keep the Commission's archives, and place its offices and staff at the disposal of the Commission.

2. If the fact-finding proceedings are held at a place other than The Hague, the Commission may, in consultation with the International Bureau, appoint a secretary.

3. The Commission may determine the locale of the fact-finding proceedings within the country agreed upon by the parties. It may hold meetings for consultation among its members at any place it deems appropriate, having regard to the circumstances of the fact-finding.

4. The Commission may meet at any place it deems appropriate for the inspection of goods, property, documents, or sites, or for the interrogation of witnesses. The parties shall be given sufficient notice to enable them to be present at such inspection.

5. For purposes of the activities contemplated in paragraphs 2-4 of this article, the Commission or the International Bureau shall, where necessary, seek the permission of, and any requisite assistance from, the country in which these activities are to be undertaken.

Article 7
Representation and Assistance

The parties may be represented or assisted by persons of their choice. The names and addresses of such persons shall be communicated in writing to the other party and to the Commission; such communication shall specify whether the appointment is made for purposes of representation or of assistance.

Article 8
Language

Subject to an agreement by the parties, the Commission shall determine the language or languages to be used in the proceedings. The Commission may request that any documents submitted in the course of the proceedings be accompanied by a translation into the language or languages agreed upon by the parties or determined by the Commission.

Article
Co-operation of Parties with the Commission

1. The parties shall co-operate with the Commission in good faith and shall, in particular, comply with requests by the Commission to submit written materials, provide evidence and attend meetings. All such documents submitted to the Commission shall, at the same time, be transmitted to the other party and to the International Bureau.

2. The parties undertake to make use of all means at their disposal to insure the appearance of witnesses and experts before the Commission. If witnesses or experts are unable to appear before the Commission, the parties shall arrange for their evidence to be taken before qualified officials in the place where the witnesses or experts are located, and speedily transmit the evidence thus obtained to the Commission.

3. A State that agrees to engage in fact-finding pursuant to these Rules shall be deemed to have granted its permission for the conduct in its territory of any of the activities set forth in article 6, paragraphs 2-4, and further undertakes to use all means at its disposal to provide the Commission with whatever assistance it may require in the conduct of the fact-finding proceedings, including but not limited to, ensuring the appearance or written testimony of witnesses and experts, as contemplated in paragraph 1 of this article.

4. In the event that the Commission requires the permission or cooperation of a third State, for example, as contemplated in article 6 of these Rules, the parties shall use all reasonable means at their disposal to obtain such permission and/or co-operation. A State that is a party to fact-finding undertakes to make the necessary request to the State concerned.

Article 10
Confidentiality

Unless the parties agree otherwise, or unless disclosure is required by the law applicable to a party, the members of the Commission and the parties shall keep confidential all matters relating to the fact-finding proceedings, including the investigations, hearings, deliberations and findings of the Commission. Unless the parties agree otherwise, the Commission shall meet *in camera*.

Article 11
Submission of Statements to the Commission

1. Upon its establishment, the Commission shall request each party to submit to it a brief written statement describing the general nature of the facts to be established and the points at issue. The Commission shall have the discretion to determine whether these statements are to be submitted simultaneously or responsively.

2. The Commission may request the parties to submit further written statements of their respective positions and the facts and grounds in support thereof, supplemented by any documents and other evidence that each party deems appropriate.

3. At any stage of the fact-finding proceedings, the Commission may request a party to submit such additional information as the Commission deems appropriate.

4. All documents, statements, information or evidence supplied by one party shall at the same time be provided to the other party, and a copy shall be filed with the International Bureau.

Article 12
Conduct of the Fact-finding Proceedings

1. Subject to these Rules and the agreement of the parties, the Commission may conduct the fact-finding proceedings in such manner as it considers appropriate, provided that the parties are treated with equality and that at any stage of the proceedings each party is given a full opportunity to present its case.

2. The Commission shall give the parties every opportunity to be present at hearings and investigations, and to submit documents, present evidence and have witnesses and experts called. The Commission may also take initiative in asking for documents and calling witnesses and experts. The method for obtaining oral testimony from witnesses and experts shall be determined by the Commission.

3. Unless the parties have decided otherwise, and having regard to the circumstances of the case, the Commission shall determine the scope and type of any record to be made of the hearings and other meetings of the Commission.

Article 13
Decision-making

When the Commission consists of three or five members, all decisions of the Commission shall be made by a majority of its members.

Article 14
Termination of Fact-finding Proceedings

1. Unless agreed otherwise, the fact-finding proceedings shall terminate upon the issuance of a written report by the Commission.

2. Unless the parties have agreed otherwise, the report of the Commission shall not be binding on the parties.

Article 15

The report shall be signed by the sole commissioner or the President of the Commission, as the case may be, and signed for acknowledgment by the Secretary-General. Individual opinions may be attached to the report. The report shall state in detail the facts established by the Commission, and the reason why certain facts may not be considered as having been established. Unless the parties agree to make it public, the report shall remain confidential.

Article 16
Costs

1. Upon termination of the fact-finding proceedings, the Commission shall, in consultation with the International Bureau, fix the costs of the fact-finding and give written notice thereof to the parties. The term 'costs' shall include:

(a) The fees of the commissioners, which shall be reasonable in amount;
(b) The travel and other expenses of the commissioners;
(c) The travel and other expenses of witnesses requested by the Commission;
(d) The costs of any expert advice requested by the Commission;
(e) The costs of any services of the Secretary-General and the International Bureau, including costs related to the holding of proceedings outside The Hague.

2. The costs, as defined above, shall be borne equally by the parties unless the Commission provides for a different apportionment. All other expenses incurred by a party, including those related to the written or oral testimony of any witnesses or experts that it presents, shall be borne by that party.

Article 17
Deposits

1. The Commission, on its establishment, may request the parties to deposit equal amounts as an advance for the costs referred to in article 16. All amounts deposited by the parties pursuant to this paragraph and paragraph 2 of this article shall be paid to the International Bureau, and shall be disbursed by it for such costs.

2. During the course of the fact-finding proceedings the Commission may request supplementary deposits from the parties.

3. If the required deposits under paragraphs 1 and 2 of this article are not paid in full by both parties within sixty days of a request therefor, the Commission may suspend the proceedings or may make a written declaration of termination to the parties, effective thirty days after the date of that declaration.

4. Upon termination of the fact-finding proceedings, the Commission shall render an accounting to the parties of the deposits received and amounts disbursed, and shall return any unexpended balance to the parties.

Permanent Court of Arbitration Optional Rules For Arbitration of Disputes Relating to Natural Resources and/or the Environment

Effective June 19, 2001

Section I. Introductory rules

Article 1
Scope of Application

1. Where all parties have agreed in writing that a dispute that may arise or that has arisen between them shall be referred to arbitration under the Permanent Court of Arbitration Optional Rules for Arbitration of Disputes Relating to Natural Resources and/or the Environment, such disputes shall be settled in accordance with these Rules subject to such modification as the parties may expressly agree upon in writing. The expression 'agreed upon in writing' includes provisions in agreements, contracts, conventions, treaties, the constituent instrument of an international organization or agency or reference upon consent of the parties by a court. The characterization of the dispute as relating to natural resources and/or the environment is not necessary for jurisdiction where all the parties have agreed to settle a specific dispute under these Rules.

2. Agreement by a party to arbitration under these Rules constitutes a waiver of any right of sovereign immunity from jurisdiction, in respect of the dispute in question, to which such party might otherwise be entitled. A waiver of immunity relating to the execution of an arbitral award must be explicitly expressed.

3. The International Bureau of the Permanent Court of Arbitration (the 'International Bureau') shall take charge of the archives of the arbitration proceeding. In addition, upon written request of all the parties or of the arbitral tribunal, the International Bureau shall act as a channel of communication between the parties and the arbitral tribunal, provide secretariat services and/or serve as registry.

Article 2
Notice, Calculation of Periods of Time

1. For the purposes of these Rules, any notice, including a notification, communication or proposal, is deemed to have been received when it has been delivered to the addressee through diplomatic channels in the case of a State, or by any other means by which it can be ascertained that notice has reached its destination. Notice shall be deemed to have been received on the day it is so delivered.

2. For the purposes of calculating a period of time under these Rules, such period shall begin to run on the day following the day when a notice is received. If the last day of such period is an official holiday or a non-work day in the State of the addressee, the period is extended until the first work day which follows. Official holidays or non-work days occurring during the running of the period of time are included in calculating the period.

Article 3
Notice of Arbitration

1. The party or parties initiating recourse to arbitration (hereinafter called the 'claimant') shall give to the other party or parties (hereinafter called the 'respondent') a notice of arbitration.

2. Arbitral proceedings shall be deemed to commence on the date on which the notice of arbitration is received by the respondent.

3. The notice of arbitration shall include the following:

(a) a demand that the dispute be referred to arbitration;
(b) the names and addresses of the parties;
(c) a reference to any rule, decision, agreement, contract, convention, treaty, constituent instrument of an organization or agency, or relationship out of, or in relation to which, the dispute arises;
(d) the pertinent arbitration clause or separate arbitration agreement;
(e) the general nature of the claim and an indication of the amount involved, if any;
(f) the relief or remedy sought;
(g) a proposal as to the number of arbitrators (i.e., one, three or five), if the parties have not previously agreed thereon.

4. The notice of arbitration may also include the statement of claim referred to in article 18.

Article 4
Representation and Assistance

The parties may be represented or assisted by a person or persons of their choice. The name and address of that person or persons must be communicated in writing to the other party, to the International Bureau and to the arbitral tribunal after he/she has been appointed.

Section II. Composition of the Arbitral Tribunal

Article 5
Number of Arbitrators

If the parties have not previously agreed on the number of arbitrators (i.e., one, three or five), and if within thirty days after the receipt by the respondent of the notice of arbitration the parties have not agreed on the number of arbitrators, three arbitrators shall be appointed pursuant to the appointment procedure in articles 6 to 8.

Article 6
Appointment of Arbitrators (Articles 6 to 8)

1. If a sole arbitrator is to be appointed, any party may propose to the other:

(a) the names of one or more persons, one of whom would serve as the sole arbitrator; and
(b) if no appointing authority has been agreed upon by the parties, the name or names of one or more institutions or persons, one of whom would serve as appointing authority.

2. If within thirty days after receipt by a party of a proposal made in accordance with paragraph 1 the parties have not reached agreement on the choice of a sole arbitrator, the sole arbitrator shall be appointed by the appointing authority agreed upon by the parties. If no appointing authority has been agreed upon by the parties, or if the appointing authority agreed upon refuses to act or fails to appoint the arbitrator within sixty days of the receipt of a party's request therefor, the appointing authority shall be the Secretary-General of the Permanent Court of Arbitration at The Hague (the 'Secretary-General').

3. The appointing authority shall, at the request of one of the parties, appoint the sole arbitrator as promptly as possible. In making the appointment the appointing authority shall use the following list-procedure, unless all parties agree that the list procedure should not be used, or used with such modifications as the parties may agree upon, or unless the appointing authority determines in its discretion that the use of the listprocedure is not appropriate for the case:

(a) at the request of any of the parties the appointing authority shall communicate to all parties an identical list containing at least three names;

(b) within thirty days after the receipt of this list, each party shall return the list to the appointing authority after having deleted the name or names to which it objects and numbered the remaining names on the list in the order of its preference;
(c) after the expiration of the above period of time the appointing authority shall appoint the sole arbitrator from among the names approved on the lists returned to it and in accordance with the order of preference indicated by the parties where the parties have agreed upon the order of preference;
(d) if for any reason the appointment cannot be made according to this procedure, the appointing authority may exercise its discretion in appointing the sole arbitrator.

4. In making the appointment, the appointing authority shall have regard to such considerations as are likely to secure the appointment of an independent and impartial arbitrator.

5. Where the appointing authority proposes to appoint a person not suggested by the parties, the parties shall, before such appointment is made, be consulted by the appointing authority in regard to any possible objections on the grounds of justifiable doubts as to the proposed appointee's impartiality or independence or that he or she does not possess the requisite qualifications.

Article 7

1. If three arbitrators are to be appointed, each party shall appoint one arbitrator. The two arbitrators thus appointed shall choose the third arbitrator who will act as the presiding arbitrator of the tribunal. If five arbitrators are to be appointed, the two party-appointed arbitrators shall choose the remaining three arbitrators and designate one of those three as the presiding arbitrator of the tribunal.

2. If within thirty days after the receipt of a party's notification of the appointment of an arbitrator the other party has not notified the first party of the arbitrator it has appointed:

(a) the first party may request the appointing authority previously designated by the parties to appoint the second arbitrator; or
(b) if no such authority has been previously designated by the parties, or if the appointing authority previously designated refuses to act or fails to appoint the arbitrator within sixty days after receipt of a party's request therefor, the appointing authority shall be the Secretary-General. The first party may then request the appointing authority to appoint the second arbitrator. In either case, the appointing authority may exercise its discretion in appointing the arbitrator.

3. If within sixty days after the appointment of the second arbitrator the two arbitrators have not agreed on the choice of the remaining arbitrators and/or presiding arbitrator,

the remaining arbitrators and/or presiding arbitrator shall be appointed by the appointing authority in the same way as a sole arbitrator would be appointed under article 6. Where the notice of arbitration names more than one claimant and the parties have not agreed upon a procedure of appointment, the claimants shall make a joint appointment of an arbitrator in their notice of arbitration. The appointment of the second arbitrator and the presiding arbitrator shall, subject to paragraph 5 of this article, take place in accordance with this article.

4. Where the notice of arbitration names more than one respondent and the parties have not agreed upon a procedure of appointment, the respondents shall jointly appoint an arbitrator. If, for whatever reason, the respondents do not make a joint appointment of an arbitrator within thirty days after receiving the notice of arbitration, the appointment of the second arbitrator shall take place in accordance with paragraph 2 of this article.
5. If, in the situation contemplated in paragraphs 3 and 4 above, within sixty days after the appointment of the second arbitrator the two arbitrators have not agreed on the choice of the remaining arbitrators and/or presiding arbitrator, such arbitrator(s) shall be appointed by the appointing authority in the same way as a sole arbitrator would be appointed under article 6.

Article 8

1. When an appointing authority is requested to appoint an arbitrator pursuant to article 6 or article 7, the party which makes the request shall send to the appointing authority a copy of the notice of arbitration including copies of the documents mentioned in article 3, paragraph 3(c) and (d). The appointing authority may request from any party such additional information as it deems necessary to fulfil its function.

2. Where the names of one or more persons are proposed for appointment as arbitrators, their full names, addresses and nationalities shall be indicated, together with a description of their qualifications including reference to their previous experience in the field of arbitration.

3. In appointing arbitrators pursuant to these Rules, the parties and the appointing authority are free to designate persons who are not Members of the Permanent Court of Arbitration at The Hague. For the purpose of assisting the parties and the appointing authority the Secretary-General will make available a list of persons considered to have expertise in the subject-matters of the dispute at hand for which these Rules have been designed.

Article 9
Challenge of Arbitrators (Articles 9 to 12)

A prospective arbitrator shall disclose to those who approach him/her in connection with his/her possible appointment any circumstances likely to give rise to justifiable doubts as to his/her impartiality or independence. An arbitrator, once appointed or chosen, and thereafter promptly, shall disclose such circumstances to the parties unless they have already been informed by him/her of these circumstances.

Article 10

1. Any arbitrator may be challenged if circumstances exist that give rise to justifiable doubts as to the arbitrator's impartiality or independence or if he/she does not have the qualifications agreed by the parties in their arbitration agreement.

2. A party may challenge the arbitrator appointed by it only for reasons of which it becomes aware after the appointment has been made.

Article 11

1. A party who intends to challenge an arbitrator shall send notice of its challenge within thirty days after the appointment of the challenged arbitrator has been notified to the challenging party or within thirty days after the circumstances mentioned in articles 9 and 10 became known to that party.

2. The challenge shall be notified to the other party or parties, to the arbitrator who is challenged and to the other members of the arbitral tribunal. The notification shall be in writing and shall state the reasons for the challenge.

3. When an arbitrator has been challenged by one party, the other party may agree to the challenge. The arbitrator may also, after the challenge, withdraw from his/her office. In neither case does this imply acceptance of the validity of the grounds for the challenge. In both cases the procedure provided in article 6 or 7 shall be used in full for the appointment of the substitute arbitrator, even if during the process of appointing the challenged arbitrator a party had failed to exercise its right to appoint or to participate in the appointment.

Article 12

1. If the other party or parties do not agree to the challenge and the challenged arbitrator does not withdraw, the decision on the challenge will be made:

(a) when the initial appointment was made by an appointing authority, by that authority;
(b) when the initial appointment was not made by an appointing authority, but an appointing authority has been previously designated, by that authority;
(c) in all other cases, by the appointing authority to be designated in accordance with the procedure for designating an appointing authority as provided for in article 6.

2. If the appointing authority sustains the challenge, a substitute arbitrator shall be appointed or chosen pursuant to the procedure applicable to the appointment or choice of an arbitrator as provided in articles 6 to 9 except that, when this procedure would call

for the designation of an appointing authority, the appointment of the arbitrator shall be made by the appointing authority which decided on the challenge.

Article 13
Replacement of an Arbitrator

1. In the event of the death or resignation of an arbitrator during the course of the arbitral proceedings, a substitute arbitrator shall be appointed or chosen pursuant to the procedure provided for in articles 6 to 9 that was applicable to the appointment or choice of the arbitrator being replaced. In the case of a three- or five-person tribunal, resignation by any arbitrator shall be addressed to the arbitral tribunal and shall not be effective unless the arbitral tribunal determines that there are sufficient reasons to accept the resignation, and if the arbitral tribunal so determines the resignation shall become effective on the date designated by the arbitral tribunal. In the event that an arbitrator whose resignation is not accepted by the tribunal nevertheless fails to participate in the arbitration, the provisions of paragraph 3 of this article shall apply.

2. In the event that an arbitrator fails to act or in the event of the *de jure* or *de facto* impossibility of his/her performing his/her functions, the procedure in respect of the challenge and replacement of an arbitrator as provided in the preceding articles shall apply, subject to the provisions of paragraph 3 of this article.

3. If an arbitrator on a three- or five-person tribunal fails to participate in the arbitration, the other arbitrators shall, unless the parties agree otherwise, have the power in their sole discretion to continue the arbitration and to make any decision, ruling or award, notwithstanding the failure of one arbitrator to participate. In determining whether to continue the arbitration or to render any decision, ruling or award without the participation of an arbitrator, the other arbitrators shall take into account the stage of the arbitration, the reason, if any, expressed by the arbitrator for such non-participation, and such other matters as they consider appropriate in the circumstances of the case. In the event that the other arbitrators determine not to continue the arbitration without the nonparticipating arbitrator, the arbitral tribunal shall declare the office vacant, and a substitute arbitrator shall be appointed pursuant to the provisions of articles 6 to 9, unless the parties agree on a different method of appointment.

Article 14
Repetition of Hearings in the Event of the Replacement of an Arbitrator

If under articles 11 to 13 the sole arbitrator is replaced, any hearings already held shall as far as necessary be repeated, unless the parties agree otherwise. If one of several arbitrators (including the presiding arbitrator) is replaced, unless the parties agree otherwise or the arbitral tribunal so decides, hearings already held shall not be repeated.

Section III. Arbitral Proceedings

Article 15
General Provisions

1. Subject to these Rules, the arbitral tribunal may conduct the arbitration in such manner as it considers appropriate, provided that the parties are treated with equality and that at any stage of the proceedings each party is given a full opportunity to present its case.

2. If any claimant or respondent so requests at any appropriate stage of the proceedings, the arbitral tribunal shall hold hearings for the presentation of evidence by witnesses, including expert witnesses, or for oral argument. In the absence of such a request, the arbitral tribunal shall decide whether to hold such hearings or whether the proceedings shall be conducted solely on the basis of documents and other materials.

3. All documents or information supplied to the arbitral tribunal by one party shall at the same time be communicated by that party to the other party and a copy shall be filed with the International Bureau.

4. A party invoking the confidentiality of any information it wishes or is required to submit in the arbitration, including to an expert appointed by the arbitral tribunal, shall make an application to have the information classified as confidential by notice containing the reasons for which it considers the information confidential to the arbitral tribunal, with a copy to the other party.

5. The arbitral tribunal shall determine whether the information is to be classified as confidential and of such a nature that the absence of special measures of protection in the proceedings would be likely to cause serious harm to the party or parties invoking its confidentiality. If the arbitral tribunal so determines, it shall decide and communicate in writing to the parties and the Registry under what conditions and to whom the confidential information may in part or in whole be disclosed and shall require any person to whom the confidential information is to be disclosed to sign an appropriate confidentiality undertaking.

6. The arbitral tribunal may also, at the request of a party or on its own motion, appoint a confidentiality advisor as an expert in accordance with article 27 in order to report to it, on the basis of the confidential information, on specific issues designated by the arbitral tribunal without disclosing the confidential information either to the party from whom the confidential information does not originate or to the arbitral tribunal.

Article 16
Place of Arbitration

1. Unless the parties have agreed otherwise, the place where the arbitration is to be held shall be The Hague, The Netherlands. If the parties agree that the arbitration shall be held at a place other than The Hague, the International Bureau shall inform the parties and the arbitral tribunal whether it is in a position to provide the secretariat and registrar services referred to in article 1, paragraph 3, and the services referred to in article 25, paragraph 3.

2. The arbitral tribunal may determine the locale of the arbitration within the country agreed upon by the parties. It may hear witnesses and hold meetings for consultation among its members at any place it deems appropriate, having regard to the circumstances of the arbitration.

3. After inviting the views of the parties, the arbitral tribunal may meet at any place it deems appropriate for the inspection of property or documents. The parties shall be given sufficient notice to enable them to be present at such inspection.

4. The award shall be made at the place of arbitration.

Article 17
Language

1. Subject to an agreement by the parties, the arbitral tribunal shall, promptly after its appointment, determine the language or languages to be used in the proceedings. This determination shall apply to the statement of claim, the statement of defence and any further written statements, and if oral hearings take place, to the language or languages to be used in such hearings.

2. The arbitral tribunal may order that any documents annexed to the statement of claim or statement of defence, and any supplementary documents or exhibits submitted in the course of the proceedings, delivered in their original language, shall be accompanied by a translation into the language or languages agreed upon by the parties or determined by the arbitral tribunal.

Article 18
Statement of Claim

1. Unless the statement of claim was contained in the notice of arbitration, within a period of time to be determined by the arbitral tribunal, the claimant shall communicate

its statement of claim in writing to the respondent and to each of the arbitrators. A copy of the documents mentioned in article 3, paragraph 3(c) and (d), shall be annexed thereto.

2. The statement of claim shall include a precise statement of the following particulars:

(a) the names and addresses of the parties;
(b) a statement of the facts supporting the claim;
(c) the points at issue between the parties;
(d) the relief or remedy sought.

The claimant shall annex to its statement of claim all documents it relies upon or deems relevant or may add a reference to the documents or other evidence it will submit.

Article 19
Statement of Defence

1. Within a period of time to be determined by the arbitral tribunal, the respondent or each of the respondents shall communicate its statement of defence in writing to the claimant and to each of the arbitrators.

2. The statement of defence shall reply to the particulars (b), (c) and (d) of the statement of claim (art. 18, para. 2). The respondent may annex to its statement the documents on which it relies for its defence or may add a reference to the documents or other evidence it will submit.

3. In its statement of defence, or at a later stage in the arbitral proceedings if the arbitral tribunal decides that the delay was justified under the circumstances, the respondent may make a counter-claim, or a claim for a set-off, arising out of, or in connection with, any
of the items mentioned in article 3, paragraph 3(c).

4. The provisions of article 18, paragraph 2, shall apply to a counter-claim and a claim relied on for the purpose of a set-off.

Article 20
Amendments to the Claim or Defence

During the course of the arbitral proceedings any party may amend or supplement its claim or defence unless the arbitral tribunal considers it inappropriate to allow such amendment or supplement having regard to the delay in making it or prejudice to the other party or any other circumstances. However, a claim may not be amended or supplemented in such a manner that the resulting claim falls outside the scope of the arbitration clause or separate arbitration agreement.

Article 21
Pleas as to the Jurisdiction of the Arbitral Tribunal

1. The arbitral tribunal shall have the power to rule on objections that it has no jurisdiction, including any objections with respect to the existence or validity of the arbitration clause or of the separate arbitration agreement.

2. The arbitral tribunal shall have the power to determine the existence or the validity of any legal instrument of which an arbitration clause forms a part. For the purposes of this article, an arbitration clause which forms part of such instrument and which provides for arbitration under these Rules shall be treated as an agreement independent of the other terms of such instrument. A decision by the arbitral tribunal that the instrument is null and void shall not entail *ipso jure* the invalidity of the arbitration clause.

3. A plea that the arbitral tribunal does not have jurisdiction shall be raised not later than in the statement of defence or, with respect to a counter-claim, in the reply to the counter-claim.

4. In general, the arbitral tribunal should rule on a plea concerning its jurisdiction or deal with its determination *motu proprio* of its own jurisdiction as a preliminary question. However, the arbitral tribunal in its discretion may proceed with the arbitration and rule on such a plea in its final award.

Article 22
Further Written Statements

The arbitral tribunal shall, after inviting the views of the parties, decide which further written statements, in addition to the statement of claim and the statement of defence, shall be required from the parties or may be presented by them and shall fix the period of time for communicating such statements.

Article 23
Periods of Time

The periods of time fixed by the arbitral tribunal for the communication of written statements (including the statement of claim and statement of defence) should not exceed sixty days. However, the arbitral tribunal may set longer time limits, if it concludes that an extension is justified.

Article 24
Evidence and Hearings (Articles 24 and 25)

1. Each party shall have the burden of proving the facts relied on to support its claim or defence.

2. The arbitral tribunal may, if it considers it appropriate, require a party to deliver to the tribunal and to the other party, within such a period of time as the arbitral tribunal shall decide, a summary of the documents and other evidence which that party intends to present in support of the facts in issue set out in its statement of claim or statement of defence.

3. At any time during the arbitral proceedings the arbitral tribunal may call upon the parties to produce documents, exhibits or other evidence within such a period of time as the tribunal shall determine. The arbitral tribunal shall take into account any refusal to do so as well as any reasons given for such refusal.

4. The arbitral tribunal may request the parties jointly or separately to provide a nontechnical document summarizing and explaining the background to any scientific, technical or other specialized information which the arbitral tribunal considers to be necessary to understand fully the matters in dispute.

Article 25

1. In the event of an oral hearing, the arbitral tribunal shall give the parties adequate advance notice of the date, time and place thereof.

2. If witnesses are to be heard, at least thirty days before the hearing each party shall communicate to the arbitral tribunal and to the other party the names and addresses of the witnesses it intends to present, the subject upon and the languages in which such witnesses will give their testimony.

3. The International Bureau shall make arrangements in consultation with the parties for the translation of oral statements made at a hearing and for a record of the hearing if either is deemed necessary by the tribunal under the circumstances of the case, or if the parties have agreed thereto and have communicated such agreement to the tribunal and the International Bureau at least thirty days before the hearing or such other period before the hearing as the arbitral tribunal may determine.

4. Hearings shall be held *in camera* unless the parties agree otherwise. The arbitral tribunal may require the retirement of any witness or witnesses during the testimony of other witnesses. Taking account of the views expressed by the parties, the arbitral tribunal is free to determine the manner in which witnesses are examined.
5. Evidence of witnesses may also be presented in the form of written statements signed by them.

6. The arbitral tribunal shall determine the admissibility, relevance, materiality and weight of the evidence offered.

Article 26
Interim Measures of Protection

1. Unless the parties otherwise agree the arbitral tribunal may, at the request of any party and having obtained the views of all the parties, take any interim measures including provisional orders with respect to the subject-matter of the dispute it deems necessary to preserve the rights of any party or to prevent serious harm to the environment falling within the subject-matter of the dispute.

2. Such interim measures may be established in the form of an interim award. The arbitral tribunal shall be entitled to require appropriate security for such measures.

3. A request for interim measures addressed by any party to a judicial authority shall not be deemed incompatible with the agreement to arbitrate, or as a waiver of that agreement.

Article 27
Experts

1. After having obtained the views of the parties, the arbitral tribunal may upon notice to the parties appoint one or more experts to report to it, in writing, on specific issues to be determined by the tribunal. A copy of the expert's terms of reference, established by the arbitral tribunal, shall be communicated to the parties.

2. The parties shall give the expert any relevant information or produce for his/her inspection any relevant documents or goods, subject to the provisions for confidentiality in article 15, paragraphs 4 to 6, that he/she may request of them. Any dispute between a party and such expert as to the relevance and appropriateness of the required information or production shall be referred to the arbitral tribunal for decision.

3. Upon receipt of the expert's report, the arbitral tribunal shall communicate a copy of the report to the parties who shall be given the opportunity to express, in writing, their

opinion on the report. A party shall be entitled to examine any document subject to article 15, paragraphs 4 and 5, on which the expert has relied in his/her report.

4. At the request of any party the expert, after delivery of the report, may be heard at a hearing where the parties shall have the opportunity to be present and to interrogate the expert. At this hearing any party may present expert witnesses in order to testify on the points at issue. The provisions of article 25 shall be applicable to such proceedings.

5. The Secretary-General will provide an indicative list of persons considered to have expertise in the scientific or technical matters in respect of which these Rules might be relied upon. In appointing one or more experts pursuant to paragraph 1 above, the arbitral tribunal shall not be limited in its choice to any person or persons appearing on the indicative list of experts.

Article 28
Failure to Appear or to Make Submissions

1. If, within the period of time fixed by the arbitral tribunal, the claimant has failed to communicate its claim without showing sufficient cause for such failure, the arbitral tribunal shall issue an order for the termination of the arbitral proceedings. If, within the period of time fixed by the arbitral tribunal, the respondent has failed to communicate its statement of defence without showing sufficient cause for such failure, the arbitral tribunal shall order that the proceedings continue.

2. If one of the parties, duly notified under these Rules, fails to appear at a hearing, without showing sufficient cause for such failure, the arbitral tribunal may proceed with the arbitration.

3. If one of the parties, duly invited to produce documentary evidence, fails to do so within the established period of time, without showing sufficient cause for such failure, the arbitral tribunal may draw appropriate inferences from such failure and make the award on the evidence before it.

Article 29
Closure of Hearings

1. The arbitral tribunal may inquire of the parties if they have any further proof to offer or witnesses to be heard or submissions to make and, if there are none, it may declare the hearings closed.

2. The arbitral tribunal may, if it considers it necessary owing to exceptional circumstances, decide, on its own motion or upon application of a party, to reopen the hearings at any time before the award is made.

Article 30
Waiver of Rules

A party who knows that any provision of, or requirement under, these Rules has not been complied with and nevertheless proceeds with the arbitration without promptly stating its objection to such non-compliance, shall be deemed to have waived its right to object.

Section IV. The Award

Article 31
Decisions

1. When there are three or five arbitrators, any award or other decision of the arbitral tribunal shall be made by a majority of the arbitrators.

2. In the case of questions of procedure, when there is no majority or when the arbitral tribunal so authorizes, the presiding arbitrator may decide on his/her own.

Article 32
Form and Effect of the Award

1. In addition to making a final award, the arbitral tribunal shall be entitled to make interim, interlocutory, or partial awards.

2. The award shall be made in writing and shall be final and binding on the parties. The parties undertake to carry out the award without delay.

3. The arbitral tribunal shall state the reasons upon which the award is based, unless the parties have agreed that no reasons are to be given.

4. An award shall be signed by the arbitrators and it shall contain the date on which and the place where the award was made. Where there are three or five arbitrators and any one of them fails to sign, the award shall state the reason for the absence of the signature(s).

5. Separate or dissenting opinions (if any) shall be in writing and signed by the dissenting arbitrator or arbitrators.

6. The award may be made public only with the consent of all the parties.

7. Copies of the award signed by the arbitrators shall be communicated to the parties by the International Bureau.

Article 33
Applicable Law

1. In resolving the dispute, the arbitral tribunal shall apply the law or rules of law designated by the parties as applicable to the substance of the dispute. Failing such designation by the parties, the arbitral tribunal shall apply the national and/or international law and rules of law it determines to be appropriate.

2. This provision shall not prejudice the power of the arbitral tribunal to decide a case *ex aequo et bono*, if the parties expressly agree thereto.

Article 34
Settlement or Other Grounds for Termination

1. If, before the award is made, the parties agree on a settlement of the dispute, the arbitral tribunal shall either issue an order for the termination of the arbitral proceedings or, if requested by both parties and accepted by the tribunal, record the settlement in the form of an arbitral award on agreed terms. The arbitral tribunal is not obliged to give reasons for such an award.

2. If, before the award is made, the continuation of the arbitral proceedings becomes unnecessary or impossible for any reason not mentioned in paragraph 1, the arbitral tribunal shall inform the parties of its intention to issue an order for the termination of the proceedings. The arbitral tribunal shall have the power to issue such an order after receiving the views of the parties thereon, unless a party raises justifiable grounds for objection.

3. Copies of the order for termination of the arbitral proceedings or of the arbitral award on agreed terms, signed by the arbitrators, shall be communicated to the parties by the International Bureau. Where an arbitral award on agreed terms is made, the provisions of article 32, paragraphs 2 and 4 to 6, shall apply.

Article 35
Interpretation of the Award

1. Within sixty days after the receipt of the award, any party, with notice to the other party or parties, may request that the arbitral tribunal give an interpretation of the award.

2. The interpretation shall be given in writing within forty-five days after the receipt of the request. The interpretation shall form part of the award and the provisions of article 32, paragraphs 2 to 6, shall apply.

Article 36
Correction of the Award

1. Within sixty days after the receipt of the award, any party, with notice to the other party or parties, may request the arbitral tribunal to correct in the award any errors in computation, any clerical or typographical errors, or any errors of similar nature. The arbitral tribunal may within thirty days after the communication of the award make such corrections on its own initiative.

2. Such corrections shall be in writing, and the provisions of article 32, paragraphs 2 to 6, shall apply.

Article 37
Additional Award

1. Within sixty days after the receipt of the award, any party, with notice to the other party or parties, may request the arbitral tribunal to make an additional award as to claims presented in the arbitral proceedings but omitted from the award.

2. If the arbitral tribunal considers the request for an additional award to be justified and considers that the omission can be rectified without any further hearings or evidence, it shall complete its award within sixty days after the receipt of the request.

3. When an additional award is made, the provisions of article 32, paragraphs 2 to 6, shall apply.

Article 38
Costs (Articles 38 to 40)

The arbitral tribunal shall fix the costs of arbitration in its award. The term 'costs' includes only:

(a) the fees of the arbitral tribunal;
(b) the travel and other reasonable expenses incurred by the arbitrators;
(c) the costs of expert advice and of other assistance required by the arbitral tribunal;

(d) the travel and other expenses of witnesses to the extent such expenses are approved by the arbitral tribunal;
(e) any fees and expenses of the appointing authority as well as the fees and expenses of the Secretary-General and the International Bureau.

Article 39

1. The fees of the arbitral tribunal shall be reasonable in amount, taking into account the complexity of the subject matter, the time spent by the arbitrators, the amount in dispute, if any, and any other relevant circumstances of the case.

2. When a party so requests, the arbitral tribunal shall fix its fees only after consultation with the Secretary-General.

Article 40

1. Each party shall bear its own costs of arbitration. However, the arbitral tribunal may apportion each of such costs between the parties if it determines that apportionment is reasonable, taking into account the circumstances of the case.

2. When the arbitral tribunal issues an order for the termination of the arbitral proceedings or makes an award on agreed terms, it shall fix the costs of arbitration referred to in article 38 and article 39, paragraph 1, in the text of that order or award.

3. No additional fees may be charged by an arbitral tribunal for correction of its award under articles 35 to 37.

Article 41
Deposit of Costs

1. The International Bureau, following the commencement of the arbitration, may request each party to deposit an equal amount as an advance for the costs referred to in article 38, paragraphs (a), (b), (c) and (e). All amounts deposited by the parties pursuant to this paragraph and paragraph 2 of this article shall be directed to the International Bureau, and disbursed by it for such costs, including, *inter alia*, fees to the arbitrators, the Secretary-General and the International Bureau.
2. Security for the costs of interim measures shall be directed to the International Bureau and disbursed by it upon order from the arbitral tribunal.
3. During the course of the arbitral proceedings the International Bureau may request supplementary deposits from the parties.
4. If the requested deposits are not paid in full within sixty days after the receipt of the request, the arbitral tribunal shall so inform the parties in order that one or another of them may make the required payment. If such payment is not made, the arbitral tribunal may order the suspension or termination of the arbitral proceedings.
5. After the award has been made, the International Bureau shall render an accounting to the parties of the deposits received and return any unexpended balance to the parties.

Permanent Court Of Arbitration Optional Rules For Conciliation Of Disputes Relating To Natural Resources And/Or The Environment

Effective April 16, 2002

Article 1
Scope of Application

1. These Rules apply to conciliation of disputes relating to natural resources and/or the environment. For the purposes of these Rules, 'conciliation' means a process whereby parties request a third person, or a panel of persons, to assist them in their attempt to reach an amicable settlement of their dispute relating to natural resources and/or the environment. The characterization of the dispute as relating to the environment or natural resources is not necessary for application of these Rules, where all the parties have agreed to settle a specific dispute under these Rules.

2. Such disputes shall be conciliated in accordance with these Rules subject to such modification as the parties may, at any time, expressly agree upon in writing, unless such modification is excluded by the agreement under which the dispute arises or the agreement to conciliate. The expression 'agree upon in writing' includes provisions in agreements, contracts, conventions, treaties, the constituent instrument of an international organization or agency or reference upon consent of the parties by a court. For the purposes of this and all following articles, 'writing' may include electronic methods of communication in accordance with accepted international practice.

Article 2
Commencement of Conciliation Proceedings

1. The party initiating conciliation shall send to the other party, with a copy thereof to the International Bureau of the Permanent Court of Arbitration (the 'International Bureau') a written invitation to conciliate under these Rules, including as appropriate:

(a) the names, addresses and telephone, or other communication references of the parties to the dispute and of the representative of the party filing the invitation; In this and all following articles, the term 'conciliator' applies to a sole conciliator or all conciliators where more than one are appointed, and the term 'conciliation commission' means a sole conciliator or all conciliators where more than one are appointed.
(b) a reference to the agreement under which this invitation arose;
(c) a reference to any rule, decision, agreement, contract, convention, treaty, or instrument of an organization or agency, under which the dispute arises;

(d) a reference to the general nature of the dispute which led to the invitation.

2.

(a) Conciliation proceedings commence when the other party accepts the invitation to conciliate, or when the invitation reaches the other party in the event there is an obligation to conciliate.
(b) If the party initiating conciliation does not receive a reply within thirty days from the date on which it sends the invitation, or within such longer period of time as specified in the invitation, it may elect to treat this as a rejection of the invitation to conciliation. The initiating party shall inform the other party of any such decision.

3. The International Bureau shall take charge of the archives of the conciliation commission (as meant in article 4) unless the parties otherwise agree. In addition, upon written request of the parties or the conciliation commission, the International Bureau shall act as a channel of communication between the parties and the conciliation commission, provide administrative and secretariat services, and/or serve as Registry.

Article 3
Number of Conciliators

There shall be one conciliator unless the parties agree on three or five conciliators. As a general rule, where there is more than one conciliator, they ought to act jointly.

Article 4
Appointment of Conciliators

1.

(a) In conciliation proceedings with one conciliator, the parties shall endeavour to reach agreement on the name of a sole conciliator within sixty days after commencement of the conciliation proceedings;
(b) In conciliation proceedings with three conciliators, each party appoints one conciliator within sixty days after commencement of conciliation proceedings, communicating the name of the conciliator to the other party and the International Bureau, and within thirty days thereafter, the two conciliators thus appointed shall choose a third conciliator to act as president of the conciliation commission;
(c) In conciliation proceedings with five conciliators, each party appoints two conciliators within sixty days after commencement of conciliation proceedings, communicating the names of the conciliators to the other party and the International Bureau, and within thirty days thereafter, the four conciliators thus appointed shall choose a fifth conciliator to act as president of the conciliation commission;
(d) If after sixty days, as set out in sub-paragraphs (a), (b) and (c) above, the parties have not agreed on a sole conciliator, or a party has not appointed its conciliator, the

Secretary-General of the Permanent Court of Arbitration (the 'Secretary- General') shall notify the parties and make such appointment within thirty days;
(e) In addition, if after thirty days, as set out in sub-paragraphs (b) and (c) above, the party-appointed conciliators have not chosen a president, the Secretary- General shall notify the parties and make such appointment within thirty days.

2. Parties may enlist the assistance of an appropriate institution or person in connection with the appointment of conciliators. In particular,

(a) A party may request such an institution or person to recommend the names of suitable individuals to act as conciliator; or
(b) The parties may agree that the appointment of one or more conciliators be made directly by such an institution or person.
(c) If the person or institution enlisted in this article refuses to act or fails to appoint the conciliator within sixty days of a party's request therefor, the parties shall endeavour to reach agreement on the name of a conciliator within thirty days.
(d) If, after thirty days, as set out in sub-paragraph (c) above, the parties have not agreed on a sole conciliator, or a party has not appointed its conciliator, the Secretary-General shall make such appointment within thirty days.

3. Parties may also enlist the assistance of the Secretary-General in connection with the appointment of conciliators. In particular:

(a) A party may request the Secretary-General to designate an institution or person to perform the function set forth in paragraph 2(a) of this article;
(b) The parties may request the Secretary-General to designate an institution or person to perform the function set forth in paragraph 2(b) of this article; or
(c) The Secretary-General may be the 'person' performing the functions set forth in paragraphs 2(a) and (b) of this article, pursuant to a request or agreement.
(d) When designated as appointing authority, the Secretary-General will make appointments within thirty days after such designation.

4. For the purpose of assisting the parties and the person or institution performing the functions set out in paragraphs 2(a) and (b) of this article, the Secretary-General will make available a list of persons considered to have expertise in the subject-matter of the dispute at hand.

5.

(a) In disputes between more than two parties, parties having the same interest shall appoint their conciliator to the commission jointly by agreement pursuant to this article.
(b) Where two or more parties cannot reach agreement on the appointment of a conciliator or conciliators within a period of sixty days after commencement of

conciliation, the conciliator shall then be appointed within thirty days by the Secretary-General.

6. In recommending or appointing individuals to act as conciliator, the institution or person making such appointments shall have regard to such considerations as are likely to secure the appointment of an independent and impartial conciliator and, with respect to a sole, third, or fifth conciliator, shall take into account the need of appointing a conciliator of a nationality other than the nationalities of the parties. The parties may request that the conciliator sign an impartiality declaration indicating any past or present professional, business, or other relationships with the parties.

Article 5
Submission of Statements to Conciliator

1. The conciliator, upon appointment, shall request each party to submit a brief written statement describing the general nature of the dispute and the points at issue. Each party shall send a copy of its statement to the other party and the International Bureau.

2. The conciliator may request each party to submit a further written statement of its position and the facts and grounds in support thereof, supplemented by any documents and other evidence that such party deems appropriate. The party shall send a copy of its statement to the other party and the International Bureau.

3. At any stage of the conciliation proceedings the conciliator may request that a party submit additional information.

Article 6
Representation and Assistance

The parties may be represented or assisted by persons of their choice. The names and addresses of such persons are to be communicated in writing to the other party, the conciliator, and to the International Bureau; such communication is to specify whether the appointment is made for purposes of representation or of assistance.

Article 7
Role of Conciliator

1. The conciliator assists the parties in an independent and impartial manner in their attempt to reach an amicable settlement of their dispute.

2. The conciliator will be guided by principles of objectivity, fairness and justice, giving consideration to, among other things, the rights and obligations of the parties and the

circumstances surrounding the dispute, including any previous practices between the parties. The conciliator will make proposals to preserve the respective rights of the parties, and to prevent and/or mitigate serious harm to the environment falling within the subject-matter of the dispute.

3. The conciliator may conduct the conciliation proceedings in such a manner as the conciliator considers appropriate, taking into account the relevant law and circumstances of the case, the wishes the parties may express, including any request by a party that the conciliator hear oral statements, and any special need for a speedy settlement of the dispute.

4. The conciliator may propose the appointment of one or more experts to report on specific issues, after having obtained the views of the parties. The conciliator may enlist the services of the Secretary-General who will provide an indicative list of persons considered to have expertise in the scientific or technical matters in respect of which these Rules might be relied upon.

5. The conciliator may, at any stage of the conciliation proceedings, make proposals for a settlement of the dispute. Such proposals need not be in writing and need not be accompanied by a statement of the reasons therefor.

Article 8
Communication Between Conciliator and Parties

1. The conciliator may meet with the parties, or may communicate with them orally or in writing. The conciliator may communicate with the parties together or with each of them separately, subject to prior notification of the intention to meet separately with the other party.

2. The conciliator shall fix the location of any meetings after consulting with the parties. The conciliator may request the International Bureau to arrange for the place where such meetings will be held.

Article 9
Disclosure of Information

When the conciliator receives information concerning the dispute from a party, the conciliator *may* disclose the substance of that information to the other party in order that the other party may present an explanation. However, when a party gives any information to the conciliator subject to a specific condition that it be kept confidential, the conciliator shall not disclose that information to the other party.

Article 10
Co-operation of Parties with Conciliator

The parties shall in good faith co-operate with the conciliator and, in particular, shall endeavour to comply with requests by the conciliator to submit written materials, provide information and attend meetings.

Article 11
Suggestions by Parties for Settlement of Dispute

Each party may, on its own initiative or at the invitation of the conciliator, submit to the conciliator suggestions for the settlement of the dispute.

Article 12
Settlement Agreement

1. When it appears to the conciliator that elements of a settlement exist which would be acceptable to the parties, the conciliator will formulate the terms of a possible settlement and submit them to the parties for their observations. After receiving the observations of the parties, the conciliator may reformulate the terms of a possible settlement in the light of such observations.

2. If the parties reach agreement on a settlement of the dispute, they draw up and sign a written settlement agreement. If requested by the parties, the conciliator draws up, or assists the parties in drawing up, the settlement agreement.

3. The parties by signing the settlement agreement put an end to the dispute and are bound by the agreement.

4. The conciliator may propose the establishment of an implementation committee upon written agreement of the parties to the settlement agreement, to assist the parties in implementing the settlement agreement. If the parties agree on the establishment of an implementation committee, the parties may request the assistance of the conciliator in any aspect of its establishment. The implementation committee may:

(a) request the parties to provide periodic reports on implementation to the committee and parties to the settlement agreement;
(b) review reports provided by the parties and communicate results of the review to other parties to the settlement agreement;
(c) monitor implementation of the settlement agreement according to procedures to be determined by the parties;

(d) determine a list of indicative measures meant to facilitate implementation and propose such measures to a party determined not to be meeting its obligations under the terms of the settlement agreement.

Article 13
Confidentiality

Unless the parties agree otherwise, or disclosure is required by a court or tribunal of competent jurisdiction, the conciliator, the parties and all other persons involved in the conciliation shall respect the confidentiality of the conciliation and may not use or disclose to any outside party any information concerning, or obtained in the course of, the conciliation. 'Information' for the purpose of this article includes, but is not limited to, views expressed, suggestions, arguments and admissions made, and positions taken by the parties or the conciliator during the conciliation. Each such person shall sign an appropriate confidentiality agreement and shall keep confidential all matters relating to the conciliation proceedings. Confidentiality extends also to the settlement agreement, except where its disclosure is necessary for purposes of implementation and enforcement.

Article 14
Termination of Conciliation Proceedings

The conciliation proceedings are terminated:

(a) by the signing of the settlement agreement by the parties, on the date of the agreement; or
(b) by a written declaration of the conciliator, after consultation with the parties, to the effect that further efforts at conciliation are no longer justified, on the date of the declaration; or
(c) by a written declaration of the parties addressed to the conciliator to the effect that the conciliation proceedings are terminated, on the date of the declaration; or
(d) by a written declaration of a party to the other party and the conciliator, if appointed, to the effect that the conciliation proceedings are terminated, on the date of the declaration, unless there is an obligation to conciliate, in which case the procedure of the underlying agreement will prevail.

Article 15
Resort to Arbitral or Judicial Proceedings

The parties undertake not to initiate, during the conciliation proceedings, any arbitral or judicial proceedings in respect of a dispute that is the subject of the conciliation proceedings, except that a party may initiate arbitral or judicial proceedings where, in its opinion, such proceedings are necessary for the preservation of and/or the interim protection of its rights.

Article 16
Competence of the Conciliation Commission

Where there is an obligation to conciliate, a disagreement as to whether the conciliation commission has competence shall be decided by the conciliation commission. Any objection that the conciliation commission has no competence shall be raised as early as possible, and in any case not later than the date of the submission of the written statement mentioned in article 5, paragraph 1.

Article 17
Costs

1. Upon termination of the conciliation proceedings, the conciliator fixes the costs of the conciliation and gives written notice thereof to the parties. All costs related to the conciliation proceedings should be reasonable in amount. The term 'costs' includes only:

(a) the fee of the conciliator;
(b) the travel and other expenses of the conciliator;
(c) the travel and other expenses of witnesses requested by the conciliator with the consent of the parties;
(d) the costs of any expert advice requested by the conciliator with the consent of the parties;
(e) the cost of any assistance provided pursuant to article 2, paragraph 3 and article 4, paragraphs 2 and 3 of these Rules;
(f) the costs of any services of the Secretary-General and the International Bureau of the Permanent Court of Arbitration.

2. The costs, as defined above, are borne equally by the parties unless the settlement agreement provides for a different apportionment. All other expenses incurred by a party are borne by that party.

Article 18
Deposits

1. The conciliator, upon appointment, may request each party to deposit an equal amount as an advance for the costs referred to in article 17, paragraph 1, which are expected to be incurred.

2. During the course of the conciliation proceedings the conciliator may request

supplementary deposits in an equal amount from each party. Before agreeing to provide initial or supplementary deposits, the parties may request an estimate of the costs including items listed in article 17, paragraph 1(a) to (f).

3. If the required deposits under paragraphs 1 and 2 of this article are not paid in full by both parties within thirty days, the conciliator may suspend the proceedings or may make a written declaration of termination to the parties, effective on the date of that declaration.

4. Upon termination of the conciliation proceedings, the conciliator renders an accounting to the parties of the deposits received and returns any unexpended balance to the parties.

5. The conciliator may request the International Bureau to perform the functions set out in paragraphs 1 to 4 of this article.

Article 19
Role of Conciliator in Other Proceedings

The parties and the conciliator undertake that, unless the parties agree otherwise, the conciliator will not act as an arbitrator or as a representative or counsel of a party or other person involved in the conciliation, in any arbitral or judicial proceedings in respect of a dispute that is the subject of the conciliation proceedings. The parties also undertake that they will not present the conciliator as a witness in any such proceedings.

Article 20
Admissibility of Evidence in Other Proceedings

Subject to the general provisions of article 13, the parties undertake not to rely on or introduce as evidence in arbitral or judicial proceedings, whether or not such proceedings relate to the dispute that is the subject of the conciliation proceedings:

(a) views expressed or suggestions made by the other party in respect of a possible settlement of the dispute;
(b) admissions made by the other party in the course of the conciliation proceedings;
(c) proposals made by the conciliator;
(d) the fact that the other party had indicated its willingness to accept a proposal for settlement made by the conciliator.

Guidelines For Adapting The Permanent Court Of Arbitration Rules To Disputes Arising Under Multilateral Agreements And Multiparty Contracts

The various Permanent Court of Arbitration optional arbitration rules can be adapted for use in resolving disputes arising under a multilateral treaty or convention (e.g., Optional Rules for Arbitrating Disputes between Two States;

Optional Rules for Arbitration Involving International Organizations and States) or a multiparty contract (e.g., Optional Rules for Arbitrating Disputes between Two Parties of Which Only One Is a State;

Optional Rules for Arbitration between International Organizations and Private Parties).

All of the provisions in the Rules are appropriate, except that modifications are needed in the mechanisms for naming arbitrators and sharing costs.

Particular care should be taken in drafting the provisions for appointing arbitrators where there may be so many parties in the arbitration that the tribunal would be of impractical size or structure if each party appointed an arbitrator. One solution sometimes considered in multiparty arbitrations is for the parties to agree that the appointing authority will designate all of the arbitrators if the parties do not do so within a specified period.

Modifications may also be needed in the provisions for sharing the costs of the arbitration. It is recommended that parties that contemplate including an arbitration provision in a multilateral agreement or multiparty contract consult in advance with the Secretary- General Permanent Court of Arbitration concerning the drafting of that provision, in order to ensure that the proposed modifications are appropriate in the context of the Rules and that the functions of the Secretary-General and the International Bureau can be carried out effectively.

Cont'd

Reduction of armament

During the Hague Conferences there was no concrete agreement reached related to the reduction of armament, but the conferences placed this theme on the international calendar. Furthermore there were some related declarations adopted. The declaration about biosecurity got elaboration in the Protocols of Geneva (1949) and in the Chemical Weapons Convention (1993). In this last convention the Organization for the Prohibition of Chemical Weapons (OPCW) has been established. This Organization has to check on compliance on the prohibition of a certain category of weapons (as well to use as to produce this weapons) and they also have to make sure to destroy all existing weapons. That's why the reduction of armament as started during the Hague Conference is still important for today's International Law.[27]

Humanitarian War Law

The third core area of the Hague Conferences is concerning Humanitarian War Law. As well the first as the second conference reached results on the area, laws and customs of war on land and adaption to maritime warfare. Mainly the laws and customs of war on land are currently considered to be part of common law.[28] The Martens Clause is still mentioned in this common law.

Offences against the laws and customs of war, known as 'Hague Law' because of their roots in the 1899 and 1907 Conventions, are codified in the 1993 Statute of the International Criminal Tribunal for the Former Yugoslavia and in the Statue of the International Criminal Court.[29] The decision to settle the Yugoslavia Tribunal in the Hague under 'Hague's law' strengthens the prospect of the Hague Humanitarian city.[30] This development was crowned when the International Court was also established in the Hague.[31]

The development of Humanitarian War Law, started as a core area of (the first) Hague Conference, turned out to be a pillar of today's International Law.

---

[27] E.P.J. Myjer, 'Honderd jaar Haagse vredesconferentie: Heeft Den Haag eindelijk een profiel?', *NJB* 1999/852.

[28] E.P.J. Myjer, 'Honderd jaar Haagse vredesconferentie: Heeft Den Haag eindelijk een profiel?', *NJB* 1999/852.

[29]< http://catdir.loc.gov/catdir/samples/cam033/00069751.pdf>.

[30] E.P.J. Myjer, 'Honderd jaar Haagse vredesconferentie: Heeft Den Haag eindelijk een profiel?', *NJB* 1999/852.

[31] Rome Statute of the International Criminal Court 1998.